Exile, Ostracism, and Democracy

Exile, Ostracism, and Democracy

THE POLITICS OF EXPULSION
IN ANCIENT GREECE

Sara Forsdyke

PRINCETON UNIVERSITY PRESS

PRINCETON AND OXFORD

ISBN: 0-691-11975-9

Library of Congress Cataloging-in-Publication Data

Forsdyke, Sara, 1967–
Exile, ostracism, and democracy : the politics of expulsion in ancient Greece / Sara Forsdyke.
p. cm.
Includes bibliographical references and index.
ISBN 0-691-11975-9 (cloth : alk. paper)
1. Exile (Punishment)—Greece—Athens—History.   2. Power (Social sciences)—
Greece—Athens—History.   3. Political crimes and offenses—Greece—Athens—
History.   4. Democracy—Greece—Athens—History.   5. Athens (Greece)—Politics and
government.   I. Title.

JC75.E9F67 2005
364.6'8—dc22   2004065773

British Library Cataloging-in-Publication Data is available

For Finn, Thomas, and Sophie

CONTENTS

Acknowledgments   ix

Chronology   xi

Abbreviations and Conventions   xiii

INTRODUCTION
Problems, Methods, Concepts   1

CHAPTER ONE
Setting the Stage
Intra-elite Conflict and the Early Greek Polis   15
     Continuity and Change: Social Diversity in Dark Age Greece   17
     The Eighth Century and the Rise of the Polis   18
     Conclusion   28

CHAPTER TWO
The Politics of Exile and the Crisis of the Archaic Polis
Four Case Studies: Mytilene, Megara, Samos, and Corinth   30
     Archaic Poetry and History: A Methodological Introduction   32
     Mytilene   36
     Megara   48
     Samos   59
     Corinth   69
     Conclusion   77

CHAPTER THREE
From Exile to Ostracism
The Origins of Democracy in Athens, circa 636–508/7   79
     The Politics of Exile in Archaic Athens: Cylon, Draco, and the
         Trial of the Alcmeonidae   80
     The Beginnings of Change: Solon   90
     A New Type of Politics: Pisistratus and Sons   101
     An End to the Politics of Exile: Cleisthenes and the
         Democratic Revolution   133
     Conclusion   142

CHAPTER FOUR
Ostracism and Exile in Democratic Athens   144
     The Procedure of Ostracism   146
     Ostracism as a Symbolic Institution   149

Ostracisms in Fifth-Century Athens 165
Other Forms of Exile under the Athenian Democracy 178
Exile and the Oligarchic Revolutions of 411 and 404 181
Conclusion 204

CHAPTER FIVE
Exile and Empire
Expulsion in Inter-State Politics 205
Athenian Control and Limitation of Exile: The Erythrae Decree 207
Further Regulation of Exile: The Chalcis Decree 210
A Judicial Decree? 223
Thucydides, Isocrates, and the Legitimacy of Athenian Power 226
Exile and the Tyrant City: A Critique of Athenian Power 232
Exile and the Mythical Past: The Defense of Athenian Power 234
Conclusion 239

CHAPTER SIX
Exile in the Greek Mythical and Historical Imagination 240
Myth, History, and Social Memory: Approaching the Greek
   Historical Imagination 242
Exile in the Democratic Tradition 244
Exile in the Anti-Democratic Tradition 267
Conclusion 276

CONCLUSION 278

Appendix One: The Date of the Athenian Law of Ostracism 281

Appendix Two: Ostracism outside Athens 285

Appendix Three: Exile in Spartan Myth and History 289

Bibliography 301

Index Locorum 327

General Index 334

ACKNOWLEDGMENTS

THIS study originates in Princeton PhD dissertation, but has been completely rewritten and expanded. I would like to acknowledge, however, the support and guidance I received from the members of the Classics Department during my years at Princeton. In particular, Josh Ober not only provided a brilliant example of intellectual energy and insight, but was a model of conscientious and empathetic mentorship.

I owe a great deal to my colleagues in the Department of Classical Studies and the Department of History at the University of Michigan. It is a great privilege to be surrounded by such a group of diverse, talented, and energetic scholars. I have frequently availed myself of their knowledge and advice, and they have always responded with great generosity. In particular, I would like to thank Benjamin Acosta-Hughes, Sue Alcock, Don Cameron, John Cherry, Derek Collins, Beate Dignas, Bruce Frier, Sally Humphreys, Sabine Mac-Cormack, David Potter, Ruth Scodel, and Ray Van Dam. I owe a particular debt of gratitude to Sharon Herbert, who as chair provided support in important ways. I would also like a acknowledge the department's talented graduate students. Their inquisitiveness and critical thinking have provided further stimulus to broaden and deepen my thoughts.

I would like to thank the members of the Classics Department at the University of Chicago for their hospitality during a year of leave (2000–2001). In particular, I benefited from the kindness and learning of Danielle Allen, Shadi Bartsch, Chris Faraone, Jonathan Hall, and James Redfield. A symposium on the ritual aspects of ostracism held in Chicago in May 2001 was particularly helpful for clarifying my thoughts on the relation between ostracism, religion, and magical practices.

I am grateful to the following scholars who have read chapters in advance or answered my inquiries: Susan Alcock, Ryan Balot, Stefan Brenne, Paul Cartledge, Walter Donlan, Antony Edwards, Lisa Nevett, Robin Osborne, Walter Scheidel, Ruth Scodel, James Sickinger, and Peter Siewert. Robert Chenault read through the entire manuscript with an eagle eye, and saved me from many errors and inconsistencies. I thank Charles Myers and Jennifer Nippins of Princeton University Press for their expert and friendly editorial assistance.

An earlier version of parts of chapters 2, 3, and 4 appeared in article form as "Exile, Ostracism, and the Athenian Democracy" in *Classical Antiquity* 19 (2000): 232–63. For permission to reprint this material, I thank the University of California Press.

Finally, friends and family. Among the many good friends that I have made in my academic career, the opportunity to discuss work and life with Ryan Balot and Sarah Harrell has been invaluable to me. Einer, Oddbjorg, Helena, and Per Larsen have followed the progress of my work from afar, and I thank them for their kind support. My parents, Pat and Don Forsdyke, always encouraged me to follow my interests, even when these took me in unexpected directions. I am grateful to them, and to my three sisters, Ruth Polly, and Charlotte, for their love and support, particularly in difficult times.

My deepest gratitude goes to my husband, Finn Larsen. Although he has not read a word of this book, his love, companionship, and many sacrifices have made its writing much easier. I dedicate the book to him, and to our two children, Thomas and Sophie, for all they have given me.

CHRONOLOGY

Bronze Age	3000–1150 BCE
Dark Age	1150–750 BCE
Archaic period	750–500 BCE
Classical period	500–323 BCE
Hellenistic period	323–30 BCE

ABBREVIATIONS AND CONVENTIONS

Abbreviations of ancient authors' names and of the titles of their works are used according to S. Hornblower and A. Spawforth, eds., *The Oxford Classical Dictionary*, 3rd edition (Oxford, 1996). In rendering Greek names and places, I have used Latinized forms, except in cases where the Greek form is in common use. All translations are my own unless otherwise noted. I have usually translated Greek into idiomatic English, but occasionally I have adopted slightly awkward English translations in the interest of rendering the Greek as accurately as possible. All dates are B.C.E. unless otherwise noted.

Ostraca are cited according to two recent editions:

Brenne   S. Brenne, "Teil II: Die Ostraka (487–ca. 416 v.Chr.) als Testi-monien," in P. Siewert, S. Brenne, B. Eder, H. Heftner, and W. Scheidel, eds., *Ostrakismos-Testimonien*, vol. 1, Historia Einzelschriften 155 (Stuttgart, 2002), 36–166. (Cited by testimonium number and ostracon number in this collection: e.g., T1/135 = testimonium 1, ostracon number 135.)

Lang   M. L. Lang, *Ostraka*, vol. 25 of *The Athenian Agora* (Princeton, 1990).

Where these editions overlap, I give both reference numbers.

The following abbreviations are used for standard reference works:

ATL	B. D. Merritt, H. T. Wade-Gery, and M. F. McGregor, *The Athenian Tribute Lists*, 4 vols. (Cambridge, MA, 1939–53).
Campbell	D. A. Campbell, *Greek Lyric*, vol. 1, *Sappho and Alcaeus* (Cambridge, MA, 1982).
Davies, APF	J. K. Davies, *Athenian Propertied Families, 600–300 BC* (Oxford, 1971).
DK	H. Diels and W. Kranz, eds., *Die Fragmente der Vorsokratiker*, 6th ed., (Berlin, 1951–52).
Hignett, HAC	C. Hignett, *A History of the Athenian Constitution to the End of the Fifth Century B.C.* (Oxford, 1952).
HCT	A. W. Gomme, A. Andrewes, and K. J. Dover, *A Historical Commentary on Thucydides*, 5 vols. (Oxford, 1945–81).

Rhodes, *CAAP*   P. J. Rhodes, A *Commentary on the Aristotelian* Athenaion Politeia (Oxford, 1981 [with addenda 1993]).

FGrH   F. Jacoby, ed., *Die Fragmente der griechischen Historiker*, 3 vols. in 7 (Berlin, 1923–30; Leiden, 1940–58).

IC   M. Guarducci, ed., *Inscriptiones Creticae*, 4 vols. (Rome, 1935–50).

IG   *Inscriptiones Graecae* (Berlin, 1873–).

IK [with place name]   *Inschriften griechischer Städte aus Kleinasien* (Bonn, 1972–).

Jeffery, *LSAG*   L. H. Jeffery, *The Local Scripts of Archaic Greece* (Oxford, 1961; rev. ed. 1990, with supplement by A. W. Johnston).

Kassel-Austin, *PCG*   R. Kassel and M. Austin, eds., *Poetae Comici Graeci*, vols. 1–3 (Berlin, 1983–2001).

LSJ   H. G. Liddell, R. Scott, and H. S. Jones, A *Greek-English Lexicon*, 9th ed., rev. (Oxford, 1996).

Maidment   K. J. Maidment, ed., *Minor Attic Orators*, vols. 1 and 2 (Cambridge, MA, 1953–54).

ML   R. Meiggs and D. Lewis, eds., A *Selection of Greek Historical Inscriptions to the End of the Fifth Century BC*, rev. ed. (Oxford, 1988).

RE   A. von Pauly, G. Wissowa, and W. Kroll, eds., *Real-Encyclopädie der klassischen Altertumswissenschaft* (Munich, 1893–).

Tod   M. N. Tod, ed., A *Selection of Greek Historical Inscriptions*, 2 vols. (Oxford, 1946–48 [reprint with new material 1985]).

TrGF   B. Snell, R. Kannicht, and S. Radt, eds., *Tragicorum Graecorum Fragmenta*, 4 vols. (Göttingen, 1971–85; vol. 1, 2nd ed. 1986).

West   M. L. West, ed., *Iambi et Elegi Graeci ante Alexandrum Cantati*, 2 vols. (Oxford, 1971 [rev. ed. 1998]).

Exile, Ostracism, and Democracy

Introduction

PROBLEMS, METHODS, CONCEPTS

> When we cannot get a proverb, or a joke, or a ritual, or a
> poem, we know we are on to something. By picking at the
> document where it is most opaque, we may be able to
> unravel an alien system of meaning. The thread might
> even lead into a strange and wonderful world view.
> —Robert Darnton, *The Great Cat Massacre*

PERHAPS no ancient Greek practice is more opaque to us than the Athenian institution of ostracism. Scholars have repeatedly labeled it bizarre, intrinsically paradoxical, and exotic. If we follow Darnton's exhortation (1984: 5), however, our puzzlement is not a cause for dismay, but a signal of fertile territory for the acquisition of a new perspective on the ancient Greek past. In many ways, I hope that the study that follows validates Darnton's claim. By investigating ostracism, I have sought to open new perspectives not simply on one particular practice, but on broader attitudes and developments in Greek culture and society. In particular, I hope that by exploring the historical origins and cultural and ideological meanings of ostracism, I shed new light on such central topics as the rise of the polis, the origins of democracy, and the relation between historical events, cultural practices, and the ways that society represents itself to itself.

THE ARGUMENT

The main argument of this book is that there was a strong connection between exile and political power in archaic and classical Greece, and that this relation had a formative effect on the institutional and ideological development of the Greek city-states (πόλεις, poleis). Specifically, I argue that in the archaic period (c. 750–500), elites engaged in violent competition for power and frequently expelled one another from their poleis. I label this form of political conflict the "politics of exile," and I suggest that it was particularly unstable, since exiled elites often called on foreign allies to help them return to their poleis and expel their opponents in turn. Many of the institutional developments of the archaic poleis can be viewed as attempts by elites to prevent violent conflict over power and the political instability that it

1

caused. By instituting formal public offices and establishing laws, for example, elites attempted to enforce the orderly rotation of political authority among themselves. These attempts at elite self-regulation, however, were ultimately unsuccessful in preventing violent intra-elite conflict, although they played an important role in strengthening the civic structures of the early Greek poleis (chapters 1 and 2).

It was at Athens during the sixth century that a more permanent solution was found to the problem of exile (chapter 3). As a consequence of particularly frequent episodes of expulsion during the late seventh and sixth centuries, first Solon and then Pisistratus attempted to stabilize their polis by encouraging non-elites to play a role in the allocation of political power. By prompting non-elites to intervene in conflict between elites and to place their support behind a particular elite group, these leaders aimed to prevent the frequent changes of power that resulted from violent conflict solely between narrow groups of elites. I argue that Pisistratus was particularly successful in activating non-elite support on his side through his skillful use of the civic institutions, rituals, and cultural symbols of the Athenian community. Furthermore, Pisistratus departed strongly from earlier practices when he allowed his political opponents to remain in Athens and enjoy a measure of prestige during his tyranny.

Despite the gains made by Pisistratus in tempering violent intra-elite conflict, the problem of exile reemerged with particular intensity in Athens between the death of Pisistratus's son Hipparchus in 514 and the democratic revolution in 508/7. I argue that the revolution by which the democracy was established was a direct outcome of a particularly violent episode of intra-elite politics of exile. In brief, during the revolution of 508/7, the Athenian masses intervened decisively in the struggle between rival elite groups. By placing its support on the side of one elite group and driving the other into exile, the demos (people: δῆμος) asserted its control over decisions of exile. Furthermore, since political power and the power to expel one's opponents were one and the same in archaic Greece, the action of the demos in taking over decisions of exile was equivalent to its assumption of political power. The politician Cleisthenes essentially recognized this equivalency when, following the demos's action, he proposed the reforms by which the democracy was established. Among Cleisthenes' reforms was the institution of ostracism (chapter 3).

In sum, I argue that both democracy and the institution of ostracism were responses to the destabilizing effects of intra-elite politics of exile. Yet the institution of ostracism was not simply a democratic form of an elite practice (chapter 4). Through the institution of ostracism, the Athenians reenacted in symbolic terms their decisive intervention in violent intra-elite conflict during the democratic revolution and thus reminded elites of their fundamental power in the polis. Even more important, through ostracism, the Athenians found a mechanism for distinguishing—in both practice and ideology—democratic rule from the forms of elite rule that had preceded it. In contrast to intra-elite politics of exile, ostracism was a particularly limited and lawful form of exile. Whereas elites in the archaic period had violently expelled one another en masse, the democratic institution of ostracism allowed for the expulsion of a single individual per year for a limited period of time. The limited nature of democratic ostracism was important in at least two ways. First, by expelling only a single individual for a fixed period of time, the Athenians avoided the destabilizing effects of the mass expulsions of the archaic period. Second, the moderate use of the power of expulsion, as represented by the institution of ostracism, was a potent symbol of the moderation, justice, and legitimacy of democratic rule in contrast to the forms of rule that had preceded it (tyranny, oligarchy). This ideology carried over into the Athenians' imperial practices and ideologies, since exile, moderation, and justice are linked together in the justification of Athens' relations with other Greek states (chapter 5).

The relation between exile, ostracism, and justice is key to understanding the role of exile in the mythical and historical imagination of the ancient Greeks (chapter 6). Although exile certainly played a prominent role in Greek mythical and historical traditions before the democracy, the forms in which many of these traditions are preserved reveal the influence of the role of exile in the legitimation of democratic rule. I argue that the Athenian democracy appropriated and transformed earlier traditions of exile in order to reinforce a distinction between the just and unjust use of political power. While the Athenian democracy prided itself on its benevolent reception of exiles from other poleis (for example, in Athenian versions of the myth of the Heraclidae), the democracy characterized non-democratic regimes, such as tyranny and oligarchy, in part through the topos of mass expulsions. The delegitimization of non-democratic forms of rule through the theme of exile is particularly evident in traditions concerning archaic Greek tyrants (for example, Periander of Corinth) and in fourth-century representations of the oligarchic revolutions of 411 and 403. Analysis of these traditions shows that the historical experience of exile under these regimes was adapted and expanded to serve as a key criterion of unjust rule. Furthermore, examination of the criticisms of democratic rule made, for example, by Thucydides and Aristotle reveals the importance of the theme of exile in the debate about the best form of government in late fifth- and fourth-century Athens.

Methods and Approaches

In addition to this specific argument about the role of exile in the political development and historical imagination of the ancient Greeks, I hope that this book makes a contribution to the debate about ways of doing history. In particular, the first chapter—which at first may seem ancillary to the central argument made in later ones—is presented in the conviction that the social, political, and cultural development of Greece in the later archaic and classical periods (c. 500–323) can be fully understood only against the background of earlier developments. In chapter 1 I argue that intra-elite competition was an important factor in the earliest phases of the development of the polis. This argument then provides the background for my claim in subsequent chapters that intra-elite competition in the form of violent politics of exile played a fundamental role in the institutional and ideological development of the later archaic and classical polis.

Chapter 2 then analyzes the role of exile in the political development of four geographically dispersed poleis. By considering the communities of Greece in their full regional diversity, both common patterns and significant divergences can be identified. In this chapter, I argue that four poleis—Mytilene, Megara, Samos, and Corinth—demonstrate that the politics of exile was a common feature of the archaic polis. The various ways in which these poleis responded to the problem of exile, moreover, provide the context for understanding the unique role of exile in Athenian political development, as I argue in subsequent chapters.

Methodologically, chapters 1 and 2 attempt to integrate material evidence into the more conventional text-based study of Greek history. In order to make sense of the relatively mute archaeological data, furthermore, I make critical use of anthropological theories of social evolution and state formation. Although anthropological theories should not be used as templates into which the material evidence for early Greece is forced, they can nevertheless provide suggestive patterns of development against which the relatively scanty evidence can be analyzed. In these chapters, I demonstrate that although many of the larger communities of early Greece underwent similar processes of increasing social and economic stratification and formalization of state structures roughly between 1150 and 750, by the late eighth century the polis was only a very weak form of "state" in the anthropological sense. Specifically, I show that as late as the last half of the sixth century, features of non-state societies—in particular, personal and rapidly changing alliances between elites ("factions," in anthropological terms)—were the dominant political force in the polis, and were the structural basis for the particular form of politics that developed.

Even more important than the consideration of Greek historical development in its full chronological depth and geographical diversity, however, this study aims to strike a balance between diachronic, event-oriented historiography and synchronic inquiries into questions of identity, ideology, and social history. I argue that it is only by considering the dynamic relation between historical events and the ways in which a society represents these events to itself through its practices and ideologies that we can hope to gain insight into ancient Greek experience and understanding of the world. The conviction not only that events shape practices and ideologies but that practices and ideologies impact events is a product of recent trends in a variety of academic fields and is ultimately informed by theoretical work in sociology, political theory, and anthropology.[1] In particular, the work of Michel Foucault, Pierre Bourdieu, and Anthony Giddens has resulted in new emphasis on how practices and ideologies both reflect the political order of society as constituted through its historical development and can themselves actively transform the structures of society.[2] In the work of these theorists, in other words, there is a reflexive relation between political or institutional history and social or ideological history (*histoire des mentalités*). In particular, social practices and ideologies themselves are given new and active roles in the explanation of historical change.

This study reflects the new orientation in historical scholarship in several ways. First of all, I argue that exile was important in Greek political history not simply as a historical event that determined Greek institutional development. Rather, I show that through a dynamic process both exile events and their later representation in the historical imagination of the ancient Greeks impacted the practices, ideologies, and further historical development of Greek society. To be more specific, I contend that the historical event of exile, and even more important, the conceptual and ideological categories that resulted from group reflection on the experience of exile, had a significant role in the creation of the group identities, group behaviors, and hence group responses to later historical conditions. For example, I argue that the institution of ostracism was both a response at the level of practice to prior historical events (archaic politics of exile; the democratic revolution) and a symbol that served at the level of ideology to define Athenian group identity and shape later Athenian group behavior. Through the institution of ostracism, not only did the Athenians define themselves in relation to the past history of exile by linking political power with control over decisions of exile, but they also marked themselves off from that prior history in both ideology and practice by using the power of expulsion with moderation. Indeed, democratic restraint in the use of exile as a political tool, I suggest, was motivated as much by the need to demarcate ideologically democratic rule from non-democratic forms of rule as by the practical need to avoid the destabilizing consequences of more extreme uses of the power of expulsion. Similarly, I argue in chapter 5 that Athenian restraint in the use of exile as a penalty against non-Athenians was as important in the justification of Athenian imperial power as it was in its practical effects of quelling civil war between democrats and oligarchs in the cities of the Athenian alliance.

In this way, exile events of the historical past and their representation in the collective practices and ideologies of the Athenians not only responded to

---

[1] For a useful summary of the impact of these theorists on historical practice, see Burke 1992. For their impact on contemporary political sociology, see Nash 2000.

[2] Foucault 1965, 1980, 1990; Bourdieu 1980/1990; Giddens 1984.

one another but helped to transform Athenian political identities and practices under the democracy. In sum, by examining a specific cultural practice (exile/ostracism) in its full historical and ideological depth, one not only can see how events, practices, and ideologies interact to form the patterns of history, but can also gain new perspectives on some central developments in Greek history: in particular the origins, practices, and ideologies of democracy in classical Athens.

Exile, Boundaries, and Group Identity

One might still ask, Why exile? Why choose to investigate exile if it is simply one example of the many ways in which historical events, social practices, and ideologies interacted to reproduce and transform Greek society? To answer this question we can turn to recent work in a number of academic fields on group identity and interaction through the formation of boundaries, both conceptual and physical. Sociologists, political theorists, historians, and anthropologists have recognized that societies tend to create conceptual boundaries through their myths and norms.[3] These myths and norms work by defining in positive terms who "we" are, but frequently by also defining "what we are not." Archaeologists, in turn, have borrowed the idea of the importance of conceptual boundaries and applied it to the physical features of a community's landscape. In particular, the role of "culturally specific symbols in border areas" has been found to be especially fruitful in understanding how groups define themselves and negotiate conflicts with one another.[4]

It is the contention of this study that historical events themselves, and the conceptual or ideological categories that result from group reflection on historical experience, are a form of boundary and play a significant role in the creation and negotiation of group identities. I argue that exile events and their representation are a particularly powerful form of boundary, since the act of expulsion constitutes a concrete expression of group identity through the physical removal of what the community "is not." For example, the earliest known Athenian law, the anti-tyranny law dating to the seventh century, enjoined all Athenians to expel the tyrant from the community. This law not only began to shape the political identity of the Athenian community by demanding the exclusion of a particular type of political actor, but also combined this

---

[3] The work of Foucault (e.g., 1965, 1990) has been very influential on the study of identity politics. For historical studies of national identity formation, see Hobsbawm and Ranger 1983, B. Anderson 1991. For ancient Greece, see Boegehold and Scafuro 1994; J. Hall 1997, 2002; G. Anderson 2003. For the importance of boundaries to the formation of communities, see A. Cohen 1985.

[4] Hodder 1982, 56–57, 84–85. In Greek archaeology, see de Polignac 1984/1995, Spencer 1995b.

conceptual definition of what the Athenians "were not" with an actual act of physical separation, thus vividly enacting the creation of community through the exclusion of an "other." In a similar sense, the expulsions perpetrated by the oligarchs at the end of the fifth century not only defined in concrete terms the exclusivity of their politics by physically removing the majority of the population from the center of political power, but also, following the restoration of the democracy, served as a powerful negative example in the collective identity of the democracy in the fourth century.

Defining Exile

It is important to be clear at the outset about what forms of expulsion constitute the substance of this book's analysis, since exile has many forms in both ancient and modern societies.[5] Exile in the broadest terms can denote any separation from a community to which an individual or group formerly belonged. Exile in the strictest sense involves a physical separation from the place where one previously lived. In the modern era, however, we know of many cases of what is called "internal exile," in which an individual or group is removed from the immediate surroundings but not expelled from the country altogether.[6] Similar cases are known in the ancient world, such as the exile of Pisistratus after his first attempt to become tyrant, when he was probably driven out of the city center but continued to reside near Brauron in Athenian territory.[7] In the civil war at Corcyra in 427, moreover, oligarchs established themselves outside the city center and waged war on the democrats in the polis from there.[8] In Athens during the oligarchic revolution of 403, likewise, the oligarchs banished the mass of the citizenry from the city center but not from Athenian territory as a whole.[9]

Thus physical separation from the geographical territory controlled by the political community does not seem to be of primary importance in defining exile. We may further ask whether any physical separation at all is necessary in defining it. Can one be in exile within one's own community? Many

[5] See Tabori 1972 for an attempt to survey exile from the earliest written records to the modern era. Tabori notes, moreover, that exile is "not a human invention" but occurs in the animal kingdom (39–40). The most comprehensive study of exile in ancient Greece is Seibert 1979. Earlier studies include Lécrivain 1919, Balogh 1943, Telschow 1952, Fischer 1963, Heisserer 1971, Karavites 1971. For more specialized studies of different types of exile (political, judicial, religious) in ancient Greece, see n. 12 below. For exile in the Roman world, see most recently Claassen 1999, Kelly 1999, S. Cohen 2002. For the theme of exile in Greek literature, see Seibert 1979, Sultan 1999, Tzanetou, *Staging* (forthcoming).

[6] The banishment of Soviet dissidents to Siberia is a notable example.

[7] Hdt. 1.60, with arguments below in chapter 3.

[8] Thuc. 3.85.3.

[9] Xen. *Hell.* 2.4.1, Lys. 25.22, with the arguments below in chapter 4.

literary critics recognize the category "inner exile" as a way of describing the alienation of a writer or artist from his native community.[10] Although this category may seem to yield too loose a definition of exile, in that it can apply to everybody in some sense, it is nonetheless useful in allowing us to connect those who are physically separated from their country with those who, even while present, suffer a sort of internal exile due to their loss of certain abstract attributes of community membership. This condition may entail loss of belief in communal norms or loss of political rights of community membership. While I will be concerned primarily with cases in which there is some degree of physical separation of the exile from his native community, I will include certain other cases in which there is a loss of political membership in the community without physical separation from it.[11]

This brings us to another set of distinctions that may be relevant in defining exile, namely whether it is always a political phenomenon or whether it may be divided into categories according to its ostensible causes (e.g., political exile, religious exile, judicial exile, economic exile).[12] For Greece, we shall immediately see that the lines between politics, religion, law, and economy are blurred and that exile is always, both in its causes and in its effects, a political phenomenon. Arguably this claim holds for the modern world as well and is fundamental to the nature of exile. Indeed, I shall argue that decisions about who is included or excluded from a community are always bound up with political power and that, in some sense, political power is the power to determine who shall and who shall not be a member of a community. In Greece in the archaic period, for example, elites gained political power by expelling their rivals from their poleis. Moreover, I argue that the Athenian demos gained power in part through assuming the power of expulsion. Finally, at the end of the fifth century, Athenian oligarchs maintained power by banishing (as well as killing) their democratic opponents.

Even when expulsions in Greece were not overtly political, political motives may be inferred.[13] The expulsion of the Alcmeonidae on the grounds of religious pollution was probably motivated by the desire of their political rivals, the Cylonians, to remove them from political power.[14] The exile of Alcibiades,

[10] See, e.g., Tabori 1972, 31–32; Tucker 1991, xiii–xiv.

[11] For example, the "internal exile" of the Athenian demos during the oligarchic revolution of 411, discussed in chapter 4 below. As Gehrke (1985, 214) has noted, there is an equivalency between exile and disenfranchisement because of the relation between landholding and citizenship in the ancient world.

[12] A number of specialized studies analyze specific categories of exile. For political exile in the context of civil war, see Gehrke 1985. For religious exile, see R. Parker 1983. For judicial exile, see Usteri 1903; Busolt 1920, 230–38; Kahrstedt 1934, 88–128; Grasmück 1978. For ostracism, see Brenne 2001, Siewert 2002.

[13] See the comment of Grasmück 1978, 19n.32: "Oft sind auch Straftat und politische Absicht nicht voneinander zu trennen, z.B. im Falle der Verbannungen der Alkmeoniden."

[14] See below, chapter 3.

although ostensibly a result of his involvement in religious transgressions, was evidently precipitated by the desire of his political opponents for his removal.[15] In fact, the use of religious and other grounds for political expulsions was so well recognized in the fifth century that the Athenians, in their attempts to regulate the political affairs of their allied cities, specified that all crimes resulting in sentences of exile were to be allowed appeal to Athens.[16] Even where political motives may not be inferred for judicial sentences of exile, such sentences were political insofar as it was the political authority of the state that decided which acts were to result in the removal of a person from the community.

Another important criterion for my definition of exile is whether this was a result of compulsion or could be freely chosen. A basic distinction may be drawn between those who are forced into exile by decree of the political authority of the state, by judicial sentence of banishment, or by fear of persecution or prosecution, and those who choose to emigrate in order to seek economic or other opportunities. In defining exile, I shall limit myself to those who were compelled by force or fear to leave their homelands, since these cases seem most bound up in the political development of the polis. For example, I shall not include the foundation of new settlements (colonization) unless these were the result of political conflict between rival groups within the community.[17] Similarly, I shall not include cases of displacement or deportation due to external aggression unless the external forces were called in by the political authorities of the state (or their opponents) in a situation of internal conflict.[18]

A final distinction to be drawn in defining exile is whether it is imposed on an individual or on a group. While this distinction may seem to be rather one of degree than of essence, we shall see that it was fundamental to the Athenians' understanding of the legality and legitimacy of an expulsion. Banishment of citizens en masse was considered typical of the arbitrary behavior of tyrants and oligarchs in the attempt to maintain power in a polis. The banishment of individuals by judicial sentence, on the other hand, was considered characteristic of democratic regimes that followed lawful judicial procedure to maintain order and justice in society.[19]

Finally, something should be said of the vocabulary of exile in the ancient sources, a topic bearing directly on the forms of exile experienced in the ancient world. The most basic words relating to exile—φυγή, φεύγειν,

[15] See below, chapters 4 and 6.

[16] See below, chapter 5.

[17] For example, Cypselus, tyrant of Corinth, is alleged to have sent out his enemies on colonizing expeditions in order that he might rule the rest more easily (Nic. Dam. *FGrH* 90 F 57). See chapters 2 and 6 below, where I argue that the conceptualization of colonization as a tyrannical tool for eliminating political opposition is a product of later ideologies.

[18] As in the case of the seven hundred families expelled by Sparta at the request of the Athenian Isagoras, Hdt. 5.72.1 (below, chapter 4). See also the expulsions perpetrated by oligarchs and democrats in the civil wars of the fifth century discussed below in chapter 5.

[19] See below, chapters 4 and 6.

φυγάς—mean "flight" or "banishment," "to flee" or "to go into exile" (leave one's homeland), and "fugitive" or "exile," respectively. It is important to note a fundamental ambiguity in these words between "flight," which can be voluntary, although it is usually accompanied by the threat of force, and "exile" as a result of a decree or sentence of banishment.[20] Accordingly, we are sometimes uncertain whether the use of these words involves an actual sentence of exile or instead flight out of fear of future prosecution or violence. The case of the historian Thucydides is a famous example, as we cannot be certain whether he was sentenced to exile or fled out of fear of prosecution for his failure to save Amphipolis.[21] Sometimes the context makes clear which is meant, as for example in the expression "to sentence to exile" (φυγῇ ζημιοῦν)[22] or the use of the verb φεύγειν in Draco's homicide law.[23] As we shall see, however, the difference between flight out of fear of persecution or prosecution and an actual decree of banishment is usually not important, since formal sentence would typically follow flight (since flight was taken to be an indication of guilt), and often the two occurred simultaneously.

A special category of judicial exile was denoted by a different term, ἀτιμία, which in the archaic period meant literally "loss of honor," and resulted in loss of protection from the community.[24] A person sentenced to ἀτιμία could be killed by any member of the community, and the killer was not required to provide compensation. (The killer was εὐαγής, "guiltless," and the victim died νηποινεί, "without compensation.") The result of such a sentence was that the person subject to ἀτιμία was compelled to flee the country in order to avoid being killed. Thus a sentence of ἀτιμία was effectively a sentence of exile. Often the family of the person subject to ἀτιμία was included in the sentence.[25]

Over time the meaning of ἀτιμία changed, coming to designate loss of certain political rights rather than a sentence of physical exile. By the end of the fifth century, a citizen sentenced to ἀτιμία lost the right to attend the assembly, enter temples or the agora, hold office, or be a member of the council or a juror.[26] Ἀτιμία in the stronger sense "outlawry" continued to exist as a penalty for certain serious crimes such as establishing a tyranny or overthrowing the democracy, but

[20] Cf. Seibert 1979, 2–3; Gehrke 1985, 216–17; LSJ s.vv. φεύγειν, φυγάς, φυγή.

[21] Thuc. 5.26.5; cf. Kahrstedt 1934, 99. See also below, chapter 4, on Themistocles' exile.

[22] Cf. Thuc. 4.65.3.

[23] IG 1³ 104.

[24] Standard discussions of the term ἀτιμία include: Harrison 1971, 169–76; Hansen 1976, 54–98; MacDowell 1978, 73–75. See Vleminck 1981 for a good summary of the older debate and a sensible argument regarding the development of the meaning of ἀτιμία.

[25] Ἀτιμία appears in archaic laws as a penalty for three offenses: for changing Draco's homicide law (Dem. 23.62); for attempting to establish a tyranny or aiding in the establishment of a tyrant (Ath. Pol. 16.10); for remaining neutral in civil strife (Ath. Pol. 8.5). In addition, ἀτιμία was evidently the penalty for intentional homicide, as is shown by Solon's amnesty law (Plut. Sol. 19.4), where those who are subject to ἀτιμία for murder are not covered by the amnesty.

[26] Andoc. 1.73–79.

different terms, such as the phrase "Let him die with impunity" (νηποινεὶ τεθνάτω), were used to designate this penalty.[27]

The discussion of ἀτιμία brings up an important ambiguity in the penalties for various crimes in Athenian law, if not in Greek law in general. Ἀτιμία essentially involved a sentence of outlawry. If the person sentenced to ἀτιμία was discovered in Athenian territory, then he could be killed with impunity. If he fled from Athenian territory, however, he could continue to live in exile unharmed. Similarly, a person sentenced to death could flee the country and avoid being killed. Thus there was an equivalency between sentences of death and sentences of exile. This is evident in such cases of treason as those of Hipparchus and Themistocles, who fled from sentences of death and lived out the rest of their lives in exile.[28] The case of Socrates, who was sentenced to death but had the opportunity to flee before the penalty was exacted, is another famous example.[29] Thus it is not surprising that the penalty for intentional homicide is variously designated as death, ἀτιμία, or ἀειφυγία,[30] "exile for life."[31]

Other words commonly used to designate the act of fleeing or being driven from the polis into exile are compounds of χωρέω, διδράσκω, ἔρχομαι, and βαίνω, and διώκω, ἐξελαύνω, ἐκβάλλω, ἐκπίπτω, and φυγαδεύω. The former group usually designates flight, and the latter forceful expulsion, but again the terms can be used interchangeably for the same event and therefore can refer to both phenomena.[32] When an expulsion is made on religious grounds, special vocabulary may be used, such as ἀγηλατέω, "drive out the pollution."[33] In tragedy, where exiles are often central characters and exile a central theme, the words ἀπόπολις or ἄπτολις (without a polis) are used to designate the state of being an exile, in addition to the more usual φυγάς.[34] The parallel word used in prose is ἄπολις.[35]

FURTHER DEFINITIONS: ELITE VERSUS NON-ELITE

Although the term "elite" can be used in contemporary sociology to designate anyone who enjoys a privileged status of whatever kind, in this book I use the

---

[27] Andoc. 1.96–97 (the decree of Demophantus, passed in 410/09).

[28] See below, chapter 4.

[29] Pl. *Cri.* 44b–c, *Ap.* 36b; D.L. 2.40–42; and below, chapter 6.

[30] See, for example, the sentence imposed on the Alcmeonidae for their killing of the suppliants during the suppression of Cylon's coup (*Ath. Pol.* 1) and Demosthenes' summary of penalties for intentional homicide (Dem. 21.43).

[31] Dem. 21.43 lists side by side death, exile for life, and confiscation of property as the penalties for intentional homicide. See also Solon's amnesty law (Plut. *Sol.* 19.4) in n. 25 above.

[32] Gehrke 1985, 216.

[33] Hdt. 5.72, Soph. *OT* 402, Thuc. 1.126.

[34] Aesch. *Ag.* 1410; Soph. *OT* 1000, *OC* 208, *Tr.* 647.

[35] Hdt. 7.104.4, 8.61.1. Also used in tragedy: e.g., Soph. *OC* 1357, *Phil.* 1018.

term more narrowly to designate those who possess some form of political privilege.[36] In ancient Greece, political privilege was based on the claim to some combination of wealth, good birth, divine favor, and excellence (ἀρετή) in some socially recognized attainment, whether prowess in battle, political skill, or some other cultural practice.[37] In archaic Greece, elite privilege entailed a monopoly on public officeholding, and hence I sometimes designate this group the "ruling elite." In classical Greece, the elites continued to monopolize political leadership, though political power no longer rested in their hands.[38] By definition, all those who were not among the elite were non-elite.

By focusing on the two categories elite and non-elite, I do not mean to deny the importance of the middle—that is, the large group of individuals who held a modicum of the markers of status. This group is often equated with the hoplites, the mass of citizens who had a moderate amount of property and participated in military and civic affairs (e.g., the assembly, civic cult).[39] Certainly the bulk of citizens must have fallen into this category. Far from eliding this group, I view it as the most important and dynamic element of the non-elites. That is to say, though I include the poor among the non-elite, I imagine that it was often the middling citizens who were the most active among the non-elite in the developments that I discuss in this book.[40]

Finally, it is important to emphasize that the boundaries between elite and non-elite were fluid.[41] In the archaic period, changes in wealth, in particular, could lead to entry into elite status (Solon's property classes) or demotion from it.[42] Similar changes in the group constituted by the term "elite" took place in the classical period, as is clear from the comic outcry against a new group of political leaders whose wealth was based not on land but on manufacturing.[43]

IDEOLOGY, SYMBOLS, AND ORAL TRADITION

Throughout this book, I refer to the collective beliefs of various political groups (poleis as a whole, democrats, oligarchs) as their "ideology." Since this

---

[36] For the generality of the term in modern sociology, compare recent studies of the "media-elite" (Goldberg 2003) or even the "criminal elite" (on white-collar crime: Coleman 1994). For discussion of the term "elite" in ancient history, see Ober 1989a, 11–17, 192–205, 248–59.

[37] My definition, therefore, combines features of the Marxist concept of class and the Weberian concept of status.

[38] See Ober 1989a for a now classic analysis of how the Athenian democracy managed to avoid the so-called iron law of oligarchy despite its continued dependence on elite leadership.

[39] On the middling hoplites, see Spahn 1977; Hanson 1995; I. Morris 1987, 1996; Raaflaub 1997b, 1999.

[40] See especially my discussion of the democratic revolution below in chapter 3.

[41] Cf. Connor 1994 on the fluidity of social boundaries (particularly between citzen and non-citizen).

[42] See, for example, Solon fr. 15 West; Theognis 57–58, 315–18 West.

[43] Rosenbloom 2002; and chapter 4 below.

term is both anachronistic and notoriously vague, a brief explanation of my usage is necessary.[44] In short, I use "ideology" to refer to the set of beliefs used by a particular group to explain and justify their worldview. A key feature of any ideology is the use of shared symbols having both a cognitive and an emotive element.[45] A well-known example of a shared symbol of the Athenian political community is the concept of tyranny.[46] Intellectually, the Athenians understood tyranny as a particular political system that stood in opposition to the principles of the democracy. In addition, the figure of the tyrant re-presented all sorts of transgressions of normative social and political values and therefore evoked powerful emotions of fear, anger, and disgust.[47] To-gether the intellectual and emotional elements of the figure of the tyrant served as a powerful collective symbol that helped integrate the democratic political community and articulate the basis of its shared political views.[48] In the course of this book, I demonstrate that the concept of exile was an ani-mating symbol in both democratic and oligarchic ideology, and that attention to the use of this symbol in these competing ideological systems sheds light on the political debates of fifth- and fourth-century Athens.

I frequently use the term "oral traditions" or simply "traditions" to refer to oral or written accounts of an aspect of the collective beliefs or ideologies of competing groups in ancient Greece. These traditions are therefore the par-ticular forms (stories, myths, accounts of the past) through which the shared symbols were invoked and the collective beliefs articulated by particular groups in ancient Greece.

EXILE AND PERIODIZATION IN GREEK HISTORY

Finally, a word should be said about the ending point of this study. In terms of historical narrative, the study ends circa 399, with Socrates' refusal to go into exile in the aftermath of the oligarchic revolutions. In terms of its analysis of the ideology of exile, however, the study extends down to the last third of the fourth century, when Aristotle wrote his treatise the *Politics*. Yet it might well be pointed out that neither did the phenomenon of exile disap-pear with Socrates' refusal of exile in 399, nor did the ideological debate

---

[44] For the origins of the term "ideology" in the aftermath of the French Revolution, see McLellan 1995, 5–6.

[45] On the use of symbols to articulate group identity, see A. Cohen 1985 15–21. On symbols, culture, and ideology see Geertz 1973, 14–17, 87–141, 193–233.

[46] See Raaflaub 2003a for recent discussion.

[47] Wohl 2002, however, argues that the tyrant was also an object of desire.

[48] As A. Cohen 1985 shows, symbols do not necessarily have shared meaning for all members of a community. While the majority of the Athenians seemed to have understood tyranny as the antithesis of democracy, for a small subset of elite critics of the democracy, tyranny was in certain respects the symbolic equivalent of radical democracy: see Ober 2003, and below, chapter 6.

about exile end with Aristotle's treatise. Indeed, fourth-century Greece was so replete with exiles that in 324 Alexander the Great issued a decree for the restoration of all exiles as a means of stabilizing the Greek poleis under his control.[49] Furthermore, many later writers, most notably Plutarch, took exile as their subject and debated its pros and cons.[50] The choice to end this study with the trial of Socrates and the treatise of Aristotle, therefore, is a product of my specific interest in ancient democratic history and theory, as well as my partially subjective judgment about what constitutes a meaningful unit of analysis in Greek history.[51]

Nevertheless, I hope that my choice is not wholly without justification, and I offer two forms of defense for my ending point (or points). First, despite the continuing history of exile in the fourth century, I suggest that the oligarchic revolutions of the late fifth century and, in particular, democratic restraint in the use of exile following the restoration of the democracy were the most important turning points in the Athenians' own understanding of the meaning of exile. As I show in chapter 6, the Athenians of the fourth century constantly turned to the exile events of the late fifth century, as well as earlier traditions of exile (for example, in myth and in their memories of archaic tyranny and the democratic revolution of 508/7), in order to think through the problem of the best form of rule. Second, despite the plethora of post-Aristotelian treatises concerning exile, these later works engage less with the functions of exile in the debate about the political organization of Greek poleis than with the impact of the experience of exile on the physical and psychological well-being of individuals. In sum, for the purpose of understanding the role of exile in the political development and historical imagination of the ancient Greeks, the late fifth and the late fourth century form the most suitable ending points.

---

[49] Tod 201; cf. Rhodes and Osborne 2003, 85.

[50] Plut. *On Exile* (*Mor.* 599a–607f).

[51] On the problem of periodization in ancient history and the inevitable selections and subjectivities that it involves, see Golden and Toohey 1997.

Chapter One

SETTING THE STAGE

Intra-elite Conflict
and the Early Greek Polis

> [T]here is really no way to understand archaic Greece
> without plunging into the revolutionary ferment of the
> eighth-century Aegean. Further, there is no way to interpret
> the eighth-century transformation without exploring the
> Dark Age, and no way to make sense of Athens without
> putting it into a broader geographical context.
> —Ian Morris

> [T]he state is not necessarily the kind of highly integrated
> information-processing subsystem the systems theorists
> would have us believe. Instead, the formal, functional, and
> dynamic properties of the state are outcomes of the often
> conflictive interaction of social actors with separate
> agendas, both within and outside the official structure
> of the decision-making institution.
> —R. E. Blanton

THIS chapter and the next attempt to answer Ian Morris's call (1998, 70: the first epigraph above) for a chronologically deep and geographically broad approach to Greek history. In this chapter, I explore the origins and nature of the early Greek polis in order to establish the conditions that form the basis for my argument about the role of exile in later Greek political development. In chapter 2 below, I provide four case studies of geographically dispersed poleis, each demonstrating the central role of (what I term) the "politics of exile" in the development of the archaic polis. These two chapters, in turn, provide the deep historical context and comparative basis for my specific argument about exile in Athenian political development, which follows below in chapters 3 to 6. In these chapters I argue that Athens both shares and diverges from the Panhellenic patterns identified in chapters 1 and 2. In particular, I argue that Athens' unique response to the problem of exile helps to explain both the origins of democracy and the unique institutional and ideological form that it took.

Analysis of the deep historical context of exile is particularly important because the so-called Dark Age (c. 1150–750) and the early Archaic Period have recently been subject to new discoveries and new interpretations, which have radically challenged our understanding of early Greek socio-political organization.[1] In this chapter, I build on the insights of this recent work, but also diverge from it in certain respects. Specifically, my work on exile in the later archaic and classical periods led me to a new perspective on the earlier archaic period. In line with my central argument (outlined above, "Introduction") that democracy was the unexpected outcome of a particularly intense episode of intra-elite politics of exile, I lay emphasis on the role of intra-elite competition as a driving force in the earlier development of the polis. While intra-elite competition in early Greek history has hardly gone unnoticed in contemporary scholarship, more stress has recently been placed on other factors (especially class conflict and the emergence of a middling ideology) as catalysts to, or symptoms of, the emergence of the polis.[2] Although I do not deny the relevance of these factors, I argue that many features of the early polis can also be understood as the unintended "outcomes of the often conflictive interaction of social actors with separate agendas" (Blanton 1998, 140: the second epigraph to this chapter).

I find support for this interpretation from recent comparative and theoretical work on state formation, specifically in two of its results. First, theorists of early state formation have recently argued that archaic states are not simply products of a rational process of increasing social complexity in response to systemic forces such as population growth, pressure on resources, and the consequent need for greater integration and formalization of social organization. Rather, these scholars argue that archaic states are also by-products of intra-elite competition for power.[3] While giving due consideration below to the difference between primary state formation (in reference to which most of these theories are formulated) and secondary state formation (the case of archaic Greece), I borrow from these insights to show that the institutions of the early poleis can be seen in part as the medium by which elites either pursued or attempted to regulate their own on-going struggles for power.

Second, I argue that the development of the early poleis was not linear and progressive but cyclical and discontinuous. As recent critiques of

[1] I. Morris (e.g., 1987, 1991, 1996, 1998, 2000) has had the most influence, though C. Morgan (e.g., 2003), R. Osborne (e.g., 1996a), Raaflaub (1991, 1993, 1997a, 1997b), Snodgrass (1971, 1980, 1987, 1993), Whitley (1988, 1991a, 1991b), and many others are also extremely important.

[2] For intra-elite conflict as a key factor in archaic Greek political development, see, for example, R. Osborne 1996a, 187–97; Raaflaub 1997b, 57. For class conflict and the emergence of a middling ideology, see especially I. Morris 1987, 177; 1996.

[3] Brumfiel 1992, 1994; Blanton et al. 1996; Blanton 1998. For the debate about the role of social agents in archaeology generally, see Dobres and Robb 2000. Flannery 1999 responds to the challenge of these theorists by arguing for the integration of process (systemic forces) and agency (individual social actors). Earle 1997, though adopting a broadly neo-evolutionary framework, focuses on power strategies among elites. See also Mann 1986 for the importance of competition for power among leaders as the cause of socio-political change.

neo-evolutionary social anthropology point out, the simple model of development from egalitarian, non-stratified communities to stratified, hierarchical states is refuted by the evidence for considerable cycling between higher and lower forms of social organization as well as the retention of earlier social forms in later ones.[4] With regard to the early Greek poleis, I show that despite the evidence for the emergence of some features of a state in the eighth and seventh centuries (civic religion, formal public offices), non-state or extra-state social formations (especially personal relations between elites) continued to have a decisive impact on the development of the polis. This observation has crucial implications for my argument about exile, since I argue in later chapters that the rapid formation and dissolution of alliances between rival elites was the social context in which violent intra-elite politics of exile developed.

In sum, the sketch of Dark Age and early archaic Greek political development that I provide in this chapter emphasizes features of early Greek socio-political organization that establish the context for my argument about exile in later chapters. It goes without saying that this introductory survey does not aim to be comprehensive and can only hint at the complexity of the evidence and issues involved.[5]

CONTINUITY AND CHANGE: SOCIAL DIVERSITY IN DARK AGE GREECE

It is important to stress at the outset that the emergence of the archaic Greek polis was a case of secondary rather than primary state formation. This distinction is important because the archaic Greek poleis arose in the context of considerable holdovers from the previous Bronze Age era of Greek civilization.[6] For example, scholars have noted that the continued presence of at least the terminology of certain Bronze Age social and political institutions (e.g., "brotherhoods," φρατρίαι, and "kings," βασιλεῖς) and cults (e.g., Dionysus, Demeter), as well as types of material culture (e.g., pottery styles). Moreover, new discoveries of large structures dating to the tenth and ninth centuries (most famously at Lefkandi), as well as reassessments of the implications of burial evidence, have resulted in arguments for a much more populous and complex Dark Age society than was previously envisioned.[7] The recognition of continuity provides an important warning that early Greek social organization cannot be interpreted in terms of linear evolution from simple to complex social formations, as some models of primary state formation suppose.

[4] Mann 1986, 38–39; Ferguson 1991; Yoffee 1993.

[5] I provide guidance to the bibliography in the footnotes for those wishing to explore the issues in greater depth.

[6] See S. Morris 1992 for a forceful argument for continuity. See Foxhall 1995 for continuity in agricultural regimes.

[7] I. Morris 1987, 2000.

On the other hand, the evidence for discontinuity is also significant. Most strikingly, archaeology attests to the drastic reduction in the number of sites in the twelfth and eleventh centuries.[8] Even when allowance is made for the possible archaeological invisibility of large numbers of people in this period, it is still generally agreed that population levels, and in consequence social complexity, were reduced across much of Dark Age Greece:[9] some sites were occupied continuously and thus may have maintained considerable social complexity, but many other sites were abandoned. In the tenth century new sites begin to appear, although it is not until the eighth century that settlement numbers and sizes increase dramatically.[10] Consideration of the evidence for discontinuity, therefore, suggests that some of the communities of Dark Age Greece may have experienced trajectories of increasing social complexity, as postulated by social-evolutionary models.

Putting the evidence for both continuity and discontinuity together, scholars have adopted a compromise position: some Bronze Age social institutions, cults, and material culture did persist, but they were put to new uses in the changed conditions of post-Mycenaean Greece.[11] Population did drop and then rise again, but not with the same consequences in different regions and sites across Greece. Specifically, some communities (e.g., Athens) maintained some social complexity in the eleventh century, and grew markedly more populous and complex in the eighth century. Other communities were reduced to simpler forms of association, and became only slightly more complex by the eighth century (e.g., Nichoria). Where new communities sprang up, some experienced population growth and increasing social complexity before collapsing and disappearing (e.g., Nichoria, Lefkandi, Zagora). Others (e.g., Sparta) grew into major powers of the later archaic and classical periods. In sum, an important consequence of recent research has been the recognition of the different ways that the communities and regions of Greece adapted to the new conditions, and the consequent acknowledgment of the social diversity of Dark Age Greece.[12]

The Eighth Century and the Rise of the Polis

Against the background of a socially diverse Dark Age, scholars have identified several factors as crucial for the emergence in the eighth century of the early

[8] Snodgrass 1971, 360–65; 1993, 37 (the latter publication adding the evidence of more recent survey evidence).

[9] Scheidel 2003, 122.

[10] See I. Morris 1987, 157 (fig. 54), for the evidence from Attica, Corinthia, and the Argive plain.

[11] The prime example is the role of the kings (βασιλεῖς): see Drews 1983; Carlier 1984; Donlan 1989, 1994.

[12] The phrase "social diversity" is borrowed from the important article of Whitley 1988. See also Farenga 1998.

state form that modern historiographers call the polis.[13] Among the changes, a rise in population, the establishment of civic sanctuaries both in the center of settlements and on the periphery, and changes in the burial record have taken pride of place.[14] For the most part, these changes have been interpreted as symptoms of a new civic ethos by which a collectivity of relatively equal citizen-soldiers articulated their collective identity and power in the newly forming communities of eighth-century Greece.[15] While scholars acknowledge the leadership of a group of wealthy and powerful families, they argue that, in contrast to Dark Age leaders, these elites were compelled to earn their status through service to the entire community. Although I agree that the eighth-century changes indicate the emergence of a new civic ethos, I lay emphasis on the role of competition between elite leaders themselves in promoting this and other changes in early Greek social organization and ideology. Rather than viewing the eighth-century changes as a consequence of pressure from below or as a response to the middling ideology of a newly politically aware group of non-elite citizens, I view the early polis in part as the means by which elite social actors attempted to maximize their own power and minimize the power of rival elites. The advantage of my emphasis on intra-elite competition is that it explains how some features of a state could emerge out of the social formations of Dark Age Greece, but also accounts for the relative weakness of the new civic institutions as opposed to the elites that continued to dominate until well into the sixth century. In what follows, I review some of the major features of the eighth-century polis and show how they can be explained, at least in part, by intra-elite competition.

Population Size and Social Organization

Anthony Snodgrass first identified population growth as crucial to the changes that gave rise to the eighth-century polis. Snodgrass used the evidence for a sharp rise in burial and settlement numbers to argue for a dramatic growth in population across Greece in the eighth century.[16] Despite Ian Morris's 1987 critique of Snodgrass's methodology for its assumption of a direct relation between archaeological remains and population size, historians still accept that in the eighth century there was substantial population growth.[17]

[13] For a critique of modern historians' use of the term "polis," see Gawantka 1985.

[14] See Snodgrass 1980, de Polignac 1984/1995, and I. Morris 1987, respectively, and discussion below.

[15] Some scholars add the Homeric epics as evidence of this phenomenon (e.g., Scully 1990; Bowden 1993; Raaflaub 1997a, 1998c; Hammer 1998, 2002), despite the elite bias of the poems. (See, e.g., I. Morris 1986, Thalmann 1998.) For discussion, see Seaford 1994, Haubold 2000. Wilson 2002 relates the themes of ransom and revenge in the *Iliad* to elite competition for status in the seventh and sixth centuries.

[16] Snodgrass 1980, 15–24.

[17] I. Morris 1998, 75. Snodgrass (1987, 1993) acknowledges the validity of Morris's critique but still claims significant population growth in the eighth century. R. Osborne (1996a, 74–82),

Social anthropologists have long considered population size to be a prime indicator and indeed a causal factor for socio-political organization.[18] Crudely put, the greater the population density, the more complex the social organization. It was partly on the basis of such theories linking population size to social organization that Snodgrass posited the emergence of the early state form of the polis in the eighth century.[19] According to this view, as the population of some communities (e.g., Athens, Argos, Corinth) rose from the hundreds to the thousands, these societies underwent a transition to early statehood. Key features of this transition according to anthropological and sociological theory include the emergence of economic classes (stratification) and the creation of formal leadership positions.[20]

Yet there are problems with this theory as applied to archaic Greece. First, as already mentioned, Morris has demonstrated that eighth-century population growth was not nearly as dramatic as Snodgrass first posited. If Morris is correct, then some communities of Dark Age Greece had already reached the critical mass of population that social anthropologists associate with state formation. Second, the two main criteria for the early state, namely economic stratification and formalization of leadership positions, are hard to determine with any precision from the evidence available for eighth-century Greece (mainly burials and the Homeric epics). Third, and perhaps most important, anthropologists themselves have come to recognize the inadequacy of evolutionary typologies, since historical societies seldom conform to ideal types. Indeed, it is now recognized that economic stratification exists "even in the early phases of evolutionary trajectories leading to early states," and that leadership in both state and non-state societies often involves elements of both achieved (informal) and inherited (formal) status.[21]

A final recent critique of evolutionary models of state formation seems apposite to archaic Greece and points to a more fruitful path for understanding early Greek socio-political development. Theories of social evolution such as the one outlined above generally see the state as a product of systemic forces

---

however, argues for slow and steady population growth from the tenth century onwards. Scheidel 2003 similarly refutes the notion of an eighth-century population explosion and demonstrates the implausibility of annual growth rates of 4 percent (Snodgrass 1980) or even 1.9 percent (Tandy 1997). Nevertheless, Scheidel's argument for a modest 0.25-percent growth rate from the tenth to the fourth century allows for both short-term and regionally specific higher growth rates (e.g., of up to 1 percent). Survey archaeologists have demonstrated the increase in number of settlements from the tenth century onwards, but the implications of this increase for absolute population figures is at present unclear: see R. Osborne 2004.

[18] See Johnson and Earle 2000 for a standard typology. Fried 1967 uses different terminology but offers a similar model.

[19] Snodgrass 1980, 24–25. Conversely, Snodgrass himself (1971, 1993) argues against social complexity in Dark Age Greece on the basis of population size.

[20] See, for example, Johnson and Earle 2000, 245–51; Runciman 1982.

[21] Yoffee 1993, Ferguson 1991. The quotation comes from Yoffee 1993, 62.

such as population growth, pressure on resources, and the consequent need to integrate the community and protect its resources from outsiders through warfare.[22] Recently such "systems" theories of state formation have come under attack as inadequately accounting for the role of human actors ("agents") in socio-political change.[23] Theorists espousing this latter view see the state not as the adaptive outcome of the need to balance populations and resources, but as "contingent and negotiated, the composite outcome of strategy, counter-strategy and the unforeseen consequences of human action."[24]

With regard to archaic Greece, the view of the state as a product of population growth and pressure on resources has come to seem inadequate, not least because survey archaeology has demonstrated that there is no evidence of any absolute pressure on resources until the end of the sixth century at the very earliest.[25] In light of the lack of evidence for population pressure, new explanations must be found not only for the emergence of the polis in the eighth century, but also for territorial wars and the explosion of new settlements abroad. I demonstrate in the following sections how social actors, particularly groups of elites competing for power and status, help to explain not only the features of the early polis, but also early Greek warfare and the foundation of new settlements.

Sanctuaries and Burial

Several scholars have pointed to the construction of civic sanctuaries both in polis centers and on the periphery of their territories as indicating the emergence of the polis. Snodgrass argued that the construction of monumental temples in the center of the polis is evidence of fairly advanced state structures able to initiate and coordinate projects requiring considerable resources.[26] De Polignac, on the other hand, argued that the construction of temples on the borders between poleis was a mechanism by which newly forming poleis defined their territories and articulated their collective identities through ritual processions from periphery to center.[27] In general, the evidence for monumentalization of civic sanctuaries and increased dedicatory activity at these sites has been interpreted as an indication of the new focus on the collectivity

[22] Johnson and Earle 2000, 23–37, integrating factors of conflict and cooperation in their model of the development of social complexity. See Carneiro 1970 for a strong statement of the conflict model. Haas (1982, 128–29) has argued that although the evidence for prehistoric state formation slightly favors the conflict model over the cooperation model, the two should not be considered mutually exclusive.

[23] See references in n. 3 above.

[24] Brumfiel 1992, 559.

[25] Foxhall 1997 summarizes the evidence powerfully.

[26] Snodgrass 1980, 58–62. Cf. R. Osborne 1996a, 101–2.

[27] De Polignac 1984/1995. For discussion of this controversial thesis, see de Polignac 1994, J. Hall 1995, Mossé 1995, Strøm 1995; Langdon 1997, 122–24.

at the expense of particular elite families.[28] Moreover, Snodgrass first observed that the increase in dedications at sanctuaries was correlated with a decline in the wealth of individual graves.[29] It is generally accepted that this change reflects constraints placed on elite display by the community.[30] Yet another way of looking at the shift in wealth from private grave to public sanctuary is that elite individuals willingly shifted their resources to sanctuaries because these sites represented a new, more potent venue for gaining status. By displaying their wealth at sites frequented by the community as a whole, and indeed (in the case of extra-urban and Panhellenic sanctuaries) by the wider Greek world, elites gained a powerful new tool in their quest for status both within and beyond their communities.[31]

Indeed, although the construction of monumental temples is often assumed to be a project initiated by and for the community as a whole, it perhaps makes more sense to view them as a product of the need of elites to gain status on an ever widening scale. In fact, it is precisely when smaller communities of leaders and followers merge into larger communities (poleis) that more powerful symbols of status are required. By promoting symbols of collective unity such as cults of patron deities, elites created a potent new context for the display of status. Both anthropological theory and the later literary record can be used to support this interpretation. As Elizabeth Brumfiel argues in regard to New World political development, monumental architecture is often an indication of a competitive situation whereby elites attempt to create and/or reinforce both vertical bonds with followers and horizontal bonds with potential elite allies.[32] With regard to archaic Greece, the relation between public building projects and intra-elite competition is most visible in the case of late archaic Athens, where elite families engaged in public construction projects both within the polis (e.g., Pisistratid construction of fountain houses, altars, and temples) and beyond (e.g., the Alcmeonid reconstruction of the Temple of Apollo at Delphi) as a means of gaining

[28] The evidence of hero cult is sometimes also adduced as an indication of collective polis identity. For discussion, see Snodgrass 1980, 38–40; and 1982; Bérard 1982; de Polignac 1984/ 1995, 128–49; Malkin 1987, 1993; I. Morris 1988; Whitley 1988, 1995; Alcock 1991 (for the role of hero cult in the crisis of the post-classical polis); Antonaccio 1993/1998, 1995. Antonaccio (1995, 6), however, distinguishes between hero cult and tomb cult, and argues, following Malkin (1987, 261–66) that hero cult post-dates the rise of the polis, which "uses heroes to focus civic and political identity." See Boedeker 1993/1998 for a fascinating application of this idea to the case of the bones of Orestes and Spartan civic identity.

[29] Snodgrass 1980, 52–54.

[30] R. Osborne 1996a, 101.

[31] De Polignac 1984/1995, 11–13. As R. Osborne (1996a, 101) says in reference to Panhellenic sanctuaries: "to make a display in burial was to make a display to a local community; to make a display in some sanctuaries, if not all, was to make a display to a wider Greek world."

[32] Brumfiel 1994, 11. Snodgrass's (1986) theory that temple construction is a form of peer-polity interaction can be adapted to indicate a competitive situation between polis elites rather than poleis as collectivities.

political support from elites and non-elites in their on-going struggle for power within the polis.[33]

In sum, the construction of monumental temples and the increase in dedicatory activity are not necessarily signs of the dominance of a new collectivity of polis citizens over the self-aggrandizing and self-interested activities of elites. Rather, elites continue to pursue their individualistic quest for power within the new civic structures; indeed, elites may have been responsible for the promotion of formerly local cults to their new civic role. By transforming these cults, elites established a new arena for the display of status to the wider community—a useful tool in their competition with other elites. On this interpretation, state institutions such as civic sanctuaries and non-state associations such as alliances between particular elite leaders and their followers co-evolve and co-exist—a fact that helps to explain the continuing importance of intra-elite alliance formation and dissolution in later archaic Greek history, as we shall see.

Finally, a word must be said about burial. As I have already noted, Snodgrass, Morris, and others have argued that changes in the burial record in the late eighth century indicate restrictions on elite display in favor of the new ideal of a community of politically equal citizens.[34] In addition to the decline in the wealth of graves in the late eighth century, these scholars point to the shift in the location of burials from within the settlement to outside the habitation area. As Robin Osborne puts it, "it is tempting to see the exclusion of burials from the central and prominent areas as [non-elite] control on one aspect of display by the elite."[35] Yet one may well wonder whether this and other changes in the burial record reflect not constraints placed on the elite by the non-elite community but instead a shift of interest of the elite from the rather limited context of burial to the more powerful symbolic context of the collective sanctuary.[36] Indeed, the central civic sanctuaries where elites displayed their wealth and status (most strikingly in the form of bronze tripod cauldrons) were at least as prominently located as the earlier elite burials within the settlement.[37]

Brief consideration of the changes in the burial record at Athens (the case most discussed) strengthen this interpretation.[38] First, as James Whitley has observed, despite the general decline in the wealth of graves in the late eighth

[33] I make this argument fully in Forsdyke, "Peisistratus" (in prep. a).

[34] Snodgrass 1980, 54; I. Morris 1987; R. Osborne 1996a. Whitley 1991b points to the increased diversity of grave goods and the decline in surface visibility of the grave as further indications of the breakdown of social rationing of goods by the elite.

[35] R. Osborne 1996a, 84.

[36] Compare R. Osborne 1996a, 101, as cited above in n. 31.

[37] For the bronze tripod cauldrons, see Hurwit 1998, 93.

[38] I rely on I. Morris 1987, Whitley 1991b, and Houby-Nielsen 1992 for the descriptions of burial changes that follow.

century, there continue to be some rich graves.[39] If there were indeed communally enforced restrictions on displays of wealth, one would expect all graves to conform to the same standard. Furthermore, although overall the wealth of graves themselves diminishes, by 700 a new feature of burials, the offering trench, allows for conspicuous consumption in the form of ritual destruction of wealth. Finally, despite the decline in the surface visibility of the grave itself in the late eighth century, by the seventh century graves are marked by mounds, and by the sixth century mudbrick tombs and funerary sculpture begin to appear. Morris has interpreted the seventh-century changes at Athens as a regression to a more hierarchical social organization. More plausibly, however, a number of scholars have interpreted the changes as a sign of the ongoing quest for new ways to assert elite status in the context of fierce intra-elite competition for power.[40] In this light, one might well wonder whether Whitley's observation of an increasing diversity of grave goods in the late eighth century is less a sign of the breakdown of elite exclusivity and the emergence of an egalitarian polis than an indication of intensified competition for power among the elite in a newly consolidating polis community. Indeed it is precisely in the context of the consolidation of smaller communities into a single larger entity that we would expect older markers of status to cease to have meaning and new, more powerful means of displaying status to be found. It is in this context that the creation of, and focus on, new collective symbols of the polis (civic sanctuaries) is most readily explicable.[41]

Agriculture and Trade, Warfare and Colonization

In addition to the changes in burial and cultic activity, scholars have pointed to the beginnings of territorial wars, as well as the foundation of new settlements abroad, as indications of a fairly developed state structure able to coordinate collective warfare and organize the resettlement of portions of its population abroad. Moreover, with regard to warfare, scholars have argued that the existence, by the late eighth or early seventh century, of fighting in massed ranks of heavily armed infantry indicates the central place of a group of citizen-soldiers in the political structure of the early polis.[42] In short, early warfare and the foundation of new settlements abroad have been taken as clear indications of an integrated state structure serving the needs of the mass of non-elite citizens, particularly in the acquisition or defense of agricultural land.

---

[39] Whitley 1991b. In particular, rich female burials continue. Although the metal wealth of graves declines, graves still contain faience, ivory, and luxury goods from the East.

[40] Houby-Nielsen 1992, 1995, 1996; R. Osborne 1996a, 85.

[41] The restrictions placed on funerary display in later archaic legislation are best explained as designed to curb violent intra-elite conflict, as is argued by Seaford 1994, 74–86.

[42] Raaflaub 1999, 134–37, with earlier scholarship.

Although I would not wish to deny the existence by the late eighth century of certain polis-wide communal structures capable of acting in concert for collective purposes (e.g., the assembly, tribal divisions), it is still possible to stress the role of intra-elite competition both in the creation of these institutions and in the activities that they perform. In what follows, I briefly indicate the role of elite rivalry in the formation of the institutional structure of the polis that we know best, Athens. Following this argument, I turn to early Greek warfare and colonization to show how these phenomena can be interpreted, at least in part, as functions of the quest of individuals (particularly the elite) for wealth and status, rather than as collective responses to problems of land hunger or overpopulation.

Recent studies of the material evidence for Dark Age and early archaic Attica suggest that, following a contraction of settlement in the early eleventh century, the Attic countryside was resettled from the center.[43] The motivation for movement back into the countryside appears to have been the desire to exploit the resources—particularly agricultural—of Attica.[44] Indeed, some of the richest graves from this period come from outside Athens.[45] The pattern of movement from center to periphery, as well as similarities in the contents of wealthy burials in Athens and Attica, suggests that there was at least a loose unity between the two even from the early Dark Age.[46] By the seventh century, ties between Athens and Attica were made more formal through the creation of public offices for which elites from throughout Attica were eligible.[47] In addition, at this time previously existing local cultic and real or fictive kinship groups—for example, the tribes (φυλαί) and brotherhoods (φρατρίαι)—were appropriated and adapted to new collective institutions of the polis.[48] The question remains, What prompted the formalization and regularization of relations between elites and local groups in Attica, and to what degree were personal and local ties undermined by this process?

[43] Whitley 1991b, 55–57; R. Osborne 1994a. Whitley 1991b summarizes the evidence (chap. 3) and provides a useful catalogue of settlement and burial evidence for Athens and Attica, with publication data (appendix).

[44] Mazarakis-Ainian 1995 (on Lathouriza).

[45] Coldstream 1977, 133–34; cited by Whitley 1991b, 57. The evidence of tomb cult (votive dedications at Mycenaean tombs) is sometimes drawn in as evidence of tension over land in local communities of Attica as a result of internal colonization: see Snodgrass 1982, Whitley 1988.

[46] Whitley 1991b, 56–57; R. Osborne 1994a.

[47] For the association of the earliest known Athenian archons (e.g., Pisistratus [669/8], Miltiades [664/3], and Megacles [?632/1]) with particular regions in Attica, see below, chap. 3.

[48] Through this formulation, I acknowledge that it is likely that these groups existed before the emergence of the polis but were put to new uses within the polis context. Some scholars have argued that the φυλαί and φρατρίαι were creations of the eighth-century polis: Andrewes 1961a, 1961b; Bourriot 1976; Roussel 1976. For discussion, see Donlan 1985; R. Smith 1985; Manville 1990, 55–69; J. Hall 1997, 4–16. Nagy (1990a, 276–93) defends the traditional view of the Indo-European roots of the φυλαί and φρατρίαι.

Two features of the early polis—public offices and written law—suggest that intra-elite competition was one cause of the creation of formal polis institutions. As Lin Foxhall notes, the earliest surviving archon list from Athens looks "like rivals in the playground taking turns."[49] That is to say, the creation of public offices was a mechanism for ensuring the orderly rotation of power among rival elites. Moreover, it has been widely noted that many of the earliest written laws are directly concerned with the orderly rotation of public office among elites, or seem to deal with the consequences of violence arising from intra-elite competition for power.[50] It seems that one major aim of the earliest written laws, then, was to affirm the rules for rotation of public office, which were apparently being repeatedly transgressed.[51] By putting these laws in physical form and by invoking the authority of the gods either explicitly on the stone or by placing the stone in a sanctuary, communal and divine support were brought to the fragile public offices of the early polis.[52] I argue in chapter 3 that written law was ultimately unsuccessful in regulating violent intra-elite conflict; nevertheless, it did have the unintended consequence of strengthening collective polis identity and institutions, a precondition for the later active participation of non-elites in the regulation of conflict among the elite. The important point here, however, is that both formal public offices and early written law were, at least in part, responses to the problem of intra-elite conflict in the early polis.[53]

Another symptom of intensified competition among the elite for status and power in the early polis is a rise in the number of settlements in Attica in the eighth century.[54] It is likely, as already mentioned, that this internal colonization was motivated by a desire to exploit the agricultural resources of Attica. Since there is no sign of overpopulation or that the landscape had reached its

---

[49] Foxhall 1997, 120.

[50] ML 2 (= van Effenterre 1994, 81: Dreros); IC 4:14 (= van Effenterre 1994, 82: Gortyn). Van Effenterre also argues that a very fragmentary law (IC 2:12.4 [= van Effenterre 1994, 83: Eleutherne]) also concerns the iteration of office. A more complete inscription (IK Erythrae 17 [= van Effenterre 1994, 85: Erythrae]), dating somewhere between the mid-sixth and early fifth century, concerns the iteration of office of the apparently important posts of the guardians of the marshes and secretary. Early Athenian law also supports this interpretation: see my discussion of the early anti-tyranny law (Ath. Pol. 16.10) and Draco's homicide law (IG 1³ 104) in chapter 3 below.

[51] R. Osborne 1996a, 189–90, 192–93. For early law as an ad hoc response to particular crises of the archaic polis, see Holkeskamp 1992, 1999.

[52] See Thomas 1992 on the significance of publication of law and its placement in sanctuaries. Recent research, moreover, has undermined the view that written law was a response to the demand for the democratization of justice: see Gagarin 1986, 121–26; Thomas 1992, 67. Compare R. Osborne (1996a, 187) on early law: "This is *elite self-regulation*, motivated not by any sense of overwhelming injustice but by a concern about which individuals have power" (my italics).

[53] Compare Foxhall 1997, 120: "At one level the ragged bundle of institutions we call the 'state' in Archaic Greece are little more than the concrete outcome of the attempt to resolve these [i.e., intra-elite] tensions."

[54] Whitley (1991b, 199–201) shows that the number of sites triples in the late eighth century.

carrying capacity, it is likely that the increased pace of movement into the surrounding territory was a product not simply of population growth, but of the desire to increase agricultural productivity for market trade.[55] Indeed, it is precisely in the late eighth century that there is evidence for Athenian involvement in overseas trade. Athenian amphoras (the so-called SOS amphoras) dating from the late eighth to the first half of the sixth century have been found in a large number of sites throughout the Mediterranean and beyond.[56] It is likely that these amphoras contained olive oil, but it is possible that they were also used to transport other agricultural products, including wine and grain.[57]

Although the question of which social classes engaged in market trade is complex, it is likely that the prime movers in these developments were the elite, since they had the resources both to increase the exploitation of the land (animals, seed corn, dependent labor) and to build ships to transport the surplus production. The fact that Athenian agricultural products seem to have been exchanged for luxury or semi-luxury goods (not subsistence needs) also suggests that elite needs lie behind the increase in production and trade.[58] Though I lay stress on elite needs in these developments, it is likely that some portion of other social classes also benefited from increased agricultural production and expanded trade networks.[59] By the sixth century, moreover, there are signs in several poleis of a group of wealthy citizens who begin to demand the privilege of eligibility for public offices formerly restricted to the older ruling elite.[60] Nevertheless, my point here is that the eighth-century phenomena of increased numbers of settlements in the countryside and the corresponding increase in production for market trade can be taken not simply as indications of increased population and the consequent need to increase agricultural production, but also as symptoms of the elite drive for wealth and status in the newly consolidating polis community.

[55] I make this and the following arguments more extensively in Forsdyke, "Land" (forthcoming).

[56] Johnston and Jones 1978. See Gras (1987, 1995) and Whitbread (1995) for recent discussion.

[57] Foxhall 1998. Solon's law (Plut. Sol. 24.1) forbidding the export of agricultural produce except for olive oil implies that other products besides oil were being exported prior to his legislation. By the mid-sixth century the number of SOS amphoras declines, but there is a marked increase in exports of Attic fine pottery—which, as R. Osborne 1996b argues, is a sign that Athenian products continued to be distributed widely throughout the Mediterranean in the sixth century.

[58] The term "semi-luxury" is from Foxhall 1998. Foxhall argues that Athenian imports would have included highly prized wheat, metals, timber, fish, and luxury manufactured goods.

[59] The poor, however, were directly harmed by these and related trends: see below, chapter 2 on Megara and chapter 3 on Solon. For a comparative example of the enrichment of non-elite farmers as a consequence of elite-driven changes in the economy, see Underdown (1985, 24–28) on early modern England. See also Foxhall 1998, who stresses that even non-elites had access to luxuries and semi-luxuries, although in smaller quantities than the elites.

[60] The best evidence is Solon's property classes, which replace birth with wealth as the criterion for public office. (See below, chapter 3.) Furthermore, some archaic poetry (especially in Solon and Theognis) may be interpreted as elite repudiation of a class of newly wealthy non-elite: see below, chapters 2 and 3).

If we turn back to two further features of the eighth-century polis—new settlements abroad (colonization) and territorial wars—they too can be explained, at least in part, as consequences of intra-elite competition for wealth and status.[61] To begin with, it is increasingly recognized that these developments were not a product of overpopulation and land hunger;[62] rather, individual adventurism in the pursuit of gain may lie behind them.[63] As in the case of the internal colonization of Attica (and other poleis' territories), moreover, it is likely that the elites were on the forefront of the push for wealth and profits, since it was they who had both the incentive (status competition) and the resources to exploit the new territories and new opportunities for market trade. Once again, some non-elites certainly benefited from new settlements and the acquisition of territory, but it was not non-elite subsistence needs driving these movements.

Similarly, if, as I have argued, the recolonization of Attica during the Dark Age was led by elites in order to create agricultural surplus for purposes of market trade, then it is likely that elite interests were also at stake in the territorial wars of the eighth century and later. In other words, elites had a clear interest in organizing mass armies to defend polis territory, and therefore early territorial wars can be explained, at least in part, as a consequence of the need of elites to protect or increase the agricultural land under their control.[64] Naturally, non-elites had an interest in defending their lands as well, a fact that made it easier for elites to create a communal army. Nevertheless, the elites' quest for wealth in order to engage in status rivalry with one another may have been a primary cause of the increased settlement of Attica, the formation of polis-wide citizen armies, the beginnings of territorial conflict between rival polis communities, and new settlements abroad.

Conclusion

In this chapter I have briefly surveyed the principal explanations for the emergence of the polis in eighth-century Greece. While not denying the relevance of the chief factors cited by other scholars (e.g., population growth, class conflict, the emergence of a middling ideology), I lay emphasis on the role of intra-elite conflict as a driving force behind the political developments of this period. I have argued that the defining features of the early polis—a rise in settlement evidence, monumental civic sanctuaries, changes in burial

[61] For a survey of early Greek settlements abroad, see Graham 1982. For early Greek warfare, see Raaflaub 1999.

[62] De Angelis 1994, Foxhall 1997, R. Osborne 1998.

[63] For early settlements abroad as a product of the pursuit of gain, see R. Osborne 1998, 257–59, 268.

[64] Even in the case of the Spartan conquest of Messenia, it is unlikely that subsistence needs explain the drive to acquire new territory. For discussion, see appendix 3 below.

practices, territorial wars, citizen armies, new settlements abroad, formal public offices, written law—can all be related to intra-elite competition for power in the newly forming communities of late Geometric and early archaic Greece.

My emphasis on intra-elite competition in the earliest phases of the polis sets the stage for the principal argument in subsequent chapters, namely that intra-elite competition in the form of violent intra-elite politics of exile was a key factor in later archaic political developments, especially the emergence of democracy in late sixth-century Athens. Before turning to Athens, however, I present in chapter 2 case studies of four poleis, Mytilene, Samos, Megara, and Corinth. I demonstrate through these examples that the problem of intra-elite politics of exile was a Panhellenic phenomenon, evoking divergent responses in different communities of archaic Greece. Nevertheless, in each case, the problem of intra-elite competition ultimately resulted in a strengthening of communal or state structures at the expense of elite power.

Chapter Two

THE POLITICS OF EXILE AND THE CRISIS
OF THE ARCHAIC POLIS

Four Case Studies: Mytilene, Megara, Samos, and Corinth

IN chapter 1, I argued that intra-elite competition was a key factor in the emergence and early development of the polis. In this chapter, I demonstrate that conflict between elites in archaic Greece often took the form of violent expulsions, and that this manner of conducting politics led to frequent changes of power as rivals exiled one another and fought one another to return. The four case studies, therefore, establish the broad context against which the role of exile in Athenian history is analyzed in subsequent chapters. I argue in the following chapters that the bizarre institution of ostracism, and indeed the Athenian democracy itself, can be best understood as Athens' unique response to the Panhellenic problem of exile.

More specifically, these comparative examples demonstrate that although violent intra-elite conflict was a common feature of the archaic polis, there was nothing inevitable about the development of democracy as a response. For example, at Mytilene, intra-elite factionalism was resolved through the establishment of a tyrant, Pittacus. Although a significant number of non-elites seem to have played a role in Pittacus's election, their action did not lead to an overturning of elite leadership in favor of popular rule. At Megara, a combination of violent intra-elite competition and rapid socio-economic change provoked the ruling elites to be extra responsive to the needs of non-elites (e.g., through Return of Interest legislation). This strategy seems to have forestalled major changes to elite rule. At Samos, intra-elite competition resulted in the emergence of the tyrannical family of Polycrates, who maintained power through limited expulsions of their rivals and, more important, by forging good relations with the rest of the Samian elite. Similarly, at Corinth, the Bacchiads and then the Cypselids ruled successfully by expelling their most immediate rivals, and by otherwise ruling benevolently. In all four cases, then, tyranny or oligarchy, not democracy, was the end product of intra-elite conflict.

In "Archaic Poetry and History" below, I discuss the problem of our sources for archaic Greek history. Specifically, this section examines the relation between the poetry produced in archaic Greek poleis and the history of those poleis. I argue that, despite the tendency of local poetic traditions to adapt to Panhellenic poetic norms, not all elements of the original performance context are lost. On this basis, I argue that the poems can reveal some aspects of the social, political, and cultural conditions of specific Greek poleis in the archaic period.

In the section "Mytilene" below, I turn to the polis of that name. Here I demonstrate that the material and textual evidence for archaic Mytilene suggests that intra-elite competition both furthered the political development of the polis and led to a crisis in the late seventh century. In particular, textual evidence for a dramatic series of expulsions and returns involving rival elite groups reveals that archaic Mytilene suffered the destabilizing consequences of intense intra-elite politics of exile. Remarkably, this crisis was resolved through the apparently spontaneous intervention of the Mytilenean people in the conflict between elites. Although this solution to the problem of exile anticipated by a century similar events in Athens, as I argue in chapter 3, the action of the Mytilenean people did not permanently alter the political structure of the Mytilenean polis. In contrast to the Athenian case, the action of the Mytilenean demos did not overthrow elite forms of rule (tyranny, oligarchy). Nevertheless, the intervention of the Mytilenean demos in intra-elite politics of exile served as a powerful warning to the elites of the consequences of letting their rivalry threaten the well-being of the polis as a whole.

The next section turns to the case of Megara. Here I argue that the poetry of Theognis as well as anecdotes about early Megarian history in Aristotle and Plutarch reveal that Megara was also suffering from violent intra-elite conflict in the seventh and sixth centuries. In contrast to ancient and modern analyses of early Megarian history, however, I show that both the tyranny of Theagenes in the late seventh century and the frequent changes of regime in the sixth century were not the product of conflict between elites and non-elites (class conflict), but rather a result of violent intra-elite conflict. I argue that Theagenes' slaughter of the cattle of the rich was not an act designed to appeal to oppressed non-elites, as Aristotle claims, but rather an example of the typical violence and destruction of property associated with violent intra-elite politics of exile. More important, I argue that modern acceptance of ancient claims that a radical democracy was installed in sixth-century Megara is based on misreadings of social rituals of inversion involving elites and non-elites. Comparative examples from other pre-modern societies show that descriptions of popular revelry involving social inversion at Megara were misinterpreted by Aristotle and Plutarch as typical instances of democratic social disorder (ἀταξία). While I do not deny that there were strong economic tensions between elite and non-elite Megarians as a result of population growth and new market opportunities, I argue that these tensions were resolved through economic measures (for example, the so-called Return of Interest) rather than democratic reforms. In sum, the frequent changes of power in archaic Megara are best explained as products of violent intra-elite politics of exile rather than non-elite rebellion against elite rule.

In the next section, I examine the case of archaic Samos, showing that the overthrow of an oligarchy of landowning elites (the so-called geomoroi) and the subsequent struggles for power among a smaller group of elites associated with the family of the tyrant Polycrates indicate that Samos, like Mytilene and Megara, was suffering from intense intra-elite conflict in the late seventh and sixth centuries. Nevertheless, I argue that the relative dominance of the family of Polycrates throughout the sixth century is best explained by the tyrants' cultivation of alliances with a fairly broad section of the elite. Contrary to ancient accounts of mass expulsions perpetrated by Polycrates against the Samian population, I argue that exile affected only the elites—and a small fraction of them, at that. As I demonstrate in chapter 6, traditions of mass expulsions under archaic tyrants are best explained as products of fifth- and fourth-century (democratic) representations of tyranny. In reality, Polycrates and his predecessors, Syloson and Aiakes, largely abstained from expelling their opponents. Furthermore, these tyrants engaged in policies that appealed to elites and non-elites alike, such as those facilitating trade or enhancing civic cult. In this way, the Samian tyrants maintained their power in the polis without the apparent need for radical political change.

The case of Corinth is examined in the penultimate section of this chapter. As with Samos, despite literary traditions of mass expulsions perpetrated by the Bacchiad oligarchy and its successor the Cypselid tyranny, the evidence suggests that only small numbers of elites went into exile under these regimes. Critical examination of the material and textual evidence for the Cypselid tyranny shows that, while the tyrants banished some members of the Bacchiad family, their general manner of rule was favorable to both elite and non-elite Corinthians. The longevity of Cypselid rule, and indeed of the oligarchies that preceded and followed that family's tyranny, suggests that ruling elites in Corinth largely managed to circumvent the destabilizing effects of intra-elite politics of exile by enticing rival elites to cooperate with their regime.

Archaic Poetry and History: A Methodological Introduction

The case studies presented below rely heavily (but not solely) on literary evidence, particularly archaic poetry, in order to reconstruct political events of the seventh and sixth centuries. The use of archaic poetry to understand the historical development of archaic poleis is particularly problematic, not only because of the allusive nature of the genre but, more important, because the poets partook of common literary conventions and themes, which may have had little to do with the time and place of any particular poet. In the most extreme form of this view, Gregory Nagy has argued that the poetry preserved under the names of Hesiod and Theognis, for instance, represents the adaptation of various local poetic traditions to a Panhellenic form, in which common features have been emphasized and local peculiarities have dropped out. While this thesis has long been accepted in regard to the Homeric texts, Nagy has extended it to apply not only to the hexameter and elegiac poets but also to the lyric poets. According to Nagy, the increased intercommunication between poleis in the Greek world beginning in the eighth century allowed for increased communication between local poetic traditions, and hence the assimilation of local traditions to Panhellenic norms.[1]

Nagy's model presents obvious problems for the use of archaic poetry to reconstruct the history of a particular polis or poet. As Ian Morris puts it, the model has two implications for historians: "First, . . . we can only approach the main body of texts synchronically. . . . Second, we cannot reconstruct specific events."[2] I will argue that Morris is only partly correct in each of these statements: that is, even according to Nagy's model, the texts can be understood diachronically, at least in part, and we may see in them some reflection of the historical conditions of their original composition. To some extent, this claim must be proved in regard to the specific problems associated with the poetry of each of the major poets discussed below, but some general points may be made that apply to all archaic Greek poetry.

First of all, Nagy's model does not refute altogether the historical existence of the archaic poets or the characters in their poems (e.g., Perses, Pittacus, Cyrnus). Rather, Nagy argues that the historical characters have been transformed into generic ones, and that the figure of the poet is absorbed by the tradition.[3] In other words, Nagy's model allows for an original poet and performance, but cautions that much of the historical distinctiveness of the original poem has been sacrificed to the aim of achieving Panhellenic status, a process of assimilation that took place over time through repeated recomposition in performance. Thus Nagy writes in regard to Pindaric lyric: "though each of Pindar's victory odes *was an occasional composition, centering on a single performance, each containing details grounded in the historical realities of the time and place of performance*, still each of these victory odes aimed at translating its occasion into a Panhellenic event, a thing of beauty that could be replayed by and for all Hellenes for all time to come."[4]

The acknowledgment of the existence of a historical poet and original performance opens up the possibility of remnants of the original performance being not fully elided in the process of adaptation to Panhellenic forms. In other words, although the historical aspects of the poem and poet may be downplayed in favor of the generic aspects, these features do not

[1] Nagy 1990b, especially 52–115.
[2] I. Morris 1996, 26–27.
[3] Nagy 1990b, 79.
[4] Nagy 1990b, 114 (my italics).

disappear altogether.[5] Nagy, in fact, is fully aware that even the process of transformation of local traditions into a common tradition does not prevent the survival of local variations within the common one.[6] Similarly, the work of Jan Vansina on the oral traditions of modern Africa has shown that the process of adapting past traditions to present conditions often leaves relics of earlier traditions within their current counterparts.[7] These remnants of earlier traditions or, in the case of archaic Greek poetry, remnants of local traditions provide a window through which the historical context of the original poem can, at least in part, be reconstructed.

Second, we might note that the generic features of archaic poetry are themselves a form of historical evidence for the worldview of the Greeks in the archaic period, and therefore may provide clues to the broad historical context in which they arose. As Leslie Kurke and Ian Morris have shown, the very similarities of theme in the songs of the archaic poets are significant for understanding in broad terms the ideologies or "competing systems of value" within the archaic poleis.[8] These scholars argue that all archaic poetry can be classified as adhering to either an elitist tradition or a middling tradition, and that these traditions reflect tensions arising from the changing social, economic, and political conditions of the archaic poleis. Although I will contest certain aspects of this interpretation below, their general point is extremely important: the shared topoi of archaic poetry evolved because they were meaningful to a large number of poleis over a long period of time;[9] these topoi were meaningful, furthermore, because they reflected the shared experience of these poleis. We might note besides that since the aim of this

[5] This corresponds with the conclusion reached by Robin Lane Fox (2000, 37) in his discussion of the problem of the corpus of Theognis: "It is wrong to argue that poetry addressing local circumstances could not be widely received elsewhere: we need only to think of Alcaeus or Attic comedy. A balanced view is preferable. The poems do sometimes refer to events in the poet's own city and to specific mishaps elsewhere, but not so pervasively that they could not travel and appeal beyond their context."

[6] Nagy 1990b, 60n.42: "This is not to say, of course, that the convergent version may not be complex, containing multiformities within its overarching uniformity." Nagy's whole methodology, moreover, depends on the ability to detect earlier and later layers of tradition, as well as local and Panhellenic versions, and thus he uses the term "stratigraphy" (e.g., p. 76). Nagy considers that the epic cycle, for instance, not only represents local traditions as opposed to the Panhellenic traditions of Homer, but also preserves earlier layers of tradition as opposed to the more rapidly evolving traditions of Homer (pp. 70–79).

[7] Vansina 1985, 118–25. See, for example, p. 122: "Social change often leads to additions, not to suppression, leaving older variants intact. Items that tend to be suppressed leave traces." See also Forsdyke 1999 for the application of Vansina's model to oral traditions in Herodotus.

[8] Kurke 1992; 1994; 1999, 19–23; I. Morris 1996, 27–28.

[9] See, for example, Nagy 1990b, 67: "What is particular to Megara alone...tends to be shaded over; what is shared by Megara and by a wide variety of other city-states is highlighted." While Nagy is particularly interested in myth and ritual, the principle is valid with regard to the political themes and values of archaic poetry. See Nagy 1985.

chapter as a whole is to provide a generalized historical context of archaic Greek political development against which the better-documented history of Athens may be drawn, the Panhellenic character of much archaic poetry is an asset, not a loss.

Two further points can be made regarding the connections between archaic poetry and history. First, it is generally agreed that archaic lyric and elegy were performed in a symposiastic setting.[10] Since we know that the symposium was an important part of elite social and political life, and that the elites held political power in the archaic poleis, it is likely that the poems performed in this context were "deeply embroiled in the political, social and economic issues of the day."[11] That is not to say that all the poems must be understood in strictly political terms. Certainly, many of the poems relate to general issues, such as youth and old age, man's relationship with the gods, and the joys of food and drink. It is easy to imagine that such poems were performed as entertainment in symposia by generations of elites.[12]

Yet it is equally undeniable that many poems reveal, in their specific details, clear links with the social, economic, and political problems of particular poleis at particular points in time. The boundary markers (ὅροι) of Solon (fr. 36 West) are one such example. Since such poems must also have been performed repeatedly in symposiastic settings over time (and thus survived to be recorded),[13] we must imagine that references to the details of the specific historical circumstances of their composition must have been dealt with in one of two ways by later performers and audiences. Either references to the specific historical circumstances of the original composition were downplayed in favor of the generic themes, or specific historical references in the poems were given equal prominence with the generic themes and served as part of the oral tradition of the history of the community. Since we know that oral traditions tend to slough off elements that are no longer meaningful to their audiences, we must imagine that the historically specific details were meaningful because they served to maintain memories of the history of the community.

[10] E. Bowie 1986, 1990. For the symposiastic setting of Alcaeus's lyric, see Rösler 1980; and below.

[11] Kurke 1992, 92.

[12] See especially Theognis 239–43, where the poet foresees that his songs about Cyrnus will be performed at future symposia. Solon fr. 27 West, on the ten periods of a man's life, is a good example of a poem that may have been performed, not necessarily verbatim, repeatedly over time. On the kinds of symposiastic recitation and of games of capping, which presumably would have drawn on a shared body of inherited poetry, see Collins 2004.

[13] Lane Fox (2000, 45) reminds us, however, that even given the role of the symposia in the oral transmission of archaic poetry, these poems must have circulated in written form by the sixth century at the latest. Friis Johansen (1993, 26–29) argues that the idea of a seal in Theognis presupposes a fixed written text, and on this ground proposes that Theognis is to be dated in the sixth century, not the seventh as West (1974, 65–71) proposes. Friis Johansen also argues that the linguistic evidence for lines 19–38 suggests a date no earlier than c. 550.

This brings up a final point. The historical ties between poetry and polis can often be confirmed by later sources. It is certainly true that later sources often had nothing more than the poems themselves to go on, and often reconstructed the historical context of the poems anachronistically according to their own times and places. Yet not only did later ancient sources usually have more of the original poems to interpret than we do, but these sources often had access to other sources for the traditions and history of the archaic poleis. This fact is clear from later sources' use of certain archaisms. For example, the terms "sixth-parters" (ἑκτήμοροι) and "Shaking-off of Burdens" (σεισάχθεια) preserved in Aristotle, and "Return of Interest" (παλιντοκία) preserved in Plutarch, suggest that these authors had access to additional traditions no longer available to us.[14] More broadly, whole anecdotes preserved in later sources (particularly Aristotle and Plutarch) regarding the political history of various poleis often show signs of their origins in archaic oral traditions and thus can help provide the context in which links can be made between history and poetry. A good example of such an anecdote is Aristotle's account of the slaughter of the cattle of the rich in Megara, which, even if it is not historical, I argue reflects both the primary basis of wealth among the Megarian elite and tensions between elites in the archaic period.[15]

MYTILENE

The city of Mytilene, on Lesbos, provides the first example of the role of exile in the political development of the archaic poleis. Not only did the elites of archaic Mytilene utilize exile as a means of competing for power, but the continual back-and-forth movement of elites from power to exile so destabilized the polis that it precipitated a crisis of the political order. A few features of the geography and history are helpful for putting Mytilene's problem of exile in its local context.

Lesbos is located on the eastern edge of the Greek world, and thus hovers in the borderland "between East and West."[16] A natural consequence of this location is that its culture shares as much with the non-Greek cultures of the Troad and northwestern Anatolia as it does with mainland Greece and the Aegean.[17] Despite the obvious difference provided by geography, however,

---

[14] *Ath. Pol.* 2, 6; Plut. *Quaest. Graec.* 18 (*Mor.* 295d).

[15] *Pol.* 1305a8–28; and see my discussion below.

[16] This phrase is applied to Lesbos by Spencer 1995a. Much of the material in the following paragraphs is drawn from Spencer's important article, which brings together previously unpublished and obscurely published archaeological evidence for Lesbian culture and history from the Bronze Age to the early Iron Age.

[17] One of the best examples of the blending of Eastern and Western culture in Lesbos may be found in cultic practice. In Lesbos in general and Mytilene in particular, the joint worship of the

Lesbos seems to have experienced some of the major developments of late Bronze Age and early Iron Age Greece. The Bronze Age settlements of Lesbos were destroyed or abandoned from the fourteenth through twelfth centuries and were resettled in the early Iron Age. Greek tradition held that Lesbos was settled by Greeks from Boeotia and Thessaly, a tradition confirmed by dialectal similarities between these regions. Mytilene and Pyrrha appear to have been the first sites settled, soon followed by Methymna and Antissa. Finds from the other two poleis of Lesbos, Eresus and Arisbe, have so far been dated only to the archaic period. It is unclear whether this pattern of settlement reflects successive waves of colonization from mainland Greece or the original colonists of Mytilene and Pyrrha subsequently migrated to the other settlements.

What is clear from the material record is that during the early archaic period, there was a strong drive to acquire agricultural land. First, it is noteworthy that each of the six poleis of archaic Lesbos controlled a portion of the arable plains of the island.[18] Moreover, Herodotus tells us that at some time in the archaic period, Methymna annexed Arisbe, thereby reducing the number of poleis on the island to five.[19] Methymna's choice to annex Arisbe rather than its other neighbor, Antissa, seems to have been motivated by Arisbe's possession of the largest arable plain on the island.[20] The settlement of the Troad from Lesbos, furthermore, and conflict between Mytilene and Athens over Sigeum in the late seventh century confirm the drive to acquire land.[21]

A further indication of the importance of land in archaic Lesbos is a group of nineteen monumental stone towers and enclosures in prominent locations in the rural landscape. Nigel Spencer has argued that these towers had a largely symbolic function at both the intra- and the extra-polis level.[22] Noting the expensive and prestigious style of masonry employed in their construction, Spencer argues that the elites of the Lesbian poleis built them "as status symbols ... marking social differentiation within the polis."[23] The location of these status symbols on

---

Greek god Apollo and the Anatolian goddess Cybele is attested both by Alcaeus (fr. 129 Campbell) and by epigraphical evidence (Spencer 1995a, 296–99). See also the dual foundation stories discussed below.

[18] See the map of the poleis and plains in Spencer 2000, 69.

[19] Hdt. 1.151.2.

[20] Mason (1993, 230), who suggests that the annexation of Arisbe by Methymna was a consequence of Mytilene's exclusion of Methymna from colonial expansion in the Troad. See also Spencer 1995b, 38.

[21] Settlement of the Troad from Lesbos: Spencer 1995b, 38, citing Strabo 13.1.58 and 13.2.1, and modern studies of the archaeology of this area that reveal cultural ties between Lesbos and this region. See also Mason 1993, 226–29. Conflict between Mytilene and Athens over Sigeum: Strabo 13.1.38–39, Hdt. 5.94–95, D.L. 1.74, Diod. Sic. 9.12.1, with discussion by Spencer 2000, 78–79.

[22] Spencer 1995b. See also Mason (1993, 230) on the towers as testimony of inter-polis competition for land.

[23] Spencer 1995b, 37.

the margins of the polis territories, rather than in the center of the settlement, seems significant and may be related the importance of land as the basis of elite wealth. Spencer has argued that the marginal location of the towers may also be explained by inter-polis rivalry, in particular over the resources of the land. Extending François de Polignac's theory of the role of rural cult structures in defining the polis geographically, Spencer argues that the towers served a symbolic function in delineating and laying claim to the polis territory.[24]

The question remains, however: What lies behind the drive for land? In accordance with the general analysis outlined above in chapter 1, I suggest that the competition and conflict over land in archaic Lesbos was fueled not simply by population growth but by elite competition for wealth and status in the newly consolidating polis communities. Several pieces of evidence support this interpretation. First is the evidence for trade in agricultural goods.[25] Lesbian gray-ware amphoras, which were used to transport wine and other agricultural products, have been found widely distributed throughout the Mediterranean Basin, from the Black Sea to Sicily to North Africa.[26] Furthermore, Herodotus mentions that the Mytileneans were the only ones among the Aeolians to participate in the founding of the Hellenion at Naucratis, the trading port for the Greeks in Egypt.[27] Strabo tells us that both Alcaeus and Charaxus, the brother of Sappho, spent time in Egypt; in the case of the latter, we are explicitly told that he was engaged in bringing Lesbian wine to Naucratis.[28]

The presence of Eastern luxuries in the archaeological remains from Lesbos suggests that Mytilenean elites traded agricultural products for luxury goods from the East.[29] Furthermore, Leslie Kurke and Ian Morris have noted the prominence of references to Eastern luxuries in the poetry of Sappho and Alcaeus and have suggested that elites made use of their access to Eastern luxuries to assert their status and thus legitimate their claim to power in the polis.[30] Unfortunately, the burial record—one of the most likely sources of evidence for elite use of foreign luxuries—is poor for Mytilene (as it is for most of the Lesbian poleis).[31] Not-

---

[24] Spencer (2000, 72) adds the cult sites of Apothiki and Klopedi to his catalogue of symbolic markers of polis territory. The idea that cultic centers on the margins of the polis territory are symbolic markers of territory is derived from the work of de Polignac 1984/1995, discussed above in chapter 1.

[25] Spencer (2000, 75–78) collects the literary and documentary sources for Mytilenean trade.

[26] Spencer 1995a, 301; 2000, 78, with map of the distribution of Lesbian amphoras on p. 77.

[27] Hdt. 2.178.2. Mytilenean presence in Naucratis is confirmed by epigraphical evidence: see Spencer 2000, 76, with n. 15.

[28] Strabo 1.2.30, 17.1.33. For Mytilene's natural endowments for maritime trade (double harbor, abundant timber for ship construction); see Mason 1993, 228–29.

[29] For Eastern luxuries in Lesbos, see Spencer 1995a, 292–93.

[30] Kurke 1992, 93 (following Mazzarino 1947); 1994; I. Morris 1996.

[31] For the burial record at Mytilene, see Spencer 1995a, 279–81, 295. The primary problem for archaeologists is that the modern settlement overlies the ancient one in all but two of the Lesbian poleis, and hence the finds tend to be limited to what turns up in modern construction

withstanding, Nigel Spencer has made ingenious use of some negative evidence to suggest that elite access to foreign luxury was the primary mode of elite legit-imation in archaic Mytilene, noting the absence of both monumental towers in the hinterland and elaborate architecture in the city center.[32] If towers and civic architecture played a role in the assertion of elite status in other poleis, then the absence of such monuments in Mytilene suggests that Mytilenean elites had al-ternative sources of prestige.[33] The obvious source of distinction for Mytilenean elites, Spencer surmises, is their access to Eastern luxuries through trade.[34]

For further evidence regarding the socio-political organization of Mytilene, we must turn to the literary sources. Chief among these sources are, of course, the poems of Sappho and Alcaeus. The works of these two poets display some of the tendencies toward Panhellenization so problematic for understanding the history of particular poleis. For instance, the presence of themes and dic-tion that occur in poetry from the rest of Greece calls into question the his-torical specificity of the poems and the extent to which they preserve the form and content of their original performances.

Nevertheless, one reason for believing that the extant poems of Sappho and Alcaeus do in fact preserve the form of their original performance is their dialect. Unlike the poems of Theognis, which are preserved in the Panhel-lenic koine of the Ionic dialect as opposed to Theognis's native Doric, the poems of Sappho and Alcaeus remain in the Lesbian poetic dialect.[35] The question of the content of the poems and its relation to the original performance context and historical situation is more complex. Wolfgang Rösler has argued that the lack of explanation of the details of the historical situation in the poems of Alcaeus means that the poems assume this knowledge in their audience, and thus that the poems have been preserved as they were performed for their original audience, the group of elite male companions (ἑταιρεία) of Alcaeus.[36]

---

projects. For an exception, see the relatively well-known burials at Antissa, discussed by Spencer (1995c), who shows that there is clear evidence for elite display of wealth through dedications at an ancestor/hero cult in one of the cemeteries at Antissa.

[32] Spencer 2000, 78–79. For the evidence for architecture in Mytilene, see Spencer (1995a, 277–303; 2000, 73–75), who notes (2000, 75) that columns have been found on the acropolis, but since no foundations have been found, it is unclear whether these are votive columns or belong to a "more substantial structure."

[33] Spencer (2000, 73) does note, however, that Mytilene is relatively isolated from the other Lesbian poleis by distance and a mountain range, and therefore may have had little need to engage in symbolic competition with other poleis and their elites through building towers.

[34] It is important to note that Spencer (1995a, 292–93) shows that Mytilene is no more pro-minent than other Lesbian poleis in terms of number of finds of Eastern origin. Yet the archaeo-logical record is meager, at least in the current state of excavations; hence the finds may not be representative.

[35] This is not to say that the dialect of the poems is purely the vernacular Lesbian form of Aeolic. A. Bowie (1981, 47–178) shows that the poetic dialects of Sappho and Alcaeus reveal the influence of Ionic, as well as that of the "poetic dictions of other early Greek poets, both epic and lyric."

[36] Rösler 1980, 33–56.

Yet one might argue in response to Rösler that the lack of explanation of the details of the historical situation is the result of precisely the type of Panhellenization of local poetic traditions that Nagy hypothesizes. Nagy might respond to Rösler's argument that there would be no need to explain the historical details (for instance, the references to Pittacus as "the son of Hyrrhas") once the poems had reached Panhellenic status, because the specific historical situation no longer mattered to a Panhellenic audience. A Panhellenic audience would read the historical characters and actions of Alcaeus's poetry generically—that is, as typical instances of intra-elite conflict—regardless of the particular historical persons involved and the particular historical details of Mytilene in the late seventh century. The poet Alcaeus and his opponent Pittacus became, for a Panhellenic audience, generic figures in the Panhellenic theme of intra-elite conflict. Ian Morris in fact makes this argument when he writes: "A man singing Alcaeus took the part of the betrayed one, trying to recreate an ideal, homogeneous world by casting out the traditional enemy, just as Archilochus cast out Neoboule the 'fickle one,' Hipponax cast out Boupalos the 'big-dick,' and Demosthenes was to cast out Aeschines with accusations of servile origin. If we take anything from these stories at face value, we may be seriously misled."[37]

It is difficult to judge whether the lack of explanation of the historical context of Alcaeus's poetry is a result of its preservation as originally performed to the knowing audience of Alcaeus's companions, as argued by Rösler, or whether this feature is due to the fact that the poems exist as they were performed to a Panhellenic audience, which understood the poetry in generic terms. I would argue that the evidence of dialect slightly tips the balance in favor of Rösler's explanation.[38] Yet is it necessary to choose between explanations? It is possible to argue that the poems of Alcaeus as we have them reflect both the historically specific context of their original performance, *and* their ability to be translated—that is, be meaningful—to a Panhellenic audience. That is to say, the poems can be read historically, as alluding to the specific historical situation of Alcaeus and his associates, but also generically, as reflecting the concerns and social struggles of elites across the Greek world. Certainly, one must attribute the survival of the poems of Sappho and Alcaeus precisely to their ability to relate to issues of Panhellenic concern, in particular the subject of intra-elite conflict.[39]

If we can indeed read the poems of Alcaeus and Sappho at least in part

[37] I. Morris 1996, 27.

[38] Kurke (1992, 91–92; 1994, 67–68) accepts the idea that the poems of Alcaeus and Sappho originated and were composed for performance at a symposium before "a closed aristocratic *hetaireia*."

[39] Aristophanes' *Wasps* 1222–48 shows not only that lines of Alcaeus's poetry (fr. 141 Campbell) were sung in symposia in different times and places, but that the poetry was meaningful in contexts of political conflict regardless of the specific historical details. Repeated performance of the poems of Alcaeus in symposia is attested in Athen. 15.693f–694a.

historically, what can they tell us about the political history of Mytilene in this period? Later sources preserve anecdotes about archaic Mytilenean history that help to piece together the evidence of the poems. The most striking feature of politics in Mytilene revealed by these sources is the frequency of intra-elite conflict and the politics of exile in the polis's history. In fact, the poems of Alcaeus became known as Τὰ Στασιωτικά in later tradition because of the prominence of the theme of civil unrest (στάσις).[40]

Prior to the mid-seventh century, a single elite family, the Penthilidae, held a monopoly on political power in Mytilene. According to tradition, the Penthilidae were descended from Orestes and led the Aeolian migration to Lesbos.[41] It is likely that, partly on the basis of these claims of heroic ancestry, this family held power in the form of a monarchy or narrow oligarchy, perhaps not unlike that of the Bacchiadae at Corinth. (See below.)

Around the middle of the seventh century, the exclusive rule of the Penthilidae ended. Aristotle tells us that "when the Penthilidae were going around striking people with clubs, Megacles and his friends [φίλοι] attacked and killed them."[42] Since in later times brutality toward the people was one of the topoi of the illegitimate rule of tyrants, we must be wary of accepting Aristotle's explanation of the overthrow of the tyranny. Indeed, within Aristotle's treatise, this anecdote appears as just one among many instances of brutal and arrogant tyrannical behavior.[43] The evidence for the continued dominance of the elite in Mytilene, and even the untarnished prestige of the family of the Penthilidae itself, suggests that the end of the monarchy was less a product of rebellion against elite rule than a response to the demands of a wider group of elites for a share of power.[44] By downgrading the former monarchs to the status of just one among many leading families, the elites of Mytilene created the conditions for sharing power among themselves. This power-sharing arrangement was most likely achieved through the institutionalization of public offices, a characteristic of the political development of many poleis at this time.[45] The

---

[40] Strabo 13.2.3.

[41] Hellanic. *FGrH* 4 F 32; Anticlid. *FGrH* 140 F 4; Strabo 9.2.3, 13.1.3; Paus. 3.2; schol. *in* Eur. *Rhes.* 251. An alternative tradition suggests that the non-Greek figure of Makar first colonized the island: *Il.* 24.544; Diod. Sic. 5.57.2, 5.81.3. The dual tradition of colonization may reflect the habitation of Lesbos by both Greeks and non-Greeks of northwest Anatolian origin: Spencer 2000, 39–40.

[42] Arist. *Pol.* 1311b27–29.

[43] Clubs, moreover, were associated with the bodyguard of the tyrant, and are prominent in fifth-century accounts of the tyranny of Pisistratus. See chapter 3 below.

[44] The marriage of Pittacus (on whom see below) to a member of the family of the Penthilidae is mentioned in Alcaeus fr. 70 Campbell and D.L. 1.81.

[45] Page (1955, 179n.1) suggests that the earliest civic office at Mytilene was the office of prytanis (πρύτανις, "president"), such as is attested in archaic Miletus (Arist. *Pol.* 1305a15). Sappho alludes to such an institution in one of her poems (no longer extant) when she "praises her brother Larichus because he poured the wine for the Mytileneans in the town hall [πρυτανεῖον]." (Athen. 10.425a).

primary aim of the earliest civic offices, as argued above in chapter 1, was to prevent the domination of power by any single elite family and to allow for the rotation or sharing of power among elite families. Certainly, some of the basic institutions of the polis as seen in other parts of the Greek world existed in Mytilene by the end of the seventh century, since Alcaeus mentions a council (βόλλα) and a regularly convened assembly (ἀγόρα καρυζομένα).[46]

Tradition remembered the overthrow of the Penthilidae in the form of a single event characterized by the typical features of elite conflict, including violent removal of one elite group (the Penthilidae) by another (Megacles and his friends). One might doubt that the change from monarchical rule to rule by a coalition of elite families was achieved through one violent event, as the tradition so neatly records. Historically, it is likely that a series of events—not necessarily all violent—led to the evolution of the political institutions of Mytilene as we see them at the time of Alcaeus.[47]

The next events of Mytilenean history suggest that civic institutions, such as annually rotating public offices, were inadequate curbs to the desire of particular elite factions to dominate the polis. Sometime after the overthrow of the Penthilidae, a tyranny was established by one Melanchrus.[48] We know nothing about this figure besides the fact that he was reviled by Alcaeus in his poetry, and was later overthrown by a coalition of elites consisting of one Pittacus and the brothers of Alcaeus.[49] It is likely that Melanchrus belonged to one of the leading elite families of Mytilene, just as did his opponents Pittacus and the family of Alcaeus. Pittacus's elite status is demonstrated by his marriage into the family of the Penthilidae.[50] Alcaeus's status may be inferred from his composition of poetry for performance in a symposium. In other words, Melanchrus, Pittacus, and the family of Alcaeus were not outsiders seeking power but insiders seeking to ensure their continued influence in and/or domination of the polis.

It is likely that Melanchrus was killed or banished from Mytilene, since we hear no more of him. It is unclear whether Pittacus and the brothers of Alcaeus thereafter restored rule by a broad-based coalition of elites or whether they too sought exclusive power themselves. Strabo, certainly, was suspicious of Alcaeus's aims, stating that "Alcaeus reviled equally Pittacus, Myrsilus, Melanchrus, and the Cleanactidae, but he himself was not innocent of such attempts to overthrow the constitution" (13.2.3). The fact that a new tyranny

[46] Alc. fr. 130 Campbell, cited below.

[47] See Thomas 1989, 133–44, on the phenomenon of "telescoping" a series of events into one event in oral traditions.

[48] D.L. 1.74; *Suda* s.v. Πιττακός; Strabo 13.2.3; Alcaeus fr. 331: "Melanchrus, worthy of respect to the city." This is likely to be ironic (as suggested by Campbell 1982, 371), since we are told by Strabo that Alcaeus reviled Melanchrus elsewhere in his poetry.

[49] D.L. 1.74, *Suda* s.v. Πιττακός.

[50] See n. 44 above.

was formed shortly thereafter around the person of Myrsilus suggests that Pittacus and the brothers of Alcaeus may have restored rule by a coalition of elites.[51]

The struggle between the new tyrant Myrsilus and the ruling coalition headed by Pittacus and the brothers of Alcaeus is the subject of several allegorical poems of Alcaeus, according to an ancient commentary.[52] These poems describe a ship tossed in a storm at sea, a common metaphor for the state in archaic poetry.[53] The metaphor suggests that the struggle was violent and might result in either the death or the exile of one or the other faction (fr. 6.1–14, trans. Campbell 1982, 239):

> This wave in turn comes (like?) the previous one, and it will give us much trouble to bale out when it enters the ship's [*lacuna*] Let us strengthen (the ship's sides) as quickly as possible, and let us race into a secure harbor; and let soft fear not seize any of us; for a great (ordeal) stands clear before us. Remember the previous (hardship): now let every man show himself steadfast. And let us not disgrace (by cowardice) our noble fathers lying beneath the earth.

Though the papyrus becomes increasingly fragmentary following these lines, the connection with Myrsilus seems confirmed by the subsequent phrases (27–28) "monarchy . . . let us not accept (μοναρχίαν . . . μ]ηδὲ δεχωμ[)."

If we follow the logic of the allegory, we may take the immediate threat ("this wave") as Myrsilus's attempt at tyranny, while the reference to a previous wave may allude either to an earlier attempt by Myrsilus or to the tyranny of Melanchrus. A second poem echoes this use of the image of waves to describe successive attacks on the political order of the state. Notably, this second poem makes a pun on the word στάσις, which can mean both "direction" and "political strife" (fr. 208, trans. Campbell 1982, 321–23):

> I fail to understand the direction [στάσις] of the winds: one wave rolls in from this side, another from that, and we in the middle are carried along in company with our black ship, much distressed in the great storm. The bilge-water covers the masthold; all the sail lets the light through now, and there are great rents in it; the anchors are slackening; the rudders . . .

It is possible that the successive waves battering the ship of state refer to repeated attempts of Myrsilus to establish a tyranny, as mentioned above. This interpretation is made more likely by the fact that Myrsilus was at one point exiled by the coalition of elites headed by Pittacus and Alcaeus's brothers, since one of Alcaeus's poems was apparently "addressed to the person who

---

[51] For the tyranny of Myrsilus, see fragments of a poem and commentary cited by Page 1955, 179–81.

[52] Page 1955, 181–97. Heraclitus, *Alleg. Hom.* 5, also attests that the poem concerns the tyrannical conspiracy of Myrsilus.

[53] Page 1955, 181.

provided a boat for Myrsilus's return [εἰς τὴν Μυρσίλου κάθοδον].[54] This would suggest that Myrsilus was initially expelled on attempting to seize power and later returned from exile, successfully establishing a tyranny. It is likely that Myrsilus's success in the later attempt was a result of his acquisition of support (financial and military) from foreign sources during his exile.

Yet Myrsilus's success must not have been wholly dependent on foreign support, since we learn from Alcaeus that Pittacus defected to the side of Myrsilus before or after the latter's victory. We learn of this event at a later point in the struggle, when Alcaeus (and presumably his brothers) have themselves been forced into exile. From his haven in exile, Alcaeus prays for revenge against Pittacus and Myrsilus (fr. 129, trans. Campbell 1982, 299):

> Come, with gracious spirit hear our prayer, and rescue us from these hardships and from grievous exile [ἀργαλέας φύγας]; and let their Avenger pursue the son of Hyrrhas [Pittacus], since once we swore [ἀπώμνυμεν], cutting [τόμοντες] . . . , never (to abandon?) any of our comrades [τῶν ἑταίρων], but either to die at the hands of men who at that time came against us and to lie clothed in earth, or else to kill them and rescue the people from their woes [δᾶμον ὑπὲξ ἀχέων ῥύεσθαι]. But Pot-Belly did not talk to their hearts; he recklessly trampled the oaths underfoot and devours our city [δάπτει τὰν πόλιν ἄμμι] . . . not lawfully [οὐ κὰν νόμον] . . . grey . . . written . . . Myrsilos . . .

Though Alcaeus complains that Pittacus broke their oath by joining the victors and avoiding death, we might note that Alcaeus similarly broke his oath and avoided death by fleeing into exile. The papyrus commentary on Alcaeus's poetry tells us that Alcaeus and his associates fled to Pyrrha, the nearest city on Lesbos.[55] The commentator refers to this period of exile as "the first exile," implying that Alcaeus's faction attempted to return and was exiled again sometime after this.

We learn of this attempt to return and the second exile from a passage in Aristotle's *Politics* in which historical examples of "elected tyrants" (αἰσυμνῆται) are listed. Apparently Alcaeus and his brother Antimenides tried to return to Mytilene by force, and in response the Mytileneans elected Pittacus as tyrant to fight off the exiles. Although the former tyrant Myrsilus had probably died by this time (fr. 332 Campbell), this does not fully explain the extraordinary action of the Mytileneans in electing Pittacus as tyrant in response to the attempted return of the exiles. A closer examination of the passage in Aristotle is therefore warranted (Arist. *Pol.* 1285a32–38):[56]

---

[54] A fragment of a commentary on a poem of Alcaeus (cited by Page 1955, 180) mentions that "the poem is addressed to one Mnamon, who provided a boat for Myrsilus's return. He also mentions that Alcaeus does not blame [Mnamon] for this."

[55] Page 1955, 179.

[56] See also D.L. 1.75, Strabo 13.2.3, Plut. *Sol.* 14.7.

[An αἰσυμνήτης] is, to speak simply, an elected tyranny.... For example, the Mytileneans once elected [εἵλοντο] Pittacus to resist the exiles [πρὸς τοὺς φυγάδας] who were led by Antimenides [the brother of Alcaeus] and Alcaeus the poet.

Aristotle then cites Alcaeus himself (fr. 348 Campbell) for proof that Pittacus was made tyrant by universal consent:

They have made the lowborn Pittacus tyrant [ἐστάσαντο τύραννον] of that spiritless and unfortunate polis, and all together they praise him greatly [μέγ᾽ ἐπαίνεντες ἀόλλεες].

There are problems with accepting Aristotle's claim for the popular election of Pittacus.[57] First of all, there are differences between Aristotle's claim and the fragment of Alcaeus that he cites in support of it. Aristotle says, "the Mytileneans once elected Pittacus [as tyrant]," whereas the fragment says that "they all together" established Pittacus as tyrant. Besides the differences in the verbs used, the subject of the verb ἐστάσαντο in the fragment is unspecified. The adjective ἀόλλεες need not refer to the Mytileneans as a whole, since it can be used of small groups, and may in fact refer to Pittacus's faction.[58] Finally, the term αἰσυμνήτης is not otherwise attested at Mytilene or anywhere else with the meaning that Aristotle gives it, except in later sources who base their usage on the passage in Aristotle.[59]

It seems impossible, therefore, to confirm Aristotle's claim that the Mytileneans as a whole established Pittacus as tyrant.[60] Yet several pieces of evidence suggest that something unusual happened at Mytilene, and may confirm Aristotle's report. Our sources tell us that the election of Pittacus resulted in the defeat of the exiles and a period of peace, which lasted at least until Pittacus's abdication of power ten years later.[61] Furthermore, Pittacus became one of the Seven Sages, and many of the stories associated with him have a markedly antielitist bent.[62] While it is likely that most of these stories derive from the trans-

[57] Page (1955, 238) and Rösler (1980, 30) both accept Aristotle's claim that the Mytilenean demos elected Pittacus, although they consider the term αἰσυμνήτης to be anachronistic. For criticism of this view, see Romer 1982.

[58] In Homer, the adjective is often used of the Trojans or Argives grouped "all together" (e.g., Il. 5.98, 12.443, 15.312), a usage that would imply that Alcaeus did use the term to refer to the Mytileneans collectively as a people. Yet Homer also uses the adjective of smaller groups: e.g., Il. 9.89, the council of elders; Od. 3.165, all Nestor's ships; Od. 3.412, all Nestor's sons; Od. 4.448, all the seals. It is possible, therefore, that Alcaeus used the adjective to describe the "whole" of Pittacus's faction.

[59] Romer 1982.

[60] One might, however, note that Aristotle presumably had access to more of Alcaeus's poetry than we possess, as well as other sources for early Mytilenean history, such as the history of Lesbos written by Hellanicus.

[61] D.L. 1.75. In fact, our sources record no further political upheavals in Mytilene until the fifth century, though this is most likely due to the deficiencies of our sources.

[62] D.L. 1.74–83.

formation of the historical Pittacus into the legendary figure of a wise man (an appropriation of a local tradition by a wider, Panhellenic one), this transformation may have been based on some historical kernel in which Pittacus was remembered for his enhancement of the civic order in response the threat of intra-elite violence.

The stability of Mytilene following Pittacus's election, as well as the traditions that gathered around Pittacus demonstrating his wise rule, seems to suggest that something unusual happened in Mytilene, and this unusual element may indeed have been the intervention of non-elites in the conflict between rival elite factions. The fact that Pittacus was not overthrown by a rival faction of elites, and ruled for ten years, suggests that he may have had the support of a group of citizens that went beyond the traditional elite grouping of the family and its immediate political allies. But what evidence is there, besides this event, that non-elite Mytileneans had the potential to act collectively against elites in the political sphere?

The review of the archaeological evidence presented above suggested that elite power was based on wealth derived from landownership and trade. Overseas trade, moreover, was used to reinforce the status of elites vis-à-vis non-elites, since the Eastern luxuries obtained thereby served as symbols of elite status, which marked them off from non-elites. Yet there must have been further effects of the increased production and expanding trade networks of archaic Mytilene that are not as readily visible in the archaeological or literary record. Although I suggested above that elites were the ones primarily involved in agricultural production for trade, it is likely that some non-elites also benefited from the new economic opportunities. First, it is possible that non-elites sometimes sailed the ships owned by elites and, if they were lucky, enriched themselves at the same time as the owners.[63] Among the mass of small landowners that made up the majority of the population, moreover, some must have been more successful than others in increasing production for market trade. It is possible, therefore, that some portion of the non-elites was becoming wealthier and laying claim to elite symbols of power.

There is some evidence that the economic expansion of the eighth through sixth centuries may have created a new class of wealthy non-elites, and that this group may have put some pressure on the traditional elite to justify their power in the community. A fragment of Sappho in fact seems to reflect elite resentment over the challenge provided by the wealthy non-elite: "Wealth without virtue is no harmless neighbor. The blending of both brings the height of happiness" (fr. 148, trans. Campbell 1982, 161).[64] In the face of the

[63] For the idea that archaic trade was conducted by agents of the elite, see Humphreys 1978, 167–68; Cartledge 1983, 6.

[64] Kurke (1992, 101) interprets this fragment as "an aristocratic attack on *arrivistes*" and (p. 94) describes the social context as follows: "In a period when various factors cause a broader distribution of wealth and political influence, threatening the power monopoly of the elite,

emergence of a group whose wealth rivaled that of the old elite, new means had to be found to distinguish elite from non-elites and thus legitimize elite claims to status and power. One common way of reaffirming the distinction was the claim that virtue, not wealth alone, was the quality that distinguished elites and gave them the right to superior status and power. We see this theme recur in the poetry of Theognis and Solon, suggesting that the rapidly changing economic conditions were causing problems for traditional elites through-out the Greek world.[65] Under these conditions, it is likely that at least some wealthy non-elites of Mytilene could have asserted their right to determine the political shape of Mytilene when intra-elite factionalism was threatening the stability of the state.

What of the non-elites of Mytilene? Is there any basis for believing that they may have had the political self-consciousness to intervene in intra-elite con-flict, as Aristotle implies that they did? Unfortunately, there is no direct evidence for the conditions of the lowest stratum of Mytilenean society in the archaic period. Given the drive for land and wealth discussed above, however, it is likely that the poor were forced into increasingly exploitative relations with the wealthy, as apparently happened in early sixth-century Athens and Megara. Yet, as I argue below, although the poor of Athens and Megara may have protested their worsening economic situation, there is no indication that they sought political reform. If the poor had any role in electing Pittacus, therefore, then this was likely a result of a summons by their elite patrons, who sought to defend themselves against violent attack by a rival elite faction.

The key point emerging from my analysis is that intra-elite conflict, and specifically the politics of exile, was a prominent political feature of archaic Mytilene. Moreover, I have argued that the instability caused by frequent attacks on the city by exiled elites provoked some non-elites to intervene in politics for the first time. In establishing Pittacus as tyrant, these non-elites put their support behind one elite group and forced the other to retreat into exile. Despite the potential implications of this action for the role of non-elites in politics, however, this event does not seem to have altered the formal distribution of political power. Indeed, the fact that Pittacus ruled as tyrant for ten years before laying down his power suggests that the action of the non-elites was not motivated by the desire to change the political structure of Mytilene, but aimed only to restore stability to the polis.

Nevertheless, Strabo tell us that "Pittacus used the monarchy to overthrow the dynasties and then gave back independence to the polis."[66] Diogenes

---

conscious forms of aristocratic display become more and more prominent in reaction. And as *nouveaux riches* non-aristocrats acquire the wealth to compete in the different arenas of display, money is no longer the distinguishing factor: style of expenditure becomes all-important."

[65] See chapter 1 above and the discussions below of Megara (in this chapter) and Athens (chapter 3).

[66] Strabo 13.2.3.

Laertius similarly says that Pittacus "held power for ten years and brought the constitution into order."[67] While we cannot infer from these late sources that anything like popular rule was inaugurated following the intervention of non-elites in the violent conflict between elites, we might imagine that henceforth elite ambitions were more strongly tempered by the need to preserve the stability of the polis, so as not to provoke similar displays of non-elite power. Nevertheless, the action of non-elites in breaking the cycle of the politics of exile must have strengthened their self-consciousness of collective identity and potential power. Even if this power was not often exerted, the memory of the events surrounding Pittacus's election must have served as a powerful warning to elites of the political potential of the masses.

MEGARA

Megara provides the second example of the role of the politics of exile in the development of the archaic poleis. Not only did elite factions experience frequent exile and return, but episodes of exile are strongly correlated with key turning points in Megarian political development. Before turning to this argument, a few comments must be made about the problematic nature of the evidence for archaic Megara.

Our evidence for archaic Megara is primarily textual, since very little archaeological evidence is available.[68] The textual evidence for the political history of Megara presents both advantages and disadvantages in comparison to the evidence for other archaic poleis. On the one hand, the poetry preserved under the name Theognis of Megara was subject to the processes of Panhellenization, and thus arguably informs us very little about the specific history of Megara in a particular time period. On the other hand, a number of anecdotes about archaic Megarian history are preserved in later sources. Not only are these sources apparently independent of Theognis's poetry, but it is likely that they are based on genuine Megarian historical traditions.[69] The chief problems with these anecdotes are their anachronistic understanding of earlier Megarian history and the difficulty of determining the period of Megarian history reflected in them.

[67] D.L. 1.75.

[68] The dearth of material evidence for archaic Megara is a result of the fact that the modern town of Megara sits directly on top of the ancient settlement and the consequent lack of major excavation projects (Legon 1981, 25–26).

[69] Okin 1985 shows that our two main sources of anecdotes about archaic Megara, Aristotle's *Politics* (which drew from his now lost *Constitution of the Megarians*) and Plutarch's *Quaestiones Graecae*, both probably relied on local Megarian historians for their accounts. Four writers of local Megarian history are known, all dating to the fourth or third centuries B.C.E.: Praxion, Dieuchidas, Hereas, and Heragoras (*FGrH* 484–86; Picirilli 1975).

More serious problems arise regarding the relation between the poetry of Theognis and Megarian history. Besides the ahistoricizing effects of Pan-hellenization, there are three further features of Theognis's poetry that make historical interpretation problematic.[70] First, the poetry preserved under Theognis's name can be dated on internal grounds anywhere from the second half of the seventh century to the first half of the fifth. Thus it is clear that poetry composed by other poets came to be preserved under Theognis's name. This raises the second problem, namely: Assuming that there was an original, historical Theognis, when did he live? Third, which of the almost fourteen hundred lines of poetry can be attributed to this historical Theognis? In re-sponse to the difficulties of determining the answers to these last two prob-lems, a number of scholars have declared it futile to attempt to link the poetry with a historical poet or a specific period of Megarian history. Rather, these scholars argue, it is better to approach the poet as a persona and the poetry as generic, reflecting "the crystallization of archaic and early classical poetic traditions emanating from Megara."[71]

In response to the serious difficulties of connecting Theognidean poetry to the historical development of Megara, the following approach seems best. First, I rely on the anecdotes about Megara in Plutarch and Aristotle, and not the poetry of Theognis, for the reconstruction of a basic narrative of Megarian political history. Second, I use the poetry of Theognis to illustrate some of the ideological tensions and patterns of events in archaic Megara, rather than specific historical events.[72] I hope that this approach will account for both the reality of historical change in archaic Megara and the generic expression, in the poetry of Theognis, of the tensions arising from this historical change.[73]

Before turning to the sources for Megarian political history, a brief overview of Megarian history from the end of the Bronze Age through Geometric times is needed to put the later developments in context. Megara was occupied in the Bronze Age and suffered decline in the twelfth century, just as did other

---

[70] Nagy 1985 notes that Theognidean poetry is preserved in the Ionic dialect, and not in Megara's native Doric. According to Nagy, this is a clear sign that the poetry as we have it was intended for a Panhellenic audience.

[71] Cobb-Stevens et al. 1985, 2; Nagy 1985; Figueira 1985a. The following statement of Cobb-Stevens et al. (loc. cit.) is particularly revealing of the approach of these scholars: "Efforts to create a political biography of Theognis—such as correlating the warnings about the dissolution of the polis with a specific bout of partisan strife or the lamentations on an exile's plight with a historical banishment of the poet—yield an impoverished reading of the corpus." For a con-trasting view of the possibility of a historical reading of the poetry, see Lane Fox 2000.

[72] For the poetry of Theognis as a reflection of the ideology of the Megarian elite, see Nagy 1985, Figueira 1985a.

[73] E. Bowie (1997, 62) accepts (with some modifications) West's (1974) distinctions between portions of the text as more or less genuine. Most important, he accepts that lines 19–254 contain a high proportion of verses that may "have been plausibly and even correctly ascribed by [the] compiler to Theognis." For a similar view, see Lane Fox 2000.

Mycenaean settlements.[74] Tradition records that Megara was reoccupied by settlers known as Dorians during the Dark Age.[75] Dialectal and cultic similarities with other poleis (in particular Argos) confirm that the resettlement of Megara was in some way connected with the movement of Greek speakers in the Peloponnesus, though not necessarily from areas beyond it.[76] Moreover, as Irad Malkin and others have shown, traditions such as that of the Dorian Invasion reflect complex processes by which the various local communities negotiated their relations with one another and with the land.[77] Tensions over land between the local communities of the Megarid and surrounding areas must have resulted in considerable fluidity of populations and boundaries. We know from Plutarch that the Megarid was initially settled in five villages (κῶμαι), Heraea, Piraea, Megara, Cynosura, and Tripodiscus.[78] Insofar as these villages can be located, it seems that the two westernmost, Heraea and Piraea (including the important cult site of Perachora), came under Corinthian control by the late eighth century.[79]

It is likely that tensions with Corinth over land precipitated the "coming together" or synoecism of the village communities into the polis of Megara.[80] The populations of the villages of the western Isthmus may at this time have migrated eastward to the centrally located village of Megara.[81] The combined populations and settlements that constituted the new polis of Megara were organized into tribes, for which the three Dorian names were adopted (Hylleis, Pamphyleis, and Dymaneis).[82] As emphasized in chapter 1 above, whether or not tribes existed before the polis, in the eighth century they were put to new use as units of polis organization.[83] It is interesting to note that the

[74] Legon 1981, 42–43.

[75] Hdt. 5.76; Paus. 1.39.4–5; Strabo 9.1.7, 14.2.6.

[76] Legon 1981, 45–46. J. Hall (1997, 56–65) analyzes the traditions regarding the Dorian invasion and shows that they have less to do with original migrations than with the assimilation of various distinct myths of origin into common traditions.

[77] Malkin 1994a; J. Hall 1997, 56–65; Salmon 1984, 48.

[78] Plut. Quaest. Graec. 17 (Mor. 295b–c).

[79] See Legon (1981, 49–51) for the evidence linking these villages to the western Isthmus. The date of the Corinthian take-over is contested, with some placing it in the tenth century and others in the eighth. (See Figuiera 1985b, 265, for summary of debate.) As N. Jones (1987, 96) points out, however, there is no need to connect Plutarch's account of the villages with the political structure of the Megarian polis. C. Morgan (1994, 131) notes that the proximity of the western promontory of Perachora to Corinth make it most likely that Corinth was connected with the area from very early times.

[80] In this regard, the conflict theory of state formation proposed by Carneiro 1970 seems to fit the Megarian case.

[81] Figueira 1985b, 266. Legon (1981, 60–70) proposes that the migration of population from these districts helps to explain Megarian colonization in the late eighth century. Even if the date of the Corinthian take-over could be determined precisely, Megarian colonization was probably a result of a variety of factors: see below.

[82] For the Dorian tribes, see IG 4² 1.41; 7.70, 72.

[83] See N. Jones 1987 (95–96) for the distinction between the tribes as a polis unit and the villages as pre-polis settlement organization.

polis of Megara defined itself in opposition to its neighbors (as the polis-"ethnic" Megara proclaims), but also emphasized its ties to its Peloponne-sian neighbors through the adoption of the Dorian tribes and through cultic activities, especially the cults of Apollo and Hera. This double-sided aspect of early Megarian identity reflects the complex situation of Dorian and non-Dorian populations in a contested landscape.[84]

Although the early polis may have been ruled by a single king, it is likely that by the seventh century a small group of elites ruled through rotating public offices and a council.[85] Subsequent events—namely the seizure of power by a tyrant, Theagenes, in the last quarter of the seventh century—suggest the existence of intense intra-elite competition for power in archaic Megara. It is precisely under conditions of such violent conflict over power among elites that public offices emerged in the rest of Greece. (See chapter 1 above.)

Yet it is notable that Aristotle viewed Theagenes' rise in terms of a conflict between elites and non-elites. Aristotle regarded Theagenes as a demagogue (δημαγωγός) and champion of the people (προστάτης τοῦ δήμου). Aristotle believed that Theagenes won power by gaining the trust of the common people. As evidence, Aristotle cites the fact that Theagenes slaughtered the sheep of the rich before becoming tyrant. According to Aristotle, this act was Theagenes' pledge to the poor that he stood on their side, and not with the rich and powerful.[86]

It is worth separating the part of Aristotle's report that probably represents Megarian tradition (Theagenes' slaughter of the sheep of the rich) from the interpretation that Aristotle places upon this act (that Theagenes was the champion of the poor). Aristotle's interpretation clearly derives from the ex-perience of classical democratic politics, in which the consent of the masses (ὁ δῆμος) was necessary for elite rule.[87] While it is clear that there were tensions between rich and poor in archaic Megara (see below), it is unlikely that the poor were politically self-conscious enough to be the basis for a tyrant's claim to power. In terms of archaic politics, the most plausible context for the slaughter of the sheep of the rich would have been violent intra-elite com-petition for power, which often resulted in the expulsion of one group of elites by another. As Hans van Wees has argued, Megarian politics (as viewed

---

[84] In addition to the tribes, we hear of a further subdivision of the polis population, the ἑκατοστύς or "hundred" (IG 4² 1.42). The evidence for this subdivision is too poor to determine exactly how it related to the tribes and the other organs of communal organization; see N. Jones 1987, 96.

[85] There is no direct evidence, but such a change is likely based on similar transitions in the rest of Greece at this time. (See above, chapter 1.) Legon (1981, 55–58) adduces the existence of magistracies based on Hellenistic inscriptions from Megarian colonies. Paus. 1.43.3, moreover, associates the construction of a bouleuterion with the transition from monarchical rule to annually rotating magistracies.

[86] Pol. 1305a8–28.

[87] Compare my discussion of classical traditions about Pisistratus in chapter 3 below.

through the generalizing lens of Theognis's poetry) "suggests that violent struggles among the élite were common and invariably involved groups of people going into exile or fighting their way back.... therefore, power and property must have changed hands constantly as it was abandoned, seized, and recovered."[88]

The violence and frequent exile and return of elites in archaic Megara are prominent features of subsequent episodes in archaic Megarian history, as we shall see momentarily. I want to suggest, however, that these elements are reflected already in the context of Theagenes' tyranny, and in particular in the episode of the slaughter of the sheep. In other words, Theagenes did not perform this act as a public demonstration of his animosity toward the rich, as Aristotle has it, but did so in the course of his violent confrontation with his elite rivals. This interpretation of the episode better fits the context of violent intra-elite competition implicit in Theagenes' seizure of tyrannical power. In Megara, as at Mytilene, it appears that the creation of public offices was insufficient insurance against attempts at domination by a single elite leader.

Theagenes' act also reveals something of the basis of elite wealth in archaic Megara. In most archaic poleis, elite wealth was based on control of the largest portions of arable land. Landownership was undoubtedly the basis of elite status in archaic Megara, but given the nature of the landscape of the Megarid, the land would have included rocky highlands suitable for sheep grazing, as well as a portion of the main arable plain.[89] By the classical period, the Megarians were well known for their export of woolen garments, and it is likely that the seeds of this trade go back to the archaic period.[90] The fact that Megara was in the forefront of the movement to found new settlements abroad may confirm early Megarian interest in market trade.[91]

Indeed, if the movement to found new settlements was fueled by the elites' drive to wealth, as argued above in chapter 1, then these settlements are further evidence of intra-elite competition in the early Megarian polis. Given the paucity of arable land and metal deposits in Megara, moreover, trade in grain and metals would have been particularly profitable.[92] Presumably, the chief export exchanged for these goods was Megarian wool, and possibly garments. It is likely, therefore, that the sheep slaughtered by Theagenes were in fact being raised for the export trade in wool and garments.[93]

[88] Van Wees 2000, 66.

[89] Legon 1981, 22–25.

[90] Ar. *Ach.* 519, *Pax* 1003; Xen. *Mem.* 2.7.6; D.L. 6.41.

[91] For early Megarian colonies, see Figueira 1985b, 275.

[92] Legon 1981, 78–79.

[93] The prosperity of this period is indicated by investment in civic buildings. Traces of the foundations of an archaic temple have been found on one of the two hills that formed the core of the ancient city. In addition, although the present remains of the so-called Fountain House of Theagenes date only to the fifth century, it is likely that an archaic fountain house existed on the site, as tradition records (Paus. 1.40.1: Gotte 2001, 309).

Although I have argued that the elites were the prime movers behind early Megarian activity overseas, it is likely once again that some non-elites also took advantage of the opportunities for gain created by the expanding market for trade. There is some evidence that a new class of wealthy non-elites began to threaten the social and political dominance of the traditional elite in archaic Megara. The alarm of the traditional elite over the new claims to status and power made by wealthy non-elites is one of the prominent themes of Theognis's poetry (53–58 West):[94]

> Cyrnus, this city is still the city, but the people are different.
> Those who before knew neither justice nor law
> and wore out the goathide cloaks on their backs
> while grazing like deer outside the city,
> these now are honorable, son of Polypaïs.
> And those who were honorable before are now base.
> Who can bear to see it?

Consonant with this hysteria over the new nobles of the polis is a second theme of Theognidean poetry: the assertion of the legitimacy of the traditional elite on the grounds of moral superiority rather than wealth (145–46, 149–50):

> Take counsel with yourself about living a reverent life with modest means
> rather than growing rich by seeking money unjustly.
>
> . . . .
>
> The gods give money even to a wholly base man,
> Cyrnus, but a portion of excellence attends only a few.

The appearance of a new class of wealthy non-elites was not the only socioeconomic change in archaic Megara. An anecdote reported by Plutarch reveals that by the early sixth century some Megarians were so indebted to the wealthier citizens that there was a great deal of social unrest.[95] The most likely causes of the worsening conditions of the poor were population growth and increasing production for market trade. As Ian Morris has argued in relation to Solonian Athens, "population growth produced a situation where landowners would actually want to get rid of some of their sharecroppers, or else renegotiate the terms of dependency. No doubt most landowners felt constrained by custom and by patriarchal obligations towards 'their' *hektē-moroi* ["sixth-parters," sharecroppers]. But. . . . [t]he implication of much of Solon's poetry is that new market opportunities were transforming the ideology of gain."[96] As we have seen, a similar transformation of "the ideology of

---

[94] For this interpretation of Theognis, see, for example, Redfield 1986, 52–57.

[95] Plut. *Quaest.Graec.* 18 (*Mor.* 295c–d). It is generally believed that Plutarch drew his material on Megara from Aristotle's (lost) *Constitution of the Megarians*: Robinson 1997, 115n.184; Okin 1985, 14.

[96] I. Morris 2002, 36. See also Forsdyke, "Land" (forthcoming).

gain" is apparent in the reactionary poetry of Theognis. The practical consequences of this transformation may have been that the rich increased the size of their herds and appropriated larger portions of the grazing land. Poorer Megarians may have found their access to the land restricted, and so may have fallen into more oppressive debt and dependency relationships with the wealthy.

By the mid-sixth century, tensions between rich and poor had apparently created such unrest that a radical solution had to be found. The solution reached was the Return of Interest (παλιντοκία), by which creditors were required to return the interest on loans made to the poor.[97] This measure for the relief of the poor is quite similar to that enacted by Solon at approximately the same time in Athens. Known as the Shaking-off of Burdens (σεισάχθεια), Solon's measure entailed seemingly even more radical relief, since it canceled debts altogether (Arist. Ath. Pol. 6.1). In both cases, however, these measures were remedies for the economic distress of the poor. The measures do not imply that the poor were concerned with anything other than economic relief, or that they sought to overturn the rule of the elite.

Plutarch, however, presents the episode of the Return of Interest as part and parcel of dramatic constitutional changes in sixth-century Megara. Specifically, Plutarch claims that the measure was enacted by a radical democracy, which had taken power not long after Theagenes' tyranny. According to Plutarch, after the tyrant Theagenes was overthrown, the Megarians briefly adopted a sound government (ἐσωφρόνησαν κατὰ τὴν πολιτείαν, Mor. 295d). Whatever the exact form of this constitution (presumably oligarchic), it did not last long.[98] According to Plutarch, a radical democracy (ἀκόλαστος δημοκρατία, Mor. 304e) was next established at Megara. Under this radical democracy a number of injustices were perpetrated by the poor against the rich (Quaest. Graec. 18, Mor. 295c–d):

> Then, as Plato says, the demagogues, serving as wine stewards, poured out too much unmixed freedom [ἄκρατον ἐλευθερίαν], and the Megarians were corrupted and behaved with wanton violence [ἀσελγῶς] toward the rich. For example, the poor went to the houses of the rich and demanded to be hosted and feasted sumptuously. And if the poor did not receive the hospitality that they demanded, then they treated the rich with violence [πρὸς βίαν] and insolence [μεθ' ὕβρεως]. Finally they made a decree that they should get back the interest that they had given to their creditors, and they called the measure the Return of Interest [παλιντοκίαν].

While it is likely that there were rapid changes of power between elite factions in the period following the overthrow of Theagenes' tyranny,

---

[97] Plut. Quaest. Graec. 18 (Mor. 295c–d); cf. 59 (Mor. 304e–f).

[98] On prudence (σωφροσύνη) in elite ideology, see North 1966, Donlan 1980.

Plutarch's claim that a radical democracy was installed appears to be based on his source's interpretations of Megarian traditions rather than on the Megarian traditions themselves. Plutarch's source for this anecdote was probably Aristotle's lost *Constitution of the Megarians*.[99] For Aristotle, Megarian traditions describing the violent and insolent behavior of the poor toward the rich represented a clear example of the kind of social disorder (ἀταξία) that he and other political theorists associated with radical democracy.[100] Thus, although we can be reasonably certain that the specific term παλιντοκία derives from a genuine Megarian historical tradition and refers to historical legislation addressing the problem of debt, we must be skeptical of Plutarch's claim that a radical democracy existed in sixth-century Megara.[101]

As was stated already, legislation addressing the problem of debt is not unparalleled in early sixth-century Greece. Just as the Shaking-off of Burdens in Athens is not usually associated with the advent of democracy (let alone radical democracy), neither should the Return of Interest at Megara be so interpreted.[102] Furthermore, the demands made by the Megarian poor to be feasted by the rich, as well as the violent treatment that the poor apparently meted out to their social superiors if they were not given sufficient hospitality, reflect the kinds of social rituals of inversion that are typical of agricultural economies in pre-modern societies.[103] Such rituals usually take place at festival times and involve the temporary inversion of the social order.[104]

[99] On Plutarch's source, see n. 95 above.

[100] For Plutarch's dependence on concepts borrowed from anti-democratic theory, note especially his use of Plato's metaphor (*Rep.* 562d) of unmixed wine to describe the effects of unlimited freedom, his description of the Megarian democracy as unbridled (ἀκόλαστος), and his use of the terms ἀσελγῶς, βία, ὕβρις, and ἀταξία to characterize the period of democratic rule (*Quaest. Graec.* 59, *Mor.* 304e–f), Each of these concepts is paralleled in earlier anti-democratic thought, including Herodotus 3.81 ("the insolence of the unbridled democracy," δήμου ἀκολάστου ὕβριν); Thucydides' descriptions of the ignorant and irrational behavior of the Athenian masses (e.g., 2.65; 3.36–49; 6.1, 8–26, 60–61); pseudo-Xenophon's attribution of ἀκολασία and ἀταξία to democracy (*Ath. Pol.* 1.5); Aristotle's explanations of how democracies are overthrown ("as a result of the wanton violence of the leaders of the people," διὰ τὴν τῶν δημαγωγῶν ἀσέλγειαν, *Pol.* 1304b20). See also pseudo-Xenophon 1.13–14 for the idea that the demos appropriates the wealth of the rich for itself. For further development of the anti-democratic parallels, see Forsdyke 2005.

[101] *Pace* most modern historians, who accept the claims of Aristotle and Plutarch. See Robinson 1997, 114–17.

[102] Since fourth-century Athenians, including Aristotle, regarded Solonian Athens as a democracy (see Hansen 1990b), this contradiction would not have existed for them.

[103] The bibliography is extensive. For anthropological studies, see Gluckman 1956, 109–36; 1963, 110–36; Turner 1969, 166–203. Historical studies: Davis 1975, 97–151; E. Thompson 1975, 1993; Burke 1978, 201–2; Darnton 1984, 75–104; Underdown 1985; Nissenbaum 1996; Penčak et al. 2002. For parallels in ancient Greece, see Forsdyke 2005.

[104] One possible venue of such rituals of reversal was the dramatic festivals. It is notable that Aristotle credits Megara with the invention of comedy (*Poet.* 1448a). This suggests not only that Megara may have had a vibrant comic tradition already in the archaic period, but that Aristotle

Historical parallels from early modern Europe show that such ritual reversals are usually non-revolutionary, allowing for the release of tensions created by the hierarchical social order, and thus functioning as a safety valve for the status quo. The comparative examples also suggest, however, that festival revelry can turn particularly violent in periods of rapid social and economic change. Interestingly, the early modern examples suggest that festival violence aims to reassert traditional or customary norms in the face of change.

The comparative examples help to explain Plutarch's reports of the behavior of the Megarian poor toward the rich. I suggest that traditional rituals of social inversion between the wealthier members of the community and their poorer dependents took a particularly violent turn when population growth and the new opportunities for market trade contributed to the breakdown of traditional relationships of mutual reciprocity between wealthy landowners and their poorer dependents. Ritual feasting of the poor by the rich affirmed the latter's moral obligation to redistribute some portion of their wealth to the poorer members of the community from whose labor they profited. When prosperous (elite and non-elite) Megarians began to appropriate more land for themselves and to ignore their traditional obligations toward the poor, such rituals of feasting may have escalated into more violent, riotous behavior. Through these riots, the poor protested the breakdown of the traditional order. It is likely that these social protests led to the Return of Interest legislation. In sum, Plutarch's anecdote may reflect actual changes in the economic relations between rich and poor in archaic Megara. As in the case of Solonian Athens, however, there is little reason to believe that the poor demanded or were granted political power as a result.[105]

If there was no radical democracy in archaic Megara, what sort of government existed after the overthrow of the tyrant Theagenes?[106] It is likely that elites continued to struggle for dominance in the polis following the tyranny. For a short while the system of public offices was reaffirmed under what Plutarch (following Aristotle) calls "sound government." Yet intense competition for power among elites evidently continued, since we hear of further expulsions following the period of the tyranny. Pausanias (1.40.5) mentions a group of Megarian exiles (the Dorycleans) who were accused of betraying Salamis to the Athenians. Since Salamis was captured by the Athenians shortly

---

was familiar with Megarian comic tradition. It is possible, therefore, that Aristotle learned of traditions such as the feasting of the poor by the rich from the oral traditions arising from Megarian comic festivals.

[105] The further episodes of "lack of restraint" attributed by Plutarch to the time of the "radical democracy" (temple robbery and the drowning of religious pilgrims: *Quaest. Graec.* 59, *Mor.* 304e–f), are likely to be genuine historical events that were attributed by Aristotle to the period of the democracy by way of further illustration of the injustices of democratic rule. I develop this and the other arguments presented above more fully in Forsdyke 2005.

[106] It should be noted that my argument against the existence of a democracy in archaic Megara goes against current consensus: see, e.g., Robinson 1994, 114–17; Legon 1981, 119.

before Solon's archonship of 594, the Dorycleans were probably exiles from the "sound government" that ruled briefly following Theagenes' tyranny.

Violent expulsion and return, moreover, is characteristic of several subsequent episodes in archaic Megarian history as described by Aristotle (*Pol.* 1304b35–40):

> And the democracy at Megara was also put down in a similar manner. For the demagogues, so that they might have money to distribute, exiled many of the elites until they made the exiles numerous and these returned and defeated the demos in battle and established an oligarchy.

In this anecdote, Aristotle interprets the expulsion of a group of elites as a further example of the unjust rule of the supposed democracy at Megara. Yet it is very unlikely that the elites of Megara were exiled in such numbers that they were able to return and defeat the Megarian demos as a whole. A much more plausible interpretation of this episode, given what we know of the politics of exile in other archaic poleis, is that one group of elites exiled another, and then in turn was banished by the returning exiles. Aristotle anachronistically interprets this situation as a conflict between elites and leaders of the people, and suggests that under a radical democracy the elites were in exile. As we shall see in chapter 6, the idea that democracies expel their best citizens became part of anti-democratic ideology in the late fifth and fourth centuries. Aristotle may have been influenced by this ideology in his interpretation of traditions of exile in archaic Megara.

The aftermath of the episode as reported by Aristotle seems to confirm that the conflict was between elites, not between these and non-elites. According to Aristotle, the returning exiles made participation in their fight to return the criterion for eligibility for public office: "[There are various criteria of eligibility] such as by wealth or birth or virtue or some other such qualification, as at Megara, where those who shared in the return from exile and fought against the people [were eligible]" (*Pol.* 1300a18–19). If the struggle really had been between the elites and the Megarian non-elites en masse, then the much more straightforward criteria of birth or wealth would have been adopted by the returning elites after their overthrow of the democracy. Instead, since both the returning exiles and their opponents were elites, the returning group adopted the criterion of participation in the fight to return from exile as the ground for eligibility for public office.

The prominence of the theme of exile in the poetry of Theognis is a further indication that exile was a frequent experience of elites in archaic Megara (332a–b, 341–50, 1197–1202 West):[107]

> There is no dear and faithful companion for an exile,
> and this is the most grievous part of exile.

---

[107] The last line quoted below (1202) is corrupt, although Nagy (1985, 64) offers an interpretation based on parallels with Hesiod's *Works and Days*.

. . . .

O Olympian Zeus, accomplish my timely prayer:
give me something good to suffer instead of evils.
May I die if I do not find some relief from my troubles,
and may I give sorrows in return for sorrows.
For this is my lot. And not yet has retribution appeared for those
men who hold my property, having stolen it by force.

. . . .

I heard the voice of a bird calling shrilly, son of Polypaïs
—this is the messenger for men of the season for plowing;
but it wounds my black heart,
since other men possess my fertile fields,
and my mules do not drag the light plow
because . . . sea voyage.

Many attempts have been made to attribute the theme of exile in the poetry to
the personal experience of the historical Theognis during a specific episode in
the history of archaic Megara.[108] Yet given the difficulties of relating poem
and poet to historical events, it is best to interpret the theme of exile as a
reflection of the generalized experience of the Megarian elite in the archaic
period.[109] I suggest that exile was a common experience among the elite from
at least the time of Theagenes' tyranny in the late seventh century and throughout the sixth.

The idea that archaic Megara was ruled by a narrow group of traditional
elites who engaged in often violent competition for power does not exclude the
idea that certain wealthy non-elites were beginning to infiltrate their ranks. This
is certainly what Theognis's (albeit exaggeratedly reactionary) poetry suggests.
Furthermore, elite rule is not incompatible with measures for the economic
relief of the poor, as is clear from the enactment of the παλιντοκία. In fact, I
would argue that it was precisely the traditional elite who proposed such a
measure as a way both of stabilizing discontent among the lower classes and of
affirming their moral superiority over the wealthy non-elites. Traditionally,
elites had been bound by a code of reciprocity toward their social inferiors. In
the new conditions of expanding economic opportunity, the old system was
breaking down, and was gradually being replaced by a more formal mechanisms of credit and debt. One way by which the elite attempted to gain legitimacy in the eyes of the community would have been to present themselves as

[108] West (1974, 66–71) relates the theme of exile to Theognis's own banishment, which he
places in the late seventh century at the time of the tyrant Theagenes. Legon (1981, 116–19) and
Lane Fox (2000) place Theognis's exile in the sixth century at the time of the rule of the "radical
democracy."

[109] It is remarkable that many of the lines on exile appear outside the core of lines considered
most likely to be those of the historical Theognis.

the just protectors of the community (much as Alcaeus tried to do at Mytilene; see above) through their care for the poor.[110]

Hans van Wees has recently suggested that there was no "aristocracy of birth" in archaic Megara. Van Wees draws parallels with the Sicilian and American Mafia to show that "violent competition for power and property made it impossible to sustain any kind of closed elite."[111] According to van Wees, this was the case because non-elites could easily become wealthy through the violent appropriation of wealth. While it should be clear from the argument presented above that I agree that violent competition was the prime mover to political change, I would argue that far from there being no hereditary elite in archaic Megara, it was primarily among this group that the violent competition for power took place. This is certainly what comparative evidence from other, better-documented archaic poleis would suggest. Insofar as there are signs of the breakdown of the closed order of the Megarian elite, this would have been caused both by the new opportunities for profit created by market trade, as discussed above, and by intra-elite competition itself. Under conditions of intense intra-elite competition, different groups among the elite may have been anxious to present themselves as the true guardians of the polis. It is in this context that the ruling elites may have enacted such measures as the παλιντοκία to provide relief for the poor, or allowed for more regular meetings of the popular assembly to provide some voice to the newly wealthy non-elites. We have no direct evidence for the latter democratizing gesture, but some such moderate measure might account for Theognis's exaggerated complaint that those who had been rustic farmers were becoming honorable in the city.

In conclusion, I suggest that the little evidence we have for the political development of archaic Megara illustrates that intra-elite conflict and the politics of exile were its key features. Both the tyranny of Theognis and the frequent changes of regime in late seventh- and sixth-century Megara are best explained (*pace* Aristotle and Plutarch) as outcomes of intra-elite conflict. In contrast to the Mytilenean case, however, the instability caused by intra-elite conflict apparently did not provoke direct intervention by non-elites. It is possible that the modest measures taken by elites to respond to non-elite concerns helped preserve elite rule even in the face of violent intra-elite conflict.

Samos

Samos provides a third example of the role of exile in the political development of the archaic poleis. From the end of the seventh century to the end of the sixth,

---

[110] Comparative examples of relief for the poor in early modern Europe support this interpretation: see Davis 1975, 28–29, 37; E. Thompson 1993, 199–200, 243–44, 300–301, 303; and Forsdyke 2005 for further discussion.

[111] Van Wees 2000, 53.

Samian elites engaged in violent competition for power. This struggle frequently resulted in the exile of one group of elites by another, and the attempt to return to power by force, often backed by foreign allies. A brief sketch of the prehistory of Samos is useful for putting these later developments in context.[112]

Archaeological evidence confirms that Samos was occupied in the Bronze Age, and it is likely that there was some disruption of settlement between the late Bronze and early Iron Age.[113] Samos was resettled in the early Iron Age from mainland Greece, an event known as the Ionian Migration. Like the so-called Dorian Invasion of the Peloponnesus, the myth of migration to Ionia simplifies a complex process of resettlement and growth following the destruction of Mycenaean civilization. In one tradition, Athens is claimed as the mother city of the Ionians.[114] Yet it is clear from other traditions that the settlers came from a number of regions of mainland Greece, and that they often took local women as wives.[115] It is possible that non-Greeks from Caria on the Anatolian mainland formed some portion of the pre-migration population of Samos, and that they were assimilated into the social organization of the immigrants.[116]

However mixed the population of early Iron Age Samos, the population was at some point organized according to the four Attic and two Ionian tribes.[117] This (re)organization took place probably at the time of the formation of the polis, an event that occurred by the eighth century. The primary indication of the emergence of the polis is the construction of the first temple at the Heraeum (the First Hecatompedon) shortly after 800.[118] I argued above in chapter 1 that archaic temple construction was a product of the needs of the elite to find more powerful arenas for asserting status in the newly consolidating polis community. It is likely, therefore, that elites promoted the construction of the Heraeum as a way of creating a focus for communal identity, which could then serve as a forum for elite display.

Another indication of intra-elite competition in archaic Samos is the abundant evidence for Samian involvement in trade involving luxury goods. The

[112] I am indebted to Shipley's (1987) excellent study of Samos for the summary of the early settlement history and archaeology of Samos that follows.

[113] Shipley 1987, 26–27. As Shipley points out, the area of the Heraeum shows the clearest evidence for a disruption, since dedications begin to be found at the site of this Bronze Age settlement only in the ninth (or possibly tenth) century.

[114] Herodotus asserts that the most genuine of the Ionians set out from the prytaneion of the Athenians (1.146.2, 147.2) and hold the Apaturia (1.147.2). Cf. Solon's claim (fr. 4 West) that Athens was "the oldest land of Ionia." J. Hall (1997, 55) argues that the idea of Athens as mother city was formulated in the late fifth century as an ideological support to the Athenian-led alliance of Ionian cities.

[115] Alternative traditions trace the origins of the Ionians to Messenia, Achaea, and Thebes. (J. Hall 1997, 51–52). Hdt. 1.146.1 adds a number of other groups to the settlers of Ionia. For discussion, see also Thomas 2001, 225–26.

[116] Shipley 1987, 27.

[117] N. Jones 1987, 195. The evidence comes from the late seventh-century Samian colony of Perinthus; see N. Jones (1987, 286) for references.

[118] Coldstream 1977, 97.

Samians were legendary for the strength of their navy in the sixth century, and Thucydides dates the origins of Samian sea power to the visit of the Corinthian shipbuilder Ameinocles in the late eighth century.[119] Samos's participation in several battles in the late eighth century further confirms the strength of the Samian fleet already in the early archaic period.[120] Since there was no distinction between merchant craft and warships in this period, it is likely that these ships were first constructed and most often used for trading activities.

The location of Samos also facilitated active involvement in trade. Eighth-century pottery from Euboea suggests that Samos was a major stop on the trade route to the eastern Mediterranean. Already in the eighth century, Samos was the recipient of bronzes and metalwork from Attica, the Peloponnesus, and the Cyclades. Similarly, bronze figurines, carved ivories, and terra-cottas from Phrygia, Cyprus, northern Syria, and Persia confirm the flow of goods from the East.[121] Regular trade with Egypt is attested from the seventh century by the presence of Egyptian bronze figurines and carved ivories.[122] Herodotus, moreover, recounts the tale of the Samian trader Colaeus (mid-seventh century), who was en route for Egypt when he was blown off course and made a fortune trading in the West.[123]

In exchange for these luxury goods from the East and the West, the Samians offered the fruits of their fertile landscape: "oil, wine, cereals, wool, textiles, leather and perhaps Samian earth."[124] An excavated shipwreck of Ionian, possibly even Samian origin dating to around 600 confirms trade in olive oil and wine: olive pits and Samian amphoras were found on board.[125] In addition, the acquisition of some territory on the mainland opposite the island in the late eighth century seems to have been primarily motivated by the desire to provide further surpluses for trade. This area, encompassing the peninsula formed by the ridge of Mount Mycale, became known as the Peraea ("Land Opposite") and provided additional resources of arable land, pasture, and timber.[126] A different but also trade-related explanation is likely for the two earliest Samian colonies located on the rocky coast of Cilicia opposite Cyprus. The strategic location in combination with the lack of agricultural opportunities suggests that these Samian settlements served as outposts for trade with Cyprus and the Levant.[127]

As argued previously in relation to Mytilene, it is likely that the elites were the first to take advantage of the new opportunities for trade due to their interest in acquiring luxury items to enhance their status and prestige at home and abroad.

[119] Hdt. 3.39, 122; Thuc. 1.13.3–6.
[120] The so-called Meliac War, discussed below, and a battle with Aegina reported by Hdt. 3.59.4, probably dating to the late eighth century: Shipley 1987, 37–38.
[121] Shipley 1987, 42–48, Kyrieleis 1993.
[122] Shipley 1987, 56–57.
[123] Hdt. 4.152.
[124] Shipley 1987, 45.
[125] The ship, found at Giglio, off the west coast of Italy, is discussed by Shipley 1987, 61.
[126] Shipley 1987, 31–37, 47.
[127] Shipley 1987, 41–42, 47.

The necessity of producing agricultural surplus for trade, moreover, illuminates the basis of elite wealth: land. The agricultural basis of wealth is confirmed by the title of the ruling elites who held power by about 700, the geomoroi, "those who have a share of the land."[128] The regime of the geomoroi was an oligarchy of these landowning elites, who probably shared power through rotation of public office. Prior to the oligarchy of the geomoroi, a monarchy had existed similar to that of other Greek poleis of the time.[129] Presumably the opening up of power to the elites as a whole was a solution to rivalry for power between the family of the king and a small group of wealthy elites. Thucydides says that four hundred geomoroi were exiled by the people in 411, and their number may have been somewhat smaller in the archaic period.[130]

As in the cases of Mytilene and Megara, the elites were probably not the only ones to benefit from the expanding opportunities for overseas trade. Ambitious non-elites might also have taken advantage of the new opportunities to produce surplus for trade or taken their chances as agents of the elites in trading voyages. As Sally Humphreys has pointed out, the whole crew of the Samian trader Colaeus dedicated the bronze cauldron at the Heraeum, a fact suggesting that they all shared in the profits of the voyage.[131] The prospect of wealth from trading may have lured many non-elites into trade.

Although there must have been a large group of non-elites who worked small plots of land and/or were dependent laborers for the wealthy, we know almost nothing of them. Graham Shipley argues that the western side of the island was exploited agriculturally well before we have evidence of permanent settlement there in the Hellenistic period.[132] We can therefore imagine that the mass of non-elite farmers commuted from the polis center to small, possibly scattered plots in the hinterland. Interestingly, non-elite religious behavior in the form of modest dedications at the Heraeum, such as plain wooden bowls and wood and terra-cotta statuettes, is the one sphere in which the lives of the common people are detectable in the material record.[133]

With this outline of the social organization and economic basis of the early Samian polis in mind, we can now turn to the evidence for Samian political development. As we have just seen, by about 700 an oligarchy composed of landowning elites (the geomoroi) had replaced monarchical rule. The geomoroi ruled continuously until the last decades of the seventh or the

---

[128] Thuc. 8.21, Plut. *Quaest. Graec.* 57 (*Mor.* 303f–304c).

[129] Hdt. 3.59.4 mentions King Amphicrates, who ruled at the time of the war with Aegina, probably in the late eighth century.

[130] *Pace* Shipley (1987, 40), who believes that the geomoroi were even more numerous in the archaic period and that Thucydides' number represents the survivors of the preceding periods of tyrannical and democratic rule. I will argue that the tyrants sprang from the geomoroi themselves and to a large degree did not harm their fellow elites: see below.

[131] Hdt. 4.152.4; Humphreys 1978, 168.

[132] Shipley 1987, 231–47.

[133] Kyrieleis 1993, 141.

beginning of the sixth century, when a number of factors destabilized their rule. First, the Cimmerian invasions in the second half of the seventh century had lasting effects on Samos's claim to the Peraea. Following the withdrawal of the Cimmerians, the Prieneans laid claim to the area, and the Samians engaged in a series of battles to try to reclaim it. In one battle, a thousand Samians were killed by the Prieneans.[134]

Also in the late seventh century, the Samians established a series of new settlements at Amorgos and in the Propontis. These settlements seem to have been motivated by the same desires that drove the earlier settlements: arable land and the expansion of trade.[135] The desire for arable land suggests that there were tensions over land in Samos, which may have been exacerbated by the threat to Samian control of the Peraea. The desire for increased trade contacts reflects the continued drive of the elites to acquire luxury goods, as well as the expanded opportunities for non-elites to gain wealth. The second wave of Samian settlements abroad, therefore, probably reflects social and economic currents that may have destabilized the rule of the traditional landowning elite.

It was in fact Samos's settlement at Perinthus in the Propontis that served as a catalyst to the overthrow of the geomoroi. According to Plutarch, the Megarians (who were also active settlers of the Propontis) attacked Perinthus.[136] The geomoroi sent out nine generals in command of thirty ships to deal with the situation. Although two of the ships were destroyed by lightning, the Samian generals successfully defeated the Megarians and took six hundred of them captive. Following this successful action, the generals decided to overthrow the geomoroi. With the help of the Megarian captives, the generals surprised the geomoroi in council and killed them. Since the generals were themselves appointed by the geomoroi and presumably came from the same ruling group, their coup represented an attempt to establish more exclusive power for themselves. Despite Plutarch's claim that the generals aimed to liberate the polis (τὴν πόλιν ἐλευθερῶσαι), it is likely that their rule represented the replacement of a narrow oligarchy by one even narrower. That this change reflects competition for power within the elite is confirmed by the aftermath of the generals' coup: the seizure of power around 590 by a single general, named Syloson.

Syloson was general in a war against the "Aeolians," by which Plutarch probably means Mytilene.[137] Syloson's rule, like the rule of the nine generals and of the geomoroi before them, was a still more extreme form of elite rule, the narrowest possible: a tyranny. Syloson's seizure of power, therefore, was

---

[134] Plut. *Quaest. Graec.* 20 (*Mor.* 295f–296b).

[135] Shipley 1987, 50–52.

[136] Plut. *Quaest. Graec.* 57 (*Mor.* 303f–304c).

[137] Syloson also may have been one of the otherwise unnamed nine generals who fought at Perinthus, as Shipley suggests (1987, 53).

the result not of popular discontent with elite rule, but rather of intra-elite competition for power.[138] It seems that the unstable conditions of the late seventh and early sixth centuries provided opportunities for victorious generals to seize exclusive power.[139] It is anachronistic to say that the tyrant Syloson was a popular leader, or that he exploited popular discontent with the rule of the geomoroi.[140] The apparent ease with which Syloson (and later his successors) gained power seems to suggest that the non-elite were not particularly concerned about which elite group held power. Rather, it is likely that power circulated among a small group of elites, who used violence to seize power from one another.

Syloson and his descendants ruled Samos with few interruptions for the better part of the sixth century. Around 560 Syloson was succeeded by his son Aiakes, who in turn was succeeded by the most famous of the Samian tyrants, Polycrates, who ruled from the mid-540s to 522.[141] Given the background of intense rivalry among the geomoroi for power, one must ask why the family of Polycrates was able to rule for three generations. The first key to the tyrants' success was their control of the Samian military forces. Both Thucydides and Herodotus mention the legendary strength of Polycrates' navy (see above), and Herodotus (3.39.3) reports that Polycrates had a force of one hundred ships. Although we know very little about the organization of fleets in the archaic period, it is likely that Polycrates' control of the navy meant little more than his successful construction of personal alliances with the group of elites who owned ships and were willing to put them to use in the service of the community. Therefore, although in formal terms the rule of Polycrates and his predecessors represented a narrowing of the oligarchy of the geomoroi, the tyrants were successful in part because of their ability to maintain the informal cooperation of a broad group of their fellow elites—that is, the majority of the geomoroi.[142]

Some of this cooperation must have been won through the uses to which the tyrants put the ships. Though Herodotus reports that Polycrates conquered most of the islands and many of the cities on the mainland, it is likely that he and his predecessors mostly conducted raiding missions, by which they

[138] Syloson's elite status is indicated not only by his tenure of the generalship but by his father's name, Calliteles, which has aristocratic associations.

[139] Pisistratus, among other archaic tyrants, also used the generalship to launch his bid for tyranny: see chapter 3.

[140] Shipley (1987, 53) argues for this interpretation based on Polyaenus's report (6.45) that Syloson was chosen general because he seemed to be a friend of the people (δημοτικός). Polyaenus's anecdote is clearly part of a later anti-tyrannical tradition by which tyrants are represented as deceiving the people and thereby gaining power. (See below, chapter 3.) These anti-tyrannical traditions presume a mass of common people politically self-conscious enough to need to be deceived into accepting a tyrant.

[141] For the dates, see Shipley 1987, 74–80.

[142] R. Osborne (1996a, 276) reaches a similar conclusion.

enriched themselves.[143] One use to which the tyrants put this wealth was the enlargement and elaboration of the Heraeum. Under Syloson, the Hecatompedon was demolished and replaced by a much larger and more elaborate temple known after its chief architect, Rhoecus. The size of the temple (52.5 m × 105 m) and its multiple rows of columns on all sides served as a grand expression of the glory of sixth-century Samos, and it became the model for temples and tyrants elsewhere.[144] Following the loss of the Rhoecus temple in a fire, a second, even larger temple was built under Polycrates.[145] It is likely that such public symbols of Samian greatness helped to unite elites and non-elites behind the rule of the tyrants.[146]

In addition to the temples, the tyrants oversaw a number of further building projects that must have helped to cement their popularity with elites and non-elites alike. For example, a harbor mole was constructed, which increased the size of the harbor and protected the ships from southerly winds.[147] They also built a long tunnel that brought water into the city from a spring more than a kilometer away. Several other archaic tyrants engaged in public water projects (Theagenes of Megara; the Pisistratids of Athens), and these constructions served as advertisements of their service to the community.

The fact that the tyrants treated their fellow elites well is further suggested by the fact that Samian elites continued to acquire and display expensive foreign- and Samian-made luxury items. Although it has often been suggested that archaic tyrants curtailed elite display as a sort of populist policy, there is little evidence for this assertion.[148] At Samos, some of the most spectacular pieces of

[143] Hdt. 3.39.4; with Shipley 1987, 71, 94–95. The dedication of a statue of Hera by a member of the tyrant family from plunder (σύλη) during his tenure of public office c. 500 (ML 16) reveals the connection between Samian piracy and the physical magnificence of the sanctuary of Hera.

[144] The Artemisium at Ephesus appears to imitate the form of the Rhoecus temple. Similarly, the enormous Temple of Zeus at Athens, though unfinished, was intended as a symbol of the status of Athens and its tyrants in the late sixth century: see below, chapter 3.

[145] It was this temple that Herodotus saw, although he mistakenly claims that Rhoecus was the architect (3.60.4).

[146] The explanation for tyrannical building projects (such as those of Polycrates) given by Arist. *Pol.* 1313b24—namely that such projects are designed to keep the people too busy and poor to engage in political affairs—is anachronistic, because it assumes a desire of the people to engage in politics. The explanation is therefore clearly a product of fourth-century political theory. On temples and tyrants, see chapter 3 below.

[147] Hdt. 3.60; with Shipley 1987, 76–77.

[148] Keesling 2003 demonstrates this masterfully for Athenian dedications on the acropolis during the Pisistratid tyranny. Shipley (1987, 91) accepts the orthodox view that both Polycrates of Samos and Lygdamis of Naxos curbed aristocratic display, as does Stewart (1986, 67–68). Cf. B. Mitchell 1975, 84–85. The primary positive evidence comes from later literary sources: Arist. *Oec.* 1346b17, where Lygdamis is said to have put the confiscated scuptures of exiled elites up for sale; Hieronymus of Rhodes *apud* Athen. 13.602a, where Polycrates is said to have torn down the wrestling schools on the grounds that conspiracies against tyrannies were often formed among pederastic couples active there. Keesling shows that the anecdote about Lygdamis actually implies not that the tyrant prevented the display of the statues, but only that he tried to profit by selling

eastern Ionic sculpture were set up along the Sacred Way to the Heraeum during the rule of the tyrants. In particular, a youth (kouros) three times life-size made of Samian black-veined marble and dating to around 580 is a masterpiece of archaic sculpture.[149] Although the number of surviving sculptures begins to decline after about 540, it is possible that the most popular medium in this period was bronze, and bronze sculptures are less likely to survive.[150] Furthermore, there is no evidence of decline in other categories of artifact such as fine pottery and smaller metalwork.[151]

The satisfaction of the majority of elites and non-elites with the rule of the tyrants, and their willingness to let power rest within the family, is perhaps further indicated by the way in which Polycrates gained tyrannical power. As we have seen, Polycrates was preceded in power by his grandfather Syloson I and his father, Aiakes I. Yet Herodotus reports that Polycrates gained power after rising up in revolt (ἐπαναστάς) and that he seized power with a force of fifteen hoplites.[152] Shipley suggests that the geomoroi had regained power and that Polycrates rose up and overthrew them.[153] Yet this explanation is unlikely for several reasons. First, Polycrates would have needed a larger force than fifteen hoplites to overthrow the geomoroi, who numbered in the hundreds. Second, Herodotus reports that although Polycrates at first held power with his two brothers, Pantagnotus and Syloson II, he later killed Pantagnotus and exiled Syloson.[154] Given this intra-familial rivalry for power, the idea that Polycrates initially rose up and seized power from his own father, Aiakes I, is not implausible. Polycrates' initiative against his father may have been prompted by the question of succession, since Aiakes had three sons and there were besides other branches of the family who might have been interested in power.[155] For

them. Presumably the new owners of the statues were not restricted from displaying them. Regarding Polycrates' alleged destruction of the wrestling schools, a case can be made that this charge is a product of anti-tyrannical propaganda spread initially by the elite exiles from Polycrates' reign (see below) and later incorporated into Panhellenic anti-tyrannical traditions (see below). Shipley's (1987, 85–90) summary of the archaeological record refutes his own belief that Polycrates prevented his fellow elites from engaging in displays of their wealth and status.

[149] For this statue, see Kyrieleis 1993, 149–52; 1996. Other examples of similar statues under the tyrants include the Louvre youth of c. 570–550 and a youth of imported marble of c. 520.

[150] Shipley 1987, 84.

[151] Cf. Shipley 1987, 89: "The evidence indicates a higher level of achievement and a greater availability of fine goods. The quality of artistic endeavor did not fall. Even the spectacular seventh-century advances in crafts and technology were surpassed, and more and more luxury items were made from imported raw materials."

[152] Hdt. 3.48, 120. The anecdote reported by Polyaenus 1.23 regarding Polycrates' seizure of power is clearly a topos that became attached to a number of archaic tyrants: cf., e.g., Arist. Ath. Pol. 15.4–5 on Pisistratus; Polyaenus 6.45 on Syloson I.

[153] Shipley 1987, 72.

[154] Hdt. 3.39.

[155] For example, the Aiakes who made the dedication in ML 16. Meiggs and Lewis believe that he was not a member of the line of tyrants.

our purposes, however, the important point is that the wider group of elites, the geomoroi as a whole, and for that matter non-elites were largely oblivious to the violent struggles for power within the tyrannical family.

Yet despite the case for widespread support of tyrannical rule, there is evidence for at least a small group of elite opponents of the tyrants in the second half of the sixth century. Herodotus tells us that Polycrates sent "those of the citizens whom he most suspected of revolution" away on forty triremes so that they might die while fighting for Cambyses in Egypt.[156] Many details of the story are suspect, since, as we shall see in chapter 6, they conform to the fifth-century stereotype of the tyrant's brutal treatment of his fellow citizens. Nevertheless, it is clear that some elite Samians went into exile under Polycrates and sought Spartan aid to attempt to return by force and overthrow the tyranny. The appeal to Sparta was probably facilitated by personal ties of guest-friendship (ξενία) between Samian and Spartan elites, an inference that confirms the status of the exiles as elites.[157] These dissidents were probably only a small fraction of the geomoroi, most of whom were content with the rule of the tyrants.[158]

Despite their small numbers, the exiles managed to persuade the Spartans to help them, and, according to Herodotus, the Spartans sent a large military force (στόλος μέγας).[159] The fact that this large force failed to take Samos further confirms the general support that Polycrates enjoyed among the Samians who remained.[160] Herodotus states that many of the Samians themselves (αὐτῶν Σαμίων) fought together with Polycrates' foreign allies against the Spartans.[161] Polycrates' foreign allies were probably gained through his guest-friendship ties with Lygdamis, tyrant of Naxos.[162] As for Polycrates' Samian forces, it is most likely that they were composed of shipowning elites and moderately wealthy non-elites who could afford hoplite arms.

Following the unsuccessful siege of Samos by the Spartans, the exiles must have realized the futility of their attempts in the face of the strong support enjoyed by Polycrates. The exiles therefore gave up the attempt to return and

---

[156] Hdt. 3.44–47.1, 54–59.

[157] Ties of guest-friendship involving gift exchange are attested in Spartan dedications found at the Heraeum going back at least to the seventh century. See especially Cartledge 1982, 252–54.

[158] The forty triremes would then be part of the fifth-century elaboration of the story, which exaggerated the number of citizens treated brutally by the tyrant. See chapter 6 below.

[159] Hdt. 3.44.1, 46.2, 54.1.

[160] Herodotus's report (3.45.4) that Polycrates imprisoned the children and wives of the Samians in shipsheds and threatened to burn them if anyone betrayed the island to the exiles is a fifth-century explanation of why the Samians failed to overthrow the tyranny: see chapter 6 below.

[161] Hdt. 3.54.2. Compare Hdt. 3.45.3 on the exiles' initial, unsuccessful attempt to return, stating that Polycrates commanded "a great number of allied and mercenary troops as well as native [Samian] archers."

[162] Polyaenus 1.23.2. Both tyrant and exiles, therefore, made use of foreign allies to further their aims at maintaining or gaining power in Samos.

settled at Cydonia, in Crete, after some years of wandering.[163] We hear of
another group of exiles from Samos during Polycrates' reign, who are said to
have founded Dicaearchia (later Puteoli), between Naples and Cumae.[164]
The philosopher Pythagoras also probably went into exile during the tyranny
of Polycrates and for this reason spent most of the rest of his life in Italy.[165]

Following the death of Polycrates at the hands of the Persian satrap Or-
oetes, the character of politics changed to some degree due to the predominant influence of outside powers on the internal political situation in Samos.
Elite groups still gained and lost power through violence, but they began to
rely largely on Persia and, in the fifth century, on Athens for military support.
Thus following the death of Polycrates (itself a product of Persian interfer-
ence), Polycrates' exiled brother Syloson II gained the support of the Persian
king Darius in his bid to regain power in Samos.[166] A tradition arose that
Syloson's rule was so harsh that Samos became barren of people. Herodotus
records that the Persians went through Samos with a dragnet and handed over
to Syloson an empty island. These traditions can be explained as later elab-
orations of the theme of the destructiveness of the tyrant toward his own
people, and would have been important in later times for excusing the actual
lack of resistance to Syloson by the majority of elites and non-elites. Under
Syloson II and his successor Aiakes II, as under Polycrates, a small number of
elites may have gone into exile. Herodotus mentions a group of Samians "of
the Aeschronian tribe" living at Oasis in Libya in his own day, who may have
left Samos under these later tyrants.[167]

In sum, the history of Samos in the archaic period reflects the same violent
struggle for power among a narrow group of elites that we have seen in other
archaic poleis. Indeed, the oligarchy of the geomoroi seems to have gradually
disintegrated in the face of violent coups by smaller and smaller groups of
elites. Finally, the tyrannical family of Polycrates managed to maintain power
by exiling small numbers of diehard opponents, and by building informal
alliances with the majority of the geomoroi. Although economic expansion
and new market opportunities may have led to the enrichment of some non-
elites, there is little sign that they played a role in arbitrating the violent
struggles for power among elites. The only exception to this claim is the
Spartan attack on Polycrates, which seems to have prompted many Samians
to take up arms against exiles backed by a foreign foe. Whether or not this

[163] Hdt. 3.57.9.

[164] Eusebius *ad* Abraham 1489 (= 526 B.C.E.); cf. B. Mitchell 1975, 87.

[165] Aristoxenus frr.12, 16 Wehrli; Strabo 14.638; D.L. 8.3; Iamblichus, *Life of Pythagoras* 6.28.

[166] Hdt. 3.142–48. Polycrates' secretary Maeandrius briefly held power before he was exiled by
Syloson and the Persians.

[167] Hdt. 3.26. These exiles are probably to be equated with the Samians who joined the exiled
Arcesilaus III of Cyrene as mercenaries and fought to restore him (Hdt. 4.162–64): cf. Shipley
1987, 106.

action had longer-term implications for the distribution of power in Samos is obscured by the predominant role that Persia began to play in Samian affairs after the death of Polycrates.

CORINTH

The case of Corinth provides a final example of the role of violent intra-elite conflict in archaic politics. Both the oligarchy of the Bacchiads and the tyranny of the Cypselids used expulsion as a tool to secure power. As in the cases of Megara and Samos, non-elites apparently played little role in mediating intra-elite conflict, and both the oligarchy of the Bacchiads and the Cypselid tyranny were successful in maintaining elite rule.

A brief review of the prehistory of Corinth will help to put these later events in context. Most of the villages of the Corinthia show signs of abandonment or destruction at the end of the Bronze Age, and the region began to be resettled around 900.[168] Analysis of literary traditions suggests that although the early Corinthians had a their own local foundation legend, it was adapted early on to fit into the twin myths of the Dorian Invasion and the Return of the Heraclidae, which probably originated at Argos and Sparta, respectively.[169] Thus Corinth may have been resettled independently of the other major poleis of the Peloponnesus, and only later have been assimilated into the Dorian tradition.[170] Similarities in cultic practices and dialect between Corinth and the other Dorian cities may correspondingly be later adaptations rather than the result of genetic ties.[171] It was probably only during the eighth century that the population of Corinth was organized according to the three Dorian tribes.[172] It is likely that the early population of Corinth was made up of both newcomers and the thinly scattered residue of earlier inhabitants of the Corinthia.[173]

---

[168] Salmon 1984, 39–48.

[169] Salmon 1984, 38; J. Hall 1997, 56–65. The main sources for the traditions are Thuc. 1.24.2, 4.42.2; Paus. 2.4.3; Diod. Sic. 7.9.2. Hall notes the oddness of the fact that, according to Diodorus's version of the tradition, the founder, Aletes, did not accompany the returning Heraclidae, but was invited to rule following the conquest. One might also note that the tradition reported by Diodorus is at pains to reconcile the supposed Heraclid origins of Aletes with the fact that his descendants were known as Bacchiads, not Heraclidae. The solution to this inconsistency was to invent a later King Bacchis, whose fame was so great that his descendants became known not as Heraclidae but as Bacchiadae. Salmon notes, furthermore, that in one version (schol. Pind. *Nem.* 7.155a) the foundation of Corinth has nothing to do with the Return of the Heraclidae.

[170] C. Morgan (1994, 137) suggests that this assimilation took place in the eighth century on the basis of the role of the Oracle of Zeus at Dodona in the foundation myth.

[171] See J. Hall (1997, 111–81) for these arguments about cult and dialect. *Contra*: Salmon 1984, 51–53.

[172] N. Jones 1987, 97. The existence of the Dorian tribes at Corinth is inferred from their presence at the Corinthian colonies of Syracuse and Corcyra. See N. Jones 1987 for references.

[173] There is evidence of continual occupation at Corinth itself from the late Bronze Age.

Changes in the material record dating to the eighth and seventh centuries suggest not only that the Corinthian polis formed and strengthened during this time, but that rivalry among elites played a major role in these developments. The first major sign of polis formation and intra-elite competition is change in cultic behavior. Although the cult site of Isthmia dates back to the eleventh century, it is only in the eighth century that evidence for formal dining appears, as well as bronze tripods and other valuable display items.[174] Similar evidence appears at Perachora in the eighth century, and, in addition, a small apsidal temple was constructed there at this time.[175] Given the evidence for conflict with Megara over this territory, it is possible that the temple served to lay claim to the region for Corinth.[176] More important for my purposes, I suggest that the burst of cultic activity at both sites in the second half of the eighth century is a sign of intensified status competition among elites in the newly consolidating polis community.[177]

A second indication of intra-elite competition comes from the record of strong Corinthian involvement in trade. The strategic position of Corinth, with its access to both the Aegean and the Adriatic, naturally favored capitalization on the expanding trade networks connecting the East and the West. Corinthian pottery dating to the early eighth century has been found in sites scattered up and down the Adriatic seaboard, and further finds at Pithecusae dating to about 760 show that the Corinthians were trading in the West well before they established settlements there.[178] By the seventh century, Corinthian trade was booming. Although pots are the most archaeologically visible sign of Corinthian trade, they probably comprised only a small part of Corinthian exports.[179] More important were textiles, roof tiles, stone, timber, terra-cotta sculptures, olive oil, wine, perfumes, and metalwork.[180] In return for these goods, Corinthians probably received metals, corn, and salted or dried fish.[181]

---

[174] C. Morgan 1994, 124–28. The role of formal dining may be parallel to that of funeral feasts in elite burials. As burial becomes less effective in projecting status to the ever widening polis community, funeral feasts are transferred to a sanctuary context, where displays can be made and reciprocal relations enforced among a much wider group. Rabinowitz 2004, however, relates the shift to the importance, in the early polis, of neutralizing the symbolically potent activity of dining by removing it from an elite individual's residence.

[175] C. Morgan 1994, 129–30.

[176] De Polignac 1994, 15. Conflict with Megara: Plut. *Quaest. Graec.* 17 (*Mor.* 295b–c). See also my discussion of Megara above.

[177] C. Morgan (1994, 133, 140) alludes to this idea. Cultic activity in Corinth proper intensified only c. 680, when the first stone temple was built (C. Morgan 1994, 138).

[178] Salmon 1984, 85–91. For the earliest Corinthian settlements abroad (Syracuse c. 733 and Corcyra c. 720–700), see Graham 1982, 160–62.

[179] R. Osborne 1996b.

[180] Salmon 1984, 101–27.

[181] Salmon 1984, 128–31.

As with other poleis active in commerce, it was most likely the elites who initially had the motives and means to engage in trade.[182] Foremost among the motives for overseas trading would have been the desire for wealth and luxury goods—sources of symbolic capital that could be used to acquire or reinforce status and power in the consolidating polis.[183] The importance of textiles and timber as goods for exchange, moreover, suggests that landownership would have been the primary basis of wealth for Corinthian elites. It is possible that Corinthian elites were appropriating large portions of land at the expense of non-elites, since Aristotle reports that Pheidon was one of Corinth's earliest lawgivers, and that he was concerned with the distribution of land among citizens.[184] Although Aristotle does not make clear the exact terms of Pheidon's legislation, the passage indicates that there was inequality in landholdings and that there was enough discontent to prompt legislation in this area.

If we turn to the political organization of Corinth, there are further signs of intra-elite competition as a key factor in the development of the polis. Tradition held that, after the overthrow of the monarchy, the annual office of prytanis was created.[185] It is likely that there were other public offices, such as the office of polemarch, which Cypselus allegedly held before he seized the tyranny.[186] (See below.) These offices rotated among a group of two hundred elites known as Bacchiadae.[187] The creation of annually rotating public offices must have been a response to the demands of this wider group of elites for a share in political power. The small size of the Bacchiad oligarchy, however, attests to the limited range of discontent with the monarchy. The Bacchiadae ruled for almost a century, and despite the evidence for tensions over land, there seems to have been little discontent with the manner of rule or political structure of the polis during this time.

Although a later source reports that the tyrant Cypselus repatriated those who were forced into exile under the Bacchiads, it is unlikely that there were many exiles.[188] Those who did go into exile were probably just the relatives and associates of the former monarchs. The longevity of Bacchiad rule suggests that the majority of elites remained and were content with the narrow oligarchy. Moreover, the period of Bacchiad rule (roughly 750–650) was one of rapid expansion of

[182] Dion. Hal. *Ant. Rom.* 3.45 tells the story of Demaratus of the ruling Bacchiad family, who apparently grew rich through trade with Etruria. For the archaeological evidence for Corinthian trade with Etruria, see Salmon 1984, 106, 114.

[183] The story of Demaratus (see n. 182 above) illustrates the potential role that wealth acquired through trade could play in struggles for political power.

[184] Arist. *Pol.* 1265b12–16. Aristotle does not give a date for Pheidon's legislation, but Salmon (1984, 63) believes he must have legislated before the tyranny of Cypselus.

[185] Diod. Sic. 7.9, Paus. 4.4.

[186] Compare also the office of βασιλεύς, which the Bacchiad Patrocleides held before being assassinated in Cypselus's coup (below, n. 191).

[187] Hdt. 5.92β.1.

[188] Nic. Dam. *FGrH* 90 F 57.7.

trade, a fact that suggests a vigorous elite, not one subject to widespread expulsions. The construction of the Sacred and Cyclopean fountain houses during this time further reflects the strength and prosperity of Corinth under Bacchiad rule.[189]

As in other poleis, however, the mechanism for sharing power through the rotation of public offices was ultimately unsuccessful in preventing the seizure of exclusive power by an even smaller faction among the elites. In the mid-seventh century, a Bacchiad named Cypselus seized sole power.[190] Herodotus is silent about how Cypselus seized power, but Ephorus (as preserved in Nicolaus of Damascus) probably comes close to the truth when he reports that Cypselus "gathered a group of associates [ἑταιρικόν] and killed Patrocleides, who held the office of king [βασιλεύς, basileus]."[191] This report conforms with the pattern of violent seizure of power by small groups of elites that is apparent in other archaic poleis. As we shall see, Cypselus's seizure of power entailed not only the occasional murder of political opponents but, more important, their expulsion from the polis. Before I analyze this aspect of Cypselid rule, however, several important methodological issues must be dealt with.

In attempting to understand the manner of Cypselid rule we are confronted by twin problems of interpretation. First of all, the traditions concerning these tyrants have been influenced by the role of the tyrant as a negative exemplum in fifth-century democratic ideology.[192] Thus Cypselus and especially Periander became paradigmatic models of the evil tyrant. As such, all sorts of actions are attributed to them that may have little to do with the historical Corinthian tyrants: in Herodotus's account, for example, these tyrants banish, murder, and confiscate the property of many Corinthians.[193] The second problem with the traditions concerning the Corinthian tyrants is that they have been influenced by fourth-century political theory, by which tyrants are anachronistically understood as champions of the people who overthrow the repressive rule of the elites.[194] Thus in Ephorus's version of the Cypselid tyranny, Cypselus is a "friend of the people" who overthrows the "hubristic and brutal Bacchiads."[195]

---

[189] Salmon 1984, 59.

[190] The traditions (Hdt. 5. 92, Nic. Dam. FGrH 90 F 57) are very confused about Cypselus's status. On the one hand they assert that he was born of a lame mother and a non-Bacchiad father, hence implying that he was from a marginalized branch of the Bacchiads. On the other hand, it is claimed that he was polemarch before becoming tyrant. Both versions represent attempts to explain why Cypselus seized power from the oligarchy of which he was a part. The only historically sound item in the traditions is that Cypselus was in fact a member of the ruling elite. Cf. Oost 1972, 16.

[191] Nic. Dam. FGrH 90 F 57.6. The title "king" presumably was one of the magistracies established under Bacchiad rule.

[192] Forsdyke 1999, 2001; and chapter 6 below.

[193] Hdt. 5.92.ε.2. Cf. Nic. Dam. FGrH 90 F 57.7, where Cypselus is said to have banished "whoever was not a close friend [φίλος]."

[194] Arist. Pol. 1310b12–32.

[195] Nic. Dam. FGrH 90 F 57.4; cf. 57.6, where "the people" make Cypselus king. See also Arist. Pol. 1315b28–30.

Despite these seemingly contradictory representations of the Corinthian tyrants, a case can be made that both of them preserve some elements of the
historical tyranny.[196] In particular, Herodotus's account of political expulsions
under the Cypselids probably reflects the actual expulsion of the formerly ruling
Bacchiads, but not the expulsion of a wider group of citizens as Herodotus
implies. Reinterpretation of Herodotus's account along these lines not only fits
the pattern of archaic politics visible in a number of poleis, but also accords with
references to exiled members of the Bacchiad oligarchy scattered throughout
our sources. The most famous we hear of is the Bacchiad Demaratus, who went
to Etruria and became the father of one of the early kings of Rome.[197] Plutarch
mentions that the Bacchiads fled to Sparta.[198] Ephorus, by contrast, claims that
the Bacchiads went to Corcyra.[199] Finally, Plutarch mentions a Bacchiad
named Archias who founded Syracuse about 733.[200] Although Plutarch claims
that Archias's exile was a result of the death of a young boy in Corinth, it is likely
that he left because of the political struggle surrounding Cypselus's coup. In this
case, it is possible that the foundation of a new settlement abroad was a direct
consequence of intra-elite struggles for power in the newly forming polis.[201]

It is noteworthy that in each of these traditions, those exiled under Cypselus are members of the Bacchiad oligarchy. This suggests that, apart from
the Bacchiads themselves, the majority of the citizens remained in Corinth
and were content with Cypselid rule. The expansion of the number of exiles
to include the entire citizen body (as in Herodotus's account) is easily explained as a product of the later desire to vilify tyranny through reference to
the abuses perpetrated on the citizenry as a whole.[202]

Ephorus's positive version of the tyranny may reflect the general contentment
of Corinthians—elite and non-elite alike—under Cypselid rule.[203] A key factor

---

[196] Compare R. Osborne (1996a, 192–97), who similarly analyzes the Corinthian tyranny in
terms of "good tyrant/bad tyrant" traditions. Osborne, however, is more pessimistic than I that
these traditions preserve some elements of the historical tyranny.

[197] Dion. Hal. Ant.Rom. 3.46–47.

[198] Plut. Lys. 1.2.

[199] Nic. Dam. FGrH 90 F 57.7. There are traces of Corinthian exiles in Macedonia and
Caunia as well. See Berve (1967, 523) for references. Salmon 1984 does not trust the sources for
Bacchiad exiles anywhere except Corcyra.

[200] Plut. Love Stories (Mor. 772e–773b).

[201] See Malkin (1994b, 2) for the idea that the new settlements were products of the internal
struggles surrounding the formation of the polis. Malkin nevertheless believes the settlers were "in-
ferior groups" from the mother polis, not the elite. Other new settlements founded under the Cypselids
include Ambracia, Leucas, Anactorium, Apollonia, Epidamnus, and Potidaea. Ephorus explained
these settlements as places where Cypselus deported his political opponents (Nic. Dam. FGrH 90 F
57.7). Although this explanation is a product of the later anti-tyrannical ideologies, as I argue in chapter
6 below, it does suggest that intra-elite conflict lay behind early Corinthian settlements abroad.

[202] See Forsdyke 1999 and chapter 6 below for detailed analysis of Herodotus's version along
these lines.

[203] Compare my analysis of similar traditions about Pisistratus below in chapter 3.

in this contentment may have been the continued prosperity of Corinth, which is reflected in the numerous building projects of the time. During Cypselus's reign a temple of Apollo was built in Corinth, as well as a temple to Poseidon at Isthmia. In addition, the first fortification wall for the city dates to this period.[204] Periander, on the other hand, not only constructed a massive temple to Olympian Zeus but undertook projects designed to enhance Corinthian trade: the harbor at Lechaeum and the causeway by which ships could be transported across the Isthmus.[205] It is likely, furthermore, that Periander was responsible for building fountain houses for the springs of Pirene and Glauce, projects that would not only have enhanced Corinthian civic pride, but would have advertised his own status and power in the community.[206]

Periander's role in patronizing the poet Arion might also be mentioned in this regard.[207] Arion is credited with the invention the dithyramb, a choral song in honor of the god Dionysus. It is often claimed that Dionysus was a popular god, and that the promotion of festivals in his honor was part of the anti-elite policies of the archaic tyrants.[208] Yet such civic festivals would have been enjoyed by elites and non-elites alike, and would have played a role not only in creating civic unity, but also in articulating status differences between elites and non-elites. It was on the occasion of these festivals, after all, that elites had an opportunity to put themselves on display, and especially to demonstrate their services to the community.[209]

In addition to the archaeological evidence for the economic and cultural efflorescence of Corinth under the tyrants, some literary traditions suggest that tyrannical rule was viewed favorably by both elites and non-elites. The first oracle recorded by Herodotus presents Cypselus as the man who would overthrow the monarchic Bacchiads and "set Corinth right" (δικαιώσει Κόρινθον).[210] Ephorus says that Cypselus "ruled mildly and did not keep a bodyguard."[211] According to some, Periander was one of the Seven Sages, a status according well with his known role in inter-polis arbitration.[212] Aristotle, moreover, reports that Periander was neither unjust nor hubristic.[213]

Traditions recording the tyrants' services to non-elites are best explained as responses to potentially destabilizing economic troubles of the poor, rather

---

[204] For the temples, see Salmon 1984, 180; C. Morgan 1994, 140. For the fortification wall, see Salmon 1984, 220–21.

[205] Salmon 1984, 180.

[206] Salmon (1984, 201) notes, however, that the dates of construction are unclear.

[207] Hdt. 1.23.

[208] Andrewes 1956, 113–14; Salmon 1984, 201–2.

[209] For these arguments, see chapter 3 below on Pisistratus's cultural politics.

[210] Hdt. 5.92β.2, Diod. Sic. 7.9.6.

[211] Nic. Dam. FGrH 90 F 57.8.

[212] Periander as one of the Seven Sages: Nic. Dam. FGrH 90 F 58.4, D.L. 1.98. Periander as arbitrator between Mytilene and Athens over Sigeum: Hdt. 5.95.2.

[213] Arist. fr. 611.20 Rose.

than as part of an aim to become the "leaders of the people" (δημαγωγοί). The latter interpretation of the tyrants' actions is easily dismissed as anachronistic, since it assumes the political self-consciousness of the masses. Rather, the scant evidence that Ephorus provides for Cypselus's demagogic actions suggests that he had the limited aim of relieving economic distress. Ephorus reports that Cypselus became greatly loved by the people because he was the best of the magistrates then in power. Among his good deeds was the decision not to imprison those who owed fines (ἐπιτιμίαι), but to accept sureties and remit the portion of the fine that would have gone to himself as presiding magistrate.[214] While the details of this act of generosity are not reliable, the idea that Cypselus gave some form of economic relief to those who owed fines is not implausible. We hear of a measure to return interest to the poor in archaic Megara. (See above.) In archaic Athens, moreover, Solon canceled the debts of the poor, and Pisistratus gave them loans. (See below, chapter 3).

Economic relief of the poor may be further reflected in Ephorus's report that Cypselus reenfranchised those who had been disenfranchised under the Bacchiads.[215] While it is difficult to reconstruct the status that lies behind Ephorus's terms ἄτιμος (disenfranchised) and ἐπίτιμος (enfranchised), it is possible that these were the poorest members of the community, who had lost their land, and hence their citizenship, as a result of indebtedness to wealthier landowners.[216] In the case of Athens, Solon is said not only to have reaffirmed the citizenship of such destitute Athenians but to have actually brought them back home after they were sold into slavery abroad. (See chapter 3 below.) We cannot hope to recapture the detailed history behind the traditions regarding Cypselus's actions, but together they suggest that Cypselus (and possibly Periander)[217] responded to the economic distress of the Corinthian poor and won some popularity among the non-elites for doing so.

Beyond these meager inferences about the nature of Cypselid rule, the rest of the specific claims about the policies of the tyrants made by our sources seem to be derived from fifth- and fourth-century conceptions of tyranny.[218] For example, although the Cypselids did make elaborate dedications at Panhellenic sanctuaries (as was typical among families of their power and prestige), these were probably not made, as Aristotle has it, to keep the people busy and poor.[219] This interpretation of the dedications, as well as the claim that

---

[214] Nic. Dam. *FGrH* 90 F 57.5.

[215] Nic. Dam. *FGrH* 90 F 57.7.

[216] For the meaning of ἀτιμία in archaic and classical Greece see above, "Introduction."

[217] Arist. fr. 611.20 (Rose) reports that Periander collected no other taxes besides the market and harbor taxes.

[218] Salmon 1984, 195–205.

[219] Arist. *Pol.* 1313b18–22. Cypselid dedications at Delphi included a bronze palm tree (Plut. *Mor.* 164a, 299e–f, 724b) and a treasury (Hdt.1.14.2; Plut. *Mor.* 164a, 400d–e). For Cypselid dedications at Olympia (a colossus of gold; the Chest of Cypselus), see Salmon 1984, 228, with references.

the Cypselids forbade people from living in the city and from remaining idle, are all based on the anachronistic assumption that non-elites will seek a political role if they are not kept busy with work.[220] Similarly, the idea that Periander banned luxury, including the acquisition of slaves, assumes that elites are hostile to tyrants and therefore need to be suppressed through restrictions on their ability to engage in displays of conspicuous consumption.[221] As we have seen, there is good reason to believe that the majority of elites were content with Periander's rule. Furthermore, the Cypselid dedications themselves seem to attest that the tyrants were not hostile to the traditional forms of elite display in themselves, but rather were concerned to make sure that their own displays were the most extravagant.[222]

The success of the Cypselids in keeping the majority of elites and non-elites content is evident in the longevity of their rule. Aristotle lists the Cypselids as the second longest-lived tyranny, behind that of the tyrants of Sicyon.[223] According to Aristotle, Cypselus was tyrant for thirty years, and Periander for forty-four. Nevertheless, Periander's successor, Psammetichus, ruled for only three years before being overthrown.[224] Our sources are not helpful in illuminating reasons for the fall of the tyranny. Ephorus says that some of the Corinthians got together and killed the tyrant, thus "liberating the polis."[225] Plutarch claims that the tyranny was overthrown by the Spartans as part of a policy of ridding Greek cities of absolute rulers.[226] Both explanations assume that the overthrow was motivated by a desire for freedom and a recognition of the injustice of tyranny. As we have seen, these are assumptions based on later conceptions of the tyrants.

Deeper insight into the reasons for the end of the tyranny can be gained from the nature of the constitution set up following Psammetichus's murder. Although the evidence for this constitution is scant and difficult to interpret, it seems an oligarchy was formed that was even narrower than the Bacchiads'. A group of nine advance councilors (πρόβουλοι, probouloi) was established,

---

[220] Ban on living in the city: Arist. fr. 611.20 Rose, D.L. 1.98; cf. Arist. *Ath. Pol.* 16.2–3, 5 (on Pisistratus), *Pol.* 1311a8 (on tyrants in general). Ban on idleness: Nic. Dam. *FGrH* 90 F 58.1.

[221] Arist. fr. 611.20 Rose. Salmon (1984, 200) accepts that Periander banned luxury, pointing to the possible corroborating evidence of Hdt. 5.92 on Periander's burning the clothes of the women of Corinth (discussed below in chapter 6). For evidence that the archaic tyrants did not suppress elite display, see the section "Samos" above and, on Pisistratus, "A New Type of Politics" below in chapter 3.

[222] It might also be noted that Periander's active promotion of trade through the construction of the harbor and the causeway is contrary to the aim of banning luxury, since it was through trade that the elites gained the wealth and especially the metals that allowed for such luxury.

[223] *Pol.* 1315b12–30.

[224] Psammetichus was Periander's nephew: Nic. Dam. *FGrH* 90 F 60.1. The story of Periander's troubled relationship with his son Lycophron and his death at the hands of the Corcyreans, as told by Hdt. 3.50–53, is discussed below in chapter 6.

[225] Nic. Dam. *FGrH.* 90 F 60.1.

[226] Plut. *On the Malice of Herodotus* 19 (*Mor.* 859c–d).

along with a council of small size, possibly numbering eighty.[227] The existence of probouloi, along with the small size of the council, indicates the oligarchic nature of the new political structure.[228] More significant, the narrowness of this oligarchy suggests that opposition to the tyrants was formed among a small circle of elites who sought to redistribute power among themselves. Despite Ephorus's claim that the demos played a role in dismantling the tyranny, it is likely that the overthrow was accomplished by a narrow group of elites interested in gaining exclusive power for themselves.[229] These elites presumably reestablished in modified form the system of public offices established by the Bacchiads. Although we know nothing of the means of selecting these magistrates, it is likely that public offices were shared among the narrow group of elites who had overthrown the tyranny.

Despite the narrowness of the new regime, there is good reason to believe that the new oligarchs ruled moderately. The principal evidence for this claim is the extraordinary stability of their regime:[230] the oligarchs were in power from the mid-sixth to the mid-fourth century. Although Psammetichus had been murdered in the coup, and although his immediate associates may have fled into exile, the oligarchs apparently did not seek to maintain power through widespread terror and expulsions.

In sum, the history of archaic Corinth again illustrates the prevalence of violent intra-elite conflict. At Corinth, as at Megara and Samos, power changed hands as one elite faction drove another into exile and was exiled in turn. The Cypselid tyrants managed to hold on to power with relative success, however, by expelling some members of the Bacchiad oligarchy but otherwise ruling relatively benignly. The case of Corinth, like those of Mytilene, Megara, and Samos, therefore, shows how tyrants both used expulsions to secure power and took steps to ensure that the same tool could not be turned against themselves.

CONCLUSION

The detailed study of four archaic Greek poleis has shown how intra-elite competition, particularly the politics of exile, contributed to the instability of the archaic Greek poleis in the late seventh and sixth centuries. In all four

[227] The principal text is Nic. Dam. *FGrH* 90 F 60.2. For the interpretation of the size of the council, much depends on the reconstruction of Will (1955, 609–15), whereby nine councilors are chosen from each of the eight tribes. For the eight tribes, see *Suda* s.v. πάντα ὀκτώ. These tribes presumably replaced their Dorian counterparts either under the tyrants or under the new oligarchy itself. The significance of the new tribes for the political organization of Corinth, however, remains obscure. For a full discussion of the evidence for the civic organization of Corinth, see N. Jones 1980; 1987, 97–103.

[228] Salmon 1984, 234.

[229] Nic. Dam. *FGrH* 90 F 60.

[230] Salmon 1984, 236.

cases, rival elites vied for power at least in part by expelling their rivals. I have argued that these power struggles were waged largely among the elites, with little or no intervention of non-elites. The two possible exceptions—the role of non-elites in the election of Pittacus and in the defense of Samos against the exiles backed by Sparta—seem to be discrete incidents, which did not fundamentally change the balance of power between elites and non-elites. Indeed, in all four case studies, violent intra-elite conflict seems to have resulted in the strengthening of elite rule (i.e., in the form of a tyranny) rather than in its overthrow.

It is against this background that I examine the case of Athens in the next chapter. I show that Athens paralleled the development of the other archaic poleis in many ways, but ultimately diverged from the common pattern. Specifically, the Athenian case demonstrates the destabilizing effects of rampant intra-elite politics of exile, but also the dramatic steps taken by both elites and, ultimately, non-elites to avoid these consequences and end the practice of the politics of exile. The case of Athens demonstrates that a permanent solution to the problem of exile in archaic Greece could be found only through the greater involvement of the non-elites in the allocation of political power between elites. In Athens, this solution resulted not only in an end to the politics of exile but in the establishment of democratic rule.

Chapter Three

FROM EXILE TO OSTRACISM

The Origins of Democracy in Athens, circa 636–508/7

In chapter 2 I demonstrated that intra-elite politics of exile was a common phenomenon in archaic Greece. In this chapter, I argue that Athenian political development in the later archaic period both replicates the Panhellenic pattern of violent expulsions and returns, and begins to diverge from it. In particular, I argue that the relatively plentiful evidence for the development of Athens in the later archaic period demonstrates that political competition between rival groups of elites ("factions" in the anthropological sense) was the catalyst for the further development of the civic structures of the Athenian state and the enhancement of Athenian civic identity. Through the promulgation of laws, in particular, Athenian elites attempted (unsuccessfully) to moderate violent intra-elite competition, and to prevent themselves from being exiled. The indirect result of these laws, however, was to strengthen the civic structures of the state (in particular the mechanisms for the regulation of disputes) and to articulate more formally the legal and ideological basis of membership in the Athenian community (citizenship).

The actions of Solon and Pisistratus are particularly important in this regard. Solon attempted to avoid violent intra-elite competition for political office by introducing the lot for the selection of magistrates. More important, Solon saw that violent conflict between elites could be prevented only through the greater participation of non-elites in the allocation of political power. I argue that through his so-called law on stasis, Solon enjoined non-elites to intervene in intra-elite conflict. By encouraging non-elites to put their support on one side or the other, Solon hoped to prevent the rapid changes of power that resulted from competition between narrow groups of elites.

Although Solon was unsuccessful in moderating violent intra-elite competition, I argue that the later sixth-century tyrant Pisistratus developed Solon's strategy in a way that was much more effective in preventing violent intra-elite strife. I argue that Pisistratus was both an active participant in intra-elite politics of exile and the source of a new, more inclusive mode of conducting politics. Through his skillful use of the civic institutions, rituals, and cultural symbols of the Athenian community, Pisistratus was successful in activating non-elite support on his side in the struggle. Moreover, during his final tyranny, Pisistratus departed from the norm of intra-elite politics of exile by allowing his elite rivals to remain in Athens and enjoy positions of prestige. In both these ways, Pisistratus enhanced the collective unity of elite and non-elite Athenians and stabilized his position of power.

Despite the considerable advances made by Pisistratus in ending violent intra-elite competition, I show that a new round of the politics of exile broke out following the death of Pisistratus's son Hipparchus in 514. I argue that violent intra-elite competition for power was renewed with increased intensity in this period, and provided the context for the ultimate overthrow of elite power and the foundation of democracy in 508/7. I show that a crucial feature of the events by which the Athenian masses took over political power at this time was their intervention in intra-elite politics of exile. By actively giving their support to one elite group (led by Cleisthenes) and by expelling another group of elites (led by Isagoras), the Athenian masses established themselves as the arbiters of who was to be included and who excluded from the polis. I argue that this assumption of control over decisions of exile was equivalent to the usurpation of political power, since power in the archaic polis was largely a function of the ability to expel one's opponents. Cleisthenes' inclusion of the institution of ostracism among the reforms by which democratic power was established in Athens, I argue, constituted the symbolic recognition of the equivalency between democratic control over decisions of exile and democratic power.

The next section of this chapter examines the earliest known events of Athenian history—Cylon's attempt at tyranny, Draco's law on homicide, and the trial of the Alcmeonidae—and demonstrates that Athens, like other poleis in the late seventh century, was suffering from the instability caused by violent intra-elite politics of exile. The section entitled "The Beginning of Change" turns to the legislation of Solon. Here I show how Solon's measures to stabilize elite power anticipated the strategies of Pisistratus. The following section, "A New Type of Politics," examines the actions of Pisistratus and shows how he both played the game of exile and ultimately departed from this mode of political behavior. Finally, "An End to the Politics of Exile" examines the evidence for the democratic revolution and shows how exile and popular power were intimately linked both in the actions of the Athenian masses during the revolution and in the subsequent institutionalization of the democracy.

THE POLITICS OF EXILE IN ARCHAIC ATHENS: CYLON, DRACO, AND THE TRIAL OF THE ALCMEONIDAE

The earliest securely dated event in Athenian history is the attempt of Cylon, a member of the Athenian elite, to become tyrant circa 636.[1] Cylon was

---

[1] The main sources for the Cylonian affair are Hdt. 5.71; Thuc. 1.126.3–12; Plut. *Sol.* 12.1–9; Paus. 1.28.1, 7.25.3; schol. Ar. *Eq.* 445. For the date, cf. Rhodes, *CAAP* 81–82. Thucydides states that Cylon was a member of the elite (εὐγενής τε καὶ δυνατός), a fact clear also from his victory

supported in his bid for tyranny by a small group of elite Athenian friends, as well as Theagenes, tyrant of Megara.[2] It is clear from our sources that the ruling magistrates of Athens, and the Alcmeonid Megacles in particular, played a central role in opposing Cylon.[3] It is striking, however, that according to Thucydides' account, the Athenians as a whole (πανδημεί) resisted Cylon and his supporters and besieged them on the acropolis.[4] According to Thucydides, it was only when the Athenians tired of the siege that they granted the magistrates power to deal with the situation as they saw fit. If Thucydides' account is correct, then this episode represents the first known collective political action by the Athenian masses. Yet several factors make this interpretation unlikely.

First of all, it is noteworthy that Herodotus and Plutarch make no mention of the role of the Athenian people in resisting Cylon, reporting only the actions of the ruling magistrates against the Cylonians.[5] Second, Thucydides' claim that the Athenians handed over authority to the magistrates is phrased in the language typical of the fifth and fourth centuries, when the masses did hold formal power, and therefore may be an anachronistic rendering of the actual sequence of events.[6] Third, as we shall see shortly, subsequent Athenian history shows that the Athenian masses were not opposed in principle to the rule of a tyrant. In view of these points, it might be concluded that, if the Athenian masses did indeed participate in the resistance to Cylon, their action may have been prompted by the presence of Megarian troops rather than opposition to tyranny per se.

Franco Ghinatti has provided an alternative explanation of Thucydides' account along these lines. Ghinatti argues that Thucydides' claim of independent collective action by the Athenian masses refers simply to the fact that Megacles and his fellow magistrates summoned their non-elite dependents

---

in the Olympic Games and his marriage to the daughter of Theagenes, tyrant of Megara (Thuc. 1.126.3, Paus. 1.28.1, schol. Ar. *Eq.* 445).

[2] Hdt. 5.71.1 designates Cylon's supporters as "a group of age-mates" (ἑταιρηίη τῶν ἡλικιωτέων), the usual term for an elite social group: cf. Ghinatti 1970, 13–17, 55–58; Herman 1986, 10–12; Konstan 1997, 44–47. Thuc. 1.126.5 uses the term "friends" (φίλοι), on which see Konstan 1997, 28–31. For Theagenes' support, see Thuc. 1.126.5. In addition to Theagenes, Cylon may have been supported by the authorities at Delphi, who advised him on the timing of his coup (Thuc. 1.126.4).

[3] Herodotus and Thucydides differ in the title of the magistrates of Athens at this time. Herodotus (1.71.2) calls them πρυτάνιες τῶν ναυκράρων, whereas Thucydides (1.126.8) uses the more familiar classical title ἄρχοντες. This difference is not important for my argument. On the role of the πρυτάνιες τῶν ναυκράρων in the early Athenian state, see Billigmeier and Dusing 1981; Gabrielson 1985; Jordan 1992; Lambert 1993, 251–61; Wallinga 2000; Lenz, "Did Athens Have Archons: before Solon?" (unpublished).

[4] Thuc. 1.126.7–8: οἱ δὲ Ἀθηναῖοι αἰσθόμενοι ἐβοήθησάν τε πανδημεὶ ἐκ τῶν ἀγρῶν ἐπ' αὐτοὺς καὶ προσκαθεζόμενοι ἐπολιόρκουν.

[5] Hdt. 5.71.2, Thuc. 1.127.1, Plut. *Sol.* 12.1.

[6] Andrewes 1982, 387.

from the areas surrounding their nearby estates in order to help resist Cylon and his Megarian supporters. As Ghinatti notes, it is particularly significant that the estates of the Alcmeonidae at Alopece were close to the acropolis.[7] Thus although the Athenians as a whole may not have participated in the siege, it is possible that a sizable number of non-elites came to the support of their elite patrons in the context of what was perceived as a foreign invasion. The resistance to the Cylonian conspiracy may have been one of the rare instances, therefore, when a factional leader called on his entire faction, including non-elites, to support him in a situation of open warfare with his rivals.[8] Yet we must note that even if this was the case, Thucydides' account suggests that the role of the wider group of non-elites was short-lived and that the magistrates soon assumed the primary role in dealing with the Cylonians. We must assume therefore that the Megarian troops fled when they saw the extent of opposition to Cylon, and that the magistrates themselves then dismissed their non-elite dependents.[9]

Our sources tell us that Cylon and his brother escaped the siege and fled the city, but his supporters were left to seek sanctuary as suppliants in the temple on the acropolis and the altars of the Holy Goddesses on the Areopagus.[10] The magistrates then persuaded the suppliants to rise up from the altars, either by an assurance that they would not be killed or through the promise of a trial.[11] The magistrates then killed the Cylonians. Although Megacles and his family were later held responsible for the killings, it is likely that all the magistrates played a role in the slaughter.[12]

With the retreat of Cylon and his brother into exile, and the slaughter of Cylon's supporters, the ruling magistrates preserved their joint rule against the threat of tyranny. This episode can be viewed as a typical instance of violent intra-elite conflict over power, such as we have seen occurred throughout Greece in the late seventh and early sixth century. In this case, the potential tyrant was forced into exile, and the magistrates maintained their power. What is distinctive about this instance of the politics of exile, however, is the steps

---

[7] Ghinatti 1970, 24–25; Frost 1984, 286–87.

[8] For the rarity of action by an entire faction, cf. Nicholas 1966, 57.

[9] An alternative explanation for Thucydides' claim for popular resistance to the Cylonian conspiracy is that it is derived from oral traditions in which historical memories of three separate events were collapsed into one patriotic and democratic version (following the 508 revolution), in which the Athenians are always portrayed as collectively resisting tyrants. See Thomas 1989, 133–35, on the telescoping of historical memories.

[10] The terms used of Cylon and his brother's flight are ἐκδιδράσκουσιν (Thuc. 1.126.10) and φεύγει (schol. Ar. Eq. 445a).

[11] Herodotus and Thucydides give the former version of the magistrates' assurance; Plutarch, the latter.

[12] Thuc. 1.126.11 and Plut. Sol. 12.1 specifically state that all the magistrates participated in the killing of the Cylonians, while Hdt. 5.71.2 implies that, although the Alcmeonidae were blamed, all the magistrates were responsible.

that the magistrates took to reinforce and even extend their act of violent expulsion. Following the expulsion of Cylon, the magistrates held a trial in which he, his supporters, and their families were sentenced to outlawry (ἀτιμία). Although there is no direct evidence for the trial, an early law (θέσμιον) against tyranny, recorded by Aristotle, is presumed to have originated in such a trial:[13]

θέσμια τάδε Ἀθηναίων καὶ πάτρια· ἐάν τινες τυραννεῖν ἐπανιστῶνται [ἐπὶ τυραννίδι], ἢ συγκαθιστῇ τὴν τυραννίδα,ἄτιμον εἶναι καὶ αὐτὸν καὶ γένος.

The following is an ancestral law of the Athenians: If anyone makes an attempt at tyranny or participates in the establishment of a tyrant, both he and his family [γένος] shall be outlawed ([ἄτιμον]).[14]

The law on tyranny is an important example of how the ruling elite throughout Greece began to use written laws to reinforce the system of public offices against attempts by individual elites to establish more exclusive power for themselves. By defining the penalty for tyranny as outlawry (ἀτιμία), the magistrates both sanctioned their acts of expulsion and murder of the Cylonians, and set the penalty for future attempts at tyranny.[15] Outlawry, ἀτιμία, meant "loss of honor," and a person so sanctioned—at least in the archaic period—could be killed without penalty. In most cases, the outlaw fled into exile to avoid death.[16] In this light, this early law on tyranny could be seen as perpetuating the politics of exile through legal means. In this case, the law made the expulsion of potential tyrants normative, and indeed enjoined the whole community to take part in expelling or killing the tyrant.

On one level, this use of early law can be viewed simply as an attempt to circumvent the usual pattern of expulsion and return by setting up an impediment against the return of the Cylonians, and thus protecting Megacles and his fellow magistrates from violent expulsion in turn. In this aim, the law evidently failed, as we shall see shortly. On another level, however, the law is the first example in Athenian history of a strategy that we will see recur

---

[13] Gagarin 1981b, 74. See also *RE* 20.1 (1941) s.v. Φυγή, col. 975; Stroud 1968, 71, 80 (although Stroud follows Ostwald 1955 in arguing that the law on tyranny was part of the later code of Draco).

[14] *Ath. Pol.* 16.10.

[15] This claim glosses over several important issues that cannot be discussed in detail in this context, namely whether such laws were publicly displayed, whether these laws recorded particular judgments or general rules, and finally the implications of public display for the role of law in early Athens. For discussion of these issues, see Gagarin 1986, 51–56; Hignett, *HAC* 76–77; Ostwald 1969, 174–75; Thomas 1992. In brief, I follow Gagarin in accepting that the laws were publicly displayed and that they were written in the form of general rules. In addition, following Gagarin and Thomas, I believe that the display of written laws both implicates the community as a whole in the maintenance of the social order and makes use of the symbolic and sacred power of the written word to legitimate the decisions of the ruling magistrates.

[16] See "Introduction" above for the meaning of outlawry and its relation to exile.

frequently over the course of archaic Athenian history, namely the attempt to prevent violent conflict between elites by implicating the community as a whole in the guardianship of its political shape. By granting immunity to anyone who murdered a potential tyrant, the law encouraged all members of the community to play a role in protecting the status quo, rule by a coalition of elite families. Although it is clear from subsequent events that few beyond the elite themselves were prepared to act independently in defense of the political order, this law began the process of articulating the potential of non-elites to participate in the allocation of power between elites.

Although there is no direct evidence for the return of the Cylon, it is likely that he and his supporters were a contributing cause of the next two known events in Athenian history: the homicide law of Draco (c. 621) and the trial and expulsion of the Alcmeonidae (c. 600).[17] It is generally accepted that Draco's law on homicide was an attempt to control the escalation of violence resulting from the murder of the Cylonians by the ruling magistrates.[18] Briefly stated, it is likely that the surviving conspirators—possibly including the exiled Cylon, his brother, and any others who had fled following the massacre—returned to Athens and sought revenge by the customary means of avenging murder in seventh-century Greece: retaliatory murder unless a blood price was accepted.[19] Most cases of homicide in archaic Greece resulted in the flight of the killer from the community in order to avoid death at the hands of the victim's family.[20] The quest for vengeance by the Cylonians, therefore, would have amounted to an attempt to expel Megacles and his fellow magistrates from Athens. The quest for vengeance for murder would accordingly represent a form of the politics of exile.

Yet there is one highly significant discrepancy between the customary procedures for the prosecution of homicide and the practice of the politics of exile. In cases of exile as a result of homicide, it was always the relatives of

---

[17] IG 1³ 104. See also van Effenterre 1994, 16–23, for a recent edition of the law with commentary. Stroud 1968 provides a text with commentary and useful discussion of the historical setting in which the law originated. The extant inscription dates to 409/8, when the laws of the Athenians were revised and republished, as the decree recorded with the law shows. For the date of the original law, see Stroud 1968, 66–70.

[18] Carawan 1998, 43; Humphreys 1991; Stroud 1968, 71–72, with earlier bibliography cited in his n. 33. Note also van Effenterre's comment (1994, 5) that one of the principal aims of archaic legislation was to end stasis among elite families. Gagarin (1981a, 19–21), however, is skeptical of a direct link between the Cylonian affair and Draco's law on homicide.

[19] For the customary procedures for dealing with homicide, see Gagarin's analysis of the Homeric evidence (1981a, 5–18). Gagarin argues that although there is no direct evidence that "the method of treating homicide portrayed in the epics actually was common in pre-Draconian Athens, there are several indications in Draco's law itself that the treatment of homicide before Draco was similar to that found in the epics" (1981a, 18).

[20] Gagarin 1981a, 5–18. In a few cases, including the famous trial depicted on Achillles' shield (Il. 18.497–508), compensation is offered in place of the murder or expulsion of the killer.

the victim who sought vengeance and thus drove the killer into exile.[21] In other words, if the political rivals of Megacles and his fellow magistrates wished to use customary procedures for homicide to drive their rivals out of the polis, then they would have had to get the families of the dead Cylonians to agree to pursue vengeance against the magistrates. It is of course possible that the relatives of the murdered Cylonians were eager to prosecute the murder and/or were sympathetic to the political aims of the Cylonian conspiracy. In that case, they may have been only too glad to drive the magistrates out of Athens through the threat of retaliatory murder. There are, however, several pieces of evidence to weigh against a complete identity of interests between the opponents of Megacles and the families of the dead Cylonians.

First, as we have seen, Cylon was supported in his attempt at tyranny by a small band of elites, namely a ἑταιρηίη (Hdt. 5.71.1), which was a group of wealthy and powerful men who were not necessarily related by blood. Second, if Draco's homicide law was indeed the result of the escalation of violence arising from the murder of the Cylonians, as most scholars believe, then its provisions suggest that its central aim was to formalize through written law, and thus reaffirm, the customary practice of making the prosecution of homicide the responsibility of the close relatives of the victim. We might surmise that Draco's concern to limit the right of prosecution to the immediate family members was an attempt to prevent the political rivals of Megacles from using homicide as grounds to drive their political opponents out of Athens.

The idea that Draco's homicide law was primarily concerned to limit the right of prosecution (and of pardon) to immediate family members in order that homicide cases might not be used by distant relations or non-relatives as pretexts for the pursuit of grudges or self-interest was formulated by S. C. Humphreys in a characteristically perceptive argument.[22] Humphreys observed that the detailed enumeration of which family members are permitted to prosecute or to pardon a killer is best explained as an attempt to make it more difficult for homicides to be used to pursue some personal interest. In Draco's law, only immediate family members of the victim as far as cousin and cousin's son (μέχρ' ἀνεφσιότετος καὶ ἀνεφσιὸ, 20–21)[23] are permitted

---

[21] Gagarin (1981a, 10) notes that in cases in Homer in which the victim has no relatives, the killer is not subject to revenge killing or exile. The best example is Oedipus (*Od.* 11.273–80), who continued to rule Thebes even after he killed his father. Since Oedipus was his father's closest relative, he was under no threat of retaliation.

[22] Humphreys 1991, especially 22–25.

[23] The exact degree of relation specified by the phrase μέχρ' ἀνεφσιότετος καὶ ἀνεφσιὸ is debated. I follow the *communis opinio*, which seems to be "cousin and cousin's son" (cf. Stroud 1968, van Effenterre 1994), but I am tempted by Humphreys's argument for "uncles and first cousins" (1991, 25).

to initiate proceedings against a killer.[24] The fact that Draco's law affirms the right of prosecution as the prerogative of the immediate family members suggests that in the circumstances leading up to the legislation, homicide was being prosecuted by distant relations or non-relatives who were motivated by personal interests, possibly including political rivalry with the killers.

The law also specifies that the prosecution of the killer must be supported (συνδιόκεν) by cousins, sons of cousins, marriage relations (such as brothers-in-law, sons-in-law, fathers-in-law), and members of the brotherhood (φρά-τορες: 21-23). Thus the law not only ensures that only the closest relatives can initiate a prosecution, but requires a larger group of relatives and members of the brotherhood to share in that prosecution. As Humphreys observes: "The effect of these provisions is on the one hand to narrow the range of those who can bring accusations, and thus minimize the danger that homicide cases will be used as a cover for paying off other scores, and on the other hand to ensure that accusations are only brought by those who can secure solid backing."[25] The effect of these double requirements, we may surmise, was to make it more difficult for the political enemies of the killer to use a homicide as a means of driving their rivals out of the community.[26] Similarly, the detailed specification of who is permitted to pardon a killer seems designed to restrict the number of persons entitled to pardon, and thus again prevent distant relatives or non-relatives from interfering, possibly for political reasons, with the pardon and return of the killer.[27]

Two other features of Draco's law are noteworthy for the light they shed on the historical context and motives for his legislation. First of all, Draco's law affirms distinctions between intentional, unintentional, and justifiable homicide.[28] It is generally agreed that while the intent of the killer may have been taken into consideration in customary law, there was no formal requirement that it must be.[29] Why, then, we should ask, was Draco interested in for-

---

[24] In a detailed study, Tulin 1996 shows that the view (of MacDowell 1963) that Draco's law "enjoined" the relatives to prosecute, but did not prohibit non-relatives from leading the prosecution, is not supported by the evidence.

[25] Humphreys 1991, 24.

[26] Humphreys (1991, 24–25) makes the further fascinating observation that Draco's provisions for prosecution of homicides are similar to Solon's law obliging citizens to take sides in a situation of civil war, in that both attempt to eliminate those parties in a conflict with insufficient support and thus diffuse the crisis. For further discussion of Solon's law along these lines, see below.

[27] Humphreys 1991, 24.

[28] The question of whether the phrases ἄκων and μὲ 'κ προνοίας refer to a single category of unintentional murder, or whether the latter term refers to the more subtle concept of premeditation, is not essential to the argument presented here. For a summary of the debate, see Carawan 1998, 36–45. The section of Draco's law (lines 33–38) that dealt with forms of justifiable homicide (such as killing in self-defense, or, we may surmise, killing in the context of civil war) is the worst-preserved part of the inscription.

[29] Gagarin 1981b, 11–13; Carawan 1998, 45–49.

malizing these distinctions in written law? One obvious reason, given the historical context of the law, would be to ensure that intentionality be taken into consideration in the case of the Cylonians. Since the killing of the Cylonians could be classified as a form of unintentional or even justifiable homicide, the formalization of these distinctions in Draco's law would have increased the likelihood that Megacles and his fellow magistrates would be pardoned, or made exempt from prosecution. It is noteworthy in this regard that several scholars have proposed that the law on tyranny may have formed part of Draco's legislation.[30] Since that law, as we have seen, sanctioned the killing of a potential tyrant and his conspirators, it constituted precisely the sort of justifiable homicide that the badly preserved portion of Draco's law deals with. Even if, as was argued above, the law on tyranny pre-dates Draco's law, it is possible that Draco incorporated it in his law on homicide as one category of justifiable homicide.

I have argued that Draco's law was a response to the specific crisis of escalating violence between Cylon and his supporters and the ruling magistrates of Athens following the Cylonian conspiracy. In particular, I suggested that the magistrates appointed Draco to formulate the law on homicide in order to prevent themselves from being driven out of the polis permanently on the grounds of their murder of the Cylonians. Yet the law also had the indirect effect of strengthening the role of the community (state) as opposed to private individuals in the regulation of disputes between community members.[31] For example, the role of certain civic officials (βασιλεῖς, ἐφέται) and the wider community—notably the brotherhoods (φρατρίαι)—in the resolution of homicide disputes is established for the first time in written law.[32] Not only were the βασιλεῖς and the ἐφέται given roles in the determination of the intention of the killer and hence the nature of the penalty and the possibility of pardon, but the law required that the prosecution be initiated in a public space (ἀγορά) and that a wider group of the community (the brotherhoods) support it.[33]

[30] Ostwald 1955; Stroud 1968, 80. *Contra:* Gagarin 1981b.

[31] On this point, see Ruschenbusch 1960; Sealey 1983a.

[32] There are two views of the identity of the βασιλεῖς in Draco's homicide law and Solon's amnesty law (on which see below): either the chief magistrate titled βασιλεύς and the four tribal βασιλεῖς (ML 266; Rhodes, *CAAP* 649; Gagarin 1981a, 46–47), or else the series of annual chief magistrates called βασιλεῖς (Stroud 1968, 45–47; de Bruyn 1995, 26). The ἐφέται were a group of fifty-one men chosen from the elite. For the brotherhoods (φράτραι), see above, chapter 1.

[33] The standard view of the role of the βασιλεῖς in Draco's code is that they were responsible for pronouncing the final verdict: see, e.g., Gagarin 1981a, 47–48. Carawan (1998, 69–71), however, has recently made a strong argument that the role of the βασιλεῖς was to propose ways of settling the dispute through oaths and other tests. The standard view of the role of the ἐφέται (see, e.g., Gagarin 1981a, 47–48) is that they both determine the intent of the killer and also decide the case (διαγνῶναι). Carawan (1998, 71–75) once again disputes this interpretation and argues that the ἐφέται were responsible for determining (διαγνῶναι) first "whether the defendant is responsible for the outcome and therefore liable to the family" and second the intent of the killer, but only in cases where there were no surviving relatives. For objections to Carawan's views, see Wallace 2000.

Although many of these features probably existed already in customary law (for instance, the role of the βασιλεῖς in declaring the verdict, or the location of the trial in a public place), Draco's law gave further powers to public officials and the community at large in determining the outcome of the dispute. In particular, the role of the ἐφέται in determining the intent of the killer seems to be new with Draco's law, and gives these officials an important role in determining the likelihood that the killer will be pardoned and hence be able to return to Athens. In addition, the provision that the ἐφέται have the power to appoint a group of ten elite members of the brotherhoods to determine questions of pardon in the absence of relatives of the victim gave these officials further control over whether the killer could return. While these measures may have been intended to increase the control of the ruling magistrates and their appointees in the regulation of the dispute with the Cylonians, they had long-term implications for the role of public institutions and indeed the wider community in the regulation of private disputes.

Similarly, we might further note how Draco's law not only defines and extends the power of public officials, but also affirms the legal definition of community membership—that is, citizenship. The middle section of the preserved portion of the law concerns the protection of killers while in exile. According to this part of the law, anyone who killed a murderer who had gone into exile and who remained outside the border markets (i.e., the borders of the polis) and away from the games and Amphictyonic festivals (i.e., the Panhellenic gatherings where the killer might meet relatives of the victim) would be treated as one who kills an Athenian (ὅσπερ τὸν Ἀθεναῖον κτέναντα). This provision protects the killer who stays outside the community by permitting the prosecution of anyone who might try to kill him while in exile. As Humphreys has noted, the provision protected the killer in exile until such time as he might be pardoned—a protection that would have been important to Megacles and his fellow magistrates if they had indeed been forced into exile by the Cylonians.[34] More significant, the provision to treat a killer who remained lawfully in exile as equivalent to an Athenian insofar as his murder could be avenged implies that by this time membership in the Athenian community was invested with certain basic legal protections.[35] Draco's law, therefore, marks a first step in the development of a juridical concept of citizenship.

In sum, if indeed Draco's law was formulated in the context of continued violent confrontation between the Cylonians and Megacles and his fellow magistrates, then not only do we see the characteristic features of the politics of exile at work, but also we see that, once again, Megacles and the other magistrates tried to resolve the situation in their favor through the use of written

----

[34] For Homer, killers in exile were not immune from pursuit by the victim's relatives; for this reason they sought the protection of powerful men in other poleis (Gagarin 1981a, 10–11).

[35] Gagarin 1986, 80, 140; Manville 1990, 81.

law. By appointing Draco to draft a publicly displayed law whereby the customary procedures for homicide were enforced, new categories of justifiable
homicide were outlined, and the whole process was put under more formal
civic control, Megacles and his fellow archons attempted to prevent themselves from being driven from the polis by their political rivals. The fact that
Draco's law explicitly stated that those who committed murder before his
legislation were subject to its provisions (lines 19–20) seems to confirm that
the new law was formulated in response to the events of the previous years, in
particular the slaughter of the Cylonians by the archons.

This attempt by these magistrates and their supporters to prevent themselves from being driven from the polis through public written laws may have
been successful in the short term. The political rivals of Megacles and his
fellow archons could no longer chase them out of the polis through the threat
of retaliatory murder. Instead the Cylonians were required to submit to a publicly administered judicial system in which the persons allowed to prosecute a
murderer were severely restricted and the intent and circumstances of the
murder were taken into consideration. In response, the Cylonians took a new
tack in their campaign to drive out the ruling magistrates: they now agitated
for their expulsion on the grounds that they were polluted, since they killed
the Cylonians when they were suppliants at the altars of the gods.[36]

Religious fears of pollution were a serious concern in ancient Greece, and
the Cylonians would not be the last to try to exploit such concerns in order to
remove their opponents from the polis.[37] In fact, the fears of pollution incurred
by the archons in their actions against Cylon would be recalled at crucial times
in Athenian history in the attempt to remove key political figures from the
polis.[38] The Cylonians evidently persisted for quite some time in their claim
that the magistrates were polluted. It was only at the end of the seventh century
(c. 600) that the magistrates felt compelled again to seek a judicial means of
resolving the conflict.[39]

---

[36] The magistrates first got the Cylonians to rise from a sacred precinct on the acropolis; then
they began to slaughter them. Some of the Cylonians then fled to the altars of the Holy Goddesses
on the nearby Areopagus, where they were again set upon and killed by the magistrates. It was this
last act that caused them to be considered polluted (Thuc. 1.126.11, Plut. Sol. 12.1–2, schol. Ar.
Eq. 441a). Cf. Harris-Cline 1999 on the Cylonian affair and the topography of Athens.

[37] On Greek beliefs about the pollution incurred by the murder of suppliants, see R. Parker
1983, 10.

[38] Isagoras and the Spartan Cleomenes tried to remove Cleisthenes from Athens in 508 on the basis
of his relation to the Alcmeonid Megacles (Hdt. 5.70.2, Thuc. 1.126.12). Again in 431, the Spartans
tried to rouse animosity against Pericles because of his Alcmeonid roots (Thuc. 1.126.2, 127.1).

[39] Plutarch (Sol. 12.3) reports that the stasis was at its height at this time, and that the whole
population was divided between the two factions (τοῦ δήμου διαστάντος). Whether or not the
common people became involved in the conflict, it is evident that the fears of pollution had
reached such a peak that Epimenides, a man renowned for his expertise in religious matters, was
called upon to purify the city (Arist. Ath. Pol. 1, Plut. Sol. 12.6–12).

The ruling magistrates persuaded those who were deemed to be polluted to submit to a trial.[40] Three hundred men were chosen from among the elites to try the case, and one Myron of the deme of Phlya was prosecutor.[41] A curious fact about the outcome of the trial was that although all the magistrates at the time of the conspiracy were responsible for the slaughter of the Cylonians, only Megacles and his family, the Alcmeonidae, were found guilty at the trial.[42] The obvious explanation for this discrepancy is that the ruling elites tried to minimize the damage to their power resulting from the charges of pollution. By confining the guilt for the murder of the suppliants to one particular individual (and Megacles was the obvious choice, as both the leading magistrate at the time and by now conveniently dead), the families of the remaining archons avoided expulsion from the polis. At the trial, Megacles and his descendants were sentenced to exile in perpetuity (ἀειφυγία).[43] Megacles' bones were dug up and flung across the borders of Attica.[44] In addition, a Cretan holy man, Epimenides, was called upon to purify the city from the pollution.[45] Apparently a shrine to Cylon was also set up at this time, and it is likely that the statue of Cylon seen by Pausanias some seven hundred years later was part of this shrine.[46]

In sum, in making use of communal notions of pollution, the Cylonians had come upon a powerful tool in their attempt to expel their political rivals from Athens. Yet the ruling magistrates were not without resources in this on-going attempt to win power through the expulsion of their opponents. Not only did the magistrates manage to limit the damage by singling out the family of the Alc-meonidae, but, as is clear from subsequent Athenian history, the Alcmeonidae found a way to return to Athens by the mid-sixth century at the latest.

THE BEGINNINGS OF CHANGE: SOLON

By all accounts, the struggle for political power continued to destabilize the polis in the first decade of the sixth century. Like Draco's homicide legislation, the trial and expulsion of the Alcmeonidae failed to bring decades of conflict to a close. Of this period, our sources report that the Athenians "renewed their old conflict over the constitution" (τὴν παλαιὰν αὖθις στά-σιν ὑπὲρ τῆς πολιτείας ἐστασίασαν). and that "there was fierce political

---

[40] Plut. Sol. 12.3.
[41] Arist. Ath. Pol. 1, Plut. Sol. 12.3–4.
[42] See n. 36 above.
[43] Arist. Ath. Pol. 1; cf. Plut. Sol. 12.4, schol. Ar. Eq. 441a.
[44] Plut. Sol. 12.4.
[45] Arist. Ath. Pol. 1, Plut. Sol. 12.6–12.
[46] Paus. 1.28.

struggle, and for a long time [the Athenians] fought each other" (ἰσχυρᾶς δὲ τῆς στάσεως οὔσης καὶ πολὺν χρόνον ἀντικαθημένων ἀλλήλοις).[47]

Aristotle describes this struggle, however, as one between the common people and the elites (ὁ δῆμος, οἱ γνώριμοι) or the rich and the poor (οἱ πλούσιοι, οἱ πένητες).[48] He writes, furthermore, that when Solon was appointed archon (594), "the demos rose up in revolt against the elites" (ἀντέστη τοῖς γνωρίμοις ὁ δῆμος).[49] While it is clear from Solon's poetry and his legislation that there were significant tensions between elites and non-elites in Solonian Athens, I will argue in this section that violent intra-elite conflict remained a fundamental problem. Furthermore, I will show that Solon both affirmed previous legislation aimed at quelling violent intra-elite conflict and also came up with his own innovative measures to address the problem. Nevertheless, Solon ultimately failed to prevent further outbreaks of intra-elite violence. In the period following Solon's legislation, as we shall see, the politics of exile continued to destabilize the polis.

In emphasizing the role of intra-elite conflict in Solonian Athens, I do not seek to deny that there were social and economic tensions between elites and non-elites in this period. I have noted above in chapters 1 and 2 that population growth and new market opportunities resulted in both the enrichment of some non-elites and the impoverishment (and even enslavement) of others. I argue in this section, however, that Solon's responses to these tensions resulted only in modest modifications of the basic oligarchic structure of the polis. As a result of Solon's reforms, some of the richest non-elites gained access to political power, while the masses of middling and poor Athenians had their right to live as free residents on Attic soil affirmed in law. Although these changes themselves established some of the preconditions for the greater involvement of non-elites in politics, the aftermath of Solon's reforms shows that non-elites were far from ready to take a decisive role in ending the destabilizing politics of exile as practiced by the ruling elites. Such a development would only occur toward the end of the sixth century, when the effects of Solonian legislation, in combination with the popularizing politics of Pisistratus, had strengthened the political consciousness of the masses.

In 594 B.C.E. Solon was appointed as the chief magistrate (ἄρχων) of Athens in order to mediate the crisis.[50] Several pieces of Solon's legislation appear to respond to the problem of intra-elite violence. First of all, Solon reaffirmed Draco's homicide law, which as we have seen aimed to prevent

---

[47] Plut. Sol. 13.1, Arist. Ath. Pol. 5.1.

[48] Arist. Ath. Pol. 2.1, 5.1. Aristotle is followed in this by Plutarch (Sol. 13–14), although Plutarch also confusingly imports the tripartite struggle between Megacles, Lycurgus, and Pisistratus (derived from Hdt. 1.59.3 and Arist. Ath. Pol. 13) into this time period. Plutarch repeats the tripartite scheme again at Sol. 29.1 in the proper chronological place.

[49] Arist. Ath. Pol. 5.1.

[50] Arist. Ath. Pol. 5.2, Plut. Sol. 14.3.

charges of murder from becoming grounds for the banishment of political rivals.[51] Probably included within the law on homicide was the law on tyranny, whereby the murder of a person attempting a tyranny was to be classified as a justifiable homicide. Solon also explicitly reaffirmed that tyranny was a crime punishable by outlawry (ἀτιμία) and established in law that the crime of attempted tyranny was to be tried before the elite Council of the Areopagus.[52]

In addition to these measures reaffirming prior legislation, Solon enacted a law to restore to the polis those who had been driven out as a result of the politics of exile. In his amnesty law, Solon recalled all who were exiled before his archonship, except those who had been condemned by the established authorities on charges of murder, manslaughter, or attempted tyranny.[53] Solon's amnesty law was, in effect, a further attempt to reassert the provisions of Draco's homicide law, according to which only those condemned for specific crimes by public authorities following a prescribed procedure could be exiled. In declaring an amnesty for all the rest, Solon was allowing for the return to the polis of other exiles who may have been driven out by their political rivals.[54]

Two other items of Solonian legislation respond even more directly to the problem of intra-elite competition, namely Solon's reform of the method of selection of archons, and the so-called law on stasis (στάσις, "civil strife"). Before examining the logic of these provisions, however, it is useful to review other aspects of Solonian legislation, since these provide the necessary background for his more radical attempts to resolve the problem of intra-elite conflict. First, Solon's creation of four property classes based on wealth seems to have been a product of the demand of some wealthy non-elites for a share in political power. According to the reform, those whose annual production was above five hundred measures of grain became eligible for the highest

[51] Solon reaffirmed Draco's law on homicide: Arist. *Ath. Pol.* 7.1; Plut. *Sol.* 17.1; Ael. *VH* 8.10; Eusebius, *Chron.* 99B Helm; Dem. 23.66. The first two authors state that Draco wrote other legislation, which Solon overrode. Whereas Stroud (1968, 75–82) accepts that Draco wrote other legislation, I am skeptical about its existence. Cf. Carawan 1993, 310.

[52] For tyranny punished by outlawry, see Solon's amnesty law (Plut. *Sol.* 19.4), which explicitly exempts from the amnesty those condemned to outlawry for tyranny. For trial before the Areopagus, see Arist. *Ath. Pol.* 8.4. There is some debate about the historicity of Aristotle's claim that Solon established a new procedure for trying cases of tyranny before the Areopagus, since the language (κατάλυσις τοῦ δήμου, εἰσαγγελία) is anachronistic. Wallace (1989, 64–66), Rhodes (*CAAP* 156), and Ostwald (1955, 105) argue that there is no reason to reject Aristotle's claim, whereas Hansen (1975, 17–19) argues that the procedure of εἰσαγγελία was not used to try tyranny in sixth-century Athens.

[53] Plut. *Sol.* 19.3.

[54] It is possible that the amnesty was intended to cover the poor Athenians who had been sold into slavery abroad, as Ruschenbusch suggests (1966, 94). However, Plutarch does not mention the amnesty in relation to the poor, and in light of the specific exemptions of murder, manslaughter, and tyranny, the law seems to have been formulated with the situation of intra-elite conflict in mind.

offices, the nine archonships.[55] Lin Foxhall has calculated that in order to produce this amount of grain, a citizen would have needed between seventeen and twenty-eight hectares of land. Foxhall concludes, therefore, that only a small number of non-elites became eligible for these magistracies as a result of this reform.[56]

The next two classes of citizens, the hippeis and the zeugitae, produced three hundred and two hundred measures of grain, respectively. These production figures correspond, according to Foxhall's calculations, to ownership of considerable property and wealth: between seven and seventeen hectares of land.[57] Although Aristotle is not specific about the political rights granted to these groups, it is likely that they could hold some of the lesser offices and were eligible to sit on Solon's new Council of Four Hundred.[58] This council was to be composed of one hundred probouloi (advance councilors) chosen from each tribe, and was given the task of preparing and deliberating on matters to be brought before the assembly.[59] Although we do not know the manner of selection of the councilors, they were probably chosen through election in the tribes. While election probably favored the elites, who enjoyed prestige from their traditional roles in tribal politics, the number of councilors and the new criteria for eligibility seem designed to allow wealthy non-elites to play a role in the formulation of public policy. What is remarkable, however, is that only fairly wealthy Athenians could become councilors; the majority of Athenians would have been excluded from this probouleutic role.

The lowest property class created by Solon, the thetes, would have comprised the majority of the Athenians—all those from the moderately well-off to the very poor.[60] These citizens were given no share in political office, although their right to participate in the public assembly was formally acknowledged, perhaps for the first time.[61] Solon may have prescribed regular meetings for this assembly, but it is unlikely that he gave it any new political powers.[62] Thus

[55] Arist. *Ath. Pol.* 7.3, Plut. *Sol.* 18.1–2.

[56] Foxhall 1997, 130.

[57] Foxhall 1997, 130.

[58] I accept the historicity of the Solonian council. For the arguments, see Rhodes, *CAAP* 153–54. For a recent argument against the existence of a Solonian council, see Doenges 1996.

[59] Arist. *Ath. Pol.* 8.4, Plut. *Sol.* 19.1.

[60] Foxhall 1997, 131. See, however, Raaflaub (1996a, 1054, 1064), who believes that the majority of Athenians fell into the zeugite (hoplite) category. If Raaflaub is correct, then Solon gave a much more significant role to the majority of citizens than is allowed for in the interpretation given above. Cf. Wallace 1998, 16.

[61] Arist. *Ath. Pol.* 7.5 distinguishes the lowest class, the thetes, from the higher classes by noting that they were not eligible for any public office (ἀρχή). O'Neil (1995, 19) suggests that membership on the council was considered a public office.

[62] Regular meetings are hypothesized by Rhodes, *CAAP* 154. The new judicial role of the assembly is discussed below.

the political status of the majority of the Athenian population was not changed
by the replacement of the criterion of birth with one of wealth for public office.

An argument can be made, however, that Solon's measures to relieve the
economic distress of the poor indirectly established the foundations for the
development of a greater political role for the Athenian masses. By the time of
Solon, some poor Athenians found themselves increasingly indebted to the
rich, and as a result became their slaves or, worse, were either sold into slavery
abroad or forced to flee because of their debts.[63] In response to these problems, Solon not only freed a class of dependent laborers (ἐκτήμοροι, "sixth-
parters") from their obligations to their wealthy patrons, but canceled debts,
abolished enslavement for debt, and brought back those Athenians who had
been sold into slavery abroad.[64] By formulating these measures and by proclaiming them publicly in his poetry, Solon restored these impoverished men
to their status as full-fledged members of the Athenian community, and also
established both freedom of the person and residence on Athenian soil as
fundamental rights of Athenian citizenship. In fact, one might argue that, by
these measures, Solon furthered the process of the juridical definition of
Athenian citizenship that had begun with the legislation of Draco.[65]

It is perhaps worth dwelling a bit longer on Solon's restoration of those who
were either sold into slavery abroad or were forced to flee because of their
debts. Solon proudly proclaims his restoration of these enslaved and exiled
men in his poetry,[66] where for the first time in Athenian history freedom and
return from exile are linked together in opposition to loss of freedom and exile
as fundamental aspects of Athenian experience. The historical experience of
exile and slavery, return from exile and liberation, as well as the commemo-
ration of the experience in Solon's poetry, was the beginning of a process of the
creation of a historical memory and later an ideology (reinforced by subsequent experience) in which the freedom and return from exile of the Athenian

---

[63] Solon fr. 36.8–12 West. For the causes of this development, see Forsdyke, "Land" (forthcoming); see also "Megara" above in chapter 2.

[64] The identity of the ἐκτήμοροι mentioned by Arist. Ath. Pol. 2.2 is the subject of much
scholarly debate. Recent interpretations suggest that they were poor (possibly landless) laborers
whom the wealthy contracted to bring previously uncultivated marginal land into cultivation.
See Andrewes 1982, 380; Gallant 1982, 122; Brandt 1989; Link 1991, 22–25; Rosivach 1992;
Sancisi-Weerdenburg 1993; E. Harris 1997, 2002. For a succinct discussion of earlier scholarship on Solon and the problem of the ἐκτήμοροι, see Rhodes, CAAP 118–28. Cancellation of
debts and ban on enslavement for debt (measures known as the Shaking-off of Burdens): Arist.
Ath. Pol. 6.1, Plut. Sol. 15. See also E. Harris 2002 for the distinction between enslavement for
debt and debt-bondage, the usual term used to describe the mode of contracting debt in Solonian Athens. Repatriation of Athenians sold into slavery abroad: Solon fr. 36.8–12 West.

[65] Cf. Manville (1990, 124–56), who argues that a concept of Athenian citizenship emerges
clearly for the first time in the legislation of Solon.

[66] Domínguez-Monedero (2001, 54) notes the practical difficulties in locating and repatri-
ating such men, and suggests that Solon's claim was propagandistic, but was taken literally by
later authors such as Plutarch.

people became paradigmatic of periods when the polis was restored to good government, while slavery and exile were characteristic of periods when the polis was in crisis. Later on, of course, good government became synonymous with democracy, whereas bad government was equated with tyranny or oligarchy. At the time of Solon, however, what we see is the beginning of the crystallization of a set of associations in the collective memory of the Athenian people. These aspects of Athenian social memory became as much a part of Athenian identity and self-understanding as Solon's legislation itself.

Solon introduced a number of changes in the system of justice in order to ensure that the freedom and residence of Athenians in Attica remained inviolate. We have seen already that Draco formally affirmed the role of the people in the regulation of homicide cases by requiring prosecutors to make a proclamation in a public space. Solon took this development one step further by establishing the assembly as a place of appeal from the judicial decisions of magistrates.[67] By this measure, not only did unjustly treated Athenians have a place of recourse if they failed to get justice from elite magistrates, but a new check was placed on those magistrates' formerly absolute jurisdiction. Most significant in the long run, however, if not for Solon's immediate concerns, was the empowerment of the assembly of the people, who now had a new role in the polis. The granting of a judicial role was a significant step toward granting an independent political role to the assembly of the people, as Aristotle himself recognized.[68]

A further Solonian innovation in the judicial system was the provision that any person (ὁ βουλόμενος) could take legal action on behalf of injured persons (ὑπὲρ τῶν ἀδικουμένων).[69] By allowing anyone to prosecute on behalf of a wronged person, Solon ensured that even cases in which the injured party was unable to prosecute (e.g., when a person was enslaved or exiled) would still be heard. This measure provided a further guarantee to weak and poor Athenians that their new rights to freedom and residence in Attica would be protected. Furthermore, the law encouraged a new civic-minded attitude

---

[67] Arist. *Ath. Pol.* 9.1, Plut. *Sol.* 18.3. There is disagreement as to what archaic body is behind Aristotle's term for the court of appeal (δικαστήριον). The original word used by Solon was probably ἡλιαία, which suggests that it was the full assembly (Rhodes, *CAAP* 160; Ostwald 1986, 9–12). Some scholars, however, have argued, on the basis of Arist. *Pol.* 1274a3–5, that the ἡλιαία was a subsection of the assembly chosen by lot (Hansen 1975, 51–52; 1978; 1982; O'Neil 1995, 20). For a summary of the debate, cf. Ostwald 1986, 10 and n. 29.

[68] Arist. *Ath. Pol.* 9.1 (cf. *Pol.* 1273b35–1274a5).

[69] Arist. *Ath. Pol.* 9.1; cf. Plut. *Sol.* 18.6. Solon's use of the term "injured person" (e.g., τῶν ἀδικουμένων, τοῦ κακῶς πεπονθότος) probably covered bodily harm and abuse, such as an enslaved Athenian might suffer from his master. It would not have covered cases of homicide, in which the prosecution still had to be conducted by the victim's relatives according to the provisions of Draco's law. Thus Solon's provision would not have overridden Draco's careful attempts to regulate the prosecution of homicide, but would have encouraged civic participation in cases of physical abuse where the victim was unable to prosecute in propria persona.

among the citizens: Athenians were given responsibility for ensuring that
the aspects of Athenian citizenship identified by Solon would not be vio-
lated.[70] This encouragement of a civic spirit will be seen again in another
of Solon's laws, the law on stasis, which I discuss below.

These two measures—appeal to the assembly and prosecution by ὁ
βουλόμενος—constituted Solon's attempt to make sure that the weak and
the powerful received equal treatment before the law. Solon boasted in his
poetry of having accomplished equality of justice, and thereby having established equal protection of the law as a further aspect of Athenian identity:[71]

> I did these things with my power,
> bringing into harmony force and justice,
> and I finished them as I promised;
> and I made the laws equal for the poor man and the powerful
> [θεσμοὺς δ' ὁμοίως τῷ κακῷ τε κἀγαθῷ...ἔγραψα],
> fitting impartial justice on each
> [εὐθεῖαν εἰς ἕκαστον ἁρμόσας δίκην].

The crisis of the polis caused by the enslavement and exile of the poor
therefore resulted in the further articulation of the legal and ideological
meaning of membership of the Athenian polis. Civic membership was now
defined by personal freedom, security of residence in Attica, and the opportunity for judicial redress of infringement of these and other rights of
Athenian citizenship. The creation of new judicial procedures in order to
secure these aspects of Athenian identity had the ultimate, if not intentional,
result of strengthening the position of the common people in the polis. Thus
the legislation of Solon in response to the enslavement and exile of the poor
had a profound effect on the political shape of the polis: a newly inclusive
and more fully articulated concept of Athenian citizenship was created, and
the people collectively and individually were given new powers to check
abuses by powerful individuals, both magistrates and private individuals.

Following this review of Solon's responses to problems arising from economic changes and their long-term political ramifications, we can now return
to Solon's measures against intra-elite conflict. A case was made already that
violent strife over political power remained a fundamental problem in Solonian Athens. This interpretation is strengthened by considering two further
pieces of legislation: the reform of the method for the selection of archons and

---

[70] Plut. *Sol.* 18.6 approves of Solon's law on prosecution by a third person, identifying the
fostering of a civic attitude as the goal of the legislator: "the legislator justly accustomed the citizens
to have shared feelings as parts of one body [ὥσπερ ἑνὸς μέρη ⟨σώματος⟩ συναισθάνεσθαι] and
to feel for one another's sufferings [συναλγεῖν ἀλλήλοις]." Cf. Plutarch's remarks on Solon's law
on stasis, *Sol.* 20.1 Solon's concern for and actions on behalf of the poor make this inference about
his intentions plausible.

[71] Solon, fr. 36.15–20 West.

the law on stasis. Prior to Solon's legislation, the archons were elected in the tribes. It is likely that the elites' influence in the tribes virtually ensured their own election.[72] Solon, however, modified the procedure for election of archons in a measure that may have both increased the chances for a non-elite to gain office and circumvented violent conflict between rival candidates for office. Solon legislated that each tribe was to elect ten candidates (πρόκριτοι) and that the magistrates were to be chosen by lot from this group of forty candidates.[73] The election of a relatively large number of candidates from each tribe increased the likelihood that a non-elite (i.e., one of the rich but lower-born members of the highest property class) might be elected. The non-elite candidates would then have some chance of being chosen by the lot for the archonship (although probably less than that of their well-born counterparts, if in fact the latter comprised most of the pre-elected candidates).[74]

Nonetheless, Solon's main purpose in using the lot to choose among elected candidates may have been to prevent violent conflict between rival candidates for office. With the final selection determined by lot from a relatively large number of candidates, there was less chance of violent opposition between a few elite factions for the archonship.[75] The history of the rest of the sixth century, however, shows that this attempt to introduce a more impartial procedure for the selection of magistrates was unsuccessful in circumventing violent conflict between rival elites for office.

An even better example of Solon's attempts to resolve the problem of intra-

[72] See Arist. *Ath. Pol.* 3.1, 3.4, for the monopoly of elites on the magistracies before Solon. For election as the procedure for choosing magistrates before Solon, see Arist. *Pol.* 1273b35–1274a2. Arist. *Ath. Pol.* 8.2, however, states that before Solon magistrates were appointed by the Areopagus, and it may be that candidates for office were pre-selected by the elites in the Areopagus Council and then put forward to the tribes for automatic approval (election).

[73] Arist. *Ath. Pol.* 8.1. There is much debate over whether this measure is Solonian, mainly because it conflicts with statements of Aristotle (e.g., *Pol.* 1273b35–1274a3) that Solon maintained the aristocratic principle of election as the manner of choosing magistrates. I accept that the measure is Solonian, following Rhodes, *CAAP* 146–48. The election of candidates from the tribes still favors the elites, and the use of the lot among these elected candidates does not appreciably change this (cf. Wade-Gery 1958, 110–15). The new procedure, moreover, fits Solon's attempts to quench intra-elite conflict over the archonship: see below. For arguments that the law is not Solonian, cf. Hignett, *HAC* 29, 321–26; Hansen 1990. On election by lot in general, cf. Headlam 1933.

[74] This is the argument of Rhodes, *CAAP* 148, in accepting the measure as Solonian.

[75] Thus the lot, which came to be associated with democratic modes of distributing power, was initially a mechanism for regulating elite competition for public office. If this argument is correct, then the use of the lot for the distribution of public office originates in the archaic period as a response to intra-elite factionalism, and then is appropriated by the democracy for its own specifically egalitarian purposes. The case for interpreting Solon's introduction of the lot as a method of avoiding violent conflict among elites is indirectly supported by the comparative evidence of the city-states of Renaissance Italy. According to Peter Burke (1986, 142), "One common solution to the problem of faction was to choose office-holders by drawing lots."

elite conflict is the so-called law on stasis. The law probably ran approximately as follows:[76]

ὃς ἂν στασιαζούσης τῆς πόλεως μ[ὴ] θῆται τὰ ὅπλα μηδὲ μεθ᾽ ἑτέρων, ἄτιμον εἶναι.

Whoever does not join the side of one faction or the other in a situation of civil war shall be an outlaw.

Since the historicity of this law has been hotly debated, a defense of its authenticity must be given before proceeding.[77] The primary reason for accepting the law as genuine is that our sources regard it as "unique" to Solon and "paradoxical."[78] The fact that the law was considered paradoxical shows that it did not fit into our sources' preconceived notion of Solonian legislation and indeed that they (and their sources), far from having any ideological reasons for inventing such a law or attributing it to the famed Athenian legislator, in fact found the law inexplicable. The puzzlement of our sources suggests that the law was preserved in the tradition not because it

[76] Arist. *Ath. Pol.* 8.5. Additional sources for the law are Plut. *Sol.* 20.1; *Mor.* 823f, 550b–c; Cic. *Att.* 10.1.2; Gell. 2.12; D.L. 1.58. In the version of the law I present above, I leave off the additional phrase given in the *Ath. Pol.*, "and shall have no share in the polis [καὶ τῆς πόλεως μὴ μετέχειν]." I believe that this phrase was not part of the original law, but is Aristotle's addition and reveals his misunderstanding of the meaning of ἀτιμία in the archaic period. Ἀτιμία in the original law meant outlawry and not merely loss of political rights, as Aristotle paraphrases it. For this shift in the meaning of ἀτιμία, see above, "Introduction." Compare Arist. *Ath. Pol.* 26.4 for the use of the phrase, and the author's misunderstanding of the meaning of ἀτιμία in the tyranny law at 16.10. For the view that this phrase was part of the original law, cf. Lavagnini 1945–46, 23n.1; Rhodes, *CAAP* 158–59.

[77] The principal arguments against the authenticity of the law are: (1) it seems to incite civic violence rather than lessen it (von Fritz 1977); (2) Lysias's failure to mention the law, and indeed his denial that any such law existed, in prosecuting Philon, who was accused at his δοκιμασία of withdrawing from Attica during the civil war of 404/3 (Lys. 31.27–28; see Hignett, *HAC* 26–27; Sealey 1983b, 103–5); (3) the possibility that moderate oligarchs in the late fifth century could have fabricated the law in order to be able to cite the authority of Solon for their proposal that only those who were capable of defending the polis militarily should have political power (David 1984, 133–38; Gabba 1994, 109ff.). I believe that the following authors adequately refute these arguments: Goldstein 1972; Bers 1975, Develin 1977b; Manville 1980; 1990, 147–48.

[78] Of the many Solonian laws listed by Arist. *Ath. Pol.* 6–8, the law on stasis is the only one labeled ἴδιος. Aristotle uses the concept of uniqueness as an organizing principle in a short passage on lawgivers in book 2 of the *Politics*. Keaney 1981 argues that this designation was based on a comparative knowledge of law such as is also evident in Theophrastus's *Nomoi*. If this is correct, then we can be more confident in claiming that by the fourth century this law existed only in the Solonian tradition. Plutarch calls the law ἴδιος μὲν μάλιστα καὶ παράδοξος, but he manages to explain the law as reasonable and in accord with the desire "that the city be as one body and feel pain together," which he associates with Solonian legislation (*Sol.* 20.1; cf. 18.6 on the law that "anyone who wishes may prosecute a person who is wronged"; see also Plut. *Mor.* 550c, 823f). See also Aulus Gellius's description of his initial amazement that Solon made such a law (2.12).

fitted the ideological needs of the transmitters, but because it was historical. The fact that all sources unequivocally attribute the law to Solon strengthens the argument for authenticity, since fictitious but ideologically motivated ancient laws are frequently attributed to different lawgivers by different transmitters over time.[79]

One reason that the ancient authorities consider the law bizarre is that it appears to increase the scope of civic violence by seeking to include all citizens in the struggle rather than resolving it, as was Solon's aim according to his poetry. Yet if we consider the example of Mytilene and the context of intra-elite politics of exile, we may be in a better position to understand the intent of the law. According to my reconstruction of events in Mytilene (see chapter 2), the intervention of non-elites in intra-elite conflict actually stabilized the polis. When a large non-elite group put its support on the side of the incumbent elite faction, it was impossible for the exiled faction to overcome its opponents and restore itself to power. Thus the unstable movement back and forth between power and exile was stopped. It is possible that Solon likewise sought to prevent such destabilizing shifts of power. By requiring non-elites to take sides in a situation of political conflict between elites, Solon hoped to prevent the violent and rapid transfer of power from one elite faction to another. In particular, elites would be deterred from seeking power violently, since they would now have to face the opposition of the entire citizen body and not just a narrow group of rival elites.[80]

This may have been the aim of Solon, but subsequent Athenian history was to show that the people as a whole were not yet ready to play such a decisive role in determining the leadership of the polis. Following Solon's archonship, violent conflict between elites appears to have continued unabated, and there is little sign that non-elites played any role.[81] The time was coming, however, when the people would directly intervene in intra-elite strife and thereby establish securely the principle of their authority in political affairs. Solon was premature, but not foolishly utopian, in trying to legislate popular involvement in politics.

Despite the failure of Solon's attempt to dampen intra-elite politics of exile, his legislation did have an influence on how politics and conflict were conducted in the sixth century. By strengthening the people's judicial role in the polis and encouraging popular involvement in the resolution of political conflict, Solon forced the elite leadership to become more responsive to the demands of the lower classes. Solon himself embodied this new concern by

---

[79] For example, a law on orphans is attributed to Solon by D.L. 1.56 and to Charondas by Diod. Sic. 12.15.1. On legends about early lawgivers, see Szegedy-Maszak 1978.

[80] Grote (1851, 192–98) similarly viewed Solon's intent in the law on stasis to be the resolution of intra-elite conflict and deterrence of coup attempts. Cf. Glotz 1904, 370–71; Lavagnini 1945/46, 23–24; Piccirilli 1976, 759; W. Eder 1986, 293.

[81] Arist. *Ath. Pol.* 13; and below on Pisistratus's rise to tyrannical power.

responding directly and effectively to the crisis of the exiled and enslaved Athenians. Pisistratus followed Solon's lead by providing further economic relief to the poor, and making his leadership agreeable to the common people. The accounts of Pisistratus's rise to power, moreover, suggest that Pisistratus appealed to the people for support against his elite rivals—an act in line with Solon's provisions in his law on stasis. The key moment in the development of popular involvement in determining the political leadership of the polis, however, was Cleisthenes' appeal to the people in his struggle against Isagoras in 508/7. It is important to recognize, nevertheless, that Solon's legislation, and particularly the law on stasis, was the first step in this direction.

Following Solon's reforms, political conflict among elites continued unabated. In the fourth year after Solon's archonship (590/89), the Athenians did not elect an eponymous archon "on account of the internal conflict" (διὰ τὴν στάσιν). They were without a magistrate (ἀναρχίαν ἐποίησαν) again four years later "for the same reason" (διὰ τὴν αὐτὴν αἰτίαν).[82] Following this, an elite person named Damasias held the office of archon beyond the legal limit of his term.[83] Finally a board of ten was elected to replace the eponymous archon because of the incessant strife (διὰ τὸ στασιάζειν).[84]

Aristotle states that the board was to be composed of five Eupatridae (εὐπατρίδαι, "those of good birth"), three farmers (ἄγροικοι), and two craftsmen (δημιουργοί).[85] This formulation suggests that various social and economic classes were involved in the political strife, since the inclusion of farmers and craftsmen on the board seems to be a response to the disgruntlement of these groups over their exclusion from the archonship. Aristotle's formulation is suspect, however, because the subdivision of the non-elites by occupation seems to arise only in the fourth century.[86] Yet, since we know that the wealthiest among the non-elites were in fact made eligible for the archonship by Solon's reforms, and since Damasias's extended rule represented an abrogation of that right, it is likely that the composition of the board was divided between the ruling elites (Eupatridae) and some portion of the non-elites.[87] It must be remembered, however, that since only the wealthiest of the non-elite were eligible for the archonship, the division of the membership of the board between the elite and the wealthiest of the non-elite does not represent a concession to a demand of the non-elites as a

---

[82] Arist. *Ath. Pol.* 13.1.

[83] Damasias was probably a member of the ruling elite, since the name occurs in the magistrate list for 629/8 (Dion. Hal. *Ant. Rom.* 3.36.1; Wade-Gery 1958, 103).

[84] Arist. *Ath. Pol.* 13.2.

[85] Arist. *Ath. Pol.* 13.2.

[86] Rhodes, *CAAP* 183.

[87] Wade–Gery 1958, 102; Rhodes, *CAAP* 183.

whole for political power. Indeed, the next events of which we know in Athenian history (the strife between Megacles, Lycurgus, and Pisistratus in 561) suggest that the struggle for political power in the polis was still waged primarily between rival groups of elites rather than between elites and non-elites.[88] (See below.)

Damasias, a member of the ruling elite who held office for two years, evidently tried to establish himself as tyrant, to the detriment of rival elite families. It is significant that he was violently deposed and perhaps driven out of Athens.[89] Such treatment would conform to the specified punishment of tyrants in Draco's homicide law and Solon's provisions for tyrants, namely ἀτιμία, or permanent exile from Athens. We are not told how or by whom Damasias was deposed, but presumably the other elites joined forces to depose the would-be tyrant, just as they had deposed Cylon and as they would depose Pisistratus from his first and second tyrannies.

A New Type of Politics: Pisistratus and Sons

The next known events of Athenian history further confirm that strife between elites did not end with the reforms of Solon, and in fact continued to destabilize the polis. Despite the evident continuation of the politics of exile throughout the Pisistratid period, however, there are signs that Pisistratus introduced changes to the practice of politics. One aim of these changes was the lessening of violent confrontation between elites, and consequently the stabilization of the archaic polis. Although Pisistratus's policies did not result in immediate cessation of violence between elites, they laid the groundwork for the end of intra-elite politics of exile and ultimately the dramatic reversal of power relations between elites and non-elites that took place in 508/7.

In order to see how the Pisistratid tyranny represents both the continuation of intra-elite conflict and the beginnings of change, it is necessary to examine in detail the evidence for Pisistratus's rule. First, I briefly review the evidence for continued violence between elites. I show that violence between the elite leaders of factions continued unchanged, with little engagement of the masses of non-elites. Second, I argue that Pisistratus altered the destabilizing practice of intra-elite politics of exile by enlarging the basis of his support beyond the traditional socio-political grouping of the faction. By increasing his support to include not just his immediate elite allies and their dependents, but a larger portion of the residents of Attica, Pisistratus

[88] For the theory that the specifications for the composition of the board of ten actually specified the composition of the πρόκριτοι from each tribe from whom the magistrates were to be chosen by lot (see above on Solon), see Wade-Gery 1958, 102–3; followed by Rhodes, CAAP 183.

[89] The words used in Arist. Ath. Pol. 13.2 are ἐξηλάθη βίᾳ τῆς ἀρχῆς.

prevented his own violent ouster and also stabilized the practice of politics. By initiating the process of transforming non-elites into political actors, Pisistratus began to dismantle the destabilizing practice of intra-elite politics of exile.

Finally, I argue that Pisistratus modified intra-elite politics in a further, more fundamental way. Once Pisistratus had gained power in his final and most enduring tyranny, he disavowed the traditional politics of exile. Rather than exiling his elite rivals, Pisistratus conciliated them by allowing them to remain in the polis and even enjoy a measure of power and prestige. In this way, Pisistratus prevented his elite rivals from gathering forces in exile and returning to oust him by violent means. Although these modifications of the traditional politics of exile were not followed by Pisistratus's sons, they laid the foundations for the ground-breaking reversal of power between elites and non-elites in 508/7 and provided a precedent for the more moderate use of exile as a political tool of the democracy.

Three groups contended for power in Athens circa 561. According to our sources, one Megacles led the men of the coast, Lycurgus those of the plain, and Pisistratus those of the hills.[90] A key issue for interpreting the strife in this period is the composition of these three groups. There is definitive evidence for the elite status of their leaders. The leader of the first, Megacles, was descended from the magistrate Megacles who had suppressed the coup of Cylon in 636, and was thus a member of the leading elite family of the Alcmeonidae. Lycurgus, the leader of the second, was probably the ancestor of the fourth-century Lycurgus of the prominent elite family of the Eteobutadae.[91] Finally, Pisistratus, the leader of the third, was thought to be descended from some early kings of Athens.[92] His ancestor Pisistratus held the archonship in 669/8.[93] The fact that the sixth-century Pisistratus was a general in the war against Megara further confirms his elite status.[94]

The evidence for the composition of the wider base of these groups is, however, more problematic. The geographical designations have led some scholars to suspect that regional differences caused the population of a certain area to group together against those in other parts of Attica.[95] Aristotle, moreover, appears to provide evidence of economic and social differences between the groups when he states that Pisistratus's support was made up of the poor "who had been relieved of their debts" (οἵ ... ἀφῃρημέν-

---

[90] Hdt. 1.59.3, Arist. *Ath. Pol.* 13.4, Plut. *Sol.* 29.1. Plut. *Sol.* 13 describes the struggle between these three factions but mistakenly places it before the reforms of Solon.

[91] Davies, *APF* 348; Sealey 1960, 16; D. Lewis 1963, 22–23.

[92] Hdt. 5.65.3.

[93] Paus. 2.24.7; cf. Wade-Gery 1958, 101; Hopper 1961, 198.

[94] Hdt. 1.59.4, Arist. *Ath. Pol.* 14.1.

[95] For example, French 1959. For a full discussion of the geographical area covered by the names, see Hopper 1961.

οἱ τὰ χρέα) and "those who were not pure in descent" (οἱ τῷ γένει μὴ καθαροί).[96]

There are two chief problems, however, with the view that the three groups were divided by regional differences, status, or economic class. First, there is no clear evidence of social, political, or economic differences between the regions that gave the groups their names.[97] Each region contained elite landowners, small farmers, craftsmen, and traders. In particular, the archaeological evidence for the region of eastern Attica, the area where Pisistratus's group is said to have been based, suggests that (contrary to the view of Aristotle) the area had wealthy as well as poor residents.[98] The second major problem with the view that Pisistratus was supported by the poor is that this idea is clearly an inference derived from fourth-century political theory.[99] Aristotle understands the conflict between the three groups in terms of the theoretical schema of oligarchs, moderates, and democrats.[100] Pisistratus in this scheme is a democrat (δημοτικώτατος), and therefore he must have been supported by the poor masses, as the occurrence of a review of the citizen lists (διαψηφισμός) after his overthrow seems to confirm. Since Aristotle is clearly influenced by anachronistic theoretical constructs, and since there are more contextually plausible explanations for the review of the citizenship lists, a different cause must be found as the basis of the competing groups.[101]

A better model for understanding these groups is that of the faction as defined in modern anthropological studies.[102] According to anthropological theory, factions are "structurally and functionally similar groups which, by virtue of

---

[96] Arist. *Ath. Pol.* 13.5; cf. Plut. *Sol.* 29.1. The meaning of the phrase οἵ... ἀφῃρημένοι τὰ χρέα is debated. Does it mean "those who were freed from debt," or those formerly wealthy men who became poor due to Solon's cancellation of debts? I agree with Hopper (1961, 195; *pace* Rhodes, CAAP 188) that the former makes more sense. In this section of the *Ath. Pol.* Aristotle is trying to prove that Pisistratus was supported by lowborn and poverty-stricken individuals, and it is unlikely that those who were wealthy enough to make loans to the poor became impoverished from the loss of their outlay.

[97] Hopper 1961, 201–3; Sealey 1960, 162–75; Stein-Hölkeskamp 1989, 140–41.

[98] Frost 1990, 4, citing burial evidence in I. Morris 1987, 222–28.

[99] Cf. Cawkwell 1995.

[100] Arist. *Ath. Pol.* 13.4.

[101] The review of the citizenship lists in 510 was probably designed to remove the mercenaries and their descendants from the lists (cf. Diod. Sic. 11.72.3 on a review held at Syracuse after the overthrow of Gelon in 463 when seven thousand mercenaries were removed from the citizen lists. Cf. Rhodes, CAAP 188. I am uncertain why Hignett (HAC 133) and Davies (1977, 117) suggest that it was those foreign craftsmen who were enfranchised by Solon who were disenfranchised by the review. The Athenians would have had no motive to disenfranchise these men after the overthrow of the tyranny, and they would furthermore have been assimilated into the Athenian population by this time.

[102] For interpretations of the three groups in mid-sixth-century Athens as factions, see Hopper 1961, 205–7; Mossé 1964, 412–13; Sealey 1960, 17; Ghinatti 1970, 70; Stein-Hölkeskamp 1989, 141. For the continued importance of factions in classical Greece, cf. Strauss 1986, 17–31, though Strauss argues that "leadership, oratory, munificence and the advocacy of policy were more important than clientelism" in the organization of factions in this period.

their similarity, compete for resources and positions of power or prestige."[103] Structurally, factions are composed of an elite factional leader, his political allies from among the elite, and their non-elite followers. Factions can be conceptualized, therefore, as pyramid-shaped groupings, with a small group of elites at the top and a much larger group of non-elite followers at the bottom. The unity of the faction derives both from lateral ties between the elites at the top of the pyramid and vertical ties between the elite individuals at the top and non-elite individuals among the masses below. Ties between elites at the top of the faction are forged through social and political interactions and are designed to advance the particular political interests of the factional leader and his elite allies.[104] Ties between elites and non-elites are based on reciprocal relations of political support and economic need.[105] In these latter types of relationship, often termed patron-client relations, elites gain prestige and political influence in the community in proportion to the size of their non-elite followings.[106] Non-elites in turn gain economic support and even physical protection from the powerful elites whom they support politically.

Three features of the anthropological model of factional politics are significant for identifying the competing groups in sixth-century Athens as factions. First, factions are formed in order to further the political interests of the factional leaders. It is clear that the primary aim of the three groups competing for power in sixth-century Athens was to achieve political power for the leader of one at the expense of the leaders of the other two. According to Herodotus, Pisistratus formed the faction of the hills as a means of acquiring exclusive power or tyranny for himself (καταφρονήσας τὴν τυραννίδα).[107] Conversely, the leaders of the other two groups formed an alliance in order to remove Pisistratus and restore themselves to power in Athens.[108] Thus in sixth-century Attica, as in other archaic poleis, the primary aim of the formation of factions was to advance the political interests of their leaders.[109]

The second feature of the anthropological model of factions corresponding to the situation in sixth-century Attica is the importance of alliances between elites for the formation and dissolution of factions. Since a faction is formed in order to further the political interests of the factional leader and his elite allies, it is easily dissolved when one or more members of the elite leadership decide that their interests are better served through the formation

---

[103] Brumfiel 1994, 4.

[104] Nicholas 1966, 57; Brumfiel 1994, 3–5.

[105] Nicholas 1966, 56–57.

[106] On patron-client relations in ancient Greece, see Millett 1989, Arnaoutoglou 1994.

[107] Hdt. 1.59.

[108] Hdt. 1.60, 61.2.

[109] Cf. Stahl 1987, 61, 65. Stahl's characterization of the structure of the three groups and the nature of political conflict in sixth-century Athens is almost identical to mine, although he does not draw the parallel with anthropological models of factions.

of a new alliance.[110] The rapid formation and dissolution of factions is clearly attested in sixth-century Athens. Not only did Megacles and Lycurgus twice form an alliance in order to counter the threat to their power represented by Pisistratus's tyranny, but Megacles easily shifted his allegiance from Lycurgus to Pisistratus and back again when it appeared that his political interests were better served by alliance with his former rival.[111]

The rapid formation and dissolution of alliances is related to a third feature of factional politics that seems to fit the evidence for sixth-century Athens, namely the relative disengagement of the non-elite base of the faction in the power struggles between the elites at the top. Since factions are formed to serve the needs of the factional leaders and not the wider non-elite base, and furthermore since non-elites are not united with one another but rather only loosely associated within the faction as dependents of elite individuals at the top of the faction, it is relatively difficult for the factional leader to call on the active support of the entire non-elite base.[112] Rather, the size of a factional leader's support among the non-elite is known only indirectly through the number and prestige of his elite allies.[113] Thus in the normal course of factional politics, conflicts are waged between elite factional leaders without the active participation of the non-elite base.

Several features of our sources' accounts of the conflicts in sixth-century Athens seem to reflect the relative disengagement of the non-elite masses in the struggles between elites. In order to see this, however, we must look at each of Pisistratus's attempts to seize power in detail. I will argue that the context for each of these three attempts was factional politics and that each elite leader sought to maximize his power through the negotiation of alliances with rival elites. Although elites enjoyed the indirect support of non-elites who were bound to them by economic and other ties, non-elites seldom played an active role in the struggle for power between elites.[114] It is this last feature of factional politics that explains both the instability of power in sixth-century Athens and the strategy behind Pisistratus's unusual actions in the context of factional politics. The important point here is that the anthropological model of faction best explains both the context of Pisistratus's activities and the success of his unique strategies within this context.

Before turning to the detailed examination of Pisistratus's three tyrannies, it is worth mentioning further implications of interpreting the three competing

---

[110] Cf. Stahl (1987, 63), who notes that "die Mobilität...[ist] ei[n] charakteristische[r] Grundzug dieser Form sozialer Gruppenbildung."

[111] Hdt. 1.60.1–61.2, Arist. *Ath. Pol.* 14.3–15.1.

[112] The response of the seventh-century Athenian magistrates to the Cylonian coup (see above) may have been one of the rare instances when elites called on their non-elite supporters for active support.

[113] Nicholas 1966, 56–57.

[114] Cf. Stahl 1987, 65; Ghinatti 1970, 64.

groups in sixth-century Athens as factions in the anthropological sense. First of all, this model helps to explain the geographical names that our sources give to the competing groups. If we consider that factions are composed of elite leaders and their personal followers from among the elite and non-elite, the best explanation of the geographical names is that they reflect the location of the residences in Attica of each faction's leader and a significant proportion of his supporters.[115] These supporters would have included the factional leader's own kinsmen, the local elite population whose support he enjoyed, and the local non-elites who relied on him for economic support and protection.[116]

The idea that the geographical names reflect the location of the regions from which the faction leaders drew support is in accord with the settlement pattern of early Attica, which was recolonized by elites from Athens following the eleventh-century contraction in population. (See chapter 1.) The prime motivation for this movement was the desire of elites to exploit the agricultural and mineral resources of the countryside, in part to create surpluses for market trade. It was probably at this time, therefore, that elites gained control of large portions of the land. It is likely that a growing group of small farmers and agricultural laborers populated the small communities of Attica, and these local non-elites formed relations of mutual support with the large landowners in their areas.

There is in fact some evidence that the leaders of all three groups in sixth-century Athens had land in the Athenian countryside. Most clearly, a wide range of epigraphical, sculptural, and burial evidence suggests that the family of Megacles had land in the region of southern Attica around Sunium and Anaphlystus from very early times.[117] Textual and other evidence, moreover, links Pisistratus to the region of eastern and northeastern Attica.[118] Finally, the evidence suggests that the family of Lycurgus was based in the city deme

---

[115] Sealey (1960, 17), who argues that each of the leaders is to be viewed as "a wealthy landowner, who had the support of his local retainers." Cf. Connor 1971 and Finley 1983 for elites as leaders of small farmers who were tied to them by patronage.

[116] In Nicholas's (1966, 56) study of factions in the Indian villages of Radhanagar and Govindapur, "28 percent of the families were kinsmen of their faction leaders, 27 percent were economic dependents of their leaders; 21 percent of the supporters were resident in the neighborhood of which their faction leader was head, and 14 percent gave their support on grounds of caste; and 10 percent were families that took protection from a powerful foe by becoming supporters of one of his opponents."

[117] G. Anderson 2000 analyzes the evidence linking the Alcmeonids to this region from the early sixth century, arguing that the Alcmeonids established a base in the south only as a result of their exile from Athens in 600 B.C.E. following their role in the Cylonian conspiracy. It is quite likely, however, that Alcmeonid presence in the region goes much further back, given the relative richness of the region in the Dark Age. (See Whitley 1991b, 199–201.) If the model of the recolonization of Attica in the Dark Age is correct, it would explain the evidence for Alcmeonid residence both in the city demes of Alopeke, Agryle, and Xypete and in southern Attica.

[118] [Pl.] Hipparch. 228b, Plut. Sol. 10.3. See also the gravestone of one Aristion from the region of Brauron (Jeffery, LSAG no. 42), a name that Arist. Ath. Pol. 14.1 and Plut. Sol. 30.3 connect with Pisistratus.

of Butadae, which "would provide a very suitable home" for the leader of a faction based in the plain of Athens.[119] We may reasonably conclude, therefore, that the three groups took their names from the local bases of their factional leaders in the territory of Attica.[120]

A final feature of the anthropological model of faction is significant for understanding the nature of political conflict in sixth-century Athens. It is noteworthy that factional politics are a product of societies in which intra-class conflict between elites, rather than inter-class conflict between elites and nonelites, is the dominant factor. As Elizabeth Brumfiel puts it: "[U]nder conditions of class struggle, society is divided by horizontal cleavages that separate internally solidary and externally competing strata. This contrasts with a situation of factional competition in which society is divided by vertical cleavages that unite members of different strata and foster conflict between members of the same strata."[121] If indeed the model of faction fits the conditions of sixth-century Attica, then the model has significant implications for the degree of stratification of Athenian society at this time. Indeed the model of factional politics would suggest that sixth-century Attica was only weakly stratified, since verticial ties between elites and non-elites were stronger than horizontal ties between members of the same class. Since stratification is often identified with the emergence of early states in anthropological literature, its absence in sixth-century Attica may suggest that the state was only weakly developed at this time.[122]

If we now turn to the analysis of Pisistratus's three tyrannies, we will see that they took place within the context of violent intra-elite competition, and that Pisistratus's ultimate success is explained by his attempts to overcome the inherent instability of this form of political conflict.[123] In his first seizure of

[119] Rhodes, CAAP 187.

[120] Lavelle 2000, however, argues that the whole three-party scheme is a fiction created to obscure the role of the demos and the elites in supporting Pisistratus. Lavelle's explanation is not incompatible with my own interpretation, especially his view that demos and elites did actually support Pisistratus. (See discussion below.) I would add only that the parties are not complete fictions, since they do reflect the locations of the estates of the competing elites. Kinzl 1989 also doubts that the geographical names for the three groups reflect sixth-century conditions. Rather, Kinzl believes the names to be an inference from the broad geographical divisions of Greek poleis and mid-fifth-century regional divisions in Athens.

[121] Brumfiel 1994, 8.

[122] See chapter 1 above for anthropological models of state formation.

[123] For the importance of intra-elite conflict in the political struggles resulting in Pisistratus's three tyrannies, see Stahl 1987, 60–105. Blok 2000 takes Stahl's argument even further, arguing that Pisistratus introduced no changes to the practice of politics that had existed for centuries, namely violent conflict between elites and their closest elite allies. For Blok, "the majority of the population acted as spectators at the military and political arena" (p. 47). Stahl (1987, 63, 65), by contrast, views the final battle at Pallene as an exception to the general rule that the mass of citizens were not active in the political conflict between elites. Blok is right to emphasize the importance of intra-elite conflict to understanding Pisistratus's tyrannies, and Stahl is right to point to the gradual increase in the size of Pisistratus's following among the general population (p. 63).

the tyranny, Pisistratus is reported to have wounded himself and then driven to the center of Athens on a wagon.[124] Claiming that he was fleeing enemies who sought to murder him, he begged the Athenians to grant him a body-guard (ἐδέετό τε τοῦ δήμου φυλακῆς τινος πρὸς αὐτοῦ κυρῆσαι).[125] The Athenians, who were favorably disposed toward Pisistratus because of his ac-complishments as general in the war with Megara, granted him a personal guard. With this bodyguard, Pisistratus established himself as tyrant in Athens.

There are problems with taking our sources' versions of this event at face value. Our earliest and best source is Herodotus, who wrote in a period when tyranny was reviled throughout Greece and in particular by the democratic Athenians. In addition, Herodotus must have relied on fifth-century Athenian polis traditions for his account of the Pisistratid tyranny. Finally, it is widely recognized that Herodotus himself shaped his narratives about archaic tyrants according to his own artistic and ideological aims. Taking all these factors into consideration, it is important to note the ways that Herodotus and the oral traditions on which he relied adapted historical memories of the tyranny to fit contemporary conditions and attitudes.[126] It has been pointed out by Brian Lavelle, for example, that the representation of Pisistratus as tricking the Athenians not only draws on the trickster motif familiar in both Greek and non-Greek traditions, but has a clear purpose for fifth-century Athenians, since it effectively excuses them for their submission to tyranny.[127] It might furthermore be noted that Herodotus's version of the event assumes not only that the Athenian demos held power and had the authority to allocate publicly financed armed forces such as a bodyguard, but that they needed to be de-ceived (ἐξαπατηθείς) in order to hand over power to a tyrant.[128] Since the assembly was not the locus of political power in the early sixth century, and there is no sign of publicly organized military forces until the time of Cleis-thenes, these elements seem to be derived from fifth-century conditions.[129]

Yet other elements of Herodotus's account may have a more plausible sixth-century basis. First of all, it is noteworthy that the context of the story is one of violent intra-elite competition for power. Even if the idea of self-wounding is borrowed from folktale traditions of the trickster type, its deployment in the

---

[124] Sources for Pisistratus's first seizure of tyranny: Hdt. 1.59.4–6, Arist. *Ath. Pol.* 14.1, Plut. *Sol.* 30.1–4.

[125] Hdt. 1.59.4. Cf. Arist. *Ath. Pol.* 14.1: συνέπεισε τὸν δῆμον . . . φυλακὴν ἑαυτῷ δοῦναι τοῦ σώματος.

[126] Herodotus's relation to the oral traditions of the archaic period is discussed in chapter 6. See also Forsdyke 1999, 2002. For a penetrating discussion of the adaptation of traditions about the tyranny in accordance with fifth-century values, see Lavelle 1993.

[127] Lavelle 1991, 1993, 2000.

[128] Cf. Stahl (1987, 62), who is skeptical that the assembly had the power to grant Pisistratus a bodyguard.

[129] On the Athenian military before Cleisthenes, see Frost 1984. On early Greek territorial conflict, see above, chapter 1.

story of Pisistratus's seizure of power is possible only because violence between elite rivals for power was a conceivable occurrence.[130] Furthermore,
even if the Athenians did not grant Pisistratus a bodyguard, the idea that
Pisistratus might have required such a guard suggests that it was not incon-
ceivable that Pisistratus might suffer physical harm from his elite rivals.
Herodotus's report of Pisistratus's speech to the assembly seems to reflect the
form that this intra-elite violence often took: exile on threat of death. According to Herodotus, Pisistratus claimed that he "had fled his enemies
[ἐκπεφευγὼς τοὺς ἐχθρούς], who wished to kill him [ἀπολέσαι]." Pisistratus's response to the attempt of his enemies to kill him was flight, but—
befitting the trickster motif—Pisistratus fled *into* the city rather than out of it,
as was usual in cases of intra-elite violence. In two later confrontations with
his elite rivals, as we shall see, Pisistratus's flight took the usual form of exile
from the city. The general point here is that this story reflects the basic condition of sixth-century Athenian politics, namely violent confrontation between rival elite leaders who drove each other into exile through threat of
violence and death.

In addition to the general context of the accounts, a further detail
may reflect sixth-century conditions. The term κορυνηφόροι (club bearers)
is unusual, being used only with regard to Pisistratus among all the references to tyrants' bodyguards in our sources.[131] Since the oral traditions would
have been much more likely to have adopted the regular term for a bodyguard (δορυφόροι, "spear bearers") if they had invented this detail, it is likely
that this term reflects a genuine memory of Pisistratus's attempt at tyranny in
561. Since we have already determined that it is unlikely that the Athenians
in the assembly had the power to grant Pisistratus a bodyguard, and that there
were no publicly armed forces at this time, we are left with the questions,
Who were the club bearers, and what use did Pisistratus make of them in his
first tyranny?

In answer to these questions, we might first note that, even if we dismiss the
idea that Pisistratus wounded himself and thereby secured the bodygaurd with
which he seized power, it is still possible that Pisistratus made some sort of
appeal to the Athenians in the assembly.[132] Given the context of violent intra-

---

[130] For self-wounding as a typical means of deception in Greek literature, cf. Odysseus's self-
wounding at Troy (*Od.* 4.244–46) and Zopyrus's self-wounding at Babylon (Hdt. 3.154).

[131] Lavelle 1992a, 78n.1, collects the references to tyrants' bodyguards.

[132] Since the motif of an appeal to the people recurs in Pisistratus's later attempts at tyranny
(see below), it is possible, as Heleen Sancisi-Weerdenburg suggests, that this element is a result
of the tendency of oral traditions to interpret, or even invent, earlier events according to the
paradigm of later events. On this phenomenon, cf. Thomas 1989, 131–54. Sancisi-Weerdenburg
(2000b, 101–5) proposes that Pisistratus's first and second tyranny attempts are "nothing more
than an historiographical construction" based on the variant stories told in oral traditions illustrating Pisistratus's deceptive character. While I would not throw out the first and second
tyrannies entirely, Sancisi-Weerdenburg is right to point out this possibility.

elite competition for power, Pisistratus may indeed have presented himself before the Athenian people with complaints about the threats made against him by his elite rivals. In this context, Pisistratus will have reminded the Athenians of his services in the war with Megara, as Herodotus tells us, and attempted to rally public opinion on his side.[133]

What of the club bearers then? H. W. Singor has argued, on the basis of comparative evidence from several other poleis, that the term κορυνηφόροι refers to men from the non-hoplite classes, as opposed to the hoplite-armed δορυφόροι (spear bearers) of other tyrants.[134] We might note, furthermore, that in the context of violent confrontation between elite factions, it is not implausible that Pisistratus employed a small group of men of low social origins to serve as a personal bodyguard. In other words, the club bearers may have been gathered by Pisistratus for his own protection, not granted to him by the Athenians in the assembly.[135] It is likely that these men were either an ad hoc group from the city, as Herodotus seems to suggest, or some of his personal dependents from the area around his estates at Brauron.[136] The term "club bearers," therefore, may reflect the informal, ad hoc nature of Pisistratus's private bodyguard before his seizure of power, rather than the publicly financed spear bearers of successful tyrants. In either case, the low social origins of the club bearers may have given rise to the tradition that Pisistratus was supported by the poor. In fact, the club bearers would have been a small privately organized force gathered for personal protection and

---

[133] Aristotle records that Aristion made the proposal for a bodyguard to the assembly (Ath. Pol. 14.1). Since the name Aristion is attested epigraphically in the region of Brauron, it is possible that Aristion was an elite ally of Pisistratus who took a leading role in rallying public support for him against his rivals (Rhodes, CAAP 200).

[134] Singor 2000. The main evidence is the use of this term to designate a class of poor men at Sicyon (Theopompus, FGrHist 115 F 176, Pollux 3.83, Steph. Byz. s.v. Ξίος) and the use of a parallel terms such as κονίποδες of lower classes at Epidaurus and Argos as well as of Pisistratus's bodyguard (schol. Ar. Lys. 665–68 = Arist. fr. 394 Rose). Stahl (1987, 62), by contrast, suggests that the club bearers were drawn from Pisistratus's inner circle of elite allies and in particular were young men of elite status who carried clubs in imitation of Heracles, who represented the ideal elite warrior. This interpretation depends on belief in an association between Pisistratus and Heracles (Boardman 1972, 1984), which is now doubted: see R. Osborne 1983/84, Cook 1987, Blok 1990.

[135] The grant of a bodyguard may be supported by Solon fr. 11 (West), in which Solon chastised the Athenians for allowing themselves to be tricked into giving one to Pisistratus: "For you yourselves elevated these men by giving them a means of defense, and because of this you acquired evil slavery," αὐτοὶ γὰρ τούτους ηὐξήσατε ῥύματα δόντες, καὶ διὰ ταῦτα κακὴν ἔσχετε δουλοσύνην. Yet there are both textual problems (the reading of ῥύματα vs. ῥύσια) and questions of interpretation (Does the fragment refer to Pisistratus? Or to Draco?) that compromise the use of the fragment as evidence for Pisistratus's tyranny. See Rihll 1989 for a recent discussion of this fragment. See Lavelle 1992a for an argument that the body-guards of archaic tyrants (and Pisistratus in particular) were composed of natives rather than foreigners.

[136] Hdt. 1.59.5 says that the bodyguard was chosen from among the townspeople (οἱ ἀστοί).

cannot be taken as indicative of wider non-elite support as the basis of Pisistratus's power.[137]

In sum, if Pisistratus did indeed present himself before the Athenians in the assembly in 561, it is likely that he made a case that he was being treated violently by his political rivals and put his private force of club bearers on display to prove it. The elites and non-elites in the assembly may have voiced some sympathy for Pisistratus, but will neither have been deceived by him nor granted him a bodyguard. The main effect of this public display may have been to spread the word that a former hero of the campaign against Megara was being treated roughly by other powerful men. This event may have planted the seeds for widespread (i.e., non-elite) sympathy for Pisistratus over his rivals, which helped him become tyrant briefly in 561 and is visible in his later attempts at tyranny.

The analysis above suggests that Pisistratus claimed the tyranny in 561 in part on the basis of a public display of the violent actions (murder, expulsion) threatened against him by his rivals. Yet this ploy for power was ultimately unsuccessful, since he was driven into exile by his rivals shortly after seizing power.[138] The brevity of Pisistratus's first tyranny suggests that the sympathy he gained from the Athenians in the assembly was not sufficient to prevent rival elite leaders from expelling him by force. In other words, Pisistratus may have gained some passive support, but this did not translate into active and enduring willingness on the part of the Athenians to engage in violent confrontation with rival elite leaders on his behalf. Clearly, the Athenians as a whole were not yet sufficiently politicized to take an active role in the conflict between elites over political power.

I argue below that Pisistratus's success in his final and most enduring tyranny lay in his effective translation of broad popular approval into active military support in the violent confrontation with his elite rivals. Pisistratus's appeal to the Athenians in the assembly in his first tyranny therefore marks the beginning of his attempt to convert the formerly passive Athenian masses into active participants in the violent contest for power between elites. More significant, perhaps, Pisistratus's actions in his first tyranny demonstrate that he sought

---

[137] Cf. Lavelle (1992a, 81n.18), who notes that most late sources claim that Pisistratus's bodyguard numbered three hundred (Polyaenus 1.21.3; schol. Pl. *Rep.* 566b) but Plut. *Sol.* 30.3 gives the number as fifty.

[138] The words used for the expulsion of Pisistratus from power are ἐξελαύνουσι, ἐξελάσαντες (Hdt. 1.60.1), and ἐξέβαλον (Arist. *Ath. Pol.* 14.3). Since Herodotus seems to distinguish this first period of exile from the second by stating that in the second exile Pisistratus "abandoned the country completely" (ἀπαλλάσσετο ἐκ τῆς χώρης τὸ παράπαν, 1.61.2), it is possible that Pisistratus retreated only to his estates at Brauron during the first exile. The ease with which Pisistratus was summoned back by Megacles following his first exile might seem to confirm this. See G. Anderson 2000 for the argument that Pisistratus and other elites maintained residences in exile in Attica itself. Although our sources are vague about chronology, Rhodes (*CAAP* 198) suggests that Pisistratus was in power from 561 to 560 or 559.

support beyond the typical base of factional politics, his personal followers and their dependents. Rather, Pisistratus appealed for the active support of the Athenians at large. Pisistratus's second tyranny attempt again illustrates how he began to plant the seeds for this active participation of a broad section of the Athenian populace in the violent struggle for power between elites.

Following Pisistratus's expulsion by his rivals Megacles and Lycurgus, these two factional leaders themselves quarreled. Megacles then sent a message to Pisistratus offering him power on the condition that he marry Megacles' daughter.[139] Megacles and Pisistratus then devised a ploy to restore Pisistratus to Athens. Dressing up a tall woman by the name of Phye in the costume of the goddess Athena, they mounted her on a wagon and drove her into Athens. Before arriving in Athens, Megacles and Pisistratus sent messengers ahead of them to announce to the Athenians that they should receive Pisistratus benevolently, since the goddess Athena was honoring him above all men and was conveying him to the acropolis. When Pisistratus and the woman arrived in Athens, the Athenians were persuaded that the woman was Athena, and they received Pisistratus back.

Elements of this story seem to contradict one another and raise the suspicion that the historical facts of Pisistratus's second tyranny have been expanded and adapted in ways that fit the fifth-century conditions of Herodotus's informants. On the one hand, the first part of the story seems to describe the typical means of negotiating power between elites in factional politics in the sixth century. Megacles broke off his alliance with Lycurgus as a result of a quarrel and formed a new alliance with Pisistratus. Herodotus's use of the verb στασιάζειν (1.60.1) suggests that the quarrel concerned the allocation of power between them. Megacles then offered Pisistratus power, and they sealed the deal with a marriage between Pisistratus and Megacles' daughter. We are not told by our sources what happened to Lycurgus, but presumably he withdrew into exile when he saw that the balance of power was against him. All is in accord with factional politics: alliances between elites are easily formed and broken, and power is gained and lost with little involvement of the wider base of the faction.

The second part of the story is more puzzling. First of all, the story of Phye dressed as Athena assumes that the Athenians needed to be deceived into allowing Pisistratus to return and hold tyrannical power.[140] This assumption not only contradicts the first part of the account, in which Megacles offers Pisistratus power on his own initiative, but again anachronistically assumes that the Athenians as a whole had the authority to allocate power between elite leaders. A further difficulty in the story is signaled by Herodotus's own incomprehension of how the Athenians could be deceived by the ploy: he cannot understand how

---

[139] Sources for Pisistratus's second tyranny: Hdt. 1.60.2–5, Arist. *Ath. Pol.* 14.4.

[140] Hdt. 1.60.3. Cf. Herodotus's repeated use of the verb μηχανάομαι to describe Pisistratus's actions in this episode.

such a trick would have been successful among the Athenians, who of all the Greeks were most renowned for their cleverness (1.60.3).

Recent scholarship has tried to get around these difficulties by rereading the episode without the assumption that the sixth-century Athenians were deceived by the ploy. W. R. Connor, in particular, has employed insights from cultural anthropology on the role of ritual and ceremonial in civic life to show that the parade with the girl dressed as Athena was not a ploy designed to dupe the Athenians but rather an instance of a shared drama by which the Athenians expressed their consent to Pisistratus's rule through reference to shared cultural symbols.[141] According to this interpretation, while Pisistratus did employ cultural symbols to his advantage, the Athenians were not fooled by the woman dressed as Athena but, by their willing participation in the ceremony, showed their acceptance of Pisistratus.

Connor's brilliant interpretation of the episode solves Herodotus's problem of the gullibility of the Athenians. Yet even Connor's solution suggests that the assent of the Athenians as a whole was necessary for Pisistratus's assumption of tyrannical power.[142] If we rid ourselves of this assumption, then we might consider the parade with Athena not as the means by which Pisistratus gained tyrannical power, but as a means by which the unity of the Athenian community was reenacted under the auspices of the patron goddess of the polis — following Pisistratus's seizure of power. In other words, the primary aim of the ceremonial procession was not to gain the Athenians' acceptance of Pisistratus as tyrant. Popular consent was not necessary for Pisistratus's assumption of power. Rather, the ceremonial procession on the occasion of Pisistratus's return from exile and assumption of tyrannical power was an opportunity for the expression of communal unity under Athena and—only indirectly— under Pisistratus's leadership.[143]

Several details of the anecdote are in accord with this interpretation. Most important, Herodotus's narrative suggests that it was Pisistratus and Megacles

---

[141] Connor 1987, 40–50. See also Sinos 1993/1998 and Blok 2000, with their summaries of older scholarship. Sinos and Blok both interpret the procession as a form of military triumph, which drew attention to Pisistratus's divine support. Yet this explanation ignores the problem raised by Connor: that Athena does not escort Pisistratus back to Athens, but rather Pisistratus escorts the goddess. See below.

[142] Cf. Connor 1987, 44: "The ceremony thus served as an expression of *popular consent*— two-way communication, not, as so often assumed, mere manipulation" (my italics).

[143] This interpretation solves the problem identified by Bassi (1998, 178) and Blok (2000, 18), namely that Connor's interpretation requires us to believe that Herodotus and his informants were unable to understand a shared cultural pattern of traditional religious processions. On my interpretation, the puzzlement of Herodotus and his sources is explained by their assumption that the ploy was the means by which Pisistratus deceived the Athenians and seized power. Without this assumption, Herodotus and his informants would have recognized the event as a traditional collective ritual. The separation of Pisistratus's assumption of power from the collective ritual, furthermore, solves the problem of the lack of comparative cases entailing the "change of a political persona non grata into a popular leader" (Blok 2000, 19).

who were driving the chariot, and thus escorting Athena back to Athens: "Dressing up the woman in full armor, they [Megacles and Pisistratus] mounted her on the chariot, and after directing her to strike a pose that would make her appear most seemly, they drove into the city."[144] Aristotle, who explicitly draws his version of this event from Herodotus and other accounts, specifically mentions that it was Pisistratus who drove the chariot while Athena rode as passenger (παραβάτης).[145] Unlike ancient kingship rituals in which the goddess escorts a king and thereby gives divine sanction to his rule, in this episode, Pisistratus escorts the goddess. As Connor argues: "The reversal is eloquent, perhaps even programmatic. Pisistratus is not seizing the kingship but serving as the subordinate and helper of Athena."[146] If Pisistratus and Megacles intended the procession with Athena to serve as the means by which Pisistratus claimed tyrannical power, why would they have reversed the kingship ritual? The answer must be that the procession was not the means by which Pisistratus seized power, but a collective ritual by which the Athenians honored Athena and thereby expressed their civic unity under her divine protection.

Pisistratus's public self-representation as a leading worshipper and servant of the patron goddess is of course significant for his claim to power within the community. In order to understand the symbolism of Pisistratus's role in the parade, it is best to compare the event with other civic and religious rituals, as Connor has pointed out. The most obvious comparative evidence is the ritual associated with the cult of Athena on the acropolis. Significantly, this cult was refounded on a grander scale shortly before Pisistratus's second seizure of power, when the Greater Panathenaea was established (566).[147] Included in the grander civic version of the festival were musical and athletic competitions, a procession from outside the city to the acropolis, the presentation of a robe to Athena, and a sacrifice and feast.[148]

Several features of the Panathenaic procession are significant in relation to Pisistratus's escort of Phye dressed as Athena. First of all, the movement of the

---

[144] Hdt. 1.60.4. The words of the messengers in Herodotus's narrative, however, suggest that it was Athena leading Pisistratus back. This discrepancy suggests that there was no single authoritative version in fifth-century Athens. I suggest that representation of Pisistratus and Megacles as drivers is more fitting in the context of sixth-century politics.

[145] Arist. Ath. Pol. 14.4.

[146] Connor 1987, 45–46. G. Anderson (2003, 67–76) has developed this point in a different direction, arguing that Pisistratus escorted Athena back to her temple on the acropolis after the establishment of a new temple, which replaced an older, seventh-century structure. Megacles' and Pisistratus's aim, according to Anderson, was to reclaim the cult of Athena for themselves in contrast to Lycurgus's family, the Butads, who dominated the cult. If this explanation is correct, then Megacles and Pisistratus were unsuccessful, since the Butads continued to dominate the cult in the sixth, fifth, and fourth centuries. It should be noted that Anderson's interpretation depends on the dates for the temples on the acropolis, a problematic topic discussed briefly below.

[147] For the date, see Davidson 1958, 26–29. An annual festival for Athena certainly existed at least by late Geometric times; cf. Hom. Il. 2.549–51.

[148] For an excellent general account of the Panathenaea, see Neils 1992.

Panathenaic procession from the periphery of the city (Dipylon Gate) to the Temple of Athena on the acropolis parallels Pisistratus's route from country-side to city center in his procession with Phye.[149] Herodotus reports that Phye came from the village of Paeania, northeast of the city, a detail that accords with Pisistratus's probable residence at Brauron following his explusion by Megacles and Lycurgus in 560.[150] Yet the more significant part of the route would have been the last part of the trip from outside the city to the acropolis. Even though Pisistratus may have begun from the direction of Brauron and Paeania in the east, he may in fact have added to the symbolic resonance of his procession by entering through the Dipylon Gate, in the northwest, and fol-lowing the route of the Panathenaic procession to the acropolis. Whether or not Pisistratus followed this precise route, nonetheless there is a clear echo of the Panathenaic procession in the route from country to city (ἐς τὸ ἄστυ, Hdt. 1.60.4) and then up to the acropolis (ἐς τὴν ἀκρόπολιν, 1.60.5).[151]

A second parallel between the Panathenaic procession and Pisistratus's pro-cession with Phye dressed as Athena is its symbolism of collective worship and service to the goddess. In both processions, elites and commoners joined together in honoring the goddess. In the Panathenaic procession, diverse segments of the population (including metics and women) marched together, and thus the procession was an occasion when the entire community put itself on display.[152] Similarly, in Pisistratus's procession, the Athenians joined in honoring the god-dess by offering prayers (προσεύχοντο, Hdt. 1.60.5) to Phye dressed as Athena. Within the context of this exercise in collective self-representation, moreover,

[149] The route of the Panathenaic procession from the Dipylon Gate to the acropolis was probably established by the mid-sixth century at the latest: cf. R. Parker 1996, 92. The main evidence is a broad mid-sixth-century ramp leading to the acropolis, which seems designed to fit the purposes of the Panathenaic procession (Hurwit 1998, 106; Eiteljorg 1993, 9). Robertson (1998, 290–95), however, argues that the route from the Dipylon Gate replaced an earlier pro-cessional way from the southeastern part of the city only shortly before 510 B.C.E., when (Thuc. 6.57.1 attests) Hippias marshaled the procession at the Dipylon Gate.

[150] Hdt. 1.60.4, Arist. Ath. Pol. 14.4.

[151] Further evidence for the idea that Pisistratus did indeed follow the route of the Panathenaic procession is the fact that during the final tyranny the Pisistratids showed clear interest in the symbolic importance of the Panathenaic Way. The construction of the Altar of the Twelve Gods and the Southeast Fountain House can be securely attributed to the Pisistratids, and these monuments clearly mark two points along the processional way. Pisistratus's building activity in the area of the classical agora, as well as in other areas of the city, demonstrates that the tyrants were interested in inserting themselves into the symbolic spaces of the city. See Forsdyke, "Peisistratus" (in prep. a).

[152] For the idea of public processions as an opportunity for collective self-representation, see Darnton's (1984, 107–43) stimulating analysis of the procession générale in eighteenth-century Montpellier. It should be noted that the evidence for the composition of the marchers in the Panathenaic procession dates primarily to the classical period, and thus it is uncertain whether non-elites participated in earlier processions. Even if only elites processed in the sixth century, as may be suggested by an early sixth-century vase (see Maurizio 1998, 301–2), it is still likely that non-elites participated as observers. The inclusion of metics in the procession must certainly post-date the creation of that status sometime after Cleisthenes' reforms.

the elites enjoyed a special status. In the Panathenaic procession, elite families were accorded particularly prominent positions in the sequence of offerings. For example, women from elite families served as ἀρρηφόροι (bearers of sacred things) and κανηφόροι (basket bearers), and a women from the elite family of the Praxiergidae bore the sacred πέπλος (cloak) and presented it to the goddess.[153] In a similar fashion, Pisistratus granted himself a prominent role in the collective worship of Athena by presenting himself as her chariot driver in a procession to her sanctuary on the acropolis.

In sum, like other civic and religious rituals of the early Athenian state, the parade with Athena would have had a dual purpose: it served to articulate and strengthen collective identity, and to grant the elites a prominent place in the social order. I argued in chapter 1 above that the construction of monumental temples was a product of the needs of elites to create more powerful contexts for displaying status in the newly forming polis. While this development apparently took place already in the late eighth century in some poleis, it is significant that only in the sixth century in Athens do we have clear signs of it. The first monumental temple of Athena was constructed on the acropolis in the second quarter of the sixth century, and as we have seen, the cult of Athena developed into a grand civic occasion through the foundation of the Panathenaea at about this same time. Sixth-century Athens, therefore, shows clear signs of the strengthening of civic institutions and rituals at precisely the time when competition between elite leaders for power appears to be most intense.

Pisistratus's role in the promotion of civic cults is difficult to determine; the evidence is not adequate. Recently scholars have revised earlier reconstructions in which Pisistratus and his sons were credited with all the major sixth-century developments, from the construction of temples on the acropolis to the transformation of the agora into a civic space.[154] Despite the claims of

[153] Neils 1992, 17, 23; with Ar. *Lys.* 641–47 Thuc. 6.56–57. The family of the Eteobutadae supplied the priestess of the cult of Athena Polias (Garland 1984, 92) and must have had a prominent position in the festival. It is perhaps significant that this priestess dressed up as the goddess and appeared before newly wedded girls in the nuptial ceremony known as the Protelaea (Garland 1984, 93). Wohl 1996 and Maurizio 1998 emphasize the privileged position of the elite in the Panathenaic procession. On the privileges of elite families in Athenian religion generally, see R. Parker 1996, 56–66.

[154] The bibliography is extensive. For critiques of the older scholarship and recent interpretations, see the essays collected in Coulson et al. 1994 and Sancisi-Weerdenburg 2000c, and the books of Shapiro 1989 and Angiolillo 1997. For temples on the acropolis, see Hurwit 1998, 106–17; Childs 1994. For the agora, see Shear 1994; R. Osborne, "Did Democracy Transform Athenian Space?" (forthcoming); Forsdyke, "Peisistratus" (in prep. a). Recent scholarship has questioned the attribution of the City Dionysia to Pisistratus and has emphasized the democratic elements of tragedy (e.g., Connor 1989, Winkler and Zeitlin 1990, R. Osborne 1993). For rebuttals of Connor's argument, see Sourvinou-Inwood 1994 and Versnel 1995. West 1989 acknowledges the imperfections of the evidence for the early chronology of Attic tragedy, but concludes nevertheless that it is most likely that the festival developed under Pisistratus. For the role of tragedy under the democracy, see also the debate in Griffin 1998 and Seaford 2000.

one ancient source that Pisistratus founded the Panathenaea, it is likely that a coalition of leading elites, including Hippocleides, the eponymous archon of 566, played a role in its foundation.[155] Pisistratus may have had a hand in this and other sixth-century innovations, but he was not alone. The important point, however, is that Pisistratus's procession with Phye is one concrete instance in which we can see Pisistratus initiating an occasion for the expression of shared communal identity and at the same time presenting himself as leader of the community. While rituals such as the Panathenaic procession and Pisistratus's procession with Phye were not the actual means by which the elites gained power, they served as opportunities for the elite to present themselves to the community as leaders in the enactment of the social and cultural order.

This analysis suggests that Pisistratus's procession with Phye was not in fact unique or unusual and that it had meaning for the Athenians precisely because it invoked parallel or similar civic rituals. Indeed it is the role of such rituals in enacting civic identity under elite leadership that helps us understand how Pisistratus extended his support beyond his faction to include the Athenians as a whole. By initiating the parade with Athena, Pisistratus not only provided an opportunity for the Athenians to express their collective identity through shared cultural symbols, but also indirectly presented himself as the leading servant of Athena and the polis as a whole. Pisistratus's self-presentation before the Athenian people in this symbolically powerful role, like his self-presentation as beleaguered war hero in his first tyranny attempt, would have continued the process by which he inserted himself in culturally significant ways into the popular consciousness.

It is important to stress that the Athenians did not directly assert their support for Pisistratus's tyranny by participating in the ceremony, but that rather they were reminded through the ceremony of Pisistratus's service to the community. Pisistratus's cultivation of the public persona of servant to the city in his first and second tyranny attempts marks the steps by which he began to activate public opinion on his side in his struggle with his elite rivals. Nevertheless, it is clear that in the second tyranny attempt, as in the first, popular sympathy was not a decisive factor in the violent struggle for political power between rival elites. Less than one year after his return to power, Pisistratus was again driven into exile by a renewed alliance between Megacles and Lycurgus. Herodotus reports that during Pisistratus's second period of exile, he left Attica altogether and withdrew to Eretria.[156] The ease with which Pisistratus gained and then lost power shows once again that the real struggle was waged between small groups of allied elites without the active engagement of the Athenian masses. As we shall see, it was only in Pisistratus's final and most enduring

---

[155] Pisistratus as founder: schol. Arist.Or. 13.189.4–5. Hippocleides as magistrate: Euseb. Chron., Olympiad 53.3–4 (i.e., 566/5); Marcellin. Vita Thuc. 2–4.

[156] Hdt. 1.61.2.

tyranny that non-elite support played a significant role in the violent confrontation between elites.

Pisistratus's third and most successful tyranny illustrates the dual nature of
his practice of politics. On the one hand, he gained power in his final tyranny
largely through the traditional means of intra-elite competition, namely the
violent seizure of power from his elite rivals with the military support of fellow
elites in other poleis. On the other hand, the success of Pisistratus's seizure of
power was due in part to widespread elite and non-elite support both at the
time of his military victory and throughout the length of his long rule. This
support was achieved in part through his successful promotion of civic institutions under his leadership, but perhaps more remarkably through his failure
to take reprisals (i.e., banish) his vanquished elite rivals. Breaking with traditional intra-elite politics of exile, Pisistratus did not expel his rivals from the
polis, but rather allowed them to continue to enjoy some measure of power
and prestige. These latter features of his rule not only contributed to the
stability of his power, but also laid the groundwork for a more collaborative,
more broadly based mode of politics. In this sense Pisistratus's final tyranny
can be seen as the forerunner of the inclusive, democratic politics formally
instituted after the overthrow of the tyranny.

The evidence for Pisistratus's reliance on the traditional means of intra-elite
politics is quite clear. Following his expulsion at the hands of Megacles and
Lycurgus for the second time, Pisistratus spent eleven years in exile gathering
money and men in order to restore himself to power in Athens by force.[157] He
first crossed over to Eretria, on Euboea, and from there he set out for the
Thermaic Gulf in the north of Greece. Aristotle says that Pisistratus founded a
settlement at Rhaecelus, in northwest Chalcidice, and it is possible that Pisistratus gave up temporarily on his hopes for power in Athens and contented
himself with ruling a new city, as other ousted elites had done before him.[158] It
is more likely, however, that Pisistratus was lured to the Thermaic Gulf by
reports of the growing prosperity of the area, and that his aim in making a settlement there was to gather resources for his return to Athens.[159]

Certainly Pisistratus's activities after founding Rhaecelus suggest that he
was motivated by the need for money and resources to make his return by
force to Athens. Leaving the Theramaic Gulf, Pisistratus crossed over to the
area of the Strymon River and Mount Pangaeum, known for gold and sil-
ver mines. Aristotle says that Pisistratus spent his time in this area "making
money transactions and hiring mercenaries" (χρηματισάμενος καὶ στρα-

---

[157] Hdt. 1.61.2–4, Arist. Ath. Pol. 15.1–3.

[158] For example, the Samian aristocrats who, after failing to overthrow Polycrates, eventually
founded a colony at Cydonia, in Crete (Hdt. 3.59.1; and above, chapter 2).

[159] Baba (1990, 1–23) argues on the basis of the rich burial finds at Sindus (near modern
Thessaloniki) that Pisistratus was informed of the wealth of this area by the Eretrians, who were
active overseas traders and colonizers.

τιώτας μισθωσάμενος).[160] He also drew on his connections with elites in other areas of Greece for support, most notably Theban elites, the exiled Naxian tyrant Lygdamis and his supporters, and the ruling elites at Eretria.[161]

The accounts of the battle of Pallene, by which Pisistratus defeated his opponents and was restored to power at Athens, reveal that although he had considerable military support from foreign allies and mercenaries, he also enjoyed the active support of a large group of Athenians.[162] Herodotus reports that when Pisistratus and his foreign allies arrived on the coast of Attica at Marathon, they were joined by a large group of Athenian supporters (1.62.1):

> When Pisistratus and his supporters were setting up a camp in this region [i.e., Marathon], a number of partisans from the city arrived [οἵ τε ἐκ τοῦ ἄστεος στα-σιῶται ἀπίκοντο], and others from the country villages flowed in [ἄλλοι τε ἐκ τῶν δήμων προσέρρεον]. For these men, tyranny was more welcome than freedom.

Herodotus's use of the verb προσέρρεον suggests that the influx of supporters from the country villages was considerable. In addition, Herodotus's specification that Pisistratus's Athenian supporters came both from the city and from the countryside seems to indicate that Pisistratus enjoyed fairly widespread support among the Athenians. By contrast, Herodotus specifies that the Athenians who opposed Pisistratus came from the city alone, and thus were probably a smaller group comprised of Pisistratus's immediate political opponents (Megacles and Lycurgus) and their elite allies.[163] Herodotus's scornful comment that the supporters of Pisistratus preferred tyranny to freedom not only betrays the influence of this fifth-century ideological distinction on Herodotus and his sources, but also suggests that Herodotus and his sources did not invent these details about the size of Pisistratus's Athenian following for ideological reasons. Indeed, fifth-century Athenians might have preferred to obscure or eliminate this embarrassing detail from their tradition, since it revealed that a large number of their ancestors welcomed a tyrant to Athens. The fact that the traditions preserved this inconvenient detail suggests that Pisistratus did in fact enjoy widespread support.

The significant point here is that despite Pisistratus's eleven years in exile, he not only enjoyed widespread approval among the Athenians but also was able to rely on their active support in his confrontation with his elite opponents. While it is important not to exaggerate the extent of this support—

[160] Arist. Ath. Pol. 15.2. Lavelle 1992b refutes the common assumption that Pisistratus gained control of mines in this region (cf., e.g., Davies, APF 453), arguing that such control would have required considerable and continuous use of force given the strength of the Thracian inhabitants of the area. Rather, Lavelle suggests that trade and the temporary exploitation of the agricultural and mineral resources by force were the basis of Pisistratus's resources from this region.

[161] Hdt. 1.61.3–4, Arist. Ath. Pol. 15.2.

[162] Sources for the battle of Pallene: Hdt. 1.62.1–64.3, Arist. Ath. Pol. 15.3.

[163] Hdt. 1.62.2, Ἀθηναίων δὲ οἱ ἐκ τοῦ ἄστεος; cf. 63.1, Ἀθηναῖοι δὲ οἱ ἐκ τοῦ ἄστεος.

the actual participants in the battle of Pallene must have been elites and the wealthier men among the non-elites—the battle still demonstrates that Pisistratus was able to draw on a larger base of active support than was typical in intra-elite politics of exile. Rather than relying only on the narrow group of elites that comprised the leadership of a single faction (as Megacles and Lycurgus evidently did), Pisistratus drew supporters from outside his immediate faction, including those from the city and the diverse villages of Attica. How did Pisistratus gain this wider following? The answer must be that Pisistratus's prior successful public presentation of himself as a leader in the civic spaces of Athens (agora, acropolis) on those occasions when the Athenian community "represented itself to itself" (assembly meetings, festivals) both served to strengthen the Athenians' sense of their own collective political identity and created bonds between Pisistratus himself and this wider community.[164] The anedotes regarding Pisistratus's first and second seizures of tyranny, as analyzed above, are clear instances of such community building under Pisistratus's direction. We must imagine that these were not the only occasions on which Pisistratus used civic institutions and ideologies to present himself as the legitimate leader of the community.

Despite the evidence for widespread Athenian support of Pisistratus's claim to power, it is noteworthy that the traditions about Pallene, like the traditions about Pisistratus's first and second tyrannies, utilized the trickster motif to help excuse the Athenians for their submission to a tyrant.[165] In the battle of Pallene, Herodotus reports that Pisistratus and his supporters attacked their opponents after lunch, when they were relaxing at dice or taking a nap (1.63.1). Furthermore, Pisistratus is credited with a clever ploy to prevent the Athenians from gathering together to resist him (1.63.2):

> When [the defeated Athenians] were in full flight, Pisistratus devised a clever ploy [βουλὴν σοφωτάτην...ἐπιτεχνᾶται] so that the Athenians might not still gather together and might be dispersed [ὅκως μήτε ἁλισθεῖεν ἔτι οἱ Ἀθηναῖοι διεσκεδασμένοι τε εἶεν]. Mounting his sons on horses, he sent them forward. When they overtook the fugitives, they spoke what Pisistratus had ordered. [Pisistratus's sons] commanded [the Athenians] to take courage and to return each to his own home.

Herodotus's language in this passage reveals that the tradition has been shaped to portray the Athenians as victims of Pisistratus's deception.[166] Furthermore, the rest of Herodotus's account goes on to suggest that in addition to deception, Pisistratus used force to keep the Athenians in submission. After killing some Athenians in the battle and forcing others into exile (1.64.3), Pisistratus

[164] The phrase "represented itself to itself" is borrowed from Darnton 1984, 120.

[165] Lavelle 1991.

[166] Compare Herodotus's use of the verb ἐπιτεχνάομαι with his earlier use of the verb μηχανάομαι to describe Pisistratus's ruse with the girl dressed as Athena.

secured his regime not only through the money and men from his foreign allies but also by taking hostages from the children of the Athenians who remained (1.64.1–2). In these features of Herodotus's account, we see all the elements of the fifth-century construction of tyrannical rule, in particular his use of deception and force to keep the people in submission.[167]

Yet despite the heavy overlay of fifth-century ideological notions of the nature of tyrannical rule, the detail of Pisistratus's appeal to the Athenians to disperse and return home may reflect a historical memory of his leniency toward his opponents. In particular, this detail may reflect the fact that Pisistratus did not drive his opponents into exile following his victory at Pallene. Indeed, despite elite family traditions to the contrary, the documentary and literary evidence shows that elite families did not go into permanent exile under his tyranny, and that they often held positions of prestige and power under his regime. A brief review of this evidence will demonstrate this point.

Most important among the supposed exiles during the Pisistratid tyranny are the Alcmeonidae. According to Herodotus, this family went into exile immediately upon Pisistratus's victory at Pallene in 546 and remained in exile until the overthrow of the tyranny in 510.[168] A fragment of an archon list, however, shows that Cleisthenes, a prominent member of the family, was the eponymous archon in 525/4, during the tyranny of Pisistratus's sons.[169] While it is still possible that the Alcmeonidae were in exile during Pisistratus's tyranny and only returned after his death in 529/8, this is unlikely for several reasons. First of all, if Pisistratus had banished the Alcmeonids, then it is unlikely that his sons would have been more lenient, especially in the uncertain period following their father's death. Second, Cleisthenes' tenure of the archonship under Pisistratus's sons suggests a close collaboration between the Alcmeonidae and the tyrants rather than a lengthy exile. Third, the Alcmeonids had been willing to collaborate with the Pisistratids on prior occasions, as Megacles' alliance with Pisistratus in his second tyranny shows.

It is likely, therefore, that the Alcmeonidae did not go into exile following Pallene as Herodotus claims, but instead accepted Pisistratus's offer of reconciliation and continued to enjoy power in Athens. The tradition that they spent the entire period of the tyranny in exile probably arose as a result of the family's attempt to distance itself from the tyranny after the founding of the democracy. The invention of a lengthy exile under the tyrant was facilitated

---

[167] For discussion of the ideological construction of the tyrant in classical Greece, see chapter 6 below.

[168] Alcmeonidae go into exile after Pallene: Hdt. 1.64.3, Plut. Sol. 30.6. Alcmeonidae in exile for the length of the tyranny: Hdt. 6.123.1, (Ἀλκμεωνίδαι) οἵτινες ἔφυγον...τὸν πάντα χρόνον τοὺς τυράννους. Return of the Alcmeonidae in 510: Hdt. 5.62.2.

[169] ML 6.

by the family's actual (brief) exile by Pisistratus's son Hippias following the death of Hipparchus in 514, when Hippias seems to have reverted to the politics of exile. (See below.) In addition, the expulsion of the Alcmeonidae and their restoration in the events preceding the foundation of the democracy in 508/7, as well as Cleisthenes' prominent role in the foundation of the democracy itself, would have provided further substance to the family's claim that they were in exile for the length of the tyranny. (See below.) In short, Athenian oral traditions, and the Alcmeonid family tradition in particular, extended the brief periods of exile at the end of the tyranny and in the years preceding the foundation of the democracy to cover the length of the tyranny and thus to reinforce their claim to have opposed the tyrants and to have been champions of democracy.[170]

The evidence for the exile of other prominent elites during Pisistratus's rule is ambiguous at best, and in fact suggests that many acquiesced and cooperated with the tyrant. The accounts of various members of the family of the Philaïdae are illustrative. Herodotus suggests that the Philaïd Miltiades the Elder left to found a new settlement in the Chersonesus because he was hostile to Pisistratus and wanted to be free from his rule.[171] Yet the fact that Miltiades' nephew Miltiades the Younger was eponymous archon in 524/3 suggests that the family was in favor with the tyrants and held considerable power and prestige.[172] Herodotus states as much when he notes that although Pisistratus "held all the power," Miltiades the Elder was also powerful (ἐδυνάστευέ γε καὶ Μιλτιάδης), having won a victory in the four-horse chariot race at Olympia and being of an established elite family.[173] It is likely, therefore, that Miltiades founded the new settlement in the Chersonesus not out of hostility to Pisistratus, but rather for the usual reasons:

[170] Bicknell 1970. On Athenian family traditions and their propensity to exaggerate their hostility to the tyrants and extend or invent periods of exile under the tyrants, see Thomas 1989, 139–54. On the other hand, G. Anderson (2000, 401–4) accepts the exile of the Alcmeonidae and other elite families following Pallene. Anderson's main interest is in explaining the dual residences of many Athenian elite families in city and country demes; he argues that the rural residences are a result of the exile of these families under the tyranny. The residence of Athenian elites in rural Attica may date much farther back than the sixth century, however, and can be explained by the migration of elites into the Attic countryside in the Geometric period. See chapter 1 above.

[171] Hdt. 6.35.3. The date of Miltiades' departure is uncertain. It is generally dated c. 560–556: i.e., after Pisistratus's second assumption of power. This conjecture is based on Apollodorus's date for the fall of Croesus (546), since Croesus is said by Hdt. 6.37 to have rescued Miltiades from the Lampsacenes after he founded the colony in the Chersonesus. Davies (APF 299), however, accepts Herodotus's chronology (1.59.1, 62), whereby Croesus fell after the battle of Pallene in 546 and Miltiades set out for the Chersonesus after 546.

[172] ML 6, Hdt. 6.36.1. Some scholars suggest that Miltiades the Elder was head of an officially (i.e., by Pisistratus) sanctioned colonizing mission: J. Smith 1989, 44–45; Cawkwell 1995, 79–80; Baba 1990, 18.

[173] Hdt. 6.35.1.

adventurism and the pursuit of personal profit.[174] It was only the hostility to tyranny of a later age that caused Miltiades' family to revise its history to reflect these changed circumstances.[175]

The story of Cimon, half-brother of Miltiades the Elder and father of Miltiades the Younger, is ambiguous. On the one hand, Herodotus says that Cimon went into exile under Pisistratus (Κίμωνα ... φυγεῖν ἐξ Ἀθηνέων Πεισίστρατον). On the other hand, Herodotus reports that Cimon dedicated his second victory at Olympia (c. 532) to Pisistratus, and because of this gesture he was allowed to return to his property in Athens (κατῆλθε ἐπὶ τὰ ἑωυτοῦ ὑπόσπονδος). Cimon subsequently won a third victory at Olympia, and afterward he was murdered by Pisistratus's sons, according to Herodotus.[176] The contradictory nature of these stories suggests that later family traditions struggled to make the best of irrefutable evidence that Cimon had been in favor with the tyrant for at least some portion of Pisistratid rule. Indeed the idea that Pisistratus allowed an Olympic victor to live in Athens, albeit one who dedicated a victory to him, suggests that he was not afraid to let potential rivals to power enjoy prestige.[177] It is not unlikely that Cimon enjoyed uneven relations with the tyrant, just as Megacles had before him. Nevertheless, later Philaïd family tradition manipulated the facts of Cimon's history, including his Olympic victory (which Cimon probably did dedicate to Pisistratus, although perhaps not in a bid to return from exile) and his mysterious death at the time of the rule of Pisistratus's sons, in order to illustrate the family's hostility to tyranny.

The story of Miltiades the Younger has already been touched upon. According to Herodotus he was sent out to the Chersonesus by the sons of Pisistratus in order to replace his brother, who had been killed in war against the Lampsacenes.[178] We may well doubt whether Pisistratids were involved in the decision of the younger Miltiades to settle in the Chersonesus. Nevertheless Herodotus's account is revealing in its many contradictions. Although he says that Miltiades was treated well in Athens before he went out to take up control of the Chersonesus, Herodotus cannot understand this fact, given that Miltiades' father, Cimon, was supposedly killed by Pisistratus's sons.[179] An obvious explanation of this discrepancy is that Cimon was

[174] See chapter 1 above for this explanation of early settlements abroad. The proximity of the Chersonesus to the metal-rich Strymon Valley may have influenced Miltiades' choice of location: cf. Baba 1990.

[175] J. Smith (1989, 44–45) and Cawkwell (1995) suggest that the story of the Philaïd family in Herodotus derives from Miltiades the Younger's defense in his trial in 493. Miltiades was being prosecuted for tyranny in the Chersonesus, and at this time would have been eager to explain away his grandfather's foundation of the settlement as a product of his hostility to tyranny.

[176] Hdt. 6.39.1, 103.1–4.

[177] The probable dates of Cimon's Olympic victories are 536, 532, and 528: Davies, *APF* 300.

[178] Hdt. 6.39.1.

[179] Hdt. 6.39.1: the Pisistratidae "treated Miltiades well while he was in Athens, as if they did not know how his father, Cimon, was killed."

not killed by the sons of Pisistratus, and that this detail is an invention of later Philaïd family tradition.

Another elite individual who possibly went into exile under Pisistratus's rule is Callias son of Hipponicus, of Alopece. Callias is said by Herodotus to have bought the property of Pisistratus when the latter went into exile, and to have done "many other things that showed his hostility" to the tyrant.[180] Seibert, in fact, surmises that Callias went into exile in fear of Pisistratus when he returned to power in 546.[181] However, objections can be made to this thesis. First, the colorfulness of the story of Callias's purchase of the tyrant's property suggests that it may well have been fabricated as part of Callias's family tradition in order to vividly illustrate the family's hostility to tyranny at a later time. Second, the assumption that Callias fled Athens when Pisistratus returned to power is out of step with the evidence for the continued residence of a number of elite families in Athens, and their tenure of important positions in his regime.

In addition to the evidence of Cleisthenes' and Miltiades' archonships, a number of ancient sources attest to the fact that Pisistratus did not alter the system of public offices in Athens and in fact continued to let rival elites hold these and other prestigious positions. Even Herodotus, whose account shows many signs of the revision of traditions about the tyranny according to fifth-century democratic values, notes that in Pisistratus's first tyranny, "he did not disturb the existing public offices and did not change the laws, but rather he ruled according to the established ways and ordered things in a fine and proper manner."[182] Thucydides extends this period of constitutional rule to the length of the tyranny, noting that the only modification to the prevailing order was that the tyrants always placed one of their own people among the archons.[183] Thucydides is in fact adamant in countering popular notions that the tyrants were disliked by the Athenians, and argues that it was only after the death of Hipparchus in 514 that the tyranny became repressive and unpopular.[184]

The evidence of the collaboration of prominent elites with the tyrants, and the testimony of our sources besides about the constitutionality of the tyrants' rule, suggests that Pisistratus was in fact lenient toward his elite rivals following his victory at Pallene, and did not expel them from the polis.[185] Rather, he encouraged his rivals to remain in Athens, and even allowed his former rivals

---

[180] Hdt. 6.121.2.

[181] Seibert 1979, 15, 417 and n. 80.

[182] Hdt. 1.59.6.

[183] Thuc. 6.54.5–6. For the tyrants' adherence to the laws, see also Arist. *Ath. Pol.* 16.8.

[184] Thuc. 6.59.2. For Thucydides' self-conscious stance in opposition to popular traditions about the tyranny (including those reflected in Herodotus), cf. 1.20–21, 6.54.1. For the onset of repressive tyranny at the time of Hipparchus's assassination, see also Arist. *Ath. Pol.* 16.7, 19.1.

[185] Cf. Ghinatti 1970, 81; Stein-Hölkeskamp 1989, 145–48; Cawkwell 1995, 78.

to hold prestigious public offices. The idea that Pisistratus allowed rival elites to enjoy prestige and prominence in the city receives some confirmation from the evidence for the continued role of the elite in the Panathenaic procession. Thucydides reports that Hipparchus sought to insult Harmodius by dismissing his sister from among the basket bearers in the procession (6.56.1; cf. *Ath. Pol.* 18.2). This anecdote therefore reveals that elite families continued to enjoy prestige from their leading role in this civic ritual even under the tyrants. Furthermore, despite older claims that there was a decline in the number of dedications on the acropolis under the tyrants, more recent scholarship has shown that elites continued to make dedications and thus to exercise this traditional opportunity for elite display.[186]

Pisistratus's tactic of conciliating his elite rivals by allowing them to hold positions of power and prestige not only calls into question the accuracy of the ancient sources' applying the term "tyranny" (ἡ τυραννίς: e.g., Hdt. 1.59.3, 60.1, etc.) to his regime, but is also highly significant for understanding the success and duration of his rule in his final tyranny. By rejecting the politics of exile and enticing his rivals to remain in Athens and cooperate in his regime, Pisistratus avoided creating groups of hostile elite exiles, eager to attack the polis with the aid of their allies in other poleis. Just as the frequent expulsion and return of rival elites destabilized the archaic polis in the seventh and early sixth centuries, Pisistratus's restraint in the use of exile was a key to the stability of his regime in the late sixth century. Although Pisistratus's sons did not follow his example, as we shall see, Pisistratus's rejection of the politics of exile provided a vivid example to the later democracy of the benefits of a policy of moderation in the use of exile. In sum, one important factor in the stability of both Pisistratus's final tyranny and the fifth-century democracy was their departure from the practice of the politics of exile. The steps by which the democracy echoed Pisistratus's moderate use of exile is the subject of the next section. Before turning to this topic, a few more points can be made regarding Pisistratus's innovations in the use of political power.

Aristotle records several measures by which Pisistratus united a large number of the non-elites under his leadership.[187] First, Pisistratus gave loans to the poor, in the same manner that local elites must have given loans to the small farmers in their neighborhoods.[188] Through this measure, Pisistratus

---

[186] See Keesling 2003 for revisions of Raubitschek's 1949 view that there was a decline in dedications on the Athenian acropolis under the tyrants. The question of the motives of elite dedications on the acropolis is of course complex, and elite self-promotion is not the only factor involved. As Keesling points out, political interpretations of the dedications tend to neglect the personal and religious elements of the practice.

[187] Aristotle's understanding of the purpose of these measures is contrary to the interpretation presented here and can be shown to be a product of fifth- and fourth-century ideas about tyrannical rule: see chapter 6 below.

[188] Arist. *Ath. Pol.* 16.2. On the nature of Pisistratus's loans and the meaning of the verb προδανείζειν, see Wyse 1892, Migeotte 1980, Chambers 1984, Sancisi-Weerdenburg 1993.

not only created bonds between himself and many small farmers of Attica, but also detached the small farmers from local elites by removing their economic dependence on them.[189] This measure therefore contributed to the breakdown of traditional patron-client relationships and created a more unified population, which looked directly to the tyrant for economic support in times of need.[190] A second measure would have reinforced this trend toward unification of Attica under the leadership of Pisistratus, namely the establishment of a board of judges who traveled through Attica to settle disputes.[191] Prior to this innovation, we may surmise, small disputes were brought before local elites, who sat as arbitrators. The replacement of local arbitration with justice administered by representatives of the tyrant would therefore once again have detached non-elites from local elites, and unified the small farmers of Attica under the leadership of Pisistratus.[192]

Pisistratus's creation of new civic institutions such as centralized loans and deme judges parallels his use of other civic institutions to break down older factional loyalties and unite the populace under his leadership. These measures, like the construction of civic buildings and the enhancement of civic rituals, would have created a greater sense among the non-elite of their collective identity as Athenians.[193] Although Pisistratus's aim in furthering these institutions and rituals was primarily to gain broad-based, active support for his on-going struggle against his elite rivals, his actions in the civic sphere had the ultimate effect of increasing non-elites' self-awareness as a political group. In other words, through their quest for broad-based non-elite support, Pisistratus and his fellow elites played a vital role in enhancing Athenian collective identity and dismantling the older factional model of politics. Under Pisistratus, the new civic identity and structures were still closely associated with the tyrant's personal leadership, but as we shall see, it was not long after the fall of the tyranny that the Athenian masses became an independent political force.

In sum, the evidence for Pisistratus's final tyranny suggests that his success was due to his ability to gain the support of large numbers of elites and non-elites. Pisistratus gained the support of the elites by renouncing the politics of exile, and by allowing them to share political power and prestige. Furthermore, Pisistratus gained the support of a large group of non-elites by utilizing and furthering civic structures to enhance non-elite collective

---

[189] Finley 1983, 47–48; Millett 1989, 23; Stein-Hölkeskamp 1989, 146.

[190] Stein-Hölkeskamp 1989, 153; Hornblower 1992, 6–7.

[191] Arist. *Ath. Pol.* 16.5.

[192] Cf. Hignett, *HAC* 115; Rhodes, *CAAP* 216. The new deme judges may have provided a more impartial system of justice, since they would have no personal interest in the dispute.

[193] For the debate about Pisistratus's role in the development of civic festivals such as the Panathenaea, the City Dionysia, and the cult of Demeter, see above. Although the evidence for the origins of these festivals is inadequate, and older scholarship tended to assume Pisistratus's role in their founding, it is still most likely that Pisistratus, along with other elites, played some role in the elaboration of these festivals into grand civic events.

identity and unite them under his rule. Pisistratus's success in attracting a large group of non-elite supporters not only contributed to the disappearance of the older divisions of the population into elite-led factions, but began the process by which the Athenians were transformed into an active political force. His success in gaining the support of elites and non-elites must be the historical basis for Aristotle's claim that "the majority of both the elites and the non-elites wished [him to rule]. For he enticed the former through social intercourse and the latter through financial help. He treated both well."[194]

Following Pisistratus's death in 528, his elder son, Hippias, assumed power and ruled until his overthrow in 510.[195] The length of Hippias's rule suggests that he followed the stabilizing policies of his father, namely the repudiation of the politics of exile and the cultivation of a broad base of support among elites and non-elites alike. The testimony of Thucydides seems to support this view, at least for the first fourteen years of Hippias's rule, down to the murder of his brother, Hipparchus, in 514. Thucydides tells us that, despite popular assumptions, Hippias was not disliked by the majority of Athenians. He adds that the tyrants (presumably referring to the family as a whole) ruled with integrity and intelligence. In support of this claim, Thucydides notes that the tyrants did not exact large payments from the citizens, but nevertheless adorned the city beautifully, conducted foreign wars, and made the customary sacrifices. Thucydides further claims that the tyrants ruled according to the laws, with the exception that they ensured that one of their own held one of the archonships.[196]

Since Thucydides' assertions about the benevolence of the tyrants run contrary to what we would expect from fifth-century oral traditions regarding the tyranny, it is most likely that they reflect historical memories of Hippias's good rule, which would have been preserved in part as a result of the physical monuments erected by Pisistratus's sons. Indeed Thucydides (6.54.5–6) refers generally to the tyrants' beautification of the city and makes direct use of several of the tyrants' monuments to prove that Hippias and not Hipparchus was tyrant.[197] Archaeological and literary evidence confirms that the

---

[194] Arist. *Ath. Pol.* 16.9. A number of historically doubtful anecdotes preserved by Aristotle may reflect genuine memories of Pisistratus's ability to appeal to the Athenians through speeches. Aristotle classifies Pisistratus among the tyrants of old who were demagogues (δημαγωγοί; *Pol.* 1305a8–29) and recounts a story of how he disarmed the people while haranguing them with speeches (δημηγορῶν: *Ath. Pol.* 15.3–5). On the latter episode, see Keaney (1992, 108), who notes the narrative balance achieved between Pisistratus's disarming of the people at 15.4–5 and Solon's arming of the people at 8.5. It is unlikely that Solon fr. 11.7–8 (West) refers to Pisistratus, but it is significant that the poem was associated with Pisistratus in later tradition (Plut. *Sol.* 30.3). This association is based on the view that Pisistratus was a skilled orator.

[195] Sources for Hippias's tyranny: Hdt. 5.55–62; Thuc. 1.20, 6.54–59; Arist. *Ath. Pol.* 17–19, *Pol.* 1311a36.

[196] Thuc. 6.54.5–6.

[197] Thuc. 6.54.6–55.1.

sons of Pisistratus built fountain houses, altars, and even temples throughout the city.[198] The construction of public monuments, like the enhancement of civic rituals (cf. Thucydides' reference to Pisistratid performance of the customary sacrifices), was one way that the sons of Pisistratus inserted themselves into the symbolic spaces of the community, and in these activities we see a clear continuation of Pisistratus's own manner of rule.[199]

In all, it seems that Hippias followed the practices of his father for most of his years in power. He allowed the elites to continue to enjoy prestige and power through officeholding and their role in civic rituals.[200] Hippias also continued to broaden his support among the non-elite through both direct financial assistance and his leading role in the development of the civic structures and rituals of the community. This changed with the murder of his brother, Hipparchus, in 514. Although later traditions tended to associate the murder of Hipparchus with the end of the tyranny and even the advent of democracy, our sources make clear that Hippias ruled for four more years following Hipparchus's murder, and that it was several years after the end of the tyranny that democratic institutions were introduced.[201] Thucydides' account in particular shows that the murder of Hipparchus was not initially the result of hatred of tyranny per se, but that a conflict over thwarted love escalated into an attempt to overthrow the tyranny.[202] The attempt failed, however, and as a result, Hippias changed his manner of rule and resorted once again to the politics of exile.

Herodotus notes that, following the death of Hipparchus, Hippias ruled in a harsher manner toward the Athenians and that the Alcmeonidae and other Athenians were in exile.[203] Although we have already refuted Herodotus's claim that the Alcmeonidae were in exile throughout the tyranny, it is clear that they and some other elites did in fact go into exile after Hipparchus's murder.

---

[198] For a summary of the evidence, see Forsdyke, "Peisistratus" (in prep. a).

[199] Similarly, Thucydides' reference to Pisistratid taxes (6.54.5) seems to be best explained as a reference to the low interest that Pisistratus and his sons demanded in return for the loans given to needy farmers throughout Attica (Arist. *Ath. Pol.* 16.2–6; Sancisi-Weerdenburg, 1993). Finally, Thucydides' reference to Pisistratid wars (6.54.5) must include Pisistratus's successful campaign against Megara before his first tyranny (Hdt. 1.59.4), the war against Mytilene for control of Sigeum (entrusted to Pisistratus's son Hegesistratus: Hdt. 5.94.1), and the conquest of Naxos (Hdt. 1.64).

[200] For officeholding under the Pisistratids, see ML 6, discussed above in the section "A New Type of Politics."

[201] For an excellent discussion of the complex traditions concerning the liberation of Athens, see Thomas 1989, 238–82.

[202] Thucydides (6.54.3, 56.2–3) emphasizes that Harmodius and Aristogeiton were angered as a result of Hipparchus's attempt to seduce Harmodius and Hipparchus's subsequent insult to Harmodius's sister by denying her a place in the Panathenaic procession. Nevertheless, Thucydides also asserts that Harmodius and Aristogeiton's anger led to an attempt to overthrow the tyranny.

[203] Hdt. 5.62.2.

Thucydides echoes Herodotus's claim that the tyranny became harsher after Hipparchus's murder and reports that Hippias went so far as to murder many Athenians.[204] Although Thucydides' claim that many Athenians were murdered may be exaggerated under the influence of later representations of the harshness of tyrannical rule, the retreat of the Alcmeonids into exile was probably a result of the threat to their lives if they remained.[205] In short, just as the period before Pisistratus's final tyranny was characterized by violent competition between rival elites for power, so the final stages of Hippias's tyranny saw a return to such practices. Aristotle sums up the situtation in the following way: "After [Hipparchus's murder], the tyranny became much harsher. For [Hippias] was distrustful and bitter toward everyone. He took revenge for his brother and executed and expelled many men [πολλοὺς ἀνῃρηκέναι καὶ ἐκβεβληκέναι]."[206]

Pisistratus's son Hippias seems to have forgotten the pragmatic behavior of his father, and resorted to the traditional politics of exile to maintain his power in the polis. Just as Pisistratus's rejection of the politics of exile helped stabilize his regime, so Hippias's relapse into the old practice of exile destabilized his. Herodotus tells us that the Alcmeonidae and other exiles attempted to return by force and overthrow Hippias.[207] Despite Aristotle's claim that Hippias expelled many men, however, it is likely that exiles were a small group composed of Hippias's elite rivals, namely the Alcmeonidae and other leading elite families.[208] The claim in fourth-century oratory that the Athenian people as a whole (δῆμος) was in exile under the Pisistratids, moreover, is a product of the influence of the experience of exile under the Thirty Tyrants on traditions about the Pisistratid tyranny, as Rosiland Thomas has demonstrated.[209]

When the initial attempts to overthrow Hippias by force failed, the exiles took steps to gain support from elites in other poleis in a manner typical of the politics of exile.[210] The Alcmeonidae turned to Delphi, where they

---

[204] Thuc. 6.59.2.

[205] See chapter 6 below for the representation of tyrannical rule. The account of Hippias's disarmament of the Athenians at Thuc. 6.58 may also be influenced by popular representations of tyrants as deceptive; cf. on Pisistratus above in the section "A New Type of Politics."

[206] Arist. Ath. Pol. 19.1.

[207] Hdt. 5.62.2; Ar. Lys. 664–67; Arist. Ath. Pol. 19.3; schol. Ar. Lys. 665–66; Phot. s.v. λυκόποδες; Suda s.v.v. ἐπὶ Λειψυδρίῳ μάχη and λυκόποδες.

[208] The drinking song recorded by Arist. Ath. Pol. 19.3 confirms that the exiles at Leipsydrium were elites. Not only were such songs sung at symposia held by the elite, but the song explicitly praises the exiles' good birth. The word εὐπατρίδας (of good birth) is especially revealing, since it was the term that the elite used of themselves in archaic Athens. Andocides, who belonged to a prominent Athenian family, claimed his ancestors were among the exiles and fought against the tyrant (1.106). Ghinatti (1970, 78) describes the exiles at Leipsydrium as consisting of the Alcmeonidae and their closest elite allies.

[209] Thomas 1989, 131–54, 252; and chapter 6 below.

[210] The principal sources are Hdt. 5.62–63 and Arist. Ath. Pol. 19.

had long enjoyed influence.[211] After helping the Delphians to rebuild the Temple of Apollo following its destruction by fire, the Alcmeonidae persuaded them to pressure the Spartans to help overthrow the tyranny at Athens.[212] The influence of Delphi was necessary to persuade the Spartans, because the Pisistridae had guest-friendship ties with them.[213] Herodotus tells us that the Spartans obeyed the oracle because they thought that the will of the gods took precedence over the considerations of men.[214] It is possible that guest-friendship ties between the Alcmeonidae and certain Spartans, such as the leader of the first Spartan expedition, Anchimolus, also played a role in persuading Sparta to attack the tyrants. The existence of such ties may be inferred from Herodotus's report that after the failure of the first expedition, Anchimolus was given a tomb in Alopece, where the Alcmeonidae are known to have had estates.[215] It is also possible that the Spartans were motivated to attack the Pisistratidae by the tyrants' alliance with Argos.[216]

Hippias responded to the exiles' use of Spartan forces by summoning his own foreign allies in turn. Hippias relied on a force of one thousand Thessalian cavalry (and a cunning strategy) to repel the Spartans and the exiles.[217] The Spartans then sent a second, larger force headed by one of their kings, Cleomenes.[218] This second Spartan force defeated Hippias's Thessalian allies and marched on the city. Herodotus observes that the Spartans were joined in their

---

[211] Hdt. 6.125 records that Alcmeon helped the Lydians at Delphi in 547. The Alcmeonidae were also given a leading role in the First Sacred War for control of Delphi, which is dated to 591/0 by the Marmor Parium. Although modern historians are skeptical about the historicity of this war (Robertson 1978, Frost 1984), the tradition may still reflect historical memories of an association between the Alcmeonidae and Delphi. Robinson (1994, 365n.6) notes in addition that Cleisthenes consulted the Delphic Oracle for the names of the ten new Athenian tribes: Arist. *Ath. Pol.* 21.6.

[212] There has been a great deal of scholarly debate regarding the relation between the reconstruction of the temple and Herodotus's claim that the Alcmeonidae persuaded the oracle with money (5.63.1). The best interpretation of this episode is that of Stahl (1987, 121–33), with the modifications of Robinson 1994. Stahl argues that the building of the temple was an act of elite self-promotion in the context of intra-elite competition for prestige. By rebuilding the temple, the Alcmeonidae hoped not only to enhance their influence at Delphi, but to compete with the tyrants who built an altar of Pythian Apollo in Athens, rendered service to Delian Apollo (Hdt. 1.62.4), and engaged in other extravagant building projects. Robinson shows that Herodotus's claim that the Alcmeonidae persuaded the oracle with money refers to the temple construction itself. Thomas (1989, 249–50) rightly notes that the allegation that the Alcmeonidae corrupted the oracle is problematic for the view (argued most influentially by Jacoby 1913, 413; 1949, 161) that Herodotus relied on Alcmeonid sources.

[213] Hdt. 5.63.2, 90.1, 91.2; Arist. *Ath. Pol.* 19.4.

[214] Hdt. 5.63.2.

[215] Hdt. 5.63.4.

[216] Arist. *Ath. Pol.* 19.4, Hdt. 1.61, How and Wells 1912 *ad.* 5.63.2.

[217] Hdt. 5.63.2, Arist. *Ath. Pol.* 19.5.

[218] Hdt. 5.64.1, Arist. *Ath. Pol.* 19.5.

siege of the Pisistratids by "those Athenians who wished to be free."[219] This phrase is a deliberate echo of Herodotus's earlier comment about the large numbers of Athenians who supported Pisistratus at Pallene, for whom "tyranny was more welcome than freedom."[220] From the perspective of Herodotus and his fifth-century sources, just as the number of the tyrant's supporters was disappointingly large in 546, so the number of opponents of the tyrant in 510 was disappointingly small. Herodotus's phrase therefore confirms what we already suspected: the tyrants were overthrown by a small group of elite exiles who summoned the Spartans to expel the tyrants from the polis and from power.

The exiles and their Spartan allies were successful, and the Pisistratids left Attica, retreating to Sigeum, on the Hellespont.[221] It seems that the Alcmeonidae and the other returning exiles expelled only the immediate family of Hippias, since some relatives and friends of the Pisistratids remained in Athens and later became the first victims of the democratic institution of ostracism.[222] Aristotle claims that the Athenians initially allowed these men to remain following the expulsion of the Pisistratids in accordance with the "customary leniency of the demos" (τῇ εἰωθυίᾳ τοῦ δήμου πραότητι, Ath. Pol. 22.4). I argue below in chapters 4 and 6 that Aristotle's claim reflects the later historical reality (which soon developed into an ideology) of the democracy's moderate use of exile as a political tool. In this passage (and at Ath. Pol. 16.10), Aristotle misapplies the historical and ideological association between democratic rule and moderation in the use of exile to the period before the democracy. In 510, the Athenian demos as a whole had nothing to do with the expulsion of the Pisistratids. As we have seen, the tyrants were expelled by the Spartans at the behest of a small group of elite exiles. In this context of violent competition between small groups of elites, Cleisthenes and the other returning exiles needed to expel only the immediate family of the tyrants to secure their power in the polis.

The Alcmeonidae and the other exiles thus expelled their rivals, simultaneously regaining power and winning return from exile for themselves. Once again, political power was achieved primarily through expulsion of rivals, and the action of the returning exiles rearticulated the equivalency between the power to expel and political power. Conversely, loss in the game of the politics of exile entailed expulsion and loss of political power. The intimate relation between exile and political power would be on display several more times in the next few years, and, I will argue, helped to shape the institutions and ideology of the revolutionary new form of rule—democracy—that emerged as a result.

[219] Hdt. 5.64.2.

[220] Hdt. 5.62.1.

[221] Hdt. 5.64.2–65.5, Arist. Ath. Pol. 19.5–6.

[222] In addition to the friends of the tyrants mentioned in Arist. Ath. Pol. 22.4, it is possible that Isagoras, the later opponent of Cleisthenes in 508/7, was also an associate of the tyrants (cf. Arist. Ath. Pol. 20.1) and was allowed to remain in Athens following the expulsion of the Pisistratids.

Yet despite the renewed relation between power and exile, the returning exiles sought some means of gaining public legitimacy for their expulsion of their rivals. The Pisistratids, after all, had gained significant passive and even active support from a large number of Athenians during the lengthy final period of their rule. The returning exiles began the process of altering the collective memory of the tyrants by erecting a stone pillar on the acropolis proclaiming the injustice (ἀδικία) of the tyrants (Thuc. 6.55.1). By placing a physical monument in the sacred center of the polis, the exiles made use of the symbolic authority of the polis deity to gain communal sanction for their act of expulsion.[223] In addition, the Alcmeonidae and other returning exiles probably invoked the archaic tyranny law by which the tyrants and their immediate family were subject to outlawry (ἀτιμία)—a penalty that entailed permanent exile from Athens.[224] In this way, the returning exiles made use of law to implicate the community in their act of expulsion, just as had their seventh-century ancestors before them. Although these legal measures could not ensure the active participation of the community in the defense of the new order, they at least began the process of altering the image of the tyrants in the collective memory. The erection of statues of the tyrannicides at about this time, and the emergence of drinking songs celebrating their deed, seems to indicate that the returning exiles were successful in their campaign to present the overthrow of the Pisistratids as a heroic act against an unjust regime.[225]

The Alcmeonids' attempts to legitimize the expulsion of the family of Pisistratus, however, were ultimately ineffective in deterring a renewal of the politics of exile. Just as in earlier times, so also, following this later bout of the politics of exile, the actions taken by the returning exiles to give official sanction to their expulsion of their elite rivals through written laws did not deter the attempts of these exiles to return. Not long after their expulsion, the Pisistratids attempted to return by force by pressuring their guest-friends the Spartans. According to Herodotus, it was the Spartans who took the initiative to reinstall the tyrants, since they were worried about the growth of Athenian power following the overthrow of the tyranny and thought that the tyrants might help to keep Athens weak and subordinate to Sparta.[226] This version of Spartan

---

[223] On the relation between written documents, monuments, and sacred space, see Thomas 1992, 146.

[224] Usteri 1903, 40–41; Busolt 1920, 235. For the law on tyranny, see the section "The Politics of Exile" above.

[225] On the cult of the tyrannicides, see Taylor 1991. For the drinking songs, see Athen. 695a–b. The descendants of the tyrannicides were also permitted to dine at public expense in the prytaneion (IG 1³ 131), an honor reserved for benefactors of the polis. The idea that the tyrannicides-as-liberators version of the overthrow of the tyranny was promoted by an anti-Alcmeonid faction and specifically by Themistocles' faction is no longer considered plausible: Thomas 1989, 238–51. Rather, both the tyrannicides-as-liberators version and the Spartans/Alcmeonids-as-liberators version would have circulated together in the popular tradition and helped to legitimize the new order.

[226] Hdt. 5.91.

motives for the restoration of the tyrants is clearly a later Athenian construction based on an ideological association between freedom and civic strength.[227] It is more likely that the exiled Pisistratids themselves actively sought to return to Athens by force and used various arguments to convince the Spartans to help restore them. Foremost among these arguments would have been the demonstration of Alcmeonid corruption of the oracle at Delphi (κιβδήλοισι μαντήοισι, Hdt. 5.91.2), which had caused the Spartans to ignore their ties of guest-friendship with the Pisistratdae. Hippias no doubt also promised to put Athens at the service of the Spartans (ὑποχειρίας παρέξειν τὰς Ἀθήνας) should he regain power.

Ultimately, despite Hippias's lobbying, the Spartans were unable to get the support of their allies for a mission against Athens. Hippias, however, never gave up the attempt to return to power in Athens. Although his Macedonian and Thessalian allies gave him cities to settle in, Hippias returned to Sigeum and began to lobby the Persians to restore him to Athens (Hdt. 5.94.1, 96). The Persians were presumably unmoved by Hippias's promises to make Athens subordinate to Persia in return for helping to restore him to power in Athens. In 510, Athens was not a significant power worthy of the attention of the Persian empire. Nevertheless, twenty years later, a very elderly Hippias was among the Persian forces that landed at Marathon (Hdt. 6.107). The colorful story of Hippias's losing a tooth on his return to Attic soil reflects later knowledge that despite his rigorous efforts to return to power and expel his opponents, his attempts were ultimately unsuccessful.

The Spartans' expulsion of the Pisistratids following their long rule changed the balance of power in Athens. New rivalries broke out among the remaining elites, and a new round of the game of exile began. The period between the end of the tyranny and the foundation of the democracy was one of violent intra-elite competition and frequent expulsions and returns from exile. Yet the legacy of the enlightened politics of Pisistratus was not completely lost. As we shall see in the next section, the steps that Pisistratus took toward transforming the non-elite masses into an active force in the struggle between elite leaders, and the astuteness of another member of the elite—Cleisthenes—in following his example, were seeds from which a new form of politics grew.

An End to the Politics of Exile: Cleisthenes and the Democratic Revolution

The events surrounding the overthrow of the tyranny and the foundation of democracy in Athens have been the subject of continuous lively debate

---

[227] See Forsdyke 2001; and chapter 6 below.

among historians.[228] An important issue of contention is the reliability of our sources, all of which date from the second half of the fifth century and later.[229] Indeed, Kurt Raaflaub has suggested that our principal sources, Herodotus and Aristotle, are so corrupted by later assumptions and ideology that the history of the transition to democracy may not be recoverable.[230] Most scholars take a more moderate position, arguing that, with careful consideration of the nature of the oral traditions upon which our sources relied, something can be learned about these crucial events. Within this latter branch of scholarship, several positions are taken on Herodotus's sources. Some argue that his account is a product of Alcmeonid family tradition, which was eager to emphasize their personal role in expelling the tyrants and founding the democracy.[231] More recently, scholars have emphasized the diversity of Herodotus's oral sources, arguing that his account reflects not only elite family traditions, but also wider polis or popular traditions.[232] At stake in these differing views of the oral basis of our sources' accounts is nothing less than the role of the Athenian demos itself in the foundation of the democracy.

In this section, I argue that exile was a crucial feature of the events surrounding the foundation of the democracy and that an appreciation of the interplay between exile and political power leads to a new, more satisfactory explanation of our sources' accounts of the transition to democracy. I argue that a key feature of the events that resulted in the adoption of democratic political organization was the intervention of non-elites in intra-elite politics of exile and the usurpation by non-elites of control over expulsion. By intervening and ultimately resolving the violent struggle between competing elites, non-elites simultaneously asserted their control over decisions of exile and signaled a fundamental change in the balance of power between elites and non-elites. I argue that independent non-elite intervention in intra-elite politics of exile was the necessary precondition for the assumption of political power by the Athenian masses. In the next chapter, I show that the democratic institution of ostracism symbolized the key role that non-elite control over decisions of exile played in the transition to democratic rule.

Before turning to these arguments, a brief summary of our sources' accounts of the events leading to the foundation of the democracy is necessary.

---

[228] The biblography is extensive. For recent debate, see Ostwald 1988; W. Eder 1988; Ober 1993/1998; Raaflaub 1998a, 1998b; Forsdyke 2000, 2002.

[229] Of the principal sources for the reform, Herodotus probably relied primarily on oral traditions (Thomas 1989, 4), whereas Aristotle and other fourth-century sources may have made use of documentary evidence, possibly even the laws of Cleisthenes themselves: cf. Wade-Gery 1958, 135–40.

[230] Raaflaub 1998a, 41; 1998b, 87–88.

[231] Influentially argued by Jacoby (1913, 413; 1949, 161) and still followed by Lavelle 1993, among others.

[232] Thomas 1989; Forsdyke 2002.

Following the expulsion of the tyrants, Cleisthenes, a member of the Alcmeonid family, and Isagoras, a member of another leading elite family, contended for power (ἐστασίασαν, Hdt. 5.66.2) in Athens. Cleisthenes was getting the worse of the struggle, until he took the people into his alliance (τὸν δῆμον προσεταιρίζεται).[233] Cleisthenes next created a new tribal system, which formed the basis of the democracy.[234] In response, Isagoras, now faring the worse, called for help from his guest-friend King Cleomenes of Sparta. Following the instructions of Isagoras, Cleomenes sent a demand to Athens for the expulsion of Cleisthenes and his elite allies (οἱ συστασιῶται, 5.70.2) on the grounds that they were polluted as a result of their families' role in the murder of the Cylonians. Cleisthenes and his associates then withdrew from Athens, and Cleomenes arrived in Athens with a small force. Again following the instructions of Isagoras, Cleomenes proceeded to expel a further seven hundred Athenian families from Athens. Cleomenes then attempted to disband the council and establish Isagoras and three hundred of his associates in power. The council resisted, however, and, in rapid succession, Isagoras and the Spartans retreated to the acropolis, and the Athenian masses (Ἀθηναίων οἱ λοιποί, τὸ πλῆθος) besieged them.[235] After three days, the Spartans withdrew under truce; Isagoras and his Athenian supporters were either killed or exiled. Finally, the Athenians recalled Cleisthenes and the seven hundred families expelled by Isagoras.[236]

This brief summary makes clear that the violent expulsion of elites by their rivals was a key feature of the events leading to the democratic reforms. Yet in order to appreciate the connection between intra-elite competition, exile, and the assumption of political power by the Athenian people, three points must be stressed. The first point is that, up until the dramatic uprising by the Athenian masses, the events amount to a particularly intense bout of intra-elite politics of

---

[233] Hdt. 5.66.2. Cf. Aristotle's phrase "brought the people over to his side" (προσηγάγετο τὸν δῆμον, Ath. Pol. 20.1). The meaning of these phrases is contested and is further discussed below in this section. Here I provide a provisional translation.

[234] Aristotle delays mention of the specific detail of the tribal reforms until after his description of the Spartan intervention (see below), but by suggesting that the promise of democratic reforms was the basis of Cleisthenes' initial appeal to the people, he implies that Cleisthenes proposed the tribal reforms at the time when he first gained their support: "Cleisthenes brought the people over to his side by handing over power to the masses," ὁ Κλεισθένης προσηγάγετο τὸν δῆμον ἀποδιδοὺς τῷ πλήθει τὴν πολιτείαν: Ath. Pol. 20.1. The crucial issue of the timing of the tribal reforms is discussed below.

[235] Hdt. 5.72.2 reports that first Isagoras and the Spartans seized the acropolis, and then the Athenian masses gathered together. Arist. Ath. Pol. 20.3 reverses the order of these events: the masses gather together, and then Isagoras and the Spartans seize the acropolis. Ober 1993/1998 presents arguments for following Aristotle's sequence. The exact order is not crucial for my interpretation.

[236] Hdt. 5.72.4 adds the detail that the Athenians condemned Isagoras and his associates to death. Yet Herodotus himself (5.74.1) records the later attempt of Isagoras to return to power with Spartan help.

exile. The second point is that, although Cleisthenes tried to change the nature of this struggle when he "took the people into his alliance," he was not immediately successful, since subsequently he was easily expelled by Isagoras and a small force of Spartans in a manner typical of intra-elite politics of exile. The third point is that, in the rapid sequence of events beginning with Cleisthenes' expulsion and ending with his recall from exile by the Athenian people, a remarkable thing happened: the Athenians engaged in a collective uprising against the Spartans' attempt to install Isagoras and his associates in power. There are serious questions as to whether this uprising was a leaderless popular revolt and whether it represented the first independent political act by the Athenian masses. (See below.) In my view, these questions are best answered in the affirmative, but the more important point for my purposes is that at the same time as the Athenian people took control over political power in the polis (as evidenced by the democratic reforms that followed their uprising), they also took control over decisions of exile. In expelling Isagoras and the Spartans, and in recalling Cleisthenes and the other exiles, the Athenian people not only intervened in intra-elite politics of exile, but rearticulated the fundamental connection between exile and political power.

Each of these points must be taken up in some detail, since my interpretation involves several modifications to prevailing scholarly views. To begin with the nature of the struggle between Isagoras and Cleisthenes, I argue that current interpretations (following the lead of our fifth- and fourth-century sources) take a too modernist, institutionalist view of the nature of the struggle. Rather, I argue that the initial struggle between Isagoras and Cleisthenes should be viewed as a typical instance of intra-elite politics of exile, and that this is the context in which Cleisthenes' formation of an alliance with the people should be interpreted.

In order to follow this argument, it is best to begin with the difficult problem of what the phrase "took the people into his alliance" (τὸν δῆμον προσεταιρίζεται, Hdt. 5.66.2) means in terms of late sixth-century politics. As mentioned already, our fifth- and fourth-century sources suggest that the alliance was formed on the basis of the promise of democratic reforms. Aristotle bluntly states that "Cleisthenes brought the people over to his side by handing over power to the masses" (ὁ Κλεισθένης προσηγάγετο τὸν δῆμον ἀποδιδοὺς τῷ πλήθει τὴν πολιτείαν).[237] The sequence in Herodotus is a bit more complex. At the beginning of his narrative he seems to suggest that there was a temporal distinction between Cleisthenes' gaining popular support and his enactment of tribal reforms: "Cleisthenes brought the people into his alliance [τὸν δῆμον προσεταιρίζεται]. And afterwards [μετὰ δέ], he divided the Athenians into ten tribes instead of the previous four."[238] Yet

[237] Arist. Ath. Pol. 20.1.
[238] Hdt. 5.66.2.

Herodotus also implies that Cleisthenes brought the people into his party by enacting the tribal (democratic) reforms, since he follows his digression on Cleisthenes' reforms with a restatement of the fact that he got the support of the people, suggesting that the reforms were both the basis of the people's support and the means by which Cleisthenes initially won ascendancy over his rival Isagoras.[239]

Modern scholars have largely followed the implications of Aristotle and Herodotus that the basis of Cleisthenes' support by the people was his promise of democratic reforms.[240] Yet the discrepancy between Herodotus's initial statement (5.66.2) and his restatement (5.69.2) may indicate that there was confusion in his oral sources about the timing of Cleisthenes' acquistion of popular support and his enactment of the tribal reforms. Indeed it is easy to see how oral traditions of the fifth and fourth centuries might tend to collapse the distinction between Cleisthenes' appeal for popular support and his enactment of tribal reforms. In the eyes of later Athenians, it was only natural to assume that Cleisthenes brought the people into his alliance by enacting the tribal reforms whereby democratic government was realized. Yet the fact that Herodotus seems to preserve some memory that Cleisthenes gained popular support first and only then embarked on the changes that heralded the advent of democracy, may indicate that the democratic reforms were not the basis of his initial appeal to the people.

There are further reasons for doubting that the democratic reforms were the basis of Cleisthenes' appeal to the people. In the context of sixth-century society and politics, it is unlikely that he would have spontaneously offered the masses political power, without some prior action by them demanding power or demonstrating their competency to assume it. A dramatic act illustrating the people's right to political power may be found in the events following Cleisthenes' gaining of their support, not before. Furthermore, it is unlikely that in the immediate crisis of intra-elite conflict, Cleisthenes would have proposed a complex plan of political reform as the basis of his appeal for the support of the people.[241] That appeal must have been more simple and immediate. Comparison of our sources' accounts of this event with

[239] Hdt. 5.69.2.

[240] Wade-Gery 1958, 142; Andrewes 1977, 246–47; Rhodes, CAAP 244; Ostwald 1988, 306–7 (cf. 1969, 153–57); Ober 1993/1998, 218; 1998, 72; Raaflaub 1997b, 39. Rapke (1988, 49–50), interestingly, does separate Cleisthenes' attainment of popular support from his democratic reforms, suggesting that Cleisthenes gained popular support by offering citizenship to the craftsmen and mercenaries enfranchised by Solon and Pisistratus, respectively. In my view, these groups would not have been large enough to be a major factor in Cleisthenes' attainment of popular support. Cf. Lavelle 1992a on the temporary role that foreign mercenaries played in the establishment of Pisistratus's final tyranny.

[241] Ostwald 1969 avoids this problem by arguing that Cleisthenes used the general slogan "equality of political rights" (ἰσονομία) rather than a specific program of reforms.

previous episodes of intra-elite politics of exile suggests a different basis for
Cleisthenes' alliance with the people.

Herodotus and Aristotle mention that Cleisthenes was being worsted (ἐσσ-
ούμενος, Hdt. 5.66.2; ἡττώμενος, *Ath. Pol.* 20.1) in the struggle with Isagoras
before he appealed to the people. If Isagoras was following the code of intra-
elite politics of exile (as later events prove that he was), then Cleisthenes was
under threat of being expelled from the polis.[242] Just as Pisistratus had been
repeatedly compelled to leave the polis by his elite opponents, Cleisthenes may
also have been under threat of expulsion. Like Pisistratus in his first attempt at
tyranny, Cleisthenes may have appealed to non-elites in order to prevent his
expulsion. Finally, just as Pisistratus had expected and won sympathy from
non-elites because of his role in an earlier war with Megara, Cleisthenes could
have based his appeal on his role in overthrowing the tyranny when it had
become oppressive. In other words, Cleisthenes' support may have been based
on his past activities, and not on the promise of future democratic reforms. It is
furthermore likely that Cleisthenes' support at this stage was similar to Pisistratus's, namely an ad hoc group of non-elites who were representative of but
not co-extensive with the people as a whole.

This reconstruction is of course impossible to prove, but it has at least two
points in its favor over previous interpretations. First, it reconstructs the history behind the tradition in accordance with what we know of the historical
conditions (intra-elite politics of exile) and previous elite behavior in such
conditions (Pisistratus). Indeed, up to and including the Spartan Cleomenes'
intervention, the struggle between Isagoras and Cleisthenes was in conformity
with a well-established pattern of elite infighting. What was different in 508/7
was the response of the non-elites to Cleomenes' attempt to establish a narrow
oligarchy, as I argue below. A second point in favor of my reconstruction is
that it not only follows our sources' accounts in general, but also takes into
account distortions of the tradition attributable to fifth- and fourth-century
assumptions and values. It would have been easy for later Athenians to re-
interpret the events that brought about the foundation of the democracy as a
response to the thwarting of the people's desire for a democratic constitution.

The next stage of events further suggests that Cleisthenes' alliance with the
people was not based on the promise of democratic reforms, and that Cleisthenes did not yet have widespread non-elite support. According to our sources,
Isagoras countered Cleisthenes' appeal to the people by calling on his Spartan
guest-friend King Cleomenes to help him expel Cleisthenes and his elite
allies (οἱ συστασιῶται, Hdt. 5.70.1) from Athens. When Cleomenes, following the instructions of Isagoras, called for the expulsion of Cleisthenes
and his allies on the grounds that they were polluted, Cleisthenes and his

---

[242] The verb ἐσσοῦμαι is the usual term for defeat in battle in Herodotus (e.g., 1.82.3), and
thus Herodotus's usage here may easily refer to a violent defeat.

associates withdrew from the city without protest. Despite the fact that Cleisthenes "took the people into his alliance," therefore, Cleisthenes could not rely on the non-elites to take an active role on his behalf. Like Pisistratus in his first tyranny attempt, Cleisthenes had apparently gained some sympathy from a group of non-elites in his struggle against Isagoras, but this was not sufficient to ensure the active participation of non-elites in a bout of intra-elite politics of exile.

Furthermore, the fact that Cleomenes subsequently arrived in Athens with only a small military force (οὐ σὺν μεγάλῃ χειρί) suggests that Isagoras was expecting affairs to proceed as they did in traditional intra-elite politics of exile and did not expect widespread non-elite opposition, as he might have if Cleisthenes had promised, and the people actively desired, democratic reforms.[243] Finally, Cleomenes' subsequent expulsion of seven hundred Athenian families shows that he considered Cleisthenes' support to be limited to elite families and perhaps their most powerful non-elite allies.[244] In sum, Isagoras appears not to have expected Cleisthenes to have widespread and sustained support, as he might have expected had Cleisthenes won popular support on the basis of the promise of democratic reforms.

Up to this point, then, affairs were proceeding as they had in earlier instances of intra-elite politics of exile; it was the next stage that saw a divergence from the traditional pattern of events. According to our sources, Cleomenes attempted to disband the council and to establish Isagoras and three hundred of his associates in power, thus establishing a narrow oligarchy.[245] Our sources differ as to what happened next. Herodotus says that when Cleomenes tried to disband the council and establish an oligarchy, the councilors resisted (ἀντισταθείσης δὲ τῆς βουλῆς). Cleomenes and Isagoras and their faction then occupied the acropolis. Next, the rest of the Athenians ('Αθηναίων δὲ οἱ λοιποί), with one accord (τὰ αὐτὰ φρονήσαντες), besieged Isagoras and the Spartans there.[246] Aristotle, however, says that when Cleomenes tried to

---

[243] Hdt. 5.72.1; cf. C. Meier 1990, 64. We might compare this small force with the larger one (στόλῳ μεγάλῳ) that Sparta sent to depose Polycrates of Samos approximately fifteen years earlier: Hdt. 3.54.1. Presumably, in the Samian case, the Spartans expected formidable opposition from Polycrates' mercenaries and native soldiers: Hdt. 3.45.3; cf. 3.54.2.

[244] The number seven hundred is quite large, and therefore must include some non-elites. On the other hand, it is possible that this figure is exaggerated, as has been suggested to me by Kurt Raaflaub in correspondence.

[245] The sources do not specify exactly which council Isagoras tried to disband. It could be either the Areopagus Council, the Solonian Council of Four Hundred, or a proto-Cleisthenic Council of Five Hundred. Most scholars agree that, even if Cleisthenes had already passed his reforms, the Cleisthenic council will not formally have existed yet (Rhodes, CAAP 246). If it was the Areopagus council, then we would expect a different outcome from its victory than the establishment of democracy. I therefore favor the view that it was the Solonian council (with Rhodes, loc. cit.). This council would have been composed of both elites and wealthy non-elites: see above.

[246] Hdt. 5.72.2, Arist. Ath. Pol. 20.3.

dissolve the council and establish the oligarchy, the council resisted, the masses gathered together, and only then did Cleomenes and Isagoras seize the acropolis. The timing of the intervention of the demos is at issue in the two accounts. In Herodotus's scenario, the "rest of the Athenians" act only after the council has resisted, and this sequence of events has been taken to indicate that elite members of the council led the resistance. According to this view, although some non-elites certainly played a role in resisting Isagoras, they did so merely at the behest of their elite leaders.[247] Alternatively, Josiah Ober has interpreted the events as a mass popular uprising and argues that there is no evidence for elite leadership in response to Isagoras and the Spartans.[248]

Two questions need to be resolved in deciding between these rival interpretations. First, what was the historical sequence of events behind our two accounts? And second, what was the role of non-elites in the resistance to Isagoras and the Spartans? The first question is the simpler. It seems clear that oral traditions would have favored the amalgamation of the resistance of the council and the people in order to make the resistance look like a democratic response to the imposition of an oligarchy. The fact that Herodotus and, to a lesser degree, Aristotle make a distinction between the resistance of the council and the resistance of the "rest of the Athenians" suggests that there was indeed a gap between the council's initial resistance and the response of a wider group of citizens. It is probably accurate, therefore, to say that this wider group of citizens did not resist until Cleomenes and Isagoras seized the acropolis.

What then does this sequence of events imply about the role of non-elites in the resistance? Were the councilors primarily elites, and did they lead the revolt? Who were "the rest of the Athenians," and what were they responding to? How important was their resistance in the ultimate outcome of events? To begin with, whether we are talking about the Solonian council or a proto-Cleisthenic council, it would have been made up of both elites and non-elites. Moreover, as Ober notes, Cleomenes had expelled the leading elite rivals of Isagoras, and therefore it cannot be supposed that the resistance of the council was led by Isagoras's elite opponents.[249] Although there undoubtedly were some elites left in Athens, they were apparently not ones whom Isagoras expected to resist his coup. The resistance, therefore, must have come primarily from the non-elites, whom Isagoras did not expect to resist without prompting from rival elite leaders (i.e., the ones who were now in exile). Who were these

---

[247] Raaflaub 1998a; 1998b, especially 88, 91.

[248] Ober (1993/1998, 1998) argues that the resistance was a spontaneous, leaderless rebellion by which the demos carried out an act of political self-definition. C. Meier (1990, 64–70) offers an interpretation that is quite similar to Ober's and shares the view that the masses acted independently. R. Osborne (1996a, 294) appears to endorse Ober's interpretation: "[A] popular political revolution had been created such as no Greek city had previously known, motivated by an issue and not by loyalty to a particular person."

[249] Ober 1993/1998, 221–22; cf. W. Eder 1988, 466; C. Meier 1990, 65.

non-elites on the council? We may assume that the non-elite members con-
sisted of the better-off non-elites—probably those of hoplite standing and
above. The fact that Cleomenes and Isagoras immediately sought protection
on the acropolis, however, suggests that they faced armed resistance in considerable numbers.

What were these non-elites resisting? They were not resisting Isagoras at the
behest of his elite rivals, since these were in exile. Rather, they were acting on
their own initiative. This event therefore marks a fundamental break from past
instances of intra-elite politics of exile. Furthermore, as our sources make clear,
they were reacting to the dissolution of the council and the establishment of a
narrow oligarchy. Thus their resistance would have represented opposition to
elite forms of rule. Therefore the non-elites asserted their control over the
political structure of the community on their own initiative, not simply as
dependents of particular elite leaders, as was apparently the case in the resistance to the Cylonian affair.

Who were "the rest of the Athenians," and why did they join the resistance to
Cleomenes and Isagoras? Just as in the case of Pisistratus's appeal to the demos,
we must be suspicious of our sources' claim that "the rest of the Athenians" and
"the masses" (τὸ πλῆθος) joined in the resistance to Isagoras. This is just the
sort of distortion that the oral traditions of the fifth and fourth centuries would
have favored on the basis of anachronistic assumptions about the hostility of
the people to oligarchic rule. Nevertheless, we must also consider that the
outcome of these events was a radical restructuring of the political community
on the basis of democratic power. We might suspect therefore that a significant
number of non-elites from among the Athenian populace as a whole (again
probably the wealthier non-elites of hoplite status and above) played a crucial
role in resisting Isagoras. What prompted the non-elites to join the councilors
in their resistance? Presumably word spread quickly through the rural villages
of Cleomenes' actions and the council's response. The "rest of the Athenians"
will then have been responding, like the councilors, to the dissolution of the
council, the attempt to establish an oligarchy, and above all the occupation of
the sacred center of the city by a foreign army.

Yet the implications of their resistance went beyond these immediate factors
and represented, like the resistance of the councilors, an assertion of non-elite
control over the political order of the community. Perhaps most important for
the subsequent creation of a democratic political system was the fact that non-
elites acted independently, without elite leadership and not as mere pawns in
an intra-elite power struggle. This action therefore marked a fundamental shift
in power from the elites to the non-elite masses. It is most plausible that the
democratic reforms attributed to Cleisthenes by our ancient sources were a
response to the reality of a new balance of power between elites and masses.

So far we have established that although the first stages of the events
leading to the foundation of the democracy conformed to the pattern of

violent intra-elite politics of exile, this changed when Isagoras and the Spartans attempted to dissolve the council and establish a narrow oligarchy. At that time, a significant number of non-elite Athenians, acting independently of the elites engaged in the violent power struggle, decisively asserted their power to determine the political shape of the polis. It was in response to this decisive action that Cleisthenes created new institutions through which the newly empowered Athenian people might exercise power.

This leads us to the final and most important point for our analysis of the advent of democracy in Athens. At the same time as they asserted their control over the political order, the non-elites also took control over decisions of exile. For not only did non-elites intervene in a situation of violent intra-elite politics, but, following their siege of the Spartans on the acropolis, the Athenian masses expelled Isagoras and the Spartans and recalled Cleisthenes and the other exiles (τὰ ἑπτακόσια ἐπίστια τὰ διωχθέντα ὑπὸ Κλεομένεος μεταπεμψάμενοι, Hdt. 5.73.1).[250] By intervening in a situation of intra-elite politics of exile—by supporting one faction and sending the other into exile—non-elites asserted their control over the allocation of political power in the polis.[251] In essence, then, at the same time as the Athenians asserted their control of the political order, they also took control over decisions of exile. Moreover, through this action, the non-elites rearticulated the fundamental connection between control over decisions of exile and political power. Just as the power of expulsion was fundamental to elite power in the archaic period, so the people's usurpation of power over decisions of exile was fundamental to their assertion of political authority.

It is in this context that the democratic institution of ostracism is to be understood. Cleisthenes created the institution of ostracism at the same time as he established the institutions for the democratic exercise of political power in Athens. Through the institution of ostracism, moreover, the Athenian people exercised their control over decisions of exile and at the same time rearticulated the connection between exile and political power. Yet, as I demonstrate in the next chapter, the importance of ostracism in the functioning of the democracy went far beyond the rearticulation of the fundamental connection between exile and political power.

Conclusion

With the partial exception of the Pisistratid tyranny, Athenian elites practiced the politics of exile with great frequency in the period from the Cylonian

---

[250] Expulsion of the Spartans and Isagoras's faction: Hdt. 5.72.2, Arist. *Ath. Pol.* 20.3; cf. Ar. *Lys.* 274–82. Isagoras's escape with the Spartans: Hdt. 5.74.1. Recall of the exiles: Hdt. 5.73.1, Arist. *Ath. Pol.* 20.3.

[251] In some sense, therefore, the Athenians finally obeyed Solon's law on stasis. See the section "The Beginnings of Change" above.

conspiracy down to the foundation of the democracy (c. 636–508/7). I have argued, however, that both Solon and Pisistratus encouraged the involvement of non-elites in the negotiation of political conflict between elites as a means of moderating the politics of exile. I argued that the decisive moment in this development was the intervention of non-elites in intra-elite politics of exile in 508/7, an action that simultaneously asserted non-elite control over decisions of exile and signaled the fundamental power of non-elites in the polis—democracy. Finally, I suggested that the institution of ostracism was the institutional recognition of the intimate connection between control over exile and political power.

In the next chapter, I examine the procedure and use of ostracism in fifth-century Athens to show that ostracism stood not only as the institutional recognition and symbolic reminder of the origins of democratic power, but also as an important ideological symbol of the justice of democratic power in contrast to the elite forms of power that had preceded it. In brief, I argue that ostracism was an extraordinarily moderate form of exile, and that it functioned pragmatically to avoid the destabilizing consequences of the politics of exile, and ideologically as a symbol of the justice of democratic rule.

Chapter Four

OSTRACISM AND EXILE IN DEMOCRATIC ATHENS

THE institution of ostracism has always been a problem for students of democracy. Critics of democracy have seized on ostracism as the example par excellence of the irresponsibility and irrationality of democratic rule. The American founding father John Adams, following ancient critics of democracy, wrote: "History nowhere furnished so frank a confession of the people themselves of their own infirmities and unfitness for managing the executive branch of government, or an unbalanced share of the legislature, as this institution."[1] Similarly, ostracism is problematic even for those who are sympathetic to democracy. Such scholars view ostracism as a bizarre practice and have devised numerous explanations of its purpose.[2] Yet full understanding of the origins and nature of ostracism, I argue, shows that the institution was neither irresponsible, nor irrational, nor out of step with the practices and ideology of the Athenian democracy.

I argue that ostracism was central to the Athenians' conception of the nature of political power and its just use. The integral relation between ostracism and political power arises from the importance of exile in the exercise of power in the pre-democratic period and at the time of the foundation of the democracy. More important for the argument of this chapter and the one that follows, ostracism served as a fundamental way of marking off, in both practice and ideology, the rule of the people from non-democratic forms of rule. In this chapter, I argue that the procedures of ostracism and the occasions of its use reinforced a fundamental distinction between elite and non-elite forms of rule. Whereas power in the archaic period had been exercised through the frequent and violent expulsion of elites by their rivals, power under the democracy was exercised collectively through its the lawful institutions, with only infrequent and largely symbolic resort to the power of expulsion. The institution of ostracism symbolically articulated non-elite political power through control over decisions of exile,

---

[1] John Adams, cited by Roberts 1994b, 90. For Adams's critique as an echo of ancient criticisms of democracy, see chapter 6 below.

[2] The institution is called bizarre, for example, by L. Hall 1989, 93; Roberts 1994a, 318n.8. Develin (1977a, 16) calls the law "odd." Brenne (2001, 24) uses the adjective "extraordinary" (*aussergewöhnliche*) to describe the procedure of ostracism, and calls its introduction a "special case" (*Sonderfall*) in legal and constitutional history. Siewert (2002, 479) calls the institution "exotic" (*fremdartige*).

and simultaneously indicated the limited and lawful nature of democratic power.[3]

The next section, "The Procedure of Ostracism," provides an introductory background to the argument that follows. In the section "Ostracism as a Symbolic Institution," which follows, I argue that ostracism was the natural outcome of the strong connection between power over decisions of exile and political power both in the archaic period and at the time of the founding of the democracy. I argue moreover that ostracism served as a symbolic reminder of the origins of democratic rule and the fundamental power of non-elites to determine the outcome of intra-elite strife. In recalling the events by which democracy was founded and by symbolizing non-elite power in the polis, the institution of ostracism helped to deter violent intra-elite competition and stabilize the democratic polis. More important, I argue, the procedures and practice of ostracism in democratic Athens demonstrate a clear concern to avoid the destabilizing consequences of violent intra-elite politics of exile by allowing for only a limited and lawful form of exile.

In this same section I also argue that consideration of the procedure of ostracism as a form of collective ritual helps to explain the myriad associations and explanations for ostracism in the ancient sources. Borrowing from recent anthropological and historical studies that interpret social events and political institutions as forms of ritual, I argue that the practice of ostracism in the fifth century was not only a means of articulating and affirming the democratic social order, but also a mechanism for contesting and transforming it. Although ostracism never lost its fundamental significance as symbolizing democratic political power, I argue that, over the course of time, the Athenians used the institution to articulate competing notions of the grounds for inclusion and exclusion in the political community. In essence, ostracism became a site for the active determination and contestation of Athenian collective identity. In addition, I argue that the elaborate procedures of ostracism and the visual spectacle created by the casting of potsherds by the mass of the Athenians elevated the occasion to the level of high ritual and enhanced the symbolic meaning of the procedure.

In the next section, "Ostracisms in Fifth-Century Athens," I argue that the rarity of actual ostracisms in classical Athens is a further indication of the symbolic nature of the institution. I argue that the annual question in the Athenian assembly of whether to hold an ostracism, nevertheless, reminded elites of the people's fundamental control of both exile and political power. In this section I examine the evidence for the historical context of each of the

---

[3] Ober (1989a, 73–75) is one of the few historians to recognize the symbolic role of ostracism for the ideology of the democracy. Cf. also Rosivach 1987a, Christ 1992. These scholars do not, however, identify exile as a key problem of archaic politics, nor do they link the moderation of the institution, and the infrequency of its use, to the stability of the democracy. Finally, these scholars do not interpret ostracism as a ritual that had different symbolic meanings for different participants over time and had an important role in the negotiation of Athenian group identity.

ten known instances of actual ostracism in democratic Athens and show that
on each occasion, the institution served to resolve potentially violent conflict
between rival elite leaders and their supporters. Most notably, I argue
(contrary to ancient and modern interpretations) that the last known instance
of ostracism in Athens—the ostracism of Hyperbolus in 415—did not represent a misuse of the institution against a base scoundrel, but was a typical
instance of non-elite intervention in potentially violent conflict between rival
elite leaders and their supporters.

In "Other Forms of Exile under the Athenian Democracy" I turn to the use
of exile as a penalty in the Athenian democratic courts. Here I demonstrate
that the Athenian democracy did not use the courts as a mechanism for ridding themselves of opponents to democratic rule. Just as non-elites used expulsion moderately in their management of political power, so they did not
abuse it in their exercise of judicial power. Democratic moderation in the use
of exile in both political and judicial spheres, I argue, was an important factor in
the stability of the democracy in contrast to the elite regimes that preceded it.

Finally, in "Exile and the Oligarchic Revolutions of 411 and 404" I turn to
the oligarchic revolutions of the end of the fifth century and show that, in
contrast to the moderation of the democracy, the oligarchic leaders reverted to
the use of expulsion to secure their rule. I demonstrate that oligarchic violence, as seen especially in the resort to expulsion, was a particularly important theme in contemporary democratic ideology. Furthermore, I argue that
both actual expulsions and their representation in democratic ideology were
crucial factors in the ultimate overthrow of these regimes. The moderation of
the restored democracy, moreover, can be attributed both to the need to avoid
the destabilizing consequences of arbitrary expulsions, and to the quest for
ideological legitimacy in the highly unstable post-revolutionary conditions.

The Procedure of Ostracism

Our earliest accounts of the procedure of ostracism date from the fourth
century, so some consideration must be given to the possibility that the procedure in the fifth century differed from that given in our sources.[4] The first
step in any ostracism was that the question was put to the assembly of the
Athenians as to whether they wished to hold one.[5] Aristotle and Philochorus

[4] Sources for the procedure of ostracism: Arist. *Ath. Pol.* 43.5, Philoch. *FGrH* 328 F 30 (whose
sources were Androtion and Ephorus), Diod. Sic. 11.55.2 (whose source was probably Ephorus),
Plut. *Arist.* 7.5–6, schol. Ar. *Eq.* 855, Poll. 8.20. A red-figure kylix from the school of the Pan
Painter dating to c. 470 may depict the counting of sherds at an ostracism; cf. Brenne 2002b.
Recent discussions include Lang 1990, 1–2; Brenne 1994; 2001, 22–23; Scheidel 2002, 483–84;
Scheidel and Taeuber 2002 (on Arist. *Ath. Pol.* 43.5).

[5] Arist. *Ath. Pol.* 43.5, Philoch. *FGrH* 328 F 30.

report that the initial vote on whether to hold an ostracism took place in the principal assembly meeting (ἐκκλησία κυρία) of the sixth division of the ten-month (πρυτανεία, "prytany") political calendar.[6] Whether or not the original law of ostracism specified the timing of the vote in precisely these terms, there are at least two indirect indications that even in the fifth century the initial decision of whether to hold an ostracism occurred once annually, at approximately the same time of year.[7] First, we know of no instance of the ostracism of more than one individual per year. While this may not seem surprising, given the relative infrequency of ostracisms over the course of the fifth century (see "Ostracisms in Fifth-Century Athens," below), it is noteworthy that in the 480s, when ostracisms occurred almost annually, there are no examples of two ostracisms in a single year. This observation suggests, therefore, that there was a limit of one ostracism per year even in the early fifth century. A second indication that ostracisms were held once a year at a fixed date is found in allusions to ostracism in some of Aristophanes' plays, which were performed at the Lenaea festival, at about the time of the sixth prytany (January).[8] Particular note has been made of two passages in Aristophanes' *Knights*, performed at the Lenaea of 424, in which Aristophanes seems to suggest that the Athenians ought to ostracize the politician Cleon.[9] While neither of these pieces of evidence is decisive, they do suggest that even in the fifth century, the decision to hold an ostracism was taken once a year at a fixed time in the political calendar.[10]

[6] This would correspond to a late December–early February date: see n. 10 below.

[7] Errington 1994 has noted that the term ἐκκλησία κυρία occurs first in an inscription dating to 337/6 and has argued that the question of whether to hold an ostracism was reintroduced at this time out of fear of potential tyrants friendly to Macedon. According to Errington's thesis, it was only at this time that the question of whether to hold an ostracism was fixed in the principal assembly of the sixth prytany. Rhodes 1995 disputes Errington's argument, suggesting that the concept of an ἐκκλησία κυρία is older than its first appearance in an inscription.

[8] As Scheidel (2002, 483–84) notes, the incongruity between the political calendar of ten prytanies and the festival calendar of twelve months makes it impossible to determine the exact timing between the initial vote on whether to hold an ostracism, the Lenaea, and the actual vote of ostracism.

[9] Ar. *Eq.* 819, 855–57; with Scheidel 2002, 483–84. In addition to the passages in the *Knights*, there are allusions to ostracism in *Wasps* (947), *Peace* (681), and *Wealth* (627). *Knights*, *Wasps*, and possibly *Wealth* were performed at the Lenaea, and the *Peace* was performed at the City Dionysia, several months later.

[10] Scheidel and Taeuber (2002, 467–68) note the correspondence of a late December–early February date for the question of whether to hold an ostracism with a low point in the agricultural calendar, when the Athenians would have had more time to participate in an ostracism. In addition, they note that the election of generals occurred in the seventh prytany (Arist. *Ath. Pol.* 44.4). It is likely, furthermore, that other magistrates, including the archons, were selected by lot at the same time as the election of the military magistrates (Hansen 1991, 232). Thus, as Scheidel and Taeuber observe, it is possible that the preliminary vote as to whether to hold an ostracism affected the rhetoric of those standing for office.

If the Athenians decided to hold an ostracism, then the actual ostracism took place a short time afterwards, sometime before the eighth prytany (early March).[11] Whether or not the dates for the initial vote and the ostracism itself were fixed in these terms in the fifth century, there must always have been a delay between the initial vote and the actual ostracism. This delay would have allowed all those who wished to participate in the ostracism the time to obtain and inscribe ostraca (ὄστρακα, "potsherds") with the name of the person they wished to have expelled.[12] (The name of the procedure, ὀστρακισμός, is derived from the use of potsherds as ballots.)[13] There has been much discussion of the implications of this procedure for the literacy of the average Athenian.[14] The important issue for our purposes is whether non-elite Athenians cast independent votes. While there is some evidence for prepared ballots and organized campaigns against particular politicians, the evidence of the vast majority of the ostraca suggests that literate, semi-literate, and even illiterate Athenian citizens cast their votes independently.[15]

A well-known anecdote about the politician Aristides—although undoubtedly fabricated in order to illustrate his virtue—assumes that poor illiterate farmers might come to Athens to participate in an ostracism.[16] The story goes that at the time of Aristides' ostracism in 482, an illiterate farmer gave a potsherd to Aristides, whom he did not recognize, and asked him to inscribe it with the name

---

[11] Philoch. *FGrH* 328 F 30. While it is possible that there is a rough correlation between holding an ostracism (before the eighth prytany) and the selection of magistrates for the following year (seventh prytany or later), the imprecision of the specifications for the timing of these two events suggests that the Athenians made no formal attempt to coordinate them.

[12] Plut. *Arist.* 7.4, Diod. Sic. 11.55.2.

[13] *Etym. Magn.* s.v. ἐξοστρακισμός, Phot. s.v ὀστρακισμός. Ostraca have been found in considerable numbers, particularly in excavations in the marketplace (agora) and Potters' Quarters (Ceramicus) of Athens. For the agora ostraca, numbering approximately 1,145, see Lang 1990. For the Ceramicus ostraca, numbering approximately 8,500, see Brenne 2001, 2002a. In addition, a deposit of 190 ostraca inscribed with the name Themistocles and one with the name Cimon was found on the north slope of the acropolis (Lang 1990, 142–61). More recently, a group of "at least a dozen" ostraca was found in 1994–95 in the agora (Camp 1996). Even more recently, an additional group of "about 144" ostraca (cast mostly against Themistocles and Xanthippus) was found in 1996 in the agora and is due to be published by James Sickinger. For a preliminary report, see Camp 1999. For ostraca found outside Athens, see below, appendix 2.

[14] Harvey 1966, 590–93; W. Harris 1989, 53–55, 74–75; Thomas 1989, 1–94.

[15] Brenne (1994, 17–20) argues that the great variety of vessels and handwritings used for the majority of the extant ostraca suggests that most ostraca were prepared individually. See also Lang 1990, 10–18. Although there is some evidence for large groups of ostraca against the same person in only a few different hands (for example, the Themistocles ostraca from the north slope of the acropolis: Lang 1990, 142–61), Brenne shows that there are also examples from the Ceramicus of ostraca against different persons inscribed in the same hand. This suggests that there were neutral scribes—that is, persons who helped illiterate citizens by inscribing sherds for them; cf. Lang 1990, 161. For organized campaigns, see also below on Hyperbolus's ostracism.

[16] Plut. *Arist.* 7.5–6.

Aristides. When Aristides asked the farmer what Aristides had done to him, he replied: "Nothing. I don't even know the man, but I'm tired of hearing him everywhere called 'the Just.'" Aristides said nothing in response, wrote his own name on the ostracon, and handed it back to the farmer. Although other politicians may not have been so principled as Aristides is alleged to have been in this anecdote, the story does illustrate that even illiterate citizens might participate in an ostracism by getting others to inscribe their ballots for them.

On the day of the ostracism, an area of the central marketplace (ἀγορά, "agora") was closed off with wooden fences.[17] Ten entrances were made into the enclosure, corresponding to the ten tribes of Athens. An Athenian citizen wishing to participate in the ostracism took his potsherd to the entrance that corresponded to his tribe. The members of the council and the nine archons presided over the ostracism, presumably to ensure that each citizen voted only once, and that only citizens voted.[18] When all had voted, the ballots were collected and counted.[19] If at least six thousand votes had been cast, then the individual with the most votes was required to leave the city for ten years.[20] During the time of exile, the property of the ostracized person was left unharmed, and he could continue to draw revenues from it (καρπούμενον τὰ αὑτοῦ).[21] After ten years, the ostracized person could return to Athens and take up full citizenship rights again.[22]

OSTRACISM AS A SYMBOLIC INSTITUTION

The first key to understanding the role of ostracism in democratic Athens is to recognize the intimate connection between political power and exile in Athenian and indeed Greek history in the archaic period. Viewed in the light of the history of exile prior to and during the Athenian democratic revolution, the association between popular power and the power to expel a citizen through ostracism appears to be neither irrational nor bizarre. Indeed, the creation of a democratic procedure for the expulsion of a citizen from the polis makes perfect sense, given the historical process of the development of democratic power as a counterbalance to intra-elite politics of exile.

[17] Ar. *Eq.* 855 with scholion, Philoch. *FGrH* 328 F 30, Plut. *Arist.* 7.4, Poll. 8.19–20.

[18] Philoch. *FGrH* 328 F 30.

[19] Two red-figure pots by the Pan Painter possibly depict the collecting and counting of the votes. See Siewert et al. 2002, plates 10–12. For discussion, see Brenne 2002b.

[20] The sources are ambiguous about whether six thousand votes had to be cast in total, or against a particular candidate, for the vote to be valid. As Brenne (2001, 23) notes, the evidence for six thousand as a quorum is more sound. Following the Persian Wars, restrictions were imposed on where the ostracized might reside (Arist. *Ath. Pol.* 22.7–8), as a result of fear of collaboration with the Persians. For discussion, see Figueira 1987.

[21] Plut. *Arist.* 7.5.

[22] For the practice of ostracism outside Athens, see below, appendix 2.

As we have seen, political power in the seventh- and sixth-century polis was in some sense equivalent to the power to exile one's political opponents. Over the course of the sixth century in Athens, non-elites began to play a role in determining who was to be included and who excluded from the polis. The instability of the polis caused by incessant intra-elite politics of exile made the non-elites an appealing stabilizing force for ambitious elites and forced the non-elites to take an active role in the political struggles of the elites. Although Solon and Pisistratus played decisive roles in this movement, the moment of crystallization of the development toward greater popular involvement in politics occurred during the strife between Cleisthenes and Isagoras in 508/7. At that time, non-elites intervened decisively in the violent conflict between elites, driving Isagoras and his Spartan allies out and re-calling Cleisthenes to Athens. Through this action, non-elites simultaneously took control over decisions of exile and established themselves as the dom-inant political force in the polis.

The close connection between political power and the power to impose exile, as well as the need for popular involvement in politics to resolve conflict among elites, explains why the mechanism of ostracism, which provided for the peaceful intervention of the people in political conflict between elite leaders, was a central plank of Cleisthenes' democratic reforms.[23] By giving the Athe-nians the power to expel a citizen, Cleisthenes provided the new democracy with a practical means for the peaceful resolution of political strife between elite leaders and at the same time provided them with a mechanism for the symbolic expression of popular power through the traditional association between control over exile and political power. Moreover, by recalling the event by which non-elites simultaneously took over decisions of exile and assumed political au-thority, ostracism both served as a reminder of the potential of non-elites to intervene decisively in intra-elite conflict and symbolized popular power. Thus the institution of ostracism both recalled the past historical relation between exile and power and served as metonym for popular rule.

Recognition of the symbolic force of ostracism circumvents some of the objections that have been made to the view that it was a mechanism for the prevention and/or resolution of potentially violent political conflict between elite leaders.[24] The principal objection to this interpretation of ostracism is

[23] There has been much debate about whether ostracism is actually Cleisthenic and whether it was instituted in 508/7. Doubts have arisen because the first ostracism was held twenty years after Cleisthenes' reforms (488/7) and because Androtion (*FGrH* 324 F 6) claims that the institution was created at the same time as its first use. Despite a recent attempt to vindicate Androtion (Taeuber 2002), I follow the majority of our sources (and current scholarly consensus) in holding that the institution is Cleisthenic. For the arguments, see below, appendix 1.

[24] This view of ostracism has been suggested by, for example, Ostwald 1969, 156; 1988, 344–46; Develin 1977a, 21; Rhodes, *CAAP* 270; Petzold 1990, 163–73; Hansen 1991, 35; R. Osborne 1996a, 331–32; Mirhady 1997, 16. None of these scholars, however, recognizes the symbolic role of ostracism.

that the expulsion of a single individual at a fixed time of the year would hardly prevent the outbreak of violent intra-elite competition if elites were so inclined.[25] Indeed, we have seen on numerous occasions that laws and political institutions were inadequate checks on the propensity of ambitious elites to use force to seize power throughout the archaic period. This objection raises a significant point about the difference between the law of ostracism and previous attempts to regulate intra-elite conflict. I have argued that the law of ostracism was not simply an act of legislation or constitutional reform, but a response to the dramatic intervention of non-elites in intra-elite politics of exile. The law of ostracism, in other words, did not, ex nihilo, simply give non-elites power to expel a citizen, but recalled the events by which non-elites established their control over decisions of exile and simultaneously became the dominant political force in the community. The symbolic role of ostracism in recalling these events explains how ostracism could be an effective deterrent to violent intra-elite conflict. By reminding elites annually of the potential of non-elites to intervene decisively in violent intra-elite conflict, the institution of ostracism served as a potent symbol of the ability of non-elites to determine the outcome. This reminder of the historical basis of popular power would have deterred ambitious elites from trying to seize power by force in the traditional manner. Past experience had shown, and ostracism symbolically recalled, the ultimate impotence of intra-elite factionalism in the face of a politically active demos.

The symbolic role of ostracism in recalling the events of 508/7 is not the only answer to the question of how the institution could serve as an effective deterrent to violent political conflict between rival elites. The second key to understanding the function of ostracism is to recognize that it was a limited and lawful form of exile, as opposed to the unlimited and violent practice of intra-elite politics of exile in pre-democratic Athens. Indeed, the institution of ostracism not only symbolized the usurpation of political power by non-elites, but also signaled their lawful and moderate use of it. On a practical level, the moderate practice of ostracism avoided the destabilizing effects of intra-elite politics of exile with its mass expulsions and frequent violent attempts to return. On the ideological level, moreover, the institution of ostracism served as an important symbol of the justice and moderation of democratic rule in contrast to the non-democratic regimes that preceded it. In fact, democratic moderation in the use of exile, I would argue, not only prevented violent intra-elite conflict, but was a key factor in the stability of the democracy. In order to understand this argument, it is important to review some key features of the democratic practice of ostracism.

Both the type of exile imposed by a vote of ostracism and the procedures of ostracism itself underline the moderate nature of the institution. Perhaps the most striking illustration of that moderation is the limited nature of the form of

[25] L. Hall 1989, 93–94; Brenne 2001, 26.

exile imposed by vote of ostracism in comparison to intra-elite politics of exile. In particular, ostracism allowed for the expulsion of a single individual for the limited period of ten years. While a term of exile of ten years may not seem moderate to a modern observer, it is nevertheless vital to recall that the norm of intra-elite politics of exile entailed violent expulsion of a political leader, his associates, and their families for a potentially unlimited period of time, with total loss of property and power in Athens. Under those conditions, as we have seen, there was a great incentive for those exiled to attempt to return by force. By contrast, a person exiled by vote of ostracism not only lacked the support of a group of fellow exiles, but also was assured that he could return to Athens after ten years with his property intact and citizenship rights restored.[26]

In fact, it is clear that those ostracized not only regained their citizenship rights when they returned, but also suffered no great loss of prestige and influence in public affairs. Several victims of ostracism served in important public offices following their return. In 480, for example, when Athens was threatened by the second Persian invasion, Megacles, Xanthippus, and Aristides were recalled from exile and subsequently performed important public roles.[27] Xanthippus commanded the Athenian fleet at the battles of Mycale in 479 and Sestus in 478.[28] Aristides not only served as general at the battles of Salamis and Plataea but most famously assessed the initial tribute of the Delian League members.[29] Although we know little of Megacles' career following his ostracism in 487/6, the fact that he was ostracized again in 471 suggests that he continued to play an important role in public affairs after his first ostracism and return.[30] Cimon also returned to Athens after his ostracism, and subsequently negotiated a five-year truce with Sparta on Athens' behalf and led an Athenian expedition against Egypt and Cyprus in 454.[31]

In addition to the evidence of the later careers of formerly ostracized citizens, a number of ancient sources mention the mildness of the penalty of

---

[26] As was noted above, according to Plut. *Arist.* 7.5 an ostracized person could even continue to receive the proceeds from his property in Athens while in exile. The guarantee of security of property must have been an important condition for the wealthy citizens who were the usual candidates for ostracism.

[27] Aristides' recall: Hdt. 8.79.1, [Dem.] 26.6. Recall of the ostracized: Andoc.1.107, Arist. *Ath. Pol.* 22.7–8, Themistocles Decree (ML 23.44–48).

[28] Hdt. 8.131, 9.114–21.

[29] Hdt. 8.76, 95; Thuc. 5.18.5; Plut. *Arist.* 24.

[30] The evidence for Megacles' second ostracism comes from the testimony of [Andoc.] 4.34 and Lys. 14.39, as well as the evidence of a hoard of ostraca from the Ceramicus ("der grosse Kerameikosfund": Brenne 2001, 30). The latter appears to represent one ostracism, and in consequence of the many joins between ostraca against Megacles and against other politicians active in the 470s must be dated to 471: Brenne 2001, 31–41; 2002a, 42–43.

[31] The question of whether Thucydides son of Melesias was general after his ostracism (Plut. *Per.* 16.3) depends both on the date of his ostracism (443? 436?) and on whether he is to be identified with the Thucydides who served as general in the campaign against Samos in 440/39 (Thuc. 1.117.2). For the debate, see Krentz 1984; Phillips 1991; Brenne 2002a, 93–94.

ostracism, and emphasize that it was not a penalty for wrongdoing.[32] The comic poet Plato even jokes that ostracism was only befitting for the best citizens, when he suggests that the last known victim of ostracism, Hyperbolus, was unworthy of the penalty because of his base character:[33]

καίτοι πέπραγε τῶν τρόπων μὲν ἄξια
αὐτοῦ δὲ καὶ τῶν στιγμάτων ἀνάξια.
οὐ γὰρ τοιούτων οὕνεκ' ὄστραχ' εὑρέθη.

Although he got what he deserved,
his fate was too good for him and his slave brands.
For ostracism was not invented for men such as he.

Plato's jest is based on the fact that elites were the usual victims of ostracism and, as I will argue later, ultimately reflects anti-democratic critiques of ostracism.[34] Nevertheless, the gist of the joke is that ostracism itself gave Hyperbolus undeserved honor. Indeed the tradition that the mythical Athenian hero Theseus was ostracized suggests that ostracism became a necessary attribute of heroes in the Athenian imagination.[35] In sum, it is clear that victims of ostracism suffered no lasting damage to their prestige and that the institution was therefore an extremely moderate way of regulating intra-elite conflict. In particular, by limiting the extent of damage to the citizens chosen for expulsion, ostracism created incentives for the ostracized to wait out their term of exile rather than attempt to return by force.

The mildness of the penalty of ostracism, furthermore, goes some way toward refuting several common interpretations of the practice. One common belief is that it was aimed at preventing tyranny.[36] This idea first arises explicitly in the fourth century, and seems to be an inference from the fact that several of the earliest victims were associated with the family of the tyrant Pisistratus.[37] A number of comments on ostraca, furthermore, may be

[32] Diod. Sic. 11.55.3, 87.2; Plut. *Arist.* 7.2–4, *Nic.* 11, *Them.* 22.5.

[33] Kassel-Austin, *PCG* fr. 203.

[34] Thucydides makes a similar observation about the anomaly of Hyperbolus's ostracism in stating that he was ostracized not out of fear of his power and reputation but because he was a wretch and a disgrace to the city (8.73.3). On anti-democratic criticism of ostracism, see below, chapter 6.

[35] Carcopino 1909, 96–97. Theseus's ostracism: Ar. *Plut.* 627, Plut. *Thes.* 32–35, Theophrastus in *Suda* s.v. ἀρχὴ σκυρία. Compare also Arist. *Pol.* 1284a, in which Heracles' abandonment by the Argonauts is compared to ostracism.

[36] Carcopino 1909, 108; Bonner and Smith 1930, 193–95; Ehrenberg 1950, 544; Grasmück 1978, 24, citing Busolt 1920, 2:884. Taeuber (2002, 412) and Siewert (2002, 505) note that accusations of tyranny never occur explicitly on ostraca or in any of our ancient sources before Androtion. Errington 1994 argues that this explanation of the function of ostracism arose as a result of fear of tyranny in the 330s.

[37] Androtion, *FGrH* 324 F 6; Arist. *Ath. Pol.* 22.3–4, 6; *Pol.* 1302b15–21; Philoch. *FGrH* 328 F 30; with discussion of these sources by Taeuber 2002.

allusions to the tyrannical aspirations of the proposed candidates.[38] It is a reasonable conclusion, therefore, that tyrannical inclinations were among the justifications for ostracism. There are several objections to this thesis, however. Several scholars have observed, for example, that ostracism is an ineffective weapon against tyranny, since a potential tyrant might have enough influence to secure votes against his opponents rather than himself. Furthermore, a would-be tyrant could always resort to extra-legal means of seizing power.[39] The most decisive proof that ostracism was not designed as a weapon against tyranny, however, is that the Athenians had much harsher penalties for attempts at tyranny than the comparatively mild terms of this exile. Those suspected of aiming at tyranny in Athens were either condemned to death or banished for life along with their families. In addition, their property was confiscated by the state.[40] It is unlikely, therefore, that the Athenians would have resorted to ostracism, with its limited term of exile and its assurances of security of property and social position, to get rid of prospective tyrants.

Similarly, the mildness of ostracism discredits the modern view that the institution was designed as a weapon against traitors. The association between ostracism and treachery is based on the observation that many of its victims were suspected of connections to the Persians.[41] Strikingly, many ostraca contain references to the Persian sympathies of candidates for ostracism. For example, ostraca against Callixenus and against Leagrus explicitly label their candidates as traitors ($\pi\rho o\delta\acute{o}\tau\alpha\iota$).[42] More colorfully, no less than sixteen ostraca against Callias son of Cratius label him a Mede (i.e., a Persian).[43] On one ostracon against Callias there is even a drawing of a person (presumably Callias himself) in Persian dress.[44] On this basis, a number of scholars have proposed that ostracism was designed as a weapon against traitors.[45] Yet there are good reasons for distinguishing between ostracism and Athenian treatment of traitors.

First of all, the penalties for treason were severe. Traitors, for instance, were required to stand trial in Athens and, if convicted, were condemned to

---

[38] Brenne 2002a, 160–61.

[39] Rhodes, CAAP 270; L. Hall 1989, 93–95; Scheidel 2002, 487.

[40] The penalties for attempted tyranny dated back to the seventh century (see above, chapter 3) and were still valid in the fifth century: see Arist. Ath. Pol. 16.10, Plut. Sol. 19.4, with Ostwald 1955.

[41] The first victim of ostracism, Hipparchus, might have been suspected of treason after 490, when his relative Hippias, the former tyrant, arrived at Marathon with the Persians (Hdt. 6.102, 107). The well-known accusations of treason against the Alcmeonidae (Hdt. 6.121–24) may have influenced the ostracisms of Megacles and Xanthippus in 486 and 484, respectively. Finally, Themistocles, who was ostracized in 470, was also accused of treason: see below.

[42] Callixenus: Lang 589, Brenne T1/65. Leagrus: Brenne T1/71. For the referencing of ostraca, see "Abbreviations and Conventions" above.

[43] Brenne T1/45–61.

[44] Brenne T1/46. For the illustration, see Brenne 1992, 174 (= Siewert et al. 2002, plate 1). For several other ostraca with accusations of treason, see Brenne 2002a, 158.

[45] Burstein 1971, Schreiner 1976.

death or banished for life. Furthermore, traitors suffered total loss of property and loss of the right to burial in the territory of the polis.[46] Indeed, the Athenians were so anxious to expel all remnants of a traitor that even after his death, a traitor's bones could not be brought back for burial. Once again, it is unlikely that the Athenians would have opted for the relatively mild terms of ostracism to punish a traitor when they could impose much harsher penalties. The case of Themistocles is decisive, moreover, in demonstrating the distinction between ostracism and Athenian procedures for dealing with traitors. Themistocles was ostracized in 471/0, but was later recalled from exile in order to stand trial for treason.[47] If Themistocles' ostracism was conceived as a penalty for treachery, then the Athenians would not have later recalled him to stand trial on this charge.

These observations bring up an important interpretive problem regarding the variety of explanations of the function of ostracism provided by the ancient literary sources and the ostraca themselves. Besides tyranny and treason, our sources offer a great number of justifications for ostracism, ranging from excessive prestige and influence to adultery and incest. Themistocles' ostracism, for instance, is explained by the literary sources as a result of his excessive power and honor.[48] At least one voter, furthermore, seems to have been referring to Themistocles' prestige when he wrote on his ballot, "This potsherd is for Themistocles, of the deme Phrearrhius, on account of his honor ([τ]ιμῆς ἕνεκα)."[49] Another voter, however, apparently accused Themistocles of disreputable sexual activities, writing on his ballot, "Themistocles son of Neocles, asshole [καταπύγον]."[50] As Stefan Brenne notes, the word καταπύγον refers to engagement as the passive partner in anal intercourse, a role considered improper for an adult Athenian man.[51] Yet another voter accused Themistocles of being a pollution in the land (ὑπέγαιος ἄγος).[52]

Similarly, Megacles, against whom we have more than four thousand ostraca, is associated with a wide range of offenses. Some of the most frequent accusations against him allude to his elite status, and in particular his ostentatious wealth and luxurious lifestyle.[53] On five ostraca, Megacles is described

---

[46] For the penalties for treason, cf. Xen. Hell. 1.7.22, [Plut.] X Orat. 1 (Antiphon; Mor. 834a–b, Gorgias 82 B 11a DK, Thuc. 8.68.2 (on Antiphon), Lycurg. Leoc. 111–22.

[47] Thuc. 1.135.3, Plut. Them. 23. For the probable date of Themistocles' trial for treason, see Carawan 1987, 196. On Themistocles' ostracism, see discussion below.

[48] Dem. 23.204, Plut. Them. 22.

[49] Brenne T1/147.

[50] Brenne T1/150.

[51] Brenne 2002a, 132.

[52] Brenne T/149. The reading is, however, uncertain. See Brenne 2002a, 131–32, for discussion of the text.

[53] Pind. Pyth. 7.18–21 attributes Megacles' ostracism to envy of Alcmeonid victories in chariot racing.

as keeping horses (ἱπποτρόφος), a typical pursuit of the elite, and a sign of great wealth.[54] One ostracon against Megacles even has a skillfully rendered drawing of a horse and rider.[55] Six ostraca explicitly associate him with a woman named Coisyra.[56] Despite some confusion over which of several known Coisyras is meant, it seems that in fifth-century comedy the name Coisyra was associated with arrogance, ostentatious display, and ambition.[57] One ostracon accuses Megacles of being overly fond of money (φιλάργ[υρος]), a reference perhaps alluding to susceptibility to bribery in public office.[58] Another ostracon labels Megacles an adulterer (μοιχός).[59] Similar accusations of improper sexual relations occur in the literary sources dealing with Alcibiades' candidacy for ostracism, and in one ostracon against Cimon,[60] on which a voter wrote, "Let Cimon son of Miltiades go, taking Elpinice with him!" Since literary sources report that Elpinice was Cimon's sister and that he had an incestuous relation with her, it appears that Cimon's violation of communal sexual norms was the reason for this vote against him.[61]

The plethora of comments and even drawings on ostraca has only added to the variety of potential motives for ostracism. Several candidates appear to be accused of corruption in public office. Most eloquent is a potsherd against Xanthippus son of Ariphron, who was ostracized in 484. On this potsherd, a voter wrote an elegiac couplet accusing Xanthippus of some sort of public misconduct:[62]

Χσάνθ[ιππον τόδε] φεσὶν ἀλειτερὸν πρ[υτ]άνειον
τὄστρα[κον Ἀρρί]φρονος παῖδα μά[λ]ιστ' ἀδικῆν.

This potsherd declares that Xanthippus son of Ariphron
does the most wrong of the accursed leaders [or: that the
accursed Xanthippus wrongs the prytaneion].

The use of the adjective "accursed" (ἀλειτερός) on this ostracon and on several ostraca against Alcmeonids has raised questions about the use of

---

[54] Brenne T1/101–5. T1/103 is a ballot cast against not only Megacles, but "also his horses."
[55] Brenne T1/158.
[56] Brenne T1/95–100.
[57] Schol. Ar. Nub. 48 (= Suda s.v. ἐγκεκοισυρωμένην). Other possible connotations of this name include association with foreign lands, since Coisyra is an Eretrian name, and tyranny, since the tyrant Pisistratus had a wife called Coisyra. For discussion, see Brenne 2002a, 109–12, with references to earlier scholarship.
[58] Brenne T1/111. Again, the reading is uncertain; see Brenne 2002a, 117, for discussion. For parallel accusations of misuse of public office, see the famous ostracon against Xanthipppus cited below (Lang 1065) and an ostracon against Menon (Brenne T1/118) labeling him "most corrupt" ([δορο] δοκότατος). See Brenne 2002a, 123–24, for the reading.
[59] Brenne T1/106.
[60] [Andoc.] 4.14, Brenne T1/67.
[61] [Andoc.] 4.33, Plut. Cim. 4.4–7, Athen. 13.589.
[62] Lang 1065; see Lang 1990, 134, for these readings and references to further scholarship.

ostracism against those guilty of religious offenses that might pollute the entire community.[63] Related to this interpretation of ostracism is the idea that the procedure may be associated with scapegoating and other types of rituals for expelling pollution.[64] In these rituals, one or more persons were expelled from the community in order to purify it and prevent the gods from harming the rest of its members.[65] Failure to expel pollution from the community was thought to cause pestilence (λοιμός) and famine (λιμός). At Athens, two men of low social standing were annually expelled at the Thargelia festival, in early summer.[66] Besides the obvious parallel of an annual expulsion in both scapegoating rituals and ostracism, it is striking that a number of ostraca apparently allude to the expulsion of famine via the scapegoating ritual. Seven ostraca from the Ceramicus call for the expulsion of Famine (Λιμός).[67] One voter even added a patronymic to the personified famine, calling his candidate "Famine son of Noble Father." (Λιμός Εὐπ[ρ]-ατρίδες).[68]

In addition to these parallels between expulsion rituals and ostracism, Chris Faraone has observed similarities between the use of inscribed potsherds in an ostracism and the practice of inscribing curses on various materials (usually lead) in order to harm a personal enemy.[69] Many of these so-called curse tablets, moreover, contain names of well-known politicians, such as Demosthenes and Lycurgus.[70] Furthermore, as is the case with most extant ostraca, most curse tablets contain only the name of the intended victim, along with his patronymic or demotic. Scholars assume that the curse, which in later periods was actually written on the tablet, was originally spoken aloud. It is quite possible, therefore, that voters in an ostracism similarly uttered a curse before casting their ballots. Other tantalizing signs of the use of magic in ostracisms include the appearance of the words "black" (μέλας) and "sorcerer" (βάσκανος) on two potsherds.[71]

---

[63] Ostraca against the Alcmeonids: Brenne T1/92, 93; cf. T1/91. Compare also the ostracon against Aristides (Brenne T1/38 = Lang 44) accusing him of some sort of offense against suppliants, and the ostracon quoted above against Themistocles (Brenne T1/149).

[64] The association between ostracism and scapegoating rituals was first proposed by Gernet (unpublished paper cited by Vernant and Vidal-Naquet 1988, 436n.121) and popularized by Vernant and Vidal-Naquet 1988, 133–36, 326–27; Burkert 1985, 83. See most recently L. Hall 1989; Ogden 1997, 142–45. For objections, see R. Parker 1983; Mirhady 1997, 15.

[65] For overviews of scapegoating rituals in ancient Greece, see Bremmer 1983; R. Parker 1983, 257–80; Burkert 1985, 82–84; Ogden 1997, 15–28. On the larger category of expulsive rituals, see Faraone 2004.

[66] Bremmer 1983, 301, collects the sources.

[67] Brenne T1/75–81.

[68] Brenne T1/75. The reading is uncertain. See Brenne 2002a, 97–100, for discussion. See Faraone 2004 for discussion of rituals relating to the expulsion of famine demons.

[69] Faraone, pers. comm. For general discussion of curse tablets and binding spells in the ancient world, see Faraone 1991, Gager 1992.

[70] Faraone 1991, 16.

[71] Brenne T1/72, 73.

Finally, crude drawings of various animals, including a snake and an owl, may have magical connotations, since similar figures appear on curse tablets and magical papyri.[72]

In the face of the myriad possible associations and rationales for ostracism, scholars have adopted one of two approaches to understanding its function in Athens. The most common approach is to distinguish between an original purpose of ostracism and its later use. Scholars holding this view argue that although we can conjecture an original purpose of ostracism, our ancient sources inform us only about its later uses, which diverge from the original purpose of the law.[73] A common form of this argument is the notion that—whatever Cleisthenes' original intention in enacting the law of ostracism—the institution came to be misused in the fifth century as a tool in party strife.[74] Thus the rash of ostracisms in the 480s, for example, is often explained as a result of the machinations of Themistocles to get rid of his political opponents.[75] Similarly, Brenne argues that the wide variety of accusations on ostraca reveals the multiple uses to which the Athenians put the institution of ostracism, and not its original purpose.[76]

A second approach is to argue that the variety of explanations for ostracism in our sources can all be subsumed under a single general function, namely the punishment of wrongs toward the community. This is the view of Peter Siewert, who argues that the aim of ostracism was to punish various political, moral, and religious offenses against the community for which legal redress was impossible because of a lack either of corresponding laws or of clear proof. For Siewert, ostracism was an extra-judicial means of pressuring the elite to conform to the political and moral norms of the community. Foremost among the norms that Siewert detects behind the numerous explanations for ostracism in our ancient sources are aversion to excessive prestige and acceptance of the principle of equality among citizens.[77]

A third approach to ostracism, however, can reconcile the two positions outlined above and simultaneously account for the wide variety of explanations of ostracism in our ancient sources. This approach acknowledges that ostracism had its origins in particular historical circumstances and thus was enacted to meet specific needs, but also that ostracism was a form of collective ritual, and as such had different meanings for different participants over time.

---

[72] Snake, T1/162; owl, T1/166. For drawings on curse tablets and magical papyri, see Gager 1992, 68–69. For discussion of drawings on ostraca, see Brenne 1992; 2002a, 141–48, with plates 1–9.

[73] Scheidel 2002, 494. Cf. Rosivach 1987a, distinguishing between the use of ostracism in the fifth century and Athenian perceptions of the function of ostracism in the late fifth and the fourth century, when ostracisms were no longer held.

[74] Roberts 1994a, 29.

[75] Schreiner 1976, Taeuber 2002.

[76] Brenne 2002a, 166. Brenne (1994, 13) argues that the comments on ostraca are similar to the types of abuse found in comedy and reflect discussion and propaganda circulating among the Athenians between the decision to hold an ostracism and the actual vote.

[77] Siewert 1991, 13–14; 2002, 505–8.

I have argued above that ostracism was a response to the role of exile in the exercise of political power in the archaic period and at the time of the democratic revolution. According to this argument, ostracism served both as a practical means of resolving and deterring potentially violent conflict between elite leaders and as a symbolic expression of popular power and its just use. From its very origin, therefore, ostracism had a number of practical and ideological functions for the Athenian democracy.

Yet consideration of ostracism as a form of collective ritual helps to explain the variety of perspectives on the institution present in the ancient sources.[78] Theorists have long focused on ritual as a means of creating collective unity and articulating and affirming the social order.[79] More recently, a more complex understanding of the social role of ritual has been developed, which sees ritual as a dynamic force capable not simply of articulating and affirming the social order but also of contesting and transforming it. According to this model, ritual practices are constantly adapting to new conditions and renegotiating the rules by which the community is ordered.[80] The variety of perspectives on ostracism evident in the ancient evidence, I would argue, can be interpreted according to both the affirmative and the transformative role of ritual.

Like any collective ritual, the holding of an ostracism, and even the initial vote on whether to hold it, served as an occasion for collective activity and hence the enactment of the (political) community of the Athenians. Furthermore, it is easy to see how ostracism served as an occasion for the articulation of communal identity and cohesion. By collectively determining who was to be excluded from the community, the Athenians indirectly articulated the grounds for inclusion, and in doing so reestablished the basis for group membership. At the same time, however, it is important to recognize that the collectivity of the Athenians was not monolithic, and that different members of the community may have had different views on what constituted the grounds for inclusion in and exclusion from the community.[81] The variety of

[78] For a good overview of approaches to ritual, see Bell 1997. The interpretation of social events and political institutions as forms of ritual owes much to cultural anthropologists such as Victor Turner (e.g., 1969) and Clifford Geertz (e.g., 1973), and has been persuasively applied to riot and revelry in eighteenth-century France by Davis 1975 and Darnton 1984. Although this approach is not without its flaws (see, for example, Desan 1989), recognition of the ritualistic aspects of certain social and political practices has much explanatory force. Further important comparative studies include Moore and Myerhoff 1977, Wilenz 1985, Kertzer 1988, Boissevain 1992, Baringhorst 2001. For a reading of the procedures of the Athenian courts as rituals, see Bers 2000. For a reading of the procedures of the political institutions of ancient Rome as rituals, see Hopkins 1991. For revelry and riot in archaic Megara as a ritual, see chapter 3 above and Forsdyke 2005.

[79] This approach to ritual is often labeled "functionalism" and is a development of the theories of Emile Durkheim (e.g., 1995).

[80] This approach to ritual is associated with practice theory and the work of Pierre Bourdieu (e.g., 1980/1990).

[81] Compare Desan 1989, criticizing the approach of Davis 1975 partially on the grounds that she assumes unified communal understanding of the meaning of collective action.

comments on ostraca gives a small glimpse of the divergent grounds for
exclusion by ostracism. A further indication that there were different views is
the multiplicity of known candidates at any given ostracism (the so-called
scatter vote).[82]

The recognition that different members of the Athenian community had
different views on what constituted grounds for exclusion and inclusion does
not rule out the idea that there were collective meanings for the practice,
which transcended any individual participant. It must be recalled in this regard that the vast majority of ostraca contain no remarks at all, simply listing
the name of the candidate with his patronymic or demotic. Furthermore, the
large numbers of ostraca cast against Megacles and Themistocles suggest that
there could be considerable consensus among the Athenians as to who should
be excluded.[83] While we cannot assume that all these participants had a unified concept of what constituted the grounds for the ostracism of these individuals and indeed at least some ostraca indicate that they did not, it is not
unreasonable to assume that there was at least some common understanding
among Athenians as to who should be excluded and on what grounds.

An even more important feature of collective rituals, however, which explains
the variety of functions of ostracism in our sources, is the propensity of rituals to
adapt to changing historical circumstances and hence to take on different
meanings over time. Discussing the significance of the Lupercalia for the Ro-
mans, Keith Hopkins comments on both the diversity of meanings of ritual for
different participants and the tendency for the meaning of rituals to change over
time: "The stability of ritual forms must have disguised both radical diversity
and radical changes in meaning. . . . it seems likely that the Lupercalian rites
had different significance in each period for different sections of Rome's varied
population."[84] Hopkins goes on to argue that over the course of the thousand
years in which the Lupercalia was practiced, the ritual was transformed from a
fertility rite to the occasion for the punishment of sexually transgressive women.[85]

While I would not want to argue that the meaning of ostracism changed
quite so radically, it is likely that there were some changes in its significance

---

[82] Mattingly 1991 provides convenient charts of the known candidates at each ostracism.

[83] In addition to ostraca against Megacles and Themistocles numbering in the thousands, over
a hundred potsherds each have been found against Aristides, Hippocrates, Callixenus, Cleippides, and Menon. For the counts, see the useful chart of Brenne 2002a, 46–71.

[84] Hopkins 1991, 480–84.

[85] Another striking example of change in the meaning of a ritual can be observed in the development of what is known as rough music (charivari). This ritual involved the public humiliation
of an offender against communal norms. In the seventeenth century, the most common targets of
this ritual abuse were wives who beat their husbands. (Cf. Davis 1975, 105, 116.) Over the course of
the eighteenth century, the targets of rough music shifted from wives who beat their husbands to
husbands who beat their wives (E. Thompson 1993, 467–538). According to Thompson, the shift
reflects the decline of a patriarchal society and the rise of new respect for women as a result of
changes in the economy. For this ritual in ancient Greece, see Schmitt-Pantel 1981.

for the Athenians between the late sixth century when it was enacted and the late fourth century when it ceased to be in force.[86] In the earlier period, memories of archaic politics and the democratic revolution itself would still have been fresh, and hence we can expect that ostracism served as a potent reminder of the past history of exile and stood as the principal symbol of the power of the people through their control over decisions of exile. Nevertheless, already in the 480s, the earliest date of the ostraca, there are signs that, at least for some participants, ostracism served the broader and more generalized role of curtailing elite prestige and even articulating disapproval of the sexual and social behaviors of the elite. By the late fifth century, the date of our earliest literary testimonia for the practice, the role of ostracism in curtailing elite prestige and articulating the norm of democratic equality in social, legal, and political spheres was beginning to eclipse its historical origins and meaning. Nevertheless, as I shall argue below, the experience of the oligarchic revolutions of 411 and 404, both of which involved a renewal, in slightly modified form, of the politics of exile, reevoked the relation between exile and political power, and the historical events that gave rise to both democracy and ostracism. The events of the late fifth century, in other words, reinvigorated the role of ostracism as a symbol of past history, and in particular the relation between exile and political power.

The changes in its meaning over time are one indication that ostracism was a locus for the negotiation, if not transformation, of communal norms and collective identity. The evidence for the practice of ostracism over the course of the fifth century and the changing interpretations of the meaning of this institution in our literary sources show that the Athenians used it to articulate competing notions of the grounds for exclusion and inclusion, and hence that ostracism was a site for the active determination of collective identity. Its function as a forum for the negotiation of the correct ordering of the community is especially evident in anti-democratic critiques of ostracism and its use, as I argue below in chapter 6. These critiques reveal that democrats used the institution as a means of legitimating democratic rule, and that oligarchs responded in turn by representing ostracism as an example of the injustices of the masses against the very elite citizens who benefited them most. This ongoing debate reveals that ostracism was a potent symbol and site for the negotiation of the norms of the political community of the Athenians.

In sum, many of the problems with reconciling the evidence for the practice of ostracism can be resolved by recognizing that ostracism was a collective ritual practiced by a diverse group of Athenians over a fairly lengthy period of time. Although I believe that the fundamental significance of ostracism for the Athenians was its role as a deterrent to violent intra-elite conflict and its symbolic articulation of the power of the people, the institution took on different

---

[86] For the continued validity of the law on ostracism in the fourth century, see below.

(often less historically specific) meanings for different participants at different points in time and thus served as a dynamic locus for the active negotiation of the meaning of group membership. While later historical events helped to keep memories of the historical relation between exile and political power alive, over time the institution took on a broader meaning as a symbol of the power of the collectivity to exercise social and moral authority over the individuals within it.

I argued above that the form of exile imposed by a vote of ostracism was extremely moderate compared to previous forms of exile. The limit on the length of the exile and the protection of property and status that were provided to victims of ostracism removed the incentives for elites to attempt to overthrow the political order through violence. If we now turn from the form of exile imposed by an ostracism to the procedures for holding one, we can identify further indications of its moderate character, in clear contrast to archaic politics of exile.

As we have seen, the procedure involved an initial vote as to whether to hold an ostracism, followed several months later by the vote of ostracism itself if the first vote was affirmative. A number of scholars have commented on the significance of the two-stage procedure. Some have suggested that the delay was a deliberate device to avoid rash decisions in the assembly:[87] others have suggested that the delay allowed time for collective informal deliberation on who should be ostracized and why, not to mention the opportunity for campaigning by politicians against their rivals.[88] Although our sources indicate that there was no provision for formal accusations and defense in the courts or assembly as part of the procedure of ostracism, the evidence for common accusations against particular politicians on ostraca and in comic drama is certainly one indirect indication that there was at least some informal debate about who should be ostracized.[89] We may imagine that this informal debate among citizens took place not only in the theater, but in private (domestic) and public settings (agoras) throughout Attica.[90]

Perhaps more significant for understanding the delay between the initial vote and the ostracism itself is that it allowed time for the word to spread that an ostracism would be held, and facilitated the gathering of a group of Athenians significantly larger than the number regularly attending the assembly. In this regard, it is noteworthy that ostracism required a minimum of six thousand votes in order to be valid. Since it is likely that fewer than this number regularly attended the assembly in the fifth century, it is clear that

---

[87] L. Hall 1989, 95.

[88] Brenne 1994, 13.

[89] [Andoc.] 4.3 comments that the procedure of ostracism allows for no prosecution or defense, and criticizes the procedure as contrary to the laws of the democracy.

[90] On the informal transfer of information among the Athenian populace, see Hunter 1990, 1994; S. Lewis 1996.

the procedure of ostracism aimed to ensure the widest possible participation in the decision of exile.[91] The fact that ostracisms were held in the agora and not in the assembly, which could accommodate only about six thousand citizens in the fifth century, further confirms this fact. Finally, the conduct of the ostracism before the eighth prytany (early March) may also been intended to ensure a high turnout, since this period corresponds to a low point in the agricultural year.[92]

These various provisions for widespread popular participation helped to recreate in symbolic terms the conditions of the popular revolution of 508/7, when the Athenians en masse asserted their control over decisions of exile. More important, these provisions were a further mechanism by which the power of exile was moderated and thus distinguished from intra-elite politics of exile. The provisions for widespread participation in an ostracism ensured that democratic power over exile was exercised only when a significant number of Athenians thought it necessary. In contrast to intra-elite politics of exile, the participation of a large group of Athenians was required to make a vote of exile valid. Furthermore, the provision for broad participation prevented small groups of Athenians from manipulating the vote to ensure the expulsion of their rivals. The common idea that ostracism was manipulated by particular elite leaders in order to get rid of their rivals, therefore, ignores the ways in which its procedure was designed to facilitate maximum participation and avoid just such manipulation.

It is perhaps worth drawing a parallel here between the procedure for ostracism and the procedures for the constitution of the popular courts. As Victor Bers has recently stressed, the elaborate procedures by which the Athenians were selected to serve on juries cannot be explained wholly by the desire to avoid bribery and other types of corruption. Rather, Bers suggests that the rigmarole of the courts, with its jurors' ballots, sortition machines, colored sticks, and matching lintels over the courtroom doors, was part of an elaborate civic ritual that by its ceremonial aspect helped to increase the authority of the courts as well as alleviate anxiety about the potential for corruption.[93] Similarly, the elaborate procedures of ostracism must have contributed to its ritual and symbolic significance. First of all, the two-stage process, as well as the location in the agora, was designed to facilitate widespread participation, and would therefore have marked off the occasion from an ordinary assembly meeting. Second, the procedures for conducting the actual ostracism would have further enhanced the ritual significance of the event. As we have seen, on the day of the ostracism a section of the agora was cordoned off, and ten entrances were made. As the mass of Athenians filed into the ten entrances by

[91] On assembly attendance in the fifth century, see Hansen 1983, 1–23.

[92] See n. 10 above.

[93] Bers 2000. Cf. R. Osborne 1994b, 4–6, on the ritualization of political and legal procedures under the Athenian democracy.

tribe and deposited their ostraca, they were overseen by the archons and the members of the council. The visual spectacle of the ostracism would have elevated the occasion to one of high ritual and symbolic significance. Thus the procedure itself can be seen as a means of enhancing the symbolism of the Athenian masses as arbiters of decisions of exile.

So far we have seen that the procedures of ostracism were designed both to moderate the use of democratic power over decisions of exile and to increase the symbolic importance of the occasion. One final observation illustrates the moderate and symbolic nature of democratic ostracism: the infrequency with which the Athenians made use of the power of expulsion. We know of ten reasonably certain instances of the actual expulsion of an individual through ostracism in the course of the almost two centuries that the institution was in force.[94] Indeed, the Athenians held the first ostracism fully nineteen years after the law was first enacted.[95] Moreover, they rarely held ostracisms through-out the fifth century and never held any ostracisms at all in the fourth. Whether as a result of the effectiveness of the deterrent value of the existence of the institution, or as a result of the requirements for maximum participation or of the Athenians' own sense that the institution was largely symbolic in function, it is clear that the Athenian democracy used the power of expulsion much more moderately than the elite regimes that had preceded it (and indeed, than the oligarchic regimes that followed it, as we shall see).

There are important consequences of the democracy's infrequent use of the power of expulsion. First, we should note that even though the Athenians did not actually ostracize anyone in most years, the question of whether an os-tracism should be held continued to be asked each year in the sixth prytany. Indeed, even in the late fourth century, long after the last known instance of ostracism in 415, the question of whether to hold an ostracism was asked each year in the assembly.[96] The continued importance of the question suggests that one rationale for the two-stage procedure was to allow the annual sym-bolic expression of popular power through the annual question, without ne-cessitating the actual holding of an ostracism. The question alone served the function of recalling non-elite power over decisions of exile, and ultimately of

[94] This number includes the two ostracisms of Megacles (486, 471), which are now generally accepted: cf. Brenne 2001, 27. Historians are uncertain about the dates and historicity of our sources' claims of additional ostracisms of Alcibiades the Elder (Lys. 14.29), Menon (Hsch. s.v. Μενωνίδαι), Callias son of Didymias ([Andoc.] 4.32), and Damon (Arist. *Ath. Pol.* 27.4; Plut. *Per.* 4, *Nic.* 6, *Arist.* 1). For the ostracism of Damon, see Wallace 1994, accepting its historicity; Raaflaub 2003b, rejecting it.

[95] For this reason, ancients and moderns have posited—incorrectly in my view—that the institution was established only in the 480s, when it was first used. See appendix 1 below for the arguments.

[96] Arist. *Ath. Pol.* 43.5. For arguments against the view that in the fourth century the law of ostracism was replaced by the procedure for prosecuting unconstitutional proposals, see n. 139 below.

recalling the historical basis of non-elite power, namely the people's ability to determine the outcome of intra-elite conflict over political power.[97] Apparently, in most years, the question of whether to hold an ostracism alone was enough to deter elites from engaging in violent conflict over the political leadership of the polis.

Second, the infrequency with which the Athenians resorted to expelling an individual by vote of ostracism would have decreased the threat of a disgruntled group of exiles gathering together to attempt to make a return by force. Just as the procedural limitation of ostracism to one individual per year avoided the destabilizing consequences of the mass expulsions of intra-elite conflict, so the democracy's infrequent resort to actual ostracism decreased the threat of violent overthrow by large groups of exiles and their foreign allies. Indeed, as a corollary to my argument that intra-elite politics of exile destabilized the archaic polis, I would argue that the assumption of power over decisions of exile by the Athenian people as a whole, and their moderate and limited use of this power as exemplified in the institution of ostracism, stabilized the democratic polis. Similarly, just as Pisistratus had stabilized his regime by not banishing his rivals from the polis, so the infrequent resort of the Athenian people to banishment as a solution to political conflict ensured the stability of the democracy. As we shall see in chapter 6, the stabilizing effect of the infrequent use of exile was buttressed by the use of ostracism as a symbol of democratic moderation in the ideology of the democracy. The ideological importance of democratic moderation was especially important following the oligarchic revolutions of the late fifth century, which provided a clear example of the association between violent mass expulsions, the unjust use of power, and the instability of a political regime. (See below, "Exile and the Oligarchic Revolutions of 411 and 404.")

Ostracisms in Fifth-Century Athens

I have argued that ostracism was a largely symbolic institution designed to deter intra-elite competition by recalling the historical relation between exile and political power, particularly at the moment of the democratic revolution of 508/7. In the last section, furthermore, I argued that ostracism was highly effective, and that the Athenians seldom made use of their power over decisions of exile. Yet there were ten instances in the fifth century when ostracisms were actually held, and it is worth asking what these events can tell us about the role of ostracism under the Athenian democracy. Unfortunately, the evidence for the circumstances of the known instances of ostracism is

---

[97] Rosivach (1987a, 163) and Christ (1992) both note the symbolic significance of the question for the Athenian democracy.

slight. Nevertheless, a case can be made that in a number of these instances, conflict between rival elite leaders was particularly intense, and hence the Athenians felt the need to make use of their power of expulsion to diffuse the crisis and remind elites of non-elite power to determine the outcome of intra-elite conflict.

Ostracism was first used, and used most frequently, in the 480s. Between 487 and 482 no fewer than five persons were ostracized, a number equal to half the certain instances of the use of ostracism. The frequency of the use of ostracism in this decade may itself indicate that the city was undergoing a particularly intense period of political strife. Unfortunately, the decade between Marathon and Salamis is one of the most obscure in classical Greek history.[98] After a brief discussion of some later ostracisms for which the circumstances are marginally better known, therefore, I shall return to the earlier cases.

The first ostracism for which the circumstances may be elucidated is the ostracism of Aristides son of Lysimachus, in 482. Our sources are unanimous in reporting a strong rivalry between Aristides and Themistocles in the years before the Persian invasion of 480/79.[99] We know of several issues that came before the people in these years, and Themistocles and Aristides may have advocated rival policies in regard to them. One important issue was what to do with the money from the publicly owned mines at Maronea.[100] Another was the on-going hostilities between Athens and Aegina.[101] Themistocles proposed that the money be used to build ships to prosecute the war with Aegina.[102] The evidence points to the likelihood that Aristides opposed this policy, since he seems to have spent his period in exile on Aegina, and one ostracon accuses him of hostility toward a group of suppliants, who may have been fugitives from Aegina living in Athenian territory.[103]

These pieces of evidence together suggest that Themistocles and Aristides vied with one another for leadership of the polis. Herodotus in fact says that the rivalry between these two politicians was tied to personal animosity and hatred: "Themistocles was no friend of Aristides, but in fact a great enemy

---

[98] Badian (1971, 1) remarks: "There are—at least in internal history—practically no facts known." This is an exaggeration, and many scholars have tried to piece together the few known events of this period into a picture of internal politics. Cf. Knight 1970, Badian 1971, Karavites 1971; more recently, Rausch 1999, G. Anderson 2003.

[99] Hdt. 8.79; Plut. *Them.* 3.1–3, *Arist.* 2–3; Arist. *Ath. Pol.* 23.3, 28.2.

[100] Hdt. 7.144, Arist. *Ath. Pol.* 22.7, Harp. s.v. Μαρώνεια, Plut. *Them.* 4.1–3, Dem. 37.4.

[101] Hdt. 7.144.1, 145.1; Plut. *Them.* 4.1. See Figueira 1991, 1993.

[102] Hdt. 7.144, Arist. *Ath. Pol.* 22.7, Plut. *Them.* 4.1.

[103] Aristides resided in Aegina after his ostracism: [Dem.] 26.6; *Suda* s.v.v. Ἀριστείδης, Δαρεικούς; Aristodemus, *FGrH* 104 F 1.1.4; Hdt. 8.79.1; Plut. *Arist.* 8.2; schol. Ael. 46.194, 3:613 Dindorf. Cf. Figueira 1987, 291–94. Ostracon recording Aristides' harshness toward suppliants: Lang 44.

[ἐχθρὸν δὲ τὰ μάλιστα, 8.79.2]." Such language evokes the kind of intense private and public competition between elite leaders that often resulted in the outbreak of violent politics of exile in the archaic period. Under these circumstances, therefore, it is perhaps not surprising that the Athenians chose to hold an ostracism in order to diffuse the conflict and assert their own power to determine the leadership of the polis. In 482, an ostracism was held at which Aristides received the majority of votes.[104]

We also know something of the circumstances surrounding the ostracism of Cimon in 461. As in the case of Aristides' ostracism, it appears that Cimon was ostracized in conditions of potentially violent conflict between rival elites. Our sources record the conflict between Cimon and Ephialtes in the late 460s.[105] In 462, the Spartans had called on Athens for help against the helots and perioikoi, who had revolted.[106] Cimon argued strongly for helping the Spartans while Ephialtes opposed helping Sparta.[107] Cimon's view carried the day, and Cimon himself was sent to lead the Athenian forces against the rebels.[108] While Cimon was absent, however, Ephialtes and his supporters, including Pericles, passed a program of political reforms removing certain powers from the elite council known as the Areopagus and gave them to the democratic Council of Five Hundred, the assembly, and the courts.[109] When Cimon returned from Sparta, he opposed these reforms and tried to have them repealed.[110]

As in the case of Aristides and Themistocles, the different public policies pursued by Cimon and Ephialtes may reflect an underlying personal animosity. This hostility between the leaders is perhaps evident in the fact that in 463, Ephialtes' associate Pericles attempted (unsuccessfully) to prosecute Cimon for his conduct in office.[111] More strikingly, shortly after Cimon's ostracism, Ephialtes was mysteriously murdered.[112] It is possible, therefore, that even before Cimon's ostracism, the conflict had the potential to break out into a violent confrontation between the elite leaders and their supporters. Indeed, Aeschylus, in his play *Eumenides*, performed in 458, makes a plea for civic harmony, which apparently had not been fully achieved by Cimon's ostracism. Following a speech by Athena in which the goddess

[104] Arist. *Ath. Pol.* 22.8, Plut. *Arist.* 7.2.

[105] Arist. *Ath. Pol.* 28.2, Plut. *Per.* 9.4.

[106] Thuc. 1.102, Plut. *Cim.* 16.8, Diod. Sic. 11.63.

[107] Plut. *Cim.* 16.8–9. Plutarch's use of a quotation from the fifth-century playwright Ion of Chios (*FGrH* 392 F 14) makes it likely that his report of a fierce debate in Athens over whether to help Sparta is historical.

[108] Thuc. 1.102.

[109] Arist. *Ath. Pol.* 25.1–2; Philoch. *FGrH* 328 F 64b; Diod. Sic. 11.77.6; Plut. *Cim.* 10.8, 15.2.

[110] Plut. *Cim.* 15.3, 17.3; *Per.* 9.5.

[111] Arist. *Ath. Pol.* 27.1; Plut. *Per.* 10.6, *Cim.* 14.3–5. On the courts as a forum for the pursuit of personal feuds between elites, see R. Osborne 1985b, D. Cohen 1995.

[112] Arist. *Ath. Pol.* 25.5, Plut. *Per.* 10.7–8, Antiph. 5.68, Diod. Sic. 11.77.6.

attempts to instill respect for the Court of the Areopagus (a major bone of contention in Ephialtes' reforms), the chorus sings (976–86):

τὰν δ' ἄπληστον κακῶν
μήποτ' ἐν πόλει Στάσιν
τᾷ ἐπεύχομαι βρέμειν,
μηδὲ πιοῦσα κόνις μέλαν αἷμα πολιτᾶν
δι' ὀργὰν ποινὰς
ἀντιφόνους Ἄτας
ἁρπαλίσαι πόλεως,
χάρματα δ' ἀντιδιδοῖεν
κοινοφιλεῖ διανοίᾳ
καὶ στυγεῖν μιᾷ φρενί.

I pray that Civil War, insatiable in its desire for evils,
never rages in this city
and that the thirsty earth does not snatch from the city
the dark blood of citizens
because of the anger of Atē, the avenger;
but instead let them give joy in return
with mutually loving thought,
and let them hate with one mind.

The circumstances surrounding the ostracism of Cimon, therefore, are our clearest indication that ostracisms were held at times when there was the threat of violent conflict. The evidence suggests, in fact, that the ostracism of Cimon was only partially successful in defusing the crisis. Besides Ephialtes' murder and the evidence of Aeschylus's *Eumenides*, Thucydides (1.107.4) briefly mentions a plot to overthrow the democracy in 457. Although the plot was unsuccessful, it does seem to indicate that there was a potential for violent political conflict in this period, and even for the violent overthrow of the political order by disgruntled elites and their foreign allies.

Briefly, we might also consider the next use of ostracism, against Thucydides son of Melesias in 442 or slightly later.[113] Our sources report that Thucydides was the successor of Cimon in the leadership of a group of elites who opposed the policies of Pericles and his associates.[114] Among other policy differences, Plutarch reports that these two leaders clashed over the issue of the expenditure of the funds of the Delian League.[115] Plutarch in fact suggests that the rivalry between Thucydides and Pericles was so intense that it caused a deep rift in the city between the "party of the few" and the "party of the people." Although Plutarch probably depends for his analysis on

[113] See n. 31 above for the debate about the date of Thucydides' ostracism.
[114] Arist. *Ath. Pol.* 28.2, Plut. *Per.* 11.3.
[115] Plut. *Per.* 12.1–4, 14.1.

fourth-century sources, which tended to simplify earlier Athenian history according to a bipolar schema of democrats and oligarchs, it is not unlikely that in the 440s a major division arose between those who preferred a more conservative direction in politics and those who followed a more radical democratic path.[116] Plutarch, in fact, uses the vivid metaphor of a fault in a piece of iron to describe the rift (τομή) in the city caused by the rivalry (ἅμιλλα, φιλοτιμία) of these men. A fragment of the contemporary comic poet Cratinus, moreover, confirms that the rivalry between Pericles and Thucydides led to a substantial division among the people, since it suggests that Pericles only narrowly escaped being ostracized himself:[117]

> ὁ σχινοκέφαλος Ζεὺς ὅδε προσέρχεται
> ⟨ὁ⟩ Περικλέης τῳδεῖον ἐπὶ τοῦ κρανίου
> ἔχων, ἐπειδὴ τοὔστρακον παροίχεται.

This pointy-headed Zeus,
Pericles, goes forth with the Odeon on his head
since the ostracon has passed him by.

It was therefore under conditions of strong division and political conflict between rival elite politicians that the Athenians decided to hold the ostracism by which Thucydides the son of Melesias was exiled. Although there is no direct evidence that violence was imminent, the emergence of a strong division between the supporters of Pericles and those of Thucydides may have given rise to fears of violent conflict. The ostracism of Thucydides, however, appears to have defused the conflict, and deterred violent action. Indeed, following the ostracism, Pericles enjoyed uncontested leadership for over a decade.[118] Evidently the ostracism helped unite the citizens behind Pericles' leadership and allowed an internally unified Athens to consolidate its power in Greece. The unity of Athens under Pericles is reflected in the historian Thucydides' account of this period, which (albeit for ideological reasons) he contrasts so sharply with the period after Pericles' death.[119]

In sum, the circumstances of the ostracisms of Aristides, Cimon, and Thucydides suggest that ostracism was used in times of particularly intense political conflict between rival political leaders and their supporters. By holding an ostracism to temporarily remove one leader from the community, the

---

[116] For the bipolar model of politics in fourth-century sources, see especially Arist. *Ath. Pol.* 28.

[117] Kassel-Austin, *PCG*, Cratinus F 73 (= Plut. *Per.* 13.10). The fact that we possess only four ostraca against Pericles (Brenne 2001, 260–61) as opposed to sixty-seven against Thucydides (Brenne 2001, 302–3) is no hindrance to the view that the vote was close. Only a small fraction of the total number of votes at any given ostracism has been recovered, and therefore the known ostraca are unrepresentative samples.

[118] Plut. *Per.* 15.1.

[119] Thuc. 2.35–46, 65.

Athenians resolved a potentially violent conflict between elite leaders and reminded elites as a whole of non-elite power to determine the outcome of intra-elite strife. Two points are worth clarifying concerning the analysis so far. Our literary sources (particularly Plutarch) stress conflict between two elite leaders, usually the heads of oligarchic and democratic parties, as the context of the ostracisms of the fifth century. As already pointed out, the simplification of the situation into a struggle between democratic and oligarchic parties is probably a result of the influence of fourth-century politics and theory. The ostraca, moreover, demonstrate that votes were cast against several candidates at any one ostracism (the so-called scatter vote). It is important, therefore, to recognize that the political scene at the time of any known ostracism was probably much more complicated than we can hope to reconstruct. In all likelihood, there were a number of elite politicians who formed and reformed alliances with one another over an ever-changing series of issues as they struggled to maximize their personal influence in the state.

Similarly, it is important to stress that the interpretation of the political conditions leading to an ostracism presented above is not meant to imply that ostracism was primarily a means of deciding on a particular political issues, whether Athenian policy toward Sparta or the use of the funds of the Delian League.[120] Although the expulsion of a particular elite leader may have had the secondary effect of confirming the policies of his chief rival, this was not the primary motivation for the ostracism. Rather, ostracism was invoked at times of particularly intense competition between elite leaders, when the conflict threatened to dissolve into violence, which might overturn the institutional and ideological basis of the democracy. In these circumstances, the Athenian people made use of the institution of ostracism to diffuse the crisis by temporarily exiling one elite leader. The expulsion of an elite leader by the people served as a vivid reminder of the historical basis of popular power and, in particular, the people's ability to determine the outcome of intra-elite competition.

Further support for this interpretation of ostracism can be found in the last instance of the use of ostracism, that of Hyperbolus in 415.[121] The literary sources for this ostracism, however, are as complex as they are plentiful. We may dismiss the first problem with the sources, namely the contradiction over who were the principal candidates for the ostracism, Nicias and Alcibiades or Phaeax and Alcibiades.[122] This disagreement may be explained as the result of

---

[120] As in the interpretation of Ostwald 1988, 344–46.

[121] For recent discussion of the date of Hyperbolus's ostracism, see Heftner 2000b.

[122] Theophrastus fr. 139 states that the rivalry was between Alcibiades and Phaeax, but Plut. *Nic.* 11.7 reports that most of the sources agree that it was Alcibiades and Nicias who were the leading rivals and candidates for the people's support: cf. *Alcib.* 13.4, *Arist.* 7. [Andoc.] 4.2 and Plut. *Alcib.* 13.4, by contrast, acknowledge that there were three leading candidates for ostracism. See *HCT* 4:287 and Rhodes 1994, 93, for the view that the major candidates for ostracism were Alcibiades and Nicias. *Contra*: Mattingly 1991, 24.

later sources' attempts to fit the evidence for the ostracism into an anachro-nistic and unnecessarily simplistic bipolar model of political conflict.[123] (See above.) The evidence of ostraca and literary sources suggests that all three men, as well as several other figures, including the voters' ultimate choice, Hyperbolus, and another leading politician, Cleophon, were prominent pol-iticians and therefore serious candidates for the ostracism.[124]

A more substantial problem for our understanding of this ostracism is the view of our sources that the expulsion of Hyperbolus represented a misuse of the institution and that this fact explains why Hyperbolus was the last Athenian ever ostracized.[125] In brief, our sources claim that Alcibiades and Nicias (or Phaeax) were the leading candidates at the ostracism, but that these politicians joined forces and conspired with their supporters to ensure that a third, lesser figure, Hyperbolus, was ostracized instead. According to our sour-ces, the Athenians viewed this result as a misuse of the institution both because Hyperbolus did not belong to the traditional landed elite who were the usual victims of ostracism, and because the will of the people had been thwarted by elite politicians.[126]

Several contemporary sources do in fact affirm that there was something unusual about the ostracism of Hyperbolus. Thucydides notes that Hy-perbolus was ostracized not on the usual grounds of fear of his power and reputation (διὰ δυνάμεως καὶ ἀξιώματος), but because he was a scoundrel and a great shame to the city (διὰ πονηρίαν καὶ αἰσχύνην τῆς πόλεως, 8.73.3). Furthermore, as we have seen already, the comic poet Plato used the elite status of most victims of ostracism as the basis for a joke about Hy-perbolus, who, he suggested, gained undeserved honor by being ostracized.[127] It is noteworthy, however, that these contemporary sources say nothing about the alleged manipulation of the vote of ostracism by Alcibiades and Nicias. Indeed, this interpretation appears only in Plutarch, a relatively late source. A case can therefore be made that Plutarch (or more likely his fourth-century sources) developed the story of the manipulation of the vote of ostracism in

---

[123] Compare Heftner 2000a, who sees the disagreement in the sources as a product of later attempts to explain the "surprising" result of the ostracism.

[124] We have ostraca (albeit few) against all five of these figures: eight against Cleophon, five each against Alcibiades and Phaeax, four against Hyperbolus, and one against Nicias: cf. the chart in Brenne 2002a, 47, 55, 59, 64, 66. On the evidence for the prominent status of each of these men, see below.

[125] Modern historians have accepted the ancient interpretation: cf. Rhodes 1994.

[126] Plut. Alcib. 13.4, Arist. 7.3–4, Nic. 11. The latter reason for the Athenians' view that the institution had been abused is never stated explicitly, but it is implicit in the logic of the anecdote, in which the scheming by Alcibiades and Nicias is considered irregular. According to Plut. Alcib. 13.4 and Nic. 11.4, Hyperbolus initiated the ostracism. Plut. Nic. 11.1 states only that the conflict between Alcibiades and Nicias was so intense that an ostracism was held.

[127] Kassel-Austin, PCG, Plato Com. fr. 203, quoted above. See also Androtion, FGrH 324 F 42, stating that Hyperbolus was ostracized on account of his base character (διὰ φαυλότητα).

415 on the basis of the alleged low social origins of Hyperbolus, the observation that Hyperbolus's ostracism was the last held, and traditions about
Alcibiades' wily character. I will first take up these points, before turning to
further evidence that makes it unlikely that Hyperbolus's ostracism was a
product of elite manipulation, or that this was the reason for the failure of the
Athenians ever to hold another.

It has often been observed that the characterization of such figures as Cleon,
Hyperbolus, and Cleophon as base wretches (πονηροί) reflects a late fifth-
century ideological conflict and does not describe the actual social status of
these men,[128] who were in fact quite wealthy. What distinguished them from
the traditional ruling elite, however, was the fact that their wealth was derived
from industrial activities rather than land. Furthermore, the influence of men
such as Hyperbolus in politics was relatively recently acquired in comparison
to the members of the traditional landed elite. Hyperbolus's wealth, for example, was derived from lamp making, and he is the first (and only) member
of his family known to have held public office.[129] It was the increasing influence of these industrial elites that produced the strong reaction in our
sources for this period, primarily Thucydides and the comic poets. These
sources reflect the attempt of the landed elite to characterize themselves as the
good (χρηστοί) leaders, while denigrating their opponents as πονηροί — that
is, unscrupulous arrivistes who sacrificed the common good for their own
personal advancement.[130] Cleon, Hyperbolus, and Cleophon are even labeled
foreigners and slaves in the comic sources, despite clear evidence to the
contrary.[131] The ostraca, for example, have revealed that Hyperbolus's father
had the "good Attic name of Antiphanes."[132]

Despite the ideological origins of the characterization of Hyperbolus as a
base wretch (πονηρός), our later sources used this purported fact to explain his
ostracism. Noting that previous victims of ostracism had belonged to the
traditional landed elite, these sources inferred that the ostracism of Hyperbolus was the anomalous result of the intrigues of that same traditional
elite. This explanation was facilitated by the fact that one of the potential candidates for the ostracism was Alcibiades, who both belonged to the

[128] For a recent discussion of the ideological construct of the conflict of πονηροί and
χρηστοί, see Rosenbloom 2002. On Cleon, see Davies, APF 8674. On Cleophon, see Brenne
2001, 200. For Hyperbolus, see n. 129 below.

[129] Andoc. fr. 3.2 Maidment; Ar. Eq. 1304, 1315; Davies, APF 13910. Hyperbolus was probably
a councilor in 421/0 and served also as trierarch at around this time: Ar. Thesm. 837; with Davies,
APF 13910.

[130] See, for example, Thucydides' characterization of the post-Periclean leaders of Athens
(2.65) and especially his representation of Cleon (3.37–48). For the comic evidence, see Rosenbloom 2002. Cf. also Isoc. 8.75.

[131] For accusations of the foreign origins and servile birth of Hyperbolus, cf. Andoc. fr. 5
Maidment (= schol. Ar. Vesp. 1007); Kassel-Austin, PCG, Plato Com. fr. 203.

[132] Davies, APF 13910. For the ostraca, see Lang 308, 309.

traditional elite and was an especially clever politician. On the basis of Hyperbolus's status as a πονηρός, and Alcibiades' reputation for cleverness, the ostracism of the one was explained as the result of the other's intrigues with his fellow landed elites in order to avoid expulsion.[133] Yet as we have seen, Cleon, Hyperbolus, and Cleophon were prominent politicians, who were credible candidates for ostracism in their own right. Aristophanes himself apparently did not consider these men inappropriate candidates for ostracism, since he seems to have advocated the ostracism of Cleon in 424.[134] The evidence of the ostraca, moreover, suggests that Cleophon, another supposed base wretch, was also a serious candidate for the ostracism of 415. Although extant ostraca may not be representative of the actual number of votes against a candidate, it is perhaps significant that more have been found against Cleophon than against any of the other known candidates for this ostracism.[135] The candidacy and selection of Hyperbolus, therefore, should not be considered anomalous or a misuse of the institution. Rather, his candidacy, and that of other politicians from the so-called industrial elite, reflects the changing socio-economic origins of the leaders of the Athenian democracy in the second half of the fifth century.[136]

Further objections can be raised against our sources' explanation of Hyperbolus's ostracism as a result of elite manipulation and a misuse of the institution. First, as we have noted, although there is some evidence for organized campaigns against particular politicians, the preponderance of the evidence suggests that most Athenians voted independently.[137] Moreover, the procedure of ostracism required the participation of a minimum of six thousand Athenians. With such mass participation, it would have been difficult for elites, even if they combined their supporters, to ensure the outcome of the vote. The evidence for organized interest groups and parties in late fifth- and fourth-century assembly meetings, furthermore, does not prove that such blocs as these could determine the outcome of an ostracism.[138] As has already been noted, the average assembly meeting was smaller than the minimum number of necessary participants in an ostracism, and in any event the procedure of

---

[133] This interpretation of our sources' explanations is perhaps strengthened by the confusion over whether Nicias or Phaeax was the other elite candidate for the ostracism. The story implies collusion between Alcibiades and the other elite candidate, and Nicias was singularly inappropriate for such intrigue, since he had a reputation for honesty and selfless devotion to Athens: cf. Thuc. 7.86.5, Plut. *Nic.* 14. Nicias's inappropriateness for the role of Alcibiades' co-conspirator may explain why some sources proposed that Phaeax, and not Nicias, played this role.

[134] Ar. *Eq.* 819, 855–57; with Scheidel 2002, 483–84.

[135] For ostraca against Cleophon, see n. 125 above.

[136] See Connor 1971 on these "new politicians."

[137] Hoards of prepared ostraca number only in the hundreds: see n. 15 above.

[138] The evidence for organized political groups in the assembly, council, and courts is summarized by Rhodes 1994, 93. Hansen (1983, 220–22, 1987, 72–86; 1991, 283–87) argues that even in the assembly, elite leaders could not control the votes of their supporters.

ostracism did not allow for a formal debate in the assembly on the question of whom to ostracize. The absence of debate deprived elite speakers of the influence they might have over a large body of voters in the assembly. The only possible forum for influencing a large number of voters at an ostracism was the comic theater, but this would have been an indirect means at best, since, although elites provided funding for the comic performances, there is little evidence of their control over the content of the dramas.

A final objection to the view that Hyperbolus's ostracism was a misuse of the institution is the fact that this view is at least partly dependent on the post-facto observation that Hyperbolus's ostracism was the last use of the institution. It is highly doubtful that the Athenians of 415 recognized that this would be the last ostracism. As we have seen, the Athenians rarely held ostracisms in the fifth century. A gap of a decade or more between ostracisms would not have led the Athenians to consider the institution dead. More important, the Athenians never repealed the law of ostracism and in fact continued during the fourth century to ask the question of whether to hold an ostracism each year. The annual question suggests that the Athenians considered ostracism an active possibility throughout the duration of the democracy. Their failure to hold an ostracism, moreover, can be explained by the largely symbolic function of the institution, as I have already discussed.[139]

If we abandon the view that the ostracism of Hyperbolus was a misuse of the process and that the institution was discontinued for that reason, we may now consider other factors that may explain why the Athenians held an ostracism in 415. Once again, we find evidence for strong conflict between rival elite leaders, this time over Athenian policy toward Sicily.[140] Alcibiades advocated invasion and conquest. Nicias (probably supported by Phaeax) seems to have proposed a less aggressive policy. In Thucydides' portrayal of the debate between these politicians, the conflict is framed not only in terms of differences of policy, but also in personal terms.[141] This suggests a personal animosity between the two men, akin to what we have already observed in the circumstances of Aristides' rivalry with Themistocles, and Cimon's with Ephialtes. Although Thucydides presents the debate as a conflict between these two men and makes no mention of Hyperbolus and Cleophon in it, the prominence of these latter two in comedy, as well as their appearance

---

[139] If the arguments presented above are accepted, then Hansen's view (1991, 205–12) that the Athenians consciously replaced ostracism with the procedure for prosecuting unconstitutional decrees (γραφὴ παρανόμων) in 415 is untenable. The overlap between the role of ostracism as a weapon against the political leaders and the procedure of γραφὴ παρανόμων can be explained by the open texture of Athenian law, by which there were multiple mechanisms for prosecuting a single offense: cf. R. Osborne 1985b.

[140] Thuc. 6.8–26; Plut. Nic. 11, Alcib. 17–18. Mattingly (1991, 24) also draws the connection between the debate over Sicily and the ostracism of 415.

[141] Thuc. 6.12.2, 16.1.

on the extant ostraca, suggest that they may also have played a role in the debate. In sum, it is likely that both landed and industrial elites exploited the issue of Athens' war policy to engage in intense rivalry with one another over the leadership of the polis.

In addition to the conflict over Athens' war policy, Alcibiades' personal character and style of leadership apparently raised fears of an oligarchic conspiracy.[142] Indeed, following the ostracism of Hyperbolus and the debate over Sicily, several unusual incidents involving prominent elite youths were interpreted as threats to the democratic order. During one night following the decision to invade Sicily, the herms (statues of Hermes in public and private spaces throughout the city) were mutilated. Furthermore, it was reported that the secret rites of the Eleusinian Mysteries were being parodied in private performances among elite youths.[143] Fears ran high that Alcibiades and others were plotting the violent overthrow of the democracy, and as a result, Alcibiades was recalled from his command of the Athenian forces to stand trial in Athens.[144]

The aftermath of Hyperbolus's ostracism shows that intra-elite rivalry and threats to the democratic order were prominent concerns at that time. It is likely that these conditions lay behind the decision to hold an ostracism in 415. In these circumstances, the conduct of an ostracism would have served as a symbolic reminder of non-elite power, in particular the people's power to determine the outcome of intra-elite conflict. It is important to emphasize, however, that the ostracism of 415 was not held in order to decide Athenian policy toward Sicily (that was the role of the assembly), or to avert the threat of an oligarchic conspiracy (that was the role of the courts, as shown by Alcibiades' recall to stand trial). Rather, the ostracism of 415 was enacted as a symbolic reminder of power of the people in a time of particularly intense conflict over the leadership and political organization of the polis.

If we now turn back to the ostracisms for which the circumstances are less clear, we may imagine that in each of these instances (487, 486, 485, 484, 471, 470) there existed a situation of potentially violent conflict between elite leaders. Besides the larger context of the threat from Persia, the frequency of ostracisms in the 480s itself suggests that this was a particularly difficult time in the polis's history. No less than five ostracisms—half the total number ever held—occurred in this decade. Aristotle tells us that Hipparchus was

---

[142] Thuc. 6.15–17, 28.

[143] Thuc. 6.27–28. Recent good studies of the affairs of the herms and of the Mysteries include R. Osborne 1985c; Murray 1990b; Winkler 1990; Furley 1996; McGlew 1999; Wohl 1999, 2002.

[144] Thuc. 6.28, 53, 60–61. Rosenbloom (2002, 333) connects the ostracism of Hyperbolus with the prosecutions following the mutilation of the herms and the profanation of the Mysteries. For Rosenbloom, both events were mechanisms for pursuing the on-going conflict between traditional elites and the newer industrial elites. On Alcibiades and Athenian democracy, see most recently Gribble 1999; Wohl 1999, 2002.

ostracized in 487 and was followed by Megacles in 486, an unnamed "friend of the tyrants" in 485, Xanthippus in 484, and Aristides in 482.[145]

A more important indication of intra-elite rivalry is the change in the method of selecting archons that was passed in 487/6.[146] We have already seen that Solon introduced a new method for selecting archons in an attempt to deter violent conflict for political office among elites.[147] By Solon's new procedure, ten candidates for office were elected in each tribe, and then the nine archons were chosen by lot from these. I argued above in chapter 3 that by using the lot to determine which of the elected candidates should be chosen, Solon sought to dampen violent opposition between a few powerful elites over political office. This two-stage process for the selection of archons appears to have fallen into disuse under the Pisistratid tyranny, if not before.[148] In 487/6, this process was reinstituted, and we may surmise that, as in the time of Solon, intense rivalry between elites may have prompted its reintroduction.[149]

The reform of 487/6 may therefore reflect conditions of intense intra-elite rivalry and help to explain the ostracisms of the 480s. Similar conditions may have prevailed at the end of the 470s, when two ostracisms were held in successive years (Megacles in 471, Themistocles in 470). In this case, however, there is some scant evidence that the members of Megacles' family, the Alcmeonidae, formed one group, which may have been opposed to another elite group, possibly led by Themistocles. This argument is based primarily on the evidence for the scatter vote at the ostracism of Megacles in 471, which includes a number of relatives and associates of the family of the Alcmeo-

[145] Arist. *Ath. Pol.* 22.4. It used to be thought that Callias was the unnamed victim of ostracism in 485 (e.g., Rhodes, *CAAP* 276). This theory has been disproved by the downdating to 471 of the Megacles ostraca from the "grosse Kerameikosfund," since there are joins between these ostraca and those cast against Callias (Brenne 2001, 179–80).

[146] Arist. *Ath. Pol.* 22.5.

[147] On this measure, its aims, and the controversy over whether it was Solonian, see chapter 3 above.

[148] Cf. Arist. *Ath. Pol.* 22.5, which says that prior to the reform of 487 all archons were elected. Cf. *Pol.* 1273b35–1274a3, where Aristotle says that before Solon's reforms the archons were elected and that Solon did not change this procedure.

[149] For discussion of this reform, cf. Rhodes, *CAAP* 272–74; Hansen 1990a. Earlier important scholarship on this question includes Badian 1971, Develin 1979, Forrest and Stockton 1987. I agree with Rhodes (*CAAP* 274, *pace* Badian 1971) that the archonship was still an important office in this period, and that consequently the reform may be interpreted as a means of circumventing intra-elite conflict over these powerful positions. Hansen 1990a views the switch from election to selection by lot as a further means of democratizing the institutional structure of the polis, and thus denies the origins of this procedure in the archaic period. Hansen bases his argument on the clear association between sortition and democracy in our sources. In "Selection by Lot" (in prep. b), I suggest that selection by lot was in fact an archaic procedure, designed to circumvent intra-elite conflict over power, but was later appropriated by the democracy both as a means of arbitrating intra-elite conflict over public office and, more important, as an ideological symbol of equal access to political office.

nidae. The clearest case is that of Callias son of Cratius, who appears to have been a major candidate (based on the over seven hundred ostraca found against him), and who had connections to the Alcmeonidae.[150] Furthermore, one issue at the time of this ostracism may have been Alcmeonid ties with the Persians, since sixteen ostraca accuse Callias son of Cratius of Medism, and suspicions of Medism by the Alcmeonidae were circulating at this time.[151]

As for Themistocles, it is possible that he too was a leading candidate and principal rival of the Alcmeonids in 471, since he wielded great influence in Athens and in Greece generally following his successful leadership at Salamis.[152] His ostracism in the following year, 470, merely confirms his leading status. Herodotus makes clear that Themistocles had a number of political enemies (ἐχθροί) in Athens, and we may surmise that his great reputation further exacerbated his rivalry with other leading politicians.[153] Later sources, including Demosthenes and Plutarch, explain Themistocles' ostracism as a means of humbling a man who thought too much of himself.[154] This interpretation reflects the association between ostracism and democratic equality, which arises most strongly in the fourth century.[155] In the early fifth century, it is more likely that the cause of the ostracism of Themistocles was the envy of rival elites, which led to a situation that threatened to dissolve into violent confrontation and conflict.[156]

In sum, although the evidence is scanty and inconclusive, what little is known of the circumstances of the ten instances of ostracism in the fifth century is not incompatible with the view that ostracism was a means of resolving intra-elite conflict and asserting the fundamental power of the non-elites in the polis. According to this interpretation, ostracism served as a means of symbolizing non-elite power by recalling the historical connection between control over exile and political power, and in particular by reminding elites of the historical basis of non-elite rule, namely the people's decisive intervention in intra-elite politics in 508/7.

[150] For the Callias ostraca, see the chart in Brenne 2002a, 56. For Callias's connection to the Alcmeonids cf. Brenne 2001, 180. Other candidates at this ostracism with connections to the Alcmeonidae include Alcibiades the Elder, Megacles son of Callisthenes, Megacles Acharneus, and Xanthippus son of Hippocrates.

[151] Accusations of Medism against Callias son of Cratius: Brenne T1/46–61. In addition, ostraca from this ostracism against Habronichus (Brenne T1/41) and Leagrus (Brenne T1/71) explicitly mention treason. For Alcmeonid associations with the Persians in the aftermath of the Persian Wars, see above. It is somewhat surprising, however, and perhaps a counter-argument to the suggestion made above, that none of the numerous ostraca against Megacles accuses him of Medism.

[152] Hdt. 8.110, 112, 123–25.

[153] Hdt. 8.125. Cf. Pind. Pyth. 7.18–21 on the envy (φθόνος) against Megacles for his Olympic victories.

[154] Dem. 23.204, Plut. Them. 22.4.

[155] See Rosivach 1987a; and chapter 6 below.

[156] Accusations of treason arose after Themistocles was ostracized (Thuc. 1.135.3) and should be distinguished from the reasons for his ostracism: see above.

Other Forms of Exile under the Athenian Democracy

A central element of my argument so far is the idea that the Athenian democracy was a particularly stable form of political organization in part because it utilized the power of expulsion with moderation. Yet a case could be made that, although exile through ostracism was a mild form of exile, and although the Athenians rarely ostracized anyone, the democracy used other means to banish its political opponents unjustly. Indeed, as we shall see in the next two chapters, critics of the Athenian democracy responded to democratic claims of moderation in the use of exile by suggesting that the Athenian democracy used the courts as a means of arbitrarily and unjustly exiling citizens. A brief review of the use of the penalty of exile in the Athenian courts is therefore necessary. I will argue that the Athenian democracy—in contrast to the oligarchic regimes that followed it—did not abuse the legal institutions of the state in order to banish its opponents.

Before making this argument, a few features of the Athenian judicial system must be delineated. Judicial penalties were handed down by the Athenian people in their capacities as councilors, assemblymen, and jurors.[157] Although there is scant evidence for the transfer of legal power from the elite magistrates and Areopagus Council to popular assemblies, it is likely that these changes took place shortly after the founding of the democracy.[158] At this time, it is likely that the Council of Five Hundred and the assembly took over the powers of hearing trials for attempted tyranny and other major crimes. Previously the Areopagus Council had jurisdiction in these cases. Also at about this same time, democratic courts were created to deal with other offenses that had previously been handled by the Areopagus and the elected magistrates. These courts were strengthened at the time of Ephialtes' reforms (462), when all powers of the Areopagus were removed except its jurisdiction in homicide cases.

Most serious offenses under the Athenian democracy were punishable by a range of penalties, including death, exile, or fine. For some offenses, the penalty was fixed. For example, intentional and unintentional homicide were punished by death and exile, respectively.[159] As we have seen already, attempted tyranny was punished by ἀτιμία, in the sense of outlawry or lifelong exile from

---

[157] The bibliography on the Athenian legal system under the democracy is enormous. For a brief overview, see MacDowell 1978. Recent important treatments include R. Osborne 1985b; Ober 1989a; Hansen 1991; D. Cohen 1993, 1995; Todd 1993; Hunter 1994; Christ 1998; Johnstone 1999; Hunter and Edmonson 2000. For a sophisticated analysis of Athenian attitudes toward punishment, see Allen 2000.

[158] For an overview of the historical development of the courts, cf. Harrison 1971, 1–68; MacDowell 1978, 24–40. For recent discussion, cf. Hansen 1975, 1978, 1982, 1989b; Ostwald 1986, 47–77; Carawan 1987.

[159] Draco's law on homicide (see above, chapter 3) was republished in 409/8 during the revision of the laws that took place from 410 to 404; cf. van Effenterre 1994, 16.

the community.[160] After the oligarchic revolution of 411, moreover, attempted tyranny was expanded to include attempts to overthrow the democracy, for which the punishment was likewise ἀτιμία.[161] Treason was punished by death, although those suspected of treason often fled into exile before they could be apprehended and tried. In 508, Isagoras and his associates were condemned to death—probably on the ground of treason, since they brought a foreign army into the polis. Isagoras, however, apparently fled into exile and thus avoided punishment.[162] Similarly, Hipparchus, the first victim of ostracism, was condemned to death for treason sometime after 488/7, although he also fled into exile without waiting for a trial.[163] Finally, Themistocles fled a probable conviction and sentence of death for treason.[164]

Besides those crimes for which the penalty was fixed, there was a whole series of offenses for which the penalty was determined by vote of the jury between the alternative penalties proposed by the prosecutor and the defendant following conviction. Socrates' conviction for sacrilege (ἀσέβεια) is a clear example of this type of trial, since he was condemned to death after the jury voted in favor of the proposal of the prosecution over his own proposal of free meals in the city hall (πρυτανεῖον).[165] In cases in which the penalty was not fixed, it is often difficult to distinguish between a sentence of exile and self-imposed exile as a result of flight from Athens to avoid trial and punishment. The exile of the historian Thucydides falls into this category. Thucydides tells us that he went into exile for twenty years following his generalship at Amphipolis. Since there is no terminological distinction between legal penalty of exile and self-imposed exile in order to avoid a trial, we are uncertain whether he was condemned to exile for his failure to save Amphipolis, or whether he stayed away from Athens following this incident in order to avoid a harsher penalty of death or permanent exile.[166]

---

[160] The anti-tyranny law recorded by Arist. *Ath. Pol.* 16.10, dating back at least to the time of Solon (see above, chapter 3), was probably never repealed and may have been reaffirmed when Hippias was expelled in 510 (Ostwald 1955, 108), or at the time of Ephialtes, or at the end of the fifth century (Rhodes, *CAAP* 223).

[161] Andoc. 1.96–98 (decree of Demophantus).

[162] Hdt. 5.72.4, 74.1; and above, chapter 3.

[163] Lycurg. *Leoc.* 117.

[164] Thuc. 1.135.3.

[165] On Socrates' trial, see below, chapter 6.

[166] Other examples of flight to avoid penalty include Demosthenes (Thuc. 3.98.5) and two of the generals at Arginusae (Xen. *Hell.* 1.7.1). For Thucydides' exile, see Thuc. 5.26.5. To describe his exile Thucydides uses the words φεύγειν and φυγή, which can be used for a legal sentence of exile or for flight to avoid punishment: see "Introduction," above. The standard view is that Thucydides was sentenced to exile, but Seibert (1979, 312) argues that because of his misfortune during his generalship at Amphipolis Thucydides probably did not return home and that we cannot say whether he was later condemned to death or exile in Athens. The later bibliographical tradition reports that Thucydides was banished by the Athenians (Marcell. *Vita Thuc.* 23, 46) or was

Several cases of sacrilege (ἀσέβεια) resulted in exile either by conviction or by choice. The Alcmeonidae, around 600 B.C.E., had been sentenced to perpetual exile (ἀειφυγία) for committing sacrilege by slaughtering the Cylonians in the sanctuary on the acropolis.[167] Whether Anaxagoras, Protagoras, and Diagoras of Melos were actually tried, they probably left Athens in order to escape punishment for ἀσέβεια.[168] Socrates himself, although given the opportunity to flee, nevertheless submitted to punishment proposed by his prosecutors and was put to death.[169] Those implicated in the profanation of the Mysteries and the scandal of the herms in 415 either fled to avoid punishment or were put to death.[170] It was at this time that Alcibiades, who was implicated in the affair of the herms, fled into exile.[171]

We know of a number of generals who were tried for failure to perform their duties; their trials illustrate the range of penalties, including exile, that could be applied in these cases. Miltiades, for instance, was convicted of deceiving the demos for his failure to fulfill his promise to conquer Paros during his generalship in 489 and was punished by a heavy fine.[172] When three generals returned from Sicily in 424, they were convicted of accepting bribes and concluding a treaty when they could have conquered the island. Two were punished with exile, and the third was fined.[173] The generals who failed to pick up the dead and shipwrecked Athenians at Arginusae were sentenced to death.[174] Xenophon makes a great deal out of the fact that these latter generals were not given a regular trial, and on this basis suggests that the Athenian democracy abused its judicial power to the detriment of those elites who undertook to serve the polis as leaders. As we shall see in chapter 6, Thucydides makes a similar claim in his representation of the case of the mutilation of the herms and the profanation of the Mysteries. To Thucydides' mind, the Athenians' irrational fear of tyranny led them to trust false informers and to convict Alcibiades and other good citizens of attempting to overthrow the democracy.

---

ostracized (anonymus *Life of Thucydides* 7). The former notion is probably no more than an inference from Thucydides' own report that he went into exile, and the latter is a result of confusion between Thucydides son of Olorus (the historian) and Thucydides son of Melesias, who was ostracized in 442; see above.

[167] Arist. *Ath. Pol.* 1; and above, chapter 3.

[168] Plut. *Nic.* 23.4, D.L. 2.12–14. For discussion of these cases, see Wallace 1994.

[169] Pl. *Cri.* 44b–c, *Ap.* 36b; D.L. 2.40–42. For discussion, see below, chapter 6.

[170] Andoc. 1.2, 4, 13, 15–20, 34–35.

[171] Thuc. 6.27–29, 53, 60–61. On Thucydides' representation of Alcibiades' exile, see below, chapter 6.

[172] Hdt. 6.136. On the question of whether Miltiades was condemned by a popular court (δικαστήριον) as Herodotus claims, or by the assembly, see Ostwald 1986, 28–40; Carawan 1987; Hansen 1978, 1982.

[173] Thuc. 4.65.

[174] Xen. *Hell.* 1.7.34.

From this brief review, we can see that exile was one of a range of penalties handed down by the Athenians in their capacities as councilors, members of the assembly, and jurors. Furthermore, these penalties were often imposed on the most prominent elite citizens. On this basis, elite critics of democracy such as Thucydides and Xenophon viewed the justice handed out by the democratic courts as biased against the elite citizens of Athens. An objective evaluation of the verdicts in fifth-century trials against generals, politicians, and other citizens is probably impossible with the evidence available to us.[175] We can say, however, that apart from the irregular prosecution of the generals after Arginusae, the Athenians did not condemn citizens to exile, death, or large fines without giving them a chance to defend themselves in individual trials. If the accused chose to flee rather than stand trial, there was little for the courts to do but presume guilt and permit the fugitive to live out his self-imposed penalty of exile. If we turn, however, to the events of the oligarchic revolutions at the end of the fifth century, we find a stark contrast between the oligarchs' administration of justice and the justice meted out by the democrats. Whereas the oligarchs murdered and banished citizens en masse without trial, the democracy, after restoration, held regular trials and showed remarkable tolerance toward its political opponents.

Exile and the Oligarchic Revolutions of 411 and 404

Despite the stability of the Athenian democracy over nearly two hundred years, there were two occasions toward the end of the fifth century when the democracy was briefly overthrown. It is notable that on both occasions, the Athenians had recently suffered major military defeats, and it is clear that the strained situation following these defeats provided the opportunity for those disenchanted with the democracy to impose a new political order. In 411, following the Athenian defeat in Sicily, and again in 404, following Athens' final defeat in the Peloponnesian War, the Athenian democracy was overthrown, and a narrow oligarchy was established. I am concerned in this section with three major questions, namely to what extent the oligarchs relied on expulsions to secure their power, what role such banishments played in the ultimate overthrow of these regimes, and whether the democracy continued its policy of moderation in the use of expulsions following its restoration.

---

[175] Roberts 1982, however, tries to make this judgment and concludes that on the whole the Athenians had good grounds for punishing those whom they convicted. See also Pritchett (1974, 4–33) on trials of generals, and Burckhardt and von Ungern-Sternberg (2000) for a recent discussion of the major trials of fifth- and fourth-century Athens. Recently, scholars have avoided such objective evaluation in favor of a view of Athenian justice as form of social drama, in which the ultimate verdict is less important than the process by which collective civic values are articulated, negotiated, and contested: see, for example, Ober 1989a; D. Cohen 1993, 1995; Hunter 1994.

At first glance, the answers to these questions seem obvious. The oligarchs are reviled in our sources as perpetrators of the most extreme violations—including arbitrary mass expulsions—of the citizen body. Furthermore, the overthrow of the oligarchy of 404 is widely recognized as due to the efforts of a small but tenacious group of exiles. Finally, our sources praise the moderation of the restored democracy, in particular its restraint in imposing punishments of death, exile, and disenfranchisement on the defeated oligarchs. It might be concluded, therefore, that the oligarchs relied on mass expulsions to secure their regime, and that ultimately these expulsions led to their overthrow. By contrast, the restored democracy showed remarkable tolerance toward the defeated oligarchs and their supporters and thereby prevented further civil unrest.

Although there is some truth to this conclusion, I will argue that it represents an ideological simplification of a very complex set of events. In particular, I argue that accounts of mass expulsions under the oligarchs, as well as the praise of democratic moderation in the use of exile against the defeated oligarchs, are a product of the role of exile in the justification of democratic rule. While the oligarchs of 411 and 404 certainly did expel (and murder or disenfranchise) some opponents of their regimes, these abuses of power were more limited than our sources suggest. In 404, moreover, the movement that led to the overthrow of the oligarchs was started by a very small group of exiles, despite our sources' claims that the entire Athenian demos was in exile and returned triumphantly to overthrow the oligarchs. Finally, although it is true that the restored democracy behaved with remarkable legality in prosecuting the offenses perpetrated by the oligarchs, the heralded moderation of the democracy was itself a product of the need of the restored democracy to find ideological legitimacy in an unstable environment.[176] In sum, the case of the oligarchic revolutions provides a striking example of historical events, ideology, and practices interacting to produce the patterns of history.

Besides the ideological complexities of our sources for the revolutions outlined above, our understanding of the revolution of 411 is made even more problematic by the fact that we are largely dependent on a single source, Thucydides,[177] and he, moreover, is sympathetic with the aims of the leaders of the revolution, even if he does not approve of their methods.[178] As

---

[176] Compare Wolpert (2002, 3–4), who notes that a major problem for the historiography of the revolution of 404 is that our accounts are implicated in the "politics of reconciliation" that followed the restoration of the democracy.

[177] The other main source for the revolution of 411 is Arist. *Ath. Pol.* 29–33, which is, however, largely restricted to the constitutional details of the revolution and gives little attention to its background and actual events. Diod. Sic. 13.37–52 adds little to what we know from Thucydides.

[178] See Thucydides' patronizing comment (8.1.4) that, after the defeat of the Athenian expedition to Sicily, the people, as they were wont to do, were ready to put things in order (εὐτακτεῖν) on account of fear. Thucydides also praises the leaders of the revolution for their intelligence (Phrynichus, 8.27.5; Antiphon, 8.68.1; the oligarchs in general, 8.68.4). Finally,

we shall see, Thucydides' critical view of the post-Periclean democracy shapes his representation of the oligarchic revolution.[179] The aim of this section, therefore, is to appreciate how the historical events of the revolution are filtered through Thucydides' historiographical lens in order to promote his critical project. As we shall see below in this section and again in chapter 6, the representation of exile plays a crucial role in Thucydides' critique of the Athenian democracy.

Despite these methodological caveats, Thucydides' account reveals that the oligarchs of 411 used execution, imprisonment, and exile as means of getting rid of the most prominent opponents of their regime. Moreover, while the oligarchs seem not to have engaged in executions, imprisonment, or expulsions en masse, I suggest that their skillful use of selective violence against leaders of the opposition resulted in the effective silencing of the Athenian people and their alienation from the political process. The alienation of the Athenian people, moreover, can be termed a form of internal exile, since during this time Athenians withdrew from civic life.[180] In addition, I argue that false reports of mass executions, expulsions, and imprisonment allegedly perpetrated by the oligarchs in Athens were decisive in bringing the Athenian sailors stationed at Samos into revolt against the oligarchy. Remarkably, the sailors at Samos responded to the alleged violence of the oligarchs by constituting themselves as an independent political community, distinct from the government of the oligarchs in Athens. In essence, therefore, the sailors at Samos established themselves as the Athenian polis in exile. I argue that although the oligarchs' use of selective violence against opponents of their regime was initially successful in terrorizing the Athenian people into submission, this policy eventually backfired when exaggerated accounts of violence against the mass of Athenian citizenry brought the Athenian sailors into revolt and ultimately caused the overthrow of the regime.

Athens' dire military situation following the defeat in Sicily in 413 provided the conditions for the overthrow of the democracy in 411.[181] The cities subject to Athens were ready to revolt.[182] The Persians, moreover, joined with

---

Thucydides praises the more moderate oligarchic regime of the Five Thousand (8.97). See, however, Connor (1984, 224) for an argument that Thucydides' praise of Antiphon and the other leaders of the Four Hundred need not indicate his sympathy with the oligarchs. Connor's argument shows why it is important to distinguish between Thucydides' abstract political sympathies and his abhorrence of the actual methods by which the oligarchs of 411 secured their rule.

[179] Connor 1984 shows masterfully how Thucydides imposes his interpretation of events through selection, juxtaposition, and choice of diction, as well as overt authorial comment. For a recent discussion of Thucydides' objective stance in relation to his critical project, cf. Ober 1998, 52–121.

[180] For the concept of internal exile, see above, "Introduction."

[181] Thuc. 8 *passim*, Arist. *Ath. Pol.* 29.1, Diod. Sic. 13.34.1–3.

[182] Thuc. 8.2.2. Thucydides mentions the revolts of Euboea (8.5.1), Lesbos (8.5.2), and Chios and Erythrae (8.5.4).

the Spartans in helping the subject cities revolt from Athens.[183] A formal alliance was signed between Sparta and Persia, and, to add to Athens' difficulties, a fleet of ships arrived from Sicily under the command of the Syracusan Hermocrates in order to help the Spartans finish Athens off.[184] Despite the loss of so many men and ships in the Sicilian campaign, however, the Athenians rallied themselves, built new ships, and actively defended their empire in Ionia.[185] Opponents of the democracy in Athens nonetheless took advantage of Athens' difficult situation in order to establish an oligarchy.

According to Thucydides, the intrigues for the overthrow of the democracy at Athens began when Alcibiades, who was in exile due to his supposed involvement in the affairs of the herms and the Mysteries, realized that he would not be recalled from exile so long as democracy prevailed in Athens. Accordingly, Alcibiades enticed the commanders of the Athenian forces at Samos with the promise of Persian aid if they would get rid of the democracy.[186] Despite Thucydides' emphasis on Alcibiades' desire to return from exile as the initial cause of the movement to overthrow the democracy, it is clear that Alcibiades was not alone in working for this end. Thucydides reports that at least some of the commanders at Samos were eager for the overthrow of the democracy, hoping to gain more exclusive political power for themselves.[187] Thucydides' emphasis on Alcibiades, moreover, can be explained by his use of Alcibiades' exile as an example of the reckless and self-destructive tendencies of the Athenian democracy. As I argue below in chapter 6, Thucydides' representation of Alcibiades' exile is part of his critical agenda of demonstrating that the democracy brought about its own destruction through its unjust treatment of its best leaders.[188] By exiling their best leaders, Thucydides claims, the democracy brought about its own destruction, since worse men were left in control of Athens, and the best men (such as Alcibiades) were forced to conspire against their own polis.

Following the intrigues of Alcibiades, elite groups (ξυνωμοσίαι) in Athens began a campaign of violence against the leaders of the democracy.[189] Through selective assassinations of leading democrats and anyone else who

---

[183] Thuc. 8.5.4–8.2.

[184] Spartan alliance with Persian king: Thuc. 8.18. Arrival of the Sicilian ships: 8.26.

[185] Thuc. 8.1.3; 8.4. The Athenians defeated the first Spartan force sent out to help Chios revolt (8.10) and successfully restored Lesbos (8.22) and Clazomenae (8.23) to the Athenian alliance after they had revolted.

[186] Thuc. 8.47.2, 48.1; cf. Plut. Alc. 25.

[187] Thuc. 8.48.1. Cf. Kagan (1987, 113), who emphasizes that it was not only Alcibiades but the leaders of the forces at Samos who desired out of self-interest a change in the government at Athens.

[188] Compare Thuc. 6.15 (on Alcibiades) and 2.65 (on Pericles). Thucydides' representation of Alcbiades is complex, and is discussed in more detail below in chapter 6.

[189] Thuc. 8.54.4. On the nature of these elite groups, see Connor 1971.

was opposed to them, the oligarchs terrorized the Athenian people into silence.[190] Although the assembly and the Council of Five Hundred continued to meet, only the conspirators spoke at the meetings.[191] If anyone else dared to speak out, he was killed.[192] Thucydides (8.66.2) describes the atmosphere of fear and distrust among the people that led them to keep quiet and prevented them from opposing the political changes:[193]

ἡσυχίαν εἶχεν ὁ δῆμος καὶ κατάπληξιν τοιαύτην ὥστε κέρδος ὁ μὴ πάσχων τι βίαιον, εἰ καὶ σιγῷη, ἐνόμιζεν.

The people kept quiet and were in such a state of terror that they counted it a gain if, even keeping quiet, they suffered no harm.

With this atmosphere of terror in the city, it was an easy task for Pisander and his associates to establish an oligarchic constitution when they arrived in Athens. No one spoke out in opposition when the oligarchs proposed that a committee of ten be elected with full powers to formulate proposals for how the polis might best be governed.[194] Nor did anyone protest when, on the appointed day, in an assembly held outside the city, this committee brought forth a proposal by which four hundred men chosen by the oligarchs would rule.[195] The opposition had been silenced not only by the fear arising from the murders of prominent democrats, but also as a result of a decree prohibiting, on penalty of death, anyone from challenging the proposals by means of proceedings for unconstitutional proposals (γραφὴ παρανόμων) or impeachment (εἰσαγγελία).[196] Consequently, the measures for the establishment of the oligarchy of the Four Hundred were ratified without opposition, and the assembly was dismissed.[197]

The extent to which the Athenian people had been silenced and effectively disenfranchised by the terror resulting from the assassinations is underscored by Thucydides' account of the oligarchs' dismissal of the Council of Five Hundred. In a pointed allusion to Herodotus's account of the events leading to the founding of the Athenian democracy, Thucydides remarks that

[190] Thuc. 8.65.2.

[191] Thuc. 8.66.1.

[192] Thuc. 8.66.2.

[193] On fear and distrust in the oligarchic revolutions, see Balot 2001, 211–19.

[194] Thuc. 8.67.1. Arist. *Ath. Pol.* 31–32 offers two rather incoherent accounts of the constitutional proposals made by the oligarchs. The historicity of these accounts is doubted by some (*HCT* 5:242–46) and accepted with qualifications by others (Rhodes, *CAAP* 387–89). I follow Andrewes in rejecting these accounts and accepting Thucydides' version.

[195] Thuc. 8.67.3. Andrewes (*HCT* 5:165–67) lists possible reasons for holding the assembly outside the city at Colonus. He does not mention, however, the obvious likelihood that the unusual location would have resulted in lower than usual attendance, since some will not have heard about the special venue.

[196] Thuc. 8.67.2, Arist. *Ath. Pol.* 29.4, Dem. 24.154.

[197] Thuc. 8.69.1.

neither the council nor the rest of the Athenians resisted the oligarchs of 411: "The council said nothing in opposition and departed; the rest of the citizens did not start a revolution but kept quiet" (οἱ ἄλλοι πολῖται οὐδὲν ἐνεω-τέριζον, ἀλλ᾽ ἡσύχαζον).[198] Thucydides' negative echo of the democratic revolution of 508/7 underscores how completely the people had been terrorized into submission. One might liken the situation of the Athenian demos in 411 to a form of internal exile, since, as a result of their fear of violent reprisals, the Athenian people were effectively disenfranchised, although not physically expelled from the polis.

So far I have argued that the oligarchs of 411 executed leading democrats in order to terrify the Athenian masses into submission to their rule. In this section, I argue that the oligarchs' use of selective assassinations was transformed in contemporary democratic traditions into accounts of widespread violence against the mass of Athenian citizenry. I argue that this transformation was a product of the assimilation of the rule of the oligarchs to earlier representations of tyranny in democratic ideology. Furthermore, these misrepresentations of mass executions, imprisonments, and expulsions led the Athenian sailors on Samos to revolt from the oligarchs in Athens. Finally, I argue that the sailors at Samos constituted themselves as a polis in exile, and that this act of rebellion destabilized the oligarchic regime and ultimately led to its overthrow.

The transformation of the oligarchs' selective assassinations into accounts of widespread violence against the Athenian masses in Athenian democratic ideology is evident in Thucydides' implicitly rejecting a standard topos in representations of tyranny to characterize oligarchic rule. In a complex allusion to the representation of tyranny in democratic ideology, Thucydides accepts that the oligarchs of 411 used selective violence—including execution, imprisonment, and expulsion—to secure their rule, but rejects the evidently widespread belief that these penalties were inflicted on great numbers of Athenians (8.70.2):

κcaì ἄνδρας τέ τινας ἀπέκτειναν οὐ πολλούς, οἳ ἐδόκουν ἐπιτήδειοι εἶναι ὑπεξαιρεθῆναι, καὶ ἄλλους ἔδησαν, τοὺς δὲ καὶ μετεστήσαντο.

They put to death some men whom they considered it expedient to get rid of—though not many—and they imprisoned others, and others they exiled.

If we compare this passage with the representation of tyranny in other texts, we see that Thucydides echoes and modifies a standard topos about tyrants in his description of the oligarchs. For example, Herodotus's representation of the Corinthian tyrant Cypselus presents a similar tricolon of abuses (5.92ε.2):[199]

---

[198] Thuc. 8.70.1. Compare Herodotus's account of the democratic revolution, in which the council and the rest of the Athenians (Ἀθηναίων δὲ οἱ λοιποί) resist Isagoras's attempt to establish a narrow oligarchy (Hdt. 5.72.2; and above, chapter 3).

[199] See Forsdyke 1999; and chapter 6 below for the argument that Herodotus's portrait of Cypselus is a product of Athenian democratic ideology.

πολλοὺς μὲν Κορινθίων ἐδίωξε, πολλοὺς δὲ χρημάτων ἀπεστέρησε, πολλῷ
δέ τι πλείστους τῆς ψυχῆς.

[Cypselus] drove many Corinthians into exile, and he confiscated the property
of many, but mostly he killed people.

The parallelism between these two passages suggests that Thucydides deliberately evokes and alters the standard representation of tyranny in his description of the oligarchs. Thucydides' modification of the topos—his insistence
that the oligarchs did not kill many men—suggests that he is responding to
democratic ideology, in which the oligarchs were described using the standard
rhetorical tricolon of tyrannical abuses. In contrast to the rule of the tyrant,
Thucydides emphasizes that the oligarchs of 411 did not kill, imprison, and
exile many men, but rather used selective violence against key individuals in
order to intimidate the rest of the population into submission. In this passage,
as in a number of others, Thucydides is correcting what he considers the
ignorant beliefs of the mass of Athenians—many of which are known to us
through the text of Herodotus.[200]

That the democrats transformed the oligarchs' use of selective assassinations into accounts of widespread violence against the mass of Athenian
citizens is also evident in Thucydides' representation and critique of the false
report given by an Athenian named Chaereas to the Athenian sailors at
Samos. Chaereas had been a member of the crew of the Athenian ship
Paralus, which had been sent, following the suppression of an oligarchic
coup at Samos, to report to the Athenians about affairs on that island.[201] Not
realizing that an oligarchy had been established at Athens, the crew of the
Paralus sailed into Athens and was immediately arrested by the oligarchs.
Chaereas managed to escape, however, fled back to Samos, and reported to
Athenian sailors what had happened in Athens. Chaereas's reports of the
violence allegedly being perpetrated by the oligarchs against the Athenians
convinced the Athenian sailors on Samos to revolt from the government in
Athens and, ultimately, to establish their own democracy in exile.

Thucydides calls Chaereas's account of the situation in Athens under the
Four Hundred exaggerated and false.[202] Indeed, several elements of Chaereas's report of oligarchic violence correspond closely to the representation
of the tyrannical violence in Athenian democratic ideology. For this reason,
we may suspect that these elements of the representation of the rule of the
oligarchs have been assimilated to the representation of tyranny in order to
symbolize the illegitimacy of the regime in Athens in the most ideologically
charged terms. For example, Chaereas reported that the Four Hundred were

---

[200] Most famously, Thucydides corrects the Athenians' misconceptions about the Pisistratid
tyranny (1.20, 6.54–59).

[201] Thuc. 8.73–74.

[202] Thuc. 8.74.3.

punishing citizens with whippings.[203] The whip was regarded as appropriate for the discipline of slaves, not free citizens, and hence was a symbol of despotic rule for the Athenians.[204] Similarly, Chaereas reported that the Four Hundred were violating the soldiers' wives and children and that they intended to seize and imprison the relatives of the soldiers so that they might kill them, if the soldiers did not submit to them.[205] Again, violation of women was a key characteristic of despotic rule in democratic ideology.[206] Furthermore, although hostage taking was a common method of securing the cooperation of a conquered people, it was not considered an appropriate way of managing one's own citizenry.[207] Such treatment of one's fellow citizens was considered characteristic of tyrants, who used force to maintain their power in the city.[208]

A final feature of the rule of the oligarchs according to Chaereas's report seems to combine elements of the representation of tyrannical power in democratic ideology and a realistic assessment of the situation in Athens in 411. Chaereas reported that it was not possible to speak against those who held power.[209] Free speech was, of course, a central characteristic of democracy, and its suppression was a key symbol of an unjust and illegitimate regime.[210] Yet it is also noteworthy that this feature of Chaereas's report corresponds to Thucydides' own representation of the situation in Athens. As we have just seen, Thucydides' account shows that the oligarchs used selective violence to intimidate the Athenian masses into submission. According to Thucydides'

---

[203] The word used is πληγαί, literally "blows" but often meaning blows from a whip; cf. Xen. *Lac.* 2.8–9, where the noun πληγή and the verb μαστιγόω are used interchangeably. It is perhaps significant, however, that the Thirty Tyrants employed a force of three hundred whip bearers (μαστιγοφόροι: Arist. *Ath. Pol.* 35.1); see below.

[204] For the whip as a potent symbol of the relationship between master and slave, cf. Hdt. 4.3.4. See Hunter (1994, 154–84) on the whip and corporal punishment in general as appropriate for slaves and non-citizens only (citing Dem. 22.54–55, 24.166–67), although she finds some exceptions. For the whip as associated with the despotic rule of a Persian monarch as opposed to a democracy, cf. Hdt. 7.103.4, 223.3 (discussed in detail in Forsdyke 2001); Xen. *An.* 3.4.26.

[205] Thuc. 8.74.3.

[206] Most obviously in the constitutional debate (Hdt. 3.80.5), but also in the representation of the tyrants Periander of Corinth (3.50.1, 5.92.η.1) and Polycrates of Samos (3.45.4). See chapter 6 below.

[207] For legitimate hostage taking, see, for example, Pericles' taking hostages from the Samians when he established the democracy there in 441 (Thuc. 1.115, Diod. Sic. 12.27–28). The Persian king also took hostages from the cities of Ionia in order to secure their loyalty (Hdt. 6.99).

[208] Hdt. 1.64.1 (on Pisistratus), 3.45.4 (on Polycrates of Samos). For full discussion of this trope, see chapter 6 below.

[209] Thuc. 8.74.3.

[210] "Free speech" (ἰσηγορία), the word used by Hdt. 5.78 to designate the Cleisthenic democracy, shows the close association between the principle of free speech and democracy. For free speech as essential under the Athenian democracy, cf. Forrest 1966; Raaflaub 1980, 1983, 1985; Ober 1989a, 296–97; Forsdyke 2001.

own account, "the people kept quiet and were in such a state of terror that they counted it a gain if, even keeping quiet, they suffered no harm" (8.66.5). It seems, therefore, that at least in this aspect—the suppression of free speech at Athens—Chaereas's report had some basis in fact.

A further detail about the alleged situation in Athens is revealed in the speech of some representatives of the oligarchs who arrived in Samos in order to reassure the sailors. The representatives told the sailors that their relatives were not being abused (οὔθ' ὑβρίζονται . . . οὔτε κακὸν ἔχουσιν οὐδέν), as Chaereas had claimed, and that each remained in his home in possession of his property (ἀλλ' ἐπὶ τοῖς σφετέροις αὐτῶν ἕκαστοι κατὰ χώραν μένουσιν).[211] This reassurance suggests that, in addition to his reports of sexual and physical violence toward their wives and children, Chaereas had also claimed that Athenian citizens were being removed from their homes (and imprisoned or exiled) and that their property was being confiscated. We have seen already that Thucydides himself acknowledged that the oligarchs used murder, imprisonment, and exile to seize and maintain their power in Athens. Yet Thucydides was careful to specify that the oligarchs used selective violence against prominent democrats, rather than random violence against large numbers of citizens, in order to terrorize the Athenian masses. Chaereas apparently extended the number of victims of oligarchic violence to include the families of the soldiers at Samos—that is, a large group of the common citizenry. In doing so, he associated the rule of the oligarchs with the representation of tyranny in democratic ideology, and thus heightened the sailors' sense of the illegitimacy and illegality of the oligarchy. Chaereas's report of the violence of the oligarchs against the mass of the Athenian citizens was therefore a key factor in the decision of the sailors on Samos to revolt from their government in Athens and establish a separate democracy in exile.

Just as the Athenians in the city had become estranged from those who held power in Athens as a result of the extra-judicial murders, imprisonments, and expulsions, so the Athenians abroad became alienated from the government in Athens as a result of the reports of (both real and imagined) violence against citizens in Athens. While the Athenians at home arguably suffered a form of internal exile, the Athenians at Samos found themselves in actual physical exile from their polis. Although the sailors were at first eager to attack the oligarchs at home and restore the democracy and themselves to power in Athens (and thus act like traditional political exiles, seeking to reinstate themselves), they were restrained by their commanders, who were aware of the risk that withdrawal of the fleet from Ionia would present to their empire and the war with Sparta.[212] Caught in this strategic dilemma,

[211] Thuc. 8.86.3.
[212] Thuc. 8.75.1.

the sailors instead established a democracy for themselves at Samos and became in essence a democracy in exile.

Thucydides' narrative reveals both the strong democratic sentiments of the sailors at Samos and the extent to which the army became a separate political community in exile for as long as the oligarchy lasted at Athens. According to Thucydides, the first act of the leaders of the sailors was to administer an oath by which the sailors swore that they would be ruled by a democracy (δημοκρατήσεσθαι).[213] They administered this oath, says Thucydides, because they wanted to change the constitution of the fleet into a democracy (ἐς δημοκρατίαν βουλόμενοι μεταστῆσαι τὰ ἐν τῇ Σάμῳ). Normally a fleet operating abroad would not be thought to have a political constitution of its own, separate from its home city. The fact that Thucydides attributes a political constitution to the fleet shows that he considered it to be a self-conscious political community on its own. Furthermore, the actions of the sailors at Samos show that they indeed considered themselves to be a polis in exile. They held their own assemblies, elected their own trierarchs and generals, received ambassadors, and even recalled Alcibiades to their alternative polis.[214] Thucydides records in great detail the speeches of encouragement that were made in the assembly of the Athenian democracy at Samos. The sailors enumerated all the ways in which they were equal or superior to the government of the oligarchs at Athens, including the fact that they had possession of the fleet and hence could collect the tribute and provide their own wages. They in essence saw themselves as taking over the financial and administrative activities of the Athenian empire.[215]

Thucydides emphasizes the antagonism, yet parallelism, between the polis of Athens and the polis of the sailors at Samos:[216]

ἐς φιλονικίαν τε καθέστασαν τὸν χρόνον τοῦτον οἱ μὲν τὴν πόλιν ἀναγκάζοντες δημοκρατεῖσθαι, οἱ δὲ τὸ στρατόπεδον ὀλιγαρχεῖσθαι.

They stood in opposition to each other at this time, the fleet striving for the city to become a democracy, the city striving to make the fleet become an oligarchy.

Following the sailors' establishment of a separate polis in exile, the oligarchs in Athens began to feel insecure and took measures to shore up their position.[217]

---

[213] Thuc. 8.75.2.

[214] Assemblies: Thuc. 8.76.2, 77.1, 81.2, 86.1. Cf. Andrewes (HCT 5:268), who states that the phrase that Thucydides uses to describe the summoning of the assembly of sailors on Samos, ἐκκλησίαν ποιεῖν, is formal and is "a regular phrase for 'to call an Assembly'." Election of trierarchs and generals: 8.76.2, 82.1 (Alcibiades). Ambassadors received: 8.86.1 (representatives of the Four Hundred), 86.8 (Argive ambassadors). Recall of Alcibiades: Thuc. 8.81.1, Plut. Alc. 26.

[215] Cf. Andrewes, HCT 5:268–69; on Thuc. 8.76.2: the sailors at Samos "regard themselves as having taken over the functions of government."

[216] Thuc. 8.76.1.

[217] Cf. Thuc. 8.90.2, φοβούμενοι καὶ τὰ αὑτοῦ καὶ τὰ ἐκ τῆς Σάμου.

They renewed their attempts to seek peace with Sparta and hastened the construction of a wall at Eëtionea, in Piraeus.[218] Furthermore, tensions began to
arise among the oligarchs. According to Thucydides, the tensions were due to the
strength of the opposition in Samos.[219] A group within the oligarchy, realizing
that the oligarchy at Athens would not last long without the support of the fleet at
Samos, put themselves forward as proponents of the more moderate regime of
the Five Thousand.[220] Thucydides viewed the political platform of this faction
with skepticism, regarding their differentiation of themselves from the Four
Hundred as a shrewd exploitation of the situation in order to gain power for
themselves within a new oligarchy.[221] Without getting into the tricky problem of
the character of Theramenes, the leader of this new faction of oligarchs, it is
possible to suggest that the moderates recognized that the exclusion of all citizens from the political process was untenable in the long run, and that an expansion in the franchise was necessary if the oligarchic regime was to survive.[222]

After some maneuvering, the moderate oligarchs were successful in overthrowing the regime of the Four Hundred, and even in getting the Athenians
both at Samos and in Athens to consent to the new, broader oligarchy of the
Five Thousand. It is clear, however, that the Athenians accepted the constitution of the Five Thousand only as a necessary evil in the difficult war
situation. Indeed, as soon as the Athenians won a significant battle (at Cyzicus,
in 410), they changed their government back to a full democracy.[223] Our
sources are silent about how this change took place, but no doubt the moderates found it impossible to defend a more restricted franchise when the
external situation was less threatening—especially since the sailors at Samos
were responsible for Athens' improved situation.[224]

An important issue for our purposes is what happened to the Four Hundred
under the regime of the Five Thousand and later under the restored democracy. We have seen how the Four Hundred used selective assassination,
imprisonment, and banishment without judicial process as key means of securing political power. We might expect that the moderate regime of the Five
Thousand, and even more the restored democracy, might seek revenge for the
injustices committed against innocent citizens and might even resort to
summary execution or expulsion of the leaders of the Four Hundred. When
we examine the evidence, however, we find that far from hastily executing

[218] Thuc. 8.90.1. The problem of the exact location and extent of this wall and its purpose is
discussed by Andrewes, *HCT* 5:303–6; Kagan 1987.

[219] Thuc. 8.89.2, 89.4.

[220] Thuc. 8.89.2.

[221] Thuc. 8.89.3.

[222] On Theramenes, see most recently Kagan 1987, Lang 1992, Buck 1995, with older scholarship, especially Andrewes 1974, Harding 1974. On the nature of the regime of Five Thousand,
see de Ste. Croix 1956; Rhodes 1972.

[223] Arist. *Ath. Pol.* 34.1.

[224] Cf. Kagan 1987, 253.

those most culpable, these regimes allowed all those implicated in the regime
of the Four Hundred a fair trial according to the established laws.[225] More
important, although some of the oligarchs were convicted at their trials, as we
shall see, many were actually acquitted.

Thucydides, however, gives the impression that all the leaders of the Four
Hundred fled immediately to the Spartans at Decelea when the Athenians
voted to install the Five Thousand: "In this change of government, Pisander,
Alexicles, and their associates, and whoever was most prominent in the oli-
garchy [of the Four Hundred], immediately withdrew [ὑπεξέρχονται] to
Decelea."[226]

We know, however, from Thucydides' own narrative and other sources,
that several of the most prominent members of the Four Hundred did not
flee but remained to stand trial in Athens. Antiphon, Onomacles, and Archeptolemus were arrested and made to stand trial. The fact that these men
did not immediately flee suggests they had confidence that they would be
given a chance to defend themselves at trial and calculated that they could
give a convincing defense.[227]

A trial was held even for the corpse of Phrynichus, a leading member of the
Four Hundred who had been assassinated following the installation of the Five
Thousand.[228] Phrynichus was charged with treason, probably in relation to his
negotiations with Sparta when the sailors at Samos revolted from the government of the oligarchs in Athens.[229] A significant detail about this trial,
however, is that the dead Phrynichus was defended by two other leading
members of the Four Hundred, Aristarchus and Alexicles.[230] The role of these
figures in this trial shows that leading members of the Four Hundred not only
remained in Athens but went so far as to draw attention to themselves by
defending a prominent oligarch.[231] Aristarchus (and probably likewise Alexicles) was later tried for treason and, although given full opportunity to defend
himself, was condemned to death.[232] Michael Jameson argues that even the
leading oligarch, Pisander, remained in Athens, was prosecuted by the poet
Sophocles, was convicted, but fled before the punishment was exacted.[233]

---

[225] Cf. Ostwald 1986, 401: "It was a prosecution, not a persecution: we hear of no lynchings or
terrorism but only of orderly legal proceedings initiated soon after the new regime had been
established."

[226] Thuc. 8.98.1; cf. Lys. 13.73.

[227] Cf. Ostwald 1986, 401–2.

[228] Trial of Phrynichus's corpse: Craterus, FGrH 342 F 17; Lycurg. Leoc. 113; [Plut.] X Orat. 1
(Antiphon; Mor. 834b). Phrynichus's assassination: Thuc. 8.92.2, Lys. 13.71, Lycurg. Leoc. 112.

[229] Kagan 1987, 208.

[230] Lycurg. Leoc. 115.

[231] Cf. Jameson 1971, 552–53.

[232] Trial of Aristarchus: Xen. Hell. 1.7.28. Trial of Alexicles: Lycurg. Leoc. 115 (although
Lycurgus's reason for their condemnation is probably false: cf. Jameson 1971, 552.

[233] Jameson 1971.

It is significant that the moderate regime and the democracy that followed did not execute, imprison, or expel the extreme oligarchs without judicial process. The decree recording the procedures to be followed for the trial of Antiphon, Onomacles, and Archeptolemus, for example, specifies that they should be handed over to the courts and, if they should be convicted, that they be treated according to the law concerning traitors.[234] Xenophon's character Euryptolemus, moreover, argues against the proposal that the generals at Arginusae in 406 should be tried en masse by the people by noting that even Aristarchus, who had overthrown the democracy in 411, was given a day-long trial in which to defend himself and was granted all his other rights under the law.[235] If we may believe Lysias, finally, many of the Four Hundred were actually acquitted at their trials.[236]

Those who served lesser roles under the Four Hundred were also given trials and received lesser penalties if convicted. Lysias wrote a speech for one Polystratus, who had served as registrar for the enrollment of the Five Thousand under the Four Hundred.[237] At Polystratus's first trial he was convicted and fined. Lysias's speech is for a second trial on similar charges, for which presumably the penalty upon conviction was to be another fine. We learn from a decree of 405 granting a general amnesty to all those who were suffering partial disenfranchisement that some of the members of the Four Hundred and those who had performed any act under the Four Hundred had been sentenced to this relatively mild penalty.[238] Those convicted could not exercise certain rights, such as speaking and proposing measures in the assembly, but otherwise lived freely in the city.

There is evidence, nevertheless, that some did go into exile between the restoration of the democracy and the defeat of Athens in 404. The peace treaty between Sparta and Athens in 404 stipulated that the Athenian exiles be allowed to return: the most plausible identification of these exiles is that they were oligarchs who fled Athens out of fear of being convicted under the democracy for crimes committed under the Four Hundred.[239] These men may have fled after the decree of Demophantus was passed in 410/09 following the restoration of the democracy.[240] According to this decree, the killer of any overthrower of the democracy was declared free from any penalty. The decree was in essence a restatement of the archaic law against tyrants by which

---

[234] [Plut.] X *Orat.* 1 (Antiphon; *Mor.* 833f).

[235] Xen. *Hell.* 1.7.28.

[236] Lys. 20.14.

[237] Lys. 20.

[238] Andoc. 1.78 (decree of Patrocleides).

[239] Return of exiles as one of the terms of the peace settlement: Xen. *Hell.* 2.20. Cf. Lys. 13.73, stating that the Thirty Tyrants had all been members of the Four Hundred and had fled when the Four Hundred were overthrown.

[240] Andoc. 1.96–98, Lycurg. *Leoc.* 125, Dem. 20.59.

those who attempted to set up a tyranny or who aided in the establishment of a tyrant were declared outlaws (ἄτιμοι) in the archaic sense of the term.[241] This law meant that anyone might kill a tyrant or his associates and would not be subject to penalty.[242] The decree of Demophantus, however, expanded the definition of the crime by replacing the terms "tyrant or accomplice of a tyrant" with the expression "whoever overthrows the democracy or holds public office after the democracy has been overthrown." With this expansion of the former law against tyranny, any overthrower of the democracy, whether tyrant or oligarch, could be killed without judicial redress if he should appear in Athenian territory.[243]

By this law, an overthrower of the democracy was forced to flee from Athens in order to escape being killed and hence was de facto punished with lifelong exile from the community (ἀειφυγία). Although the law was probably not retroactive, it was a clear indication of the mood of the Athenians toward those who threatened their political order.[244] In fact it seems that one of the primary functions of the decree was to send a clear signal to all citizens who might plan to overturn the democracy in the future. For this reason, the law was made valid not only by being inscribed and publicly displayed but also by an oath taken by all Athenians by tribes and by demes.[245] In the oath, the Athenians swore to kill any tyrant or overthrower of democracy and to hold anyone who killed a tyrant or an overthrower of democracy exempt from punishment. In such a climate, it is not surprising that some oligarchs withdrew from the city.[246]

Despite the seeming severity of the decree of Demophantus, it is important to distinguish between the sanction to kill the overthrowers of the democracy passed by the restored democracy and the assassination of citizens by the oligarchs in order to preserve their regime. Whereas the oligarchs killed the most prominent of their opponents and did not submit to any form of judicial

---

[241] Ostwald 1955 draws this connection between the decree of Demophantus and the archaic law against tyrants. Archaic anti-tyranny law: Arist. *Ath. Pol.* 16, Plut. *Sol.* 19.4; and see chapter 3 above.

[242] See above, "Introduction" and chapter 3.

[243] Arist. *Ath. Pol.* 16.10, Andoc. 1.96. The decree of Demophantus updates the language of the archaic law, replacing the word ἄτιμος (which by the end of the fifth century had taken on the milder meaning "disenfranchisement") with the more explicit πολέμιος ἔστω 'Αθηναίων καὶ νηποινεὶ τεθνάτω, "Let him be an enemy of the Athenians, and let him die without judicial redress."

[244] Kagan (1987, 257) states that the law was not retroactive, but he does not give any evidence for this judgment. The fact that moderates such as Theramenes, who was implicated in the overthrow of the democracy in 411, were not subject to this law suggests that it was not retroactive.

[245] Andoc. 1.97–98, Lycurg. *Leoc.* 125–26.

[246] Similarly, the passage of a decree honoring the slayers of Phrynichus in 409 (ML 85) must have served as a further warning to the oligarchs that attempts to overthrow the democracy would be subject to the highest penalty.

review, those who murdered overthrowers of democracy or potential tyrants would have to be able to defend their actions in court if prosecuted by the relatives of the victim. In other words, the democrats granted judicial redress for murders if they were contrary to the laws of the city, whereas the oligarchs prevented the judicial process from functioning by monopolizing political power and terrorizing the citizens into submission.

In fact, we know of only one instance of judicial impropriety under the restored democracy. Following the Athenian victory in the battle of Arginusae in 406, the Athenians sought to punish the generals for their failure to rescue the shipwrecked Athenians and the bodies of the dead after the battle. In their distress at the lives lost and their inability to give proper burial to their relatives, they condemned the generals to death in a joint trial in the assembly. By failing to give the generals an opportunity to defend themselves in separate trials, the Athenians transgressed their usual principle of allowing defendants a fair trial according to the laws.[247] Although egregious, the execution of six of the generals without proper trial was a single instance of injustice, not a regular practice. In contrast, the Four Hundred, and even more so the oligarchs of 404 (the so-called Thirty Tyrants), executed citizens regularly as a means of suppressing opposition and securing their power in the city.

Only a few of the oligarchs who fled into exile in 410 are known. One Charicles, who became a prominent member of the Thirty Tyrants, probably went into exile at this time.[248] Other likely members of the Four Hundred who returned in 404 include Aristoteles, Pythodorus, Melobius, Mnasilochus, and Onomacles.[249]

I have argued that the oligarchs of 411 used selective violence to suppress opposition to their rule, and that this violence silenced the Athenian people and led to the revolt of the Athenian sailors at Samos from the oligarchy at Athens. In 404, by contrast, the oligarchs not only imprisoned, executed, and exiled key opponents of their regime, but explicitly expelled the Athenian people as a whole (ὁ δῆμος) from the city of Athens (but not the territory of

---

[247] The irregularity of this action is well brought out by the arguments of Euryptolemus in the assembly debate concerning the procedure for punishing the generals (cf. Xen. *Hell.* 1.7.16–33, esp. 19, 23–29) and in Lysias's speeches in which he continually contrasts the democracy's practice of allowing even the guilty a chance to defend themselves with the practice of the Thirty Tyrants, who executed men without trial: see below, and Lys. 12.17, 36, 82, 83; 13.12 (mock trial). Compare also the Athenians' later remorse for their action and their prosecution for "deception of the people" of the persons responsible for proposing the irregular procedure (Xen. *Hell.* 1.7.35, Diod. Sic. 13.103.1–2).

[248] Isoc. 16.42, Andoc.1.36. The exile of Critias, who became the leader of the Thirty Tyrants, seems to have been a result of sponsorship of a motion to recall Alcibiades (Plut. *Alc.* 33.1) rather than due to his membership in the Four Hundred (Rhodes, *CAAP* 429–30; Ostwald 1986, 431; *contra*, Kagan 1987, 208). Sources for Critias's exile: Xen. *Hell.* 2.3.15, 36; Arist. *Rhet.* 1375b, *Pol.* 1275b26–30.

[249] Aristoteles: Xen. *Hell.* 2.2.18. For the others, see Ostwald 1986, 460–62.

Attica). I argue that although the overthrow of the oligarchy of 404 was accomplished largely by a small group of citizen and non-citizen exiles, the democratic tradition assimilated the expulsion of the Athenian people from the city center with this small band of exiles and credited the Athenian people en masse with the overthrow of the oligarchy. Furthermore, I argue that following the overthrow of the oligarchy, moderation in the use of expulsion and other forms of punishment against the defeated oligarchs was a key feature in the stability of the restored democracy. In chapter 6 below, I show how this basic contrast between the behavior of the oligarchs and the democrats—especially with regard to the power of expulsion—was highlighted in later accounts of the oligarchic revolutions in order to strengthen the legitimacy of democracy as a form of rule.

Just as Athens' loss in Sicily had had grave consequences for the internal stability of Athens, so Athens' loss in the great war with Sparta brought about an outbreak of civic unrest.[250] The oligarchs who returned to Athens by the terms of the peace treaty with Sparta (404) led the civic disturbances by beginning to work for the overthrow of the democracy.[251] Of the exiles who returned, we know eight by name, three of whom, Critias, Charicles, and Aristoteles, became leading members of the oligarchy established shortly after the peace.[252] These former exiles were joined in their efforts to overthrow the democracy by moderates such as Theramenes, who had negotiated the peace.[253]

An assembly was held after the peace of 404 at which the Athenians voted to establish a commission of thirty men to draw up the ancestral laws by which they would be governed.[254] Several sources report that Lysander was present at this assembly, and thus may have helped to compel the Athenian people to alter their constitution.[255] The execution of the democrat Cleophon shortly before the conclusion of the peace, however, and the imprisonment of his associates, may further have intimidated the Athenians.[256] As in the case of the

---

[250] Arist. Ath. Pol. 34.3, Diod. Sic. 14.3.2–3.

[251] The terms of the peace treaty required the demolition of Athens' walls, the surrender of the fleet except twelve ships, the return of the exiles, and submission to Sparta in foreign policy: Xen. Hell. 2.2.20, Diod. Sic. 13.107.4. Several sources add to these the provision that Athens was to be ruled by the ancestral constitution (πάτριος πολιτεία: Arist. Ath. Pol. 34.3, Diod. Sic. 14.3.2, Justin 5.8.5). I follow Rhodes (CAAP 427) in the view that this was not part of the peace settlement with the Spartans; cf. Wolpert 2002, 13–15.

[252] See above, nn. 248, 249, for references to these men as exiles. For their membership among the Thirty Tyrants, cf. Xen. Hell. 2.3.2.

[253] Arist. Ath. Pol. 34.3, Diod. Sic. 14.3.3.

[254] Xen. Hell. 2.3.2, 11.

[255] Lys. 12.71.76, Arist. Ath. Pol. 34.3, Diod. Sic. 14.3.2–7. Xenophon, however, does not mention the presence of Lysander at this assembly. Rhodes (CAAP 433–34) accepts Lysias's version of events, including Theramenes' role in summoning Lysander and arguing for the oligarchy. Wolpert (2002, 18–24) argues convincingly for following Xenophon's version.

[256] On Cleophon and his associates, see Xen. Hell. 1.7.35, Lys. 13.12, 30.10–14.

oligarchy of 411, arbitrary violence against the citizens was the key to suppressing democratic opposition.[257] There was a notable difference, however.
Whereas the oligarchs of 411 used selective violence to intimidate their opponents into silence, the oligarchs of 404 engaged in acts of violence against
the mass of Athenian citizens and even resident aliens ("metics," μέτοικοι).
This widespread violence—in the form of executions, imprisonments, and
expulsions—was crucial to the formation of opposition to the rule of the Thirty
and its ultimate overthrow.[258]

According to some sources, the oligarchs began their campaign of violence
by executing those citizens who were known sycophants and others who were
agreed by all to be scoundrels.[259] It was not long, however, before the Thirty
began to execute citizens of good standing and anyone whom they thought
would be most able to mount opposition to them.[260] At about this time, the
Thirty obtained a Spartan garrison to help them police the city.[261] The em-
ployment of these Spartans, however, led to further executions of citizens
and wealthy metics, since the oligarchs needed access to their wealth so that
they might pay for the garrison.[262] It is difficult to specify how many victims
were executed, since our sources give different figures and possibly exaggerate
the number of killings.[263] Furthermore, our sources' reports of the murder of
citizens en masse seem to have been assimilated to the representation of tyrannical violence in democratic ideology. Xenophon, for instance, writes that
"the oligarchs were free to do whatever they liked [ἐξὸν ... ποιεῖν αὐτοῖς ὅ τι
βούλοιντο], and they killed many men out of personal animosity and many

[257] Wolpert 2002, 24. According to some sources, especially Lysias and Aristotle, the oligarchs
at first acted moderately and only later turned to violence when opposition to their rule began to
mount. Wolpert argues strongly against this view, pointing out that violence underpinned the
rule of the Thirty from the beginning.

[258] Wolpert 2002, 24: "Violence also fueled opposition and led to the collapse of their
regime."

[259] Xen. *Hell.* 2.3.12, Arist. *Ath. Pol.* 35.3.

[260] Xen. *Hell.* 2.3.14, 38–40; Arist. *Ath. Pol.* 35.4. In what follows, I generally prefer the
chronology of Xenophon over that of Aristotle. These sources differ over the chronology of such
major events as the summoning of the Spartan garrison, Theramenes' execution, and the occupation of Phyle by the exiles. Xenophon's chronology has been generally favored by modern
scholars on the grounds that Xenophon was a contemporary of the events; cf. Hignett, *HAC* 384–
89; Rhodes, *CAAP* 420–22. Wolpert 2002 also follows Xenophon's chronology. Krentz (1982,
131–47) has challenged this orthodoxy and has gained some adherents (e.g., Ostwald 1986, 481–
84). See Wolpert 2002, 15–24, for a summary and refutation of the arguments of these scholars.

[261] Xen. *Hell.* 2.3.13–14, 42; Arist. *Ath. Pol.* 37.2.

[262] Execution of metics and the hostility of metic class to the Thirty: Xen. *Hell.* 2.3.40. For the
execution of citizens and metics without trial by the Thirty, cf. Lys. 12.17, 36, 39, 48, 82, 83, 96;
13.14, 45.

[263] Isoc. 7.67 and 20.11 give the number 1,500. Aeschin. 3.235 and Arist. *Ath. Pol.* 35.4 say
that the Thirty killed over 1,500. A scholion on Aeschin. 1.39 reports that Lysias stated in a (lost)
speech that 2,500 were killed. For clearly exaggerated accounts of the number of killings under
the Thirty, see chapter 6 below.

for the sake of their money [πολλοὺς μὲν ἔχθρας ἕνεκα ἀπέκτεινον, πολλοὺς δὲ χρημάτων]."[264] Not only is the freedom to do as one likes (without subjection to judicial review) a feature of tyrannical rule according to democratic ideology, but the repetition of the phrase "many men" in a description of violent acts against the citizenry is paralleled in many descriptions of tyrannical violence, as we have just seen in the representation of the rule of the oligarchs of 411.[265]

Despite the evident impact of democratic ideology on these formulations, however, we know of a number of concrete instances of executions and flight into exile (presumably out of fear of arrest and execution), and it is likely that the numbers of victims ran into the hundreds, if not thousands.[266] Lysias and his brother Polemarchus, for example, wealthy metics, were targets of the Thirty. Polemarchus was seized and executed, but Lysias escaped and fled to Megara.[267] Xenophon, in a speech that he assigns to the moderate Theramenes, suggests that the violence of the Thirty against the citizens and metics led to both the flight of large numbers of citizens from Athens and the beginning of the formation of opposition to their rule (*Hell.* 2.3.38–42): "When I saw many men in the city becoming hostile to the government and many men becoming exiles [πολλοὺς . . . φυγάδας γιγνομένους], it did not seem to me best to banish [φυγαδεύειν] either Thrasybulus or Anytus. For I knew that thus the opposition would be strong." Despite the vagueness of Xenophon's claim that many men were going into exile as a result of the executions and imprisonment of leading opponents of the Thirty, it is not implausible that some hundreds of Athenian residents (citizen and noncitizen) left Attica out of fear of the extra-judicial executions conducted by the Thirty, as the case of Lysias illustrates.[268]

In addition to the men who apparently fled Attica out of fear of the extra-judicial executions conducted by the Thirty, we know that the Thirty also explicitly banished from the city of Athens all who were not among a group of three thousand citizens whom they enrolled to share power with them.[269] Xenophon, in fact, suggests that the Thirty expelled the citizens not only

[264] Xen. *Hell.* 2.3.21.

[265] Freedom of the tyrant to do as he likes: Hdt. 3.80.3. For a tyrant's violent acts against the mass of the citizenry, see below, chapter 6. The claim that the oligarchs disarmed the whole populace except the Three Thousand (Xen. *Hell.* 2.3.20, Arist. *Ath. Pol.* 37.2) is similarly suspect, since besides the difficulty of performing such an act it is a characteristic feature of the rule of tyrants: cf. Arist. *Ath. Pol.* 15.4–5 (on Pisistratus), *Pol.* 1311a10.

[266] Wolpert (2002, 22) suggests that 1,500 Athenians and many more non-Athenians were killed by the Thirty.

[267] Lys. 12.6–17.

[268] See also Diod. Sic. 14.5.7.

[269] Decree of banishment from the city: Xen. *Hell.* 2.4.1, Lys. 25.22, Isoc. 7.67, Diod. Sic. 14.32.4; cf. Justin 5.9.3. Enrollment of the Three Thousand: Xen. *Hell.* 2.3.17–19, Arist. *Ath. Pol.* 36.1.

from the city but also from their estates in the countryside. He adds that when the exiles gathered at Piraeus, the Thirty drove them out even from there (*Hell.* 2.4.1). In Xenophon's account, therefore, the Thirty's decree entails expulsion from all Attic territory, not just the city.

There are good reasons, however, for rejecting Xenophon's claim that the decree of the Thirty entailed banishment from all Attica. As Peter Krentz has pointed out, it would have been difficult for the Thirty to have expelled such a large group of Athenians from such a large mass of land. In addition, it would have been "shortsighted . . . to throw so many Athenians into the hands of their opponents."[270] That the Thirty did not intend to create a large group of exiles beyond the borders of Attica is demonstrated by the fact that the Spartans, probably at the request of the Thirty, sent out a proclamation forbidding the Greek cities from harboring Athenian exiles and ordering them to deliver up any exiles to the Thirty.[271] A final argument against the idea of a decree of expulsion from Attica is the similarity of this feature of Xenophon's representation of the Thirty to the representation of tyrannical rule in democratic ideology. As we shall see further in chapter 6 below, the idea that tyrants (and non-democratic regimes in general) banish large groups of citizens from their territory was a topos of fifth-century democratic ideology. It is more likely that, although the Thirty banished the citizens from the city proper, they did not expel them from Attica altogether. Indeed, an act of expulsion from the city alone fits more accurately with the political program of the Thirty. Expulsion from the city proper confirmed in physical terms the exclusion of the mass of Athenian citizens from the political process.[272]

While most residents of the city fled to Piraeus and other regions of the Athenian territory following the decree of the Thirty, a number of Athenians also decided to go into exile in non-Athenian lands at this time. The presence of Athenian exiles is attested in Thebes (and throughout Boeotia), Corinth, Megara, Argos, Chalcis, and Oropus.[273] It is likely that these were the exiles whom the Thirty tried to extradite through the aforementioned proclamation of the Spartans. By forbidding the Greek cities to harbor Athenian exiles, the

---

[270] Krentz 1982, 64–66; 1995, 139–40. It should be pointed out that Krentz's purpose in refuting Xenophon's claim is to show that the Thirty in fact banished the Athenians from the city in order that the citizens might return to the land and become perioikoi (περίοικοι, "dwellers round about") on the Spartan model. This argument then forms part of Krentz's larger project of demonstrating that the Thirty were modeling their new constitution after Sparta's. Although the oligarchs were certainly admirers of Sparta, I am skeptical of the notion that the expulsion of the citizens from the city can be explained as a product of their attempts to create a second Sparta.

[271] Din. 1.25, Diod. Sic. 14.6.1, Justin 5.9.4, Lys. 12.95, Plut. *Lys.* 27.2–4; cf. Krentz 1982, 84–85.

[272] Wolpert (2002, 22) notes that the decree had the effect of "disenfranchising practically the entire population of Athens."

[273] Thebes and Boeotia: Diod. Sic. 14.6.3, Justin 5.9.4, Plut. *Lys.* 27.5–6, Din. 1.25. Corinth: Aeschin. 2.147–48. Megara: Xen. *Hell.* 2.4.1, Lys. 12.17. Argos: Diod. Sic. 14.6.2, Justin 5.9.4, Dem. 15.22. Chalcis: Lys. 24.25. Oropus: Lys. 31.9, 17. Cf. Krentz 1982, 69.

Thirty tried to prevent the exiles from utilizing foreign resources to return and overthrow their regime. Although the Spartans managed to intimidate some Greek cities into obeying their proclamation, the Argives and Thebans did not comply. Indeed it was from Thebes, and with Theban support, that a group of exiles set out in order to overthrow the Thirty.[274]

It is widely acknowledged that, despite later claims that the Athenians went into exile en masse and fought to overthrow the Thirty, only a small number of exiles, many of them non-citizens, began the movement by which the Thirty were finally overthrown. As Andrew Wolpert has argued eloquently, the idea that the whole Athenian people suffered exile and collectively returned to overthrow the Thirty was an important fiction that helped to reconcile the divisions among the Athenian citizenry following the rule of the Thirty.[275] Furthermore, as I argue below in chapter 6, this fiction of collective exile and resistance was a product of the assimilation of this event to earlier historical experiences of exile. The key point for my current purposes is that the democratic exiles, however small in number, played a crucial role in destabilizing the regime of the Thirty. More important, I argue that in contrast to the extrajudicial murders and mass expulsions of citizens perpetrated by the Thirty, the restored democracy was markedly restrained in its treatment of the defeated oligarchs. As I argue below in chapter 6, the stark contrast between the behavior of the oligarchs and that of the democrats both renewed and strengthened the association between exile and illegitimate rule already present in democratic ideology.

Whereas the Spartan king Pausanias played a crucial role in ending the rule of the Thirty, it was the actions of a small group of exiles that set in motion the chain of events leading to the restoration of the democracy. Our sources differ as to the number of exiles who set out from Thebes, but a number between fifty and one hundred seems plausible.[276] Thrasybulus was among these exiles, but few others can be identified.[277] The exiles took up a position at Phyle, a naturally fortified place in the southern foothills of Mount Parnes.[278] At Phyle, they were reinforced by some three hundred to five hundred mercenaries hired by the exiled metic Lysias.[279] Shortly afterwards the exiles and mercenaries gathered at Phyle numbered seven hundred men, with more exiles joining them daily.

Growing alarmed, the Thirty marched out against the men at Phyle with the Three Thousand and the cavalry. After an unsuccessful attack, a sudden

---

[274] Diod. Sic. 14.32.1, Justin 5.9.8–9, Plut. *Lys.* 27.4; cf. Lys. 12.96–98.

[275] Wolpert 2002, 75–136. See also Thomas 1989, 132–54, 252–54, for the topos of the people in exile; and chapter 6 below.

[276] Krentz 1982, 70 and n. 4; Wolpert 2002, 24.

[277] Krentz 1982, 72–73.

[278] Cf. Ober 1985, 116, 145–47.

[279] Justin 5.9.9, Oros. 2.17.9, [Plut.] *X Orat.* 3 (Lysias; *Mor.* 835f); cf. Krentz 1982, 73 and n. 11.

snowstorm forced them to retreat. While they retreated, they suffered some losses from guerrilla attacks by the exiles at Phyle.[280] Soon afterwards the Thirty sent out the Spartan garrison to invest the exiles at Phyle, but the Spartans were routed by the men at Phyle in an early morning attack. Shaken by these losses, the Thirty established Eleusis as a place of refuge for themselves if they should need it. They took captive three hundred Eleusinians and brought them to Athens for execution.[281]

Meanwhile the number of exiles gathering at Phyle was growing, and shortly after the execution of the Eleusinians more than a thousand men set out from Phyle under Thrasybulus and occupied Piraeus.[282] When the Thirty marched out against them, the exiles retreated to the more easily defensible hill of Munychia, in Piraeus. Although the forces of the Thirty were better equipped and more numerous, the exiles held a superior position and were reinforced by light-armed fighters from the area around Piraeus.[283] In the ensuing battle the exiles were victorious. Two of the Thirty, Critias and Hippomachus, were killed, as were also one of the ten governors of Piraeus and seventy others who fought with the Thirty.

The victory of the exiles at Munychia shook the adherents of the Thirty in the city. These men from the city voted to depose the Thirty and elected ten men to rule in their place.[284] The remaining members of the Thirty then retreated to their refuge at Eleusis. Meanwhile the exiles in Piraeus were joined by even more men. These exiles were both citizens and metics who had fled to Piraeus and nearby cities when the Thirty had begun purging the city of opposition.[285] The exiles increased enthusiasm for their cause by promising citizenship to non-citizens if they fought with them.[286] Since honorary grants of citizenship could normally be conferred only by the

---

[280] Xen. *Hell.* 2.4.2–3.

[281] Xen. *Hell.* 2.4–8; Diod. Sic. 14.32.4; Lys. 12.52, 13.44.

[282] Xen. *Hell.* 2.4.10, Arist. *Ath. Pol.* 38.1, Diod. Sic. 14.33.2.

[283] Xen. *Hell.* 2.4.11–12, Diod. Sic. 14.33.2. Middleton 1982 argues that a significant number of the light-armed troops were Thracians.

[284] Xen. *Hell.* 2.4.23, Diod. Sic. 14.33.5.

[285] Xen. *Hell.* 2.4.25, Diod. Sic. 14.33.3–4, Arist. *Ath. Pol.* 38.3.

[286] Xen. *Hell.* 2.4.25, Arist. *Ath. Pol.* 40.2. Xenophon states that Thrasybulus offered equal taxation with citizens (ἰσοτέλεια) to the foreigners who fought with him, whereas Aristotle says that the offer was of citizenship (πολιτεία). We have a decree dating to 401 (IG 2² 10) granting some honor to some men who participated in the three stages of the resistance to the oligarchs, namely the return from Phyle, the battle at Munychia, and the stay in Piraeus. The inscription is lacunose in the places where the exact status of the persons honored and the nature of the honor are specified. Scholarly opinion is divided. Some favor the idea that citizenship was offered and granted to foreigners who fought with Thrasybulus (Whitehead 1978, 1984, 1986); others, that citizenship was granted to a small group while the rest were given equal taxation rights (M. Osborne 1981–82, 1:37–41, 2:26–43); still others, that only equal taxation rights were offered (Krentz 1982, 110–12; 1986). Harding 1987 offers a different interpretation of the decree, arguing that it granted freedom and equality of taxation to slaves who fought with the democrats.

Athenian assembly, the exiles were acting as the political authority of Athens.[287] As in 411, the exiles and their supporters at Piraeus constituted a distinct political community for themselves, separate from the Thirty and the Three Thousand in the city. The sources denote the two groups by geographical position, "those in the city" (οἱ ἐν ἄστει) and "those in Piraeus" (οἱ ἐν Πειραιεῖ). These terms mark the geographical separation of democrats from the political center but, more important, reflect the status of the men of Piraeus as exiles within their own territory—internal exiles.[288]

For a while, the two sides engaged in inconsequential skirmishes. When the Thirty called on the Spartans to send new forces, however, the fortunes of the exiles began to turn. The Spartans besieged the exiles by land and sea, and the exiles found themselves cut off from food supplies.[289] At this point, Pausanias, one of the dual kings of Sparta, marched out to Athens with a large army. His purpose in acting is given variously in the sources, but we may be certain that a desire not to let Athens become subject to his political rival Lysander was one of his motives.[290] Pausanias's actions suggest a desire to resolve the conflict in such a way as to restore independence and internal concord to Athens.

Pausanias began by commanding the exiles to return to their homes.[291] When this proved ineffective, he attacked the exiles without notable result. A guerrilla attack on Pausanias's forces by the exiles escalated into a full-scale battle, in which the exiles were defeated.[292] Following this victory, Pausanias sought to bring about a reconciliation between the exiles at Piraeus and the men in the city. The terms of the reconciliation were that the two sides should be at peace with one another and that each should return to his home except the surviving members of the Thirty and those immediately implicated in their regime: the Ten, who ruled Piraeus, and the Eleven.[293] These latter men, and anyone who wished of those who remained in the city under them, were permitted to emigrate to Eleusis, where they could manage their affairs autonomously. Those who decided to emigrate would not be permitted to

[287] For the procedures for grants of honorary citizenship, see M. Osborne 1981–82, 1:6.

[288] E.g., Xen. *Hell.* 2.4.26–27, Arist. *Ath. Pol.* 38.3–4. Ostwald (1986, 490) notes that "all our sources describe the two parties as 'city people' . . . and 'Piraeus people,' . . . which shows . . . [how the Thirty] had split the state geographically as well as ideologically." It is this division that the fiction of the people in exile was aimed to elide, as is shown by Wolpert 2002.

[289] Xen. *Hell.* 2.4.26–29.

[290] Jealousy of Lysander: Xen. *Hell.* 2.4.29, Diod. Sic. 14.33.6. Sympathy for the cause of the exiles: Lys. 18.10–12, Justin 5.10.4. Cf. Krentz 1995, 150: "less emotional motives such as respect for allies' independence and a desire to avoid military entanglements far from home were also probably involved."

[291] Xen. *Hell.* 2.4.31.

[292] Xen. *Hell.* 2.4.31–34.

[293] Xen. *Hell.* 2.4.38, Diod. Sic. 14.33.6, Arist. *Ath. Pol.* 38.3–4. The Eleven were in charge of the prison and executions, and thus were implicated in the crimes of the Thirty.

enter the city, and those who remained in the city would not be allowed to go to Eleusis except to celebrate the Mysteries. Those who wished to emigrate were given twenty days to leave. A person could at any time remove himself from the roll of the emigrants and return to the city, after which he could stand for public office in the city if he wished. At this point, therefore, it appeared that the civil war would be ended through the creation of two separate states within Attic territory. This solution, however, lasted only a short while. In 401, the Athenians became suspicious of the men at Eleusis because they were hiring mercenaries.[294] The Athenians then set out to put down the forces of the men at Eleusis and executed their generals when they came for a conference in the field. After this, the Athenians in the city persuaded the men at Eleusis to be reconciled with them. The men at Eleusis then returned to Athens, and the two parties lived together as fellow citizens.[295]

Perhaps the most important feature of the reconciliation was the oath that the Athenians took to ensure the peace. In this oath, the Athenians swore "not to remember past wrongs" (μὴ μνησικακεῖν). The amnesty was to cover all citizens, including any members of the Thirty, the Eleven, and the governors of Piraeus if they rendered account for their conduct in office in proceedings held by the restored democracy.[296] The body under which they were submitted to scrutiny, moreover, was to be composed of those who had taxable property.[297] In other words, they would render account before a sympathetic board, among whom members of the Three Thousand would be present.[298]

Thus the first settlement, by which the oligarchs of 404/3 were allowed to emigrate to Eleusis (with full rights and protections) and live separately from the Athenians in the city, was soon replaced by full reconciliation and restoration of citizens to the city. It seems that the democrats behaved moderately and justly toward their former oppressors. All the oligarchs except the ringleaders were given general amnesty, while even former members of the Thirty and their closest associates were permitted to live in Athens if they submitted to scrutiny for their conduct in office. We do hear of some exiles in the period after 401, but these were probably remaining members of the Thirty who had committed grave crimes and thought it safer not to return to Athens, where they would be tried for murder.[299]

Although the events of 404/3 were sometimes brought up in speeches before the political and judicial bodies of Athens in the years that followed the reconciliation, it appears that the former exiles did not take vengeance on

---

[294] Xen. Hell. 2.4.43.
[295] Xen. Hell. 2.4.43, Arist. Ath. Pol. 39.4.
[296] Amnesty: Xen. Hell. 2.4.43; Lys. 25.28; Andoc. 1.81, 90; Arist. Ath. Pol. 39.6.
[297] Arist. Ath. Pol. 39.6.
[298] Ostwald 1986, 499, citing Cloché 1915, 268–72.
[299] Lys. 12.35, 25.24; Krentz 1982, 123.

those who remained in the city under the Thirty.[300] Aristotle even reports that after the settlement a person who tried to stir up memories of the events of 404/3 was brought before the council and sentenced to death. This punishment was meant to serve as an example to others not to break their oath of amnesty.[301] Thus the rule of the restored democrats of 404, like that of the democrats of 410, was characterized by leniency toward the former oligarchs and the rule of law. As I argue below in chapter 6, the sharp contrast between the behavior of the restored democracy and the rule of the oligarchs both recalled and reinvigorated the connection between non-democratic regimes and exile in Athenian democratic ideology.

Conclusion

In this chapter, I have argued that the Athenian democracy used the power of expulsion with moderation and that this moderation contributed to both the stability of the democracy and its ideological legitimacy. The democratic institution of ostracism served as a practical mechanism for deterring intra-elite strife and was a key symbol of democratic moderation in the use of the power of expulsion. Following the oligarchic revolutions of the late fifth century, moreover, the contrast between elite forms of rule and democratic rule became even more marked. Borrowing from earlier democratic traditions linking exile with tyranny, the Athenians represented the oligarchs' use of violent expulsions as a key indicator of the injustice of their regime. Finally, I argued that the ideological construction of exile in the representation of oligarchic rule was an important factor in the formation of opposition to that rule, as well as in the construction of Athenian collective identity following the restoration of the democracy. In the next chapter, I show how the Athenians extended the practice and ideology of exile to their management of their relations with other Greek poleis, in particular the cities of the Athenian alliance.

---

[300] Xen. *Hell.* 2.4.43, Arist. *Ath. Pol.* 40.3; with modern judgments by Ostwald 1986, 510–11; Krentz 1982, 120; Wolpert 2002, 48–71.

[301] Arist. *Ath. Pol.* 40.2.

Chapter Five

EXILE AND EMPIRE

Expulsion in Inter-State Politics

I argued in the previous two chapters that the Athenian democracy put an end to violent intra-elite politics of exile by usurping control over decisions of exile and using this power with moderation—in particular through the institution of ostracism. Moreover, in the last chapter we saw that in contrast to the oligarchs who seized power at the end of the fifth century, the restored Athenian democracy used the power of expulsion with moderation. In this chapter, I turn to the wider Greek world of the fifth century and examine Athens' use of the tool of exile in the management of its relations with other Greek poleis. For although it might be recognized that the Athenian democracy used the power of expulsion with moderation in the domestic sphere, there are signs that it was less restrained in its relations with its allies.

Indeed, we know of a number of cases where the Athenians did expel a population en masse from its territory and settle Athenian or other colonists on the territory.[1] Furthermore, the Athenians, like a number of other major powers of the time (e.g., Sparta, Persia) frequently intervened in conflicts between oligarchs and democrats in various Greek poleis in order to install regimes sympathetic to themselves. In doing so, they sometimes expelled en masse those who were hostile to their own interests. It might be said, in fact, that major powers such as Athens contributed to the development of a new type of politics of exile in the Greek states of the fifth century. In this form of the practice of expulsion, rival groups of oligarchs and democrats appealed to outside powers for aid in expelling (and often killing) their political opponents.[2]

---

[1] For example: Histiaea, 447/6 (expulsion of Histiaeans and settlement of Athenian colonists on their land, Thuc. 1.114.3–4); Potidaea, 432 (expulsion of the men, women, and children and settlement of Athenian colonists on the land, Thuc. 2.70.3); Aegina, 431 (expulsion of men, women, and children, Thuc. 2.27.1); Mytilene, 427 (execution and enslavement according to the original decree, Thuc. 3.36.2–4; but trial and execution only of the most culpable, who numbered less than a thousand, according to the second decree, Thuc. 3.49.1–50.1); Torone, 422 (men sent to Athens, women and children enslaved, Thuc. 5.3.4); Scione, 421 (men killed, women and children enslaved, land given to the Plataeans, Thuc. 5.32.1); Melos, 416 (men whom they captured were killed, the women and children enslaved, and Athenian colonists sent to settle the land, Thuc. 5.116.4). Enslavement of the women and children essentially meant their expulsion, since they would be sold abroad, although it is possible that some were bought as slaves by the colonists.

[2] The civil war at Corcyra in 427 is the classic example (Thuc. 3.69–85). Although Thucydides makes much of the rampant killings of oligarchs by democrats, he also makes clear that a

205

While I do not wish to deny that the Athenian democracy engaged in the violent expulsion of entire populations as well as specific political groups within Greek poleis during the fifth century, I draw attention in this chapter to a neglected aspect of Athenian foreign policy, namely the ways in which the Athenian democracy sought to regulate and dampen the politics of exile in allied Greek poleis. I argue that if we pay close attention to Athenian decrees concerning relations with other Greek states, we see that the Athenians in fact took steps to reassure allied Greek states that they would not engage in violent mass expulsions and that all decisions of exile would be made through regularized political and legal procedures in both the allied state and Athens. I argue that the guarantees that the Athenians made to allied states with regard to exile were motivated both by the desire to lessen the possibility of violent civil conflict and thus stabilize Athenian relations with these states, and by a desire to represent Athenian power in the Greek world as just in comparison to that of its rival Sparta. In other words, just as the Athenian democracy set limits on the use of exile as a political tool within its own body politic in order to stabilize the polis and justify democratic power internally, so, in Athenian relations with other states, the Athenians used the power of expulsion with moderation as a means of stabilizing their alliance and justifying Athenian influence and power in the external world.

In order to make the argument that the Athenians engaged in a policy of moderation as well as brute force in their relations with other Greeks, I examine several Athenian decrees concerned with exile in the Greek poleis.[3] These decrees are usually interpreted as indications of imperialistic usurpation of control over decisions of exile, among other penalties (e.g., execution, disenfranchisement), in allied Greek states.[4] I argue, by contrast, that attention to the ideological associations of the language of the decrees, as well as the

---

number of the oligarchs fled into exile (3.85). See also Athenian intervention in Samos in 441 and 411, when the Athenians helped the Samian people expel oligarchs and establish a democratic government (Thuc. 1.115–17, 8.21; IG 1³ 96, cited below). In 441, moreover, the exiled Samian oligarchs called on another great power for aid, namely the Persians. Compare also the case of Epidamnus, where the democrats expelled the oligarchs, and then appealed to the great powers of Corcyra and Corinth for aid against the exiles (Thuc. 1.24–30). Athenian intervention in the internal struggles of Boeotian and Euboean poleis, furthermore, may have contributed to the creation of the groups of Boeotian and Euboean exiles who helped to defeat Athens at Coronea in 446 (Thuc. 1.113 and "Further Regulation of Exile" below in this chapter).

[3] Athens' dual strategy of force and moderation is in fact schematized in Thucydides' representation of the debate at Athens concerning the punishment of the Mytileneans following their revolt in 428 (3.37–48). In this debate the rival speakers, Cleon and Diodotus, make the case for force and moderation, respectively. Cleon's policy entailed the wholesale execution or expulsion of a rebellious population from its territory. Diodotus's policy required the punishment only of those most culpable of instigating the revolt, and only after a trial at Athens.

[4] For this complaint among ancient critics of the Athenian empire, see [Xen.] Ath. Pol. 1.14, 16, cited below. Meiggs 1972 is an example of this view in modern scholarship: see discussion below.

manner in which they were displayed, shows that the Athenians were not simply taking control of decisions of exile in order to help their friends and harm their enemies, as ancient and modern critics maintain, but were utilizing the political institutions, vocabulary, and visual imagery of the Athenian democracy itself to place quite remarkable limitations on their own use of the power of expulsion. I argue that the aim of this skillful use of the symbolic vocabulary of the Athenian democracy was to represent Athenian power in the Greek world as legitimate and just. In "Exile and the Mythical Past" below in this chapter, I show how late fifth- and fourth-century literary texts reveal that Athenian moderation in the use of exile served to symbolize the justice of Athenian power.

ATHENIAN CONTROL AND LIMITATION OF EXILE: THE ERYTHRAE DECREE

Evidence for Athenian control and limitation of exile in allied states is found in one of the earliest known Athenian inscriptions concerning Athens' relations with its allies, namely the decree concerning the Erythraeans.[5] Although the date of the decree is uncertain, most editors place it in the late 450s or early 440s.[6] In the first part of the decree, the Athenians set forth guidelines for establishing a council, which was to share some features with the Athenian Council of Five Hundred.[7] Most significant for my purposes, however, is that the Athenians required the new councilors to take an oath in which they swore not only to remain loyal to the Erythraean and Athenian demoi, but in addition neither to "receive back any of those who are in exile" nor "banish anyone who remains" in the city without the consent of the Athenian council and people (IG 1³ 14.26–29):

[5] IG 1³ 14. The original inscription was found near the Erechtheum and copied by a French traveler in the first part of the nineteenth century before being lost. For a recent edition and discussion of the decree, see Koch 1991. Other important editions and discussions include Highby 1936, ATL 2 D 10, ML 40. See Koch 1991, 61, for full bibliography.

[6] IG 1³ 14 prefers to leave the date uncertain. Meiggs (1972, 422) assigns the decree tentatively to 453/2 on the basis of a restoration of the archon's name. Koch (1991, 61–63) summarizes the arguments for dating (the evidence of the tribute lists, the restoration of the archon's name, the tone and contents of the decree) and argues that these are all indecisive. He nevertheless places the decree between 453 and 445. In dating this and other Athenian decrees, I adopt the earlier chronology accepted by most scholars. Mattingly (1963, 1992, 1996) has argued that many decrees traditionally dated to the mid-fifth century need to be redated to the last quarter of the fifth century. His arguments have been accepted by some scholars (e.g., Vickers 1996). The date of the decree is not crucial to the general argument presented here.

[7] The new council was to be chosen by lot from among citizens who were at least thirty years old. Membership on the council more than once in four years was forbidden. On the basis of these guidelines for the new council, many scholars infer that the Athenians required that the Erythraeans establish a democracy: cf., e.g., Meiggs 1972, 113. D. Lewis (1984, 59), however, is skeptical, and I prefer to leave open the question of the constitutional arrangements for Erythrae.

- - - τὸν φ[υγάδ]ον [κατ]αδέχσομαι οὐδ[ὲ] ηένα οὔτ' - - - - - - - - -
[ἄλλο]ι πείσο[μ]α[ι τὸν ἐς] Μέδος φε[υ]γό[ντο]ν ἄνευ τ̑ε͂[ς] βο[λ̑ες τ̑ες]
['Αθε]ναίον καὶ τ̑ο [δ]ε͂μο [ο]ὐδὲ τὸν μενόντον ἐχσελ̑ο [ἄ]ν[ευ] τ̑ες β[ολ̑ες]
τ̑ες 'Αθεναίον καὶ τ̑ο δε͂μο.

I will not receive back any of those who are in exile with the Persians, nor will I obey another [who orders me to do so] without [the consent of] the Athenian council and the people, nor will I banish anyone who remains without [the consent of] the Athenian council and people.

The stipulation concerning exile in the oath suggests that Erythrae had been embroiled in civil war entailing the politics of exile. Evidently, the group currently in exile was supported by the Persians, while the group in power was supported by Athens. It is likely that Athenian support of the latter group had resulted in its ascendancy over its rivals. The defeated opposition then sought refuge with the Persians, compelled either by force or by fear. The Athenians evidently deemed that the return of the exiles or the augmentation of the exiles by new expulsions would threaten the stability of Athens' settlement with Erythrae. They therefore required that any future decisions of exile be approved by the Athenian council and people. On the most simple reading, then, the Athenians effectively removed control over decisions of exile from the Erythraeans.

Indeed, Russell Meiggs interprets the clause concerning exile accordingly: "Athens has presumably intervened to drive out the Medizers and retains firm control of the political purge."[8] This interpretation, however, seems unbalanced. Meiggs emphasizes only Athens' control of decisions of exile, and not the limitations imposed on that control. This latter aspect of the decree arises from the phrase "without [the consent of] the Athenian council and people" (ἄνευ τ̑ε͂[ς] βο[λ̑ες τ̑ες] | ['Αθε]ναίον καὶ τ̑ο [δ]έμο, 27–28). Although it is difficult to determine the precise procedures that must be followed if the Erythraeans wish to receive back one of the exiles or banish one of their citizens, it is clear that a petition must be made to the Athenians as a whole, as embodied either in the assembly or in the courts.[9] In other words, it was not sufficient that the Erythraeans petition the Athenian officials in Erythrae—for example, the supervisor (ἐπίσκοπος) or the garrison commander (φρούραρχος)—in order to get permission to receive or expel one of their citizens.[10] This requirement is significant in several regards.

First of all, by requiring that all decisions of exile in Erythrae be approved by the Athenians as a whole, as embodied politically in the council and the assembly, the Athenians indicated that such decisions would not be hasty and arbitrary, but would be made through a regular procedure by which the most authoritative

[8] Meiggs 1972, 113.
[9] On the role of the courts in regulating exile in the allied cities, see the discussion of the Chalcis Decree below.
[10] Both these officials are attested for Erythrae in *IG* 1³ 14 and 15.

bodies of the state were consulted. This requirement must have served to reassure the Erythraeans that there would be no sudden new outbreak of the politics of exile with the support of Athenian officials and forces in Erythrae, since future decisions of exile would be subject to a regularized political and/or judicial procedure in Athens. Just as the replacement of arbitrary expulsions at Athens with the democratic procedure of ostracism had dampened the politics of exile and stabilized the state, the requirement that the Erythraeans get the approval of the Athenian people before expelling a citizen would have moderated the politics of exile at Erythrae and stabilized the political situation there.

The case for seeing the clause about exile in the oath of the Erythraean council as an attempt by Athens to moderate the politics of exile is strengthened by comparison with the Chalcis Decree, which I will discuss below. Before I do so, however, there are a few more observations concerning the Erythrae Decree that further the case for seeing the decree as aimed at the moderation of the politics of exile. Following the oath to be taken by the Erythraean council, the decree continues with provisions regarding judicial penalties at Erythrae. In this part of the decree, the Athenians seem to confirm the right of Erythraean courts to impose penalties of death, exile, and the confiscation of property (*IG* 1³ 14.29–32): "If an Erythraean kills another Erythraean, let him be put to death, if he is convicted (ἐὰν [γν]οσθεῖ) [8 *letters*] convicted, let him flee the whole [territory] of the Athenians and their alliance; and let his property be confiscated for the public treasury of the Erythraeans." In this part of the decree, the Athenians confirm the right of the Erythraeans to impose major legal penalties on their own citizens, including expulsion, if such penalties are imposed by a court of law (ἐὰν [γν]οσθεῖ).[11] Just as in the oath the Athenians were concerned to moderate the politics of exile through providing a regularized procedure for political decisions of exile, so here the Athenians are concerned that major judicial punishments such as exile are the result of proper legal procedure.[12] Both sections of the decree therefore reinforce procedural rules. In the part of the decree just cited, the Athenians, indeed, seem eager to reinforce decisions of exile made through Erythraean judicial procedures by extending the range of the penalty of exile to the whole territory controlled by Athens and its allies.

It is perhaps fitting to emphasize here that I am not arguing that Athens pursued a policy of moderation toward Erythrae because of moral considerations. Rather, Athens' policies were dictated by self-interest (τὸ ξύμφορον).[13] The Athenians judged that a policy of moderation would be more effective in keeping the allies loyal. Specifically, Athenian control over decisions of exile and guar-

---

[11] Although commentators assume that an Erythraean court is meant by this phrase, the language leaves open the possibility that an Athenian court is meant.

[12] The decree thus seems to make a distinction between political and judicial exile.

[13] Thuc. 3.47.5 (cf. 40.4); see once again Thucydides' representation of the debate concerning Mytilene (3.37–48), where both Cleon and Diodotus agree that self-interest rather than compassion (οἶκτος) should be the guiding principle of Athenian foreign policy.

antees of regularized procedures set limits on the destabilizing politics of exile in Erythrae and were designed to keep Erythrae both stable and loyal. Moreover, the use of a policy of moderation also had ideological value as well, as I argue below, since Athens' moderate use of political expulsions became an important symbol of the just exercise of Athenian power in the fifth and fourth century.

FURTHER REGULATION OF EXILE: THE CHALCIS DECREE

Shortly after the settlement of the affairs of Erythrae, the Athenians faced a major crisis in mainland Greece. In 446, Athens was defeated at Coronea in Boeotia by a group of Boeotian and Euboean exiles along with the Locrians.[14] This defeat meant loss of the influence in Boeotia that Athens had gained in 458/7 with the victory over the Spartans at Oenophytae.[15] Furthermore, shortly after the defeat at Coronea, the entire island of Euboea revolted from the Athenian alliance. Ironically, it is quite likely that Athens' policies in Boeotia and Euboea in the 450s contributed directly or indirectly to the creation of the groups of Boeotian and Euboean exiles who brought about the crisis in 446.[16] Nevertheless, I argue in this section that despite the Athenians' possible role in creating the group of hostile exiles who then helped to defeat them, a decree concerning Athens' relations with Chalcis following the suppression of the revolt of Euboea demonstrates that the

[14] Thuc. 1.113.

[15] Thuc. 1.108.

[16] Meiggs (1972, 99–100; cf. 176), for example, infers from the participation of Boeotian troops in an Athenian campaign in Thessaly shortly after 458/7 that Athens had required Boeotian cities to participate in Athens' foreign policy and had "promoted elements that might be expected to favor Athens, and [kept] in check hostile elements by requiring hostages and exiling the irreconcilable." With regard to the Euboean exiles, there is some highly controversial evidence that Euboea, along with Andros and Naxos, may have received Athenian cleruchs c. 450. Some late sources claim that Athenian cleruchs were established in Euboea by the Athenian general Tolmides, presumably after the expulsion of some Euboean landholders (Diod. Sic. 11.88.3, Paus. 1.27.5; cf. Plut. *Per.* 7.8). For the view that Euboea did receive cleruchs on confiscated land, see Meiggs 1972, 121–24. Isoc. *Paneg.* 107–9, on the other hand, takes it as fact that cleruchs were *not* established on Euboea as they were in Scione. Furthermore, the Athenian decree of 446 concerning Chalcis mentions "foreigners in Chalcis," an ambiguous phrase taken by some to refer to Athenian cleruchs (*IG* 1³ 40.52–57). Fornara 1978, however, argues that these foreigners are not cleruchs but "simply Athenian citizens who lived in Chalcis." The archaeological evidence (Green and Sinclair 1970) for the presence of Athenians on Euboea is inconclusive as to whether the Athenians were cleruchs or simply Athenians living abroad. The cause of Tolmides' mission to Euboea is unknown, although it is possible that civil war in the Euboean cities in the 450s made Euboean loyalty to Athens uncertain and prompted Tolmides' campaign. Meiggs (1972, 123–24) suggests that the establishment of a cleruchy was intended to stabilize the situation by providing support to the pro-Athenian factions in the cities. The Athenians may have been settled on land confiscated from Euboeans who were exiled either by their pro-Athenian opponents or by the Athenians themselves.

Athenians attempted to stabilize relations with the cities of Euboea in the future by placing limits on their own power to expel Euboean citizens.

Before making this argument, a brief review of Athens' management of the aftermath of the revolt of Euboea is necessary. From the literary sources we know that, at the outbreak of the revolt, Pericles crossed over to Euboea with an army, and, after a quick return to Athens to deal with a Peloponnesian invasion led by the Spartan king Pleistoanax, subdued the whole of Euboea.[17] The Athenians then came to terms with most of the cities on the island, but expelled the Histiaeans from their homes and resettled their land. Plutarch tells us that the harsh treatment of the Histiaeans was due to their execution of the crew of an Athenian ship that they had captured.[18] The relative leniency with which the rest of Euboea was treated indeed suggests that there must have been something particularly offensive to the Athenians in the behavior of the Histiaeans during the revolt.

From inscriptions we learn some of the details of the settlements that Athens made with Eretria and Chalcis. Unfortunately, only the decree concerning Chalcis is well preserved.[19] Meiggs writes of the decree: "Chalcis has been punished severely and no important concessions are made."[20] Examination of the contents of the decree, however, reveals that Meiggs's judgment is again one-sided. Just as in the Erythrae Decree the Athenians strive to exert some restraint on the politics of exile, so in the Chalcis Decree they show similar concern to pursue a policy of moderation, especially in banishments.[21]

First of all, it is remarkable that by the terms of the Athenian decree concerning Chalcis not only are the Chalcidians to swear an oath of loyalty to the Athenian people, but the Athenian council and jurors are to swear an oath to the Chalcidians. Indeed, the oath of the Athenians comes first in the decree, ahead of the Chalcidians'.[22] It was usual in an inter-state peace treaty

[17] Thuc. 1.114, Diod. Sic. 12.7, Plut. *Per.* 22–23. Plutarch's claim that Pericles also expelled the wealthy landowners, the Hippobotae, from Chalcis and established a cleruchy there at this time is plausibly explained as confusion with the events of 506 recorded by Herodotus (5.77.2–3); cf. Fornara 1978, 44–47. This confusion is also evident in Ael. *VH* 6.1, as argued by Fornara.

[18] Plut. *Per.* 23.2.

[19] *IG* 1³ 40.

[20] Meiggs 1972, 118. Cf. Balcer 1978, 35: "not a generous concession"; cf. ML p. 141.

[21] See now Ostwald 2002 for a similar reinterpretation of the Chalcis Decree as an example of Athenian moderation. Ostwald focuses particularly on the question of whether Athens imposed political restrictions on Chalcis, and concludes that Athens did not interfere with Chalcidian political autonomy.

[22] The only other attested instance of an Athenian oath in a decree following a revolt is in the Athenian decree of 439/8 concerning the Samians (*IG* 1³ 48). It is likely, however, that the Athenians swore an oath to the Eretrians in their settlement with Eretria after the revolt of Euboea (*IG* 1³ 39.1–3). In other Athenian settlements with subject states, only the oath of the subject state is attested, although this may have more to do with the fragmentary condition of the decrees than the non-existence of Athenian oaths to the subject states. See, for example, *IG* 1³ 14 and 15 (Erythrae) and 37 (Colophon).

for both parties to swear to abide by its terms.²³ In the Chalcis Decree, therefore, Athens appears to take a stance toward the Chalcidians more akin to an inter-state agreement between independent states than to a dictation of terms to a defeated rebellious subject. Indeed, the Athenians make a number of promises in their oath that read more like attempts to pacify the Chalcidians than to punish them (*IG* 1³ 40.3–16):

> The council and the jurors of Athenians are to swear the following oath: I will not banish Chalcidians from Chalcis [οὐκ ἐχσελῶ Χαλκιδέας ἐχ Χαλκίδος], nor will I destroy the city [οὐδὲ τὲν πόλιν ἀνάστατον ποέσο], nor will I disenfranchise any private citizen [οὐδὲἰδιότεν οὐδένα ἀτιμόσο] or sentence to exile [οὐδὲ φυγῆι ζεμιόσο] or arrest [οὐδὲ χσυλλέφσομαι] or kill [οὐδὲ ἀποκτενῶ] or confiscate the property [οὐδὲ χρέματα ἀφαιρέσομαι] of anyone without trial [ἀκρίτο οὐδενός] without the [consent of] the Athenian people [ἄνευ τὸ δέμο τὸ Ἀθεναίον], nor will I put to vote a motion against [anyone] without prior notice [οὐδ' ἐπιφσεφιῶ κατὰ ἀπροσκλέτο], either against the [Chalcidian] people [κατὰ τὸ κοινῶ] or against any private individual [κατὰ ἰδιότο οὐδὲ ἑνός]; and, if an embassy arrives, I will bring it before the council and the people [προσάχσο πρὸς βολὲν καὶ δῆμον] to the best of my ability within ten days when I am president [hόταν πρυτανεύο]. I will uphold these things (ταῦτα δὲ ἐμπ[ε]δόσο) if the Chalcidians continue to obey the Athenian people (Χαλκιδεῦσιν πειθομένοις τῶι δέ[μ]οι τῶι Ἀθεναίον).

Besides the fact that the Athenians swear an oath at all, two further points in the contents of the oath are remarkable. First, it is significant that the Athenian oath is taken by the Athenian council and jurors. Second, the Athenians appear to guarantee the Chalcidians some sort of due process before exacting any severe penalties. Before elaborating on these two points, however, the contents of the oath must be clarified. Two distinct categories of action are outlined in the oath.²⁴ The first category concerns actions that may be taken against the Chalcidians as a whole (Χαλκιδέας, ll. 4–5; κατὰ τὸ κοινο, l. 11). In this regard, the Athenians pledge not to expel the Chalcidians en masse (οὐκ ἐχσελῶ Χαλκιδέας ἐχ Χαλκίδος, ll. 4–5) or destroy their city (οὐδὲ τὲν πόλιν ἀνάστατον ποέσο, ll. 5–6).²⁵ The second category concerns actions against individual Chalcidians (ἰδιότεν οὐδένα, l. 6; κατὰ ἰδιότο οὐδὲ ἑνός,

---

²³ See, for example, *IG* 1³ 83.26–28, with Thuc. 5.47.8–11 (Athenian treaty with the Argives, Mantineans, and Eleans of 420).

²⁴ Cf. Balcer 1978, 37.

²⁵ For the translation of the verb ἐχσελῶ as referring to a political act following defeat in war, see Koch 1991, 514n.6, with examples cited there. Balcer (1978, 35), on the other hand, takes the verb as a reference to judicial exile. This is odd, since Balcer himself (see n. 24 above) recognizes that a distinction is made between political actions against the Chalcidians as a whole and judicial actions against individual Chalcidians. Judicial exile is distinguished from political exile in the inscription through the use of the distinct phrase φυγῆι ζεμιόσο.

ll. 11–12). In this regard, the Athenians pledge neither to disenfranchise, nor sentence to exile, nor arrest, nor kill, nor confiscate the property of any individual. The Athenians therefore distinguish between political penalties enacted against the city as a whole and legal penalties against individual citizens.

The Athenian pledge to refrain from these categories of action is qualified by the phrases ἀκρίτο οὐδενὸς and ἄνευ τô δέμο τô Ἀθεναίον (ll. 9–10). These phrases are crucial to the interpretation of the decree, although their exact meaning and relation to one another is not immediately clear. The meaning of the adjective ἀκρίτο is clarified through its usage in Athenian texts. As noted by Balcer, Rhodes, and others, the adjective ἄκριτος "connotes the legal meaning 'without trial in the proper form' and was regularly used in Athenian cases where the verdicts of the Boule [council] were not confirmed by a Heliastic [popular] court."[26] In other words, someone who is punished ἄκριτος is not given the chance to defend himself before a popular court. Moreover, grammatically the phrase ἀκρίτο οὐδενός depends (as a possessive genitive) on the last clause of the second set of actions (i.e., legal penalties against individuals): "nor will I confiscate the property of anyone without a proper trial." The phrase ἀκρίτο οὐδενός, therefore, seems to refer to an individual's right to trial before a popular court.

The phrase ἄνευ τô δέμο τô Ἀθεναίον, on the other hand, could be taken to qualify not only actions against individuals as heard in the popular courts, but also those against the Chalcidian people as a whole. In regard to the latter category of actions (mass expulsion, destruction of the city), the phrase would mean that the Athenians pledged that these actions could be taken only by decree of the people (and not by the council or the Athenian officials on hand in Chalcis). This sense is strengthened by the later clauses in which the Athenians pledge not to bring a motion to vote without prior notice, and to bring a Chalcidean embassy before the council and people within ten days.[27] In these clauses, the Athenians are promising not only that decisions concerning the Chalcidian people will be taken by the Athenian people as a whole, but that the Chalcidians will be given the opportunity to present their side through a hearing in the council and assembly.

If we take the phrase ἄνευ τô δέμο τô Ἀθεναίον as qualifying not only the first category of actions against the Chalcidian people as a whole, but also the second category of penalties against individual Chalcidians, then the phrase would refer to the will of the Athenians as enacted through the popular courts, a meaning foregrounded, as we have seen, by the use of the adjective

---

[26] Rhodes 1972, 180; Balcer 1978, 37–38; with references to Lys. 22.2, Arist. Ath. Pol. 40.2. See also Xen. Hell. 1.7.25 on the trial of the generals in 406.

[27] These two clauses of the oath apply strictly only to the Athenian councilors, not the jurors, since it was the councilors who had the responsibility to bring a motion to vote (ἐπιφσεφιô) and to bring embassies before the council and assembly. Cf. Balcer 1978, 43.

ἄκριτος. The idea that through both phrases the Athenians guarantee individual Chalcidians due process of law before a popular court is strengthened by consideration of the rider to the decree proposed by one Archestratus (*IG* 1³ 40.70–76):

> Archestratus proposed . . . trials [τὰς εὐθύνας]²⁸ between Chalcidians [Χαλκ-ιδεῦσι κατὰ σφῶν αὐτόν] are to take place in Chalcis [ἔναι ἐν Χαλκίδι] just as [trials] between Athenians take place in Athens [καθάπερ Ἀθένεσιν Ἀθεναίοις], except [in cases in which the penalties are] exile, death, and disenfranchisement [πλὲν φυγὲς καὶ θανάτο καὶ ἀτιμίας]; concerning these, appeal [ἔφεσιν]²⁹ to the Heliaea of the Thesmothetae [ἐς τὲν ἐλιαίαν τὲν τῶν θεσμοθετῶν] at Athens is to be allowed according to the decree of the people [κατὰ τὸ φσέφισμα τῶ δέμο].

Leaving aside other issues for the moment, the rider provides for a trial in the Heliaea (ἠλιαία, popular courts of Athens) for Chalcidians who become subject to the severest penalties.³⁰ Thus the rider corresponds to the second category of actions pledged by the Athenians in their oath, namely not to impose the severest penalties on individual Chalcidians without due process of law before a popular court. We may conclude, therefore, that the Athenians guarantee by their oath both a fair hearing before the Athenian people to a Chalcidian delegation before issuing a decree of mass expulsion of Chalcidians or destruction of Chalcis, and the right to a trial in an Athenian popular court for any Chalcidian subject to the penalties of dienfranchisement, exile, arrest, death, or confiscation of property. Meiggs dismisses these concessions as not important, presumably because the Athenians retain the power to exact these penalties if they so decide. I contend, however, that Meiggs overlooks the symbolic and ideological, not to mention practical, significance of these Athenian pledges.

The significance of these pledges is evident from three considerations. First of all, as I noted above, the oath is to be sworn by the Athenian councilors and jurors. This brings the oath sworn to the Chalcidians in line with the oaths sworn annually by the Athenian councilors and jurors to the Athenian citizens themselves. Second, and not unrelated to the first point, is that

---

²⁸ Most scholars accept that the term εὐθύνας must refer to any trial, and not strictly to the Athenian procedure for examining a magistrate at the end of his term. Cf. de Ste. Croix 1961, 271; Balcer 1978; Meiggs 1972. Gomme (*HCT* 1:342), however, argues for the more restricted meaning.

²⁹ I accept de Ste. Croix's arguments (1961, 271–72) for interpreting ἔφεσιν as "appeal"; cf. Harrison 1971, 191; Meiggs 1972, 224–25.

³⁰ The phrase "Heliaea of the Thesmothetae" was the archaic way of referring to the Athenian popular courts. See Balcer 1978, 109–10, with references there in n. 23; Rhodes 1972, 168–69; Hansen 1989c. The phrase is also used in the Coinage Decree of 449 (*ATL* 2 D 14, ML 45). The use of the term "Heliaea" alone may be found in the Clinias Decree of 448/7 (*IG* 1³ 34.39, 71) and in the tribute reassessment decree of 425/4 (*IG* 1³ 71.49).

the Athenians extend their own political and judicial processes to the Chalcidian people. Just as the Athenian councilors and jurors swore annually to follow the laws and decrees of the Athenian people in their conduct of political and judicial affairs, so they swore an oath to the Chalcidians to allow the same political and judicial procedures to govern their behavior toward Chalcis and the Chalcidians. Third, the significance of the fact that the Athenian decree describing the provisions of the Athenian oath to the Chalcidians was inscribed and prominently displayed in both Chalcis and Athens should not be underestimated. By publicly displaying not only Chalcis's duties toward Athens but also Athens' toward Chalcis, the Athenians represented themselves to the Chalcidians and to themselves as a just and moderate imperial power. The inscribed stone would have served as a physical monument to the just relations between Athens and its allies and as a reference point for the oral dissemination of this representation in the public spaces of Athens, Chalcis, and other subject states. Each of these three points must be taken up individually.

It is unusual in extant decrees for the Athenian councilors and jurors together to be required to swear an oath.[31] Christian Koch ascribes the participation of the jurors to the need to have a large body of oath takers corresponding to the male citizenry of Chalcis, who are required to take the Chalcidian oath.[32] Jack Balcer notes, more importantly, the parallels in content between the Athenian oath to the Chalcidians and the councilors' and jurors' oaths, and comments on the appropriateness of having the council and jurors swear an oath regarding political and judicial procedures.[33] Although Balcer explicates the textual and substantive parallels between the oaths, however, he does not recognize the full significance of having the Athenian councilors and jurors swear an oath to Chalcidian citizens just as they swear an oath to the citizens of Athens.[34]

The Councilors' Oath (Bouleutic Oath) at Athens is traditionally dated to 501/0, though its contents were subject to additions of a later date.[35] One of

[31] The only parallel is the very uncertain reconstruction of IG 1³ 11.6–7 (Athenian treaty with Egesta) by Bradeen and McGregor 1973, 71–81. Cf. Koch 1991, 155–57. It is not unusual for the council to swear an oath on behalf of the Athenian people. See, for example, IG 1³ 76.8–9 (Athenian decree concerning the Bottiaeans), where the council, the generals and "the rest of the magistrates" swear an oath; IG 1³ 83.26–28, with Thuc. 5.47.8–11 (Athenian treaty with the Argives, Mantineans, and Eleans of 420), where the council and the deme magistrates swear the oath.

[32] Koch 1991, 156.

[33] Balcer 1978, 33.

[34] Balcer 1978, 37–45. Note Balcer's comment on the contents of the Athenian oath in the Chalcis Decree (p. 35): "This was not a generous concession but rather the explicit implementation of Athens' imperial power."

[35] The traditional date for the introduction of the Councilors' Oath is given by Arist. Ath. Pol. 22.2 as the archonship of Hermocreon (501/0).

the chief pieces of evidence for the content of the Councilors' Oath is an
inscription that appears to be part of the laws concerning the council inscribed during the revision of the laws in 409.[36] The archaic language of
some of the clauses indicates that these provisions are much older than the
date of this revision. On the basis of various complicated historical arguments, scholars have dated the provisions in the inscription to the early fifth
century at the latest: that is, earlier than the oath in the Chalcis Decree.[37]
Although the fragmentary state of the inscription, as well as the archaic
language, makes the precise content of the provisions in the decree uncertain, it is clear that it restricts the powers of the council. Of primary importance is the restriction on the council's power to impose major penalties
on the citizens without the consent of the Athenian people.

In a legible part of the inscription, the Council of Five Hundred[38] is
forbidden either to declare or to end war, impose a penalty of death, or impose a θοά (heavy fine?) on an Athenian "without the Athenian people in

---

[36] IG 1³ 105.

[37] I accept Rhodes's arguments (1972, 170–207) that the law restricting the powers of the
council dates to the time of Ephialtes' reforms, when the Council of Five Hundred took over
judicial powers formerly accorded to the Areopagus. Rhodes argues that the law was a response
to the fear that once the Areopagus's judicial powers were transferred to the Council of Five
Hundred at the time of Ephialtes, the Council of Five Hundred "might start to amass ἐπίθετα."
Ostwald (1986, 30–40) argues, however, that the law originally was formulated in the early fifth
century before the reforms of Ephialtes in order to restrict the ability of the Areopagus Council
to inflict the severest penalties on the citizens. Ostwald hypothesizes that when judicial powers
(except in homicide cases) were removed from the Areopagus Council and given over to the
Council of Five Hundred and the popular courts by the reforms of Ephialtes in 462, the law
restricting the powers of the Areopagus Council was retained for the Council of Five Hundred,
despite the fact that this council had never had power to inflict these penalties. Ostwald dates the
law to the early fifth century on the basis of the evidence for the roles of the assembly and
popular courts in several early fifth-century trials, and the idea of a parallelism between political
equality before the law (ἰσονομία), where no political decisions were valid without the approval
of the Athenian people, and the judicial equality implied by the law. While this last argument is
tempting, the locus of early fifth-century trials is highly controversial. Carawan 1987, following
Hansen 1975, 1980, argues for a pre-Ephialtic division of powers between the Areopagus and
demos "whereby the assembly directly controlled treason trials and the council prosecuted
official misconduct." Ryan 1994 has pushed back the date of the law in the inscription even
further, arguing, among other things, that the phrase ἄνευ τô δέμο τô 'Αθεναίον πλεθύοντος
indicates the possibility of appeal of judicial decisions made by the magistrates, including the
Areopagus Council, to the people, a right attributed to Solon in our sources (Arist. Ath. Pol. 7.1,
Pol. 1274a1–22). It is not necessary for my argument to pin down the date of origin of the
restrictions on the powers of the council; I need only to show that they predate the Chalcis
inscription. I am, however, tempted by Ryan's attempt to date the law to Solon's time on the
basis of the archaic language.

[38] Although the subject of the prohibitions is not evident because of the fragmentary state of
the inscription, it is assumed to be the Council of Five Hundred based on the references to this
council elsewhere in the inscription and the use of the term ἐπιφσεφιô ("I will put to the vote"),
which is most appropriately used of this council. Cf. Rhodes 1972, 196.

assembly" (ἄνευ τô δέμο τô Ἀθεναίον πλεθύοντος).[39] This last phrase is
repeated eight times in the extant portions of the inscription. We cannot help
but notice the similarity of the phrase to those found in the decree con-
cerning Erythrae (ἄνευ τê[ς] βο[λêς τêς] | [Ἀθε]ναίον καὶ τô [δ]έμο) and that
concerning Chalcis (ἄνευ τô δέμο τô Ἀθεναίον). While the exact meaning
of the phrase ἄνευ τô δέμο τô Ἀθεναίον πλεθύοντος is difficult to determine, it is generally agreed that the provision is designed to prevent the
council from imposing serious penalties on Athenian citizens without the
consent of the people.[40] This consent would have been obtained either in
a judicial session of the assembly (ἡλιαία) or in a popular court (δικαστήριον).

It is clear, therefore, that by the mid-fifth century, the phrase ἄνευ τô δέμο
τô Ἀθεναίον πλεθύοντος denoted reference to a popular court, with the court
standing by synecdoche for the Athenian demos itself.[41] Other clauses of the
Councilors' Oath, known to us through literary sources, confirm the essential
role of that oath, namely to ensure that the council remained subject to the
will of the highest authority of the state, the Athenian people. Specific clauses
known only from fourth-century versions of the oath, for example, include the
promise not to imprison any Athenian who provides three sureties, and "not to
exile, imprison, or kill anyone without trial."[42] Although these clauses may not
date to the fifth century, they are in line with the general thrust of the earlier
inscriptional evidence. The most general clauses of the oath known from
fourth-century sources, moreover, namely to deliberate according to the
laws,[43] and to deliberate in the best interests of the polis and people,[44] further

---

[39] I borrow this translation from Rhodes 1972, 197. It is possible, as suggested by Cloché (see
Rhodes 1972, 197, for this summary of Cloché's arguments), that the phrase means "plenary assembly," i.e., an assembly with at least six thousand present, as required for a vote of ostracism. Note the law
cited by Dem. 24.45 forbidding annulment of the penalty of outlawry (ἀτιμία) or release from debt to
the gods or the city without a vote of amnesty (ἄδεια) by six thousand Athenians voting by secret ballot.
Cf. also the law cited by Dem. 24.59 forbidding the establishment of a law for a specific person unless
six thousand Athenians vote by secret ballot. Rhodes accepts that by the end of the fifth century the
popular courts were considered to represent the δῆμος πληθύων in judicial matters. Cf. Carawan
1987, 169n.5: "The phrase [δῆμος πληθύων] may best be understood as requiring a decree of the of
the assembly for capital offences, whether tried before the assembly or the court."

[40] Cf. IG 1³ 105: "lex, qua cavetur ne res gravissimae sine populi voluntate agantur."

[41] Most scholars accept that the popular courts (δικαστήρια) not only represented the will of
the people but were considered equivalent to the people practically and ideologically (Ober
1989b; Ostwald 1986, 34; Rhodes 1972, 197–98). The concept of synecdoche as applied to the
relation between the courts and the people is Ober's (1989b). Hansen (1987, 101–7; 1989b),
although agreeing that the courts represented the people, does not allow that the popular courts
were in any sense considered to be equivalent to the people.

[42] Dem. 24.147, [Andoc.] 4.3, cited and discussed below in regard to the Jurors' Oath. See
Rhodes 1972, 194, for a complete list of known clauses of the Councilors' Oath.

[43] Xen. Mem. 1.1.18.

[44] Lys. 31.1, [Dem.] 59.4.

support the idea of a limitation on the powers of the council in favor of the authority of the Athenian people as a whole.

The parallelism between the roles of the Councilors' Oath in Athens and the oath of the Athenian councilors and jurors to Chalcis should now be clear. In both cases, the Athenian magistrates swore to defer all decisions about the most severe penalties inflicted on citizens to the highest authority of the state, the Athenian people. In doing so, they confirmed the right to full legal procedure under the auspices of the Athenian people, whether the people judged the case themselves in the assembly or a popular court rendered judgment on behalf of the people. Thus the Athenian council makes the same pledge to the Chalcidians as it does to its own citizens.

Apart from the Councilors' Oath, we know that Athenian jurors also swore an oath (the Heliastic or Dicastic Oath) before being empaneled.[45] The date of the introduction of the Jurors' Oath is uncertain, although it is likely that its main clauses go back to the first half of the fifth century, when the popular courts began to play a prominent role in judicial decisions.[46] In essence, the jurors swore that they would conduct a fair trial in accordance with the laws. Key provisions of the oath include, for example, the promises to vote according to the laws and decrees of the Athenian people and the Council of Five Hundred, to listen to both sides of the case, not to accept bribes, and to vote on the issue at hand only.[47] The annual Jurors' Oath at Athens, therefore, pledges a proper trial in the popular courts, just as did the annual Councilors' Oath in regard to the most severe penalties. Both oaths, moreover, are echoed in the Chalcis Decree through the pledges made to the Chalcidians by precisely these same bodies.

In an even more striking parallel with the Chalcis Decree, the most complete extant version of the Jurors' Oath contains, among other things, a promise not to recall the exiles or banish anyone contrary to the established laws and decrees of the Athenian people and council:[48]

οὐδὲ τοὺς φεύγοντας κατάξω, οὐδὲ ὧν θάνατος κατέγνωσται, οὐδὲ τοὺς μένοντας ἐξελῶ παρὰ τοὺς νόμους τοὺς κειμένους καὶ τὰ ψηφίσματα τοῦ δήμου τοῦ Ἀθηναίων καὶ τῆς βουλῆς οὔτ' αὐτὸς ἐγὼ οὔτ' ἄλλον οὐδένα ἐάσω.

Neither will I recall those in exile or those who have been condemned to death, nor will I exile those who remain, contrary to the established laws and decrees of the Athenian people and council. Neither will I myself [do these things], nor will I permit anyone else [to do these things].

---

[45] Isoc. 15.21.

[46] Sources for the oath, however, date only from the fourth century onward. See Harrison 1971, 48, for full references.

[47] Dem. 24.149–51.

[48] Dem. 24.149.

Furthermore, in a speech purportedly given by an opponent of Alcibiades in 417/6 (when Alcibiades was a candidate for ostracism) but probably written in the early fourth century, the speaker suggests that the promise not to exile, imprison, or kill anyone without proper trial was part of both the Jurors' Oath and the Councilors' Oath at Athens:[49] "For [in the oaths] you swear neither to banish [μήτε ἐξελᾶν] nor to imprison [μήτε δήσειν] nor to kill [μήτε ἀποκτενεῖν] anyone without trial [μηδένα ... ἄκριτον]."[50] It is tempting to argue that this provision goes back to the beginnings of the democracy in the late sixth and early fifth centuries, since, as I argued in earlier chapters, arbitrary exile in the pre-democratic period played a formative role in the practices and ideology of the democracy. It is likely, however, that this clause of the Councilors' Oath and the Jurors' Oath was inserted only after the oligarchic revolution of 403, when individuals were notoriously banished, executed, or had their property confiscated without trial.[51] Nevertheless, the parallel with the oath of the Athenians in the Chalcis Decree is striking. Furthermore, as noted above, the Councilors' Oath certainly included a prohibition against the imposition of the death penalty without proper trial before a popular court. It is plausible that the other major penalties (exile, disenfranchisement, confiscation of property) were included in the lost clauses of the inscription, where only the phrase "without the people in assembly" remains. The jurors' annual oath to judge according to the laws and decrees of the people and council will certainly have covered the major penalties of death, exile, and disenfranchisement in principle, even if these cases were not explicitly singled out in the oaths already in the fifth century as they certainly were in the fourth.

In sum, the fact that the Athenian councilors and jurors swore to the Chalcidians that all cases of death, exile, and disenfranchisement would be judged by regular legal procedures under the auspices of the Athenian people brings this oath into line with those sworn by these same bodies to the Athenian citizens themselves. Substantively and symbolically, the Athenians therefore placed the Chalcidians on a par with their own citizens, extending to the Chalcidians privileges that were central to their own conception and practice of democratic citizenship.

Finally, we should consider the implications of the fact that the decree was to be inscribed and prominently displayed in both Chalcis and Athens. The

---

[49] The speaker actually refers to the People's Oath (ὁ ὅρκος τοῦ δήμου), not the Jurors' Oath (ὁ ἡλιαστικὸς ὅρκος), as was the usual expression. There is little doubt, however, that the Jurors' Oath is meant. For a recent discussion of the date of the speech, see Heftner 2001.

[50] [Andoc.] 4.3.

[51] Most scholars view the clause on exile as post-403: Harrison 1971, 48; MacDowell 1978, 44; Hansen 1991, 182; Todd 1993, 54. Balcer (1978, 40–43) argues that the clause on exile was part of the Jurors' Oath by the mid-fifth century, on the basis of the parallel between the oath to the Chalcidians and [Andoc.] 4.3. See above, chapter 4, for arbitrary executions, expulsions, and confiscations of property under the oligarchs.

fact that the decree was displayed is significant for how the Athenians wished to have their actions interpreted. I argue that the decree's manner and site of publication show that the Athenians wished to represent their settlement with the Chalcidians to themselves and to the Greek world as one between equals, and as just and divinely sanctioned.

The Chalcis Decree, like many another, specifies the means, procedure, and location of its publication (*IG* 1³ 40.57–63): "The secretary of the council is to inscribe this decree and the oath on a stone stele and have it erected on the acropolis at the expense of the Chalcidians, and the council of the Chalcidians is to inscribe and erect [the decree and the oath] in Chalcis in the Temple of Olympian Zeus."

The acropolis at Athens was obviously the most conspicuous and revered part of the city. The Temple of Olympian Zeus at Chalcis was presumably also a prominent and sacred location in Chalcis. In Athens, the acropolis, along with the agora, was the location of most public inscriptions, including treaties between states, victory dedications, praises of benefactors, and denunciations of public wrongdoers, including debtors to the state. Since the city could, and did, keep records on less permanent materials, which were not publicly displayed, it is clear that the inscriptions on stone in prominent public places were meant to be known and viewed by the people of Athens, including citizens, metics, and visiting foreigners.[52]

In her illuminating work on literacy and orality in ancient Greece, Rosalind Thomas raises the question of whether these inscriptions were actually read. She shows that some inscriptions, especially lists, were meant to be consulted, and there is some evidence that individuals did actually go up to the acropolis to examine them.[53] Thomas argues, however, that the most important function of public inscriptions was their use as symbolic memorials to past events and decisions of the Athenian people. Whether or not they actually read the inscriptions, the people of Athens knew the contents orally through participation in the assembly or by word of mouth.

The dimensions of the Chalchis Decree—as of most decrees—would have made it easily legible for a person standing on the ground.[54] Regardless of whether the Chalcis Decree was actually read, however, the contents may have been represented symbolically in a relief on the stone that originally capped the inscription.[55] This relief may have shown a symbol of Chalcis or

---

[52] See Sickinger 1999 for a study of records not inscribed on stone, arguing that uninscribed documents were more numerous and important for the functioning of Athenian society than inscribed documents.

[53] Thomas 1992, 74–100,128–57.

[54] Lawton 1995, 10–11. One well-known exception is the tribute lists, which were too large to be consulted with ease.

[55] Balcer (1978, 84–85) posits the existence of a relief based on a calculation of the size of the capping stone. *IG* 1³ 40 also suggests that the capstone may have been adorned by a relief

Euboea (a patron deity or cow, for example) along with one of Athens (for instance, Athena or an owl).[56]

A good example of an extant Athenian inscription with such a relief is the Athenian decree concerning the Samians of 405/4 (IG 1^3 127), where the two cities are represented by their patron goddesses, Athena and Hera. The two goddesses clasp right hands, a gesture that Carol Lawton interprets as symbolic both of the particular agreement and of a "more general unity and accord."[57] Lawton argues, furthermore, that the handshake (δεξίωσις) "portrays the allies as equals and their relationship with Athens as harmonious and reciprocal."[58] The goddesses are equally prominent in the relief and, although Athena has some of her military equipment at her side (helmet, spear, shield), these items are not in active use. Both goddesss stand in a relaxed pose. A passerby would easily have been able to identify the parties to the agreement from the portrait of Athena with her well-known attributes and the depiction of a second goddess combined with the reference to the Samians in the title to the decree. If Lawton's analysis is correct, moreover, the viewer would have interpreted the monument as an indication of the equal and fair relationship between Athens and Samos.

We cannot assume that the same symbolism existed on the Chalcis Decree as on the Samos Decree, since the Samians enjoyed great favor with the Athenians for their loyalty to Athens through the difficult final stages of the war with the Peloponnesians. Indeed, in the decree concerning Samos, the Athenians grant Athenian citizenship to the Samians. Nevertheless, if my interpretation of the contents of the Chalcis Decree has any validity, then the Athenians, far from treating the Chalcidians as defeated rebels, were in fact extending to them certain privileges intimately tied to their own concept of citizenship. Under such circumstances, it is not unlikely that the decree contained a relief, similar to the relief on the Samos Decree, symbolically representing Athens and Chalcis as harmonious and equal partners. Viewers of the decree, therefore, might have perceived this symbolism, without necessarily reading the decree. The location of the monument in sacred precincts in both cities, moreover, and the possible use of religious symbolism in the relief would have linked the contents of the decree to the gods, reinforcing the message of the just and indeed divine legitimacy of the agreement.[59]

The function of the published inscription, further more, is not limited to its role as a physical reminder of the agreement between the two cities. Thomas

---

("fortasse anaglypho ornatus"). The presence of a capping stone is suggested by the existence of cuttings on the top side of the decree. On the symbolic and allegorical functions of Attic document reliefs, see Lawton 1995, 26–30.

[56] See Balcer 1978, 85, for suggestions for the Chalcis Decree; Lawton 1995, 39–63, for a catalogue of the iconography used to represent cities in documentary reliefs.

[57] Lawton 1995, 30, 36.

[58] Lawton (1995, 36) suggests, however, that this equality was a "convenient fiction."

[59] Lawton 1995, 26–27.

shows that public writing served not so much as a means of administration as
"to protect and confirm the values of the city."[60] Drawing largely on evidence
for lists of public offenders and benefactors, which were often displayed on the
acropolis, Thomas argues that inscriptions were "exemplary texts displayed for
the improvement and encouragement of the rest of the citizenry." Inscriptions
could also serve a more imperialistic function, serving as symbols of Athenian
power to both citizens and non-citizens. The Chalcis Decree can be interpreted
in the light of both these functions. In particular the double aspects of the
contents of the decree in indicating not only Athenian power but also Athens'
just use of that power, as discussed above, seem to serve both these functions.
The Chalcis Decree confirms not only Athenian power but also Athenian
values. The decree sends a message to citizens and non-citizens alike of both
Athens and Chalcis that Athens is guided by justice in its dealings with its allies.
This message played an important part in the Athenians' justification of their
power abroad, as we shall see.

One way of illustrating the double function of the Chalcis inscription in
demonstrating Athens' power and justice is to compare it to other famous
inscriptions on the acropolis. Indeed, it is remarkable that some of the best-
attested monuments on the acropolis mark not only Athens' increasing power
but also the Athenians' just use of that power. It makes eminent sense,
moreover, that they placed such public affirmations of the justice of their
actions in the sacred center of their own city and their allies'. By associating
these representations of Athenian actions with the divine patrons of each city,
the Athenians lent religious legitimacy to their acts.[61]

One of the best-known, but no longer extant, monuments on the Athenian
acropolis was the bronze four-horse chariot dedicated by the Athenians to
Athena from one-tenth of the ransom obtained after their defeat of the Boeotians and Chalcidians in 506. Herodotus records the inscription on the base
of the sculpture:[62] "Having subdued the tribes of the Boeotians and Chalcidians by their feats in war, the sons of the Athenians quenched their hubris
[ἔσβεσαν ὕβριν] with gloomy iron bonds. With a tenth [of the spoils], [the
Athenians] dedicated these horses to Athena." While the monument obviously attests to the military might of the Athenians, it also advertises their just
use of this power. The Athenians represent themselves as having "quenched
the hubris" of the Boeotians and Chalcidians, suggesting not only that the
actions of their opponents were contrary to pious respect for the gods, but also
that they themselves are the gods' avengers.[63] Athenian piety is, moreover,
signaled by the use of part of the spoils in glorification of Athena. The

[60] Thomas 1992, 139.

[61] Thomas 1992, 146. Compare Bers 2000 on the religious legitimacy given to the courts
through elaborate rituals.

[62] Hdt. 5.77.4.

[63] For the semantics of ὕβρις, see Fisher 1992.

sculpture itself, with its expensive metal and careful craftsmanship, would have displayed to onlookers the wealth and power of Athens as well as its devotion to the gods. Through this monument in the sacred center of the city, the Athenians interwove the notions of Athenian power, justice, and piety.

The Athenian tribute lists are another well-known monument from the Athenian acropolis attesting to Athenian power and piety. Thomas has well observed that these huge stones—they were definitely not designed to be read with ease—with their long lists of subjects and tribute amounts were more suited as a symbol of the vast size and power of the Athenian empire than as a useful reference for the details of Athenian imperial finances. The fact that the stones record the one-sixtieth of the tribute dedicated to Athena, moreover, suggests that this monument was a symbol not only of Athenian power, but of the pious ends toward which the empire was directed. By displaying in the sacred center of the city the one-sixtieth of the tribute dedicated to Athena, rather than the fifty-nine-sixtieths devoted to other purposes, the Athenians again linked their political and military activities with their piety and hence lent religious legitimacy to their empire.[64]

The Chalcis Decree can be viewed along similar lines. It too was placed on the Athenian acropolis, and it too interwove the dual notions of Athenian power and justice. The location and physical aspects of the inscription served to reinforce the ideological message of its contents. The location linked Athenian actions with the gods, as may also have the relief on the capstone. The content, with its oaths (also sworn on penalty of divine sanction) and its guarantees of regularized political and judicial procedures, indicated the limits on Athenian power, as well as the fact of Athens' power over its subjects.

A JUDICIAL DECREE?

Even if the Chalcis Decree can be viewed as an attempt by Athens to pursue a policy of moderation, on what grounds can we extrapolate from this specific case to Athens' policy toward its empire as a whole? Several scholars have made the case for the existence of a generalized judicial decree, by which Athens removed power over decisions of death, exile, and disenfranchisement from its subjects and required such cases to be decided in Athenian courts.[65]

[64] See Smarczyk 1990 for Athens' use of religion in the administration of empire. See also Boedeker and Raaflaub 1998 on art and empire.

[65] Balcer (1978, 119–42) makes the most forceful and thorough case, arguing not only for the existence of a judicial decree covering the whole Athenian empire but for its early date (c. 450). De Ste. Croix (1961, 270–71) outlined some arguments for the existence of such a decree, but left the date open, placing the decree "before the last years of the Empire." Meiggs (1972, 225) warns against generalizing from the Chalcis Decree to an overall imperial decree, but accepts that by 424 (his date for [Xen.] *Ath. Pol.*) cases involving the major penalties were required to be brought before Athenian courts in the first instance.

While no such judicial decree survives, its existence can be inferred from references in inscriptions and literary sources.

The best evidence for the existence of a generalized judicial decree is the Athenian inscription of 412 concerning Samos, in which the Athenians grant the Samians power over decisions of death, exile, and confiscation of property as a reward for their loyalty to Athens in overthrowing an oligarchy:[66]

> The Samian people are to be praised because they freed themselves by overthrowing the existing oligarchy and banishing those Samians who brought in the Peloponnesians to Samos and Ionia (Σ]αμίον τὸς ἐπάγοντας Πελοποννεσίος ἐπὶ Σάμον καὶ τὲν Ἰονίαν ἐχσέβαλον)... and if the Samian people condemn some men to death or exile or confiscation of property ([ἐὰν δέ τινον καταγνôι ὁ δ]ῆμος ὁ Σαμίον θάνατον ε͂ φυγὲν ε͂ δέμευσιν χρεμάτον), let [the decision] be valid [κύριον ἔστο]... It is permitted also to the Athenian people to condemn them to exile and death and confiscation of property, if it is necessary.

Apparently the fact that the Samian people had taken action to expel the oligarchs when Athens' fortunes were at a low ebb had led the Athenians to trust the Samian people and to entrust to them the power over the major penalties, especially exile. Since we have no decree by which these powers had been stripped from the Samians in the first place, we must conjecture that Samos had been covered by a generalized judicial decree valid for all the allies.[67]

The case for a generalized decree is strengthened by literary sources. In Antiphon's speech *On the Murder of Herodes*, the speaker accuses his opponents of condemning to death and killing a man themselves "when it is not even permitted to a city [οὐδὲ πόλει ἔξεστιν] to punish a man with death [οὐδένα θανάτῳ ζημιῶσαι] without the [permission of] the Athenians [ἄνευ Ἀθηναίων]."[68] Although the man in question was a slave (and thus probably not covered by an Athenian decree), Antiphon appears to be appealing to a general principle of Athenian imperial administration. Moreover, the phrase ἄνευ Ἀθηναίων evokes the phrases used in the decrees concerning Erythrae and Chalcis, as well as the Councilors' Oath.

Finally, a passage from the *Constitution of Athenians* attributed to Xenophon (henceforth pseudo-Xenophon) appears to allude to a generalized judicial decree regulating exile. The author points out the importance of judicial control to the Athenian people's management of allied states:[69]

[66] IG 1³ 96.

[67] It is possible that Athens removed power over major penalties after the supression of the revolt led by oligarchs in 439. Yet neither Thuc. 1.115–17 nor Diod. Sic. 12.27.2–28.4 mentions these terms. Such terms may have been outlined in a decree settling the affairs of Samos in 439 (IG 1³ 48), but the decree is fragmentary, and the extant portions do not cover judicial terms.

[68] Antiph. 5.47.

[69] [Xen.] *Ath. Pol.* 1.16.

The Athenian people seem to plan badly, since they force the allies to sail to Athens for judicial proceedings. But [the Athenians] point out in turn how the Athenian people benefit by this. . . . [For] sitting at home, without making any sea voyages, they govern [διοικοῦσι] the allied cities, and they protect the democrats and destroy their enemies in the courts [τοὺς μὲν τοῦ δήμου σῴζουσι, τοὺς δ' ἐναντίους ἀπολλύουσι ἐν τοῖς δικαστηρίοις]. But if the allies were to hold trials at home, they would destroy those of their own people who were especially friendly to the Athenian people, since they are hostile to the Athenians.

In this same context, the author writes:[70]

[The Athenians] disenfranchise the elites and confiscate their property and exile them and kill them [τοὺς μὲν χρηστοὺς ἀτιμοῦσι καὶ χρήματα ἀφαιροῦνται καὶ ἐξελαύνονται καὶ ἀποκτείνουσι], whereas they promote the interests of the lower class [τοὺς δὲ πονηροὺς αὔξουσιν].

Granted that the author of this work is a biased witness writing a polemical treatise, nevertheless he bases his critique on what we have already seen to be a generalized principle of Athenian imperial rule, namely that Athens removed power over decisions of death, exile, disenfranchisement, and the confiscation of property from the allied cities.[71] The combined evidence therefore suggests that the Athenians did indeed enact some sort of generalized decree regulating the major penalties. Nevertheless, this decree is not to be taken as asserting control over the means to conduct political purges in the allied cities. Rather, as I argued above, the Judicial Decree was a means for Athens to moderate civil conflict in the cities by reassuring subjects that the highest penalties—including exile—would be exacted from citizens only through regularized political and legal procedures.

Although the scanty evidence for a judicial decree gives little grounds for determining the date when it was introduced, a case can be made for placing it in the 440s around the time of the Chalcis Decree. In this decade, Athens experienced a number of revolts from her alliance, which led to a decrease in the tribute assessments of a number of states and the signing of the Thirty Years' Peace with Sparta.[72] There is good reason to suppose, therefore, that Athens sought to stabilize its alliance further through passage of a judicial decree at this time.

[70] [Xen.] Ath. Pol. 1.14.

[71] Balcer (1978, 119–42) adduces other, less decisive evidence for the Judicial Decree, especially Ar. Av. 1422–32 and the phrase κατὰ τὸ φσέφισμα τõ δέμο in the rider to the Chalcis Decree. Balcer takes the phrase as a reference to the lost Judicial Decree, not to the main part of the decree containing the oaths, as other commentators do: cf. Meiggs 1972, 225; ML 52, p. 143. It is worth noting that the terms of the Chalcis Decree were probably applied to Eretria as well; cf. IG 1³ 39.

[72] See Meiggs 1972, 152–204, for a summary of these events.

One obstacle, however, to interpreting the Judicial Decree and in particular the Chalcis Decree as moderate measures is the cumulative evidence
of other decrees that have traditionally been taken as repressive. The prime
example of such decrees is the so-called Coinage Decree of circa 449.[73]
Recently, however, Thomas Figueira has challenged the standard interpretation of the Coinage Decree, arguing that the traditional reconstruction and
interpretation of this decree on the basis of parallel evidence from inscriptions found in different parts of Athens' empire has been shaped by a preconceived notion of the strong hand that Athens allegedly used to manage
her empire.[74] Figueira proposes instead that "the Coinage Decree was not an
enactment that worked to any marked parochial advantage of the Athenians.
Nor did it constitute a major tightening of imperial control to the disad-
vantage of the allies. Rather . . . this psephism [decree] probably acted to
codify and order prevailing circumstances or to encourage their more de-
sirable features."[75] If Figueira is correct, then we might question whether
modern scholarly reconstructions and interpretations of other inscriptions
regarding Athens' relations with its allies have similarly been colored by the
Thucydidean notion of Athens as a harsh (tyrannical) imperial power. My
interpretation of the Erythrae and Chalcis decrees above seems to lend
support to this milder view. If we remove our preconceived notion that the
Athenians ruled their empire repressively, then we are better able to see how
these decrees further a policy of moderation designed to enhance allied
cooperation with Athenian power.[76]

THUCYDIDES, ISOCRATES, AND THE LEGITIMACY OF ATHENIAN POWER

Athens' use of harsh penalties against its allies as well as its attempts to use
moderation in the management of the empire gave rise to a heated debate,
both in Athens and abroad, about the justice and legitimacy of Athenian
power. We have just seen that control of and moderation in the use of exile
were key factors in Athens' management of its empire. We should therefore
expect Athens' behavior in regard to exile to have played a key role in the

[73] *ATL* 2. D 14, ML 45.

[74] Arguably the traditional interpretation is a result of the influence of Thucydides. Cf., e.g.,
Thuc. 1.98.4–99.2: "After this, the Athenians fought with the Naxians, who had revolted, and
they set up a siege. This was the first allied city to be enslaved contrary to established practice.
Afterwards each of the other allies was enslaved when the occasion arose. Among the causes of
the revolts, the greatest were the failure to produce the right amount of tribute and ships, or the
failure to provide any at all. For the Athenians were exacting [ἀκριβῶς ἔπρασσον] and grievous
[λυπηροί], applying force [προσάγοντες τὰς ἀνάγκας] to those who were not accustomed or
willing to suffer."

[75] Figueira 1998, 15.

[76] See now also Ostwald 2002 for an interpretation of the Chalcis Decree along these lines.

debate about the justice of the empire. This is in fact the case, although since we have no sources that directly record this debate, we must collect a broad variety of evidence in order to piece together the key terms of the debate, from inscriptions, ancient historians, tragedy, and fourth-century funeral orations.

We have already seen how the inscriptions that Athenians erected in Athens and in the cities of their allies were designed not only to curtail the politics of exile but to project an image of Athens as a just and moderate imperial power. We also saw that a critic of the Athenian democracy, pseudo-Xenophon, referred to Athens' control of decisions of death, exile, and citizenship in the allied cities as a sign of the injustice (albeit shrewd pragmatism) of the Athenian people. If we turn now to our best contemporary source for this period, Thucydides, we can trace these two sides of the debate even further. Athens' policy of political and judicial regulation of exile, in fact, served as a key term in the arguments of both Athens' supporters and its detractors.

Thucydides is a difficult source: we must not take his representations of events, and especially speeches, as wholly accurate. Yet it is equally inappropriate to dismiss all elements of Thucydides' account as products of his own political, didactic, and artistic purposes. Parallels between ideas, concepts, and arguments in Thucydides' history and those in a variety of other sources have the best chance of being reflections of the actual debates and arguments in Athens.

The debate at Sparta in book 1 is a good place to start. The Corinthians call a meeting of Sparta and its allies in order to consider whether Athens' actions are grounds for declaring war. The Corinthians argue the case for going to war. Although they famously spend much of their speech comparing the Spartan and the Athenian character and criticizing the Spartans for their slowness and caution, their central claim is that Athens is guilty of wrongdoing (ἀδικία) toward the rest of the Greeks.[77] The Corinthians use strong language to condemn Athenian behavior: "We are being treated insolently (ὑβριζόμενοι) by the Athenians."[78] In a later speech, the Corinthians elaborate on this characterization of Athenian behavior, calling Athens a tyrant city insofar as it enslaves other Greeks.[79]

A delegation of Athenians that happens to be present at Sparta on other business is given the role of defending Athenian behavior. Their defense not only reveals the ways that the Athenians justified their behavior abroad, but provides further details of the accusations that were being made against Athens. The Athenians begin by rejecting the notion that they are making a defense plea in a legal court, asserting that they have two aims in their speech. First, they are concerned to show the gravity of the consequences if the Spartans and

[77] Thuc. 1.68.3.
[78] Thuc. 1.68.2.
[79] Thuc. 1.122.3, 124.3.

their allies make the wrong decision (i.e., declare war on Athens). Second, they intend to show that Athens deserves what it possesses (Thuc. 1.73.1). It is this latter goal that is important for our inquiry.

The Athenians base their claim to worthiness on three arguments. The first is that Athens' service to Greece in the Persian Wars justifies its leadership.[80] The second argument is that Athens did not seize the leadership by force but assumed it at the request of the allies.[81] Finally, and most important, the Athenians argue that although they have maintained their empire because of a natural desire to look after their own interests, they wield power more justly than the Spartans would in the same position, and more justly than is necessary in relation to their strength.[82] This last argument reveals that the Athenians justified their empire partly through the relative moderation of their exercise of power (Thuc. 1.76.1–4):

> If you [Spartans], by remaining behind, had grown hated in your leadership just as we have, we know well that you would not have become less grievous [λυπη-ρούς] to the allies and that you would have been forced either to rule forcefully [ἄρχειν ἐγκρατῶς] or risk danger to yourselves.... Those men are worthy to be praised who, using their human nature so as to rule others, are more just [δι-καιότεροι] than their power [requires them to be]. We think therefore that others, if they should take up our power, would show that we are moderate [μετριάζομεν]. Lack of trust rather than praise surrounds us unreasonably [οὐκ εἰκότως] because of our reasonableness [τοῦ ἐπιεικοῦς].

This claim of Athenian moderation corresponds well with what we have inferred from the inscriptional evidence. There the Athenians represented themselves as just and moderate through the use of regularized political and legal procedures. It is on the basis of precisely this aspect of Athens' imperial administration that the Athenians in Thucydides then proceed to justify themselves (1.77.1–3):[83]

> For both because we come off the worse [ἐλασσούμενοι] in court cases with our allies deriving from judicial agreements [ταῖς ξυμβολαίαις πρὸς τοὺς ξυμμάχους δίκαις] and because we required that legal decisions [τὰς κρίσεις] be made among ourselves by means of equal laws [ὁμοίοις νόμοις], we are viewed as being overly fond of going to court [φιλοδικεῖν].[84] And no one asks

---

[80] Thuc. 1.73.4–74.4. This is a common topos in oratory, particularly that recalling the past glories of Athens, such as funeral orations. Cf. Loraux 1986.

[81] Thuc. 1.75.2.

[82] Thuc. 1.75.3–76.4.

[83] My translation incorporates elements of the translations offered by de Ste. Croix 1961, Meiggs 1972, and Hornblower 1991. On "seeking a greater share" (πλεονεκτεῖν), see Balot 2001.

[84] As Hornblower (1991, 122) notes, "This is a difficult sentence." Cruxes include the meaning of ξυμβολαίαις δίκαις and of φιλοδικεῖν, as well as the question of whether a single type of case is mentioned, or two different types. I follow the now standard line, first argued by de Ste. Croix

why this reproach is not made of others elsewhere who rule empires and are less moderate [μετρίοις] than us toward their subjects. For justice is not required of those to whom it is permitted to use force [βιάζεσθαι γὰρ οἷς ἂν ἐξῇ, δι-κάζεσθαι οὐδὲν προσδέονται]. But our allies, accustomed to associate with us as equals [ἀπὸ τοῦ ἴσου ὁμιλεῖν], if they suffer something beyond what they think necessary in either judgment or power on account of our empire or some such thing, are not grateful for not being deprived of more, but bear it worse that they have been deprived of something than if from the beginning we dis-regarded the law [ἀποθέμενοι τὸν νόμον] and openly sought a greater share [φανερῶς ἐπλεονεκτοῦμεν].

The Athenians argue that, although some people (e.g., pseudo-Xenophon) criticize them for compelling the allies to come to Athens for trials, they are in fact more deserving of rule precisely because they allow the allies to enjoy legal and political equality (ὁμοίοις νόμοις, ἀπὸ τοῦ ἴσου ὁμιλεῖν) and are therefore moderate (μέτριοι). Here we catch glimpses of Athenian imperial ideology as we have already detected it in inscriptions. The passage from Thucydides, as well as the implications of the display of the Chalcis inscrip-tion just discussed, suggests that the Athenians believed that such provisions as we saw in the Chalcis Decree could plausibly be represented to the allies as a sign of Athens' justice, and thus it supports my interpretation of the Chalcis Decree as representative of Athens' policy of moderation. It is unlikely that Athens could plausibly make the argument that these provisions were just and moderate if they were overtly using their power over decisions of death, exile, and disenfranchisement in order to help their friends and harm their enemies arbitrarily in the allied states. The Athenians, in Thucydides' representation, suggest by contrast that the judicial measures were intended to allow legal procedures, not force, to govern their relations with their allies.

Pseudo-Xenophon, on the other hand, puts a negative spin on Athenian judicial relations with the allies, arguing, as do many modern historians, that Athens usurped control of major penalties in order to have control over

---

(1961, 95–96), that ξυμβολαίαι δίκαι are cases arising from interstate judicial agreements, which include a broad variety of legal cases and not just those having to do with commercial agreements. Along with de Ste. Croix (p. 97), I also take the verb φιλοδικεῖν in its regular sense, "love to litigate." In regard to the question of whether two distinct types of cases are being discussed, I agree with Meiggs (1972, 232–33), who argues: "It seems unlikely that the Athenians at Sparta would have limited themselves to defending Athenian ξυμβολαί when so much imperial juris-diction had no connection at all with ξυμβολαί," and therefore that "[i]n the second clause the Athenians are admitting that they have transferred some cases to Athens, but then (whereas in many allied courts there is no real justice) in Athens the laws are the same for all." In this regard, de Ste. Croix (p. 100) is less convincing in his argument that the Athenians limit their defense to Athenian sufferings in regard to interstate judicial agreements precisely because their conduct in these was unimpeachable, whereas in other cases Athens used its power to intrude unfairly on allied autonomy. Hornblower (1991, 122–23), however, sides with de Ste. Croix in arguing that only one specific type of case (those arising from interstate judicial agreements) is mentioned.

political purges in the subject states. Implicit in this view is the idea that the judicial regulations are simply an ideological screen for ruthless imperialism. I argue by contrast that we have to take the Athenian pledges in the Chalcis Decree more seriously, accounting for the practical, ideological, and symbolic significance of the particular bodies that swear the oath, the language of the oath, and finally the symbolism of the manner of its display in Athens.

I would argue, moreover, that the passage from Thucydides reflects the ideology and symbolism of the oaths of the Athenians to the Chalcidians. The Athenians in Thucydides say that they require legal decisions to be made in Athens with "equal laws," and that they allow their allies to associate with them "as equals." Political equality and, in particular, equality before the law (ἰσονομία) were fundamental tenets of the Athenian democracy.[85] I argued that in the Chalcis Decree the Athenians practically and symbolically extended privileges to the Chalcidians that were central to their own concept of citizenship, particularly the right to a fair trial. The passage from Thucydides reflects this interpretation of the decree by using the same central tenets of Athenian democracy to describe Athenian relations with their allies.

If we turn to a later source, we see many of these claims echoed and further delineated. Isocrates' orations *Panegyricus* and *Panathenaicus* were written much later than the Peloponnesian War, yet it is clear that he is influenced by fifth-century arguments about the Athenian empire.[86] Isocrates' principal goal in the *Panegyricus* is to unite the Greek states to fight against the Persians. His method of achieving this goal, however, is to show that Athens deserves to lead the Greeks.[87] Thus Isocrates' aim corresponds precisely with that of the Athenians at Sparta in Thucydides' debate. Indeed, Isocrates draws a direct link between Athens' moderate rule during the fifth century and its claim to leadership in the fourth: "Even as before our city justly (δικαίως) ruled the sea, so now not unjustly (οὐκ ἀδίκως) Athens claims leadership."[88]

After surveying a series of Athens' services to Greece in the legendary past (to which we shall return later), Isocrates considers Athens' more recent claims to good service. He doles out equal praise to Athens and Sparta for their actions during the Persian Wars, but objects to the complaints made about Athens' behavior following the wars (*Paneg.* 100):

> After [the Persian Wars], some criticize us, saying that when we took over the rule of the sea, we became the cause of many evils for the Greeks; and they reproach us in

---

[85] The concept of equality before the law goes back to Solon: see above, chapter 3. For ἰσονομία under the democracy, see Ostwald 1969. For the Athenian concept of equality generally, see Cartledge 1996, Raaflaub 1996b, Roberts 1996.

[86] Loraux (1986, 65, 67, 74) in her stimulating study of the epitaphios argues that Isocrates' lists of deeds justifying the greatness of Athens must ultimately derive from fifth-century funeral orations.

[87] *Paneg.* 15–18.

[88] *Paneg.* 20.

their speeches with the enslavement of the Melians and the destruction of the people of Scione [τόν τε Μηλίων ἀνδραποδισμὸν καὶ τὸν Σκιωναίων ὄλεθρον].

Isocrates responds to these criticisms with two general points, which are identical to those made by the Athenians in Thucydides' account. First, Isocrates argues that Athens was relatively moderate in the use of its power. Although a few enemy states admittedly suffered harsh penalties, loyal states remained unharmed. Isocrates argues, second, that Sparta was much less moderate in the exercise of power (*Paneg.* 102):

> Second, if some others had managed the same situation more leniently [πραό-τερον], then they might reasonably censure us.

Specifically, Isocrates points to the Athenian practice of holding trials at Athens, alleging that, in comparison, the Spartans arbitrarily exacted the harshest penalties on citizens from subject cities without proper trials (*Paneg.* 113–14):

> In addition to the other accusations, they dare to speak about the trials once held at Athens [περὶ τῶν δικῶν καὶ τῶν γραφῶν τῶν ποτε παρ' ἡμῖν γενομένων], when they themselves have put to death without trial [ἀκρίτους ἀποκτείναντες] more men in three months than this city tried [ἔκρινεν] during the whole length of her empire. And who could recount the banishments [φυγάς], the civil strife [στάσεις], the overturning of the laws [νόμων συγχύσεις], and the changes of constitutions [πολιτειῶν μεταβολάς], or the outrages against children [παίδων ὕβρεις], the abuses of women [γυναικῶν αἰσχύνας], and the seizures of property [χρημάτων ἁρπαγάς]?

While Isocrates obviously refers to Spartan activities after the Peloponnesian War in making this argument, his central claim that the Spartans are less moderate in the exercise of power than the Athenians goes back to the same fifth-century justifications of the Athenian empire that we saw in Thucydides.

The same justifications and criticisms are evident in the *Panathenaicus*, a long speech in praise of Athens written in Isocrates' old age. Isocrates takes as his task an enumeration of Athens' services to Greece.[89] This speech thus echoes his proof of Athens' worthiness to lead in the *Panegyricus*, as well as the speech of the Athenians in Thucydides. Again, his argument turns on the idea that although both Athens and Sparta committed atrocities, Athens nevertheless used her power more moderately and mildly (μετριώτερον καὶ πραότερον) than Sparta, which was harsher and sharper (πικροτέραν καὶ χαλεπωτέραν).[90] Again Isocrates recounts the standard criticisms of Athens, among which the treatment of the Melians, Scionians, and Toronians, as well as the trials held in Athens, are foremost. Isocrates focuses on the trials held at Athens and argues that Sparta killed more Greeks without trial (πλείους Λακεδαιμόνιοι τῶν

[89] *Panath.* 35.
[90] *Panath.* 56 and 65, respectively. See also *Panath.* 90, 121.

Ἑλλήνων ἀκρίτους ἀπεκτόνασι) than were brought to trial and judgment in Athens (τῶν παρ' ἡμῖν . . . εἰς ἀγῶνα καὶ κρίσιν καταστάντων) from the time of the founding of the city.[91]

Furthermore, in response to the idea that Athens alone exiled Greeks and destroyed their cities, Isocrates points to two events, one in the early archaic period and one during the Peloponnesian War, when Sparta was responsible for the expulsion of Greeks and the destruction of a Greek state. The Spartans drove out the Messenians from their land in the archaic period and executed the Plataeans in 427.[92] Athens by contrast, notes Isocrates, found a new home for the Messenians and allowed the Plataeans to take up Athenian citizenship.[93] Isocrates' reference to an event in the distant past to justify Athens' current behavior is not an isolated instance, as we shall see, in fifth-century imperial ideology. Indeed, the even more remote mythical past was called on to support Athens' power. In "Exile and the Mythical Past" below in this chapter, I will show that the idea that Athens benevolently received the exiles from other Greek states was a prominent part of Athenian imperial self-justification.

The parallels between the defense of Athens in Thucydides and Isocrates, as well as the inscriptional evidence discussed above, suggest that the Athenian use of trials at Athens for the major penalties of death, exile, and disenfranchisement was a focal point both for criticisms of Athenian imperial rule and for Athens' own justification of it. Key to Athens' justification was the lawful—that is, with regularized political and legal procedures—and moderate (μετρίως, πράως) use of the major penalties, especially exile and death.[94]

EXILE AND THE TYRANT CITY: A CRITIQUE OF ATHENIAN POWER

At this point we must turn to fifth-century representations of tyrants in order to detect the full valence and symbolism of the Corinthian claim that Athens

---

[91] *Panath.* 66; cf. 181.

[92] *Panath.* 91, 93, respectively. It is perhaps significant that a defense of Sparta given by one of Isocrates' former students, as reported by Isocrates in the same speech, not only included the familiar claim that Sparta enjoyed a stable constitution (cf. Hdt. 1.65) but also specified that Sparta did not suffer civil war, murders, and unlawful banishments (φυγὰς ἀνόμους), among other misfortunes rampant in other Greek states (*Panath.* 259).

[93] *Panath.* 94.

[94] Lysias's account of the period between the end of the Persian Wars and the end of the Peloponnesian War in his funeral oration (2.55–60) reveals a perspective similar to the evidence of Thucydides and Isocrates in proving that "the Athenians alone of the Greeks deserve to be leaders of the Greeks" (57). Lysias claims that Athens used its power justly to make her allies free from faction (ἀστασιάστους), not allowing the many to be slaves to the few, but compelling all to live in equality (τὸ ἴσον ἔχειν ἅπαντας, 56). Lysias claims that Athens did not enslave any Greek city and draws a strong contrast with Sparta's behavior after Aegospotami. When the Spartans took over the leadership of the Greeks, Lysias claims, they enslaved the Greek cities and set up tyrants in them.

was a tyrant city. As we have seen, the Corinthians described Athens as a tyrant city insofar as it enslaved the other Greeks, and the Athenians responded with the claim that they in fact allowed their allies to interact with them as equals, not subjects. An association with slavery, however, does not exhaust the ideological connotations of the concept of tyranny. As I argue below in chapter 6, one of the primary characteristics of tyranny according to fifth-century Athenian democratic ideology was its arbitrary expulsion of citizens from the community. The question to be answered in this section is whether this association between tyranny and exile is evoked in the metaphor of Athens as tyrant city.[95]

According to the portraits of tyranny presented in Herodotus, tyrants were associated with the arbitrary expulsion of citizens from the community. In particular, the Corinthian tyrants Cypselus and Periander were singled out for their violent expulsion and execution of citizens and the confiscation of their property.[96] It is striking that these three abuses ascribed to Cypselus are precisely those of which Athens was accused as imperial leader, and in reference to which the Athenians boasted of behaving more justly than others. It is clear, therefore, that this tricolon of penalties—exile, confiscation of property, death—formed a central topos in Athens for the legitimation and criticism of the use of power both internally and externally. The metaphor of the tyrant served as a symbol of the immoderate and illegal use of power both within the state and beyond it. In particular, the tyrant's expulsion and murder of citizens and the seizure of their property were central points of reference.

Aristotle's discussion of the story of Periander's advice to his fellow tyrant Thrasybulus of Miletus further illustrates the parallel between tyranny and empire.[97] As Aristotle notes, the story of Periander and Thrasybulus notoriously associated tyranny with the removal of citizens from the community through the vivid image of the tyrant cutting down the tallest ears of corn in a field.[98] Aristotle, however, argues that it is not just tyrants who get rid of their rivals in this way, but also democracies and oligarchies. In order to justify this claim, Aristotle argues that the democratic institution of ostracism was equivalent to the tyrannical practice of removing the tallest ears of corn, since "ostracism works in the same way, as a means to remove the outstanding citizens and exile them."[99] Most significant for our current purposes is the third

---

[95] Two other characters in Thucydides—Pericles and Cleon—use the same metaphor to describe Athens. Strictly speaking, as noted by Macleod 1983, Cleon uses the term τυραννίς as a metaphor ("your empire is a tyranny," 3.37.2), and Pericles merely employs a simile ("your empire is like a tyranny," 2.63.2). For discussion of the tyrant-city metaphor, see Raaflaub 1979, Tuplin 1985, and chapter 6 below.

[96] Hdt. 5.92ε–η, discussed fully in chapter 6 below.

[97] Arist. *Pol.* 1284a26–b34.

[98] Hdt. 5.92.ζ, discussed fully in chapter 6 below.

[99] Arist. *Pol.* 1284a35–37, discussed fully in chapter 6 below.

parallel drawn in this passage. Aristotle argues that just as tyrants and democrats arbitrarily exile citizens, so imperial powers get rid of their most
powerful rivals. In drawing this comparison, Aristotle continues the imagery
of the tyrant cutting down the tallest ears of corn, with the difference that this
time the corn represents whole states rather than individual citizens (*Pol.*
1284a38–b4):

> And those who have power over cities and races do the same thing [i.e., get rid of
> the outstanding citizens]. For example, the Athenians did this to the Samians,
> Chians, and Lesbians. For as soon as [the Athenians] had strong control of their
> empire, they brought them low [ἐταπείνωσαν αὐτούς], contrary to their agree-
> ments. And the Persian king used to cut down [ἐπέκοπτε] the Medes and the
> Babylonians and the others who thought highly of themselves because they once
> had an empire.

The terms "brought low" and "cut down" obviously draw on the imagery of
the Thrasybulus anecdote, and (as I argue more fully below in chapter 6) the
comparison with ostracism shows that Aristotle understood this imagery to
symbolize the removal of citizens through exile. In applying the anecdote to
the practices of empires, therefore, Aristotle draws on the association between tyranny and exile in democratic ideology. Just as tyrants arbitrarily
exile citizens from their states in order to maintain power, Athens arbitrarily expels citizens from subject states in order to better control its empire.
It is likely that the Corinthians intended to evoke the same association between tyranny and arbitrary expulsion when they labeled Athens a tyrant city.

Exile and the Mythical Past: The Defense of Athenian Power

If critics of Athenian imperial behavior utilized associations between tyranny
and exile to link Athens' empire with tyranny, the Athenians did not sit idle in
the ideological struggle. The Athenians themselves drew on the mythical past
to counter the very claim that Athens was unjust in its practice of exile. By
citing mythical examples of Athenian justice in contrast to the injustices of
other states toward exiles, Athens found a powerful tool in the debate about
the legitimacy of Athens' empire.[100]

Two myths were especially important in Athens' claims, namely the myth
of the Heraclidae and the myth of autochthony. These stories were recounted
in Athenian tragedy and in state funerals, and were even used as arguments in
interstate negotiations. The relevance of these mythical stories to fifth-century
concerns seems obscure at first. If, however, we bear in mind the terms of the
debate about the legitimacy of Athens' leadership over the Greeks outlined in

---

[100] The relation between myth, history, and ideology is discussed fully in chapter 6 below.

the last two preceding sections, then the stories suddenly have relevance. Indeed, in these myths, the Athenians justify their power on precisely the same grounds as outlined above—namely the claim to be more moderate and just in the use of power than other states, and in particular to be protectors of exiles from other states, rather than perpetrators of exile.

The myth of the Heraclidae was told in fifth-century tragedy and frequently evoked in oratory, especially in speeches during inter-state negotiations and in funeral orations. In the latter two types of speeches, the Athenians were concerned to justify their pre-eminent position in Greece.[101]

A good example of the Athenians' use of the myth of the Heraclidae is the account given by Herodotus of the dispute between the Tegeans and the Athenians over which of them deserved to be positioned on one of the wings in the battle against the Persians at Plataea.[102] The Tegeans lay claim to the position on the basis of their king's legendary defeat of Hyllus, the leader of the Heraclidae, in single combat at the Isthmus, thus preventing the return of the Heraclidae to the Peloponnesus. The Athenians respond to the Tegean claim in kind, citing equally legendary exploits of the Athenians (9.27.2):

> When the Heraclidae, whose leader [the Tegeans] claim to have killed at the Isthmus, had been driven out by all the Greeks whom they reached [ἐξελαυνομένους ὑπὸ πάντων Ἑλλήνων ἐς τοὺς ἀπικοίατο] in their flight from slavery to the Myceneans [φεύγοντες δουλοσύνην πρὸς Μυκηναίων], we alone received them [μοῦνοι ὑποδεξάμενοι] and with their help put an end to the brazen behavior [ὕβριν] of Eurystheus by defeating those who then held power over the Peloponnesus.

Euripides' *Heraclidae*, usually dated to the beginning of the Peloponnesian War, similarly focuses on the exile of the Heraclidae as a key feature of Eurystheus's injustice and the Athenian reception of the Heraclidae as a key indication of Athens' justice. The speaker is Iolaus, a companion of the children of Heracles (12–20, 31–33):

> When their father left the land,
> Eurystheus at first wanted to kill us.
> But we ran away [ἐξέδραμεν], and although we lost our city,
> our lives were safe. So we are in exile [φεύγομεν], wandering,
> exchanging one city for another.
> For in addition to the other wrongs, Eurystheus
> dared to commit this further misdeed against us [τόδε ὕβρισμα ... ὑβρίσαι]:

---

[101] Aeschylus wrote a tragedy on the Heraclidae (now lost; cf. *TrGF* 3:190–93), as did Euripides. For the evocation of the myth in funeral orations, cf. Lys. 2.11–16; Pl. *Menex.* 239b6; [Dem.] 60.8; Isoc. *Paneg.* 52–56, *Panath.* 194–96 (all probably borrowing this material from fifth-century funeral orations: see n. 86 above).

[102] Hdt. 9.26–28.1.

wherever we are staying, he finds out and sends
heralds to demand our surrender, and he shuts us out of the land [ἐξείργει
χθονός].
Thus deprived of all of Greece [πάσης δὲ χώρας
Ἑλλάδος τητώμενοι],
we, having come to the neighborhood of Marathon [i.e., Athens],
sit at the altars of the gods as suppliants.

In the course of the drama, the Athenians offer refuge to the Heraclidae,
despite Eurystheus's threats and eventual attack, and are praised by Iolaus for
their benevolent treatment of the exiles (303–6, 315–19):[103]

> For we,
> having fallen into this extremity of misfortune, found
> these men [the Athenians] friends and kinsmen, who alone of all the inhabited
> Greek land stood up for these children [the Heraclidae].
>
> You [the Heraclidae] ought to honor them [the Athenians],
> for they took on a formidable land...
> as enemy on our behalf,
> looking out for wandering beggars [πτωχοὺς ἀλήτας].
> And they did not hand us over, nor did they drive us out from their land
> [ἀπήλασαν χθονός].

Athens's reception and protection of exiles from other lands was, of course,
a theme in many other myths as recounted in Athenian tragedy, and is
connected with the more general theme of Athens as protector of the
weak.[104] The centrality of the theme of exile in the topos of Athenian benevolence toward the weak, however, and the importance of exile in the
critique and justification of Athens' empire help to explain the importance of
these myths about exiles in the fifth century. We might compare this ideological construction with what historians of Renaissance Italy call the "myth
of Venice." The fourteenth-century poet Petrarch articulates some of the
elements of this myth in a passage that shows striking similarities with what
we might call the "myth of Athens": "The august city of Venice rejoices; the
one home today of liberty, peace, and justice, the one refuge of honorable

---

[103] The final line (319) is deleted in Diggle's (Oxford, 1984) edition of the text.

[104] For full discussion of this theme in tragedy, see Tzanetou, *Staging Citizenship* (forth-
coming). Examples of dramas concerning Athenian protection of exiles include Aeschylus's
Eumenides, Sophocles' *Oedipus at Colonus*, and Euripides' *Heracles, Heraclidae*, and *Medea*.
Compare also Aeschylus's *Suppliants*, especially 605–24 and 942–44, where the connection
between a democratic political system and the benevolent treatment of exiles is emphasized. For
Athenian protection of the weak, see Eur. *Heracl.* 175, *Supp.* 337–41, 379–80; Xen. *Hell.* 6.5.45;
Pl. *Menex.* 244e; Isoc. *Paneg.* 52–58, *Peace* 138.

men, the one port to which can repair the storm-tossed, tyrant-hounded craft of men who seek the good life."[105]

If we turn now to the myth of autochthony, we can see a similar relation at work between the themes of exile and Athenian justice. The myth of autochthony is discussed most fully in fourth-century funeral orations, but it probably existed long before.[106] Scholars have noted the various functions that the myth of autochthony played in fifth-century Athens, including the claim to chronological priority in relation to other poleis, the enhancement of citizen identity and unity vis-à-vis non-citizens, and the affirmation of the political equality of all citizens.[107] The Athenian myth of autochthony, however, also shows a further interest in representing Athens as a state that did not engage in expulsions of its own citizens or citizens of other states and in fact received exiles from other states benevolently.[108] In this way, the Athenian myth of autochthony echoed Athens' claims to just leadership of the Greeks through its moderation in the use of exile, and would have served to counter criticisms of Athens' imperial behavior based on the unjust use of exile.

Thucydides cites the myth in the introduction to his history. His main aim in this section of his introduction is to show that the mobility of the early Greeks prevented them from accumulating resources and becoming as powerful as the Greeks of his own day. Athens serves as a negative example for his general point about Greece, since according to the myth of autochthony, the Athenians inhabited Attica from the beginning and by receiving exiles from other cities became a powerful state (1.2.5–6):

The same men always inhabited Attica [ἄνθρωποι ᾤκουν οἱ αὐτοὶ αἰεί], for the most part, since Attica was without civil strife [τὴν Ἀττικὴν ... ἀστασίαστον οὖσαν] because of the infertility of the soil.[109] And a not inconsiderable proof of this is that Athens grew an account of immigration [διὰ τὰς μετοικίας] in a way different from other states. For the most powerful men who were expelled from other states [ἐκ ... τῆς ἄλλης ... Ἑλλάδος ... ἐκπίπτοντες] due to war or faction migrated to the Athenians [παρ' Ἀθηναίους ... ἀνεχώρουν], since they thought Athens a secure land, and they became citizens [πολῖται γιγνόμενοι] and made

---

[105] Petrarch, *Letters*, p. 234, cited by Muir 1981, 22.

[106] Most scholars assume that the myth goes back at least to the eighth century (cf. Hom. *Il.* 2.547–48), but Rosivach 1987b argues that it dates only to the fifth century. According to Rosivach, the earliest reference to the autochthony of the Athenian people as a whole is Soph. *Aj.* 202; (cf. also Hdt. 1.56.3, 7.161.3). For the myth of autochthony in fourth-century funeral orations, cf. Pl. *Menex.* 237b1–239a4; Isoc. *Paneg.* 24–25, *Panath.* 124; [Dem.] 60.4–6.

[107] Rosivach 1987b, 302–5; Loraux 2000, 13–27.

[108] Rosivach (1987b, 303) notes the connection between the myth of autochthony and the unique moral quality of the Athenians that leads them to protect the oppressed.

[109] Note the contrast with Herodotus's version of early Athenian history, where the city is plagued by faction (1.59–64, discussed above in chapter 3 and below in chapter 6). Herodotus contrasts the stability of Sparta to that of Athens. For further discussion of this contrast, see M. Meier 1998, 45–47.

Athens more populous. As a result the Athenians later sent out colonies to Ionia, since Attica was not sufficient.

Thucydides' argument brings out two essential points of the myth of autochthony in the fifth century, namely the permanence of the Athenians on Attic soil and the reception in Athens of exiles from other states. On the surface, these two points seem contradictory, since the same men cannot have always inhabited Attica if new citizens were constantly accepted from elsewhere.[110] Yet myths are able to accommodate inconsistencies and, in any case, reflect the changing needs of the Athenians over time.[111] The idea of autochthony would certainly have helped the early Athenians claim possession of their land, and the idea of the reception of outsiders would have helped the growing community accommodate the reality of constant influxes of newcomers. In particular, elites who did not belong to the exclusive ruling group of the Eupatrids could claim descent from leading families in other states and hence lay claim to prestige in Athens.[112] By the fifth century, autochthony could be claimed for all Athenians, thus granting them a degree of noble ancestry in accordance with the prevailing democratic ethos. The idea of the early reception of powerful immigrants from other states, on the other hand, conveniently legitimized the origins of Athenians with obvious foreign connections.[113]

Yet the significance of these two elements of Thucydides' version of the myth can be pushed further, since they correspond to the known use of the theme of exile in the justification of Athens' power in the fifth century. As we have seen, the Athenians constantly evoked the myth of the Heraclidae to assert their justice and hence their claim to leadership of the Greeks. A key element of the myth was the unjust banishment of the Heraclidae from the Peloponnesus and their reception in Athens. The fifth-century Athenians justified their leadership of the Greeks in part through the idea of their more just treatment of exiles in the mythical past. The myth of autochthony seems to draw on this same theme, showing that the early Athenians did not drive out others in order to found their city but in fact received and protected exiles from other states.[114] Moreover, while the citizens of other states suf-

---

[110] Cf. Lys. 2.17 for a variation avoiding this essential contradiction: "The beginning of our existence was just. For we did not, as did many others, settle in a foreign land by gathering together from all over and expelling others, but we are autochthonous and hold the same land as both mother and fatherland." Note, however, that Lysias still links justice and failure to expel others from their land.

[111] For discussion of this point, see below, chapter 6.

[112] Consider, for example, the Pisistratid family, incorporated into the Athenian ruling class from early archaic times but tracing its ancestry back to the Neleids of Pylos (Hdt. 5.65.3).

[113] Cf. Pl. Menex. 237b1, 238b7: note especially the parallelism drawn between ἰσογονία and ἰσονομία.

[114] Cf. Lysias's version of the myth of autochthony, cited in n. 110 above. Lysias places specific emphasis on the fact that the Athenians did not need to banish others to settle their land,

fered exile because of civil strife and war, Athens was "without civil strife," and hence its citizens enjoyed peaceful residence on their land. The idea that its population grew in part through the reception of exiles from other states furthers Athens' claim to be a more just power, since those who were driven out from other states found friendly welcome there. In short, I suggest that one reason for the continued importance of the myth of autochthony in fifth-century Athens was its role in distinguishing Athens from Sparta in regard to the potent issue of exile.[115] The Spartans notoriously drove out the indigenous people of Laconia and Messenia in order to found their state, and were known in the fifth century for their expulsions of strangers (ξενη-λασίαι).[116] The Athenians, in contrast, drew on the mythical past to show that they neither inflicted exile on others nor refused the entreaties of exiles from other states.

CONCLUSION

In this chapter I have argued for a parallelism between Athens' practice and ideology of exile in its internal and external relations. I argued that just as the Athenian democracy took control of decisions of exile among its own citizens, so did it also among its allied states. Yet I showed that part of the aim of taking control of exile both internally and externally was to end or at least dampen the politics of exile. Moreover, Athenian restraint in the use of exile not only stabilized political conflict in Athens and in its allied states, but served as an important tool in the justification of democratic power at home and Athenian power abroad. In the next chapter, I examine more closely the role of the theme of exile in the justification of Athenian democratic power by examining the representation of exile in a number of literary texts. I argue that exile played a significant role in the internal debate about the justice of democratic rule just as it did in the debate about the legitimacy of empire.

---

and cites this as evidence of Athens' "just beginning" (ἡ ἀρχὴ τοῦ βίου δικαία) in contrast to that of "many other peoples." Cf. also Saxonhouse (1986, 256) on the myth of autochthony: "A city of autochthonous origins gives the appearance of peaceful origins. The violence at the beginnings of cities is glossed over if a people inhabit a land from which their ancestors sprang. The inherent injustice, the taking from others of what is theirs, entailed in the founding of cities is ignored."

[115] Loraux (2000, 15) also associates the myth of autochthony with Athenian ideological conflict with Sparta.

[116] On the Spartans' expulsion of the Messenians, see Isoc. *Panath.* 91, discussed above, in which Isocrates responds to criticism of Athens by pointing out that Sparta banished the Messenians. For the role of exile, including ξενηλασία, in Spartan history and ideology, see appendix 3.

Chapter Six

EXILE IN THE GREEK MYTHICAL AND
HISTORICAL IMAGINATION

In the last two chapters, I argued that the historical experience of exile shaped the ways that the Athenian democracy conceptualized and exercised political power. In these chapters we saw that the Athenian democracy's moderate use of exile both internally (as symbolized in the institution of ostracism) and externally (as represented in imperial decrees) was key both to Athens' internal stability and to the maintenance of its empire. In this chapter, I turn back to the internal politics of Athens to examine more closely the role of exile in the ideological validation of democratic rule. The central claim of this chapter is that the historical experience of exile shaped both Athenian memories of the past and its justifications of the present order. In order to make this claim, I show how Athenian democratic traditions appropriated earlier Panhellenic traditions illustrating the relation between exile and the illegitimate use of power. These traditions were retold in Athenian democratic lore in order to contrast the violent and irresponsible rule of non-democratic regimes to the moderation of the democracy. I demonstrate that exile was a key term in this ideological construct by illustrating its prominence both in democratic representations of non-democratic regimes (especially tyranny), and in the responses of critics of the Athenian democracy to democratic practice and ideology.

The next section, "Myth, History, and Social Memory," discusses the functions of mythical and historical traditions in Greek society as a way of methodologically grounding the analysis that follows. Integral to this discussion are both the importance of the memory of the past in the justification of the present order, and the recognition that different groups within society maintain different versions of the past in order to further their own social, political, and ideological agendas. Here I draw a distinction between the versions of the past preserved by the Athenian people at large (ὁ δῆμος), as the dominant power in fifth-century Athens, and those preserved by an important subgroup within Athenian society, namely elite critics of popular rule. A key issue in this division between democratic and anti-democratic traditions is how these competing ideologies are reflected in the texts that are our sources for Greek memories of the past (e.g., historical prose, tragedy, oratory). While tragedy and oratory are generally recognized as important sources for Athenian democratic ideology, I argue that a number of narratives in Herodotus's *Histories* also reflect aspects of Athenian democratic tradition.

Next, "Exile in the Democratic Tradition" examines the democratic representations of that phenomenon. I begin with the representation of tyranny in Herodotus's *Histories*, showing that although Herodotus's representations of tyrants (Cypselus and Periander of Corinth, Polycrates of Samos, Pisistratus of Athens) reveal traces of their origins in elite oral traditions of the archaic period, their form in the *Histories* is shaped by fifth-century Athenian democratic ideology, in particular by the role of exile in the justification of democratic rule. Specifically, I show that the theme of exile is emphasized and expanded in the democratic tradition in order to illustrate the harmful effect of non-democratic regimes on the entire citizen body. Whereas elite traditions of the archaic period noted that tyrants often killed or exiled and confiscated the property of their elite rivals, democratic traditions suggest that the people as a whole suffer these penalties under tyranny. The ideological association between tyranny and mass expulsions served both to delegitimize non-democratic rule (and, conversely, legitimize democratic rule) and to excuse and explain the Athenians' submission to the Pisistratid tyranny.

In this section, I also compare Herodotus's account of the tyrant Periander's troubled relationship with his son Lycophron against Athenian versions of the myth of the Heraclidae in tragedy and oratory. I argue that Periander's relationship with his son serves as a metonym for a tyrant's relations with the citizen body. Periander's progressive expulsion of his son first from his home, then from the homes of all other Corinthians, and then from Corinth altogether reflects the role of exile in the representation of tyranny in democratic ideology. By comparing Herodotus's account of Periander with Athenian versions of the myth of the Heraclidae, moreover, I show that both stories borrow in similar ways from the trope of exile in democratic ideology. Finally, I turn to the representation of the oligarchy of 403 in Xenophon's *Hellenica* and in fourth-century oratory. I show that representations of the oligarchy are also shaped by the role of exile in democratic ideology, and in particular by the connection between non-democratic regimes and mass expulsions.

In the next section, "Exile in the Anti-Democratic Tradition," I examine the response of critics of the democracy to the construction of exile in democratic ideology. I focus on three examples. First, I show how Thucydides and Xenophon shaped their representations of the banishment of Alcibiades in order to equate the democracy with a tyranny through its unjust banishment of its best citizens. Second, I argue that Plato's representation of the trial of Socrates similarly responds to the representation of the tyrant in democratic ideology by suggesting that the democracy behaved like a tyrant in forcing Socrates either to flee into exile or to accept the punishment—death—meted out to him by the democratic jury. Finally, I examine Aristotle's discussion of ostracism. Aristotle, like Thucydides, Xenophon, and Plato before him, equates democracy with a sort of tyranny, but focuses specifically on ostracism as a practice representative of the tyrannical tendencies of the democracy.

Aristotle's discussion, I argue, illustrates the centrality of exile, and in particular ostracism, in both the justification of democracy and in anti-democratic responses to democratic ideology.

MYTH, HISTORY, AND SOCIAL MEMORY: APPROACHING THE
GREEK HISTORICAL IMAGINATION

It is widely recognized that a society's memories of the past are largely determined by the utility of that past in the present. In other words, what a society chooses to remember is a product of which memories serve a socially useful function in the present. A society's memory of its past, moreover, is not a constant entity but is continually reshaped as the needs of society change, and as the past is put to different uses by various groups within the society.[1] As many have pointed out, in this continual reshaping of memories of the past, forgetting is as important a process as remembering. As groups within society tailor their memories of the past to current needs, elements of the past that do not serve a useful function, or work against a group's needs, are de-emphasized, and often drop out of its narrative of the past altogether. Conversely, other elements of the past are emphasized, and sometimes even invented, in order to make the past more socially useful in the present.[2]

In this chapter, I examine the ways in which two different groups within Athenian society adapted mythical and historical traditions about exile in order to further their political agendas. The first group with which I am concerned is naturally the Athenian democracy itself, which, through its multiple forums for collective deliberation and self-representation (the assembly, courts, theater, civic rituals and festivals) articulated a common version of the past that, at least in part, validated the principle of democratic rule. Democratic versions of the past, moreover—what Rosalind Thomas terms "the official polis tradition"—formed the master narrative of Athenian history in the fifth and fourth centuries. It is generally well recognized that the versions of the past that are presented in many of the central texts of the fifth

---

[1] It is important to recognize that the term "social memory" implies a unified consciousness among all members of society. Rather, it is more useful to think in terms of a large number of competing memories among different groups within society. There may at any one time be a version of the past enjoying relative dominance in a society, but this is never to the exclusion of multiple counter-versions of the past that circulate among sub-groups within society (e.g., families, or specific classes or status groups, such as the elites of late fifth-century Athens). For the competing types of oral tradition in ancient Greece, see Thomas 1989.

[2] The bibliography on social memory is vast. I cite only a few recent studies for the general principles outlined above: Hobsbawm and Ranger 1983, Vansina 1985, Assmann 1992, Fentress and Wickham 1992, Le Goff 1992, Hartog and Revel 2001. For studies of social memory in Greek and Roman antiquity, see, for example, Thomas 1989, Gehrke and Möller 1996, Alcock 2002.

and fourth centuries (for example, tragedy and oratory) reflect, at least in part, this dominant democratic tradition.[3] To this catalogue of democratic texts, I would add Herodotus's *Histories*. Since the relationship of the *Histories* to Athenian democratic traditions is less well recognized in current scholarship, and since its narratives form the backbone of my explication of the democratic tradition of exile, I must say a few words on this topic.

The presence of Athenian democratic versions of the Greek past in Herodotus's *Histories* has gone unrecognized for two principal reasons. First, Herodotus has suffered through comparison with his successor Thucydides, who has long been considered the political historian, and whose history is much more clearly bound up with the vicissitudes of the Athenian democracy in the fifth century.[4] Second, and more important, Herodotus was not an Athenian, and it was for a long time widely accepted that his knowledge of Athenian history was derived from elite families such as the Alcmeonidae and the circle of Pericles, who propagated a partisan and elitist version of the Athenian past.[5] Recently this view has come into question, and many now recognize that Herodotus used not simply family traditions alone but the wider polis or popular traditions of the democracy.[6] As I have argued in several previous publications, many features of Herodotus's narratives concerning the past both of Athens and of other poleis and cultures can best be explained by positing Herodotus's familiarity with Athenian democratic ways of representing the past.[7]

Against the dominant democratic tradition of fifth- and fourth-century Athens, a competing group of memories of the past can be identified. These competing versions can be attributed to a small subgroup of the Athenian population, namely elite critics of popular rule.[8] Although it is not always easy to neatly classify a given author or text as anti-democratic (see, for example, the

[3] For tragedy, see, for example, Goldhill 1988, 1990; Winkler and Zeitlin 1990. The association between tragedy and democracy is not universally accepted: see Griffin 1998, with the responses of Seaford 2000 and Rhodes 2003. For oratory, see, for example, Loraux 1986, Wolpert 2002.

[4] To the extent that scholars have considered Herodotus's relationship with Athens, they have usually focused on the question of his views of Periclean Athens and the Athenian empire. See, for example, Moles 2002, with earlier bibliography. Recent works that take Herodotus's political thought seriously include Raaflaub 1987, 2002; Saxonhouse 1996; N. Thompson 1996; Forsdyke 2001, in press.

[5] Jacoby 1913, 237–38, 413; 1949, 152–58. See Lavelle 1993 for a recent version of this theory.

[6] Thomas 1989 is fundamental for this reassessment of Herodotus's sources.

[7] Forsdyke 1999, 2001, 2002. It is important to stress that I do not wish to underestimate the complexity of Herodotus's *Histories*, or to suggest that Herodotus was simply a mouthpiece of the Athenian democracy. Rather, I seek to identify one strand in some of the narratives of the *Histories* that has previously been neglected. Compare Kurke (1999, 333) on the multiplicity of types of oral traditions present in the *Histories*: "Herodotus appears to preserve competing, sometimes even contradictory logoi from oral informants across a whole spectrum of socioeconomic and ideological positions."

[8] See Ober (1998, 14–51) for a general and theoretical account of this critical community.

discussion of Xenophon's *Hellenica* below), it remains clear that in broad outline such authors as Thucydides, Plato, and Aristotle often express criticisms of democratic rule, which probably derive from arguments circulating among a small circle of elites who were disenchanted with it. As we shall see, the criticisms of democratic rule made by these authors in fact not only reveal anti-democratic traditions of exile but also reflect, through their emphasis on exile, the importance of this theme in democratic traditions.

EXILE IN THE DEMOCRATIC TRADITION

The best way to illustrate the role of the theme of exile in Athenian democratic ideology is to examine the representation of tyranny in the democratic texts listed above.[9] In this section I examine Herodotus's representation of three archaic tyrannies (the Cypselids of Corinth, Polycrates of Samos, and Pisistratus of Athens). I argue that Herodotus's accounts of these tyrannies reflect democratic appropriations of archaic anti-tyrannical traditions. In both the earlier traditions and their democratic transformations, arbitrary expulsions play a central role in the characterization of tyranny. In the case of the tyrant Periander of Corinth, I demonstrate that Herodotus's account is influenced by another great exile narrative—the myth of the Heraclidae, as it is told in Athenian democratic traditions. Finally, I turn to the representation of the Thirty Tyrants in Xenophon and oratory, showing how their quasi-tyranny was assimilated to earlier democratic traditions through exaggerating and emphasizing the number of people exiled by their regime.

Herodotus's narrative concerning the Corinthian tyrants Cypselus and Periander is embedded in a larger account of the origins and early successes of the Athenian democracy.[10] I have argued in previous publications that this larger context reveals the democratic ideological origins of Herodotus's version of the story of the Corinthian tyrants.[11] I argued that several details of Herodotus's narrative demonstrate slippage between an earlier archaic tradition in which rival elites were the victims of the tyrant's brutality, and a

---

[9] For the role of the tyrant in Athenian democratic ideology, see recently Raaflaub 2003a, with earlier bibliography. See also Wohl (2002, 215–69), who argues that tyranny was both an object of repudiation and an object of allure, and as such had a vital role in animating the beliefs and emotions by which the democracy was sustained.

[10] Scholarly discussion of Herodotus's representation of tyranny is extensive: see Dewald 2003 for a summary. Some argue that tyranny is always a bad thing for Herodotus (e.g., Lateiner 1989, Raaflaub 2003a). Gray 1996 argues that Herodotus's representations of tyrants are adapted to fit specific contexts in his *Histories*, and do not conform to a stereotype. Dewald 2003 argues that Herodotus's Eastern despots are paradigmatic examples of the evils of tyranny, while Greek tyrants play a more ambiguous role. For the etymology and semantic range of the word τύραννος in Greek literature, see V. Parker 1998.

[11] Forsdyke 1999, 2001.

democratic version in which the entire citizen body suffers from the tyrant's injustices. In this section and those that follow, I demonstrate that arbitrary expulsions were a key feature of the representation of tyranny in Athenian democratic ideology.

The immediate context for Herodotus's account of the Corinthian tyrants is a proposal by the Spartans to restore the sons of the tyrant Pisistratus to power in Athens. The Corinthian Socles objects to this proposal and describes the brutal rule of the Corinthian tyrant Cypselus as an example of the evils of tyranny (5.92ε.2):

πολλοὺς μὲν Κορινθίων ἐδίωξε, πολλοὺς δὲ χρημάτων ἀπεστέρησε, πολλῷ δέ τι πλείστους τῆς ψυχῆς.

He drove many Corinthians into exile, and he confiscated the property of many, but mostly he killed people.

Three facts—besides the rhetorical style of the sentence—lead us to suspect this statement is a highly selective and indeed thoroughly tendentious representation of Cypselus's rule. First, this wholly black picture of the tyranny conflicts strikingly with Socles' earlier account of an oracle predicting that Cypselus would bring justice to Corinth.[12] Second, the existence of positive traditions about the Corinthian tyrants in other sources suggests that Herodotus or his sources selected, and perhaps even invented, these negative features for their representation of tyrannical rule.[13] Finally, and most important, a combination of textual and archaeological evidence suggests that there was no mass expulsion or elimination of citizens following the overthrow of the Bacchiad oligarchy.[14] I argued above in chapter 2 that the longevity of the tyrannical regime was probably a result of its good relations with fellow elites and masses alike. It is unlikely, therefore, that Cypselus perpetrated mass expulsions and executions of citizens as Herodotus's account alleges.

Yet Herodotus's claim about the brutality of Cypselus's reign is not wholly without historical basis. As I argued above in chapter 2, there is some evidence of limited expulsions and executions under the tyrants. According to Nicolaus of Damascus, Cypselus seized power by killing the Bacchiad Patrocleides, who held the office of king.[15] Furthermore, numerous sources attest to the expulsion of the former ruling oligarchs, the Bacchiads.[16] Thus if

---

[12] Hdt. 5.92β.2, quoted and discussed above in chapter 2.

[13] For positive accounts of the Cypselid tyranny, see Nic. Dam. *FGrH* 90 F 57 on Cypselus; F 58 4 and D.L. 1.98 on Periander as one of the Seven Sages. For Periander as arbitrator between Mytilene and Athens over Sigeum, see Hdt. 5.95.2.

[14] The evidence is discussed above in chapter 2.

[15] Nic. Dam. *FGrH* 90 F 57.6. The title "king" presumably was one of the magistracies established under Bacchiad rule.

[16] The sources are discussed above in chapter 2.

there is any historical basis to Herodotus's account of Cypselus's brutal treatment of the Corinthians, it lies in the tyrant's treatment of the former ruling oligarchs—that is, his elite rivals. On this basis, we may surmise that the Bacchiads, the elite opponents of the tyrant, were the original source of the traditions asserting that the tyrants used expulsions and murder in order to gain and retain power in Corinth. Yet here we can observe a discrepancy between the historical experience that gave rise to these traditions—namely the tyrant's treatment of rival elites—and Herodotus's representation of tyrannical brutality. Indeed, Herodotus suggests that it was not just the elites who were the victims of the tyrants' brutal actions. Rather, he asserts that the entire citizen body of the Corinthians suffered murder, expulsion, and the confiscation of property at Cypselus's hands.

The inconsistency between the historical basis of tyrannical brutality (against elite rivals to the tyrant) and its later representation (against the Corinthians as a whole) is best explained as a product of the appropriation by the democracy of the traditions of the elite opponents of the tyrant, in this case the Bacchiads. The traditions of these elite rivals were concerned to delegitimize the tyranny and legitimize rule by a coalition of elites, in part by illustrating their unjust treatment by the tyrant. Democratic traditions, on the other hand, utilized the figure of the tyrant to legitimize democratic rule, and hence were concerned to demonstrate tyrannical brutality not simply toward rival elites but toward the citizenry at large. Thus the historical victims of tyrannical brutality were eclipsed by the citizen body as a whole in democratic traditions.

This slippage between archaic elite traditions and later democratic traditions, as well as the thematic importance of expulsion as the means by which tyrants gain and retain power, is even more visible in the next portion of Socles' speech, where he turns to the rule of Cypselus's son Periander.[17] In this well-known episode, Periander learns the arts of tyrannical brutality by consulting with a fellow tyrant, Thrasybulus of Miletus. According to Herodotus's version of this story,[18] Periander sent a messenger to Thrasybulus in order to learn how he might rule Corinth most securely and best (ὄντινα ἂν τρόπον ἀσφαλέστατον καταστησάμενος τῶν πρηγμάτων κάλλιστα τὴν πόλιν ἐπιτροπεύοι).[19] Thrasybulus led the messenger into a field and proceeded to cut back and throw away the ears of grain that protruded above the rest (τινὰ ... τῶν ἀσταχύων ὑπερέχοντα). He did this until he had destroyed the most beautiful and tallest part of the crop (τὸ κάλλιστόν τε καὶ βαθύτατον τοῦ ληίου). Without saying a word, he sent the messenger back to Periander. When the messenger reported Thrasybulus's peculiar behavior,

---

[17] For full analysis of this portion of the speech, see Forsdyke 1999.

[18] With the two tyrants' roles reversed, the story also appears in Arist. Pol. 1284a26–33 and 1311a20–22, discussed below.

[19] Hdt. 5.92ζ.2.

Periander understood that he was being advised to kill the most outstanding citizens (τοὺς ὑπερόχους τῶν ἀστῶν φονεύειν).[20]

Up to this point in the story, the imagery and language suggest that the elites—"the ears of grain that protruded above the rest," "the most beautiful and tallest part of the crop," "the most outstanding citizens"—were the victims of the tyrant's brutality. These features of the story suggest, therefore, that this portion of the narrative originated in the anti-tyrannical traditions of the elite opponents of the tyrant in the archaic period. Yet the story does not stop there. In Herodotus's version of the anecdote, Periander responds to the advice of Thrasybulus not by simply killing the most outstanding citizens, but by performing a wide range of abuses against the Corinthian citizens as a whole—men and women alike. Foremost among his abuses are the murder and expulsion of any citizens who remained following Cypselus's purges (5.92η.1):[21]

> Periander then set about performing every sort of misdeed against the citizens [ἐς τοὺς πολιήτας]. For he finished off whatever Cypselus had left behind in the way of killing [κτείνων] and banishing [διώκων], and in one day he stripped naked all the women of Corinth [πάσας τὰς Κορινθίων γυναῖκας] on account of his wife, Melissa.

The striking contrast between the imagery of the anecdote in which Thrasybulus cuts down the ears of grain that stick out above the rest and the tyrant Periander's response to this symbolic advice—widespread violence against all Corinthian citizens—demonstrates how archaic elite anti-tyrannical traditions were appropriated and adapted by the democracy. In democratic versions, tyrannical violence affects all the citizens, not just the elite.

In the next section of this chapter, I argue that Aristotle's comparison of Thrasybulus's action with the democratic procedure of ostracism suggests that cutting down and throwing away the ears of grain was widely seen as symbolic of the tyrant's use of expulsion as a political tool. Before I turn to Aristotle's discussion, I will examine several further examples of the tyrannical use of expulsion as a means of gaining and maintaining power.

In book 3 of his *Histories*, Herodotus describes the reign of the Samian tyrant Polycrates (3.39–60). The connection between this digression on Samian history and the main subject of the narrative at this point—the Persian conquest of Egypt—is only loosely justified by a chronological coincidence between the invasion of Egypt by the Persian king Cambyses and a Spartan expedition to depose the Samian tyrant. On this basis, however, Herodotus describes how Polycrates rose to power, how he conquered a number of

[20] Hdt. 5.92ζ.3–η.1.
[21] Herodotus specifies, furthermore, that both free women and slave women were stripped (5.92η.3).

Greek poleis, how he gained and lost an alliance with the Egyptian king Amasis, and how he warded off the Spartan invasion. Finally, Herodotus winds up his discussion of archaic Samos by describing a number of its marvelous structures, including a water channel, a harbor mole, and an enormous temple of Hera.

My concern with Herodotus's narrative is primarily with the description of how the tyrant gained and maintained power. On the first point, Herodotus is brief, but the parallelism with his narrative of the Corinthian tyrants is clear (3.39.1–2): "Polycrates had power in Samos after rising up in revolt. At first he held power jointly with his brothers, Panagnotus and Syloson, but later he gained sole power in Samos by killing [ἀποκτείνας] one brother and exiling [ἐξελάσας] the other." Although this account is probably based on a historical coup of Polycrates against his own family (see chapter 2 above), Herodotus's blunt phrasing recalls the representation of the manner of rule of the Corinthian tyrants. In both cases, the tyrants' use of execution and expulsion is highlighted. Moreover, as we shall see later, this representation of Polycrates' treatment of members of his own family can be taken as metonymic for his treatment of the citizen body as a whole. Before we turn to this argument, however, it is worth pointing out further parallels between Herodotus's narrative of the Corinthian tyrants and his narrative of Polycrates' manner of rule.

According to Herodotus, the Spartans mounted an expedition against Polycrates at the behest of a group of Samian exiles. As we saw above in chapter 2, these exiles were probably a small group of elite rivals of the tyrants who withdrew into exile or were actively expelled in the struggle for power in archaic Samos. Yet Herodotus gives a more colorful account of how these men came to be exiled, simultaneously suggesting that they were a much larger group than is historically likely. According to Herodotus (3.44), Polycrates secretly sent a message to the Persian king Cambyses asking that he request a Samian contingent for his invasion of Egypt. Cambyses complied, and Polycrates then selected those of the Samian citizens (τῶν ἀστῶν) whom he most suspected of dissent and sent them on forty triremes to Egypt, instructing Cambyses not to send them back (μὴ ἀποπέμπειν). The exiles, however, did not reach Egypt, but on realizing what Polycrates had done sailed back to Samos and attacked him. When the exiles failed to defeat the tyrant, they sailed to Sparta to request support in overthrowing him.

As in the case of the Corinthian tyrants, Herodotus's account of tyrannical expulsions probably is based on the traditions of the tyrant's elite rivals, a small group of whom may in fact have gone into exile under his regime. Yet Herodotus's account expands this small group of elite exiles to a larger group of potential opponents, who not only fill forty triremes and constitute a credible allied force for Cambyses' Egyptian campaign, but attempt to overthrow Polycrates by themselves. It is likely that this shift from a small group of elite opponents to a large group of Samian citizens is a product of the appropriation of elite traditions of exile by later democratic traditions. In these latter, I suggest, a tyrant's expulsion of innocent citizens is symbolic of the injustice of non-democratic regimes.

Parallels between the story of Polycrates and other accounts of the illegitimate rule of tyrants confirm this relation. Specifically, the trick by which Polycrates expels a large group of opponents to his regime is paralleled not only in Herodotus's account of Egyptian ruler Apries, but also in later accounts of the Corinthian tyrant Cypselus's rule. According to Herodotus, King Apries sent a large force of Egyptians to aid the Libyans in their struggle against the Greek colony of Cyrene. In the ensuing battle, almost the entire Egyptian force perished. The destruction of this large Egyptian force was the cause of a rebellion against Apries, reports Herodotus, since the Egyptians believed that Apries had deliberately sent them away into a clearly bad situation in order that they might perish and he might rule the rest of the Egyptians more securely (Αἰγύπτιοι... δοκέοντες τὸν Ἀπρίην ἐκ προνοίης αὐτοὺς ἀποπέμψαι ἐς φαινόμενον κακὸν ἵνα δὴ σφέων φθορὴ γένηται, αὐτὸς δὲ τῶν λοιπῶν Αἰγυπτίων ἀσφαλέστερον ἄρχοι).[22] In this tradition, a historical battle of Egyptians against Greeks is transformed into an example both of tyrannical brutality against citizens and of tyrannical trickery on a par with Polycrates' deception.

More specifically, Apries' alleged motive for sending away a large group of Egyptians to fight in a remote battle—namely his desire to get them killed so that he could rule the rest of Egyptians more securely—recalls the themes and language of Herodotus's account of the tyrant Periander of Corinth. As we saw above, Periander consulted Thrasybulus about how he might rule Corinth most securely and best (ὅντινα ἂν τρόπον ἀσφαλέστατον καταστησάμενος τῶν πρηγμάτων κάλλιστα τὴν πόλιν ἐπιτροπεύοι). Periander was advised to kill the leading citizens, and in response the tyrant set about murdering and banishing the Corinthian citizens en masse.

A further variation on this same theme is evident in a tradition about the Corinthian tyrant Cypselus. According to Nicolaus of Damascus, whose source was probably the fourth-century historian Ephorus, Cypselus deported to settlements abroad anyone who was not a friend in order that he might rule the rest more easily (εἴς τε ἀποικίαν ἐξῆγε τοὺς μὴ φίλους, ὅπως ἂν ῥᾷον ἄρχοι τῶν λοιπῶν).[23] In this case, expulsion to settlements abroad replaces service in the army as the means by which the tyrant gets rid of a large number of his own citizens and secures his rule over the rest of the population. It is likely that the theme of expulsion as the means by which a tyrant secures his power has been superimposed on traditions describing Corinthian settlements abroad.

[22] Hdt. 2.161.4, 4.159.5–6.
[23] Nic. Dam. FGrH 90 F 57.

In sum, each of these tyrants is depicted as using expulsion and extermination as means of maintaining his power in the polis. Although as I demonstrated above in chapter 2 many archaic Greek tyrants did in fact expel (and occasionally kill) their elite rivals as part of the struggle for power in the poleis of archaic Greece, in these traditions we see how accounts of elite exile—and even battle narratives and accounts of new settlements abroad— are transformed into instances of mass expulsions and executions by which the tyrant, either by force or by deception, is represented as maintaining his rule over an unwilling citizenry.

Herodotus's depiction of the tyrant Pisistratus of Athens is a further example of this pattern. Herodotus's account of Pisistratus's final seizure of tyranny reveals the ways that the Athenians in the fifth century tried to accommodate the inconvenient fact of widespread popular support of the tyranny into their democratic traditions.[24] Indeed many of the apparent contradictions in Herodotus's account are explicable as results of the attempt of fifth-century democratic traditions to disguise the fact of widespread Athenian support for the tyranny.[25] The most obvious way in which the tradition tries to accomplish this is to suggest that Pisistratus tricked the Athenians into submitting to his rule. Not only does Pisistratus win the battle of Pallene by attacking his opponents while they are having lunch, but he also deploys a clever ruse to prevent the Athenians from rallying together to renew their resistance (1.63.2):

> When [the defeated Athenians] were in full flight [φευγόντων], Pisistratus devised a clever ploy [βουλὴν σοφωτάτην . . . ἐπιτεχνᾶται] so that the Athenians might not still gather together and might be dispersed [ὅκως μήτε ἁλισθεῖεν ἔτι οἱ Ἀθηναῖοι διεσκεδασμένοι τε εἶεν]. Mounting his sons on horses, he sent them forward. When they overtook the fugitives [τοὺς φεύγοντας], they spoke what Pisistratus had ordered. [Pisistratus's sons] commanded [the Athenians] to take courage and to return each to his own home [ἀπιέναι ἕκαστον ἐπὶ τὰ ἑωυτοῦ].

By presenting the Athenians as duped by the tyrant into returning home, Herodotus and his fifth-century sources imply that the Athenians would have continued to resist the tyrant had they not been tricked into dispersing.[26] But this explanation contradicts the first part of the narrative, where Herodotus

[24] For the popularity of the Pisistratid tyranny, see above, chapter 3.

[25] For this argument, see also Lavelle 1993; Bassi 1998, 144–91.

[26] Compare Herodotus's use (1.59.1) of the participle διεσπασμένον (scattered) to describe the condition of the Athenians under Pisistratid rule. This explanation of the means by which Pisistratus prevented opposition to his rule from forming anticipates one of the mechanisms for the maintenance of tyrannical rule in Arist. Pol. 1311a10, namely the expulsion of the people from the city and their dispersal (διοικίζειν). Aristotle's formulation of this feature of tyrannical rule may in turn may be a product of memories of the expulsion of the people from the city by the Thirty Tyrants in 403: see chapter 4 above.

makes clear that Pisistratus's opponents were comprised of a small group of elites from the city, and that by contrast a large group of Athenians from throughout Attica came out in support of him.[27] Yet in his narrative of the battle itself, these divisions of the Athenian citizenry are elided, and Pisistratus's opponents are designated simply as "the Athenians" (Hdt. 1.63.1–2). The most plausible explanation of this shift is that the theme of tyrannical trickery, which in Athenian democratic ideology served to show how tyrants imposed their rule on an unwilling citizenry, was superimposed on earlier traditions concerning the battle of Pallene, in which the actual extent of popular support for Pisistratus was preserved.[28]

A second contradiction in Herodotus's narrative reveals how the theme of mass expulsions under the tyranny was superimposed on earlier traditions regarding Pisistratus's final seizure of absolute power. Immediately following the account of Pisistratus's clever ruse by which the Athenians were deceived into dispersing, Herodotus reports that the tyrant also prevented further resistance to his rule both by maintaining a strong foreign military force in the city and by taking hostages from among the children of the Athenians. Since foreign mercenaries and hostage taking are both paralleled in other accounts of tyrannical rule, we may suspect that these elements of Pisistratus's tyranny have been adapted from the representation of the tyrant in anti-tyrannical traditions. Indeed, Brian Lavelle has recently argued that it is highly unlikely that Pisistratus had the resources to maintain a significant foreign military force in Athens during his tyranny.[29] Furthermore, as we saw above in chapter 3, Pisistratus's so-called bodyguard was probably comprised of a handful of low-born native Athenians rather than trained foreign mercenaries.

More interesting is the claim that Pisistratus took hostages from among the children of the Athenians, which not only is paralleled in Herodotus's account of how the Samian tyrant Polycrates quelled resistance to his rule, but also is connected to the theme of exile in both tyrannical narratives. According to Herodotus's version of the Samian tyranny, when Polycrates found himself under attack by the men whom he had exiled, he took hostage the children and wives of the Samian citizens who remained under him (3.45.4):

> In order to prevent the citizens who remained under him [τῶν ὑπ' ἑωυτῷ ἐόντων πολιητέων] from betraying him to the returning exiles [τοὺς κατιόντας], Polycrates crowded together in shipsheds their wives and children and threatened to burn them up, shipsheds and all.

---

[27] Pisistratus's opponents are labeled "those from the city" (1.62.2, 63.1), whereas his supporters are said to have arrived from the city and to have "poured forth" from the country villages (1.62.1). For discussion, see above, chapter 3.

[28] On the tendency of oral traditions to preserve traces of earlier versions, see Vansina 1985, 118–23; Thomas 1989, 143; Forsdyke 1999.

[29] Lavelle 1992a.

Similarly, Herodotus (1.64.1) reports that Pisistratus

> took hostage the children of those Athenians who remained and did not imme-
> diately flee into exile [τῶν παραμεινάντων ᾿Αθηναίων καὶ μὴ αὐτίκα φυγό-
> ντων], and he put [the children] on Naxos. For he had conquered this island and
> had handed it over to Lygdamis.

Besides the evident parallelism in the ways that Polycrates and Periander
are represented as preventing resistance to their rule, Herodotus's claim regarding Pisistratus's use of hostages presents some contradictions to his
earlier narrative. As we have just seen, according to Herodotus's narrative,
the Athenians were prevented from fleeing into exile following the battle of
Pallene and were tricked into dispersing to their homes. Yet in his use of
the theme of hostages, Herodotus implies that a number of Athenians did in
fact flee when he states that Pisistratus took hostages from among the
children of those Athenians who remained and did not immediately flee (τῶν
παραμεινάντων ᾿Αθηναίων καὶ μὴ αὐτίκα φυγόντων, 1.64.1). The best explanation for this contradiction is that it is caused by the collision of several
different aspects of the representation of tyranny in democratic ideology—
tyrannical trickery, dispersal of the citizenry, hostage taking, and expulsion.

   In the final part of Herodotus's narrative, the theme of tyrannical trickery
again collides with the theme of tyrannical expulsions (1.64.3): "Thus Pisistratus ruled as tyrant over the Athenians, some of whom died in battle [ἐν
τῇ μάχῃ ἐπεπτώκεσαν], and others of whom fled into exile [ἔφευγον ἐκ τῆς
οἰκηίης] along with the Alcmeonidae."

   As in his summary statements about the rule of Cypselus and Periander
of Corinth, Herodotus's final summation of Pisistratus's tyranny focuses on
mass death and exile as the primary features of a tyrant's rule. As I demonstrated above in chapter 3, the theme of mass expulsions under the
Pisistratid tyranny is echoed not only in Alcmeonid claims to have been in
exile for the entire length of the tyranny, but in the claims of other elites
that they or their ancestors were exiled under the tyrants. Indeed, in its most
extended form, the tradition of tyrannical expulsion included the entire
citizen body: "When the tyrants ruled the city, and the people were in exile
[ὁ δῆμος ἔφευγε]...."[30]

   As I argued above in chapter 3, there is little evidence to support these
assertions of mass expulsions under the Pisistratids. In fact the evidence
suggests that Pisistratus disavowed traditional intra-elite politics of exile and
allowed his rivals not only to remain in Athens but to enjoy positions of
power and prestige. The only evidence for expulsion, indeed, is the exile of
the Alcmeonidae in the brief period between the death of Hipparchus in
514 and the overthrow of the tyranny in 510. It seems that this brief period

---

[30] Andoc. 1.106. Cf. Thomas 1989, 139–44.

of the Alcmeonids' exile was not only retrojected onto the entire length of the tyranny but was extended to include a much larger group of Athenians. By suggesting that a large group of citizens was forced into exile under the tyranny, the Athenians both implied that they did not acquiesce in the rule of the tyrants and excused themselves for their failure to overthrow them.

More important, by representing the tyrants as perpetrating mass expulsions, the Athenians found a powerful motif for the justification of democratic rule. The arbitrary expulsions by the tyrants highlighted the contrast with the democratic exercise of political power as represented by the institution of ostracism. As I argued above in chapter 4, ostracism served as a reminder of the close link between power over decisions of exile and political power in the archaic polis and at the time of the founding of the democracy. Moreover, ostracism stood as a symbol of the limited, moderate, and lawful use of power by the Athenian democracy, in contrast to the elite regimes that had preceded it. In this ideological construction, the figure of the tyrant as the perpetrator of violent expulsions of the mass of Athenian citizenry served as a powerful negative example. It is in this light that the theme of exile in Herodotus's narrative of Pisistratus's final tyranny, as well as in his narratives of other archaic tyrants, should be viewed.

One further example should confirm my reading of the democratic resonances of the theme of exile in Herodotean tyrant narratives: the story of Periander's troubled relationship with his son Lycophron.[31] This story is embedded in Herodotus's narrative of the Spartan expedition against the Samian tyrant Polycrates discussed above, and is ostensibly mentioned to explain why the Corinthians joined the Spartans in attacking him. According to Herodotus, Periander's conflict with his son was the original cause (via a long chain of events) for Corinthian hostility toward Samos. While this is the ostensible motivation for Herodotus's narrative, the thematic significance of the story of Periander and his son for the representation of tyranny in both Panhellenic and Athenian democratic traditions provides an even deeper purpose. In particular, consideration of the theme of exile in this story reveals parallels not only with the representation of tyrants in Herodotus but also with Athenian traditions about mythical tyrants as told in tragedy and other representations of the legendary past.

I begin with a summary of Herodotus's narrative. The conflict between Periander and Lycophron began with Periander's murder of his wife, Melissa. Soon afterwards, Periander's two sons were summoned to visit their maternal grandfather, Procles, tyrant of Epidaurus. Procles asked the boys if they knew who had killed their mother. The elder son thought nothing of the question. The younger son, Lycophron, however, realized that his father was the murderer. As

<hr />

[31] Hdt. 3.50–53.

a consequence, on his return to Corinth, Lycophron decided not to speak to his father. Despite Periander's attempts to converse with him, Lycophron would say nothing. Herodotus's representation of what happened next must be quoted in full (3.50.3–52.2):

> Finally Periander grew angry with his son and banished him from his home [ἐξελαύνει ἐκ τῶν οἰκίων]. After banishing this son [ἐξελάσας δὲ τοῦτον], Periander then inquired of his elder son what their grandfather had said to them. This son answered that their grandfather had received them hospitably, but that he did not remember what Procles had said when he sent them back. Periander responded that it was impossible that Procles had not said anything to them, and pressed his son with inquiries. The elder son then remembered and told Periander [what Procles had said]. Periander took this to heart and determined not to display any weakness. He therefore sent a messenger to the place where his son who had been banished by him [ὁ ἐξελασθεὶς ὑπ' αὐτοῦ παῖς] was living and forbade them to receive his son in their homes [ἀπηγόρευε μή μιν δέκεσθαι οἰκίοισι]. Whenever his son was driven out [ὁ δὲ ... ἀπελαυνόμενος] and went to another house, he was driven out from this house also [ἀπηλαύνετ' ... καὶ ἀπὸ ταύτης], since Periander threatened those who received him and ordered them to shut Lycophron out [ἀπειλέοντός τε τοῦ Περιάνδρου τοῖσι δεξαμένοισι καὶ ἐξέργειν κελεύοντος]. On being driven out [ἀπελαυνόμενος], Lycophron went to the home of one friend after another [ἐπ' ἑτέρην τῶν ἑταίρων]. These friends received [ἐδέκοντο] Lycophron into their homes, although they were afraid, since Lycophron was the son of Periander. Finally, Periander issued a decree [κήρυγμα] saying that whoever received Lycophron into their home [ὑποδέξηταί μιν] or spoke to him would owe a fine to Apollo. Because of this decree [κήρυγμα], no one was willing to speak to Lycophron or accept him into their homes [οἰκίοισι δέκεσθαι].

Later, when Periander took pity on his homeless son, he tried to win him back by reminding him that he could enjoy the privileges of the tyranny. Lycophron responded to this offer by telling his father that he owed a fine to Apollo. According to Herodotus, "Periander then realized that his son was implacable and sent him out of his sight by putting him on a ship to Corcyra [ἐξ ὀφθαλμῶν μιν ἀποπέμπεται στείλας πλοῖον ἐς Κέρκυραν]" (3.52.6).

What is striking about this long narrative of Periander's troubles with his son is the emphasis on expulsion as the primary response of the tyrant to his son's intransigence. Indeed, the words for exile proliferate and build throughout the passage. What begins as expulsion from the tyrant's own home later becomes expulsion from the homes of all the rest of the Corinthians, and finally culminates in expulsion from Corinth altogether.

Christiane Sourvinou-Inwood has noted the importance of the theme of exile in this narrative and has related it to deep mythical structures of rites of initiation, father-son hostility, and polluted murderers.[32] Sourvinou-Inwood's analysis along these lines is persuasive, since these mythical motifs all involve some form of exile. In the mythical schema of initiation, for example, young men are required to go off into the wilderness before returning to be re-integrated into the community as men. The story of Lycophron, for Sourvinou-Inwood, represents a failed initiation, since Lycophron refuses to return to Corinth and ultimately does not successfully replace his father as the mythical paradigm requires. Similarly, polluted murderers must typically leave the community until they are purified and can return. Although Lycophron does not kill his father, his hostility toward him, according to Sourvinou-Inwood, is symbolically equivalent to murder.[33] Certainly, the theme of pollution by murder is invoked in Lycophron's refusal to speak to his father, a standard feature of the treatment of polluted murderers.[34]

Despite the clear impact of these deep mythological schemata on the story of Periander and Lycophron, I suggest that Sourvinou-Inwood's analysis does not capture the full significance of the story for Herodotus's audience. Indeed, in Sourvinou-Inwood's eagerness to demonstrate (correctly) the futility of attempting to recover a historical basis—that is, actual historical events— behind the story, she dismisses too summarily the politico-historical narrative surface of the tale by focusing exclusively on its deep mythological structures. Attention to the politico-historical narrative surface of the Periander story, however, enables one to detect parallels with fifth-century Greek, and particularly Athenian, democratic traditions regarding tyrants and exile. Most important in these traditions is the idea that tyrants arbitrarily banish citizens. In Athenian democratic traditions, moreover, tyrannical expulsions are contrasted with Athens' reception and protection of those banished from other states. While many Athenian traditions could be cited for this ideological construction, I focus on Athenian versions of the myth of the Heraclidae to show that the story of Periander and Lycophron borrows not only from mythological structures relating to general social patterns such as initiation and pollution by murder, but also from myths with strong political associations for the Athenian democracy.

The first political detail of significance for the ideological meaning of the narrative is that Periander is not simply a father, but a tyrant. As such, he makes use of a state mechanism—a public decree (κήρυγμα)—to banish his son Lycophron, who threatens Periander's political legitimacy by refusing to

---

[32] Sourvinou-Inwood 1991, 244–84.

[33] Another way of looking at the role of the polluted-murderer schema in the Lycophron story is to note that in this story Periander reverses the typical structure: Periander (the actual murderer of his wife) does not go into exile, but instead treats his guiltless son like a polluted outcast. This reversal is a further example of how a tyrant "disturbs customary norms" (νόμαια κινέει πάτρια, Hdt. 3.80.5).

[34] R. Parker 1983, 125.

obey him.[35] Periander banishes Lycophron first from his home, then from the homes of others, and finally from Corinth altogether. The repetition of the narrative element of exile is significant in two respects. First, it emphasizes the tyrant's use of exile in response to dissent. As we have seen above, this is a common feature of the representation of the tyrant in Panhellenic and Athenian traditions, serving to illustrate the injustice of tyranny in contrast to non-tyrannical, especially democratic, forms of rule. The fact that Periander banishes a single citizen, and indeed his own son, moreover, does not undermine the parallelism with the other tyrant stories, where mass expulsions of largely anonymous citizens are the norm. As has often been noted, one of the primary features of tyranny in fifth-century representations is its tendency to blur the distinction between public and private. The tyrant treats his own family as ruthlessly as he might an anonymous citizen. In tragedy, the tyrant fears his own relatives and closest friends (φίλοι).[36] In Herodotus's narrative, several tyrants, including Periander and King Cambyses of Persia, murder their own kin out of fear of rebellion.[37] Moreover, it is widely recognized that narratives about relations within ruling families often symbolize the broader relations of citizens toward one another. As Carol Dougherty puts it: "There is a strong tendency in Greek narrative of all kinds to personalize public action.... Just as two brothers quarreling over status and power within an individual family can represent civic stasis in a larger sense, an individual's personal, often physical, trauma can also substitute within a tale for larger civic problems."[38] Recognition of this "tendency...to personalize public action" allows us to read the narrative of Periander's banishment of his son as metonymic for his treatment of the citizen body as a whole. Periander's banishment of Lycophron, therefore, is paradigmatic for the way a tyrant manages political dissent among the citizenry at large.

Yet the emphasis on the motif of tyrannical expulsions in the Periander story is not limited to this negative example of the tyrant's abuse of his own citizens. The repetition of words for banishment, and particularly the progression from banishment from the home of the tyrant to banishment from the polis altogether, strongly recalls another important tyrant narrative, fifth-century Athenian versions of the myth of the Heraclidae. As noted already

[35] As Sourvinou-Inwood (1991, 259) notes, a public proclamation against the killer is also a feature of the schema of the polluted killer (cf. R. Parker 1983, 125, for the evidence, especially Soph. OT 236–43).

[36] Aesch. PV 224–25. Cf. Lanza 1977, 232–36.

[37] Periander's murder of his wife: Hdt. 3.50.1. In a way Periander is also responsible for Lycophron's death: see below. Cambyses murders both his brother and his sister-wife: 3.30–32. Note especially the imagery of the lettuce, which Cambyses' sister-wife strips bare and then compares to Cambyses' treatment of his own family. See also Polycrates' treatment of his brothers: Hdt. 3.39.1–2, discussed above.

[38] Dougherty 1993, 17.

above in chapter 5, the Athenians made use of this myth at important civic occasions such as funeral orations, inter-state negotiations, and dramatic performances.[39] As we have seen, the central event of this myth is the Peloponnesian tyrant Eurystheus's unjust banishment of the children of Heracles and their reception by the Athenians. Athenian versions of the myth of the Heraclidae, moreover, show clear structural parallels with Herodotus's account of Periander. In both stories there is a progression from an initial banishment from the immediate territory of the tyrant to subsequent banishment, reinforced by decree, from the places where the exiles seek refuge.

This parallel is best illustrated by Euripides' version of the myth in his play *Heraclidae*, but is evident in all the Athenian evocations of it. In this excerpt from Euripides' play, Iolaus, a companion of the children of Heracles in exile, is speaking (12–20):

> When their father left the land,
> Eurystheus at first wanted to kill us.
> But we ran away [ἐξέδραμεν], and although we lost our city [πόλις μὲν οἴχεται]
> our lives were safe. So we are in exile, wandering [φεύγομεν δ' ἀλώμενοι],
> exchanging one city for another [ἄλλην ἀπ' ἄλλης ἐξοριζόντων πόλιν].
> For in addition to the other wrongs, Eurystheus
> dared to commit this further misdeed against us:
> wherever we are staying, he finds out and sends
> heralds to demand our surrender, and he shut us out of the land
> [πέμπων ὅπου γῆς πυνθάνοιθ' ἱδρυμένους
> κήρυκας ἐξαιτεῖ τε κἀξείργει χθονός].

Just as in the story of Periander and Lycophron, the tyrant first banishes the victims from his own territory and then issues a decree demanding that they be shut out from the places where they seek refuge. In both stories, there is a progression in severity, exile from a single place becoming exile from every place. In both stories, the words for banishment occur with striking frequency, thus emphasizing the association between exile and a tyrant's method of managing dissent. In both stories, the exiles are condemned to perpetual wandering by the tyrant's decree.

In Lycophron's case, as we saw, this perpetual wandering was ended by a further decree of banishment to the island of Corcyra. In the case of the Heraclidae, by contrast, the wandering is ended by the reception of the children of Heracles by the Athenians. The Athenians alone of all the Greeks defy Eurystheus's decree, receive the Heraclidae in their city, and fight off Eurystheus when he comes to reclaim them by force. The importance of the

---

[39] Funeral orations: Lys. 2.11–16, Pl. *Menex.* 239b6, [Dem.] 60.8. Interstate negotiations or political pamphlets designed for such purposes: Hdt. 9.27.2; Isoc. *Paneg.* 52–56, *Panath.* 194–96. Dramatic performances: *Heraclidae* of Aeschylus (*TrGF* 3:190–93) and Euripides.

myth of the Heraclidae to the Athenians is amply illustrated by its many
evocations in political speeches of the democracy in which we see not only
the wrongdoing of the tyrant Eurystheus illustrated primarily by his unjust
banishment of the sons of Heracles, but the justice of Athens illustrated
precisely by the opposite of exile, namely reception of exiles into the city. In
these versions of the myth, much is made of the fact that Athens alone
welcomed the exiles, while all the other Greek states obeyed Eurystheus's
decree and banned the Heraclidae.

For example, in Herodotus's account of the negotiations between Greek
states before the battle of Plataea in 479, the Athenians claim the right to
serve on one of the wings of the assembled Greek army. They justify their
claim over that of the Tegeans (who are also claiming the right to the
position) by recalling their service to the Heraclidae (9.27):

> It is necessary for us to show you why we have always been considered more
> distinguished than the Tegeans. When the Heraclidae, whose leader [the Te-
> geans] claim to have killed at the Isthmus, had been driven out by all the Greeks
> whom they reached [ἐξελαυνομένους ὑπὸ πάντων Ἑλλήνων ἐς τοὺς ἀπικοίατο]
> in their flight from slavery under the Myceneans [φεύγοντες δουλοσύνην πρὸς
> Μυκηναίων], we alone received them [μοῦνοι ὑποδεξάμενοι] and with their
> help put an end to the brazen behavior [ὕβριν] of Eurystheus by defeating those
> who then held power over the Peloponnesus.

In this Athenian version of the myth of the Heraclidae, not only is tyrannical injustice equated with the expulsion of the Heraclidae from all
Greek states, but Athens distinguishes itself for its reception of the exiles.
Similarly, in Athenian funeral orations, Eurystheus's expulsion of the Heraclidae not just from his own state but from all the rest of Greece is contrasted with Athens' willingness to receive the exiles and face Eurystheus
single-handedly. In Lysias's *Funeral Oration*, for example, we read the following (Lys. 2.11):

> Later on, when Heracles had disappeared, his children fled from [ἔφευγον]
> Eurystheus and were banished by all the Greeks [ἐξηλαύνοντο δὲ ὑπὸ πάντων
> τῶν Ἑλλήνων]. Though they were ashamed of this deed, they feared Eur-
> ystheus's power. When, however, the Heraclidae reached this city [Athens:
> ἀφικόμενοι εἰς τήνδε τὴν πόλιν], they sat as suppliants at the altars. Although
> Eurystheus demanded their surrender, the Athenians were not willing to hand
> them over [οὐκ ἠθέλησαν ἐκδοῦναι]. The Athenians revered the virtue of
> Heracles more than they feared for their own safety; they also thought it better to
> fight on behalf of the weak with justice [μετὰ τοῦ δικαίου] than to give in to the
> powerful and hand over those who had been wronged by them.

Athens' singular action in protecting the exiles is similarly a source of praise
in Euripides' *Heraclidae* (303–6, 315–19):

For we,
having fallen into this extremity of misfortune, found
[the Athenians] friends and kinsmen, who alone of all the inhabited
Greek land stood up for these children [οἱ τοσῆσδ᾽ οἰκουμένης Ἑλληνίδος γῆς
τῶνδε προύστησαν μόνοι].

. . . .

You [the Heraclidae] ought to honor [the Athenians],
for they took on a formidable land . . .
as enemy on your behalf,
looking out for wandering beggars [πτωχοὺς ἀλήτας].
And they did not hand us over, nor did they drive us out from their land [οὐδ᾽
ἀπήλασαν χθονός].

Further examples of Athens' role as protector of exiles from other states can be found in tragedy and even in Thucydides' Archaeology (1.2).[40] This aspect of Athenian representations of tyrannical expulsions is best related to both internal Athenian justifications of democratic rule and external justifications of Athenian imperial control. I argued above in chapter 4 that the Athenians legitimized democratic rule in part through the symbolic and ideological representation of democratic moderation in the use of exile. The institution of ostracism, in particular, was an important part of this ideological construction. By representing non-democratic regimes, and particularly both mythical and historical tyrants, as using unjust expulsions of innocent citizens in order to maintain power in the polis, the Athenian democracy found a compelling negative example for its own moderate and lawful use of political power. Furthermore, as we saw above in chapter 5, Athenian moderation in the use of exile was also ideologically important in Athenian relations with other Greek states, in particular in regard to Athenian claims to leadership of the other Greeks. By representing other states as submitting to tyrannical expulsions, and by presenting themselves as the protectors of those exiled from other states, the Athenians reinforced their claim to just leadership through appeal to both negative and positive examples.

If we turn now to the representation of the Thirty Tyrants in fourth-century sources, we will see that they are represented according to the paradigm of tyranny in democratic traditions, especially in regard to the theme

---

[40] For tragedy, see Euripides' *Medea* (where Athens shelters Medea after her exile), or Aeschylus's *Suppliants* (where Argos is the dramatic equivalent of democratic Athens and serves as place of refuge for the daughters of Danaus). For a complete discussion of the theme of exile in tragedy, see Tzanetou, *Staging Citizenship* (forthcoming). For this theme in Thucydides, see above, chapter 5. Also note Herodotus's comments on the Gephyrae, who were expelled by the Boeotians and turned to Athens for refuge. According to Herodotus, "the Athenians received them on set terms to be citizens, though they determined that they were to be excluded from a number of privileges, which I will not relate" (5.57.2; cf. 61.2).

of mass expulsions.[41] In chapter 4 above I demonstrated that the oligarchs who ruled Athens in 403 were responsible for widespread violence against the Athenian citizenry. Most important, the Thirty used extra-judicial executions and the expulsion of the mass of Athenian citizenry from the city of Athens (but not the territory of Attica) as the means by which they secured their power. Furthermore, we saw that although some Athenians did go into exile from Attica during the rule of the Thirty—and these played a vital role in the eventual overthrow of their regime—the large majority of Athenians remained and did not actively resist them. In this section, I argue that the expulsion of the mass of Athenians from the city center became conflated in Athenian memory with the actual exile in foreign lands of a small number of Athenians and metics. In other words, the historical fact of the resistance of a small group of exiles was transformed in the collective memory of the Athenians into the exile of the people as a whole and their unified resistance to the rule of the Thirty.

I will first set out the evidence for this transformation in the collective memory of the oligarchic revolution and then explore several reasons for it. In brief, I suggest that the theme of the people in exile in our accounts of the rule of the Thirty was a product of the interaction between the historical experience of exile during the revolution of 403 and prior traditions concerning the relation between the illegitimate use of political power and exile (which in turn were a product of the interaction between the earlier historical experience of exile in the archaic period and in the earlier history of the democracy). In sum, the revolution of 403 reinvigorated earlier traditions concerning the connection between exile and illegitimate rule and both helped to reshape and was shaped by these earlier traditions. It is perhaps in the representation of the Thirty Tyrants that we can most clearly see the dynamic process by which historical experience and memory interact to continually change the ways that the past is remembered.

Xenophon's account of the rule of the Thirty provides a good example of the ways that the historical expulsions during their rule were transformed, under the influence of earlier traditions of exile, into the idea that the Athenian people as a whole (ὁ δῆμος) were expelled from Attica and actively fought to resist the Thirty. In Xenophon's account, the expulsion of the people from the city center is conflated with the confiscation of the property of a small number of wealthy citizens, in such a way as to suggest that the Thirty expelled the mass of Athenians not only from the city but also from their lands and Athenian territory as a whole (*Hell.* 2.4.1):

---

[41] The application of the term "tyrant" to these rulers possibly derives from the fourth-century historian Ephorus, if indeed the first appearance of the phrase "Thirty Tyrants" in Diod. Sic. 14.3.7 reflects Ephorus's usage. The use of the term "tyrant" itself is significant for my analysis, since it suggests that the oligarchs of 404/3 were being interpreted according to the construction of the tyrant in democratic ideology. I thank Robert Chenault for drawing my attention to this point.

[Following the execution of Theramenes, the Thirty] thought they could now act as tyrants [τυραννεῖν] without fear. They then decreed that those who were not on the catalogue [of the Three Thousand] were not to enter the city [μὴ εἰσιέναι εἰς τὸ ἄστυ], and they evicted them from their estates [ἦγον ἐκ τῶν χωρίων], in order that they themselves and their friends might have these people's lands. And when [those banned from the city] fled to Piraeus [φευγόντων εἰς τὸν Πειραιᾶ], the Thirty drove many of them away from there [ἐντεῦθεν πολλοὺς ἄγοντες], and they filled both Megara and Thebes with refugees [ἐνέπλησαν καὶ τὰ Μέγαρα καὶ τὰς Θήβας τῶν ὑποχωρούντων].

Not only does Xenophon conflate the expulsion of the people from the city with the more limited confiscations of property from wealthy citizens, but he suggests that the Thirty expelled so many men from Attica that they "filled both Megara and Thebes with refugees." Moreover, through his account of successive banishments first from the city, then from their estates, and finally from Piraeus, Xenophon recalls the actions of the tyrant in democratic traditions that we have just examined. As we saw above, the tyrant Eurystheus in the myth of the Heraclidae and Periander in Herodotus's account of his relationship with his son used decrees of banishment to expel their opponents from a progressively expanding territory. It seems likely that Xenophon blurs the distinction between the Thirty's decree of expulsion of the people from the city center and the exile of a smaller group of citizens and noncitizens to foreign poleis, in order to evoke these earlier traditions concerning the relation between exile and illegitimate rulers.

Lysias similarly blurs the distinction between the expulsion of the people from the city and the exile of a more limited group of citizens to foreign places when he suggests that "the men of Piraeus" were composed not merely of those who returned from exile in foreign cities and fought to overthrow the Thirty but of all those who were banished from the city center. In this example, furthermore, we see the tyrannical paradigm of successive expulsion from one city after another that we first encountered in the myth of the Heraclidae and the representation of the rule of Periander (Lys. 12.95–97):

And I wish to say a few words to you men of Piraeus, although you are numerous. For however many of you are from Piraeus, remember the matter of your arms. For after fighting many battles in foreign lands you were disarmed not by your enemies but by these men [the Thirty] in times of peace.[42] Then recall that you were expelled from the city [ἐξεκηρύχθητε ἐκ τῆς πόλεως] that your ancestors had bequeathed to you. And finally, when you were in exile [φεύγοντας ὑμᾶς], they demanded you from the various cities [ἐκ τῶν πόλεων ἐξῃτοῦντο]. . . . And as many of you who escaped death and at great risk to your

---

[42] On the topos of tyrannical disarmament of the people, see above, chapter 3, on Pisistratus.

lives wandered to many cities [εἰς πολλὰς πόλεις πλανηθέντες] and were expelled from them all [πανταχόθεν ἐκκηρυττόμενοι], lacking in basic necessities and having left behind your children either in a hostile fatherland or in a foreign land, you came, despite many adversities, to Piraeus.

Several scholars have observed the tendency of fourth-century orators to expand the group of exiles who fought to overthrow the Thirty to include the whole population and indeed everyone who could not demonstrably be shown to have been a member of the Thirty. Rosalind Thomas, for example, has shown that elite speakers often insert themselves or their ancestors among the exiles who fought against the Thirty as a way of demonstrating their democratic sympathies.[43] Thomas's prime example of this phenomenon is a passage in pseudo-Demosthenes where the speaker falsely claims that his ancestor, one Aristocrates, was a leader among the exiles who fought to overthrow the Thirty ([Dem.] 58.67, trans. after Thomas 1989, 133):

> On behalf of the city, Aristocrates son of Scelias, the uncle of my grandfather Epichares, whose name my brother here bears, performed many fine deeds when we were at war with the Spartans. He razed Eëtionea, into which Critias and his followers were about to receive the Spartans, and he tore down the wall and led back the people from exile [κατήγαγε τὸν δῆμον].

As Thomas effectively demonstrates, here the speaker not only "conveniently omitted and forgot Aristocrates' membership of [the earlier oligarchy of] the Four Hundred," but falsely inserted his ancestor into the heroic return of the people following the overthrow of the Thirty in 403. For our purposes, this passage demonstrates how elite orators elided distinctions between the expulsion of the people from the city center and the resistance of Thrasybulus and the exiles to the Thirty. In these speakers' versions of this key moment in democratic history, the Athenians as a whole (including the speaker's ancestors) suffered exile and fought collectively to overthrow the Thirty and return to the city.

In a similar vein, Andrew Wolpert has observed the tendency of fourth-century litigants in the law courts to assimilate the jury to the exiles who fought against the Thirty.[44] For example, Isocrates, in a speech written for the younger Alcibiades, son of the more famous Alcibiades, asks the jury to sympathize with his father on the basis that he suffered exile from the city (following the affair of the herms in 415) just as they did under the Thirty in 403 (Isoc. 16.12):

> I think that my father ought rightly to obtain pardon from you. For you experienced the same misfortune as he when you were exiled by the Thirty [ὑπὸ τῶν τριάκοντ' ἐκπεσόντες]. You ought to recall how each of you was disposed and how you were minded to undergo any sort of danger in order to cease being a

---

[43] Thomas 1989, 132–38.
[44] Wolpert 2002, 91–95, especially 91n.28 for a complete catalogue of instances of this topos.

resident alien [μετοικῶν] and return to your homeland [κατελθεῖν εἰς τὴν πατρίδα] and punish those who had expelled you [τοὺς ἐκβαλόντας].

In this passage, the speaker clearly equates the jury, as representatives of the people, with the exiles who fought to overthrow the Thirty. Isocrates' use of the word for being a resident alien (μετοικῶν), as well as his use of the phrase "return to your homeland" (κατελθεῖν εἰς τὴν πατρίδα), makes clear that the speaker thinks of the jurors as having been in exile from Attica, and thus is assimilating the people to the small group of exiles who actually left Athens and under Thrasybulus's leadership fought against the Thirty to return to the polis. In doing so, the speaker effectively elides the distinction between the jury at his trial, the demos of 403 (which was expelled from the city alone and did not actively resist the tyrants), and those few who actually left Attica and returned to fight the Thirty.

Wolpert convincingly argues that the tendency of speakers to include jurors among the exiles who fought to overthrow the Thirty is not simply an attempt to flatter them and win their favor. Rather, the fiction that all Athenians shared in the exile and fought against the Thirty was a vital ideological construction by which the actual divisions among the Athenian citizens were elided and the Athenian community was reunited following the brutal civil war.[45] For Wolpert, the representation of the exiles who fought to overthrow the Thirty as the people in exile allowed the Athenians to forget that the men of the city (the Three Thousand) had supported the Thirty. This misremembrance allowed all Athenians to partake of the fiction that they had a share in overthrowing the Thirty. On the basis of the observations made above, we might add that the fiction allowed the Athenians to forget that they, the people, although banished from the city center, did not actively resist the Thirty until the smaller group of exiles had won considerable successes against them.

Although Wolpert's argument for the unifying function of the fiction of jurors as the people in exile is convincing, it is not the whole story. Comparison with earlier representations of exile makes clear that mass expulsion was already an important part of the representation of illegitimate rule in Athenian democratic ideology even before the fourth century. In particular, I argued above that the Athenians adapted archaic traditions of exile to suggest that tyrants used mass expulsions to secure their regimes. This ideological construction, I argued, played an important role in the justification of democratic rule, since the Athenians prided themselves on their moderation in the use of exile. I suggest that the emphasis on mass expulsion under the Thirty also borrows from this democratic ideological tradition.

Perhaps the best example of the influence of earlier traditions concerning tyranny and mass exile on the representation of the rule of the Thirty can be

---

[45] See Loraux 2002 for a similar analysis of the politics of remembering and forgetting in Athens.

found in Lysias's account of their injustices. In this example, we see not only that Lysias makes use of the familiar rhetorical tricolon of tyrannical abuses (here expanded to a tetracolon), but that no distinction is made between the historical sufferings of wealthy and prominent citizens and non-citizens who were killed or exiled by the Thirty and the suffering of the mass of Athenian citizens, who were expelled from the city center alone (Lys. 12.21):

οὗτοι γὰρ <u>πολλοὺς</u> μὲν <u>τῶν πολιτῶν</u> εἰς τοὺς πολεμίους <u>ἐξήλασαν</u>, <u>πολλοὺς</u> δ' ἀδίκως ἀποκτείναντες ἀτάφους ἐποίησαν, <u>πολλοὺς</u> δ' ἐπιτίμους ὄντας ἀτίμους [τῆς πόλεως] κατέστησαν, <u>πολλῶν</u> δὲ θυγατέρας μελλούσας ἐκδίδοσθαι ἐκώλυσαν.

[The Thirty] sent <u>many citizens into exile</u> with the enemy; <u>many</u> citizens they killed unjustly and deprived of burial; <u>many</u> men who had citizen rights they disenfranchised; the daughters of <u>many</u> men they prevented from being given in marriage.

We might compare this with Herodotus's representation of the rule of the archaic tyrant Cypselus, cited above (5.92ε.2):

<u>πολλοὺς</u> μὲν Κορινθίων <u>ἐδίωξε</u>, <u>πολλοὺς</u> δὲ χρημάτων ἀπεστέρησε, <u>πολλῷ</u> <u>δέ</u> τι <u>πλείστους</u> τῆς ψυχῆς.

He drove <u>many</u> Corinthians <u>into exile</u>, and he confiscated the property of <u>many</u>, but <u>mostly</u> he killed people.

It is noteworthy that Lysias both replicates the rhetorical catalogue of tyrannical abuses in the Herodotean passage and expands it. Both passages begin with expulsion, and both create the impression of an exhaustive number of victims of tyrannical violence through the repetition of the adjective "many" (πολλοί). Lysias, furthermore, expands Herodotus's rhetorical tricolon not only by mentioning those who were disenfranchised, but by noting the impact of confiscations of property on the daughters of Athenian citizens. Indeed the last element of Lysias's tetracolon both evokes the tyrannical abuse of women so common in Herodotus's portraits of tyrants, and indirectly indicates that the Thirty confiscated the property of many citizens—for this is presumably the reason why the daughters of many Athenian citizens were unable to marry: they had no dowry.[46]

It is clear from this example that earlier traditions concerning the relation of tyranny to exile influenced the representation of the rule of the Thirty in the fourth century. In particular the blurring of the distinction between the small group of exiles who fought to overthrow the Thirty and the mass of Athenians who were expelled from the city alone is explicable not simply by the need for reconciliation following the civil war, but also by the role of

---

[46] On the tyrant's abuse of women, see above.

mass expulsions in the legitimization of democratic rule. In these traditions, mass expulsions illustrated the harmful effect of non-democratic regimes on the citizen body, in implicit contrast to the moderation of democratic rule. In fact, in fourth-century traditions, the role of exile in illustrating the contrast between tyrannical brutality and democratic moderation becomes much more explicit. In particular, fourth-century traditions make much of the difference between the brutal rule of the Thirty and the restrained behavior of the democracy following its restoration in 403. Indeed, the mass expulsions of the Thirty are explicitly opposed to the moderation or mildness (πραότης) of democratic rule. For example, in a speech of Isocrates, the moderation (πραότης) of the people following the overthrow of the Thirty is contrasted with the mass executions and expulsions that the Thirty had committed (Isoc. 7.67):[47]

> No one would justly praise the mildness [πραότητα] of those men [the Thirty] rather than that of the people. For when [the Thirty] took control of the city by vote of the assembly, they killed fifteen hundred citizens without trial, and they forced more than five thousand to flee to Piraeus [φυγεῖν ... ἠνάγκασαν]. But when the democrats were victorious and returned under arms, they put to death only those most culpable for the wrongs and dealt so honorably [καλῶς] and lawfully [νομίμως] with the others that those who banished them fared no worse than those who returned [μηδὲν ἔλαττον ἔχειν τοὺς ἐκβαλόντας τῶν κατελθόντων].

The importance of moderation in the use of expulsion, in particular, as a feature of democratic moderation (πραότης) in democratic ideology becomes clear from several passages in Aristotle's *Constitution of the Athenians*. In his discussion of the first use of ostracism in Athens, for example, Aristotle notes that the Athenians' failure to expel the entire circle of relatives of the Pisistratids following the overthrow of the tyranny in 510 is an example of "the customary mildness of the demos" (*Ath. Pol.* 22.4):

> Hipparchus son of Charmus, from the deme of Collytus—a relative of Pisistratus—was the first man ostracized. . . . For the Athenians permitted the friends and relatives of the tyrants who were not immediately implicated in the revolution to continue to dwell in the polis [εἴων οἰκεῖν τὴν πόλιν], utilizing the customary mildness of the demos [χρώμενοι τῇ εἰωθυίᾳ τοῦ δήμου πραότητι].

In this passage it is clear that the failure of the people to expel the friends and relatives of the tyrants en masse is taken as the prime example of democratic moderation (ἡ τοῦ δήμου πραότης). Furthermore, it is no coincidence that Aristotle utilizes the key word πραότης in his discussion of ostracism, since,

---

[47] See also Xen. *Hell.* 2.4.13–14, 40–42, for comparison of the injustice of the Thirty with the justice of the people.

as I argued above in chapter 4, ostracism was the symbol par excellence of
democratic moderation. With an understanding of the importance of moderation in the use of exile as a primary component of the ideological construction of democratic rule, Aristotle's comment in another passage that the
Athenian laws on tyranny were mild (πρᾷοι) at the time of the Pisistratid
tyranny makes perfect sense (*Ath. Pol.* 16.10):

> The Athenian laws concerning tyranny were mild [πρᾷοι] at this time. This is true
> of the other laws, but especially the one regarding the establishment of a tyranny.
> For their law was the following: "This is an ancestral law of the Athenians: If
> someone attempts to become tyrant or if he helps establish a tyranny, he and his
> family are to be outlawed [ἄτιμον]."

The key to understanding Aristotle's view of this archaic law as especially mild
is to recognize that Aristotle misunderstands the force of its penalty of outlawry
(ἀτιμία), assuming that it means disenfranchisement (as it did in his own
time), not exile (as was the archaic meaning of the word). In other words,
Aristotle calls the archaic law on tyranny mild precisely because, as he understands it, it did not require that the tyrant go into exile. Thus this passage demonstrates again that in fourth-century democratic ideology, the
self-proclaimed moderation of the people (ἡ τοῦ δήμου πραότης) was symbolized primarily through moderation in the use of expulsion. One cannot
help but suspect that Aristotle's interpretation of this law as mild is influenced
by the contrast between oligarchic brutality and democratic moderation
during the revolutions of late fifth-century Athens. Yet considering more
broadly the history of exile and its use in democratic ideology beginning from
archaic times, this fourth-century equation between democracy, moderation,
and restraint in the use of exile is hardly surprising.[48]

So far I have demonstrated that the theme of mass expulsion (the people
in exile) under the Thirty in fourth-century traditions was a product of interaction between the actual historical experience of exile during these times
(both the expulsion of the people from the city center and the exile in foreign
lands of a small group of Athenians and metics who eventually fought to
overthrow the Thirty) and the ideological representation of exile in Athenian
democratic traditions. It was the dynamic interaction between historical
experience (in both the distant and the recent past) and the representation of
that experience in later traditions, as well as the need for unity following the
civil wars, that created the fictions of the people in exile and the people as

---

[48] See also Arist. *Ath. Pol.* 16.2–10, 19.1, for the opposition between democratic mildness
(πραότης) and tyrannical brutality—here articulated by the words τραχύτης and πικρότης,
synonyms of χαλεπότης. Here Aristotle supports his argument that Pisistratus did not rule tyrannically by demonstrating his humane (φιλάνθρωπος) and mild (πρᾶος) behavior toward the
citizens (16.2–10). In contrast, Aristotle notes Hippias's brutality (τραχύς, πικρός), as illustrated by
his execution and expulsion of many citizens (πολλοὺς ἀνῃρηκέναι καὶ ἐκβεβληκέναι, 19.1).

liberators in traditions concerning the rule of the Thirty. In fourth-century traditions, both tyrants and oligarchs are characterized by the mass expulsion of innocent citizens. Indeed, as Rosalind Thomas has shown, the concept of the people in exile under the brutal rule of the Thirty is even transferred in fourth-century traditions, directly back to the period of the earlier tyranny of Pisistratus.[49] In other words, not only did earlier traditions linking tyranny and exile influence the representation of the rule of the Thirty, as I have just argued, but fourth-century representations of the rule of the Thirty influenced subsequent representations of the Pisistratid tyranny. Thomas's prime example of this phenomenon is a passage from Andocides in which he asserts that when the tyrants (i.e., the Pisistratids) ruled Athens, the people were in exile (ὁ δῆμος ἔφευγε).[50] Similarly, in another speech also discussed by Thomas, Andocides asserts that although his ancestors could have remained on friendly terms with the tyrants, they prefered to "go into exile with the people" (ἐκπεσεῖν μετὰ τοῦ δήμου).[51]

EXILE IN THE ANTI-DEMOCRATIC TRADITION

So far I have examined the ways that Athenian democratic traditions justified democratic rule through the use of the theme of exile. In this section, I turn to four critics of the Athenian democracy to examine how they reacted to the construction of exile in democratic ideology.[52] By examining the critiques of democracy made by Thucydides, Xenophon, Plato, and Aristotle, I show that exile not only played a vital role in the defense of democracy but also served as a point of ideological contestation for its critics. In short, all four of these authors reacted to the equation between mass expulsions and non-democratic regimes by suggesting that democracy was no different from tyranny and oligarchy in resorting to unjust and unlawful expulsions.

For Thucydides and Xenophon, the exile of Alcibiades was paradigmatic of the democracy's propensity to engage in tyrannical expulsions that not only perpetrated an injustice against the best citizens but ultimately harmed the city itself, since the Athenians deprived themselves of their best leaders. Plato similarly exploits the representation of exile in democratic ideology to suggest that the Athenians simultaneously mistreated Socrates, one of their best citizens, and harmed themselves by unjustly forcing him either to flee into exile or to submit to execution. Finally, Aristotle reacts to the democratic claim to moderation by arguing that the democratic institution of ostracism is no different from the use of expulsion by tyrants and oligarchs. In

[49] Thomas 1989, 139–44, 252–53.
[50] Andoc. 1.106.
[51] Andoc. 2.26. Thomas also notes the same phenomenon in Isoc. 16.26.
[52] For a thorough analysis of ancient critics of Athenian democracy, see Ober 1998.

Aristotle's view, all three regimes unjustly use the power of expulsion to remove opponents and secure their rule. In sum, the importance of exile in the arguments of all four of these critics of democracy shows that in the late fifth and fourth centuries, exile was a key concept in the debate about the best way of ruling a community.

I begin with Thucydides and Xenophon. As indicated above, these authors do not accept the simplistic equation between non-democratic regimes (tyranny and oligarchy) and exile in democratic ideology. Rather, these historians suggest through their representation of past events that democracy is itself tyrannical, because it unjustly banishes its best citizens.[53] The prime example of this claim for both historians is the exile of Alcibiades. For Thucydides and Xenophon, Alcibiades' exile was a product of the irrational hysteria of the people, and the intrigues of Alcibiades' political opponents, rather than a consequence of his guilt in the affair of the herms or the profanation of the Mysteries.[54] Both historians, furthermore, believed that Alcibiades' exile was a major cause of Athens' defeat in the Peloponnesian War. By exiling Alcibiades, these historians claim, the Athenians deprived themselves of one of their best leaders and as a consequence were defeated in the war. Xenophon, moreover, even suggests that the overthrow of the democracy and the installation of the brutal oligarchy of 411 were direct results of Alcibiades' exile.

Thucydides' analysis of the causes and consequences of Alcibiades' exile begins with his representation of the debate over the Sicilian expedition.[55] In his recreation of this debate, Thucydides has Alcibiades' opponent, Nicias, cite Alcibiades' flamboyant lifestyle in order to suggest that he was advocating the expedition for his own personal gain rather than the good of the polis (6.12.2). While Thucydides does not deny Alcibiades' personal motives for advocating the expedition (6.15.3), he suggests that Nicias's accusations set in motion a chain of associations in the popular imagination whereby Alcibiades' lifestyle became not only an indication of his aims to win prestige and enrich himself, but also a sign of his intentions to overthrow the democracy (6.15.4):

> The majority of Athenians feared him for the great lawlessness of his personal habits and the state of mind in which he acted [τὸ μέγεθος τῆς τε κατὰ τὸ ἑαυτοῦ σῶμα παρανομίας ἐς τὴν δίαιταν καὶ τῆς διανοίας ὧν καθ' ἓν

---

[53] The idea of Athens as a tyrannical polis has long been recognized as a feature of late fifth-century representations of the Athenian empire: see, for example, Hunter 1973–74, Connor 1977, Raaflaub 1979, Tuplin 1985, Scanlon 1987, Barceló 1990. Nevertheless, the role of exile as a marker of the tyrannical inclinations of the Athenian democracy toward its own citizens has not to my knowledge been emphasized.

[54] On the affair of the herms and the profanation of the Mysteries, see R. Osborne 1985c; Murray 1990b; Winkler 1990; Furley 1996; McGlew 1999; Wohl 1999, 2002; and chapter 4 above.

[55] For recent studies of Thucydides' representation of Alcibiades, see Gribble 1999; Wohl 1999; 2002, 125–70.

ἕκαστον ἐν ὅτῳ γίγνοιτο ἔπρασσεν]. As a consequence, [the many] set them-selves against him as one aiming at tyranny [ὡς τυραννίδος ἐπιθυμοῦντι].

Thucydides' presentation of the affairs of the herms and the Mysteries, in the subsequent narrative, serves to reinforce this interpretation of the cause of popular hostility to Alcibiades and his consequent exile. Thucydides re-ports that Alcibiades' political opponents exploited accusations of his in-volvement in the affairs of the herms and the Mysteries in order to banish him from the city (ἐξελάσειαν) and enjoy political leadership themselves (6.28.2).[56] In order to do this, they incited the Athenians by saying that Alcibiades was part of a plot to overthrow the democracy (ὡς ἐπὶ δήμου καταλύσει), and they cited his undemocratic lifestyle as proof (ἐπιλέγον-τες τεκμήρια τὴν ἄλλην αὐτοῦ ἐς τὰ ἐπιτηδεύματα οὐ δημοτικὴν παρα-νομίαν, 6.28.2).

The description of the Athenians' behavior in response to these accusa-tions evokes the irrational hysteria that colors Thucydides' representations of the masses throughout his history and underlies his critique of demo-cratic rule.[57] Even more important for the present argument, the words that Thucydides uses to describe the response of the Athenians to the accusations against Alcibiades explicitly recall the features of tyrannical rule according to Athenian democratic ideology. First of all, Thucyidides evokes the fear (φόβος) and suspicion (ὑποψία) that characterize tyrannical rule in demo-cratic ideology.[58] According to Thucydides, the Athenians "received every-thing they were told with suspicion [πάντα ὑπόπτως ἀποδεχόμενοι]" and "were in a constant state of fear and looked on everything with suspicion [ἐφοβεῖτο αἰεὶ καὶ πάντα ὑπόπτως ἐλάμβανεν]" (6.53.3). Second, Thucy-dides depicts the Athenians as responding to the unverified accusations and suspicions of tyrannical plots with extreme harshness: the people "were harsh and suspicious [χαλεπὸς ἦν τότε καὶ ὑπόπτης] toward those who were accused in the affair of the Mysteries, and it seemed to them that everything was done as part of an oligarchical and tyrannical plot [ἐπὶ ξυνωμοσίᾳ ὀλιγαρχικῇ καὶ τυραννικῇ]" (6.60.1).

Not only does the concept of tyrannical harshness (χαλεπότης) represent

[56] Furley 1996 argues that the affairs of the herms and Mysteries were perpetrated by different groups with opposite political aims, but that there was a campaign to bring the crimes together and attribute them both to Alcibiades.

[57] Key passages for Thucydides' representation of the lawlessness, irrationality, and change-ability of the people include the plague narrative (2.52–53), the representation of Pericles' relationship with the people (2.58–65), the description of civil war at Corcyra (3.81–83), the Mytilenean debate (3.36–50), Cleon and the debate concerning Pylos (4.27–28), and the de-scription of the Sicilian expedition (6.1–32).

[58] See, for example, Aesch. PV 224–25, Soph. OT 584–91, Eur. Supp. 444–46 (an allusion to Hdt. 5.92). See Lanza 1977, 233–36, for a catalogue of these features of the representation of tyranny in tragedy.

the polar opposite of the democracy's self-proclaimed moderation (πραότης), but it is a feature of tyranny that Thucydides himself highlights in his description, in this same context, of the final years of the Pisistratid tyranny (6.53.3). In fact, in his digression on the Pisistratid tyranny, which falls in the middle of his description of the Athenians' treatment of Alcibiades, Thucydides aims to disprove popular assumptions about the lawlessness and brutality of tyranny by showing that for most of their rule the Pisistratids behaved lawfully and mildly (6.54.5–6). According to Thucydides, moreover, it was precisely Hippias's fears and suspicions following the murder of his brother that led him to become harsher toward the citizens (6.59.2):[59] "After this [the murder of Hipparchus], the tyranny became harsher [χαλεπωτέρα]. Hippias became more fearful [ὁ Ἱππίας διὰ φόβου ἤδη μᾶλλον ὤν] and as result both killed many citizens and looked around for a place of refuge in case of revolution."

By representing the Athenians' treatment of Alcibiades as a product of irrational fear (φόβος) and suspicion (ὑποψία), and by suggesting that the democracy acted with undue harshness (χαλεπότης) toward Alcibiades, Thucydides deliberately inverts the standard categories by which the tyrant is opposed to democracy in Athenian democratic ideology. Thucydides in effect suggests that the Athenians belied their own claim to mildness (πραότης) and behaved rather according to their own (misguided) conceptions of the harshness (χαλεπότης) of tyranny. Furthermore, by exiling Alcibiades they perpetrated the equivalent of the tyrant Hippias's unjustified and brutal killings in the final years of the Pisistratid tyranny.

Finally we should note that Thucydides states in no uncertain terms the effect of the exile of Alcibiades on the welfare of Athens. After removing Alcibiades, the Athenians "turned over their affairs to other men, and in no time at all they destroyed the city."[60] Thus, not only did the Athenians act tyrannically in causing the exile of Alcibiades, but by doing so they removed from power one of the best citizens and brought about their own destruction. There could not be a more pointed criticism of democratic rule.

If we turn now to Xenophon's representation of Alcibiades' exile, we can see that he points to some of the same conclusions about democratic rule as Thucydides. In his representation of the events of the final years of the Peloponnesian War and the oligarchic revolution of 411, Xenophon suggests, like Thucydides, that the Athenian democracy brought about its own destruction by exiling Alcibiades. The first place where we can observe Xenophon's shaping of his narrative toward this conclusion is in his description of the war in Asia Minor following the restoration of the democracy in 410. In this section of

---

[59] Compare Arist. *Ath. Pol.* 19.1, where Hippias is said to have become both suspicious of his fellow citizens (πᾶσιν ἦν ἄπιστος) and harsh (τραχύς, πικρός). As a result, says Aristotle, he murdered and exiled many citizens (πολλοὺς ἀνῃρηκέναι καὶ ἐκβεβληκέναι).

[60] Thuc. 6.15.4.

his narrative, Xenophon credits Alcibiades with Athenian successes, and is careful to show that Alcibiades was not responsible for Athenian losses.[61] In the speeches of Alcibiades' supporters, moreover, which Xenophon reports in his description of Alcibiades' triumphant return to Athens in 407, a case is made for the injustice of Alcibiades' banishment and its detrimental effect on Athens.[62]

In the view of Alcibiades' supporters, Alcibiades "was the greatest of citizens [κράτιστος . . . τῶν πολιτῶν]" and "was banished unjustly [οὐ δικαίως φύγοι]." Taking advantage of Alcibiades' absence (as leader of the Sicilian expedition) Alcibiades' enemies "robbed him of his fatherland [ἐστέρησαν τῆς πατρίδος]." Furthermore, Alcibiades had been prevented by his banishment (φυγῇ ἀπειργόμενος) from helping his fellow citizens, his kinsmen, and the whole polis when he saw them making mistakes. With Alcibiades in exile, his enemies gained power and slew the best men (ἀπολλύναι τοὺς βελτίστους);[63] the citizens then accepted these worse men as rulers because they were the only ones left and there were no better men to rule (ἑτέροις βελτίοσιν οὐκ εἶχον χρῆσθαι).[64]

In sum, through the lengthy speech that he gives to Alcibiades' supporters, Xenophon suggests that the exile of Alcibiades was a result of the machinations of his political enemies and that the exile of Alcibiades allowed worse men to lead the city, which, in turn, led to the abuses of power under the oligarchs. Thus the Athenian democracy, by allowing itself to be persuaded by Alcibiades' enemies, brought about the exile of one of its best citizens, which in turn led to the overthrow of the democracy. Xenophon, therefore, like Thucydides, sees the democracy as the author of its own destruction.

The representation of the exile of Alcibiades by Thucydides and Xenophon shows that these authors responded to use of the theme of exile in Athenian democratic ideology by reversing the usual association between non-democratic regimes and expulsion. These authors instead suggest that democracy itself was an unjust and unsound form of rule because it unfairly and irrationally exiled its best citizens, and that by doing so it caused Athens' defeat in the Peloponnesian War and brought about its own destruction.

If we turn next to Plato, we will see how he adapted this critique of Athenian democracy to explain the causes and consequences of Socrates' trial and execution.

Despite recent modifications to the scholarly view that Plato was hostile to

---

[61] E.g., the loss at Notium, *Hell.* 1.5.11–14; cf. 2.1.25, where Alcibiades foresees the loss at Aegospotami, but his strategic advice to the Athenian generals is ignored.

[62] It is noteworthy, moreover, that the speech of Alcibiades' supporters is quite lengthy, whereas that of his detractors is confined to a one-sentence summary.

[63] This is a direct reference to the rule of the Four Hundred, who used political assassinations to maintain themselves in power: see above, chapter 4.

[64] Xen. *Hell.* 1.4.13–17.

Athenian democracy, it is still generally accepted that much of his philo-sophical writing is broadly concerned with critiquing democratic practices.[65] Similarly, although there has been some challenge to the idea that Plato's negative view of the Athenian democracy was a direct consequence of the trial and execution of his teacher, it is clear that Plato's representation of this trial in the *Apology* contains some pointed criticisms of Athenian democratic practice.[66] Since this is not the place to lay out Plato's criticisms in full, I want to focus on one passage in this speech, in which Plato's representation of Socrates' trial evokes the role of exile in the justification of democratic rule as well as in its critique. Specifically, I will suggest that Plato's representation of Socrates' rejection of exile as a penalty following his condemnation recalls both the equation between tyranny and expulsion in Athenian democratic ideology and the inversion of this equation in Thucydides' critique of the Athenian democracy.

The passage in question occurs in the portion of Socrates' speech in which he must propose a penalty for himself following the vote by which he was found guilty. As was mentioned already in chapter 4 above, the penalty for Socrates' conviction on charges of impiety and corruption of the youth was not fixed by law. Rather, following condemnation, the jury decided the penalty by voting on the competing proposals made by the defense and the prosecution. Whereas his prosecutors proposed the penalty of death, Socrates suggested that he should be given free meals in the city hall (πρυτανεῖον), an honor usually conferred upon those who had performed distinguished service to the community.[67] Socrates proposed this reward on the grounds that he rendered the highest service to the Athenians (εὐεργετεῖν τὴν με-γίστην εὐεργεσίαν) by forcing them, through their conversations with him, to examine their lives critically and seek the good.[68]

Yet Plato's representation of Socrates' proposal for punishment is much more elaborate than this, including not only the claim that Socrates was actually a benefactor of the polis (εὐεργέτης) and thus deserving of reward, but also a survey (and rejection) of the standard penalties of death, impris-onment, fine, and exile.[69] It is Socrates' discussion of the penalty of exile that concerns us here. Socrates rejects the penalty of exile on the grounds that

[65] For recent discussion of Plato's criticisms of Athenian democracy, see Roberts 1994a, 71–92; Ober 1998, 156–247. For recent arguments against Plato as anti-democratic, see Saxonhouse 1996, 87–114; Euben 1997, 202–28; Monoson 2000, 111–238.

[66] See especially Monoson 2000, 118, for a challenge to standard views of the impact of Socrates' trial on Plato's view of democracy.

[67] Pl. *Ap.* 36b–e. On the prytaneion, see Miller 1978.

[68] Pl. *Ap.* 36c–d, 38a.

[69] Pl. *Ap.* 37a–e. Plato's Socrates does briefly propose a fine of one mina (the amount that he can afford) and then thirty minas (the amount that his friends offer on his behalf) at the end of this section of the speech (37b). Xenophon's Socrates, by contrast, refuses even to propose a fine (*Ap.* 23).

he will be expelled from the cities to which he might flee for the same reasons as those for which he is forced to flee Athens (*Ap.* 37c, trans. after Gallop 1997):

Should I propose banishment [φυγῆς]? Perhaps that is what you would propose for me. Yet I must surely be obsessed with my survival, fellow Athenians, if I am so illogical as that. For you my fellow citizens were not able to endure my discourses and arguments, but found them onerous and unpleasant, and for this reason you now seek to be rid of them [αὐτῶν νυνὶ ἀπαλλαγῆναι]. Will others then endure them easily? I don't think so, fellow Athenians.

Next, Socrates imagines what it would be like to wander from city to city, as each community inevitably expelled him (*Ap.* 37d):

Indeed a fine life it would be for one of my age to go into exile [ἐξελθόντι], always exchanging one city for another and always being driven out [ἄλλην ἐξ ἄλλης πόλεως ἀμειβομένῳ καὶ ἐξελαυνομένῳ]. For I know well that wherever I go, young men will listen to me speaking, just as they do here. And if I drive them away [ἀπελαύνω], they themselves will banish me [ἐξελῶσι] by persuading their elders. And if I do not drive them away [μὴ ἀπελαύνω], their fathers and relatives [will banish me] of their own accord.

The repetition of the terms for exile in this passage, and especially the notion of progressive expulsion first from Athens and then from each of the cities of Greece in turn, recalls the representation of tyrannical expulsions in Athenian versions of the myth of the Heraclidae and in Herodotus's account of Periander's relationship with his son Lycophron. I argued above that both the myth of the Heraclidae and the story of Periander utilized the theme of exile to demonstrate the brutality and illegitimacy of non-democratic forms of rule. It is striking, therefore, that Plato uses the same mythical structure of repeated banishment to imagine the consequences of a penalty of exile for Socrates. The similarity of this imaginary scenario to the representation of tyranny in these stories suggests an equation between the Athenian democracy's treatment of Socrates and the construction of the tyrant in democratic ideology. In other words, Plato's use of the theme of expulsion both recalls and inverts the connection between exile and tyranny in democratic ideology, and in this sense parallels the critiques of Thucydides and Xenophon. Most striking of all in this regard is that in contrast to Athenian versions of the myth of the Heraclidae, in which their expulsion from the cities of Greece is contrasted to the reception of the exiles by Athens, in Plato's imaginary recreation of the consequences of expulsion, not only is Socrates successively expelled from the cities of Greece, but the series of expulsions begins from Athens itself. In this way, the Athenian democracy is placed on a par with the Peloponnesian tyrant Eurystheus in the Athenian mythical imagination, since the Athenian democracy, like Eurystheus, is the source of the initial decree.[70]

I have argued so far that Thucydides, Xenophon, and Plato all borrow from and invert democratic traditions concerning the relation between exile and tyrannical rule. In the final example of this section, I turn to Aristotle's *Politics* to show that, in this as in many other aspects of his political theory, Aristotle borrowed from and made more explicit the ideas implicit in earlier Athenian democratic and anti-democratic traditions. In particular, I argue that Aristotle's discussion of the representation of the encounter between the Corinthian tyrant Periander and Thrasybulus of Miletus (such as we have encountered it in Herodotus's *Histories*) both confirms the importance of the theme of exile in the justification of democratic rule and attempts to refute the logic of its use in democratic ideology.

Aristotle mentions the story of Periander and Thrasybulus in a discussion of how political power is to be allocated in a polis. In this context, Aristotle is concerned with the problem of how to distribute power fairly in a polis, in which some individuals are superior to others in birth, wealth, or virtue.[71] Although Aristotle admits that such superior individuals have no right to greater political power, he does make an exception for men of truly outstanding virtue (ἀρετή). According to Aristotle, such men cannot be treated equally with others, since equal treatment would be unjust for them due to their unequal virtue and political ability.[72] Rather, in the best constitution, a man of outstanding virtue must be made king and obeyed by all.[73] In deviant constitutional forms (such as a democracy), however, men of outstanding virtue must be excluded, so as not to violate the principles of the constitution or fairness to the outstanding individual.[74] This is the logic of democratic ostracism, Aristotle argues. In a polis in which equality is the aim, it is necessary to remove those who are outstanding in any form of political strength.[75] Aristotle continues (*Pol.* 1284a26–37):

> Hence those who blame tyranny [τοὺς ψέγοντας τὴν τυραννίδα] and the advice of Periander to Thrasybulus are not to be thought wholly right in their censure.[76]

[70] Another example of Plato's equation between tyranny and democracy through a play on democratic representations of exile is his rewriting of the tricolon of abuses in the representation of tyranny: "Democracies come into being, I believe, when the poor are victorious and kill some of the rich, exile others, and give citizenship and political rights to the rest" (*Rep.* 557a). Here Plato changes the last term of the tricolon from "disenfranchisement" to "enfranchisement," thus underlining the contrast between the abuse of the elite and the favorable treatment of the masses under a democracy.

[71] Arist. *Pol.* 1282b14–1284a3.

[72] Arist. *Pol.* 1284a5–17.

[73] Arist. *Pol.* 1284b25–34.

[74] Arist. *Pol.* 1284a3–17.

[75] Arist. *Pol.* 1284a17–22.

[76] Note that Aristotle reverses the names of the advisor and advisee, a variation showing that the anecdote was transmitted for its ideological, not historical, significance.

For they say that Periander said nothing to the messenger who was sent to him for advice, but, by removing [ἀφαιροῦντα] the ears of grain that stood out [τοὺς ὑπερέχοντας τῶν σταχύων], leveled [ὁμαλῦναι] the field [τὴν ἄρουραν]. The messenger did not understand the meaning of this, but when he reported it to Thrasybulus, Thrasybulus understood that it was necessary to get rid of the outstanding men [τοὺς ὑπερέχοντας ἄνδρας ἀναιρεῖν]. This action is not expedient only for tyrants, however, and not only tyrants do this, but also oligarchies and democracies. For ostracism has the same effect: to cut down [τῷ κολούειν] the outstanding men [τοὺς ὑπερέχοντας] and to exile them [φυγαδεύειν].

Several aspects of Aristotle's version of the anecdote are noteworthy. First, Aristotle reverses the roles of Periander and Thrasybulus, a variation showing that the anecdote was transmitted for its ideological, not historical, significance. Furthermore, as we saw above, in Herodotus's version of the anecdote, the original imagery of the outstanding ears of grain was generalized in such a way as to suggest that the entire citizen body, and not just the elites, were victims of the tyrant's brutality. I argued that this slippage was the product of the appropriation and adaptation of an archaic oral tradition by the Athenian democracy. If I am right, then it is noteworthy that in Aristotle's version of the anecdote, the original imagery of the story is revalidated through comparison with the democratic practice of ostracism. According to Aristotle, tyrants remove the outstanding citizens (τοὺς ὑπερέχοντας ἄνδρας ἀναιρεῖν) in a manner similar to the democracy's use of ostracism, where "those who seem to stand out in power [τοὺς δοκοῦντας ὑπερέχειν δυνάμει]" are banished.[77] According to Aristotle, "ostracism has the same effect" as do tyrants, namely "to cut down the outstanding men [τοὺς ὑπερέχοντας] and to exile them [φυγαδεύειν]." In addition to refocusing attention on the elites as the victims of the tyrant's brutality (and thereby strengthening the parallel with the democratic procedure of ostracism), Aristotle adds his own modification to the imagery by using the verb ὁμαλῦναι, "to level," to describe Periander's action. By drawing attention to the level crop left behind by the tyrant, Aristotle similarly strengthens the parallel with the democratic procedure of ostracism, since the aim of democracy is equality among citizens—a level citizen body.

Aristotle, interestingly, is not wholly critical of the principle of removing outstanding citizens from the community, although he does believe that lawgivers should so construct the constitution in the first place that they have no need of such measures.[78] Aristotle argues that it may be expedient for all types of constitution—both the deviant forms such as tyranny and democracy, and correct forms such as kingship—to remove outstanding citizens from the polis.[79] What is important for Aristotle is whether these expulsions

---

[77] Arist. *Pol.* 1284a17–22.
[78] Arist. *Pol.* 1284b17.
[79] Arist. *Pol.* 1284b3–20.

are done in the interest of the community as a whole. Ostracism, Aristotle believes, was misused as a tool in political conflict between different groups in the polis (στασιαστικῶς).[80]

Aristotle's use of the Thrasybulus anecdote, therefore, is complex, involving both an acknowledgment of the occasional justice of removing outstanding citizens and a condemnation of the actual use of ostracism by the Athenian democracy. It is significant, however, that the anecdote plays a central role in Aristotle's discussion of the allocation of political power in a polis. Moreover, Aristotle takes issue with the customary use of the anecdote ("those who blame tyranny and Periander's advice": *Pol.* 1284a26–28). The fact that he cites the example of democratic ostracism to dispute this function of the anecdote suggests that it was democrats who customarily used it to justify democratic rule. Thus the discussion confirms that the Thrasybulus anecdote played a central role in democratic ideology even as late as Aristotle's time. Furthermore, Aristotle's comparison of the anecdote with the democratic practice of ostracism shows that he is both responding to the customary use of the anecdote to illustrate the injustice of non-democratic forms of government, and attempting to refute the simplistic equation between tyranny and exile by pointing to the parallelism between the anecdote and the democratic procedure of ostracism. Like Thucydides, Xenophon, and Plato before him, Aristotle contests the use of the theme of exile in Athenian democratic ideology by demonstrating that the democracy was guilty of similarly tyrannical expulsions. All four authors, therefore, collapse the distinction between tyranny and democracy in part through the theme of exile.

CONCLUSION

I have argued that the theme of exile played an important role in the ongoing debate about the best form of rule in fifth- and fourth-century Athens. In particular, I showed how the Athenian democracy appropriated and adapted earlier mythical and historical traditions of exile in order to justify democratic rule. This appropriation and adaptation is evident in accounts of historical Greek tyrannies (for example, those of Periander, Polycrates, and Pisistratus), as well as in Athenian versions of the myth of the Heraclidae. On the basis of these adaptations and appropriations, I argued that the texts in which these versions of the past are preserved—Herodotus's *Histories*, tragedy, and oratory—reflect (at least in part) Athenian democratic versions of the past. Similarly, I argued that the writings of four critics of the Athenian democracy (Thucydides, Xenophon, Plato, and Aristotle) reveal through

---

[80] Arist. *Pol.* 1284b21–22.

their representations of exile and ostracism the crucial importance of the theme of exile both in the justification of democratic rule and in elite criticism of the Athenian democracy. In sum, examination of the theme of exile in the literary tradition reveals how the historical experience of exile was transformed in the Greek imagination in order to serve as a key term in the debate about the political order of fifth- and fourth-century Athens.

CONCLUSION

I began this book by suggesting that the modern perception of ostracism as a bizarre institution indicates that we have failed to grasp the ancient cultural logic of the practice, and that by doing so, we might gain a new perspective on the ancient Greeks. After all, even Aristotle, who theorized extensively about the injustice of democracy toward its best citizens, was prepared to admit that ostracism had a certain political justice.[1] Aristotle's judgment suggests that the distinction between ancient and modern understandings of ostracism is not just a result of differing degrees of appreciation of individual rights. Rather, in the course of this book, I have suggested that the key to understanding ostracism on its own terms is to place it in its full historical and cultural context, particularly by noting its relation to other forms of exile as they existed from the early archaic times through the classical period. In addition, I placed particular emphasis on the dynamic interaction between the historical experience of exile and its representation in the imagination of the ancient Greeks.

Two of the most surprising results of this recontextualization of ostracism in its historical and imaginative dimensions have been to show, first of all, that ostracism was a relatively moderate form of exile by ancient standards. Furthermore, I show that—far from being an extreme example of the people's unfitness to rule (as American founding father John Adams claimed)—for the ancient Athenians, ostracism was a powerful symbol of the justice of democratic rule. Indeed, I demonstrated that Adams's judgment is based on the responses of ancient critics to the dominant ideology of the democracy, in which the moderation of democratic ostracism was contrasted to (what democrats represented as) the arbitrary and immoderate use of expulsion by non-democratic regimes.

By exploring the deep historical context of exile in the earliest phases of the development of the polis, I showed that the democrats' perception of the immoderation of non-democratic uses of exile was both a reflection and a distortion of past historical experience. Through four case studies, I demonstrated that elites often expelled their rivals in the quest for power in the newly formed, rapidly developing poleis of archaic Greece. The frequent expulsion of elites by their rivals—a practice that I term the "politics of exile"—created a crisis of stability for most poleis, since expelled elites frequently sought to return by force and expel their opponents in turn. In response, elites themselves

[1] Arist. *Pol.* 1284b16–18.

developed various mechanisms for curtailing violent intra-elite conflict, including the creation of formal public offices and the formulation of written
laws enforcing their orderly rotation. My study of intra-elite politics of exile,
however, does not simply confirm that intra-elite competition was a catalyst to
the institutional development of the early polis but, more important, shows
how fragile these early state structures were in the face of violent competition
between small groups of elites.

It is against this background that I develop my interpretation of ostracism
and its relation to the emergence of democracy in Athens. For Athens both
shares and diverges from the common pattern. The history of Athens from
the late seventh century shows that violent conflict between elites was a
frequent occurrence, which prompted legislation designed to curtail it (e.g.,
Draco's homicide legislation, the anti-tyranny law, and Solon's law on civil
conflict). The failure of this legislation to prevent further episodes of violent
intra-elite politics of exile is demonstrated by Pisistratus's three seizures of
tyrannical power, and even more vividly by the dramatic series of expulsions
and returns in the years immediately preceding the foundation of the democracy. While I argued that both Solon and Pisistratus laid the groundwork
for the solution to intra-elite conflict, it was only through the foundation
of democracy that a lasting remedy was found. I argued that a particularly
intense episode of the politics of exile in Athens in 508/7 provoked a dramatic intervention by the Athenian people, which in turn led to a paradigm
shift in the practice of politics.

A key feature of the events that led to the foundation of the democracy was
the Athenians' seizure of control over decisions of exile. In their dramatic
uprising, the Athenian people expelled one group of elites (Isagoras and his
allies) and recalled another from exile (Cleisthenes and his allies). This was
a striking departure from previous instances of the politics of exile, when the
masses had largely remained passive to conflicts among the elites. By assuming
control over decisions of exile, however, the Athenian people signaled that
they had come of age and were ready to assume the reins of power. The
centrality of decisions of exile to the Athenian people's assumption of power
explains why ostracism was a conspicuous part of the democratic reforms.
Through ostracism, the Athenians reenacted in symbolic terms their dramatic
intervention in intra-elite politics of exile during the events of the revolution.
Furthermore, they signaled that they were simultaneously the arbiters of
decisions of exile and the holders of supreme political power. The historical
association between power over decisions of exile and political power,
therefore, explains both the connection between ostracism and democracy and
the important role that the theme of exile assumed in the Athenian (and,
more broadly, Greek) imagination.

A key feature of my explanation of ostracism is the recognition of its symbolic role in Athenian politics. In addition to its important function of

representing democratic power through popular control of decisions of exile, it also served to mark off democratic power from other forms of rule though the particularly limited form of exile that it enacted. In contrast to earlier and non-democratic forms of expulsion, ostracism was limited to a single citizen per year for a ten-year period. Moreover, in most years, the Athenians were content simply to raise the question in the assembly as to whether they wanted to ostracize anyone, without actually deciding to do so. The moderation of democratic ostracism had a pragmatic function of avoiding the creation of large numbers of hostile exiles ready to attack the polis (a lesson of history that the oligarchs of late fifth-century Athens did not take to heart) and therefore helps to explain the stability of democratic rule. Even more important, however, the limited nature of ostracism served as a powerful symbol of democratic moderation and justice in comparison to non-democratic regimes. Indeed, the Athenians developed a vivid negative counterpart to the positive example of ostracism as a symbol of democratic moderation through representations of the mass expulsions perpetrated by historical tyrants and oligarchs. The same practical and symbolic functions of exile are evident in Athens' imperial policies and self-representations.

In closing, I want to emphasize that I am not arguing that the Athenians' use of ostracism was legitimate or just in any absolute sense. Indeed, by our standards, it seems particularly arbitrary and harsh. What I am suggesting is that the institution makes sense in its own historical context and culture, and that if we undertake to understand it in that context, we can recapture some new perspectives on the practices and imaginary of the ancient Greeks.

Appendix One

THE DATE OF THE ATHENIAN LAW OF OSTRACISM

THE date of the introduction of ostracism has been a matter of great debate among scholars.[1] The principal problem is that a fragment of Androtion conflicts with the majority of our sources, who attribute the institution to Cleisthenes.[2] Androtion, however, reports that the law of ostracism was established at the same time as it was first used against Hipparchus, a relative of Pisistratus, in 488/7. The majority of scholars have accepted that the institution is Cleisthenic and have dismissed Androtion's claim on various grounds.[3] Yet a few scholars have argued that Androtion was correct, including the authors of the most recent comprehensive study of the testimony.[4] The argument is set forth by Hans Taeuber, who demonstrates the inadequacy of previous arguments both for and against Cleisthenic authorship, and then argues that the question must be based on, first, which sources were available to Androtion and Aristotle, and second, the historical conditions that were most likely to result in the introduction of ostracism.[5] Taeuber argues reasonably that Androtion made use of documents, possibly even bronze or stone monuments, that named those ostracized and the archons of the years in which they were ostracized.[6] Aristotle, on the other hand, worked from secondary sources, primarily Androtion's *Atthis* itself.

Yet Taeuber also (plausibly) argues that both Androtion and Aristotle made inferences about the author of the law of ostracism based on the names of those first ostracized. Whereas Androtion inferred that the law was introduced in the early 480s out of suspicion of the motives of the relatives of the Pisistratidae, Aristotle went one step further and associated the law with

---

[1] See Taeuber 2002, 401–7, for a summary of the scholarship.

[2] Androtion, *FGrH* 324 F 6. Sources attributing the institution to Cleisthenes: Arist. *Ath. Pol.* 22.1–4; Philochorus, *FGrH* 328 F 30; Ael. *VH* 13, 24; Diod. Sic. 11.55.1.

[3] For example, the following scholars accept the law of ostracism as Cleisthenic: Dover 1963; Thomsen 1972, 11–60; Ober 1989a, 73–75; Hansen 1991, 35. The arguments against Androtion are summarized by Taeuber 2002, 405.

[4] Siewert et al. 2002.

[5] Taeuber 2002, 407–12.

[6] Cf. Lycurg. *Leoc.* 117–19. I am however skeptical of Schreiner's 1976 argument that the inscription mentioned by Lycurgus was a list of ostracized citizens. As I point out in chapter 4 above, ostracized citizens suffered no lasting damage to their reputation, and therefore it is unlikely that the Athenians kept permanent, publicly displayed lists of ostracized persons. Nevertheless, Schreiner's argument, followed by Taeuber 2002, for the existence of some sort of list to which Androtion had access is a reasonable inference.

Cleisthenes, who was both an opponent of the tyrants and the founder of the democracy. Thus, according to Taeuber, the author of the law was not known in the fourth century, and both Androtion and Aristotle made inferences based on the list of known victims.[7] The question then remains: Which source should we believe?

In order to answer this question, Taeuber turns to the historical context, basing his argument for following Androtion on the fact that the introduction of the lot for the selection of the archons took place in 487/6, shortly after Androtion's date for the introduction and first use of ostracism in 488/7. Taeuber argues that the timing is not likely to be accidental. Both measures had a common goal, namely "to diminish elite influence and give the demos greater say." Taeuber even suggests that Themistocles was the author of the law of ostracism in 488/7.[8]

But Taeuber's argument is not decisive. The introduction of the new procedure for selecting archons and the first use of the institution of ostracism could both be responses to the first potentially violent conflict between rival elite politicians since the democratic revolution of 508/7.[9] Furthermore, one could use Taeuber's own point about the aim of ostracism being "to diminish elite influence and give the demos greater say" as grounds for adopting a Cleisthenic date for the institution. After all, there was no greater measure taken to diminish elite influence and give the people a voice in politics than the Cleisthenic reforms themselves.

In the face of the difficulties of coming up with a decisive answer to the question of when ostracism was introduced, most recent authorities entertain both options.[10] Indeed, it must be acknowledged that plausible arguments for either date can be made on the basis of the current evidence. Yet there is one way out of this impasse, and that is by emphasizing, as I have done above in chapter 3, the crucial role of exile in the conduct of politics both before and during the events of 508/7. Specifically, if intra-elite politics of exile was the dominant mode of exercising political power in the pre-democratic polis, and if, as part of the dramatic popular uprising of 508/7, the Athenian people simultaneously took control of decisions of exile and political power, then the introduction of the institution of ostracism at this time makes perfect sense. Ostracism gave the Athenian people a formal mechanism for asserting their control over the leadership and direction of the polis by giving them the power to expel one leading politician.

If we accept that the law of ostracism is Cleisthenic in date, then we must answer one of the principal objections to this date, namely the fact that the Athenians did not hold an ostracism for twenty years after Cleisthenes' reforms.

[7] Cf. Scheidel 2002, 483.

[8] Taeuber 2002, 410. Cf. Schreiner 1976, 92, for a similar proposal.

[9] Forsdyke 2000, 256–57; and chapter 4 above.

[10] See, e.g., Pomeroy et al. 1999, 191; R. Osborne 1996a, 331–32; cf. Brenne 2001, 24.

There are two possible answers to this objection. First, I would point out that it is possible that the Athenians did in fact hold ostracisms before 488/7 and that this date reflects the first successful ostracism. That is to say, ostracisms may have been held, but because votes were insufficient in number—ostracism required a quorum of six thousand voters (see chapter 4 above)—no one was ostracized. A better response to the objection that the first ostracism was not held until 488/7, however, is to note that ostracisms were in fact infrequently held throughout the fifth century. Indeed, a twenty-year gap between uses is not unparalleled: compare the gap between Cimon's ostracism in 461 and that of Thucydides son of Melesias in 443, and the gap between this latter ostracism and that of Hyperbolus in 415.

More important, I argued above in chapter 4 that the infrequency with which the Athenians resorted to holding an ostracism is related to the symbolic and moderate nature of the institution. First, I argued that the Athenians seldom needed to hold ostracisms, because the question posed in the assembly each year as to whether they wished to hold one was a sufficient reminder to elites of the power of the people and the potential of non-elites to intervene decisively in intra-elite conflict. As a result of this annual reminder, there was seldom need to hold an actual ostracism. Second, I argued that the infrequent use of ostracism is connected to the moderate nature of the institution. Both the procedures of ostracism and the limited form of exile it imposed were designed to ensure that only individual citizens were exiled, for limited periods of time. In this way, the Athenian democracy not only avoided the destabilizing consequences of frequent expulsions, but also found a means of distinguishing the democratic use of power from the non-democratic. According to Athenian democratic ideology, ostracism symbolized the democracy's just and moderate use of political power, in contrast to the arbitrary mass expulsions of non-democratic regimes (tyranny and oligarchy). The infrequent holding of ostracisms by the Athenian democracy further strengthened democratic claims to moderation and just rule.

Finally, I should address the possibility that a procedure for exiling individuals from the polis by means of written ballots existed before Cleisthenes. This possibility has been raised by the discovery of a late Byzantine account of ostracism involving the council and the existence of a few sixth-century ostraca.[11] In addition, a few sources attest to a procedure similar to ostracism by which members of the council (probably the Areopagus) wrote down on leaves the name of a magistrate whom they thought ought to be removed from office for misconduct.[12] The procedure of petalism at Syracuse (see appendix 2), furthermore, seems to be a version of this form of expulsion using leaf-ballots.

[11] For the former account, see Keaney 1972, Develin 1985, Dreher 2000. For the ostraca, see Develin 1977a, 1985.

[12] Aeschin. 1.111–12; *Suda* s.'v. ἐκφυλλοφορεῖν, ἐκφυλλοφορῆσαι; Poll. 8.18–19.

On the basis of this evidence, it is likely that the idea of using written ballots—whether leaves or potsherds—not only existed prior to Cleisthenes' law of ostracism, but was practiced in various poleis throughout Greece. Cleisthenes' law on ostracism is simply a particular form, and the best-known example, of this general Greek practice. It is noteworthy, however, that Cleisthenes' law of ostracism involved not just expulsion from political office, as the practice of expulsion by leaves apparently did, but expulsion from the polis for ten years. Moreover, Cleisthenes' most important innovation to the general Greek practice was to make the whole people—ὁ δῆμος—the voters in an ostracism, and not just the council, as in the earlier procedure. Cleisthenes' adaptations of the generalized Greek practice were suited to the historical context of Athens in the late sixth century, as I have argued in the course of this book.

Appendix Two

OSTRACISM OUTSIDE ATHENS

EVIDENCE both literary and archaeological attests to procedures similar to ostracism in a number of poleis.[1] In this appendix, I briefly summarize the scanty evidence and provide some comment on the relatively well-documented case of petalism at Syracuse. In general, consideration of the evidence from outside Athens suggests that Athenian ostracism was simply one elaboration of a more generalized Greek practice of using written ballots—whether leaves or potsherds—as a means of determining a penalty (removal from public office or exile). Ostracism-like procedures such as petalism at Syracuse may be local versions of the general Greek practice, and are not necessarily direct imitations of Athenian ostracism.[2]

Literary evidence attests to the existence of ostracism, or similar procedures, at Argos, Miletus, Megara, Syracuse, and possibly Ephesus.[3] Unfortunately, in every case but one the sources simply state that the procedure existed, without any further comment. The one exception is Diodorus, who speaks at some length about a procedure at Syracuse, petalism, that was similar to ostracism at Athens.

PETALISM IN SYRACUSE CIRCA 454/3

According to Diodorus, the Syracusans imitated the Athenians by introducing a law similar to ostracism.[4] The Syracusan institution was called petalism (πεταλισμός), since the name of the candidate was written on an olive leaf (πέταλον), not a potsherd. Diodorus notes another difference, namely that those petalized were required to go into exile for five years rather than ten. Since Diodorus mentions no other details of the Syracusan procedure, we may assume that he thought it identical to ostracism in all other respects.[5] Indeed, Diodorus is emphatic that the purpose of the two institutions was the same, namely to curtail the influence of the powerful and

[1] Brenne (2001, 27–28) and B. Eder and Heftner (2002, 296–99) summarize the evidence.
[2] *Contra*: B. Eder and Heftner 2002, 299.
[3] Argos, Miletus, and Megara: Arist. *Pol.* 1302b18–19; schol. Ar. *Eq.* 855. For Megara, one ostracon has been found: see Kritsas 1987. Ephesus: Merkelbach 1969, 202. For Syracuse, see notes 4 and 5 below.
[4] Diod. Sic. 11.86–87.
[5] Cf. Hesych. s.v. πεταλισμός: "Petalism is ostracism using leaves."

thereby prevent tyranny. According to Diodorus, the institution was introduced in the mid-fifth century, shortly after an attempt at tyranny by one
Tyndarides.

It is likely that Diodorus had no deep understanding of ostracism, since he
provides a thoroughly conventional interpretation of its role in Athens.
Similarly, Diodorus's simplistic application of this conventional interpretation of ostracism to Syracusan petalism gives rise to further doubts. The
problem of understanding Syracusan petalism on its own terms, however, is
complicated by the meagerness of our understanding of the Syracusan political system in the mid-to late fifth century.[6] In brief, we know that the
Deinomenid tyranny was overthrown around 467, and that either an Aristotelian polity (a mixed regime, with elements of aristocracy and democracy)
or a democracy was installed. The institution of petalism itself has played a
significant role in the scholarly debate over the nature of the Syracusan
regime. For some, petalism is a key piece of evidence for a "thorough-going
democracy."[7] For others, the rapid repeal of petalism shortly after it was
introduced is viewed as clear evidence of the predominant power of
elites within the democracy.[8]

I have only a few observations to add to the debate. First, the fact that the
Syracusans used leaves and not potsherds may suggest that the practice was
not directly related to Athenian ostracism, but was derived from an older,
general Greek procedure designed to regulate magistrates in office.[9] (Cf. appendix 1 above.) If by contrast the Syracusans were in fact imitating Athenian
ostracism, we must ask why they chose to diverge from Athenian practice in
this regard. Two possibilities may be entertained: either they wished to distinguish themselves from the Athenians in this way (Berger 1989, 305), or else
the non-durability of leaves was designed to limit the long-term stigma associated with having been a candidate for petalism.

Given the parallels with other procedures utilizing leaves, as well as the
shorter term of exile, I prefer to think that petalism was not a direct imitation
of Athenian ostracism. Rather, I suggest that petalism was an elaboration of a
prieviously existing procedure, and was a mechanism for penalizing misconduct in office. The fact that Syracusan petalism was repealed shortly after
it was introduced may support this interpretation. Diodorus says that as a
result of the law of petalism, the most powerful men were exiled, and the
elite and those most capable of managing public affairs withdrew into private life. According to Diodorus, the polis was reduced to chaos as a consequence, and the law of petalism was repealed.

---

[6] See Robinson 2000, 190–97, for a summary of the evidence and scholarly debate on the
nature of the Syracusan political system in the post-Deinomenid period.

[7] Robinson 2000, 197.

[8] Berger 1989, 305–6. Repeal of petalism: Diod. Sic. 11.87.

While Diodorus's explanation of the demise of petalism betrays the influence of conventional anti-democratic ideology in its view that the exile of the best men resulted in disorder and bad governance (see above, chapter 6), it is striking that petalism, unlike ostracism, was repealed so soon after it was enacted. Again two interpretations are possible. As noted above, the transience of the institution may be a sign that the elites were powerful enough to get rid of a law that was against their interests. This answer, however, begs the question why the elites, if they were so powerful, let the law pass in the first place. A better explanation may be that, unlike ostracism, petalism was not restricted to a single vote per year, but could be held whenever there was a sentiment that a public figure was behaving inappropriately. In other words, petalism lacked a key feature of ostracism, namely infrequent use. (See above, chapter 4.) Diodorus certainly claims that petalism had a devastating effect on civic participation in Syracuse. Too frequent resort to petalism may have been the cause.

Turning now to the archaeological evidence, we note that potsherds inscribed with the names of individuals have been found from Argos, the Chersonesus, Cyrene, and Megara.

Argos

One ostracon, inscribed with the name Alcandrus and dating to the second quarter of the fifth century, has been found.[10]

Chersonesus

Jurig Vinogradov and Michael Zolotarev report that forty-five ostraca have been found from the Chersonesus.[11] The authors date the ostraca to the whole span of the fifth century. These are very similar to Athenian ostraca in form: they are inscribed on similar vessels, and they contain names with patronymics. Some of the ostraca have additional comments (e.g., accusations of sexual impropriety) that have striking parallels with Athenian ostraca.[12] In interpreting the function of these ostraca, much depends the reconstruction of political affairs in the Chersonesus. Vinogradov and Zolotarev (1999) relate the ostraca to the founding of Chersonesus Taurica, which they argue took place in 528/7. They suggest that the settlement was founded by democrats from Heraclea Pontica after a civil war. The authors

[9] Berger (1989, 305) relates the use of leaves to religious ceremony but cites no parallels.

[10] Pariente et al. 1986.

[11] Vinogradov-Zolotarev 1999, Vinogradov 2001.

[12] Vinogradov-Zolotarev 1999, 116–18. See my discussion of the significance of graffiti on the Athenian ostraca in chapter 4 above.

argue that the democrats introduced ostracism as a weapon against demagogues, who, as Aristotle tells us, had caused the overthrow of the democracy in Heraclea Pontica through their excessive expulsions of elites.[13] This
interpretation is conjectural and cannot be proved on current evidence.

Vinogradov and Zolotarev make much of the early date of some of the
ostraca, which are possibly earlier than the first attested case of ostracism at
Athens. On this basis, the authors argue that ostracism in the Chersonesus was
not an imitation of Athenian ostracism, but rather was inherited from the
colonists' mother cities, either Megara or Miletus. Although I have argued
above that the institution of ostracism dates to 508/7 and not 488/7, when it was
first used (see appendix 1 above), I concur with the authors' view that ostraca
from the Chersonesus may represent a development of similar practices in
Megara and Miletus rather than a direct imitation of Athenian ostracism.

Cyrene

Twelve ostraca have been found in the agora at Cyrene.[14] Lidiano Bacchielli
dates them on palaeographical grounds to the late fifth century. As at Athens
and the Chersonesus, the ostraca are inscribed with a name plus patronymic.
There are nine ostraca inscribed with the same name. Bacchielli argues that
the ostraca represent an instance of a single ostracism at Cyrene, not a long-
lasting law. The occasion, according to Bacchielli, was a conflict between oligarchs and democrats dating to the period 413–401 B.C.E., when a
democracy apparently existed.[15] This reconstruction, once again, cannot be
proved on current evidence.

Megara

One ostracon has been found at Megara.[16] It is inscribed with a name and
patronymic: Heraclitus son of Panchares. According to Charalampos Kritsas,
the pot type and letter forms best correspond to a date in the first quarter of
the fourth century. Yet on historical grounds, Kritsas dates the ostracon to
circa 343–338, when a democracy existed in Megara. Kritsas argues, however, that the institution of ostracism at Megara goes back as far as 460
(the date of an alliance with Athens) or 427–424 (when a democracy possibly
existed in Megara). Kritsas himself acknowledges the speculative nature of
his arguments.

[13] Arist. Pol. 1304b31–34.
[14] Bacchielli 1994.
[15] Diod. Sic. 14.34–36, Arist. Pol. 1319b1–33.
[16] Kritsas 1987.

Appendix Three

EXILE IN SPARTAN MYTH AND HISTORY

EXILE is prominent in ancient traditions about Sparta, from the myth of the exiled children of Heracles, who returned to reclaim their ancestral lands (including Laconia), to the fifth-century Spartan practice of expulsion of foreigners (ξενηλασία). The question arises, therefore, What role did exile play in Spartan political development and ideology?

The problem with Sparta—and the reason why Sparta does not form one of the major case studies of this book—is that the early development of the Spartan polis is very obscure, and no clear relation between intra-elite politics of exile and the particular development of the Spartan state can be drawn.[1] Nevertheless, in this appendix I analyze the scanty evidence and argue that the politics of exile may have played a role in Spartan political development. I also examine the use of the theme of exile in Spartan foundation myths. I argue, following recent scholarship, that myths of exile played an important role in legitimating Spartan land claims.

Next I turn to examples of the use of exile as a punishment against Spartan kings. I argue that, although the expulsion of kings served as an important mechanism for ensuring the subordination of the kings to Spartan law, nevertheless these expulsions were qualitatively different from similar sentences of judicial exile in Athens, let alone the non-judicial procedure of ostracism. The key difference between judicial expulsions at Athens and Sparta was the non-democratic nature of the Spartan judicial system. More similar to Athenian practice was the tendency of elites at Sparta—including the two kings—to use judicial exile as a means of removing political rivals.

In the final section of this appendix, I briefly discuss the evidence for the expulsions of foreigners (ξενηλασίαι) at Sparta. In accord with recent scholarship, I argue that although the Spartans did in fact expel foreigners on a number of occasions, the extent and signficance of this practice was exaggerated in traditions deriving from Athenian democratic ideology and oligarchic idealization of Sparta. In regard to Athenian democratic ideology, I argue that the expulsion of foreigners not only served as a key component in the construction of Sparta as a closed and unfree society in contrast to Athens, but also allowed the Athenians to align the Spartans with a long Athenian tradition in which unjust forms of rule (especially tyranny) were associated with arbitrary expulsions.

---

[1] For the problems with the evidence for early Sparta, see Starr 1965; Cartledge 1980/2001, 26.

Exile in Archaic Spartan Political Development

Despite the lack of any explicit evidence of intra-elite politics of exile in archaic Sparta, there are several indications that the development of the Spartan polis in this period was at least partly a product of intra-elite conflict, and possibly took the form of violent expulsions.[2] First and foremost, traditions about the origins of the Spartan political system stress the importance of civil unrest (στάσις) as a cause for the political reforms. Herodotus says that before the Lycurgan reforms, Sparta "had been the most disorderly state of all the Greeks."[3] Thucydides says that Sparta was "in a state of civil unrest [στασιάσασα] for the longest time" before the reforms.[4] Although these traditions claim that the conflict was ended with one stroke by the creation of a new political system (the Lycurgan reforms) by the eighth century at the latest, it is more likely that the Spartan constitution evolved piecemeal in response to continuing civil unrest over the course of the archaic period.[5] The question remains what kind of civil strife gave rise to the reforms, and whether intra-elite politics of exile was a particular feature of the conflict. The evidence is suggestive but not conclusive.

One might begin with the dual kingship. The existence of a joint kingship at Sparta from about 775–760 is most likely the product of the synoecism of several villages, each with its own ruling family.[6] The joint kingship represents a power-sharing arrangement between the two families and their supporters, and is presumably an institutional means of preventing violent conflict over power in the new polis. The creation of the joint kingship, therefore, was equivalent in function, if not in form, to the institutionalization of formal public offices in other archaic poleis. In the latter case, public offices rotated among elites and were designed to circumvent violent conflict over power. (See chapter 1 above.) The continuing tension between the families of the two kings throughout the archaic and classical periods, however, demonstrates

---

[2] Recent scholarship on the political development of early Sparta is extensive and includes Nafissi 1991; Thommen 1996, 2003; M. Meier 1998; Richer 1998; Link 2000; Lipka 2002.

[3] Hdt. 1.65.2.

[4] Thuc. 1.18.1.

[5] For the lack of civic unrest in Sparta after Lycurgus's reforms, see Hdt. 1.65, Thuc. 1.18. In Herodotus, the contrast been the civil unrest at Athens and the "good order" of Sparta is sharply drawn: cf. M. Meier 1998, 45–47. An interesting historical parallel for the ideological distinction between Athens and Sparta with regard to order and stability may be found in the contrast between Florence and Venice in the historical imagination of Renaissance Italy: see Muir 1981, 13–61.

[6] Cartledge 1979/2002, 88–92; 2001, 59. Cartledge (1979/2002, 92–93; 1992) argues that the village of Amyclae was incorporated into the Spartan polis later than the original four villages, and probably took place in the mid-eighth century. The story of the Minyans (Hdt. 4.145), who colonized Thera, may be a result of the unwillingness of the elites of Amyclae to subordinate themselves to the Spartan kings: Cartledge 1979/2002, 93; cf. on the Partheniae below.

that, like the institutionalization of public offices, the creation of the dual kingship was only partly successful in tempering competition between these rival elite families for power.[7] It is noteworthy nevertheless that Sparta did avoid tyranny in the archaic period, unlike many other poleis.

A second indication of the problem of intra-elite conflict in archaic Sparta is a series of reforms that can be dated roughly to the mid-seventh century. These reforms are preserved for us in the form of a document known as the Great Rhetra.[8] Foremost among the reforms enshrined in this document is the formalization of the role of the Council of Elders, which was given the power to formulate policy alongside the kings. This redistribution of power among a wider group of elites may have been a response to the claim of this wider group to a greater share of power.[9] Alternatively, the institutionalization of the role of the twenty-eight elders may have been a mechanism for diffusing potentially violent and hence destabilizing conflict between the two royal families. Similarly, Paul Cartledge suggests that the limited decision-making role granted to the Spartan people ($\delta\hat{\alpha}\mu o\varsigma$) by this same document was "a technique whereby the hoplite *damos* might formally resolve irreconcilable conflicts within the aristocratic elite, thereby helping forestall tyranny."[10] On this reading, the formalization of state structures apparent in the Great Rhetra is integrally related to the problem of intra-elite conflict.

A third possible indication of intra-elite competition for power is Sparta's aggressive territorial expansion throughout the archaic period. Traditionally, this expansion has been viewed as a sign of overpopulation.[11] Recent survey evidence, however, suggests that, as in other poleis, there was no absolute pressure on the landscape in terms of food production until the second half of the sixth century at the earliest.[12] In other words, the Spartans chose to expand externally before they had even begun to fully exploit the territory of

[7] For continued tension between kings, see Hdt. 6.52.8; and below, "Judical Penalties of Exile in Sparta."

[8] The document is recorded by Plut. *Lyc.* 6. For the difficulties of interpreting this document, see Cartledge 1980/2001, 29–36. For a new interpretation questioning the extent of power granted to the people by this document, see van Wees 1999b.

[9] The assassination of an early seventh-century Spartan king, Polydorus, by a member of the non-royal elite (Paus. 3.3.3), for example, is suggestive in this regard. Pausanias's account of Polydorus as a king popular with the masses, on the other hand, is probably shaped by later events and ideologies, most notably those of third-century Spartan politics: Cartledge 1979/2001, 115–16; *contra*, Sakellariou 1990, 77. The institutionalization of the role of the elders may be compared to the creation of the kingship itself and of formal public offices in other archaic poleis, since all were designed, on this reading, to prevent violent intra-elite conflict over power.

[10] Cartledge 1980/2001, 35.

[11] Cartledge 1979/2002, 98–100.

[12] Cavanagh et al. 1996, 151–74. Nevertheless, Cavanagh et al. (1996, 234) assume that "need rather than greed" motivated Sparta's early conquests.

Laconia itself. Given the significant challenges of trying to conquer external territories (and, in the case of Messenia, one separated from Laconia by the 2,400-m Mt. Taÿgetos), and the easy availability of land within Laconia, it is unlikely that these expansionist enterprises were undertaken simply as a means of feeding a growing population. At a minimum, the conquests were designed to assert Spartan power within the Peloponnesus through military means. It is also likely, however, that the elites who initiated this policy had an eye not only on the position of Sparta within the wider Greek world, but also on their own enrichment and prestige.

The idea that elite greed and status competition had a role in Sparta's external expansion is strengthened by recent scholarship demonstrating that land—including the newly conquered territory of Messenia—was not equally distributed among the Spartan "Ὅμοιοι (Equals), and indeed that there was significant inequality of wealth in archaic and classical Sparta.[13] Finally, the story of the Partheniae, who left Sparta and founded Taras circa 706, may reflect not only intra-elite competition for land and status in Sparta, but also one consequence of defeat in this struggle.[14]

On the other hand, as the case was with other poleis of the archaic period, intra-elite rivalry was not the only driving force of political change.[15] Underlying problems such as inequalities in wealth, and, in the latter half of the sixth century, population growth and consequent pressure on the land, probably led to tensions between elite and non-elite.[16] Most important, the drive for conquest and the consequent need to manage the helot threat required the Spartan elite to rely particularly heavily on the mostly non-elite hoplites of the *damos*.[17] It is safest to conclude, therefore, that both conflict within the elite and tensions between elites and non-elites were driving forces in the development of the Spartan political system.[18]

[13] Hodkinson 2000, 65–112, 151–86. The region of Laconia surveyed by Cavanagh et al. (1996 193–95), furthermore, demonstrates significant inequality in property sizes, ranging from small farmsteads to "villas."

[14] The main sources for the story of the Partheniae are Arist. *Pol.* 1306b30, Strabo 6.3.2 (= Antiochus, *FGrH* 555 F 13), Diod. Sic. 8.21. For recent discussion, see Cartledge 1979/2002, 106–7; Malkin 1994a, 139–42; Nafissi 1999, 251–58.

[15] One more piece of evidence for intra-elite status competition, however, is Herodotus's account of the restoration of the bones of Orestes (1.67–68), which Boedeker (1993/1998, 168–69) argues reflects an attempt to transcend elite claims to status by reclaiming a hero who belonged "to no family but to Lakedaimon as a whole."

[16] Cf. Cartledge 1980/2001, 32–33. For the possibility of rapid growth in population and pressure on the landscape in the latter half of the sixth century, see Cavanagh et al. (1996, 234), who note the rapid expansion of rural habitation sites in this period, along with Sparta's unsuccessful attempt to conquer Tegea (Hdt. 1.66–68).

[17] Tyrtaeus frr. 10–12 (West) are exhortations to Spartan hoplites to fight bravely, and may be assumed to reflect the ways that the Spartan elite motivated the non-elites to follow their expansionist policies.

[18] Cartledge 1980/2001, 38.

SPARTAN MYTHS OF ORIGINS: LAND, IDENTITY, AND THE USES OF EXILE

Among the myths relating to the origins of Sparta, the myth of the Return of the Heraclidae stands out. This myth enjoyed wide circulation throughout the archaic and classical periods and played different roles in the civic ideology of different poleis.[19] In fifth-century Athens, it served as a vehicle for celebrating Athenian justice, since the Athenians claimed to have sheltered the Heraclidae when they were unjustly expelled from the Peloponnesus. (See above, chapters 5 and 6.) The Spartans, along with the Argives and Messenians, assimilated the myth of the Heraclidae to another foundation myth—the Dorian migration—in order to explain their status as relative newcomers and to legitimate their claim to the territory they ruled. In this section, I briefly explain how the theme of exile in the myth of the Heraclidae served a legitimating function for the Spartans by creating links between themselves and the earlier inhabitants of Laconia.[20]

Unlike the Athenians, who claimed continuous occupation of their territory (see chapter 5 above), the Peloponnesians dealt with the disruption in settlement patterns following the collapse of the Bronze Age kingdoms in ways that acknowledged the gap between older and newer inhabitants of the land.[21] This gap is most evident in the myth of the Dorian migration, which viewed the populations of the Peloponnesus as descendants of a group that migrated into Greece from the region of Doris, in central Greece, following the collapse of the Bronze Age palaces.[22] Jonathan Hall suggests that through the myth of the Dorian migration, the Spartans acknowledged their recent arrival in Laconia, yet presented their appropriation of the land as divinely ordained in the mythical pattern of chosen peoples.[23]

Intertwined from an early date with the myth of the Dorian migration was a second foundation myth, the return of the Heraclidae.[24] This myth seems to have originated at Argos, though it soon was appropriated by the Spartans and adapted to the myth of the Dorian migration.[25] The reason for the adoption of the myth not only by the Spartans but also later by the Messenians was its utility in legitimating claims to territory. Rather than presenting

[19] For the origins of the myth in the archaic period, see R. Osborne 1996a, 36–37.

[20] My discussion is based on recent important discussions, including Cartledge 1992; J. Hall 1997, 2000, 2002; Malkin 1994a.

[21] Malkin 1994a, 17. On the clear gap in the archaeological record, see Cartledge 1992.

[22] The principal sources for the Dorian migration are Diod. Sic. 4.57–58, Apollod. *Bibl.* 2.8.2–4. Earlier, less extensive references to the myth include Tyrtaeus fr. 2 West; Pind. *Pyth.* 1.62–65, *Isth.* 9.3–4; Hdt. 1.56.3; Thuc. 1.12.3.

[23] J. Hall 2002, 88; *contra*, Malkin 1994a, 33. Tyrtaeus fr. 2 (West), cited by Hall, seems to attest to the idea of Laconia as a gift to the Spartans from Zeus.

[24] For the original independence of these two myths, see J. Hall 2002, 80, with earlier bibliography.

[25] For the Argive origins of the myth of the Heraclidae, see J. Hall 1997, 61–62; 2002, 81.

the new settlers as outsiders, this myth suggested that they were the legitimate inhabitants of the land, who were unjustly expelled and were rightfully restored. According to the original Argive version of this myth, the ancestors of the Argive kings, the children of Heracles, were unjustly expelled from their kingdom, and later returned to claim their patrimony. The Spartans, on the other hand, adapted the myth by duplicating the exile motif.[26] According to Spartan traditions, the Spartan king Tyndareus was expelled by Hippocoön, and was restored to his kingdom by Heracles. In thanks for this act of service, Tyndareus granted his kingdom to Heracles' descendants. Through this mythical construction, the Spartans found a mechanism both for legitimating their claim to the land by presenting themselves as the descendants of the returning children of Heracles, and for linking themselves (via Heracles' service to Tyndareus) to the pre-Dorian genealogical traditions of the Homeric epics.

In sum, the theme of exile in Spartan traditions serves to explain and legitimate the appropriation of Laconia by presenting the Spartans as returning exiles who had a legitimate claim on the land through Heracles' act of service to the former ruler. Moreover, by tracing their ancestry back to Heracles, the Spartan kings created a mechanism for asserting their primacy over the rest of the population of Laconia.[27]

EXILE IN SPARTAN FOREIGN POLICY: THE CASE OF THE MESSENIANS

Despite their self-representation as returning exiles, the Spartans' conquest of Laconia must have caused displacements of its own.[28] Though this early episode is obscure, later Spartan aggression against the neighboring Messenians, and the displacements that it caused, are relatively well remembered.[29] In particular, following the First and Second Messenian wars, displaced Messenians participated in the colonization of Rhegium and Zancle, which they renamed Messana.[30]

---

[26] Malkin 1994a, 22.

[27] R. Osborne 1996a, 36.

[28] It is remarkable, however, that the traditions emphasize the integration of the previous inhabitants with the Dorians, rather than their displacement (Paus. 2.13.1).

[29] In addition to the literary evidence cited in nn. 30–32 below, two treaties, one preserved in Aristotle, and the other in an inscription, attest to Sparta's attempts to prevent other states from receiving exiles from Messenia or other refugees from Sparta: see Jacoby 1944, Gschnitzer 1978. I thank Paul Cartledge for drawing my attention to this evidence.

[30] Strabo 6.257, Tyrtaeus fr. 5 (West), Paus. 4.14.1. Interestingly, the tradition suggests that following their defeat by the Spartans, the Messenians either went into exile (noble landowners) or were enslaved (non-nobles). This representation parallels fifth-century Athenian representations of the period of the Pisistratid tyranny, an ideological construction that helped to disguise acquiescence to tyrannical rule: see above, chapter 3. It is perhaps likely that there were rather few actual exiles—mostly elite Messenians who objected to being subordinated to Sparta—and that the majority of Messenians remained.

Furthermore, following a revolt circa 464, Messenian rebels were settled by the Athenians at Naupactus.[31] Finally, after Epaminondas's liberation of Messenia in 369, the Messenian exiles were recalled.[32] Although the number of actual exiles from Messenia during Spartan rule was probably small, the experience of exile served an organizing principle for the creation and strengthening of Messenian identity, in much the same way as the construction of the people in exile was central to Athenian democratic identity after 403.[33] (See chapter 4 above.)

JUDICIAL PENALTIES OF EXILE IN SPARTA

As in Athens, exile was one of a triad of major penalties imposed for the most serious crimes in Sparta.[34] Along with the other major penalties—death and disenfranchisement—exile was a penalty that could be imposed only in a trial before the supreme judicial authority in Sparta, the Council of Elders.[35] When the defendant in a trial was one of the kings, the ephors brought the case before the elders and joined them in judgment.[36] The use of the penalty of exile against kings, and in particular the role of the ephors in prosecuting cases against the kings, raises the important question of the role of judicial expulsion in the regulation of royal power.

In assessing the role of exile in the regulation of the kings, the same problem arises as is encountered in evaluating Athenian use of judicial exile, namely the tendency of those accused (and convicted) of serious crimes to go into exile to avoid punishment. (See above, "Introduction.") The claims of our sources that a particular king went into exile, therefore, are not necessarily evidence that he was sentenced to exile. On balance, however, it seems that failure to perform military duties on campaign as expected, and in particular the suspicion of having accepted bribes (treason), seems to have been punished by death or exile. The case of Leotychidas is representative,

[31] Thuc. 1.103.3.

[32] Paus. 4.26.5, Diod. Sic. 15.66.6; for discussion, Luraghi 2002, 63.

[33] Luraghi 2002 notes the importance of exile for the creation of Messenian identity. On the role of conquest and liberation in the construction of Messenian identity, see Alcock 1999, 2001, 2002. I do not discuss here Sparta's role in supporting factions in the Greek states during the period of Athens' hegemony: this topic is dealt with in part above in chapter 5, and is too large to discuss in this context. On the restoration of exiles (presumably pro-Spartan oligarchs) to the Greek poleis following the end of the Peloponnesian War, see above, chapter 4.

[34] For example, the penalty for unintentional homicide was apparently exile (Xen. An. 4.8.25), as at Athens: see above, chapter 3.

[35] Xen. Lac. 10.2, Plut. Lyc. 26.2, Arist. Pol. 1294b33–34. It should be noted that we know little about the Spartan judicial system before about the mid-sixth century, and it is likely that the kings had a much more important role earlier. By the mid-sixth century, justice in Sparta was administered primarly by the Council of Elders and the ephors, with the kings holding only residual judicial capacities: see Hdt. 6.57.4–5; with MacDowell 1986, 123–24.

[36] Paus. 3.5.2; with de Ste. Croix 1972, 350–53; MacDowell 1986, 128–29.

since he was caught accepting bribes on campaign in Thessaly circa 476 and was condemned to either death or exile. Either way, he fled to Tegea, and his house in Sparta was demolished.[37]

In a similar case, King Pleistoanax was accused of having accepted bribes to withdraw from Attica shortly after he invaded in 446/5.[38] It is unclear whether Pleistoanax went into exile as a result of a judicial sentence or in order to avoid the death penalty. After nineteen years in exile, Pleistoanax was restored to Sparta and his kingship through the command of the Delphic Oracle. Following his return, however, Pleistoanax's political enemies attacked him on the grounds that he had bribed the oracle to ensure his restoration.[39] This last detail suggests that political rivalries at Sparta could be pursued through the courts, and that judicial exile could be used as a means of removing political opponents from power.[40]

In 395, the Spartan king Pausanias was charged in a capital case for various failures in his military command but did not show up for his trial and fled to Tegea.[41] One of the charges against Pausanias—namely that he recovered the bodies of the Spartan dead through truce rather than through battle—evokes the Athenians' punishment of the generals at Arginusae and other punishments of Athenian generals. (See chapter 4 above.) It appears from this case that the Spartans, like the Athenians, were ruthless in prosecuting their generals for perceived failures of duty.

In assessing the function of judicial exile at Sparta, the question of the ephors' role in prosecuting such cases must be addressed. On the one hand, the creation of the ephorate in the mid-sixth century may be viewed as a mechanism to ensure that the kingship survived by preventing the abuse of power.[42] This function is apparent from the oaths exchanged monthly between kings and ephors: the kings swore to rule according to the established laws, and the ephors swore to maintain the kingship unshaken as long as the kings kept their oath.[43] On the other hand, the fact of their election from among the Spartan people as a whole (δᾶμος) suggests that the ephors served as a mechanism for collective oversight of the kings.[44] In this sense, cases of judicial exile

---

[37] Hdt. 6.71–72; cf. the case of King Agis in 418 (Thuc. 5.63), accused of failing to conquer Argos when he had the opportunity. Agis's penalty, oddly, was the demolition of his house and a heavy fine. But his case may be exceptional; cf. de Ste. Croix 1972, 351. For the symbolic significance of the razing of the house in Greek society, see Connor 1985.

[38] Thuc. 1.114.2, 2.21.1.

[39] Thuc. 5.16–17.

[40] See chapters 3 and 4 above for examples of the use of judicial exile to pursue political rivalries in Athens; see also the case of Demaratus, discussed below.

[41] Xen. Hell. 3.5.25; Strabo 8.5.5; Ephorus, FGrH 70 F 118.

[42] Cartledge 1980/2001, 35–36.

[43] Xen. Lac. 15.7.

[44] For the election of the ephors from the δᾶμος, see Arist. Pol. 1265b39–40, 1270b25–28, 1272a31–32.

in Sparta may be compared to those in Athens, albeit in Sparta collective power was asserted only indirectly through the ephors, whereas in Athens the demos made its judgment directly. It must be emphasized, however, that collective control over the expulsion of Spartan kings is in no way parallel to Athenian ostracism. The expulsion of Spartan kings was determined through a trial before a small group of magistrates, and the king was given the opportunity to present his case. Indeed, we know of a number of cases in which the king successfully defended himself, and thus avoided death, exile, or disenfranchisement.[45]

Finally, mention must be made of the famous case of the exile of Demaratus described by Herodotus.[46] In 491/0, the two Spartan kings Demaratus and Cleomenes were engaged in bitter rivalry. Herodotus attributes the beginning of the hostilities to Demaratus, who took to slandering Cleomenes while he was away dealing with Aeginetan Medism. In return, Cleomenes conspired to remove Demaratus from office. By bribing the Delphic Oracle, Cleomenes managed to get Demaratus deposed on the grounds that he was not the true son of the former king Ariston. Despite his loss of royal power, however, Demaratus still held public office in Sparta. According to Herodotus, it was only following a taunt about his reduced status that Demaratus chose to go into exile rather than endure such humiliation. The fact that the Spartans pursued Demaratus—probably out of the (justified) fear that he would go over to the Persians—confirms that Demaratus was not subject to a judicial penalty of exile. In sum, although it is unlikely that Cleomenes sought to exile him in order to win predominant power, nevertheless Demaratus's exile was the indirect consequence of intra-elite rivalry in Sparta. [47]

It should be noted, finally, that Cleomenes himself did not escape retribution. When his disreputable activities against Demaratus became known, Cleomenes either was condemned to exile or fled to avoid punishment. Either way, the Spartans soon recalled Cleomenes and restored him to his kingship, apparently out of fear of his anti-Spartan intrigues in exile. Upon his return, Cleomenes began his descent into madness and died gruesomely through self-mutilation.

XENELASIA: FACT OR FICTION?

In examining the evidence for "expulsions of foreigners" (ξενηλασίαι) at Sparta we face conflicting evidence. On the one hand, the concept of

---

[45] For example, the cases of Cleomenes (Hdt. 6.82) and the regent Pausanias (Thuc. 1.94–95, 128–34). In the case of Pausanias, Thucydides comments that there seemed to be clear evidence for his treachery (1.95.5).

[46] Hdt. 6.61–70, 73–75.

[47] Leotychidas, who replaced Demaratus, presumably would have been subordinate to Cleomenes, since the latter was responsible for putting him in power. In addition, Cleomenes was an Agiad: i.e., a member of the senior royal house.

ξενηλασία is strongly rooted in traditions about Sparta.[48] On the other hand, there is abundant evidence of close ties between Spartans and foreigners and the presence of foreigners in Sparta throughout the archaic and classical periods.[49] On the basis of this contradiction, Stefan Rebenich argues that, although there are some instances of expulsion of foreigners in Spartan history—notably the ephors' expulsion of the Samian Maeandrius circa 520, and the policy of expelling Athenians from Sparta on the eve of the Peloponnesian War—these occurred primarily in response to particular historical crises, and do not represent a continuous policy.[50] Rebenich answers the question of why the tradition of Spartan ξενηλασία was so strong by noting its utility in Athenian propaganda during the Peloponnesian War. For the Athenians, ξενηλασία served as a symbol of the authoritarian and closed nature of Spartan society, in contrast to the freedom and openness of Athenian society. (Cf. Thuc. 2.39.) Furthermore, for oligarchic Laconophiles, the expulsion of foreigners fit perfectly into their construction of the so-called Spartan mirage, since it was the means by which Lycurgus ensured that the citizens were uncorrupted by foreign ways.[51]

On the basis of my study of exile, I have one further observation to add to Rebenich's explanation of why the practice of ξενηλασία was so prominent in traditions about Sparta. I have argued that the theme of exile played a central role in Athenian democratic ideology as a result of the history of exile in the archaic period and the specific historical circumstances of the foundation of the democracy in Athens (chapters 3–6 above). I argued that the Athenians not only adopted ostracism as a symbol of the moderation and lawfulness of their democracy, but also adapted mythical and historical

---

[48] Sources for ξενηλασίαι include Thuc. 2.39 (cf. 1.144.2); Xen. *Lac.* 14.4; Ar. *Av.* 1012; Pl. *Leg.* 949e–950a; Theopompus, *FGrH* 115 F 178; Plut. *Lyc.* 27.6. Hdt. 1.65.2 seems to reflect this tradition—albeit with some difference in chronology—in saying that before the Spartans adopted their Lycurgan constitution, they did not mix with foreigners (ξείνοισι ἀπρόσμεικτοι). Similarly, Herodotus's account (3.148) of the expulsion of the Samian Maeandrius from Sparta (c. 520–515), on the grounds that he might corrupt the Spartans through his wealth, seems to be based on the tradition of ξενηλασία.

[49] Cf. Cartledge 1982; 1987, 244–46; Rebenich 1998, 344–47. Foreigners at Sparta include artists, musicians, poets (e.g., Terpander), philosophers (e.g., Anaximander), historians (e.g., Herodotus, Thucydides), not to mention politicians (e.g., Themistocles, Cimon, Alcibiades) and oligarchs and Laconophiles (e.g., Critias, Xenophon). Sparta served as a place of refuge for many of these latter when they were exiled from Athens.

[50] Rebenich (1998, 356) does concede that a number of factors contributed to the increased frequency of expulsions from Sparta in the fifth century, but also (pp. 353–54) demonstrates that other poleis, including Athens, also occasionally banished foreigners. The most prominent Athenian case is that of Arthmius of Zelea, who was an official representative (πρόξενος) of his polis in Athens and was expelled from Athens c. 461 for bringing Persian gold to Greece in order to stir up war against the Athenians: cf. Aeschin. 3.258, Din. 2.24.

[51] Cf. Xen. *Lac.* 14, Plut. *Lyc.* 27.6. For the term "Spartan mirage," see Ollier 1993 and most recently Powell and Hodkinson 2002.

traditions about exile in order to emphasize the difference between democratic and non-democratic forms of rule. In these traditions, arbitrary mass expulsions served as a key element in the representation of unjust rule, especially tyranny. If my argument is correct, then we have one further reason why the Athenians might have wished to emphasize Spartan expulsions of foreigners. By doing so, they were able to align Sparta with other unjust regimes in the mythical and historical traditions, and thereby highlight the justice and moderation of Athens.

BIBLIOGRAPHY

Abbreviations of journal titles are those listed in the frontmatter of the annual issues of *L'Année Philologique*, with a few familiar slight variations.

Alcock, S. E. 1991. "Tomb Cult and the Post-Classical Polis." *AJA* 95:447–67.
———. 1993. *Graecia Capta: The Landscapes of Roman Greece*. Cambridge.
———. 1999. "The Pseudo-History of Messenia Unplugged." *TAPA* 129:333–41.
———. 2001. "The Peculiar Book IV and the Problem of the Messenian Past." In S. E. Alcock, J. F. Cherry and J. Elsner, eds., *Pausanias: Travel and Memory in Roman Greece*, 142–53 Oxford.
———. 2002. *Archaeologies of the Greek Past: Landscape, Monuments, and Memories*. Cambridge.
Alcock, S. E., and R. Osborne, eds. 1994. *Placing the Gods: Sanctuaries and Sacred Space in Ancient Greece*. Oxford.
Allen, D. S. 2000. *The World of Prometheus: The Politics of Punishing in Democratic Athens*. Princeton.
Anderson, B. 1991. *Imagined Communities: Reflections on the Origin and Spread of Nationalism*. 2nd ed. London.
Anderson, G. 2000. "Alkmeonid 'Homelands,' Political Exile, and the Unification of Attica" *Historia* 69:387–412.
———. 2003. *The Athenian Experiment: Building an Imagined Political Community in Ancient Attica, 508–490 B.C.* Ann Arbor.
Andrewes, A. 1956. *The Greek Tyrants*. London.
———. 1961a. "Phratries in Homer." *Hermes* 89:129–40.
———. 1961b. "Philochorus on Phratries." *JHS* 81:1–15.
———. 1974. "The Arginousai Trial." *Phoenix* 28:112–22.
———. 1977. "Kleisthenes' Reform Bill." *CQ* 27:241–48.
———. 1982. "The Growth of the Athenian State." In Boardman and Hammond 1982, 360–416.
Angiolillo, S. 1997. Ο ΕΠΙ ΚΡΟΝΟΥ ΒΙΟΣ: *Appunti sulla politica culturale nell'Atene di Pisistrato e dei Pisistratidi*. Cagliari.
Antonaccio, C. 1993/1998. "The Archaeology of Ancestors." In Dougherty and Kurke 1993/1998, 46–70.
———. 1995. *An Archaeology of Ancestors: Tomb Cult and Hero Cult in Early Greece*. Lanham, MD.
Arnaoutoglou, I. 1994. "Associations and Patronage in Ancient Athens." *AncSoc* 25:5–17.
Assmann, J. 1992. *Das kulturelle Gedächtnis: Schrift, Erinnerung und politische Identität in frühen Hochkulturen*. Munich.
Baba, K. 1990. "The Macedonian/Thracian Coastland and the Greeks in the Sixth and Fifth Centuries B.C." *Kodai* 1:1–23.
Bacchielli, L. 1994. "L'ostracismo a Cirene." *RFIC* 122:257–70.

Badian, E. 1971. "Archons and Strategoi." *Antichthon* 5:1–4.

Bakker, E. J., I.J.F. de Jong, and H. van Wees, eds. 2002. *Brill's Companion to Herodotus.* Leiden.

Balcer, J. M. 1978. *The Athenian Regulations for Chalkis: Studies in Athenian Imperial Law.* Historia Einzelschriften.Wiesbaden.

Balogh, E. 1943. *Political Refugees in Ancient Greece: From the Period of the Tyrants to Alexander the Great.* Johannesburg.

Balot, R. K. 2001. *Greed and Injustice in Classical Athens.* Princeton.

Barceló, P. 1990. "Thukydides und die Tyrannis." *Historia* 39:401–25.

Baringhorst, S. 2001. "Political Rituals." In K. Nash and A. Scott, eds., *The Blackwell Companion to Political Sociology,* 290–301. Oxford.

Bassi, K. 1998. *Acting like Men: Gender, Drama and Nostalgia in Ancient Greece.* Ann Arbor.

Bell, C. 1997. *Ritual: Perspectives and Dimensions.* Oxford.

Bérard, C. 1982. "Récupérer la mort du prince: Héroisation et formation de la cité." In Gnoli and Vernant 1982, 89–105.

Berger, S. 1989. "Democracy in the Greek West and the Athenian Example." *Hermes* 117:303–14.

Bers, V. 1975. "Solon's Law Forbidding Neutrality and Lysias 31." *Historia* 24:493–98.

———. 2000. "Just Rituals: Why the Rigmarole of the Fourth-Century Athenian Lawcourts?" In P. Flensted-Jensen, T. H. Nielsen, and L. Rubenstein, eds., *Polis and Politics: Studies in Ancient Greek History Presented to M. H. Hansen on His Sixtieth Birthday, August 20, 2000,* 553–59. Copenhagen.

Berve, H. 1967. *Die Tyrannis bei den Griechen.* Munich.

Bicknell, P. J. 1970. "The Exile of the Alcmeonidai during the Peisistratid Tyranny." *Historia* 19:129–31.

Billigmeier, J. C., and A. S. Dusing. 1981. "The Origin and Function of the Naukraroi at Athens: An Etymological and Historical Explanation." *TAPA* 111:11–16.

Blanton, R. E. 1998. "Beyond Centralization: Steps toward a Theory of Egalitarian Behavior in Archaic States." In Feinman and Marcus 1998, 135–72.

Blanton, R. E., G. M. Feinman, S. Kowalewski, and P. Peregrine. 1996. "A Dual-Processual Theory for the Evolution of Mesoamerican Civilization." *Current Anthropology* 37:1–13.

Blok, J. 1990. "Patronage and the Peisistratidae." *BABesch* 65:17–28.

———. 2000. "Phye's Procession: Culture, Politics and Peisistratid Rule." In Sancisi-Weerdenburg 2000c, 17–48.

Boardman, J. 1972. "Herakles, Peisistratos and Sons." *RA,* 1972:57–72.

———. 1984. "Image and Politics in Sixth-Century Athens." In H.A.G. Brijer, ed., *Ancient Greek and Related Pottery,* 239–47. Amsterdam.

Boardman, J., and N.G.L. Hammond, eds. 1982. *The Cambridge Ancient History.* Vol. 3.3, *The Expansion of the Greek World, Eighth to Sixth Centuries B.C.* 2nd ed. Cambridge.

Boedeker, D., 1993/1998. "Hero Cult and Politics in Herodotus." In Dougherty and Kurke 1993/1998, 164–77.

Boedeker, D., ed. 1987. *Herodotus and the Invention of History.* Arethusa Monographs, 20. Buffalo.

Boedeker, D., and K. A. Raaflaub, eds. 1998. *Democracy, Empire and the Arts in Fifth-Century Athens*. Cambridge, MA.

Boegehold, A., and A. C. Scafuro, eds. 1994. *Athenian Identity and Civic Ideology*. Baltimore.

Boersma, J. S. 1970. *Athenian Building Policy from 561–560 to 404–403 BC*. Groningen.

———. 2000. "Peisistratos' Building Activity Reconsidered." In Sancisi-Weerdenburg 2000c, 49–56.

Boissevain, J. 1992. *Revitalizing European Rituals*. London.

Bonner, R. J., and G. Smith. 1930. *The Administration of Justice from Homer to Aristotle*. Vol. 1. Chicago.

Bourdieu, P. 1980/1990. *The Logic of Practice*. Trans. R. Nice. Stanford, CA. [Originally published as *Le sens pratique* (Paris, 1980).]

Bourriot, F. 1976. *Recherches sur la nature du génos*. Paris.

Bowden, H. 1993. "Hoplites and Homer: Warfare, Hero Cult, and the Ideology of the polis." In J. Rich and G. Shipley, eds., *War and Society in the Greek World*; 45–63. London.

Bowie, A. M. 1981. *The Poetic Dialect of Sappho and Alcaeus*. Salem, NH.

Bowie, E. L. 1986. "Early Greek Elegy, Symposium and Public Festival." *JHS* 106: 13–35.

———. 1990. "*Miles Ludens*? The Problem of Martial Exhortation in Early Greek Elegy." In Murray 1990a, 221–29.

———. 1997. "The *Theognidea*: A Step towards a Collection of Fragments?" In G. W. Most, ed., *Collecting Fragments/Fragmente sammeln*, 53–66. Göttingen.

Bradeen, D. W., and M. F. McGregor. 1973. *Studies in Fifth-Century Attic Epigraphy*. Norman, OK.

Brandt, H. 1989. "Γῆς ἀναδασμός und ältere Tyrannis." *Chiron* 19:207–20.

Bremmer, J. 1983. "Scapegoat Rituals in Ancient Greece." *HSCP* 87:299–320.

Brenne, S. 1992. "'Portraits' auf Ostraka." *AM* 107:161–85.

———. 1994. "Ostraka and the Process of Ostrakophoria." In Coulson et al. 1994, 13–24.

———. 2001. *Ostrakismos und Prominenz in Athen: Attische Bürger des 5. Jahrhunderts v.Chr. auf den Ostraka*. Vienna.

———. 2002a. "Die Ostraka (487–ca. 416 v.Chr.) als Testimonien (T1)." In Siewert et al. 2002, 36–166.

———. 2002b. "Rotfigurige Schale des 'Pan-Malers' (Oxford 1911.617) aus Cerveteri (470–460 v.Chr.): Auszählung der Ostraka?" In Siewert et al. 2002, 174–84.

Brock, R., and S. Hodkinson, eds. 2000. *Alternatives to Athens: Varieties of Political Organization and Community in Ancient Greece*. Oxford.

Brumfiel, E. 1992. "Distinguished Lecture in Archaeology: Breaking and Entering the Ecosystem—Gender, Class and Faction Steal the Show." *American Anthropologist* 94:551–67.

———. 1994. "Factional Competition and Political Development in the New World: An Introduction." In E. Brumfiel and J. W. Fox, eds., *Factional Competition and Political Development in the New World*, 3–13. Cambridge.

Buck, R. J. 1995. "The Character of Theramenes." *AHB* 9:14–23.

Burckhardt, L., and J. von Ungern-Sternberg, eds. 2000. *Grosse Prozesse im antiken Athen*. Munich.

Burke, P. 1978. *Popular Culture in Early Modern Europe*. New York.

———. 1986. "City-States." In J. A. Hall, ed., *States in History*, 137–53. Oxford.

———. 1992. *History and Social Theory*. Cambridge.

Burkert, W. 1985. *Greek Religion*. Trans. J. Raffan. Cambridge, MA.

Burstein, S. M. 1971. "The Recall of the Ostracized and the Themistocles Decree." *CSCA* 4:93–110.

Busolt, G. 1920. *Griechische Staatskunde*. 3rd ed. Munich.

Campbell, D. A. 1982. *Greek Lyric: With an English Translation*. Vol. 1, *Sappho and Alcaeus*. Cambridge, MA.

Camp, J. M. 1994. "Before Democracy: Alkmeonidai and Peisistratidai." In Coulson et al. 1994; 7–12.

———. 1996. "Excavations in the Athenian Agora, 1994 and 1995." *Hesperia* 65: 231–61.

———. 1999. "Excavations in the Athenian Agora, 1996 and 1997." *Hesperia* 68: 255–83.

Carawan, E. 1987. "*Eisangelia* and *Euthyna*: The Trials of Miltiades, Themistocles, and Cimon." *GRBS* 28:167–208.

———. 1993. "Tyranny and Outlawry: *Athenaion Politeia* 16.10." In Rosen and Farrell 1993, 305–19.

———. 1998. *Rhetoric and the Law of Draco*. Oxford.

Carcopino, J. 1909. "Histoire de l'ostracisme athénien." *Mélanges d'Histoire Ancienne* 25:83–266.

Carlier, P. 1984. *La royauté en Grèce avant Alexandre*. Strasbourg.

Carneiro, R. 1970. "A Theory of the Origin of the State." *Science* 169:733–38.

Cartledge, P. A. 1979/2002. *Sparta and Lakonia: A Regional History, 1300–362 BC*. 2nd ed. London.

———. 1980/2001. "The Peculiar Position of Sparta in the Development of the Greek City-State." *PRIA* 80:91–108. [Reprinted in Cartledge 2001, 21–38.]

———. 1982. "Sparta and Samos: A Special Relationship?" *CQ* 32:243–65.

———. 1983. "'Trade and Politics' Revisited: Archaic Greece." In P. Garnsey, K. Hopkins, and C. R. Whittaker, eds., *Trade in the Ancient Economy*, 1–15. London.

———. 1987. *Agesilaus and the Crisis of Sparta*. Baltimore.

———. 1992. "Early Lakedaimon: The Making of a Conquest State." In J. M. Sanders, ed., *ΦΙΛΟΛΑΚΩΝ: Lakonian Studies in Honour of Hector Catling*, 49–55. London.

———. 1996. "Comparatively Equal." In Ober and Hedrick 1996, 175–85.

———. 2001. *Spartan Reflections*. Berkeley and Los Angeles.

Cavenagh, W., J. Crouwel, R.W.V. Catling, and G. Shipley. 1996. *Continuity and Change in a Greek Rural Landscape: The Laconia Survey*. Vol. 1, *Methodology and Interpretation*. ABSA Supplementary vol. 26. London.

Cawkwell, G. L. 1995. "Early Greek Tyranny and the People." *CQ* 45:73–86.

Chambers, M. H. 1984. "The Formation of the Tyranny of Peisistratus." In J. Harmatta, ed., *Proceedings of the Seventh Congress of the International Federation of the Societies of Classical Studies* 1:69–72. Budapest.

Childs, W. A. P. 1994. "The Date of the Old Temple of Athena on the Athenian Acropolis." In Coulson et al. 1994, 1–6.

Christ, M. R. 1992. "Ostracism, Sycophancy, and Deception of the Demos: [Arist.] *Ath. Pol.* 43.5." *CQ* 42:336–46.

———. 1998. *The Litigious Athenian*. Baltimore.

Claassen, J.-M. 1999. *Displaced Persons: The Literature of Exile from Cicero to Boethius*. London.

Cloché, P. 1915. *La restauration démocratique à Athènes en 403 avant J.-C.* Paris.

Cobb-Stevens, V., T. J. Figueira, and G. Nagy. 1985. "Introduction." In Figueira and Nagy 1985, 1–8.

Cohen, A. P. 1985. *The Symbolic Construction of Community*. London.

Cohen, D. 1993. *Law, Sexuality and Society: The Enforcement of Morals in Classical Athens*. Cambridge.

———. 1995. *Law, Violence and Community in Classical Athens*. Cambridge.

Cohen, S. T. 2002. "Exile in the Political Language of the Early Principate." PhD dissertation, University of Chicago.

Coldstream, J. N. 1977. *Geometric Greece*. London.

Coleman, J. W. 1994. *The Criminal Elite: The Sociology of White-Collar Crime*. New York.

Collins, D. 2004. *Master of the Game: Competition and Performance in Greek Poetry*. Cambridge, MA.

Connor, W. R. 1971. *The New Politicians of Fifth-Century Athens*. Reprint: Indianapolis, 1992.

———. 1977. "Tyrannis Polis." In J. H. D'Arms and J. W. Eadie, eds., *Ancient and Modern: Essays in Honor of Gerald F. Else*, 95–109. Ann Arbor.

———. 1984. *Thucydides*. Princeton.

———. 1985. "The Razing of the House in Greek Society." *TAPA* 115:79–102.

———. 1987. "Tribes, Festivals and Processions: Civic Ceremonial and Political Manipulation in Ancient Greece." *JHS* 107:40–50.

———. 1989. "City Dionysia and Athenian Democracy." *C&M* 40:7–32.

———. 1994. "The Problem of Athenian Civic Identity." In Boegehold and Scafuro 1994, 34–41.

Cook, R. M. 1987. "Pots and Peisistratan Propaganda." *JHS* 107:167–69.

Coulson, W. D. E., O. Palagia, T. L. Shear, Jr., H. A. Shapiro, and F. J. Frost, eds. 1994. *The Archaeology of Athens and Attica under the Democracy*. Oxbow Monograph 37. Oxford.

Darnton, R. 1984. *The Great Cat Massacre and Other Episodes in French Cultural History*. New York.

David, E. 1984. "Solon, Neutrality and Partisan Literature of Late Fifth-Century Athens." *MH* 41:129–38.

Davidson, J. K. 1958. "Notes on the Panathenaia." *JHS* 78:23–41.

Davies, J. K. 1977. "Athenian Citizenship: The Descent Group and the Alternatives." *CJ* 73:105–21.

Davis, N. Z. 1975. *Society and Culture in Early Modern France*. Stanford, CA.

De Angelis, F. 1994. "The Foundation of Selinous: Overpopulation or Opportunities?" In G. R. Tsetskhladze and F. De Angelis, eds., *The Archaeology of Greek Colonization: Essays Dedicated to Sir John Boardman*, 87–110. Oxford.

de Bruyn, O. 1995. *La compétence de l'Aréopage en matière de procès publics*. Historia Einzelschriften 90. Stuttgart.

de Polignac, F. 1984/1995. *Cults, Territory and the Origins of the City-State*. 2nd ed. Chicago. [Originally published as *La naissance de la cité grecque* (Paris, 1984).]

———. 1994. "Mediation, Competition and Sovereignty: The Evolution of Rural Sanctuaries in Geometric Greece." In Alcock and Osborne 1994, 3–18.

de Ste. Croix, G.E.M. 1954. "The Character of the Athenian Empire." *Historia* 3:1–42.

———. 1956. "The Constitution of the Five Thousand." *Historia* 5:1–23.

———. 1961. "Notes on Jurisdiction in the Athenian Empire." Parts 1 and 2. *CQ* 11:94–112, 268–80.

———. 1972. *The Origins of the Peloponnesian War*. London.

Desan, S. 1989. "Crowds, Community, and Ritual in the Work of E. P. Thompson and Natalie Davis." In Hunt 1989, 25–71.

Develin, R. 1977a. "Cleisthenes and Ostracism: Precedents and Intentions." *Antichthon* 11:10–16.

———. 1977b. "Solon's Law on Stasis." *Historia* 26:507–8.

———. 1979. "The Election of Archons from Solon to Telesinos." *AC* 48:455–68.

———. 1985. "Bouleutic Ostracism Again." *Antichthon* 19:7–15.

———. 1989. *Athenian Officials 684–321 B.C.* Cambridge.

Dewald, C. 2003. "Form and Content: The Question of Tyranny in Herodotus." In K. Morgan 2003, 25–58.

Dietler, M. 2001. "Theorizing the Feast: Rituals of Consumption, Commensal Politics, and Power in African Contexts." In Dietler and Hayden 2001, 65–114.

Dietler, M., and B. Hayden, eds. 2001. *Feasts: Archaeological and Ethnographic Perspectives on Food, Politics and Power*. Washington, D.C.

Dobres, M.-A., and J. Robb, eds. 2000. *Agency in Archaeology*. London.

Doenges, N. A. 1996. "Ostracism and the Boulai of Kleisthenes." *Historia* 45:387–404.

Domínguez-Monedero, A. J. 2001. *Solón de Atenas*. Barcelona.

Donlan, W. 1980. *The Aristocratic Ideal in Ancient Greece: Attitudes of Superiority from Homer to the End of the Fifth Century B.C.* Lawrence, KS.

———. 1985. "The Social Groups of Dark Age Greece." *CP* 80:293–308.

———. 1989. "The Pre-state Community in Greece." *SO* 64:5–29.

———. 1994. "Chief and Followers in Pre-state Greece." In C. M. Duncan and D. W. Tandy, eds., *From Political Economy to Anthropology*, 34–51. Montreal.

Dougherty, C. 1993. *The Poetics of Colonization: From City to Text in Archaic Greece*. Oxford.

Dougherty, C., and L. Kurke, eds. 1993/1998. *Cultural Poetics in Archaic Greece: Cult, Performance, Politics*. Cambridge. [Reprint: Oxford, 1998.]

Dover, K. J. 1963. "Androtion on Ostracism." *CR* 13:256–57. [Reprinted in K. J. Dover, *The Greeks and Their Legacy: Collected Papers* 2:83–85 (Oxford, 1988).]

Dreher, M. 2000. "Verbannung ohne Vergehen: Der Ostrakismos (das Scherbengericht)." In Burckhardt and von Ungern-Sternberg 2000, 66–77.

Drews, R. 1983. *The Evidence for Kingship in Geometric Greece*. New Haven.

Durkheim, É. 1995. *The Elementary Forms of Religious Life*. Trans. K. Fields. New York.

Earle, T. 1997. *How Chiefs Come to Power: The Political Economy in Prehistory*. Stanford, CA.

Eder, B., and H. Heftner 2002. "T18–21: [Andokides] 4, 'Gegen Alkibiades'—Vorbemerkungen: Verfassershaft und Abfassungszeit der Rede." In Siewert et al. 2002, 277–301.

Eder, W. 1986. "The Political Significance of the Codification of Law in Archaic Societies: An Unconventional Hypothesis." In K. Raaflaub, ed., *Social Struggles in Archaic Rome*, 262–300. Berkeley and Los Angeles.

———. 1988. "Political Self-Confidence and Resistance: The Role of the Demos and Plebs after the Expulsion of the Tyrant in Athens and the King in Rome." In T. Yuge and M. Doi, eds., *Forms of Control and Subordination in Antiquity*, 465–75. Leiden.

———. 1991. "Who Rules? Power and Participation in Athens and Rome." In Molho et al. 1991, 169–96.

Ehrenberg, V. 1950. "Origins of Democracy." *Historia* 1:515–48.

Eiteljorg, H. 1993. *The Entrance to the Athenian Acropolis before Mnesicles*. AIA Monographs, n.s., 1. Boston.

Errington, R. M. 1994. "'Ἐκκλησία κυρία in Athens." *Chiron* 24:135–60.

Euben, J. P. 1997. *Corrupting Youth: Political Education, Democratic Culture, and Political Theory*. Princeton.

Faraone, C. A. 1991. "The Agonistic Context of Early Greek Binding Spells." In C. A. Faraone and D. Obbink, eds., *Magika Hiera: Ancient Greek Magic and Religion*, 3–32. Oxford.

———. 2004. "Hipponax Fragment 128W: Epic Parody or Expulsive Incantation?" *ClAnt* 23:209–45.

Farenga, V. 1998. "Narrative and Community in Dark Age Greece: A Cognitive and Communicative Approach to Early Greek Citizenship." *Arethusa* 31:179–206.

Feinman, G. M., and J. Marcus, eds. 1998. *Archaic States*. Santa Fe, NM.

Fentress, J., and C. Wickham. 1992. *Social Memory*. Oxford.

Ferguson, Y. 1991. "Chiefdoms to City-States: The Greek Experience." In T. Earle, ed., *Chiefdoms: Power, Economy and Ideology*, 169–92. Cambridge.

Figueira, T. J. 1985a. "The Theognidea and Megarean Society." In Figueira and Nagy 1985, 112–58.

———. 1985b. "Chronological Table: Archaic Megara, 800–500 B.C." In Figueira and Nagy 1985, 261–303.

———. 1987. "Residential Restrictions on the Athenian Ostracized." *GRBS* 28:281–305.

———. 1991. *Athens and Aigina in the Age of Imperial Colonization*. Baltimore.

———. 1993. *Excursions in Epichoric History: Aiginetan Essays*. Lanham, MD.

———. 1998. *The Power of Money: Coinage and Politics in the Athenian Empire*. Philadelphia.

Figueira, T. J., and G. Nagy, eds. 1985. *Theognis of Megara: Poetry and the Polis*. Baltimore.

Finley, M. I. 1983. *Politics in the Ancient World*. Cambridge.

Fischer, K. 1963. "Die politische Emigration in der Zeit des peloponnesischen Krieges." PhD dissertation, Hamburg.

Fisher, N. 1992. *Hybris: A Study in the Values of Honour and Shame in Ancient Greece*. Warminster.

Fisher, N., and H. van Wees, eds. 1998. *Archaic Greece: New Approaches and New Evidence*. London.

Flannery, K. V. 1999. "Process and Agency in Early State Formation." *Cambridge Archaeological Journal* 9:3–21.

Fornara, C. W. 1978. "*IG* I², 39.52–57 and the 'Popularity' of the Athenian Empire." *CSCA* 10:39–55.

Forrest, W. G. 1966. *The Emergence of Greek Democracy: The Character of Greek Politics, 800–400 BC.* London.

Forrest, W. G., and D. Stockton. 1987. "The Athenian Archons: A Note." *Historia* 36: 235–40.

Forsdyke, S. 1999. "From Aristocratic to Democratic Ideology and Back Again: The Thrasybulus Anecdote in Herodotus' *Histories* and Aristotle's *Politics*." *CP* 94:361–72.

———. 2000. "Exile, Ostracism and the Athenian Democracy." *ClAnt* 19:232–63.

———. 2001. "Athenian Democratic Ideology and Herodotus' *Histories*." *AJP* 122: 333–62.

———. 2002. "Herodotus on Greek History, 525–480." In Bakker et al. 2002, 521–49.

———. In press. "Herodotus and Politics." In C. Dewald and J. Marincola, eds., *The Cambridge Companion to Herodotus.* Cambridge.

———. 2005. "Revelry and Riot in Archaic Megara: Democratic Disorder or Ritual Reversal?" *JHS* 125.

———. Forthcoming. "Land, Labor and Economy in Solonian Athens: Breaking the Impasse between History and Archaeology." In J. Blok and A. Lardinois, eds., *Solon of Athens: New Historical and Philological Approaches.* Leiden: Brill.

———. In preparation (a). "Peisistratus, the Agora and the Development of Urban Space in Archaic Athens."

———. In preparation (b). "Selection by Lot in Athens: A Democratic Institution?"

Foucault, M. 1965. *Madness and Civilization: A History of Insanity in the Age of Reason.* Trans. R. Howard. New York.

———. 1980. *Power/Knowledge: Selected Interviews and Other Writings, 1972–1977.* Ed. C. Gordon. London.

———. 1990. *The History of Sexuality.* Trans. R. Hurley. New York.

Foxhall, L. 1995. "Bronze to Iron: Agricultural Systems and Political Structures in Late Bronze Age and Early Iron Age Greece." *ABSA* 90:239–50.

———. 1997. "A View from the Top: Evaluating the Solonian Property Classes." In L. Mitchell and Rhodes 1997, 113–36.

———. 1998. "Cargoes of the Heart's Desire: The Character of Trade in the Archaic Mediterranean World." In Fisher and van Wees 1998, 295–309.

French, A. 1959. "The Party of Peisistratus." *G&R* 6:46–57.

Fried, M. H. 1967. *The Evolution of Political Society: An Essay in Political Anthropology.* New York.

Friis Johansen, H. 1993. "A Poem by Theognis, Part II.3: Dating Theognis 19–38." *C&M* 44:5–29.

Frost, F. J. 1984. "The Athenian Military before Cleisthenes." *Historia* 33:283–94.

———. 1990. "Peisistratus, the Cults and the Unification of Attica." *AncW* 21:3–9.

Furley, W. D. 1996. *Andokides and the Herms.* BICS Supplementary vol. 65. London.

Gabba, E. 1994. "Da qualche considerazioni generali al caso della legge sull'impossibile neutralità." In G. Maddoli, ed., *L'Athenaion Politeia di Aristotele, 1891–1991: Per un bilancio di cento anni di studi.* Perugia.

Gabrielson, V. 1985. "The Naukraroi and the Athenian Navy." *C&M* 36:21–51.

Gagarin, M. 1981a. *Drakon and Early Athenian Homicide Law*. New Haven.

———. 1981b. "The Thesmothetai and the Early Athenian Tyranny Law." *TAPA* 111:71–77.

———. 1986. *Early Greek Law*. Berkeley and Los Angeles.

Gager, J. 1992. *Curse Tablets and Binding Spells from the Ancient World*. Oxford.

Gallant, T. W. 1982. "Agricultural Systems, Land Tenure and the Reforms of Solon." *ABSA* 77:111–24.

Gallop, D. 1997. *Plato: Defence of Socrates, Euthyphro, Crito*. Oxford.

Garland, R. 1984. "Religious Authority in Archaic and Classical Athens." *ABSA* 79:75–123.

Gawantka, W. 1985. *Die sogenannte Polis: Entstehung, Geschichte und Kritik der modernen althistorischen Grundbegriffe der griechische Staat, die griechische Staatsidee, die Polis*. Stuttgart.

Geertz, C. 1973. *The Interpretation of Cultures: Selected Essays*. New York.

Gehrke, H.-J. 1985. *Stasis: Untersuchungen zu den inneren Kriegen in den griechischen Staaten des 5. und 4. Jahrhunderts v.Chr.* Munich.

Gehrke, H.-J., and A. Möller, eds. 1996. *Vergangenheit und Lebenswelt: Soziale Kommunikation, Traditionsbildung und historisches Bewusstsein*. Tübingen.

Ghinatti, F. 1970. *I gruppi politici ateniesi fino alle guerre persiane*. Rome.

Giddens, A. 1984. *The Constitution of Society: Outline of the Theory of Structuration*. Oxford.

Glotz, G. 1904. *La solidarité de la famille dans le droit criminel en Grèce*. Paris.

Gluckman, M. 1956. *Custom and Conflict in Africa*. Oxford.

———. 1963. *Order and Rebellion in Tribal Africa*. London.

Gnoli, G., and J.-P. Vernant, eds. 1982. *La mort, les morts, dans les sociétés anciennes*. Cambridge.

Goldberg, B. 2003. *Arrogance: Rescuing America from the Media Elite*. New York.

Golden, M., and P. Toohey, eds. 1997. *Inventing Ancient Culture: Historicism, Periodization and the Ancient World*. London.

Goldhill, S. 1988. "Battle Narrative and Politics in Aeschylus' Persians." *JHS* 108:189–93.

———. 1990. "The Great Dionysia and Civic Ideology." In Winkler and Zeitlin 1990, 97–129.

Goldstein, J. A. 1972. "Solon's Law for an Activist Citizenry." *Historia* 21:538–45.

Gotte, H. R. 2001. *Athens, Attica and the Megarid: An Archaeological Guide*. London.

Graham, A. J. 1982. "The Colonial Expansion of Greece." In Boardman and Hammond 1982, 83–162.

Gras, M. 1987. "Amphores commerciales et histoire archaïque." *DArch* 5:41–50.

———. 1995. *La Méditerranée archaïque*. Paris.

Grasmück, E. L. 1978. *Exilium: Untersuchungen zur Verbannung in der Antike*. Munich.

Gray, V. 1996. "Herodotus and Images of Tyranny: The Tyrants of Corinth." *AJP* 117:361–89.

Green, J. R., and R. K. Sinclair. 1970. "Athenians in Eretria." *Historia* 19:515–27.

Gribble, D. 1999. *Alcibiades and Athens: A Study in Literary Presentation*. Oxford.

Griffin, J. 1998. "The Social Function of Attic Tragedy." *CQ* 48:39–61.

Grote, G. 1851. *History of Greece*. Vol. 3. London.

Gschnitzer, F. 1978. *Ein neuer spartanischer Staatsvertrag und die Verfassung des peloponnesischen Bundes*. Meisenheim.

Haas, J. 1982. *The Evolution of the Prehistoric State*. New York.

Hall, J. M. 1995. "How Argive Was the 'Argive' Heraion? The Political and Cultic Geography of the Argive Plain, 900–400 B.C." *AJA* 99:577–613.

———. 1997. *Ethnic Identity in Greek Antiquity*. Cambridge.

———. 2000. "Sparta, Lakedaimon and the Nature of Perioikic Dependency." In P. Flensted-Jensen, ed., *Further Studies in the Ancient Greek Polis*, Historia Einzelschriften 138, 73–89. Stuttgart.

———. 2002. *Hellenicity: Between Ethnicity and Culture*. Chicago.

Hall, L.G.H. 1989. "Remarks on the Law of Ostracism." *Tyche* 4:91–100.

Hammer, D. 1998. "The Politics of the *Iliad*." *CJ* 94:1–30.

———. 2002. *The* Iliad *as Politics: The Performance of Political Thought*. Norman, OK.

Hansen, M. H. 1975. *Eisangelia: The Sovereignty of the People's Courts in Athens in the Fourth Century B.C. and the Public Action against Unconstitutional Proposals*. Odense.

———. 1976. *Apagoge, Endeixis and Ephegesis against Kakourgoi, Atimoi and Pheugontes*. Odense.

———. 1978. "Demos, *Ecclesia* and *Dicasterion* in Classical Athens." *GRBS* 19:127–46. [Reprinted in Hansen 1983, 139–60.]

———. 1980. "Eisangelia in Athens: A Reply." *JHS* 100:91–95.

———. 1982. "The Athenian Heliaia from Solon to Aristotle." *C&M* 33:9–47. [Reprinted in Hansen 1989a, 219–61.]

———. 1983. *The Athenian Ecclesia: A Collection of Articles, 1976–1983*. Copenhagen.

———. 1987. *The Athenian Assembly in the Age of Demosthenes*. Oxford.

———. 1989a. *The Athenian Ecclesia*. Vol. 2, *A Collection of Articles, 1983–89*. Copenhagen.

———. 1989b. "Demos, Ekklesia, and Dikasterion: A Reply to Martin Ostwald and Josiah Ober." *C&M* 40:101–6. [Reprinted in Hansen 1989a, 213–18.]

———. 1989c. "The Athenian Heliaia from Solon to Aristotle." In Hansen 1989a, 219–62.

———. 1990a. "When Was Selection by Lot of Magistrates Introduced in Athens?" *C&M* 41:55–61.

———. 1990b. "Solonian Democracy in Fourth-Century Athens." In W. R. Connor, M. H. Hansen, K. A. Raaflaub, and B. S. Strauss, *Aspects of Athenian Democracy*, 71–99. Copenhagen.

———. 1991. *The Athenian Democracy in the Age of Demosthenes*. Oxford.

———, ed. 1993. *The Ancient Greek City-State*. Copenhagen.

Hanson, V. 1995. *The Other Greeks: The Family Farm and the Agrarian Roots of Western Civilization*. New York.

Harding, P. 1974. "The Theramenes Myth." *Phoenix* 20:101–11.

———. 1987. "Metics, Foreigners or Slaves? The Recipients of Honours in *IG* II^2 10." *ZPE* 67:176–82.

Harris, E. M. 1997. "A New Solution to the Riddle of the Seisachtheia." In L. Mitchell and Rhodes 1997, 103–12.

——. 2002. "Did Solon Abolish Debt-Bondage?" *CQ* 52:415–30.

Harris, W. V. 1989. *Ancient Literacy.* Cambridge, MA.

Harris-Cline, D. 1999. "Archaic Athens and the Topography of the Kylon Affair." *ABSA* 94:309–20.

Harrison, A. R. W. 1971. *The Law of Athens.* Vol. 2, *Procedure.* London. [2nd ed. 1997.]

Hartog, F., and J. Revel, eds. 2001. *Les usages politiques du passé.* Paris.

Harvey, F. D. 1966. "Literacy in the Athenian Democracy." *REG* 79:585–635.

Haubold, J. 2000. *Homer's People: Epic Poetry and Social Formation.* Cambridge.

Headlam, J. W. 1933. *Election by Lot at Athens.* 2nd ed. Cambridge.

Heftner H. 2000a. "Der Ostrakismos des Hyperbolos: Plutarch, Pseudo-Andokides und die *RSA* Ostraka." *RhM* 143:32–59.

——. 2000b. "Zur Datierung der Ostrakisierung des Hyperbolos." *RSA* 30:27–45.

——. 2001. "Die pseudo-andokideische Rede 'Gegen Alkibiades' ([And.] 4)—Ein authentischer Beitrag zu einer Ostrakophoriedebatte des 415 v.Chr?" *Philologus* 145:39–56.

Heisserer, A. J. 1971. "Alexander and the Greek Exiles." PhD dissertation, University of Cincinnati.

Herman, G. 1986. *Ritualised Friendship and the Greek City.* Cambridge.

Highby, L. I. 1936. *The Erythrae Decree: Contributions to the Early History of the Delian League and the Peloponnesian Confederacy.* Leipzig.

Hobsbawm, E., and T. Ranger, eds. 1983. *The Invention of Tradition.* Cambridge.

Hodder, I. 1982. *The Present Past: An Introduction to Anthropology for Archaeologists.* London.

Hodkinson, S. 2000. *Property and Wealth in Classical Sparta.* London.

Hodkinson, S., and A. Powell, eds. 1999. *Sparta: New Perspectives.* London.

Hölkeskamp, K.-J. 1992. "Written Law in Archaic Greece." *PCPS* 38:87–117.

——. 1999. *Schiedsrichter, Gesestzgeber und Gesetzgebung im archaischen Griechenland.* Stuttgart.

Hopkins, K. 1991. "From Violence to Blessing: Symbols and Rituals in Ancient Rome." In Molho et al. 1991, 479–98.

Hopper, R. J. 1961. "'Plain', 'Shore' and 'Hill' in Early Athens." *ABSA* 56:189–219.

Hornblower, S. 1991. *A Commentary on Thucydides.* Vol. 1, *Books I–III.* Oxford. [Reprinted with addenda and corrections 1997.]

——. 1992. "Creation and Development of Democratic Institutions in Ancient Greece." In J. Dunn, ed., *Democracy: The Unfinished Journey, 508 B.C.–A.D. 1993,* 1–16. Oxford.

——. 1995. *A Commentary on Thucydides.* Vol. 2, *Books IV–V.24.* Oxford.

Houby-Nielsen, S. 1992. "Interaction between Chieftains and Citizens? Seventh-Century-B.C. Burial Customs in Athens." *Acta Hyperborea* 4:343–74.

——. 1995. "'Burial Language' in the Archaic and Classical Kerameikos." *Proceedings of the Danish Institute at Athens* 1:129–91.

——. 1996. "The Archaeology of Ideology in the Kerameikos: New Interpretations of the Opferrinnen." In R. Hägg, ed., *The Role of Religion in the Early Greek Polis,* 41–54. Stockholm.

How, W. W., and J. Wells. 1912. A *Commentary on Herodotus*. 2 vols. Oxford.

Humphreys, S. C. 1978. *Anthropology and the Greeks*. London.

——. 1991. "A Historical Approach to Drakon's Law on Homicide." In M. Gagarin, ed., *Symposion 1990: Vorträge zur griechischen und hellenistischen Rechtsgeschichte*, 17–45. Cologne.

Hunt, L., ed. 1989. *The New Cultural History*. Berkeley and Los Angeles.

Hunter, V. 1973–74. "Athens *Tyrannis*: A New Approach to Thucydides." *CJ* 69: 120–26.

——. 1990. "Gossip and the Politics of Reputation in Classical Athens." *Phoenix* 44:299–325.

——. 1994. *Policing Athens: Social Control in the Attic Lawsuits, 420–320*. Princeton.

Hunter, V., and J. Edmondson, eds. 2000. *Law and Social Status in Classical Athens*. Oxford.

Hurwit, J. 1998. *The Athenian Acropolis: History, Mythology and Archaeology from the Neolithic Era to the Present*. Cambridge.

Jacoby, F. 1913. "Herodotus." *RE* Supplement band 2:205–520. [Reprinted in *Griechische Historiker* (Stuttgart, 1956), 7–164.]

——. 1944. "ΧΡΗΣΤΟΥΣ ΠΟΙΕΙΝ (Aristotle fr. 592R)." *CQ* 38:15–16.

——. 1949. *Atthis*. Oxford.

Jameson, M. H. 1971. "Sophocles and the Four Hundred." *Historia* 20:541–68.

Johnson, A. W., and T. Earle. 2000. *The Evolution of Human Societies: From Foraging Group to Agrarian State*. 2nd ed. Stanford, CA.

Johnston, A. W., and R. E. Jones. 1978. "The 'SOS' Amphorae." *ABSA* 73:103–41.

Johnstone, S. 1999. *Disputes and Democracy: The Consequences of Litigation in Ancient Athens*. Austin.

Jones, J. E., A. J. Graham, and L. H. Sackett. 1973. "An Attic Country House below the Cave of Pan at Vari." *ABSA* 68:355–452.

Jones, J. E., L. H. Sackett, and C.W.J. Eliot. 1962. "The Dema House in Attica." *ABSA* 57:75–114.

Jones, N. F. 1980. "The Civic Organization of Corinth." *TAPA* 110:161–93.

——. 1987. *Public Organization in Ancient Greece: A Documentary Study*. Philadelphia.

Jordan, B. 1992. "The Naukraroi of Athens and the Meaning of NEMΩ." *AC* 61:60–79.

Kagan, D. 1987. *The Fall of the Athenian Empire*. Ithaca.

Kahrstedt, U. 1934. *Staatsgebiet und Staatsangehörige in Athen*. Stuttgart.

Karavites, P. 1971. "Problems in the Athenian Democracy, 510–480 B.C.: Exiles—A Case of Political Irrationality." PhD dissertation, Loyola University, Chicago.

Keaney, J. J. 1970. "The Text of Androtion F6 and the Origin of Ostracism." *Historia* 19:1–11.

——. 1972. "A Late Byzantine Account of Ostracism." *AJP* 93:87–91.

——. 1981. "Aristotle, *Politics* 2.12.1274a22–b28." *AJAH* 6:97–100.

——. 1992. *The Composition of Aristotle's Athenaion Politeia: Observation and Explanation*. Oxford.

Keesling, C. M. 2003. *The Votive Statues of the Athenian Acropolis.* Cambridge.

Kelly, G. 1999. "Exilium: A History and Prosopography of Exile in the Roman Republic." PhD dissertation, Bryn Mawr.

Kertzer, D. I. 1988. *Ritual, Politics, and Power.* New Haven.

Kinzl, K. H. 1989. "On the Consequences of Following *AP* 21.3 (on the Phylai of Attika)." *Chiron* 19:347–65.

Knight, D. W. 1970. *Some Studies in Athenian Politics in the Fifth Century B.C.* Historia Einzelschriften 13. Wiesbaden.

Koch, C. 1991. *Volksbeschlüsse in Seebundangelegenheiten: Das Verfahrensrecht Athens im ersten attischen Seebund.* Frankfurt.

Konstan, D. 1997. *Friendship in the Classical World.* Cambridge.

Krentz, P. 1982. *The Thirty at Athens.* Ithaca.

———. 1984. "The Ostracism of Thoukydides, Son of Melesias." *Historia* 33:499–504.

———. 1986. "The Rewards for Thrasyboulos' Supporters." *ZPE* 62:201–4.

———. 1995. *Xenophon: Hellenika II.3.11–IV.2.* Warminster.

Kritsas, C. B. 1987. "Τὸ πρῶτο Μεγαρικὸ ὄστρακον." *Horos* 5:59–73.

Kurke, L. 1992. "The Politics of ἁβροσύνη in Archaic Greece." *ClAnt* 11:91–120.

———. 1994. "Crisis and Decorum in Sixth-Century Lesbos: Reading Alcaeus Otherwise." *QUCC* 47:67–92.

———. 1999. *Coins, Bodies, Games and Gold: The Politics of Meaning in Archaic Greece.* Princeton.

Kyrieleis, H. 1993. "The Heraion at Samos." In Marinatos and Hägg 1993, 125–53.

———. 1996. *Der grosse Kuros von Samos.* Bonn.

Lambert, S. D. 1993. *The Phratries of Attica.* Ann Arbor.

Lane Fox, R. 2000. "Theognis: An Alternative to Democracy." In Brock and Hodkinson 2000, 35–51.

Lang, M. L. 1990. *Ostraka.* Vol. 25 of *The Athenian Agora.* Princeton.

———. 1992. "Theramenes and Arginousai." *Hermes* 120:268–79.

Langdon, M. K. 1997. "Cult in Iron Age Attica." In S. Langdon, ed., *New Light on a Dark Age: Exploring the Culture of Geometric Greece*, 113–24. Columbia, MO.

Lanza, D. 1977. *Il tiranno e il suo pubblico.* Turin.

Lateiner, D. 1989. *The Historical Method of Herodotus.* Toronto.

Lavagnini, B. 1945–6. "Solone e il voto obbligatorio." *AAPal* 6:19–34.

Lavelle, B. M. 1991. "The Compleat Angler: Observations on the Rise of Peisistratus in Herodotus (1.59–64)." *CQ* 41:317–24.

———. 1992a. "Herodotus, Skythian Archers, and the *Doryphoroi* of the Peisistratids." *Klio* 74:78–97.

———. 1992b. "Peisistratus and the Mines of Thrace." *GRBS* 33:5–23.

———. 1993. *The Sorrow and the Pity: A Prolegomenon to a History of Athens under the Peisistratids, c. 560–510 B.C.* Stuttgart.

———. 2000. "Herodotus and the 'Parties' of Attika." *C&M* 51:51–102.

Lawton, C. L. 1995. *Attic Document Reliefs: Art and Politics in Ancient Athens.* Oxford.

Lécrivain, C. 1919. *L'exil politique dans l'histoire grecque.* Mémoires de l'Académie des Sciences, Inscriptions et Belles Lettres de Toulouse, 11th series, 7.

Le Goff, J. 1992. *History and Memory.* Trans. S. Rendell and E. Claman. New York. [originally published in Italian 1977.]

Legon, R. P. 1981. *Megara: The Political History of a Greek City-State to 336 B.C.* Ithaca.

Lenz, J. Unpublished. "Did Athens have Archons before Solon?"

Lewis, D. M. 1963. "Cleisthenes and Attica." *Historia* 12:22–40.

———. 1984. "Democratic Institutions and Their Diffusion." In *Praktika of the Sixth International Conference on Greek and Latin Epigraphy, Athens, October 3–9, 1982*, 55–61. Athens.

Lewis, S. 1996. *News and Society in the Greek Polis.* London.

Link, S. 1991. *Landverteilung und sozialer Frieden im archaischen Griechenland.* Stuttgart.

———. 2000. *Das frühe Sparta: Untersuchungen zur spartanischen Staatsbildung im 7. und 6. Jahrhundert v.Chr.* St. Katharinen.

Lipka, M. 2002. *Xenophon's Spartan Constitution: Introduction, Text, Commentary.* Berlin.

Loening, T. C. 1987. *The Reconciliation Agreement of 403–2 B.C. in Athens: Its Content and Application.* Stuttgart.

Loraux, N. 1986. *The Invention of Athens: The Funeral Oration in the Classical City.* Trans. A. Sheridan. Cambridge, MA. [Originally published in French 1981.]

———. 2000. *Born of the Earth: Myth and Politics in Athens.* Trans. S. Stewart. Ithaca. [Originally published in French 1996.]

———. 2002. *The Divided City: On Memory and Forgetting in Ancient Athens.* New York. [Originally published in French 1997.]

Luraghi, N., ed. 2001. *The Historian's Craft in the Age of Herodotus.* Oxford.

———. 2002. "Becoming Messenian." *JHS* 122:45–69.

MacDowell, D. M. 1963. *Athenian Homicide Law in the Age of the Orators.* Manchester.

———. 1978. *The Law in Classical Athens.* Ithaca.

———. 1986. *Spartan Law.* Edinburgh.

Macleod, C. W. 1983. *Collected Essays.* Ed. O. Taplin. Oxford.

Malkin, I. 1987. *Religion and Colonization in Ancient Greece.* Leiden.

———. 1993. "Land Ownership, Territorial Possession, Hero Cults and Scholarly Theory." In Rosen and Farrell 1993, 225–34.

———. 1994a. *Myth and Territory in the Spartan Mediterranean.* Cambridge.

———. 1994b. "Inside and Outside: Colonization and the Formation of the Mother City." In B. Augostino and D. Ridgway, eds., *Apoikia: Scritti in onore di Giorgio Buchner*, 1–9 Naples.

Mann, M. 1986. *The Sources of Social Power.* Vol. 1, *A History of Power from the Beginning to A.D. 1760.* Cambridge.

Manville, P. B. 1980. "Solon's Law of *Stasis* and *Atimia* in Archaic Athens." *TAPA* 110:213–21.

———. 1990. *The Origins of Citizenship in Ancient Athens.* Princeton.

Marinatos, N., and R. Hägg, eds. 1993. *Greek Sanctuaries: New Approaches.* London.

Mason, H. J. 1993 "Mytilene and Methymna: Quarrels, Borders and topography." *EMC* 37:225–50.

Mattingly, H. B. 1963. "The Growth of Athenian imperialism." *Historia* 12:257–73.

———. 1991. "The Practice of Ostracism at Athens." *Antichthon* 25:1–26.

———. 1992. "Epigraphy and the Athenian Empire." *Historia* 41:229–38.

———. 1996. *The Athenian Empire Restored: Epigraphic and Historical Studies.* Ann Arbor.

Maurizio, L. 1998. "The Panathenaic Procession: Athens' Participatory Democracy on Display?" In Boedeker and Raaflaub 1998, 297–317.

Mazarakis-Ainian, A. 1988. "Early Greek Temples: Their Origin and Function." In R. Hägg, N. Marinatos, and G. C. Nordquist, eds., *Early Greek Cult Practice*, 105–19. Stockholm.

———. 1995. "New Evidence for the Study of the Late Geometric–Archaic Settlement at Lathouriza in Attica." In C. Morris, ed., *Klados: Essays in Honour of J. N. Coldstream*, BICS Supplementary vol. 63, 143–55. London.

———. 1997. *From Rulers' Dwellings to Temples: Architecture, Religion and Society in Early Iron Age Greece (1100–700 B.C.).* Studies in Mediterranean Archaeology 121. Jonsered.

Mazzarino, S. 1947. *Fra oriente e occidente: Ricerche di storia greca arcaica.* Florence.

McGlew, J. F. 1993. *Tyranny and Political Culture in Ancient Greece.* Ithaca.

———. 1999. "Politics in the Margins: The Athenian Hetaireiai in 415 B.C." *Historia* 48:1–22.

McLellan, D. 1995. *Ideology.* 2nd ed. Minneapolis.

Meier, C. 1990. *The Greek Discovery of Politics.* Trans. D. McLintock. Cambridge, MA. [Abridgment of *Die Entstehung des Politischen bei den Griechen* (Frankfurt, 1980).]

Meier, M. 1998. *Aristokraten und Damoden: Untersuchungen zur inneren Entwicklung Spartas im 7. Jahrhundert v.Chr. und zur politischen Funktion der Dichtung des Tyrtaios.* Stuttgart.

Meiggs, R. 1972. *The Athenian Empire.* Oxford.

Merkelbach, R. 1969. "Das Distichon über den Ostrakismos des Xanthippos." *ZPE* 4:201–2.

Middleton, D. F. 1982. "Thrasyboulos' Thracian Support." *CQ* 32:298–303.

Migeotte, L. 1980. "Note sur l'emploi de *prodanizein.*" *Phoenix* 34:219–26.

Miles, M. 1998. *The City Eleusinion.* Vol. 31 of *The Athenian Agora.* Princeton.

Miller, S. G. 1978. *The Prytaneion: Its Function and Architectural Form.* Berkeley and Los Angeles.

———. 1995. "Architecture as Evidence for the Identity of the Early Polis." In M. H. Hansen, ed., *Sources for the Ancient Greek City-State: Acts of the Copenhagen Polis Center*, 2:201–44. Copenhagen.

Millett, P. 1989. "Patronage and Its Avoidance in Classical Athens." In A. Wallace-Hadrill, ed., *Patronage in Ancient Society*, 15–47. London.

Mirhady, D. 1997. "The Ritual Background to Athenian Ostracism." *AHB* 11:13–19.

Mitchell, B. M. 1975. "Herodotus and Samos." *JHS* 95:75–91.

Mitchell, L. G., and P. J. Rhodes, eds. 1997. *The Development of the Polis in Archaic Greece.* London.

Moles, J. 2002. "Herodotus and Athens." In Bakker et al. 2002, 33–52.

Molho, A., K. Raaflaub, and J. Emlen, eds. 1991. *City-States in Classical Antiquity and Medieval Italy.* Ann Arbor.

Möller, A. 2000. *Naucratis: Trade in Archaic Greece.* Oxford.

Monoson, S. S. 2000. *Plato's Democratic Entanglements: Athenian Politics and the Practice of Philosophy.* Princeton.

Moore, S. F., and B. G. Myerhoff, eds. 1977. *Secular Ritual.* Amsterdam.

Morgan, C. 1994. "The Evolution of a Sacral 'Landscape': Isthmia, Perachora, and the Early Corinthian State." In Alcock and Osborne 1994, 105–42.

——. 2003. *Early Greek States beyond the Polis*. London.

Morgan, K., ed. 2003. *Popular Tyranny: Sovereignty and Its Discontents in Classical Athens*. Austin.

Morris, I. 1986. "The Use and Abuse of Homer." *ClAnt* 5:81–138.

——. 1987. *Burial and Ancient Society: The Rise of the Greek City-State*. Cambridge.

——. 1988. "Tomb Cult and the 'Greek Renaissance': The Past in the Present in the Eighth Century B.C." *Antiquity* 62:750–61.

——. 1991. "The Early Polis as City and State." In J. Rich and A. Wallace-Hadrill, eds., *City and Country in the Ancient World*, 25–57. London.

——. 1996. "The Strong Principle of Equality and the Archaic Origins of Greek Democracy." In Ober and Hedrick 1996, 19–48.

——. 1998. "Archaeology and Archaic Greek History." In Fisher and van Wees 1998, 1–91.

——. 2000. *Archaeology as Cultural History*. Oxford.

——. 2002. "Hard Surfaces." In P. Cartledge, E. E. Cohen, and L. Foxhall, *Money, Labour and Land: Approaches to the Economies of Ancient Greece*, 8–43. London.

Morris, I., and B. Powell, eds. 1997. *A New Companion to Homer*. Leiden.

Morris, I., and K. A. Raaflaub, eds. 1998. *Democracy 2500? Questions and Challenges*. AIA Colloquium 2. Dubuque, IA.

Morris, S. P. 1992. *Daidalos and the Origins of Greek Art*. Princeton.

Mossé, C. 1964. "Classes sociales et régionalisme à Athènes au début du VIe siècle." *AC* 33:401–13.

——. 1969. *La tyrannie dans la Grèce antique*. Paris.

——. 1995. "Foreword." In de Polignac 1984/1995, vii–xi.

Muir, E. 1981. *Civic Ritual in Renaissance Venice*. Princeton.

Murray, O. 1987. "Herodotus and Oral History." In H. Sancisi-Weerdenburg and A. Kuhrt, eds., *Achaemenid History*, vol.2, *The Greek Sources*, 93–115. Leiden. [Reprinted in Luraghi 2001, 16–44.]

——, ed. 1990a. *Sympotica: A Symposium on the Symposion*. Oxford.

——. 1990b. "The Affair of the Mysteries: Democracy and the Drinking Group." In Murray 1990a, 149–61.

——. 2001. "Herodotus and Oral History Reconsidered." In Luraghi 2001, 314–25.

Nafissi, M. 1991. *La nascita del kosmos: Studi sulla storia e la società di Sparta*. Perugia.

——. 1999. "From Sparta to Taras: *Nomima, Ktiseis* and Relationships between Colony and Mother City." In Hodkinson and Powell 1999, 245–72.

Nagy, G. 1985. "Theognis and Megara: A Poet's Vision of His City." In Figueira and Nagy 1985, 22–81.

——. 1990a. *Greek Mythology and Poetics*. Ithaca.

——. 1990b. *Pindar's Homer: The Lyric Possession of an Epic Past*. Baltimore.

Nash, K. 2000. *Contemporary Political Sociology: Globalization, Politics and Power*. Oxford.

Neils, J., ed. 1992. *Goddess and Polis: The Panathenaic Festival in Classical Athens*. Princeton.

Nicholas, R. W. 1966. "Segmentary Factional Political Systems." In M. J. Swartz, V. W. Turner, and A. Tuden, eds., *Political Anthropology*, 49–59. Chicago.

Nissenbaum, S. 1996. *The Battle for Christmas*. New York.

North, H. 1966. *Sophrosyne: Self-knowledge and Self-restraint in Greek Literature*. Ithaca.

Ober, J. 1985. *Fortress Attica: Defense of the Athenian Land Frontier, 404–322 B.C.* Leiden.

———. 1989a. *Mass and Elite in Democratic Athens: Rhetoric, Ideology and the Power of the People*. Princeton.

———. 1989b. "The Nature of Athenian Democracy." *CP* 84:322–34. [Reprinted in Ober 1996, 107–22.]

———. 1993/1998. "The Athenian Revolution of 508/7 B.C.E.: Violence, Authority, and the Origins of Democracy." In Dougherty and Kurke 1993/1998, 215–32. [Reprinted in Ober 1996, 32–52.]

———. 1996. *The Athenian Revolution: Essays on Ancient Greek Democracy and Political Theory*. Princeton.

———. 1998. *Political Dissent in Democratic Athens: Intellectual Critics of Popular Rule*. Princeton.

———. 2003. "Tyrant Killing as Therapeutic Stasis: A Political Debate in Images and Texts." In K. Morgan 2003, 215–50.

Ober, J., and C. Hedrick, eds. 1996. *Dēmokratia: A Conversation on Democracies, Ancient and Modern*. Princeton.

Ogden, D. 1997. *The Crooked Kings of Ancient Greece*. London.

Okin, L. A. 1985. "Theognis and the Sources for the History of Archaic Megara." In Figueira and Nagy 1985, 9–21.

Ollier, F. 1933. *Le mirage spartiate*. Paris.

O'Neil, J. L. 1995. *The Origins and Development of Ancient Greek Democracy*. Lanham, MD.

Oost, S. I. 1972. "Cypselus the Bacchiad." *CP* 67:10–30.

Osborne, M. J. 1981–82. *Naturalization in Athens*. 2 vols. Brussels.

Osborne, R. 1983/84. "The Myth of Propaganda and the Propaganda of Myth." *Hephaistos* 5/6:61–70.

———. 1985a. *Demos: The Discovery of Classical Attika*. Cambridge.

———. 1985b. "Law in Action in Classical Athens." *JHS* 105:40–58.

———. 1985c. "The Erection and Mutilation of the Hermai." *PCPS* 31:47–73.

———. 1987. *Classical Landscape with Figures: The Ancient Greek City and Its Countryside*. London.

———. 1993. "Competitive Festivals and the Polis: A Context for Dramatic Festivals at Athens." In A. H. Sommerstein, S. Halliwell, J. Henderson, and B. Zimmerman, eds., *Tragedy, Comedy and the Polis*, 21–38. Bari.

———. 1994a. "Archaeology, the Salaminioi and the Politics of Sacred Space in Archaic Attica." In Alcock and Osborne 1994, 143–60.

———. 1994b. "Introduction: Ritual, Finance, Politics: An Account of Athenian Democracy." In R. Osborne and Hornblower 1994, 1–21.

———. 1996a. *Greece in the Making, 1200–479 BC*. London.

———. 1996b. "Pots, Trade and the Archaic Greek Economy." *Antiquity* 77:31–44.

——. 1998. "Early Greek Colonization? The Nature of Greek Settlement in the West." In Fisher and van Wees 1998, 251–69.

——. 2004. "Demography and Survey." In S. E. Alcock and J. F. Cherry, eds., *Side-by-Side Survey: Comparative Regional Studies in the Mediterranean World*, 163–72. Oxford.

——. Forthcoming. "Did Democracy Transform Athenian Space?" In R. C. Westgate, N.R.E. Fisher, and A.J.M. Whitley, eds., *Building Communities: House, Settlement and Society in the Aegean and Beyond*, xx–xx.

Osborne, R., and S. Hornblower, eds. 1994. *Ritual, Finance, Politics: Athenian Democratic Accounts Presented to David Lewis*. Oxford.

Ostwald, M. 1955. "The Athenian Legislation against Tyranny and Subversion." *TAPA* 86:103–28.

——. 1969. *Nomos and the Beginnings of the Athenian Democracy*. Oxford.

——. 1986. *From Popular Sovereignty to the Sovereignty of Law: Law, Society and Politics in Fifth-Century Athens*. Berkeley and Los Angeles.

——. 1988. "The Reform of the Athenian State by Cleisthenes." In J. Boardman, N.G.L. Hammond, D. M. Lewis, and M. Ostwald, eds., *The Cambridge Ancient History*, vol. 4, *Persia, Greece and the Western Mediterranean c. 525 to 479 B.C.*, 2nd ed., 303–46. Cambridge.

——. 2002. "Athens and Chalkis: A Study in Imperial Control." *JHS* 122:134–43.

Page, D. 1955. *Sappho and Alcaeus: An Introduction to the Study of Lesbian Poetry*. Oxford.

Pariente, A., M. Piérart, and J. P. Thalmann. 1986. "Travaux de l'École Français en Grèce en 1985." *BCH* 110:764–65.

Parker, R. 1983. *Miasma*. Oxford.

——. 1996. *Athenian Religion: A History*. Oxford.

Parker, V. 1998. "Τύραννος: The Semantics of a Political Concept from Archilochus to Aristotle." *Hermes* 126:145–72.

Penčak, W., M. Dennis, and S. P. Newman, eds. 2002. *Riot and Revelry in Early America*. University Park, PA.

Petzold, K.-E. 1990. "Zur Entstehungsphase der athenischen Demokratie." *RFIC* 118:145–78.

Phillips, D. J. 1991. "Men Named Thoukydides and the General of 440/39 B.C." *Historia* 40:385–95.

Piccirilli, L. 1975. *Megarika: Testimonianze e frammenti*. Pisa.

——. 1976. "Aristotele e l'atimia (*Athen. Pol.* 8,5)." *ASNP* 6:739–61.

Pomeroy, S. B., S. M. Burstein, W. Donlan, and J. T. Roberts. 1999. *Ancient Greece: A Political, Social and Cultural History*. Oxford.

Pritchett, W. K. 1974. *The Greek State at War*. Vol. 2. Berkeley and Los Angeles.

Powell, A., and S. Hodkinson, eds. 2002. *Sparta: Beyond the Mirage*. London.

Raaflaub, K. A. 1979. "Polis tyrannos: Zur Entstehung einer politischen Metapher." In G. W. Bowersock, W. Burkert, and M.C.J. Putnam, eds., *Arktouros: Hellenic Studies Presented to Bernard M. W. Knox on the Occasion of His 65th Birthday*, 237–52. Berlin.

——. 1980. "Des freien Bürgers Recht der freien Rede: Ein Beitrag zur Begriffs- und Sozialgeschichte der athenischen Demokratie." In W. Eck, H. Galsterer, and

H. Wolff, eds., *Studien zur antiken Sozialgeschichte: Festschrift F. Vittinghoff*, 7–57. Cologne.

———. 1983. "Democracy, Oligarchy, and the Concept of the 'Free Citizen' in Late Fifth-Century Athens." *Political Theory* 11:517–44.

———. 1985. *Die Entdeckung der Freiheit: Zur historischen Semantik und Gesellschaftsgeschichte eines politischen Grundbegriffes der Griechen.* Vestigia 37. Munich.

———. 1987. "Herodotus, Political Thought, and the Meaning of History." In Boedeker et al. 1987, 221–48.

———. 1988. "Athenische Geschichte und mündliche Überlieferung." In J. von Ungern-Sternberg and H. Reinau, eds., *Vergangenheit und mündlicher Überlieferung*, vol. 1 of *Colloquium Rauricum*, 197–225. Stuttgart.

———. 1991. "Homer und die Geschichte des 8. Jhs. v.Chr." In J. Latacz, ed., *Zweihundert Jahre Homer-Forschung*, 205–56. Stuttgart.

———. 1993. "Homer to Solon: The Rise of the Polis—The Written Sources." In Hansen 1993, 41–105.

———. 1996a. "Solone, la nuova Atene e l'emergere della politica." In S. Settis, ed., *I greci: Storia, cultura, arte, società* 2.1:1035–81. Turin.

———. 1996b. "Equalities and Inequalities in Athenian Democracy." In Ober and Hedrick 1996, 139–74.

———. 1997a. "Homeric Society." In I. Morris and Powell 1997, 624–48.

———. 1997b. "Soldiers, Citizens and the Evolution of the Early Greek Polis." In L. Mitchell and Rhodes 1997, 49–59.

———. 1998a. "Power in the Hands of the People: Foundations of Athenian Democracy." In I. Morris and Raaflaub 1998, 31–66.

———. 1998b. "The Thetes and Democracy (A Response to Josiah Ober)." In I. Morris and Raaflaub 1998, 87–103.

———. 1998c. "A Historian's Headache: How to Read 'Homeric Society'?" In Fisher and van Wees 1998, 169–93.

———. 1999. "Archaic and Classical Greece." In K. A. Raaflaub and N. Rosenstein, eds., *War and Society in the Ancient and Medieval Worlds*, 129–61. Cambridge, MA.

———. 2002. "Philosophy, Science, Politics: Herodotus and the Intellectual Trends of His Time." In Bakker et al. 2002, 149–86.

———. 2003a. "Stick and Glue: The Function of Tyranny in Fifth-Century Athenian Democracy." In K. Morgan 2003, 59–93.

———. 2003b. "The Alleged Ostracism of Damon." In G. W. Bakewell and J. P. Sickinger, eds., *Gestures: Essays in Ancient History, Literature and Philosophy Presented to Alan L. Boegehold*, 317–31. Oxford.

Rabinowitz, A. T. 2004. "Symposium, Community and Cultural Exchange in Archaic Sicily and South Italy." PhD dissertation, University of Michigan.

Rapke, T. T. 1988. "Cleisthenes the Tyrant Manqué." *AHB* 3:47–51.

Raubitschek, A. 1949. *Dedications from the Athenian Acropolis.* Cambridge, MA.

Rausch, M. 1999. *Isonomia in Athen: Veranderung des öffentlichen Lebens vom Sturtz der Tyrannis bis zur zweiten Perserabwehr.* Frankfurt.

Rebenich, S. 1998. "Fremdenfeindlichkeit in Sparta? Überlegungen zur Tradition der spartanischen Xenelasie." *Klio* 80:336–59.

Redfield, J. M. 1986. "The Development of the Market in Archaic Greece." In B. L. Anderson and A.J.H. Latham, eds., *The Market in History*, 29–57. London.

Renfrew, C., and J. F. Cherry, eds. 1986. *Peer Polity Interaction and Socio-Political Change*. Cambridge.

Rhodes, P. J. 1972. *The Athenian Boule*. Oxford. [Reprinted with addenda and corrigenda 1985.]

———. 1994. "The Ostracism of Hyperbolus." In R. Osborne and Hornblower 1994, 85–98.

———. 1995. "Ekklesia Kyria and the Schedule of Assemblies at Athens." *Chiron* 25:187–98.

———. 2003. "Nothing to Do with Democracy: Athenian Drama and the Polis." *JHS* 123:104–19.

Rhodes, P. J., and R. Osborne, eds. 2003. *Greek Historical Inscriptions, 404–323 BC*. Oxford.

Richer, N. 1998. *Les éphores: Etudes sur l'histoire et sur l'image de Sparte, VIIIe–IIIe siècles avant J.-C.* Paris.

Rihll, T. E. 1989. "Lawgivers and Tyrants (Solon frr. 9–11 West)." *CQ* 39:277–86.

Robb, J. E., ed. 1999. *Material Symbols: Culture and Economy in Prehistory*. Carbondale.

Roberts, J. T. 1982. *Accountability in Athenian Government*. Madison.

———. 1994a. *Athens on Trial: The Antidemocratic Tradition in Western Thought*. Princeton.

———. 1994b. "The Creation of a Legacy: A Manufactured Crisis in Eighteenth-Century Thought." In J. P. Euben, J. R. Wallach, and J. Ober, eds., *Athenian Political Thought and the Reconstruction of American Democracy*, 81–102. Ithaca.

———. 1996. "Athenian Equality: A Constant Surrounded by Flux." In Ober and Hedrick 1996, 187–202.

Robertson, N. 1978. "The Myth of the First Sacred War." *CQ* 28:38–73.

———. 1998. "The City Center of Archaic Athens." *Hesperia* 67:283–302.

Robinson, E. W. 1994. "Reexamining the Alcmeonid Role in the Liberation of Athens." *Historia* 93:363–69.

———. 1997. *The First Democracies: Early Popular Government outside Athens*. Stuttgart.

———. 2000. "Democracy in Syracuse, 466–412 B.C." *HSCP* 100:189–205.

Romer, F. E. 1982. "The AISYMNĒTEIA: A Problem in Aristotle's Historical Method." *AJP* 103:25–46.

Rosen, R., and J. Farrell, eds. 1993. *Nomodeiktes: Greek Studies in Honor of Martin Ostwald*. Ann Arbor.

Rosenbloom, D. 2002. "From Ponēros to Pharmakos: Theater, Social Drama and Revolution in Athens, 428–404 B.C.E." *ClAnt* 21:283–346.

Rosivach, V. J. 1987a. "Some Fifth- and Fourth-Century Views on the Purpose of Ostracism." *Tyche* 2:161–70.

———. 1987b. "Autochthony and the Athenians." *CQ* 37:294–306.

———. 1992. "Redistribution of Land in Solon, Fragment 34 West." *JHS* 112:153–57.

Rösler, W. 1980. *Dichter und Gruppe: Eine Untersuchung zu den Bedingungen und zur historischen Funktion früher griechischer Lyrik am Beispiel Alkaios*. Munich.

Roussel, D. 1976. *Tribu et cité*. Paris.

Runciman, W. G. 1982. "Origins of States: The Case of Archaic Greece." *Comparative Studies in Society and History* 24:351–77.

Ruschenbusch, E. 1960. "ΦΟΝΟΣ: Zum Recht Drakons und seiner Bedeutung für das Werden des athenischen Staates." *Historia* 9:129–54.

———. 1966. ΣΟΛΩΝΟΣ ΝΟΜΟΙ: *Die Fragmente des solonischen Gesetzwerkes mit einer Text und Überlieferungsgeschichte*. Historia Einzelschriften 9. Wiesbaden.

———. 1981. "Atthis und Politeia." *Hermes* 109:316–26.

Ryan, F. X. 1994. "The Original Date of the δῆμος πληθύων Provisions of IG I³ 105." *JHS* 114:120–34.

Sakellariou, M. B. 1990. *Between Memory and Oblivion: The Transmission of Early Greek Historical Traditions*. ΜΕΛΕΤΗΜΑΤΑ 12. Athens.

Salmon, J. B. 1984. *Wealthy Corinth: A History of the City to 338 BC*. Oxford.

Sancisi-Weerdenburg, H. 1993. "Solon's Hektemoroi and Pisistratid Dekatemoroi." In H. Sancisi-Weerdenburg, R. J. van der Spek, H. C. Teitler, and H. T. Wallinga, eds., *De Agricultura: In Memoriam Pieter Willem de Neeve*, 13–30. Amsterdam.

———. 2000a. "The Tyranny of Peisistratos." In Sancisi-Weerdenburg 2000c, 1–15.

———. 2000b. "Cultural Politics and Chronology." In Sancisi-Weerdenburg 2000c, 79–106.

———, ed. 2000c. *Peisistratos and the Tyranny: A Reappraisal of the Evidence*. Amsterdam.

Saxonhouse, A. 1986. "Myths and the Origins of Cities: Reflections on the Autochthony Theme in Euripides' *Ion*." In J. P. Euben, ed., *Greek Tragedy and Political Theory*, 252–73. Berkeley and Los Angeles.

———. 1996. *Athenian Democracy: Modern Mythmakers and Ancient Theorists*. Notre Dame, IN.

Scanlon, T. F. 1987. "Thucydides and Tyranny." *CSCA* 6:286–301.

Scheidel, W. 2002. "Aussagen der Testimonien über die Institution des Ostrakismos." In Siewert et al. 2002, 483–503.

———. 2003. "The Greek Demographic Expansion: Models and Comparisons." *JHS* 123:120–40.

Scheidel, W., and H. Taeuber. 2002. "T41: Aristoteles, *Ath. Pol.* 43.5 (ca. 328–325 v.Chr.)—Vorabstimmung in der Volksversammlung über die Abhaltung eines Ostrakismos." In Siewert et al. 2002, 465–71.

Schmitt-Pantel, P. 1981. "L'âne, l'adultère et la cité." In J. Le Goff and J.-C. Schmitt, eds., *Le charivari*, 117–22. Paris.

Schreiner, J. H. 1976. "The Origin of Ostracism Again." *C&M* 31:84–97.

Scully, S. 1990. *Homer and the Sacred City*. Ithaca.

Seaford, R. 1994. *Reciprocity and Ritual: Homer and Tragedy in the Developing City-State*. Oxford.

———. 2000. "The Social Function of Attic Tragedy: A Response to Jasper Griffin." *CQ* 50:30–44.

Sealey, R. 1960. "Regionalism in Archaic Athens." *Historia* 9:155–80. [Reprinted in R. Sealey, *Essays in Greek Politics* (New York, 1965).]

———. 1983a. "The Athenian Courts for Homicide." *CP* 78:275–96.

———. 1983b. "How Citizenship and the City Began in Athens." *AJAH* 8:97–129.

Seibert, J. 1979. *Die politischen Flüchtlinge und Verbannten in der griechischen Geschichte*. Darmstadt.

Shapiro, H. A. 1989. *Art and Cult under the Tyrants in Athens*. Mainz.

Shear, T. L. 1994. "'Ισονόμους τ 'Αθήνας ἐποιησάτην: The Agora and the Democracy." In Coulson et al. 1994, 225–48.

Shipley, G. 1987. *A History of Samos, 800–188 BC*. Oxford.

Sickinger, J. 1999. *Public Records and Archives in Classical Athens*. Chapel Hill.

Siewert, P. 1991. "Accuse contro i 'candidati' all'ostracismo per la loro condotta politica e morale." In M. Sordi, ed., *L'immagine dell'uomo politico: Vita pubblica e morale nell'antichità*, Contributi dell'Istituto di Storia Antica 17, 3–14. Milan.

———. 1999. "Il ruolo di Alcibiade nell'ostracismo di Iperbolo." In E. Luppino-Manes, ed., *Aspirazione al consenso a azione politica in alcuni contesti di fine V sec. a.C.: Il caso di Alcibiade*, 19–27. Alexandria.

———. 2002. "Der ursprüngliche Zweck des Ostrakismos (Versuch einer historischen Auswertung)." In Siewert et al. 2002, 504–9.

Siewert, P., S. Brenne, B. Eder, H. Heftner, and W. Scheidel, eds. 2002. *Ostrakismos-Testimonien*. Vol. 1. Historia Einzelschriften 155. Stuttgart.

Singor, H. W. 2000. "The Military Side of the Peisistratean Tyranny." In Sancisi-Weerdenburg 2000c, 107–29.

Sinos, R. 1993/1998. "Divine Selection: Epiphany and Politics in Archaic Greece." In Dougherty and Kurke 1993/1998, 73–91.

Smarczyk, B. 1990. *Untersuchungen zur Religionspolitik und politischen Propaganda Athen im delisch-attischen Seebund*. Quellen und Forschungen zur Antiken Welt 5. Munich.

Smith, J. A. 1989. *Athens under the Tyrants*. Bristol.

Smith, R. C. 1985. "The Clans of Athens and the Historiography of the Archaic Period." *EMC* 29:51–61.

Snodgrass, A. 1971. *The Dark Age of Greece: An Archaeological Survey of the Eleventh to Eighth Centuries BC*. Edinburgh. [Reprinted with addenda 2000.]

———. 1980. *Archaic Greece: The Age of Experiment*. Berkeley and Los Angeles.

———. 1982. "Les origines du culte des héros en Grèce antique." In Gnoli and Vernant 1982, 107–19.

———. 1986. "Interaction by Design: The Greek City-State." In Renfrew and Cherry 1986, 47–58.

———. 1987. *An Archaeology of Greece: The Present State and Future Scope of a Discipline*. Berkeley and Los Angeles.

———. 1993. "The Rise of the Polis: The Archaeological Evidence." In Hansen 1993, 30–40.

Sourvinou-Inwood, C. 1991. "On Herodotus 3.48 and 3.50–53." In C. Sourvinou-Inwood, *'Reading' Greek Culture: Texts and Images, Rituals and Myths*, 244–84. Oxford.

———. 1994. "Something to Do with Athens: Tragedy and Ritual." In R. Osborne and Hornblower 1994, 269–90.

Spahn, P. 1977. *Mittelschicht und Polisbildung*. Frankfurt.

Spencer, N. 1995a. "Early Lesbos between East and West: A 'Grey Area' of Aegean Archaeology." *ABSA* 90:269–306.

———. 1995b. "Multi-dimensional Group Definition in the Landscape of Rural Greece." In Spencer 1995d, 28–42.

———. 1995c. "Respecting Your Elders and Betters: Ancestor Worship at Antissa, Lesbos." *EMC* 39:45–60.

———. 1995d. *Time, Tradition and Society in Greek Archaeology*. London.

———. 2000. "Exchange and Stasis in Archaic Mytilene." In Brock and Hodkinson 2000, 68–81.

Stahl, M. 1987. *Aristokraten und Tyrannen im archaischen Athen*. Stuttgart.

Starr, C. G. 1965. "The Credibility of Early Spartan History." *Historia* 14:257–72. [Reprinted in C. G. Starr, *Essays on Ancient History* (Leiden, 1979), 134–43.]

Stein-Hölkeskamp, E. 1989. *Adelskultur und Polisgesellschaft: Studien zum griechischen Adel in archaischer und klassischer Zeit*. Stuttgart.

Stewart, A. 1986. "When Is a Kouros Not an Apollo?" In Mario del Chiaro, ed., *Corinthiaca: Studies in Honor of D. Amyx*, 54–70. Columbia, MO.

Strauss, B. S. 1986. *Athens after the Peloponnesian War: Class, Faction and Policy, 403–386 BC*. Ithaca.

Strøm, I. 1995. "The Early Sanctuary of the Argive Heraion and Its External Relations (8th–Early 6th Cent. B.C.)." *Proceedings of the Danish Institute at Athens* 1:37–127.

Stroud, R. S. 1968. *Drakon's Law on Homicide*. Berkeley and Los Angeles.

Sultan, N. 1999. *Exile and the Poetics of Loss in Greek Tradition*. Lanham, MD.

Szegedy-Maszak, A. 1978. "Legends of the Greek Law-Givers." *GRBS* 19:199–209.

Tabori, P. 1972. *The Anatomy of Exile: A Semantic and Historical Study*. London.

Taeuber, H. 2002. "Androtion *FgrHist* 324 F 6(ca. 340 v.Chr.): Die Einführung und erste Anwendung des Ostrakismos (488/7 v.Chr.)." In Siewert et al. 2002, 401–12.

Tandy, D. 1997. *Warriors into Traders: The Power of the Market in Early Greece*. Berkeley and Los Angeles.

Taylor, M. W. 1981. *The Tyrant Slayers: The Heroic Image in Fifth-Century-B.C. Athenian Art and Politics*. New York.

Telschow, K. 1952. "Die griechischen Flüchtlinge und Verbannten von der archaischen Zeit bis zum Restitutionsedikt Alexanders des Grossen (324)." PhD dissertation, Kiel.

Thalmann, W. G. 1998. *The Swineherd and the Bow: Representations of Class in the Odyssey*. Ithaca.

Thomas, R. 1989. *Oral Tradition and Written Record in Classical Athens*. Cambridge.

———. 1992. *Literacy and Orality in Ancient Greece*. Cambridge.

———. 2000. *Herodotus in Context: Ethnography, Science and the Art of Persuasion*. Cambridge.

———. 2001. "Ethnicity, Genealogy and Hellenism in Herodotus." In I. Malkin, ed., *Ancient Perceptions of Greek Ethnicity*, 213–33. Cambridge, MA.

Thommen, L. 1996. *Lakedaimonion politeia: Die Entstehung der spartanischen Verfassung*. Historia Einzelschriften 103. Stuttgart.

———. 2003. *Sparta: Verfassungs- und Sozialgeschichte einer griechischen Polis*. Stuttgart.

Thompson, E. P. 1975. *Whigs and Hunters: The Origins of the Black Act*. London.

———. 1993. *Customs in Common*. London.

Thompson, N. 1996. *Herodotus and the Origins of the Political Community: Arion's Leap*. New Haven.

Thomsen, R. 1972. *The Origin of Ostracism: A Synthesis*. Copenhagen.

Todd, S. C. 1993. *The Shape of Athenian Law*. Oxford.

Tucker, M. 1991. "Introduction." In M. Tucker, ed., *Literary Exile in the Twentieth Century: An Analysis and Biographical Dictionary*. Westport, CT.

Tulin, A. 1996. *Dike Phonou: The Right of Prosecution and Attic Homicide Procedure*. Stuttgart.

Tuplin, C. 1985. "Imperial Tyranny: Some Reflections on a Classical Greek Political Metaphor." *History of Political Thought* 6:348–75.

Turner, V. 1969. *The Ritual Process*. London.

Tzanetou, A. Forthcoming. *Staging Citizenship: Exile and Return in Athenian Tragedy*.

Underdown, D. 1985. *Revel, Riot, and Rebellion: Popular Politics and Culture in England, 1603–1660*. Oxford.

Usteri, P. 1903. *Ächtung und Verbannung im griechischen Recht*. Zurich.

van Effenterre, H. 1994. *Nomima: Recueil d'inscriptions politiques et juridiques de l'archaïsme grec*. Rome.

van Wees, H. 1999a. "The Mafia of Early Greece: Violent Exploitation in the Seventh and Sixth Centuries B.C." In K. Hopwood, ed., *Organized Crime in Antiquity*, 1–51. London.

———. 1999b. "Tyrtaeus' *Eunomia*: Nothing to Do with the Great Rhetra." In Hodkinson and Powell 1999, 1–41.

———. 2000. "Megara's Mafiosi: Timocracy and Violence in Theognis." In Brock and Hodkinson 2000, 52–67.

Vansina, J. 1985. *Oral Tradition as History*. Madison.

Vernant, J.-P., and P. Vidal-Naquet. 1988. *Myth and Tragedy in Ancient Greece*. Trans. J. Lloyd. New York.

Versnel, H. S. 1995. "Religion and Democracy." In W. Eder, ed., *Die athenische Demokratie im 4. Jahrhundert v.Chr.*, 367–87. Stuttgart.

Vickers, M. 1996. "Fifth-Century Chronology and the Coinage Decree." *JHS* 116:171–74.

Vinogradov, J. G. 2001. "Ostrakismos als strenges Kampfmittel für Demokratie im Lichte der neuen Funde aus Chersonesos Taurike." In D. Papenfuss and V. M. Strocka, eds., *Gab es das griechische Wunder? Griechenland zwischen dem Ende des 6. und der Mitte des 5. Jahrhunderts v.Chr.*, 379–86. Mainz.

Vinogradov, J. G., and M. I. Zolotarev. 1999. "L'ostracismo e la storia della fondazione di Chersonesos Taurica: Analisi comparata con gli ostraka dal Kerameikós di Atene." *Minima Epigraphica et Papyrologica* 2:111–31.

Vleminck, S. 1981. "La valeur de ἀτιμία dans le droit grec ancien." *LEC* 49:251–65.

von Fritz, K. 1977. "Nochmals das solonische Gesetz gegen Neutralität um Bürgerzwist." *Historia* 26: 245–47.

Wade-Gery, H. T. 1958. *Essays in Greek History*. Oxford.

Walker, W. H., and L. J. Lucero. 2000. "The Depositional History of Ritual and Power." In Dobres and Robb 2000, 130–47.

Wallace, R. W. 1989. *The Areopagus Council to 307 B.C.* Baltimore.
———. 1994. "Private Lives and Public Enemies: Freedom of Thought in Classical Athens." In Boegehold and Scafuro 1994, 127–55.
———. 1998. "Solonian Democracy." In I. Morris and Raaflaub 1998, 11–29.
———. 2000. Review of Carawan 1998. *BMCRev* 2000.05.02.
Wallinga, H. T. 2000. "The Athenian Naukraroi." In Sancisi-Weerdenburg 2000c, 131–46.
West, M. L. 1974. *Studies in Greek Elegy and Iambus.* Berlin.
———. 1989. "The Early Chronology of Attic Tragedy." *CQ* 39:251–54.
Whitbread, I. 1995. *Greek Transport Amphorae: A Petrological and Archaeological Study.* Athens.
Whitehead, D. 1978. "ΙΣΟΤΕΛΕΙΑ, a Metaphor in Xenophon." *Eirene* 16:19–22.
———. 1984. "A Thousand New Athenians." *LCM* 9:8–10.
———. 1986. "The Ideology of the Athenian Metic: Some Pendants and a Reappraisal." *PCPS* 32:147–48.
Whitley, J. 1988. "Early States and Hero Cults: A Reappraisal." *JHS* 108:173–82.
———. 1991a. "Social Diversity in Dark Age Greece." *ABSA* 86:341–65.
———. 1991b. *Style and Society in Dark Age Greece.* Cambridge.
———. 1995. "Tomb and Hero Cult in Archaic Greece." In Spencer 1995d, 43–63.
Wilentz, S. 1985. *Rites of Power: Symbolism, Ritual and Politics since the Middle Ages.* Philadelphia.
Will, E. 1955. *Korinthiaka.* Paris.
Wilson, D. F. 2002. *Ransom, Revenge and Heroic Identity in the* Iliad. Cambridge.
Winkler, J. J. 1990. "Phallos Politikos: Representing the Body Politic in Athens." *Differences* 2:29–45.
Winker, J.J., and F. I. Zeitlin, eds. 1990. *Nothing to Do with Dionysos? Athenian Drama in Its Social Context.* Princeton.
Wohl, V. 1996. "Εὐσεβείας ἕνεκα καὶ φιλοτιμίας: Hegemony and Democracy at the Panathenaia." *C&M* 47:25–88.
———. 1999. "The Eros of Alcibiades." *ClAnt* 18:340–85.
———. 2002. *Love among the Ruins: The Erotics of Democracy in Classical Athens.* Princeton.
Wolpert, A. 2002. *Remembering Defeat: Civil War and Civic Memory in Ancient Athens.* Baltimore.
Wyse, W. 1892. "*Prodanizein.*" *CR* 6:254–57.
Yoffee, N. 1993. "Too Many Chiefs? (or, Safe Texts for the '90s)." In N. Yoffee and A. Sheratt, eds., *Archaeological Theory: Who Sets the Agenda?* 60–78. Cambridge.

INDEX LOCORUM

Aeschines
    1.39, 197
    1.111–112, 283
    2.235, 197
    3.258, 298
Aeschylus
  Ag.
    1410, 11n34
  Eu.
    976–86, 167–68
  PV
    224–25, 256, 269
  Supp.
    605–24, 236
    924–44, 236
Alcaeus (Campbell)
    fr.6, 43
    fr.70, 41n44
    fr.129, 36nn17 and 44
    fr.130, 42n46
    fr.208, 43
    fr.331, 42n48
    fr.332, 44
    fr.348, 45
Andocides
    1.2–35, 180
    1.36, 195
    1.73–79, 10n26, 193
    1.81–90, 203
    1.96–98, 11n27, 179,
      193–94
    1.106, 252, 267
    1.107, 152
    2.26, 267
    4.2, 170
    4.3, 162, 217, 219
    4.14, 156
    4.32, 164n94
    4.33, 156
    4.34, 152
    fr.3.2, 172
    fr.5, 172
Androtion (*FGrH* 324)
    fr.6, 153, 281–82
    fr.42, 171

Antiphon
    5.47, 224
    5.68, 167
Aristophanes
  Av.
    1012, 298
    1422–432, 225n71
  Eq.
    445, 80, 82
    855–57, 146–47, 149
    1304–315, 172
  Lys.
    641–47, 116
    664–67, 129
  Pac.
    681, 147
  Plut.
    627, 147, 153
  Thesm.
    837, 172
  Vesp.
    947, 147
Aristotle
  Ath. Pol.
    1, 11n30, 89, 180
    2.1, 91
    2.2, 94
    3.1–4, 97
    5.1–2, 91
    6.1, 54
    7.1, 92, 216n37
    7.3, 93
    7.5, 93
    8.1–2, 97
    8.4, 92, 93
    8.5, 10n25, 98–100
    9.1, 95
    13.1–2, 99, 100–101
    13.4, 102, 103
    14.1–4, 102, 108, 111–14
    15.1–3, 118–19
    15.3–5, 66n152, 127n194,
      198n265
    16.2–3, 76, 125
    16.5, 126

Aristotle (*continued*)
    16.7–8, 124
    16.9, 127
    16.10, 10n25, 26n50, 83–84, 131,
        179, 194, 266
    17–19, 127–31
    18.2, 125
    19.1, 124, 270
    20, 131n222, 135–42
    21.6, 130n211
    22.1–6, 131, 153, 176, 215,
        265–66, 281
    22.7–8, 149, 152, 166–67
    23, 166
    25, 167
    27, 164n94, 167
    28, 166–69
    29–33, 182n177, 183–85
    34, 191, 196
    35, 188, 197
    36, 198
    37, 197–98
    38, 201–2
    39, 203
    40, 201, 204, 213
    43.5, 146, 164
Oec.
    1346b17, 65n148
Poet.
    1448a, 55n104
Pol.
    1265b12–16, 71
    1265b39–272a32, 296
    1273b35–274a3–5, 95, 97, 176
    1274a1–22, 216n37
    1275b26–30, 195
    1282b, 274
    1284a–b, 153n35, 233–34,
        246n18, 274–76, 278
    1285a32–38, 44–45
    1294b33–34, 295
    1300a18–19, 57
    1302b15–21, 153
    1304b20, 55n100
    1304b31–34, 288
    1304b35–40, 57
    1305a8–29, 36n15, 51–52,
        127n194
    1306b30, 292
    1311a10, 198n265, 250n26
    1311a20–22, 246n18

    1311b27–29, 41n42
    1313b18–22, 75
    1313b24, 65n146
    1315b12–30, 76
    1319b1–33, 288
Rhet.
    1375b, 195
    fr.611 (Rose), 74, 75, 76
Athenaeus
    589, 156
    602a, 65n148
    695a–b, 132
Craterus (*FGrH* 342)
    fr.17, 192
Cratinus (Kassel-Austin)
    fr.73, 169
Demosthenes
    15.22, 199
    20.59, 193
    21.43, 11nn30 and 31
    22.54–55, 188
    23.62, 10n25
    23.204, 155, 177
    24.45, 217n39
    24.59, 217n39
    24.147, 217
    24.149–51, 218
    24.154, 185
    24.166–67, 188
    26.6, 152, 166
    37.4, 166
    58.67, 262
    59.4, 217
    60.4–8, 235, 237, 257
Dinarchus
    1.25, 199
    2.24, 298
Diodorus Siculus
    4.57–58, 293
    7.9, 71
    8.21, 292
    11.55, 146, 148, 153, 281
    11.77, 167
    11.86–87, 153, 285–86
    11.88, 210
    12.7, 211
    12.15, 99n79
    12.27–28, 188, 224
    13.34, 183
    13.37–52, 182n177
    13.103, 195

13.107, 196
14.3, 196, 260n41
14.5, 198
14.6, 199
14.32–33, 198, 200–202
14.34–36, 288
Diogenes Laertius
 1.56, 99
 1.58, 98
 1.74–83, 45n62, 48
 1.98, 245
 2.12–14, 180
 2.40–42, 11n29, 180
Dionysios of Halicarnassus
 Ant. Rom.
  3.36, 100
  3.45, 71n182
  3.46–47, 73
Ephorus (FGrH 70)
 fr.118, 296
Euripides
 Heracl.
  12–33, 235–36
  175, 236
  303–19, 236
 Supp.
  337–80, 236
  444–46, 269
Gellius, Aulus
 2.12, 98
Herodotus
 1.23, 74
 1.56, 237, 293
 1.59, 102, 108–11, 118n158, 124,
  125, 128
 1.60, 7n7, 105, 111–17, 125
 1.61, 111, 117–19
 1.62–64, 119–21, 128, 130, 188,
  250–53
 1.65, 232, 290, 298
 1.66–68, 292n15
 1.151, 37n19
 2.161, 249
 3.26, 68
 3.30–32, 256
 3.39, 61n119, 64, 65n143,
  66n154, 247–49
 3.44–47, 67–68, 139n243, 188,
  247–49, 251–52
 3.48, 66n152
 3.50–53, 188, 253–56

 3.54–59, 67–68, 139n243
 3.60, 65nn145 and 147
 3.80, 188, 198, 255n33
 3.81, 55n100
 3.120, 66n152
 3.122, 61n119
 3.148, 298
 3.154, 109n130
 4.3, 188
 4.145, 290
 4.152, 61n123
 4.159, 249
 4.162–64, 68n167
 5.55–65, 127–31, 259n40
 5.65, 102, 238
 5.66, 135–38
 5.69, 137
 5.70, 89n38, 135
 5.71, 80–82
 5.72, 9n18, 11n33, 135, 139,
  179, 186
 5.73, 142
 5.74, 135n236, 179
 5.77, 211, 222
 5.78, 188
 5.91, 132–33
 5.92, 74, 186–88, 233, 245–47,
  269
 5.94, 128, 133
 5.95, 74, 245
 5.96, 133
 6.35–36, 122
 6.39, 123
 6.52, 291
 6.57, 295
 6.61–70, 297
 6.71–72, 296
 6.73–75, 297
 6.82, 297
 6.99, 188
 6.102, 154n41
 6.103, 123
 6.107, 133
 6.121–24, 124, 154n41
 6.125, 130n211
 6.136, 180
 7.103, 188
 7.104, 11n35
 7.144–45, 166
 7.161, 237
 7.223, 188

Herodotus (*continued*)
    8.61, 11n35
    8.76, 152
    8.79, 152, 166
    8.95, 152
    8.110–25, 177
    8.131, 152
    9.26–28, 235, 257–58
    9.114–21, 152
Homer
  Il.
    2.547–48, 237
    18.487–508, 84n20
  Od.
    4.244–46, 109n130
    11.273–80, 85n21
IC
    2.2.4, 26n50
    4.14, 26n50
IG
    1^3 11, 215
    1^3 14, 207–10
    1^3 15, 208, 211
    1^3 27, 221
    1^3 34, 214
    1^3 37, 211
    1^3 39, 211, 225n71
    1^3 40, 210–23
    1^3 48, 211, 224
    1^3 71, 214
    1^3 76, 215
    1^3 83, 212, 215
    1^3 96, 206, 224
    1^3 104, 10, 26n50, 84–89
    1^3 105, 216–17
    1^3 131, 132n225
    2^2 10, 201
    4^2 1.42, 51n84
IK
    Erythrae 17, 26n50
Isocrates
    4.15–20, 230
    4.24–25, 237
    4.52–58, 235–36, 257
    4.100–14, 230–31
    4.107–9, 210
    7.67, 197–98, 265
    8.138, 236
    12.35–65, 231
    12.66–259, 232, 235, 237, 257
    15.21, 218

    16.12, 262
    16.26, 267
    16.42, 195
    20.11, 197
Justin
    5.9, 198–200
    5.10, 202
Lycurgus
  Leoc.
    112–15, 192
    117–19, 179, 281
    125–26, 193–94
Lysias
    2.11–16, 235, 257–58
    2.17, 238
    2.55–60, 232
    12.21, 264
    12.95–97, 261–62
    12, 195–202
    13.12, 195–96
    13.14, 197
    13.44–52, 201
    13.71–73, 192–93
    14.29, 164n94
    14.39, 152
    18.10–12, 202
    20.14, 193
    22.2, 213
    24.25, 199
    25.22, 7n9, 198
    25.24–28, 202–3
    30.10–14, 196
    31.1, 217
    31.27–28, 98, 199
ML
    2, 26n50
    6, 121, 122
    16, 65n143, 66n155
    23, 152
    40, 207–10
    45, 214, 226
    85, 194
Nic.Dam. (*FGrH* 90)
    fr.57, 71, 73, 74, 75, 245, 249
    fr.58, 74, 245
    fr.60, 76
Pausanias
    1.27, 210
    1.28.1, 80–82, 90
    2.13, 294
    2.24.7, 102

3.3.3, 291n9
3.5.2, 295
4.4, 71
4.26, 295
7.25.3, 80n1
Philochorus (*FGrH* 328)
fr.30, 146–49, 153, 281
fr.64b, 167
Pindar
Isth.
9.3–4, 293
Pyth.
1.62–65, 293
7.18–21, 155, 177
Plato
Ap.
36b–37e, 11n29, 180, 272–73
Crit.
44b–c, 11n29, 180
Leg.
949e–950a, 298
Menex.
237–39, 235, 237–38, 257
244e, 236
Rep
562d, 55n100
566b, 111n137
Plato [comicus] (Kassel-Austin)
fr.203, 153, 171–72
Plutarch
Alc.
13, 170–71
17–18, 174
33, 195
Arist.
1, 164n94
2–3, 166
7.2–6, 146, 148–49, 152, 153,
167, 170–71
8.2, 166
24, 152
Cim.
4.4–7, 156
10–16, 167
Lyc.
6, 291
26, 295
27, 298
Lys.
1.2, 73
27.2–6, 199–200

Mor.
295c–d, 53n95, 54
295f–96b, 63n134
303f–4c, 63n136
304e–f, 54n97, 55n100
550b–c, 98–100
599a–607f, 14n50.
772e–73b, 73
823f, 98
833–34, 192–93
835f, 200
859c–d, 76
Nic.
6, 164n94
11, 153, 170–71, 174
23, 180
Per.
4, 164n94
7, 210
9–10, 167
11–14, 168
15, 169
16.3, 152n31
22–23, 211
Sol.
12.1–9, 80–82, 89
13.1, 90–91, 102n90
14.3, 91
17.1, 92
18.1–2, 93
18.3, 95
18.6, 95, 96
19.4, 10n25, 11n31, 92, 194
20.1, 98–100
29.1, 91n48, 102–7
30.1–4, 108–12, 127n194
Them.
3–4, 166
22, 153, 155, 177
23, 155
Thes.
32–35, 153
Polyaenus
1.21, 111
1.23, 66n152, 67n162
6.45, 64n140, 66n152
Sappho (Campbell)
fr.148, 46–7
Solon (West)
fr.11, 127n194
fr.15, 12n42

Solon (*continued*)
    fr.27, 35n.12
    fr.36, 35, 94, 95
Sophocles
  Aj.
    202, 237
  OC
    208, 11n34
    1357, 11n35
  OT
    236–43, 256
    402, 11n33
    584–91, 269
    1000, 11n34
  Phil.
    1018, 11n35.
  Trach.
    647, 11n34
Strabo
    6.2.57, 294
    6.3.2, 292
    8.5.5, 296
    13.2.3, 42, 47
Theognis (West)
    53–58, 53
    57–58, 12n42
    145–46, 53
    149–50, 53
    239–43, 35n12
    315–18, 12n42
    332a–b, 57–58
    341–50, 57–58
    1197–202, 57–58
Theophrastus
    fr.139, 170
Theopompus (*FGrH* 115)
    fr.178, 298
Thucydides
    1.2, 237–38, 259
    1.12, 293
    1.13, 61n119
    1.18, 290
    1.20–21, 124n184, 127, 187
    1.24–30, 206
    1.68–77, 227–29
    1.94–95, 297
    1.98–99, 226
    1.102, 167
    1.103, 295
    1.107, 168
    1.108, 210

    1.113, 206, 210
    1.114, 205, 296
    1.115–17, 188, 206, 224
    1.117, 152n31
    1.122–24, 227
    1.126, 11n33, 80–82, 89
    1.128–34, 297
    1.135, 155, 177, 179
    1.144, 298
    2.21, 296
    2.27, 205
    2.35–46, 169, 298
    2.52–53, 269
    2.58–65, 269
    2.63, 233
    2.65, 55n100, 169, 172, 184
    2.70, 205
    3.36–49, 55n100, 172, 205–6,
      209, 233, 269
    3.50, 205
    3.69–85, 205, 269
    3.85, 7n8
    3.98, 179
    4.27–28, 269
    4.65, 10n21, 180
    5.3, 205
    5.16–17, 296
    5.18, 152
    5.26, 179
    5.32, 205
    5.47, 212, 215
    5.63, 296
    5.116, 205
    6.1, 55n100, 269
    6.8–28, 55n100, 174–75, 180,
      184, 268–70, 269
    6.53–59, 116, 124, 125, 127–129,
      132, 175, 180, 187, 269–70
    6.60–61, 55n100, 175, 180, 269–70
    8.1–68, 182, 183–86, 189
    8.70, 186
    8.73–86, 153, 171, 186–90
    8.89–98, 183, 190–92
Tyrtaeus (West)
    fr.2, 293
    fr.5, 294
    fr.10–12, 292
Xenophon
  An.
    3.4.26, 188
    4.8.25, 295

Ap.
    23, 272n69
[Ath.Pol.]
    1.5, 55n100
    1.13–14, 55n100, 206n4, 225
    1.16, 206n4, 224–25
Hell.
    1.4, 271
    1.5, 271
    1.7. 179–80, 192–93, 195–96, 213
    2.1, 271
    2.2, 195–96

2.3, 195–98
2.4, 7n9, 198–204, 260–61, 265
2.20, 193
3.5, 296
6.5, 236
Lac.
    2.8–9, 188
    10.2, 295
    14.4, 298
    15.7, 296
Mem.
    1.1.18, 217

GENERAL INDEX

acropolis, at Athens, 116, 120; decrees on, 220; dedications on, 125; and ostraca, 148

Adams, J., and ostracism, 144, 278

adultery, and ostracism, 155, 156

Aegina, 166, 205, 297

Aegospotami, 271

Aeschylus, 167, 235n101, 236, 257n39

Africa, 34, 38

agency, 21. *See also* elites

Agis, 296n37

agora: at Athens, 116, 120; decrees in, 220; and ostraca, 148n13; and ostracism, 149, 162, 163–64

agriculture, in Athens, 26–28, 147n10; on Lesbos, 37–39. *See also* trade

Aiakes, 32, 64, 66

aisymnetai (elected tyrants), 44

Alcaeus, 34n5, 35n10, 38; brothers of, 42–44; poetry of, 39–45, exile of, 44

Alcibiades (the Elder): as a candidate for ostracism, 156, 170–75, 219; and democracy, 184; exile of, 8–9, 180, 184; ostraca against, 171, 177n150; ostracism of, 164n94; recall of, 190, 195n248, 271; representation of, 267–71; at Sparta, 298; trial of, 175; as trickster, 173

Alcibiades (the Younger), 262

Alcmeonidae: as candidates for ostracism, 176–77; and Cylon, 81–90, 102; and Delphi, 22, 129–30, 133; exile of, 8, 11n30, 84, 90, 121–22, 128–32, 252; family tradition of, 130n212, 134, 243; ostraca against, 156; and Persia, 177; residence of, 106; and Sparta, 130; trial of, 80, 90, 180

Alexander the Great, exile decree of, 14

Alexicles, 192

Alopece (deme), 124, 130

Amasis, 248

amnesty, 217n39; of 405 BCE, 193; of 403 BCE, 203–4. *See also* Solon

Amorgos, 63

Amphipolis, 179

Amyclae, 290

Anaphlystus, 106

Anaxagoras, 180

Anaximander, 298

Anchimolus, 130

Anderson, B., 6n3

Anderson, G., 6n3, 106, 114n146, 122n170

Androtion, 146n4, 281–82

anthropology, cultural, 113, 145; neo-evolutionary approaches, 16–17; use of in historical research, 4. *See also* factions; ritual; states

Antiphon, 182, 192–93, 224

Antissa, 37

Anytus, 198

Apollo, 254

Apries, 249

archaeology, survey, 21, 291

Archeptolemos, 192–93

Archestratus, 214

Archias, 73

archons (magistrates), at Athens, 25n47, 26, 102, 121, 127; selection of, 97, 176, 282

Areopagus Council, 82, 92, 97, 139, 168, 178, 216n37, 283

Arginusae, 180, 193, 195, 296

Argos, 50, 130, 293; and Athenian exiles, 199–200; early social organization of, 20; ostracism at, 285, 287

Arion, 74

Arisbe, 37

Aristarchus, 192–93

Aristides: ostraca against, 157n63, 160n83, 166; ostracism of, 148–49, 166–67, 176; recall of, 152

Aristocrates, 262

Aristophanes, 147, 173. See also comedy.

Aristotle, 3, 13, 31; on democracy, 55, 244, 247, 265–68, 274–76, 278; on ostracism, 233–34, 241–42, 247, 265–68, 274–76, 278, 281–82; on tyranny, 41

Aristoteles, 195; return of, 196

Arthmius (of Zelea), 298n50

asebeia (impiety), penalties for, 179–80, 272

assembly (political): at Athens, 93, 95–96, 108–10, 163, 173, 185, 208–9; 216–19; at Mytilene, 42

Athena: cult of, 112–18, 221; dedications to, 222–23; temple of, 114n146, 115–16

Athens: conflict with Megara, 102; early settlement patterns of, 25, 26; early social organization of, 18, 20; and protection of weak, 55–59, 235–39; and reception of exiles, 235–39, 255–59; regions of, 102–7; relations with allies, 205–39. *See also* democracy; empire; ideology

atimia (outlawry), 217n39; in Athenian decrees, 212–15; of Cylon, 83, 178; definition of, 10–11; 78–79; and Solon, 92; and tyranny, 194, 266. *See also* legal system

Attica. *See* Athens

autochthony, myth of, 234, 237–39

Babylon, 234

Bacchiadae, 30, 32, 69, 71–74, 77, 245; building projects of, 72

Bacchielli, L., 288

Balcer, J. M., 213, 215, 223

ballots: leaves as, 283–87; secret, 217n39. *See also* ostraca

Balot, R., 185n193, 228n83

Bell, C., 159

Berger, S., 286

Bers, V., 159n78, 163

Black Sea, 38

Blanton, R. E., 15–16

Blok, J., 113nn141, 143

blood-price, 84

bodyguard, of Peisistratus, 108–11; of tyrants, 41n43

Boedeker, D., 292

Boeotia, 37, 199, 206, 210, 222

Boule. *See* council

Bouleutic oath. *See* oaths

boundaries, and group identity, 6. See also *horoi*

Bourdieu, P., 5, 159n80

Bourriot, F., 25n48

Brauron, 110, 115

Brenne, S., 146n4, 148nn13, 15; 154nn38, 42, 43, and 44, 158, 285n1 et passim

bribery, 218; and ostracism, 156, 163, 295–97

Bronze Age, 17; on Lesbos, 37; on Mytilene, 49; at Sparta, 293

brotherhoods (*fratrai*), 17, in Athens, 25, 86–87

Brumfiel, E., 16n3, 21n24, 22, 104, 107

burial, 17, 19, 21–24; in Athens and Attica, 23–24, 25; in Mytilene, 38. *See also* funeral oration

Burke, P., 5n1, 55n103, 97n75

Burkert, W., 157

Butadae (deme), 107.

Callias, son of Cratius, ostraca against, 154, 177

Callias, son of Didymias, ostracism of, 164n94

Callias, son of Hipponicus, exile of, 124

Callixenus, ostraca against, 154, 160n83

Cambyses, 67, 247–48

Camp, J., 148n13

Caria, 60

Cartledge, P., 290–94

Cavanagh, W. et al, 291–92

Ceramicus (Potters' Quarters), ostraca from, 148nn13 and 15, 152n30, 157

Chaereas, 187

Chalcidice, 118

Chalcis, and Athenian exiles, 199; defeat of, 222

Charicles, exile of, 195; return of, 196

charivari, 160n85

Chersonesus, 122, 123; ostracism at, 287–88

children, and tyrants, 188, 205n1, 231, 251–52

Chios, 234

Christ, M., 145n3, 165n97

Cimon, (sixth-century), 152; exile of, 123–24

Cimon (fifth-century): ostracism of, 152, 156, 167–68; ostracon against, 156; and Sparta, 152, 298

citizenship, 219, 221; at Athens, 88, 94–96, 103; grants of, 201–2, 221, 232, 237

civil war. *See* stasis

class, 12n37; in Athens, 103, 107, 225; conflict between, 16, 31, 107; emergence of, 20; and states, 107. *See also* elites; non-elites

Cleippides, ostraca against, 160n83

Cleisthenes, 2, 80, 100, 121, 122, 131, 133; exile of, 135; and foundation of Athenian democracy, 133–42, 150, 279; and ostracism, 281–84

Cleomenes, 130, 135–41, 297

Cleon, 147, 172–73, 206n3, 233n95; as a candidate for ostracism, 173

Cleophon: as a candidate for ostracism, 171–74; execution of, 196 ostraca against, 171, 173

club-bearers. *See* bodyguard
Cohen, A., 6n3
Coinage Decree, 214
Coisyra, 156
Colaeus (Samian trader), 61
colonization. *See* settlements abroad
Colophon, 211
comedy, 34n5; at Megara, 55n104. *See also* Aristophanes; ostracism
Connor, W. R., 113, 183n178
Corcyra, 7, 205n2, 254
Corinth, 4, 30, 206, 227, 232–34; 244–47, 253; and Athenian exiles, 199; early history of, 20, 69–70; and exile, 32, 69–77, relations with Megara, 50, 70; temple of Apollo at, 74. *See also* Cypselus; Periander
Coronea, battle of, 206, 210
corruption. *See* bribery
council: at Erythrae, 207; at Mytilene, 42; at Megara, 51; Solonian (of Four Hundred), 93, 135, 139–40. *See also* Areopagus Council; Council of Elders; Council of Five Hundred
Council of Elders (at Sparta), 291, 295–97
Council of Five Hundred (Cleisthenic), 139–40, 164, 178, 185, 207–8, 214–19. *See also* oaths
courts, popular, 163, 178–81, 213–19, 223–25. See also *heliaea*; legal system; oaths; trials
Critias, 262, 298; exile of, 195n248; death of, 201; return of, 196
cult, in Athens, 112–18; in Corinth, 32, 70; in Megara, 51; of tombs, 25n45
curses, and ostracism, 157
Cylon, 101, 135, 141, 180; attempt at tyranny, 80–90; partisans of, 8; shrine of, 90; and Theagenes, 81
Cyprus, 61, 152
Cypselus (tyrant of Corinth), 9n17, 71–75; representation of, 186–87, 233, 241, 245–46, 249
Cypselidae, 30, 32, 69, 75–77; dedications of, 75
Cyrene, 249; ostracism at, 288
Cyrnus, 33, 35n12, 53
Cyzicus, 191

Damasias, 100–101
Damon, ostracism of, 164n94
Darius, 68
Dark Age, 15; social diversity of, 17–18

Darnton, R., 1, 55n103, 115n152, 159n78
Davis, N. Z., 55n103, 59n110, 159n78
death penalty, 182, 195, 209, 214, 216, 223–25, 233, 272–73, 295. *See also* exile; legal system
debt, at Athens, 94–96, 102–7; at Corinth, 74–75; at Megara, 53–56
Decelea, 192
deception. *See* tricksters
decrees: Athenian, 207–26, dating of, 207n6. *See also* Coinage Decree; Judicial Decree
Deinomenids, 286
Delian League, 152, 168
Delos, 130n212
Delphi, 129–30; temple of Apollo at, 130; oracle at, 296–97
Demaratus (of Corinth), 71n182
Demaratus (of Sparta), 297
demes, 119, 141
Demeter, cult of, 17
democracy (Athenian): critics of, 144, 153, 161, 178, 181–96, 224–25, 240–44, 267–76; and exile, 134–42, 270–76; foundation of 2, 30, 80, 133–43, 279, 282; and the law, 191–95; moderation of, 2–3, 5, 131, 165, 178, 182, 191–96, 203–4, 207, 209, 226, 228–32, 237, 240, 265–66, 270, 278, 280, 298–99; overthrow of, 168, 175, 179, 180–204, 268–69; and stability, 165, 178; as tyranny, 241, 267–76. *See also* ideology; ostracism
Demophantus, decree of, 11n27, 179, 193–94
Demosthenes, and curse tablets, 157
dependency: at Athens, 81–82, 94, 104–106, 126, 141; and factions, 104–7; at Megara, 54–56. See also *hectemoroi*
Desan, S., 159nn78, 81
Develin, R., 283
Dewald, C., 244n10
Diagoras (of Melos), 180
Dicastic oath. *See* oaths
Diodorus, on petalism, 285–87
Diodotus, 206n3
Dionysus, cult of, 17, 74; festival of, 116n154, 147
Dipylon Gate, 115
disarmament, 198n265, 261
disenfranchisement, 75, 182, 186, 199, 206, 212–14, 223–25, 264, 295. See also *atimia*
disorder (*ataxia*), 31; and democracy, 55

documents. *See* inscriptions
Dorian invasion, 50, 60, 293
Dorian tribes, 50
Dougherty, C., 256
dowry, 264
Draco, homicide law of, 10, 84–89, 91, 95
drinking songs, 129n208, 132
Durkheim, É., 159n79

Egypt, 38, 61, 67, 152, 247–49
eisangelia (impeachment), 185
Eleusis, 201–3
elites: agency of, 16; conflict between, 1–2, 16,
  19, 22–29, 41–48, 51–52, 56–59, 60, 62–64,
  67–68, 77–78, 79–80, 85, 91–92, 96–101,
  107–33; 166–77, 278–79, 282; definition of,
  11–12; and democracy, 184; and factions,
  104–7; and ostracism, 153, 155, 158,
  161; self-regulation of, 2, 26; restrictions
  on, 22
Elpinice, 156
empire (Athenian), 3, 190; critique of, 232–
  39; defense of, 226–32; 234–39; and
  regulation of exile, 9, 205–39; revolt from,
  183–84
Epaminondas, 295
Ephesus, ostracism at, 285
Ephialtes, 167–68, 178, 216n37
Ephorus, 72–76, 146n4, 249, 260
ephors (at Sparta), 295–97
Epidamnus, 206
Epidaurus, 253
Epimenides, 90
epitaphios. See funeral oration
equality: in Athens, 230n85, 237; between
  allies, 221, 229–30, 232–33; and ostracism,
  158, 161, 274–76. *See also* freedom of
  speech (*isegoria*); *isonomia*
equals (at Sparta), 292
Eresus, 37
Eretria, 117–19, 156, 211
Erythrae, decree concerning, 207–10
Eteobutadae, 102, 116n153
Euboea, 61, 118, 206; revolt of, 183, 210–11
Eupatridae, 100, 238
Euripides, 235–36, 257–59
Euryptolemus, 193, 195n247
Eurystheus, 235–36, 257, 273–74
events, versus ideologies, 4
execution, 183, 186–89, 193–97, 206, 212.
  See also death penalty; legal system

exile: and death penalty, 11; definition of,
  7–11; democratic use of, 2–3, 5, 146,
  178–81; demos in, 182, 189–90, 195,
  198–200, 252–53, 260–64; elite use of, 1–3;
  as judicial penalty, 8–11, 178–81, 295–97;
  literature of, 14; and oligarchy, 181–205; in
  perpetuity, 90, 180, 194; polis in, 183,
  186–89; and power, 136–43, 149–50; 240,
  279; problem of, 1–2, 4; studies of, 7n5; and
  tyranny, 245–67; types of, 7–11; vocabulary
  of, 9–11. *See also* inner exile; internal exile;
  ostracism
extradition, of exiles, 199, 236

factions: at Athens, 79, 103–7; definition of,
  103–4; dissolution of, 126; role in state
  formation, 17
famine, and ostracism, 157
Faraone, C., 157
feasting, rituals of, 55–56, 70n174
festivals, Panhellenic, 88
Figueira, T., 226
fines, 216, 272. *See also* penalties
Five Thousand (oligarchy of), 191–92
Foxhall, L., 21n25, 26, 27nn57, 58, 59, 93
Foucault, M., 5, 6n3
Four Hundred (oligarchy of), 3, 146, 161, 165,
  183–96, 262, 271. *See also* oligarchy
freedom of speech (*isegoria*), 188
funeral oration, 230n86, 234–37, 257–58

Gagarin, M., 83nn13 and 15, 84nn18, 19, and
  20, 85n21, 86, 87nn30, 32, and 33, 88nn34
  and 35
Geertz, C., 13n45, 159n78
Gehrke, H.-J., 8nn11, 12, 10n20, 11n32
generals, trials of, 180, 193, 195, 213, 295–96
geomoroi (at Samos), 32, 62–63
Gephyrae, 259
Gernet, L., 157
gerousia. *See* Council of Elders
Ghinatti, F., 81
Giddens, A., 5
Gluckman, M., 55n103
gossip, 162, 220. *See also* rumor
government, debate about best form of, 3
graphe paranomon (unconstitutional proposals), 174n139, 185
Gray, V., 244n10
Great Rhetra, 291
greed, 228–29, 292

Grote, G., 99n80
guest-friendship (*xenia*), 67, 130, 133

Hall, J., 6n3, 50n76, 60nn114 and 115, 293
Hansen, M. H., 147n10, 174n139
Harmodius, 125
hectemoroi ("sixth-parters"), 36, 53, 94. *See also* dependency
Heftner, H., 171
heliaea, 95n67, 214
Heliastic Oath. *See* oaths
Hellespont, 131
helots, 292
Hera, patron deity of Samos, 221. *See also* Samos
Heraclea Pontica, 287–88
Heracles, 110n134, 153n35, 235, 257–58, 289, 294
Heraclidae, myth of, 234–36, 241, 255–59, 261, 273, 289, 293–94
Heraclitus, son of Panchares, ostracon against, 288
Hermocrates (of Syracuse), 184
herms, mutilation of, 175, 180, 184, 268–69
Herodotus: and democratic ideology, 119, 124, 134, 235, 243; and family tradition, 243; and oral tradition, 108, 112, 119, 120, 134; sources of, 134; and Sparta, 298; and Thucydides, 243; and tyrants, 131, 185–87, 233, 241
heroes, cult of, 22n28
Hesiod, 32
hetaireia (elite male social group), 39, 81, 85, 184
Hipparchus (son of Peisistratus) 2, 80, 124, 127–28
Hipparchus (fifth century) 11, 154n41, 179; ostracism of, 175–76, 265, 281
Hippias, 122; tyranny of, 127–33, 154n41, 270
Hippocleides, 117
Hippocoön, 294
Hippocrates, ostraca against, 160n83
Hippomachus, 201
Histiaea, 205, 211
histoire des mentalités, 5
historical imagination, of the Greeks, 5, 277
history, modern methods of research, 3
Hobsbawm, E., and T. Ranger, 6n3
Hodkinson, S., 292
Homer, and the polis, 19n15; epics of, 33, 34n6

homicide, 84–85, 178, 254–55; intentional, 11, 86–7; justifiable, 87, 92. *See also* Draco
Hopkins, K., 159n78, 160
hoplites, 24, 66, 93n60, 110, 141, 292; organization of, 108. *See also* warfare
Hornblower, S., 228–29
horoi (boundary markers), 35. *See also* Solon
hostages, 121, 188
Humphreys, S. C., 85–86, 88
Hunter, V., 188n204
hubris, 189, 222, 227, 235
Hyllus, 235
Hyperbolus, ostraca against, 171; ostracism of, 146, 153, 170–75

identity: Athenian, 5, 79, 88, 94–96, 114–17, 120, 126, 145, 159–62, 237; Messenian, 295; of the polis, 19, 22; Spartan, 22n28. *See also* citizenship
ideology: definition of, 12–13; democratic, 131, 133, 138, 140–41, 144–46, 165, 182, 186–89; 196–200; 206, 219, 234, 240–67, 275–76, 278–80, 289, 298–99; elitist, 34; vs. events, 4–5, 275; imperial, 206–39; middling, 16, 19, 28, 34; and myth, 232, 234–39, 240, 242–44; and symbols, 13, 187. *See also* tyranny
impiety. *See* asebeia
imprisonment, 183, 186, 193, 195–97, 217, 219, 272. *See also* legal system
incest, and ostracism, 155, 156
industrial elite, 172. *See also* new politicians
initiation, rituals of, 255
institutions, versus ideology, 5
inner exile, 8
inscriptions: display of, 194, 215, 219–23; symbolism of, 222–23. *See also* lists; monuments
interest, return of (at Megara), 30, 31, 36, 54–56, 58, 59. *See also* debt
internal exile, 7, 183, 202
Iolaus, 235
Ionia, 189
Ionian migration, 60, 238
Ionian tribes, 60
Isagoras, 9n18, 80, 131n222, 135–142, 179, 279
Isocrates, 230–32, 262–63, 265
isonomia, 137n241, 216n37, 238n113
Isthmia, 74

Jacoby, F., 130n212, 134n231, 243
Jameson, M., 192
Johnson, A. W., and T. Earle, 20–21
judicial agreements, 228–29
Judicial Decree, 223–26
jurors. *See* courts; oaths

Kagan, D., 194n244
Keesling, C. M., 65n148, 125
Kertzer, D., 159
kings (*basileis*), 17; at Corinth, 245; at Myti-
lene, 41; at Megara, 51; at Sparta, 289–91,
295–97
Koch, C., 207–15
Krentz, P., 197–204
Kritsas, C., 288
Kurke, L., 34, 35n11, 38, 46, 243n7

Laconia, 239, 289, 291–94
landownership: in Athens, 25–28, 103; in
Corinth, 71; in Mytilene, 37–38, 46; in
Megara, 52, 54; in Samos, 62; at Sparta,
291–94. *See also* agriculture
Lane Fox, R., 34n5, 35n13
Lang, M., 146n4, 148nn13 and 15
Lanza, D., 256n36, 269n58
Lavelle, B., 108, 119n160, 134n231, 250–51
lawgivers, legends of, 99
laws: revision of, 216; at Sparta, 296; written,
26, 83n15, 279. *See also* tyranny
Lawton, C., 220–21
Leagrus, ostraca against, 154
Lefkandi, 17, 18
legal system, 178–81; penalties under, 178–80,
216–18, 272–73. See also *atimia*; death
penalty; disenfrachisment; execution;
fines
Lenaea, 147
Leotychidas, 295–96
Lesbos, 36–39, 234
Libya, 68, 249
lists, of benefactors and offenders, 222; of
ostracized persons, 281
literacy, and inscriptions, 220; and ostracism,
148–49
litigiousness, of Athens, 228
Loraux, N., 230n86, 239
lot, selection by, 97, 176, 282. *See also* Solon
Luraghi, N., 295
luxuries, 27, 38, 60–61, 71, 76; and ostracism,
155–56. *See also* trade

Lycophron, 241, 253–57
Lycurgus (sixth-century, Athenian) 102–7,
112–14, 117, 119, 120
Lycurgus (fourth-century Athenian) 102; and
curse tablets, 157
Lycurgus (of Sparta), 290–92, 298
Lygdamis (of Naxos), 65n148, 67, 119, 252
Lypercalia, 160
Lysander, 196, 202
Lysias, 193, 198, 200, 232n94, 238n114,
258–59, 261–62, 264

Macedonia, 133
magic, and ostracism, 157
Maiandrius, 298
Malkin, I., 50, 73n201, 293
Manville, B., 94n65
marathon, 119, 236
market. *See* trade
Maronea, mines at, 166
marriage, 264
medism. *See* treason
Megacles (seventh-century Athenian),
81–90, 102
Megacles (sixth-century Athenian), 102–7,
112–14, 117, 119, 120, 123
Megacles (son of Callisthenes), ostraca
against, 177n150
Megacles (son of Hippocrates): ostraca
against, 155–56, 160; ostracism of, 152,
154n41, 164n94, 176; recall of, 152
Megacles (Acharneus), ostraca against,
177n150
Megacles (of Mytilene), 41, 42
Megara, 4, 30, 75; and Athenian exiles, 199,
261; and conflict with Athens, 102, 110,
111; and conflict with Samos, 63; and
democracy, 31, 54–56; and exile, 31, 48–59;
early history of, 49–52; evidence for, 48–49;
local traditions of, 48–49; ostracism at,
285, 288
Meier, C., 140n248
Meier, M., 237n109, 290n5
Meiggs, R., 206–8, 211
Melanchrus (tyrant of Mytilene), 42
Melobius, 195
Melos, 205, 231
memory, social, 240, 242–44; and forgetting,
242, 263; and history, 260–65, 278–79.
See also ideology; oral tradition;
traditions

Menon, ostraca against, 156n58, 160n83;
    ostracism of, 164n94
mercenaries, 67, 103n101, 118–21, 137n240,
    200, 203, 251. *See also* bodyguard
Messana, 294
Messenia, liberation of, 295; Spartan conquest
    of, 28, 232, 239, 292, 294–95
metics, 196–98, 200–201, 260, 263
Methymna, 37
middling citizens, 12. *See also* ideology
Miletus, ostracism at, 285, 288
Miltiades, the Elder, 122–23
Miltiades, the Younger, 122–23, 180
Minyans, 290n6
Mnasilochus, 195
monarchy. *See* kings
Monoson, S., 272nn65 and 66
monuments, symbolism of, 132, 219–23
Moore, S. F., and B. G., Myerhoff, 159n78
Morris, I., 15–17, 19, 23, 24, 33, 34, 38, 40, 53
Muir, E., 237, 290n5
Munychia, 201
Mycale, 152
Myrsilus, 43–44
mysteries, affair of, 175, 180, 184, 268–69
myth: and exile, 235–39, 253, 257–59; and
    history, 240, 242–44, 293–94; and structur-
    alism, 254. *See also* ideology
Mytilene, 4, 30, 63, 99, 205–6; early history of,
    36–37; and exile, 31, 32, 36–48

Nagy, G., 32, 40
Naucratis, 38
Naupactus, 295
new politicians, 12. *See also* industrial elite
Nicias, 170, 174, 268; ostracon against, 171
Nichoria, 18
Nicolaus of Damascus, 245, 249
non-citizens. *See* metics
non-elites, 78; in Athens, 81–82, 93–96, 100–20,
    125–27, 134–43, 177; in Corinth, 73–76;
    definition of, 11–12; and exile, 136, 143; and
    factions, 104–7; in Mytilene, 46–48; at
    Megara, 51–56, 58; at Samos, 62, 64, 67
Notium, 271

oaths, 190, 194, 203, 207–19, 230; Councilors'
    Oath, 214–19, 224; Jurors' Oath, 214–19
Ober, J., 12n38, 134n228, 140, 145n3,
    183n179, 243n8, 267n52
Odysseus, 109n130

Oedipus, 85n21
Oenophytae, 210
offices: in Athens, 25–26, 87–88, 124–25, 128,
    147n10; and bribery, 156; in Corinth, 71;
    formal public, 2, 26, 279; in Megara, 51;
    in Mytilene, 41–42; regulation of, 26,
    286; removal from, 283–87; at Sparta,
    290–91
old oligarch. *See* Xenophon
oligarchy, 30, 181–83; and exile, 181–204;
    and the law, 194–95. *See also* Four Hun-
    dred and Thirty Tyrants
olive-oil. *See* trade
Olympia, games at, 122, 123
Onomacles, 192–93, 195
oral tradition, 13, 34–36, 82n9, 120, 127, 137,
    140–41, 215, 241, 242–43, 276. *See also*
    Herodotus
orality. *See* oral tradition
Orestes, 41; bones of, 22n28, 292n15
Oropos, Athenian exiles at, 199
Osborne, R., 23, 73n196, 167n111, 174n139
    et passim
ostraca: comments on, 153–60, 287; definition
    of, 148; drawings on, 154, 156, 158; find
    locations and quantities for, 148n13; with-
    out comments, 160. *See also* ballots and
    ostracism
ostracism: and adultery, 155, 156, 161; and
    agriculture, 147n10, 163; bouleutic (by the
    council), 283–84; and collective identity,
    159–62; and comedy, 147, 158n76, 162,
    174; and critics of democracy, 144, 161,
    233, 274–76, 278; and curse tablets, 157;
    dating of, 150n23, 281–84; definition of,
    148; elite victims of, 153, 155, 158, 161; and
    equality, 158, 161, 177; first use of, 164,
    281–82; gaps in dates between uses, 174,
    282–84; and gossip, 162; and *graphe para-*
    nomon, 174n139; and incest, 155; initial
    vote of, 146–47, 162–65; introduction of, 2,
    5, 80, 142, 164; last use of, 171–75; and
    literacy, 148–49; location of, 149, 162–64;
    and magic, 157–58; misuse of, 171; mod-
    eration of, 3, 131, 151–55, 162–65, 253,
    280, 283; modern interpretations of, 150,
    153–58 ; modern judgments of, 1, 144, 278;
    and organized campaigns, 148–49, 162,
    163, 173; outside Athens, 285–88; and
    pollution, 155–58; and prestige, 155, 158,
    161, 177; procedure of, 146–49; and

property, 149, 152; reasons for, 155–62; and recall, 152; and religious offenses, 157–58; as ritual, 145, 158–62; and rumor, 162; and scapegoating, 157; and scatter-vote, 160, 170, 176; and selection of archons and generals, 147n10; and sexuality, 155, 156, 161, 287; and spectacle, 145, 163–64; symbolism of, 2, 5, 80, 142–45; 149–65, 278–80, 283; and treason, 154–55, 177; and tyranny, 153–54, 285–86; uncertain cases of, 164n94; use of, 131, 145–46, 164–177; and violence, 168, 170, 282; and voters (number of), 149, 162–63, 173. *See also* ostraca; petalism

Ostwald, M., 170n120, 192nn225 and 227, 216n37 et passim

outlawry. *See atimia*

Pangaeum, Mount., 118

Paeania, 115

Pallene, battle of, 119–21, 124, 250–52

Pan painter, 146n4, 149n19

Panathenaia, festival of, 114–17, 125

Parker, R., 157, 255

Paros, 180

Partheniae, 292

Patrocleides, decree of, 193

patronage. *See* dependency

Pausanias, 200, 202, 296

peace treaty (of 404 BCE), conventions of, 211–12, and exiles, 193, 196

Peloponnesian War, 196, 227, Athens's defeat in, 268–71

penalties (legal). *See atimia*; legal system

Penthilidae, 41

Perachora, 50, 70

Peraea, 61, 63,

Periander (tyrant of Corinth), 3, 74; representation of, 233, 241, 246–47, 249, 274–76; and son, 253–57, 261, 273

Pericles, 167–69, 233n95, 243; ostraca against, 169n117; and revolt of Euboea, 211

Perinthus, 63

periodization, in ancient history, 13–14

perioikoi, 199

Perses, 33

Persia, 61, 175, 205, 208, 230, 234; and Athens, 113, 184; and Samos, 68–69; and treason, 154–55. *See also* Alcmeonidae; Persian Wars; Pisistratidae

Persian Wars, 166, 228

petalism, 285–87

Petrarch, 236–37

Phaeax, 170, 174; ostraca against, 171

Pheidon, 71

Philaïdae, exile of, 122–24

Philochorus, 147

Phrynichus, 182, 192; treason of, 192; death of, 194

Phye, 112–17

Phyle, 200–201

Pindar, 33

Piraeus, 191, 199–202, 261

Pisander, 185, 192

Pisistratus (seventh-century Athenian), 102

Pisistratus (sixth-century Athenian), 2, 7, 66n152, 75, 79–80, 100, 101–27, 138, 156n57, 279; and cult, 116–17; and deme judges, 126; exile of, 111, 112, 117–19; and Heracles, 110n134; and loans to the poor, 125–26; and relations with elites, 124–27; and relations with non-elites, 125–27; representation of, 241, 250–53, 267; tyranny of, 107–28; use of expulsion, 121–25; wars of, 128n199

Pisistratidae (family of Pisistratus): building projects of, 22, 65, 127–28; origins of, 238n112; ostracism of, 153, 265, 281; overthrow of, 121, 130–32, 245; and the Persians, 133; rule of, 121; and Sparta, 130, 132–33; representation of, 270. *See also* Hipparchus; Hippias

Pithecusae, 70

Pittacus (tyrant of Mytilene), 30, 33, 42–48

Plataea, 152, 232; battle of, 235, 258

Plato, 54, 55n100, 241, 244; and democracy, 267, 271–74; and exile, 272–74

Pleistoanax, 211, 296

Plutarch, 31, 54–55

poetry, archaic 30–31, 32–36; and symposium, 35

de Polignac, F., 19n14, 21–23, 38

polis, development of, 4; rise of, 18–19; egalitarian ethos of, 22–24

pollution, and exile, 11, 89, 135, 255. *See also* ostracism

Polycrates (tyrant of Samos), 30, 32, 64–69, 139n243; building projects of 65; representation of, 241, 247–49, 251–52

Polystratus, 193

poor, the: at Athens, 94–96, 102–7; at Corinth, 74–75; at Mytilene, 47; at Megara, 51, 53–56, 58–59. *See also* debt; non-elite
population, size of, 16, 17, 18, 19–21, 28, 31; in early Athens, 26–27, in Megara, 53, in Sparta, 291–92
Potidaea, 205
potsherds. *See* ostraca
power, imperial, 207. *See also* exile
praotes, (moderation, leniency), 231–32, 265–66, 270
Praxiergidae, 116
Priene, 63
processions, 21; at Athens, 113–18
property, confiscation of, 209, 214, 219, 224–25, 231, 233, 245–46, 260–61, 264. *See also* ostracism
Propontis, 63
Protagoras, 180
Psammetichus, 76–77
punishment (legal). *See atimia*; legal system
Pyrrha, 37
Pythagoras, 68
Pythodorus, 195

Raaflaub, K., 134, 244n9
razing of houses, 296
Rebenich, S., 298
reciprocity. *See* dependency; guest-friendship
reconciliation, agreement of 403 BCE, 202–4
revelry, popular, 31, 54–56. *See also* ritual
Rhaecelus, 118
Rhegium, 294
Rhodes, P. J., 213, 216n37, et passim
rich, the, 54. *See also* elite
rights, individual, 278
riots, 56, 140–41
ritual: at Athens, 113–18, 125, 128, 163; civic, 2, 21, 113; at Corinth, 74; expulsive, 157; of inversion, 31; 55–56; theories of, 159–60. *See also* ostracism
Roberts, J. T., 158n74, 181n175, et passim
Robinson, E., 286
Rome, 73
Rosenbloom, D., 172, 175n144
Rosivach, V., 145n3, 158n73, 165n97, 177n155, 237nn106, 107, and 108
Rosler, W., 39–40
rough music, 160n85

Roussel, D, 25n48
rumor, 141, 162, 183, 187, 189. *See also* gossip

Sacred War, First, 130n211
sacrilege. *See asebeia*
Sages, Seven, 45, 74
de Ste. Croix, G. E. M., 228–29
Salamis, 152, 177
Samos, 4, 30, 32, 234, 253; Athenian fleet at, 183–84, 186–91; decrees concerning, 221, 224; early history of, 60–62; and exile, 59–69; revolt of, 152n31, 206, 211; sculpture at, 66; sea power of, 61; temple of Hera at, 60, 65, 248; trade and, 60–62. *See also* Polycrates
Sancisi-Weerdenburg, H., 109n132, 128n199
sanctuaries, and the polis, 19, 21–24; dedications at, 22–23
Sappho, 38, poetry of, 39
Saxonhouse, A., 239, 272n65
scapegoating, 157
scatter-vote, 160, 170, 176
Schmitt-Pantel, P., 160n85
Scione, 205, 231
Seibert, J., 124
seisachtheia. See Solon
self-interest, 209
self-wounding, 108–9
Sestos, 152
settlements abroad, 9, 21, 25, 28; Megarian, 52; Corinthian, 70, 73, 249
sexual relations, and ostracism, 155, 156, 161; and women, 160. *See also* adultery
share-cropping. *See hectemoroi*
Scheidel, W., 20n17, 146n4, 158
Shipley, G., 62
Sicily, 180; Athenian defeat in, 183; Athenian invasion of, 174, 268
Sickinger, J., 220
Sicyon, 76
Siewert, P., 158, 281
Sigeum, 128, 131, 133
Singor, H. W., 110
slavery, 75, 94, 153, 172, 188, 201n286, 205, 224, 232n94, 233, 235, 247, 258
Snodgrass, A., 18–20, 21–22
social diversity, in Dark Age Greece, 17–18
Socles, 245
Socrates, 11, 13, 179–80, 241, and exile, 271–74

Solon, 2, 53, 79, 90–101, 216n37, 279; amnesty law of, 92; and council of, 93, 400;
and democracy, 55n102; and *horoi*, 35; and
judicial reforms, 95–96; and law on stasis,
79, 98–100, 279; poetry of, 27n60, 47,
94–96; and property classes, 12, 27n60,
92–94; and selection of archons, 96–97,
176; and "Shaking-off of Burdens"
(*seisachtheia*), 36, 54, 55, 75, 94–96
Sophocles, 192, 236
Sourvinou-Inwood, C., 254–55
space, public, in Athens, 87–88, 116, 120,
127–28, 162. *See also* agora
Sparta, 18, 205, 230–32; and aid to Samians,
67; and Athens, 130–33, 189, 191, 196–97,
199–202, 210, 225, 239; debate at, 227–29;
and conflict between elites, 290–97; and
exile, 289–99; and expulsion of foreigners
(*xenelasia*), 239, 297–99; kings of, 289–91,
295–97; and Persia, 183–84; and tyrants, 76,
247–48, 291. *See also* Messenia
Spencer, N., 36n16, 37–38, 39
Stahl, M. 104n109
stasis (civil unrest), 41, 43, 100, 168, 231–32,
237–39, 263–64, 276, 290. *See also* elites;
Solon, law on stasis
states, formation of, 4, 16–17, 20–21; leadership in, 20; Athenian, 87–88
status, 12n37, 20; in Athens, 103; competition
for, 22–23; 28, 37–38, 71, 292
Strabo, 42
Sunium, 106
sycophants, 197
Syloson (tyrant of Samos), 32, 63
symbols: and ideology, 13; and inscriptions,
219–23; and culture, 117; and oaths, 214–
19. *See also* monuments; ostracism
symposium, 35
Syracuse, 73, 285–87. *See also* petalism
Syria, 61

Taeuber, H., 158n75, 281–82
Taras, 292
Tegea, 235, 258, 292, 296
temples. *See* sanctuaries
Terpander, 298
Thargelia, festival of, 157
Thebes, 119; and Athenian exiles, 199–201,
261
Theagenes (tyrant of Megara), 31, 51–52, 54,
58, 65; and Cylon, 81

Themistocles, 11, 132n225, 154n41, 166, 282,
298; decree of, 152n27; ostraca against, 155,
160; ostracism of, 155, 158, 176–77; treason
of, 155, 177n156, 179
Theognis, poetry of, 27n60, 32, 39, 47, 48–49;
dating of, 35n13; exile of, 58
Thera, 290n6
Theramenes, 191, 194, 196
Thermaic Gulf, 118
Theseus, ostracism of, 153
Thesmothetae, 214
Thessaly, 37, 130, 133, 296
thetes, 93–96
Thirty Tyrants, 7; 146, 161, 165, 196–204,
219, 250; representation of, 3, 259–67.
See also oligarchy
Thirty Years' Peace, 225
Thomas, R., 82n9, 83n15, 122n170, 128–130,
132nn223 and 225, 134, 200n275, 220–23,
242–43, 252, 262, 267
Thompson, E. P., 55n103, 59n110,
160n85
Thrasybulus (Athenian), 198, 200–201, 263
Thrasybulus (of Miletus), 233–34, 246–47,
249, 274–76
Thucydides, son of Melesias, ostracism of,
152n31, 168–69, 180
Thucydides, son of Olorus, 3, 10, 169, 174; on
Alcibiades, 180, 241, 267–70; and autochthony, 237–38, 259; and democracy,
181–96, 244, 269–70; and empire, 226–29;
exile of, 179, 298; and Herodotus, 187; as
historical source, 227; and oligarchy,
182–82; and popular tradition, 124, 187
Tolmides, 210n16
Torone, 205, 231
towers, on Lesbos, 37–38, 39
trade: Athenian, 27–28, 53; Corinthian, 70;
Lesbian, 37–39; Megarian, 31, 52, 53, 58;
Mytilenean, 46; Samian, 32, 60–62
tradition: adaptation/appropriation of, 246–49,
275–76; and elite, 246–52; and family,
121–24, 130n212; local, 32–36; panhellenic,
32–36, 240, 253; and polis, 242–43;
popular, 134, 243. *See also* ideology;
memory; oral tradition
tragedy, and democracy, 116n154, 242–43;
and exile, 11, 235–36, 257–59
treason, 177, 179; penalties for, 154–55, 179,
192; at Sparta, 295–97
treaty. *See* peace treaty

trials, 181, 195, at Athens, 213–19; in allied states, 212–19. *See also* courts; legal system

tribes (*phylai*), in Athens, 25; Cleisthenic, 136–38, 164. *See also* Dorian tribes; Ionian tribes

tribute, 152, 190; lists of, 223; reassessment of, 214, 225

tricksters, 108, 120, 173, 248–52

Turner, V., 55, 159

Tyndareus, 294

tyrannicides, 132

tyranny: Athens as, 227, 233–34; and building projects, 22, 65, 74, 127–28; and burial, 264; and children, 188, 205n1, 231, 251–52; and disarmament, 198n265, 261; and dissent, 256; and exile, 233–67; historical, 30; and hostages, 251–52; law against, 6, 83, 87, 92, 132, 178–79, 193–94, 266; and mercenaries, 251; penalties for, 154; popular support of, 64, 75; relations with elites, 65, 73–76; representation of, 13, 32, 41, 72, 75–76, 108, 119–21, 124, 129, 186–89, 197–98, 232–34, 241, 244–67, 269–70, 280; and suspicion, 269–70; and tricks, 248–52; and women, 188, 247, 251, 253, 264. See also *aisymnetae*

van Wees, H., 51–52, 59

Vansina, J., 34, 251n28

Venice, myth of, 236

Vernant, J.-P., and P. Vidal-Naquet, 157

Vinogradov, J.-G., and M. Zolotarev, 287–88

violence, and oligarchy, 183–204. *See also* ostracism

virtue (*arete*), 12, 47, 274

voting. *See* ostracism

warfare, 21, 24–25, 28

wealth, 52–53, 59; and ostracism, 155. *See also* elites; landownership; trade

whip, as symbol, 188

Whitley, J., 16n1, 18n12, 23–24, 25nn43, 45, and 46

Wilenz, S., 159

wine. *See* trade

Wohl, V., 244n9

Wolpert, A., 182n176, 196–202, 262–63

women, 188, 205n1, 231, 247, 251, 253, 264

Xanthippus (son of Ariphron): ostracism of, 154n41, 156n58, 176; ostracon against, 156; recall of, 152

Xanthippus (son of Hippocrates), ostraca against, 177n150

xenelasia. *See* Sparta

xenia. *See* guest-friendship

Xenophon, 180, 193; on Alcibiades, 241, 267, 270–71; and democracy, 181; and oligarchy, 197–99, 241, 260–61; pseudo-, 224–25; on Socrates, 272n69; and Sparta, 298

Zagora, 18

Zancle, 294

Zeus, 293